The University of California Press
gratefully welcomes the contribution
provided by

ENTE CASSA DI RISPARMIO DI FIRENZE

toward the publication of this book.

The first volume of the California Lectura Dantis
draws on a wide range of international scholar-critics.
Each contributor presents his or her reading, in essay form,
of a canto of the *Inferno*. The *Purgatorio* and *Paradiso* volumes
will follow the same format, providing the long-awaited companion
to the three volumes of Allen Mandelbaum's verse tranlsations,
with facing Italian text, of *The Divine Comedy*.

ADVISORY BOARD

Ignazio Baldelli
University of Rome

Teodolinda Barolini
Columbia University

Charles T. Davis†
Tulane University

Giuseppe Di Scipio
Hunter College and Graduate Center, CUNY

Cecil Grayson
Oxford University

Emilio Pasquini
University of Bologna

Lea Ritter Santini
University of Münster

John A. Scott
University of Western Australia

Lectura Dantis

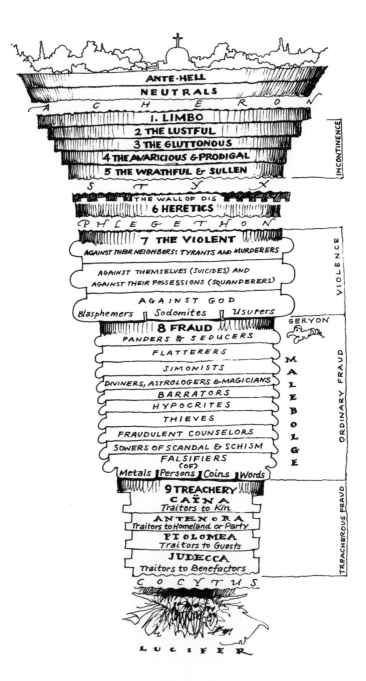

The moral topology of *Inferno*,
by Barry Moser

Lectura Dantis

INFERNO

Edited by

ALLEN MANDELBAUM

ANTHONY OLDCORN

CHARLES ROSS

UNIVERSITY OF CALIFORNIA PRESS

Berkeley Los Angeles London

*The editors have benefited much from the help of
the Wait Tower staff of Wake Forest University,
especially the unstinting care of Lily Saadé,
as well as from the editorial collaboration of
Martha Craig at Purdue University.*

University of California Press
Berkeley and Los Angeles, California

University of California Press, Ltd.
London, England

© 1998 by
The Regents of the University of California

Library of Congress Cataloging-in-Publication Data

Lectura Dantis : Inferno / edited by Allen Mandelbaum,
   Anthony Oldcorn, Charles Ross.
       p.   cm.—(California lectura Dantis ; 1)
   Includes bibliographical references and index.
   ISBN 0-520-21249-5 (alk. paper).—ISBN 0-520-21270-3 (alk.
paper)
     1. Dante Alighieri, 1265–1321. Inferno. I. Mandelbaum,
   Allen, 1926– . II. Oldcorn, Anthony.   III. Ross, Charles,
   1949– . IV. Series.
   PQ4443.L38   1998
   851´.1—dc21   98-34223
                                                             CIP

Printed in the United States of America
9 8 7 6 5 4 3 2 1

The paper used in this publication meets the minimum
requirements of American National Standards for Information
Sciences—Permanence of Paper for Printed Library Materials,
ANSI Z 39.48-1984.

This volume of the
California Lectura Dantis
is dedicated to our indispensable
colleague and peerless editor of the text
of Dante's
Divine Comedy,
the late

GIORGIO PETROCCHI

It is unthinkable
to read the cantos of Dante
without aiming them
in the direction of the present day.
They were made for that . . .
They demand the commentary
of the futurum.

OSIP MANDELSTAM

CONTENTS

Dante in His Age

ALLEN MANDELBAUM

> Possessed of every good, Florence has defeated her enemies in war and in great battles. She enjoys her fortune, her victorious pennants, her powerful people. Everywhere she reinforces and augments her power. Ardent, vigorous, she strikes down every enemy. She possesses the sea, possesses the land, possesses all of the world. Under her government, all of Tuscany has become happy. Like Rome, she sits ingathering her victories; she decides everything; she regulates everything with sure laws.

The proud Florentines inscribed this epigraph in stone on the Palazzo del Podestà (now the Bargello) around 1255. It echoed the spirit of the Florentine commune—or commonwealth or republic—during the decade of republican government from 1250 to 1260, the period of the *Primo Popolo,* or First Republic. Florence energetically reaffirmed her economic independence, was jealous of her own political establishment, and was proud of the representative democracy she had constructed. The First Republic was followed by an interval of six years of antirepublican rule, but it was restored in 1266 as the Second Republic, which lasted until the fifteenth century.

In 1265, one year before this republican restoration, Dante was born in Florence. And, as he himself lets us know (*Par.* XII, 115–117), his birth fell under the sign of Gemini, between May 14 and June 13. From the *Comedy* we learn that one of his great-grandfathers, Cacciaguida (*Par.* XV–XVII), was knighted by the emperor Conrad III and may have died in the Second Crusade in the Holy Land (1147). Though the Alighieri were certainly not among the most prominent citizens of Florence, some of them were sufficiently active politically to suffer exile in 1248 and 1260, years of bitter civil strife. Of Dante's own parents not much is known. His father, Alighiero, seems to have been a lender and money changer who accumulated fairly substantial land holdings near Florence. Dante's mother, Donna Bella (Gabriella), died early (between 1270 and 1273). His father remarried quickly and died before 1283.

Florence's network of schools was to become a significant civic achievement in the fourteenth century. But little is known of its schools in the thirteenth century—when Bologna was certainly ahead of Florence in classical training—and nothing of Dante's own early education. Whatever the quality of the formal frame of his early studies, and whether or not they had any formal frame at all, he was clearly an intense self-teacher (with reference to poetry he declares that he had learned "by himself the art of speaking words in rhyme" [*Vita nuova* III, 9]); and he surely benefited from the rhetorical and civil teachings he found in the works of Brunetto Latini (*Inf.* xv, 30–124).

Possibly around 1285 (though some date Dante's "effective" marriage later), he married Gemma Donati, to whom he had been betrothed, in accord with the customs of the time, as early as 1277. With Gemma Donati, he had at least three children: Jacopo, Pietro, and Antonia (Pietro was to become one of the most lucid commentators we have on the *Comedy*).

Unquestionably, the major event of Dante's youth was, or became, his love for Beatrice. (The historical Beatrice was very probably Bice, daughter of Folco Portinari, a close neighbor of the Alighieri; married to Simone de' Bardi, she died an early death in 1290.) Dante tells us that he first saw Beatrice, and immediately felt the force of love for her, when he was almost nine and she some eight months younger. That first vision was followed, some nine years later, by Beatrice's first spoken greeting to Dante. The Italian for the greeting or salutation she bestowed, *salute*, also means well-being, blessedness, and salvation; and Beatrice, whose name means she-who-blesses, became the essential presence in Dante's mythologizing and theologizing of love.

Dante was a searcher for final meanings; he read the events that followed his boyhood vision of Beatrice, including the event of her very early death, as an invitation to his spiritual transformation. Dante foreshadowed this transformation in the tale of his love (not least in its title announcing new life), the *Vita nuova*, an autobiographical work in poetry and prose that he compiled in 1293–1294, a few years after the death of his beloved. He fully embodied this transformation in the *Comedy*, where Beatrice is the woman who, in the first canto of the *Inferno*, sends Virgil to rescue the straying Dante from the "shadowed forest" of fear and error, and who will later lead Dante to the vision of Paradise. And when Dante first sees Beatrice—veiled—in the *Comedy*, in the Earthly Paradise at the summit of the Mountain of Purgatory, he exclaims (*Purg.* xxx, 34–39):

> Within her presence, I had once been used
> to feeling—trembling—wonder, dissolution;
> but that was long ago. Still, though my soul,
>   now she was veiled, could not see her directly,

> by way of hidden force that she could move,
> I felt the mighty power of old love.

After the death of Beatrice, Dante entered, belatedly but voraciously, a period of philosophic study. His motives were both the need for consolation and the restless, urban, unecclesiastical curiosity that characterized one who was becoming the most complete intellectual of his time. By the 1290s Dante could have drawn on three philosophical-theological schools in Florence: the school of the Dominicans, in Santa Maria Novella; of the Augustinians, in Santo Spirito; and of the Franciscans, in Sante Croce. Dante was also sensitive to many developments in Paris, the place of confluence for philosophic study in the thirteenth century. He was aware of, and may indeed have been tempted by, Aristotelian currents that saw human reason—independent of faith and grace—as having sufficient force to find God; or even by more radical Aristotelian tendencies, which saw human reason as a self-sufficient means of attaining happiness—in essence, a declaration of philosophy's complete independence from theology. (Cavalcanti, the first among Dante's friends, had probably espoused this radical position—and positions still more unorthodox.) Such philosophic temptations may be one aspect of the forest in Canto 1 of the *Inferno*.

His philosophic concerns were soon paralleled by his very active political involvement; and certainly the politics of Florence in the years around the turn of the century are an essential part of the *Infern*-al forest.

In 1289 Dante had probably participated in two important Florentine victories, the battle of Campaldino (*Inf.* XXII, 4–5 and *Purg.* v, 91–93) and the taking of Caprona (*Inf.* XXI, 94–95). After the death of Beatrice and his apprenticeship in philosophy, from 1295 on, he occupied a series of public offices on the various councils of Florence, his service culminating in a two-month tenure as one of the six priors, the principal counselors of state, in 1300. During this term of office, Dante was drawn into a conspicuous role in attempting to thwart the ambitions of Pope Boniface VIII. Boniface was the most formidable and determined figure in Italian politics in the years of his pontificate, 1294–1303. And for his attempt to thwart Boniface, Dante was to pay a heavy price. (Boniface, in turn, was to pay a heavy price throughout the *Comedy;* the very last words of Beatrice to Dante in the *Paradiso* are a ferocious condemnation of Boniface—*Par.* XXX, 148.)

Even the briefest view of Dante's political involvement—and much of the political content of the *Comedy*—requires a wider frame: the struggle for power within the Florentine republic and in Italy at large, between forces supporting the papacy and forces supporting the Holy Roman Empire. The names designating these forces were Guelph and Ghibelline (Italianizations of the German *Welf*, dukes of Bavaria, and *Weiblingen*, an ancestral castle of their opponents, the Hohenstaufen emperors). These names were said to have been imported into Florence in the wake of a family feud that erupted on Easter 1215 between the Buondelmonti and the Amidei (*Inf.* XXVIII, 106–109). But by the third and fourth decades of the century, Guelph and Ghibelline had acquired the larger resonance of pro-papal and pro-imperial political parties, respectively, in Florence.

The last Holy Roman emperor who was a major presence in thirteenth-century Italy was Frederick II. It was his death in 1250 that weakened imperial factions everywhere and allowed the establishment of the First Republic of Florence. In a city that now had a landed military aristocracy, newer merchant magnates, lower nobility, bankers, and artisans, the Guelph majority banished many Ghibellines and legislated a new balance of power. There were nobles and magnates in both parties, but the Guelphs were more sensitive to the pro-papal sympathies of the guilds—made up of artisans and smaller merchants (the *popolo* in *Primo Popolo* may mean "people," but it does not quite mean "populace")—and better able to mobilize those sympathies on their own behalf. The papacy, for its part, had every interest in encouraging city-republics responsive to the papacy's own temporal interests in central Italy. An all-embracing emperor or republics with tenaciously pro-imperial sentiments, like Pisa and Siena, could hardly support any increase in the political power of the pope.

The First Republic ended in 1260, with the defeat of the Florentine Guelphs by regrouped Ghibelline forces at the battle of Montaperti (*Inf.* X, 85–93). The Ghibelline interval lasted until 1266. In that year Manfred, Frederick II's illegitimate son, was killed at the battle of Benevento (the haunting fate of his unburied body is evoked in *Purg.* III, 112–132). With his death, pro-imperial partisans were banished from Florence, and the Second Republic restored Guelph power.

Any lingering doubts about that power were eliminated in 1289 by the battle of Campaldino (fought by Florence against Arezzo and the Ghibellines of Tuscany) and by the taking of the Pisan castle of Caprona. These were Guelph victories in which Dante, as noted above, probably took part; they marked the final disappearance from Florence of the Ghibellines.

In place of the divisions between Guelphs and Ghibellines, the 1290s, the decade of Dante's entry into politics, saw the division of the Florentine Guelphs themselves into two new factions: White and Black. The Whites (the party of Dante), led by the Cerchi family, whose considerable wealth was of relatively recent origin, tried—often ineptly—to defend the independence and the freedom of the republic from the ambitions of the pope and his French allies. The Blacks, led by the Donati, of older, aristocratic origin, appeared more ready to compromise with the ambitions of the pope in order to obtain power over Florence for themselves. Their leader, Corso Donati—distant relative of Dante's wife and brother of Dante's intimate friend, Forese Donati—was arrogant, unscrupulous, and extremely capable (for his violent end, dragged to death at the tail of a horse, see *Purg.* XXIV, 82–87).

It was precisely during the priorate of Dante that the Signoria, the ruling body of Florence, decided to free the city from factious presences, banishing—impartially—leaders of both the Blacks and the Whites. Among those banished was Dante's own friend, fellow poet, and fellow White, Guido Cavalcanti.

Eager to extend the domain of the Roman Catholic Church over Tuscany, Pope Boniface VIII, who had taken office in 1294, profited from the internal discord of Florence. Dante read the aims of Boniface and was among the first to oppose them. He tried to neutralize the secret maneuvers of Cardinal Matteo d'Acquasparta, who had been sent by the pope to Florence in May 1300. The cardinal's apparent aim was to pacify and reconcile factions in the city; in reality he intended to use those very conflicts to affirm papal influence in Florence with the open support of the Blacks.

The Signoria did not yield, and the pope finally ordered the cardinal to excommunicate all the magistrates of Florence and to confiscate their holdings. At the end of September 1300, when Dante was no longer in office, the cardinal launched an interdict denying the magistrates of Florence sacraments and Christian burial.

In 1301 Boniface decided to send Charles of Valois to Florence, again with the pretext of bringing about peace between the factions, and again with the real aim of helping the Blacks regain power and of destroying the republican constitution.

In October 1301 Dante was sent to Rome with two other representatives of the commune to ask Boniface to clarify his intentions. The pope sent the other two ambassadors back to Florence so that they might persuade the Florentines to yield to him, but he seems to have kept Dante, from whom he had most to fear, in or near Rome. In the interim Charles of Valois, helped by the Blacks, entered Florence on the first of November without encountering the opposition of the Whites. Once they had power, the Blacks levied penalties and confiscations against the most representative members of the Whites. Among these was Dante, who was asked to appear before the judges in order to defend himself from accusations formulated without proofs, of barratry, of opposition to the pope and to Charles of Valois, and of having fomented discord and imperiled peace. Dante did not present himself, and on January 27, 1302, he was condemned—in absentia—to two years of exile, to perpetual exclusion from public office, and to the payment of a ruinous fine of five thousand florins within three days. News of the condemnation reached Dante when he had not yet returned to Florence (Leonardo Bruni, Dante's fifteenth-century biographer, places him in Siena then). On the tenth of March, because Dante had not appeared, he was condemned by a new sentence to the confiscation of all his goods and to death by burning should he fall into the hands of the commune.

Thus began the exile that would keep Dante away from Florence until his death.

In exile he wandered through many cities, depended on the generosity of many lords, became aware of how hard it is "to climb and to descend the stairs of others" and how "salt-bitter is the bread" in the houses of others: the arrows of "the bow of exile" (*Par.* XVII, 55–60).

In 1303 or 1304 Dante was at the court of the Scaligers in Verona, which he refers to as his "first refuge and . . . inn" (*Par.* XVII, 70). From Verona he probably returned to Tuscany, specifically Arezzo, and then he may have spent time in Treviso, Padua, Venice, Bologna, and Reggio Emilia. In 1306 he was in Lunigiana as the guest of the Malaspina family; they charged him with handling peace negotiations with the bishop of Luni. Early and late in his exile, he was in the Casentino, and in 1308 he was in Lucca. Boccaccio and others also assign to him a stay in Paris. And even this is only a partial list of possibilities.

In every way, Osip Mandelstam is justified in wondering "how many shoe soles, how many ox-hide soles, how many sandals Alighieri wore out in the course of his poetic work, wandering about on the goat-paths of Italy."

Between 1302 and 1304 the exiled Whites, among them Dante, made a considerable number of attempts to reenter Florence, allying themselves with the long-since-exiled Ghibellines. All of their attempts failed, and Dante detached himself definitively from that "wicked, foolish company" and decided to become a party unto himself (see *Par.* XVII, 62–69 and *Inf.* XV, 70–72)—himself and his prophetic-poetic missions.

For wherever Dante went in his exile, he saw an Italy rent by internal wars and encountered other exiles banished from their cities. By Dante's time even southern Italy—once joined under a single monarch, Frederick II—had seen Sicily dissociate itself. Frederick himself, a notorious freethinker, is placed in Canto X of the *Inferno* with "Epicurus and his followers." But in his time Frederick was as formidable an emperor as Boniface, in his time, was a pope. No figure in the thirteenth century gave more flesh to that phantom resurrection of the Roman Empire of the West: the German-based Holy Roman Empire. No figure, after his death, so incited a desire for symbolic return in a successor figure. The true political unity of the Holy Roman Empire was merely a fiction by now, but it was still a fiction that had enormous motivating force as a political idea—especially for Dante.

Meditating on the cause of Italy's afflictions and divisiveness, Dante thought he had found its origin in the lack of a supreme secular head, one who could bring justice and peace among peoples. The Roman Empire was considered by Dante to have been a providential means to meet this need, as he explained in a Latin work of his exile, *Monarchia* (II, i, 2–3, see below); but since the death of Frederick II, no emperor had come again to Italy to resume the imperial crown, and thus the throne of the empire was, to all effects, vacant.

But the years 1308–1312 offered the possibility of the return of a Holy Roman Emperor to Italy. After the death of Boniface in 1303 and the brief pontificate of Benedict XI, which ended in 1305, the archbishop of Bordeaux became Pope Clement V (*Inf.* xiv, 82–88). In 1309 Clement had established himself in Avignon. Clement was a Frenchman in France, and the French were inveterately anti-imperial. Despite Clement's affiliations, he announced in 1310 the descent into Italy of the emperor Henry VII, who had been elected in 1308, and invited all to welcome Henry with honors. It was especially this news that kindled Dante's hope for imperial restoration. The emperor seemed to Dante to be a possible bringer of peace to the Italian communes, and Dante, describing himself as "a humble Italian in unmerited exile," wrote three political epistles in Latin. The first, of October 1310, to the lords and people of Italy, exhorted them to favor the task of the emperor in restoring peace. The second, of March 1311, to the Florentines, rebuked them—"the most empty-headed of all the Tuscans, crazy by nature and crazy by corruption"—for their hostility to the emperor. And the third, of April 1311, written to the emperor himself, asked him to reestablish justice and order in Florence.

Dante's hope was not to be realized. Henry was indeed crowned at Milan in 1311 and at Rome in 1312. But his siege of Florence in 1312 was allowed to lapse quickly (a glorious episode for the Florentines, but for Dante, a disaster). By then Clement, under pressure from the French, had aligned himself against Henry; and Robert of Anjou, the king of Naples, declared the throne of the empire vacant and transferred all imperial rights to the pope. On August 21, 1313, Henry died suddenly at Buonconvento, and the concrete hope of many exiles for a reconstituted empire faded definitively. (At the next election for emperor, no candidate could command sufficient consensus.)

Whether before or after the destruction of Dante's hope in Henry (somewhere in the period from 1308 to 1317—with conjectures ranging widely), Dante made plain the nature of his political ideas in a passionate pamphlet, *Monarchia* (Monarchy). With historical and philosophical arguments, Dante sustained the authority and independence of the emperor. For him the papacy and the empire were two suns, not—as some Guelphs contended—a sun and a moon; each derived its own light directly from God and was destined to illuminate all of humanity. The pope would guide men to eternal happiness, and the emperor would guide them to earthly happiness. Neither of them, however, was to usurp the task of the other. The Church must renounce all temporal power, remaining scrupulously within the spiritual realm. (This requirement accounts for Dante's vehemence against the Donation of Constantine [*Inf.* xix, 115–117]).

The urgency of Dante's political epistles and *Monarchia* was certainly heightened by the fact that the Church, though it preserved its spiritual prestige until the end of the thirteenth century, had lost the theocratic power that it enjoyed in preceding centuries. Boniface VIII had attempted in vain to resurrect the ancient universal power of the Church; but after him, and because of his policies, the Church became, with Clement V's transfer of the papacy to Avignon, an instrument in the hands of France.

At the death of Clement in 1314, some eight months after the death of Henry VII, Dante wrote another epistle, this time to the Italian cardinals assembled at Carpentras near Avignon to elect a new pope. After denouncing those who are "shepherds only in name," Dante pleads for the return of the papacy to Rome. This plea, too, proved fruitless. The Italians were expelled from the conclave; and two years later, in 1316, still another French pope, John XXII, was elected. (Much of the hope and the wormwood of Dante's years in exile are condensed in Beatrice's last words to Dante, *Par.* XXX, 133–148. There in addition to denouncing Boniface, she praises the "lofty" Henry VII and excoriates Clement.)

Perhaps because he had written the epistle to the emperor, Dante was excluded from the amnesty offered to the exiles by Florence in 1311; and when a new amnesty was granted in May 1315, Dante refused the conditions the Florentines offered as too humiliating for his conscience. In a letter to "a Florentine friend," whom the poet calls "father," Dante declared that he would never reenter Florence except under honorable conditions (*Epistola* XII, 4). On November 6, 1315—since Dante had not submitted to the conditions required to obtain amnesty—his death sentence was reaffirmed, but now it included not only Dante but his sons, who had been with him for some time.

Between 1312 and 1321, the year of his death, Dante passed from one court to another. In Verona, at the court of Cangrande Della Scala, Dante completed the final stages of his work on the *Inferno* and *Purgatorio* (possibly between 1314 and 1315). There, too, he began work on the *Paradiso,* dedicating his work-in-progress to Cangrande. From Verona he went—possibly in 1318—to Ravenna, to the court of Guido Novell da Polenta, a nephew of Francesca, the woman Dante immortalized in Canto V of the *Inferno.*

In 1319–1320 the scholar Giovanni del Virgilio invited Dante to Bologna to be crowned there as poet. In their correspondence, in Latin hexameters, Dante declined the invitation. With the completion of *Paradiso,* he explained, he hoped that he might be crowned on the banks of his "native Arno" if he "should ever return there."

In 1320 Dante did accept an invitation to return to Verona to lecture on a scientific topic. That lecture is a small treatise in Latin now known as the *Questio de aqua et terra.*

In 1321, possibly on a return voyage from an ambassadorial mission to Venice that he had undertaken at the request of Guido da Polenta, Dante fell ill. He died in Ravenna, probably in the night between the thirteenth and fourteenth of September. The complete *Paradiso* was made public posthumously.

CANTO I
The Hard Begin

LETTERIO CASSATA

Translated and edited by Charles Ross
and Anthony Oldcorn, with a foreword
by Charles Ross and Allen Mandelbaum

> When I had journeyed half of our life's way
> I found myself within a shadowed forest
>
> (I, 1–2)

Foreword

The "possessive of human solidarity" (Spitzer)—"our life's way"—links the particularity of Dante the wayfarer to the universality of humanity. And nothing in the work Dante called his *Comedy* or other works, his poems, letters, and treatises, suggests that "our" is to be understood as applying to other than both men and women. In the *Convivio* (IV, xxiii, 6–10) Dante fixes thirty-five years as the midpoint of human life, following Psalm 89:10 (90:10 in the King James), which sets seventy years as the length of our days. Thus, for Dante himself, who was born in 1265, the year 1300 accords well with the cited texts and with a passage in Isaias (38:10), "In the midst of my days I shall go to the gates of Hell."

The "shadowed" or dark forest is the way station to many images of darkness, blindness, and obscurity that obsess Hell—that realm in which the sun never appears, as it does throughout Purgatory—though Virgil, somewhat clairvoyantly, will refer to the movement of the unseen skies on the earth above as "starless" (III, 23—while *Inferno* begins at night, *Purgatorio* begins at dawn and *Paradiso* at noon). Here the forest precedes the journey through Hell. It is the dark wood of life on earth when lived in sin; it is Dante's interior wood; and it is the wood of political darkness, of Florence, of Italy, of papal corruption, of the absences of imperial authority.

At this point Dante sees the alternative to the dark forest: the "hill"—that is, the path to virtue, which leads upward. The hill is illuminated by the sun, which Dante does not see directly but whose rays stand for the light of

God's grace. Dante's access to the hill, however, is blocked by the three beasts he encounters—beasts symbolic of different aspects of human sinfulness (31–60). For most early commentators—and, after many alternate proposals, for many moderns—the leopard represents lust; the lion, pride; the she-wolf, avarice or cupidity. Whatever specific area of sin is assigned to each animal, the Italian certainly links them alliteratively to each other—*lonza-leone-lupa*—and to Lucifer in Canto XXXIII.

Not Dante, then, but the representative pilgrim whom Beatrice will finally—and for the only time—name as Dante (*Purg.* xxx, 55), finds himself blocked by wild beasts, unable to ascend the illuminated hill before him, lost in a shadowed forest, until Virgil rescues him. The author of the epic *Aeneid,* the greatest literary work of classical Roman literature, tells him that only by indirection can he find directions out. Dante calls his work a "comedy" (*Inf.* XVI, 128 and XXI, 2) because it moves from the despair of Hell through Purgatory to a paradisial vision of God. He must, says Virgil, first enter Hell.

It is not known exactly when Dante began to write the *Inferno.* But he was surely writing while in exile from Florence, and he was constructing a fiction dated before both his exile and his act of writing began. His work is therefore a product of his mature years, a lesson in adult education. To read through the *Inferno, Purgatorio,* and *Paradiso* today is to raise the same issues Dante faced after he was thirty-five. As an adult, Dante turns for insight to an author whose texts young schoolboys have pored over, often learning to dislike them and then forgetting them in later years. How do we remember or re-find in later life what we wish we had known better in our student years? For Dante to meet Virgil in middle age is exactly our situation when we confront Dante's text. However badly our teachers taught us or poorly we pay attention, they and the generations that proclaim a classic at least point us in the right direction.

Dante's problem in the first canto is to point himself in the right direction. In his fiction he has no choice: wild beasts prevent his ascent, fear in his heart freezes him. But when composing his poem, Dante had many choices, and it is the work of literary criticism to point them out. By meeting Virgil in his poem, Dante tells us whom he read for guidance. By writing in vernacular Italian, Dante broadens his audience beyond the educated male circle who knew Latin. He brings Virgil to life, just as those who write commentary lectures must try to bring Dante to life. The question is always, Did Dante succeed in his retelling? The question is the same for us. Can we bring Dante to life?

With this understanding, that Dante's animation of Virgil is the same as our problem of animating Dante, we may begin by asking, How difficult was it for Dante to begin? The answer is that Dante learned as he composed: if he sees a vision of the empyrean in the *Paradiso,* he is also a more experienced poet by then. This essay therefore looks at the difficulties of

Dante's opening, what Spenser would later call "the hard begin" (*Faerie Queene* III, iii, 21).

The Hard Begin

One of Dante's most informed and judicious Italian readers, Natalino Sapegno, denounced the first canto of Dante's *Divine Comedy*. Reluctantly, he found the unpracticed narrator in less than total command of his means and goals. The symbolism of the prologue is at times less than transparent. The narrative and dramatic technique are labored and contrived. The characters are wooden and not altogether convincing. Dante obscures his moral message. His art is unripe. And yet, Sapegno recognized that the first canto offers a solemn and arresting introduction to more than just the *Inferno*. It "presents *in nuce* the full complexity of the elements that converge" in the whole poem. "For now, the journey is more of a dream vision than a drama or a narrative. The allegory tends to be superimposed on the fantastic plot. . . . The *Comedy* must be seen as a work that takes shape as it goes along, not an organic, preconstituted block of forms and concepts." Since Sapegno's diffidence reflects that of a number of modern critics, I should like to take these reservations as my point of departure and submit several impugned passages in Dante's text to detailed analysis.

Dante's is still a manuscript culture. The absence of the smallest scrap of writing in the author's own hand, let alone a preliminary sketch or preparatory draft of the *Comedy*, forces us to reconstruct conjecturally the growth of the poem as a whole and of its individual parts, starting with this introductory canto. We must examine the letter of the text, following the principles of historical philology and textual criticism. This method will allow us to avoid the error of those interpreters who "start by discussing Dante's symbols in the abstract and bend them to fit systems arbitrarily constructed out of elements alien to the poet's own thought" (Barbi, 31). Otherwise, "exegetical criticism becomes a meaningless bandying of words, something we practitioners ought to feel slightly ashamed of" (Parodi, 322).

The Opening Allusion

In the twentieth canto of the *Paradiso,* in the sphere of Jupiter, Dante finds himself together with the soul of Ezechias, thirteenth king of Judah, whose life is narrated in three parallel biblical stories (2 Kings 18–20, 2 Paralipomenon 29–32, and Isaias 36–39). Dante does not name Ezechias but refers to him as he who "delayed his death through truthful penitence," adding "now he has learned that the eternal judgment / remains unchanged, though worthy prayer below / makes what falls due today take place tomorrow" (*Par.* xx, 51–54). From the Bible we know that when Ezechias fell gravely ill, the prophet Isaias announced his impending death. Ezechias then implored God to grant that he might live another fifteen years. Vandelli observed that Ezechias's prayer was "anything but penitent": "I beseech thee, O Lord, remember how I have walked before thee in truth, and with a perfect heart, and have done that which is good in thy sight" (Isaias 38:3). Sapegno, indeed, goes so far as to cast doubt on the traditional identification of the soul in *Paradiso* xx as Ezechias. Mattalia, however, has pointed out that the chief source for Dante's reference is in fact Ezechias's song of thanks to the Lord (Isaias 38:10–20, in particular verse 17: "thou hast cast all my sins behind thy back"). In this song, the miraculously cured king gives poignant expression to contrasting sentiments— past pain and sorrow, renewed joy and hope—that led Dante to exalt him in *Paradiso.* Dante gives him a conspicuous place among the spirits that make up the eye of the Eagle, the living symbol of Justice.

Without a doubt, the beginning of Dante's sacred song derives from the beginning of the song of Ezechias ("In the midst of my days I shall go to the gates of hell" [Isaias 38:10]). The allusion invests "the cold chronological facts with a cloak of sacrality" (F. Mazzoni, 19). It brings a grandiose, even liturgical note to the work's exordium. "Everything to come, even before the narrative begins, is wrapped in an aura of solemnity and intensity of significance that the reader cannot escape: he will be transported, as if in a trance, by the power of the narration toward unheard-of events. . . . At the same time, he will be continually cajoled—by a voice that from time to time is heard in the text, saying 'Reader!'—to open his eyes, to distinguish and analyze the various levels of meaning that assault him simultaneously" (Risset, 84–85). There is nothing strange about Dante's method. For Dante and his contemporaries were supremely knowledgeable in the language of the Scriptures and often used biblical references to confer significance on their subjects (Gilson, 74).

Like Ezechias, Dante is on the verge of dying in the prime of his life (see *Inf.* ii, 107–108 and *Purg.* i, 58–60); but then, illuminated by grace, he changes the course of his life, urging himself to shun his past and redeem the future from sin. In the "shadowed forest" he experiences, like Ezechias before him, "the bitterness of the thought of the evil he had committed and its dangers" (Tommaseo). Just as the eyes of Ezechias are described as "looking upward" (Isaias 38:14), so Dante gazes "on high" (16). Just as Ezechias "wept with great weeping" (Isaias 38:3), thereby making his prayer to God acceptable, so Dante weeps, and only his "tearfulness" (92) induces Virgil ultimately to help him with words of salvation (Matthew 5:4, "Blessed are they that mourn: for they shall be comforted"). Finally, like Ezechias, Dante goes in the midst of his days to the gates of hell and returns, restored to health by the divine will.

One source must have been instrumental in leading Dante to identify with this intrepid king and see him as the very model of the sinner who finds himself and redeems himself by means of repentance and hope. That source is the sermon that Bernard of Clairvaux devoted to the song of Ezechias (*Sermones de diversis* III, *Patr. Lat.* 183.546–551)—the same Bernard who will be Dante's guide in the closing cantos of *Paradiso*. According to Bernard's interpretation, the words of Ezechias's song signify the grace visited (*gratiae visitatio*) on the sinner whom fear of God urges toward wisdom (*qui timore Dei initatur ad sapientiam*). Dante's finding himself within the shadowed forest means more (and less) than the physical realization of his topographical whereabouts. The moral implications are paramount. "It is already a kind of sudden awakening, an arousal into light" (Pagliaro 1967, 13). "When reason stirred, he realized that till now he had been led by appetite" (Daniello). The first effect of the *gratiae visitatio* is the awareness that one is lost. It is also the first glimmer of a resolution to change.

The identification of Dante with Ezechias offers a model to the reader, who, following suit, can identify with Dante and, through him, with Ezechias himself. In the controversial letter to Cangrande, the author informs us that the purpose of his "poetic fiction" is "to remove those living in this life from the state of misery and lead them to a state of happiness" (*Epistola* XIII, 79). He offers his story as an *exemplum* to those living in this life, affirming a universal community of spiritual interest, "a protean relationship, constantly returning and renewed throughout the poem, between one man and mankind in general, between the fate of the individual and the fate of all" (Getto, 2).

This bond of solidarity between the pilgrim/poet and each of his readers (the story is told of you!, *de te fabula narratur*) is quickly established by the "our" of line 1. The universalizing passive verb of the Italian text (*era smarrita*) further suggests that the path was lost "not merely to Dante but to mankind in general" (Castelvetro), as do the two present tenses used to describe the forest (*è cosa dura* and *è amara*). Together they "suggest, not a fearful memory, but a real and present actuality" (Vandelli). The "path that does not stray" (3), was already a metaphorical topos. It is found in classical literature (Cicero, *De finibus* I, 18, 57; *De officiis* I, 32, 188) and in the Bible (Proverbs 2:13: "Who leave the right way, and walk by dark ways"; 2 Peter 2:15: "Leaving the right way that have gone astray").

The Opening Scene

Duplicity and ambiguity characterize the setting, actors, and events of the poem's opening. In the words of Croce's memorable demurral, "we find ourselves in a forest that is not a forest, we see a hill that is not a hill, we look up toward a sun that is not a sun, and we encounter three wild animals, that are and are not three wild animals" (Croce, 73). But, as Singleton for one has shown, "the layering of meaning by no means implies that Dante at the outset is under some strain and special labor to get his poem under way." Instead, "the poet is deliberately leading the reader into double vision, to place him on what he had every right to assume would be the most familiar of scenes. . . . This language of metaphor (for all the poet could anticipate of his readers) could hardly be more familiar, nor these figures more worn by use" (Singleton, 6–7).

The image of the forest had been a favorite in the patristic tradition at least since Augustine (*In Ioannem* v, tr. xvi, 6: *In hac tam immensa silva plena insidiarum et periculorum* [In this forest so immense and full of snares and dangers]). "What Dante says about the forest in which he finds himself astray is merely a figurative way of indicating his own moral aberration; . . . according to Thomas Aquinas's definition (*Summa theologica* I, 1, 10, 3), the literal meaning is not the figure in itself but what is figured by it, in other words, what the figure points to" (Barbi, 119). As Dante's son Pietro Alighieri explained, "Proceeding metaphorically, he represents his self-discovery in a shadowed forest, that is, in a state of vice . . . in which the sun of truth does not shine." A decade or so later, Benvenuto da Imola affirms that "this same forest is the vicious worldly state. . . . And he calls it 'shadowed' on account of ignorance and sin."

The dread and horror of the forest dominate the second and third tercets. The tone is established by the initial interjection *Ahi* ("Ah" [4]), "an adverb expressive of surprise or pain" (Serravalle). It is reinforced by the demonstrative *esta* ("that" [5]), which, like the Latin *iste*, is used by Christian writers, often conveying a nuance of repulsion (e.g., Leo the Great, *Sermones* LXXXII, 4: *silvam istam frementium bestiarum* [this forest of raging beasts], referring to Rome at the time of Peter's coming). The horror of the forest is such that even in recall it renews Dante's fear, and Virgil's example (*Aen.* II, 204, *horresco referens* [I shudder / to tell what happened]) guides Dante as he exploits the motif of the persistence or renewal of an emotion in memory.

Among the other motifs of the narrative, the "sleep" of line 11 signifies the eclipse of the vigilance of reason and the consequent forgetfulness of one's Maker (see Augustine, *Enarrationes in psalmos* LXII, 4: *Somnus autem animae est oblivisci Deum suum* [the sleep of the soul is to forget one's God]). The illuminated "shoulders" (16), or summit of the hill, allude to the happy state of moral freedom enjoyed in the well-ordered society, free from base desire or *cupiditas*. The "planet / which serves to lead men straight" is the sun. The "three beasts" personify "the three radical impediments identified in the First Epistle of John (2:16: *concupiscentia carnis* [the concupiscence of the flesh], *superbia vitae* [the pride of life], and *concupiscentia oculorum* [the concupiscence of the eyes], otherwise known as *cupitas* [cupidity, greed, avarice]). These images belong "to the literal, not the allegorical level" (Barbi, 75), because Dante represents his metaphoric ambience as real. But the metaphoric language gives life to space. The landscape described by Dante is the horizon of his soul.

The Poet's Statement of Purpose

After the tactical retreat of verses 4–7, where Dante expresses the horror that still assails him even when he only thinks about that forest, he responds to a possible objection on the reader's part: if memory is so unbearably bitter, why make matters worse by dwelling on it? The answer is that he may "retell the good discovered there" (8).

Sapegno explains that the "good" refers to the help sent by heaven in the person of Virgil, while the "other things I saw" refers to the three beasts soon to be described. He admits, however, that, to be perfectly accurate, none of these things are encountered in the forest. The truth is that the "good" discovered in the forest can only be the initial salvific effect of the *gratiae visitatio,* the visitation of grace, what Boccaccio called "the divine mercy [which] in the dark night of our ignorance and guilt is ready with open arms to look not at the wrongs we have committed but only at the good disposition of the soul willing to turn to receive it." Dante's entire journey, from the moment the pilgrim finds himself astray to the climactic moment in the Empyrean heaven takes place under the aegis of divine grace. "All of the good to come, of whose conquest the journey is an allegorical and fantastic representation, is potentially contained in this 'good' that Dante claims to have discovered in the forest, because it is from here that it all proceeds" (Mattalia). But "in order to treat of the good that comes from a knowledge of sin, he will describe the punishments that sin incurs" (Ottimo). The "other things," then, are the punishments of hell and not, as the accepted interpretation would have it, the three beasts, who will appear, as Virgil will appear, *outside* the forest.

This identification implies that Virgil will lead Dante to hell "through this same valley . . . but by a speculative route (*per via speculationis*)" (Benvenuto). Just as the punishment is the intrinsic effect of the transgression, so hell too is found "within the shadowed forest." It is its foundation, no less. "The single individual cannot escape from the forest . . . otherwise than through an act of sustained introspective meditation, which leads him to the very pit of the universe, compelling him to face all of the world's evil and to overcome it cathartically in a value judgment" (F. Mazzoni, 126). After attempting, presumptuously and therefore unsuccessfully, to escape by his own devices (28–60, and see II, 41–42), Dante will have to return, under Virgil's guidance, to the "shadowed forest," plunging into its depths until he reaches the very gate of hell. The site of the world to come is in this world, *in interiore homine,* in the depths of each individual conscience.

Finally, Dante's use of the past tense deserves close attention. The "good discovered" in the bitter forest is a historical fact, something singular and exceptional, disattached and separate from the basis of that dolorous picture. But the other things "that I saw" are valued in that they are now objects of Dante's recounting and a necessary premise for evoking his own salvation.

The Terrible Panic

Once he has come to his moral senses, the pilgrim is seized by a terror so intense that the blood rushes to fortify the seat of courage, flooding his heart. Understood in terms of the dynamics of medieval physiology (see Boccaccio's comment), the image of the "lake within my heart" (21) is neither precious nor contrived. It contributes, rather, to that "frightening atmosphere" that Momigliano identified as the "secret inspiration of the canto." Only the apparition of the hill lit by the rays of the sun momentarily assuages his panic fear, inspiring in him la speranza de l'altezza ("the hope of . . . climbing" [53–54]). "His fear is rightly assuaged because he conceives the hope of escaping from this forest as soon as he catches his first dim glimpse of the light of virtue" (Benvenuto).

Not even the leopard "with his speckled skin" (43) is able to extinguish that hope. But when the lion of pride appears, "head held high and ravenous with hunger" (46), fear once again takes hold. In the ensuing atmosphere of nightmarish hallucination, the very air seems "contaminated with fear" (Ungaretti). "The lion shall roar," says the prophet, "who will not fear?" (Amos 3:8). It is as if Dante's lion were to inspire even greater terror by his silence. And then the appearance of the she-wolf completely routs Dante's hope of climbing. The she-wolf of cupidity, even more than the lion of pride, literally emanates terror: in the Italian text, "fear issued from her sight" (la paura . . . uscia di sua vista [53]). For a sublime contrast to the fear in the air in line 48, we must see Paradiso XXVII, 4–5 ("What I saw seemed to me to be a smile / the universe had smiled")—a "potent and graceful image" (Torraca). Three intense images—the air that seems imbued with fear and trembling, the heavens that seem to revel, the universe that seems to smile—summarize the experience of the entire poem: a progressive conquest of spaces ever vaster and more bright, more blissful and more free.

"The Task So Quickly Undertaken" (Inf. II, 42)

The simile of lines 55–60 ("he who glories while he gains / will . . . lament") effectively expresses Dante's sadness at having lost "the hope / of ever climbing up that mountain slope." Some commentators see the subject of the simile as a miser, some see the gambler of Purgatorio VI, and others the farmer of Inferno XXIV. But the psychology of Dante's persona, that of a sinner who has found himself, does not seem comparable to a gamester or an agricultural worker. It would be better to read these lines more generally: "a man intent on achieving some goal who sees that the time is near which will deprive him of it" (Venturi, 175) or "anyone who has ever rejoiced over some acquisition" (Padoan). The terms with which the victim's predicament is evoked are in fact so broad that it might even be argued that we are dealing with a false or specious simile. This variety of simile has no precedent in classical literature, although the Bible contains a number of examples ("But I, as a deaf man, heard not: and as a dumb man not opening his mouth" [Psalm 37:14]; "I am become as a man without help" [Psalm 87:54]). Rather than calling them pseudo-similes, I prefer the term "inclusive similes," since they have the formal characteristics of a traditional simile, but with a difference. A traditional simile brings out the common characteristic linking two different objects. In an inclusive simile, the second term of comparison includes the first. The frequency of this figure in the *Comedy* underscores the exemplarity of the pilgrim Dante's role as Everyman.

The figure of Dante at this point may be illuminated by a comparison with the Greek Ulysses, who will appear among the fraudulent counselors in Canto XXVI. Dante struggles to attain the summit of the mountain that is "the origin and cause of every joy" (78), a concrete metaphor for the moral freedom achievable, however imperfectly, "in the active life (that is, in the exercise of the moral virtues)" (*Convivio* IV, xxii, 18). In contrast, the goal of Ulysses' last voyage is "the world that is unpeopled" (xxvi, 117), the island mountain of Purgatory, whose summit—though Ulysses, ironically, would be the last to know it—is in fact the seat of the Earthly Paradise.

Inspired by the sight of the "shoulders" of that "hill" "clothed" by the rays of the morning sun, Dante undertakes his journey with overhasty confidence, with the same "impetuous and unpremeditated presumption" attributed to Saint Peter in the *Monarchia* (III, ix, 9): "to which he was driven not only by the sincerity of his faith, but also, I believe, by the purity and simplicity of his nature." The words of Canto II, 42 ("the task so quickly undertaken"), must refer to this initial misplaced confidence in his own resources rather than to the obedient pilgrim's willingness to follow Virgil in the last line of the first canto ("Then he set out, and I moved on behind him"). Similarly, the "folly" attributed by Virgil to Dante in *Purg.* I, 59, refers to the pilgrim's first straying from the path and implicitly qualifies his error as one of excessive trust in his purely human capabilities. It cannot have been intellectual pride that caused Dante to lose his way in the shadowed forest, because he was in a state of somnolence. "He entered the forest when he relaxed the mental vigilance that kept him on the true path" (Pagliaro 1961, 13), "not by a willful choice of evil but out of negligent disregard of his spiritual responsibilities" (Padoan).

The Dante who, in obedience to the Divine Will, allows himself to be led by Virgil through the Otherworlds of punishment and expiation is in no way comparable to Ulysses. Not so the Dante who, fearful of being trapped forever in the forest, attempts in his folly to scale the mountain of delight, without realizing that the ascent is barred until such time as the divinely predestined Greyhound comes to slay the she-wolf of cupidity. The two are linked by their misplaced faith in their own self-sufficiency, their refusal to recognize their limitations, and their failure to seek the help of divine grace—without which a soul "may long to fly but has no wings" (*Par.* XXXIII, 15).

Virgil's Long Silence

The phrase "step by step" (*a poco a poco*) describes the slow but ineluctable retreat of Dante before the she-wolf: "he that contemneth small things, shall fall by little and little" (Ecclesiasticus 19:1). Two lines later, I prefer the reading *ruinava* to Petrocchi's *rovinava* or for that matter *ruvinava*. All three are attested in the manuscript tradition. The metrical dieresis on the epenthetic *rüinava*, however, coupled with the pair of bisyllables *basso loco* at the end of the line, opportunely slows down the rhythm, suggesting a slow and deliberate withdrawal, quite the opposite of the precipitate tumble imagined by most commentators. Dante's retreat is to spiritual *ruin,* the renunciation of salvation (D'Ovidio, 466; Mazzali, 114). "Morally, the *basso loco* (lower ground) signifies the mind's dejection for the thwarted venture and its dread of dwelling in continued misery" (Bianchi).

This is not the place to rehearse again the various allegorical explanations that have been offered of line 63, a notorious crux in Dante exegesis. They are discussed at length in my 1970 article in *Studi danteschi.* Suffice it to recognize the unfoundedness of the widespread opinion, given authority by Sapegno's repetition, that "taken literally and interpreted rationally, the characterization [of Virgil] is incongruous to the circumstances and not especially clear." The allegory remains arbitrary and obtrusive (and its interpretation controversial) only as long as Virgil's faintness is seen as a *result* of his silence. The phrase "because of the long silence," which, in Sapegno's traditional analysis, grammatically qualifies "faint" and can be "justified solely in light of the allegorical role attributed to the figure of Virgil," actually qualifies the verb "seemed." "Dante does not say that he *was* faint but that he *seemed* faint, that he [Dante], in other words, conjectured from Virgil's appearance that the latter was faint" (Andreoli). The point is Virgil's silence *now,* not his past silence. Virgil continues to remain silent in the face of Dante's clear and urgent need for his immediate help. This is what gives the pilgrim the impression that he is "faint," incapable of speaking, or at least of making himself heard: "for he who sees a need but waits to be / asked is already set on cruel refusal" (*Purg.* XVII, 59–60).

We should bear in mind, however, that Virgil, for all his "persuasive word" (II, 67), could give Dante no immediate help against the she-wolf. All he could do was to guide him on "another path" (91). Why, then, waste words? "A wise man will hold his peace till he see opportunity: but a babbler, and a fool will regard no time" (Ecclesiasticus 20:7). Dante must first

experience on his own and to the hilt the obstacles that prevent his climbing the mountain of delight, so he can assess the total inadequacy of his
own resources. Only then will he be ready to accept the idea of the otherworldly journey, beginning with the descent into hell, as his only means of
salvation. This is why Virgil did not address the retreating pilgrim. As for
the length of the silence, that is a subjective impression. "However brief it
may have been, that silence seemed mortally long to the pilgrim in his ex-
cruciating anguish" (Pézard, 341–342).

Dante cannot know the identity of the figure who suddenly appears before his eyes. Only after casting a terrified glance around him, and seeing no
one else "in that vast wilderness" (64), does he finally summon up the
strength to cry out, in the words of the contrite David, which are also the
words of any repentant sinner: "*Miserere* di me" ("Have pity on me" [65]).
But even after that humble and heartfelt cry, Virgil does not pronounce
the salutary words. He merely reveals himself to be the great poet from
Mantua, asking Dante the leading question: "But why do you return to
wretchedness? / Why not climb up the mountain of delight?" (76–77). The
question is maieutic: "having Dante confess his own impotence is the most
effective way to prepare him to accept Virgil's proposal, his invitation to the
spiritual journey that will rehabilitate Dante to the good and thereby save
him" (Del Lungo). At first the pilgrim has difficulty believing that the figure before him is really "that Virgil" (79), "our greatest muse" (*Par.* xv, 26).
Dante's shame ("fear of being dishonored through some fault" [*Convivio* iv,
xix, 10]) no doubt derives from the fact "that he did not recognize him
sooner" (Buti). His embarrassment also stems, however, from the gross
error of having believed "faint" or tongue-tied history's most eloquent
speaker, "the fountain / that freely pours so rich a stream of speech" (79–
80)! Virgil will utter his salutary words only after he has seen the sincerity
of Dante's prayers and the firmness of his determination confirmed by his
"tearfulness" (92).

The Greyhound and Italy

It was the figure of the she-wolf *cupiditas* that "generated that of the Greyhound, the swift and skilful hunter" (Torraca). "The greyhound is a breed
of dog," explains Boccaccio, "marvelously inimical to wolves: the author
declares that one of these greyhounds will come, capable of 'inflicting
painful death on her.'" Not necessarily a Greyhound with a capital letter
then, and not just any greyhound, but the one greyhound with the power
to kill the she-wolf, who, inasmuch as she is a creature of hell, "cannot die
a natural death" (Castelvetro), but only a "painful" (102)—in other words,
violent—one. An emperor, in other words: "one prince who, possessing all
things and being unable to desire anything else, would keep the kings content within the boundaries of their kingdoms and preserve among them the

peace in which the cities might rest. Through this peace the communities would come to love one another, and by this love all households would provide for their needs, which when provided would bring man happiness, for this is the end for which he is born" (*Convivio* IV, iv, 4). "For the emperor alone to Dante's manner of thinking has the institutional role of eliminating *cupiditas*" (F. Mazzoni, 131). The alliteration of the noun *veltro* with the future verb *verrà*, in enjambment, as well as the internal rhyme of *verrà* with *farà*, underscore in the Italian text the solemn and ringing tone of the prophecy: a prophecy *ante eventum*, founded not on the certainty of fact but on a fervent inner aspiration.

Dante's prediction echoes Virgil's (*Aen.* I, 286–287), cited by Dante himself in *Epistola* VII, 13:

> *Nascetur pulchra Troianus origine Caesar,*
> *imperium Oceano, famam qui terminet astris*

Then a Trojan / Caesar shall rise out of the splendid line. / His empire's boundary shall be the Ocean; / the only border to his fame, the stars.

The expression *tra feltro e feltro* ("between two felts"[105])—"one of those obscure phrases that form part of the prophetic style" (Momigliano)—succeeds in giving the prophecy "its arcane and hermetic character, rendering it more suggestive and solemn" (Grabher). Among the many conjectural glosses, many of them speculative in the extreme, I much prefer the astrological explanation, already proposed by several of the early commentators —for the Anonimo Fiorentino, for instance, the Greyhound must be "favorably complexioned by the heavenly constellations"—and perfected by Olschki (55 n.2). With the term *feltro* ("felt," a metonym for "felt headgear"), Dante indicates the distinguishing attribute of the Dioscuri, Roman deities recognizable by their cone-shaped felt caps, implying that the birth of the liberator will take place beneath the particular auspices indicated by the constellation of the *pilleati fratres*, the "felt-cap-wearing brothers," Castor and Pollux. The poet nourished a special affection for the "stars of glory" of Gemini, the "constellation steeped / in mighty force," the sign of the zodiac under which he himself was born: "all of my genius— / whatever be its worth—has you as source" (*Par.* XXII, 112–113). The idea put forward by Olschki, however, that by the Greyhound Dante intended to designate himself simply does not hold water. In the first instance, it is contradicted by the use of the future ("his place of birth *shall be*" [105; my emphasis]), which can hardly be applicable to a thirty-five-year-old. "It is further undermined by the inconsistency involved in Dante's putting himself forward as the savior of the world from the she-wolf in the very same breath in which he admits to having been bested by her on the personal level" (Figurelli, 115).

Just as in line 75 Dante's *superbo Ilïon* ("pride of Ilium") contains overtones of moral condemnation not present in Virgil's *superbum / Ilium (Aen.* III, 2–3), so here *quella umile Italia* ("low-lying Italy" [106]) may be seen as taking on a moral coloring absent from the Roman poet's *humilem . . . / Italiam (Aen.* III, 522–523). In Virgil the adjective stresses the non-mountainous nature of the Salentine peninsula as it appeared to the seafaring Trojans; in Dante, the humility of Italy, biblically transfigured, becomes a guarantee of her imminent salvation, as in Psalm 17:28: "For thou wilt save the humble people; but wilt bring down the eyes of the proud." "Proud Ilium was laid low, humble Italy will be raised up" (Pietrobono). "The liberator of the world will come when Italy is ready (see also *Par.* XXX, 136–138), in other words, when she is prepared to receive him with the humility and devotion that are his due: Italy will be saved when she becomes humble, no longer rebellious and proud, in the sight of God's Emissary" (G. Mazzoni, 184). The adjective *umile* is, then, proleptic: "Italy will be saved if and when she is free of the pride that brought Troy to her ruin" (Montanari). Not "vile" or "miserable," then, but "compliant," "meek," and therefore evangelically destined—see Matthew 5:4: "Blessed are the meek: for they shall possess the land"—to be rewarded. The idea of humility as the basis for expiation and redemption was part of the ascetic tradition inherited by Aquinas, and Bernard of Clairvaux's *Tractatus de gradibus humilitatis et superbiae* and Anselm of Aosta's *De similitudine* (99 ff.) are very close in spirit to Dante. It has been pointed out that the virtue of humility is the guiding principle in Dante's Purgatory (Tateo).

To sum up, Dante's contention is that Italy—at present anything but humble, infatuated as she is by her own "blind greediness" (*Par.* XXX, 139) and made "fierce . . . recalcitrant and savage" by the temporal power of the popes and the negligence of the German emperors (see *Purg.* VI, 76–126)—will one day humbly consent to be led and redeemed, as she was in the days of ancient Rome, by a new Caesar, by the Greyhound-Emperor ("the conqueror of raving Hesperia [i.e., Italy]," as Henry VII is called in *Epistola* VI, 12).

The Second Death

I take issue with the translator on a minor point. I interpret the Italian *grida* (117) to mean "invokes" rather than "laments." I believe, with Francesco Mazzoni, that the expression "second death" in the same line is to be read "in the technical scriptural sense of 'eternal damnation following upon the Last Judgement': all the more painful in that soul and body will be joined together again in a more complete union and hence more capable of feeling and suffering the pangs of loss (see, for this theological point, VI, 109–111: 'Though these accursed sinners never shall / attain the true perfection, yet they can / expect to be more perfect then than now'). After the Day of Judgement, in other words, the torments of the Damned will be more severe and the bliss of the Saved enhanced" (F. Mazzoni, 143). For the "second death," see Apocalypse 20:14 ("And hell and death were cast into the pool of fire. This is the second death"), repeated in 21:8, as well as Augustine, *Contra Iulianum* VI, 31. The phrase is also used in this sense by Francis of Assisi in his *Laudes creaturarum* (*la secunda morte nol farrà male* [for the second death will not harm them (31)]), not to mention Dante himself in his Latin epistle to the Florentines: "And you who transgress all laws human and divine, you whom the dread voracity of greed has caused to be ready for any wickedness, are you not even distressed by the terror of the second death *(terror secunde mortis)* . . . ?" (*Epistola* VI, 5).

As he journeys through hell, Dante will see "the ancient spirits in their pain" (116), each of whom cries out invoking the definitive damnation of the second death, "that death by which, after the general resurrection of all mankind, body and soul will be punished together in hell" (Guido da Pisa). "Resurrected on the Day of Judgement, they will be condemned body and soul for the final time; and each one cries out because in his despair he would prefer that the final sentence were already upon him" (Buti). We have only to recall what Momigliano dubbed "the first moral self-revelation of Dante's sinners, the first appalling witness to their irremediable depravation"—the all-rejecting litany of curses of III, 103–105: "they execrated God and their own parents / and humankind, and then the place and time / of their conception's seed and of their birth." In the same canto, Virgil will explain to Dante the sinners' paradoxical eagerness to cross Acheron: "because celestial justice spurs them on / so that their fear is turned into desire" (III, 125–126). "Fear is turned into desire, as it is in the man being led to the gallows: since go he must, he wants to get there quickly, having no other choice, so as to be quickly dead" (Buti). The fundamental law of hell consists precisely in this transformation of the *terror secunde mortis* into desire. "For as individuals *were* in their passions and sufferings, in their intentions and their accomplishments, so now here they are presented for ever, solidified into images of bronze" (Hegel, 1103–1104).

Some Provisional Conclusions

No other canto has attracted so many wrong-headed and implausible interpretations as the first. I take comfort in having pointed out one or two of them in this essay and, with that confidence, I would like to go a small step further and attempt to formulate a comprehensive critical judgment based on the foregoing textual analysis.

Is it true that the symbols used by Dante in Canto I are obscure or ambiguous? Is his conception provisional, tentative, and sketchy? Is there confusion and vagueness in the details? Is the psychological analysis naive by modern standards? Of course, but within certain well defined limits, first and foremost those inherent in the specifically biblical, patristic, and scholastic culture of Dante's fourteenth-century "reader," as well as those imposed by the very nature of a "work in progress," which cannot come right out and say everything all at once without risking the loss of a sense of narrative development and becoming a work of pure theology.

Apart from that, the strictures of Dante's modern critics do not seem justified. While undeniably a work *in fieri*, in the process of becoming, the *Comedy* is at the same time, and dialectically, a complex poetic structure built upon a solid base of theology and rhetoric, with no significant internal cracks or sutures. Moreover, the presumption that the work's beginning must evince the poet's inexperience and his resort to a patchwork of narrative and dramatic techniques fails to take account of the eventuality—which the rigors of exile do not appear to have precluded—of the poet's going back over his work and correcting possible incongruities and naïvetés, even though no visible traces of such a revision survive. Dante's modern critical editor, the late Giorgio Petrocchi, in fact concluded "from a series of external and internal indices" that the *Inferno*, composed between 1304 and 1308, remained "open to correction till the second half of 1314, when the author finally decided to release it" (Petrocchi, 81).

Far from lacking a narrative and dramatic dimension, the first canto falls neatly into two parts: "In the first part the author describes his ruin, in the second he illustrates the help he received for his salvation" (Boccaccio). The first part (1–60) culminates, as we saw, in the epic account of the initial attempt of the pilgrim Dante to escape the wood and scale the mountain—as reckless and taboo as the "wild flight" (XXVI, 125) of Ulysses in a later canto. The highly dramatic second part (61–136) is marked by the clash between the pilgrim's gratuitous voluntarism and the dawning of rational awareness. "We go from the brooding silence of the forest and the beasts—fearful soundless apparitions—to dialogue; from solitude to encounter—the first of the countless dramatic encounters the poem contains" (Bosco 1987, 191). The severe judgments of many modern critics seem to stem not so much from any intrinsic weakness or artistic immaturity in the poet as from the same critics' inability to comprehend these two successive moments, narrative and dramatic.

BIBLIOGRAPHY

Many of these same issues are discussed at greater length in vol. 1 of Anthony K. Cassell's monograph *Lectura Dantis Americana* (Philadelphia, 1989), which has an extensive bibliography, including an older reading of my own. My other relevant contributions include "Il disdegno di Guido," *Studi danteschi* 46 (1969): 5–49; "Il lungo silenzio di Virgilio (*Inf.* 1, 61–63)," *Studi danteschi* 47 (1970): 15–41; "morte," *Enciclopedia dantesca* 3:1038–1041 (Rome, 1971); and "Note sul testo del Canto I dell'*Inferno*," *Annali della Scuola normale superiore di Pisa*, Classe di lettere e filosofia, 3d ser., 15 (1985): 103–128. Guglielmo Gorni's *Dante nella selva: Il primo canto della "Commedia"* (Parma, 1995) appeared after this *lectura* had been consigned to the editors.

Avalle, D'Arco Silvio. *Modelli semiologici nella "Commedia" di Dante.* Milan, 1975.
Barbi, Michele. *Problemi fondamentali per un nuovo commento della "Divina Commedia."* Florence, 1955.

Bosco, Umberto. *Altre pagine dantesche.* Caltanisetta, 1987.

————. "Capaneo." *Enciclopedia dantesca,* 1:813–815. Rome, 1970.

————. *Dante vicino.* Caltanisetta, 1966.

Croce, Benedetto. *La poesia di Dante.* Bari, 1920.

Del Lungo, Isidoro. *Il Canto i dell'"Inferno."* Florence, 1904.

D'Ovidio, Francesco. *Nuovi studi danteschi.* 2 vols. Milan, 1906–1907.

Fasani, Remo. *Il poema sacro.* Florence, 1964.

Figurelli, Fernando. "Il canto i dell'*Inferno.*" In *"Inferno": Letture degli anni 1973–1976,* ed. Silvio Zennaro. Rome, 1977.

Fubini, Mario. *Metrica e poesia.* Milan, 1962.

Getto, Giovanni. *Aspetti della poesia di Dante.* Florence, 1966.

Gilson, Etienne. *Dante the Philosopher* (1939). Trans. David Moore. London, 1948.

Hegel, G. W. F. *Aesthetics: Lectures on Fine Art* (1835). Trans. T. M. Knox. 2 vols. Oxford, 1974.

Mazzali, Ettore. *Appunti sul ritmo e sui modi narrativi dell'"Inferno"* (Canti i–viii). Bari, 1921.

Mazzoni, Francesco. *Saggio di un nuovo commento alla "Divina Commedia: Inferno."* Florence, 1967.

Mazzoni, Guido. "Il Canto i dell'*Inferno*" (1914). Reprinted in *Almae luces: Malae cruces,* ed. Nicola Zanichelli, 167–186. Bologna, 1941.

Montanari, Fausto. "L'incontro con Virgilio." In *L'esperienza poetica di Dante,* 117–133. Florence, 1959.

Olschki, Leonardo. *The Myth of Felt.* Berkeley, 1949. Rewritten as *Dante poeta veltro* (Florence, 1953).

Pagliaro, Antonino. "Similitudine." *Enciclopedia dantesca,* 5:253–259. Rome, 1976.

————. *Ulisse: Ricerche semantiche sulla "Divina Commedia."* 2 vols. Messina-Florence, 1967.

Parodi, E. G. "L'ideale politico di Dante." *In Dante e l'Italia nel VI centenario della morte del poeta MCMXXI.* Rome, 1921.

Petrocchi, Giorgio. *L'ultima dea.* Rome, 1977.

Pézard, André. *Dante sous la pluie de feu.* Paris, 1950.

Risset, Jacqueline. *Dante écrivain: l'intelletto d'amore.* Paris, 1982.

Ronconi, Aurelio. *Interpretazioni grammaticali.* Rome, 1971.

Singleton, Charles S. *Dante Studies: Commedia, Elements of Structure.* Cambridge, Mass., 1949.

Spitzer, Leo. "The Addresses to the Reader in the *Commedia.*" *Italica* 32 (1955): 143–165.

Spoerri, Theophil. *Introduzione alla "Divina Commedia."* Trans. Marco Cerruti. Milan, 1966. Originally published as *Einführung in die Göttlichen Komödie* (Zurich, 1946).

Tateo, Francesco. "Umiltà." *Enciclopedia dantesca,* 5: 819–821. Rome, 1976.

Ungaretti, Giuseppe. "Commento al primo canto dell'*Inferno.*" *Paragone* 3, no. 36 (1952): 5–21.

Venturi, Luigi. *Le similitudini dantesche, ordinate, illustrate, e confrontate.* Florence, 1874.

Vignuzzi, Ugo. "Tosto (agg.)." *Enciclopedia dantesca,* 5:671. Rome, 1976.

Other names in parentheses not found in the list above are those of the authors frequently cited in the remainder of the volume and included in the General Bibliography. Among them are the classical early commentaries (Guido da Pisa, Pietro Alighieri, the Ottimo Commento, Boccaccio, Benvenuto da Imola, Francesco da Buti, and the Anonimo Fiorentino in the fourteenth century, Giovanni da Serravalle in the fifteenth, and Castelvetro and Daniello in the sixteenth) and their modern successors (Tommaseo 1865, Torraca 1915, Vandelli 1929, Grabher 1934–1936, Pietrobono 1924–30, Montanari 1949–1951, Sapegno 1955 and 1968, Mattalia 1960, Padoan 1967, Vallone and Scorrano 1986). The citations to the commentaries are *ad locum* and no page reference is included.

CANTO II

Dante's Authority

ROBERT HOLLANDER

The opening canto of the *Comedy* sweeps us into the perilous situation of its protagonist. No matter how artificial its action may seem, it is intense, focusing our attention on events and their consequences. Canto II, in comparison, is more distant and discursive. In Canto I, we were caught up with Dante in his sense of mortality, and in his vulnerability, like ours, to sin. As Canto II opens, we immediately become aware that he is a being altogether different from us, a poet:

> The day was now departing; the dark air
> released the living beings of the earth
> from work and weariness; and I myself
> alone prepared to undergo the battle
> both of the journeying and of the pity,
> which memory, mistaking not, shall show.

The moment, which prepares for an action (the descent into Hell), draws our attention to the poetic nature of the account of that descent, first by virtue of being itself a Virgilian borrowing, and second by insisting on the intervention of our poet's *mente*, or memory, between the events recorded and our reception of them. The Virgilian provenance of Dante's vigil in the darkness of evening was noted by many of the early commentators, although opinions varied as to exactly which Virgilian text lay behind Dante's (see Mazzoni, 165: *Aeneid* III, 147; IV, 522–528; VIII, 26–27; IX, 224–225). The first six verses put us in mind of poetry with their reminiscence of Virgil, not as some allegorical representative of "Reason," but as that most particular poet, author of the *Aeneid*. As he enters the poem, Virgil is addressed first by name (I, 79), then as "light and honor of all other poets" (82), as *maestro e . . . autore* (85), and finally as *poeta* (130). The first word spoken by Dante to Virgil here is, again, *poeta* (10). By the end of the canto his titles will refer to his present functions in the journey, *duca, segnore,* and *maestro* (140); indeed, these will henceforth be more used than any others (Gmelin, 59–60). Yet, at the outset, the titles that Dante gives him would imply that his having been a poet was the single most important qualification for his astonishing role as guide in a Christian poem.

As for the second matter, C. S. Singleton, who has been instrumental in reshaping our understanding of Dante's troubling claim that his poem is not a fiction, offers the following gloss to the sixth verse: "Memory will now faithfully retrace the real event of the journey, exactly as it took place. This most extraordinary journey through the three realms of the afterlife is represented, never as dreamed or experienced in vision, but as a real happening. . . . Here, then, and in the following invocation, the poet's voice is heard for the first time as it speaks of his task as poet" (1970, 22–23).

If the first canto of *Inferno* is the "canto of fear," as is often asserted (see Mazzoni, 49, with recognition of F. D'Ovidio and C. Ballerini), the second canto is the "canto of the word." The substantive *parola* occurs five times, more than in any other canto of the poem (43, 67, 111, 135, 137), as though to mirror the insistent presence of *paura* in the preceding canto, where it too occurs five times (also more than in any other). Still more indicative of the obsession with the word found in Canto II is the fact that only one other canto of *Inferno* includes a higher percentage of direct discourse. The eleventh, since it is principally devoted to Virgil's verbal diagram of Hell, opens with nine lines of description but then shifts entirely to dialogue; thus 106 of its 115 verses (92 percent) are spoken. The second canto follows hard upon; a total of 118 of its 142 verses (83 percent) are spoken, whether by Dante or Virgil. No other canto of the *Inferno* is as filled with spoken words.[1]

It has become a commonplace to assert that the first canto serves as preface to the entire *Comedy,* the second as prologue to *Inferno* (Pagliaro, 17, cites Conrad of Hirsau: "*Proemium* prefacio est operis, *prologus* quedam ante sermonem prelocutio"). This schema is probably acceptable, even if both *Purgatorio* I & II and *Paradiso* I & II constitute similar introductory units, a fact that may eventually erode the distinction. Nonetheless, by postponing his invocation to the second canto Dante would seem to be calling our attention to a structural principle of 1+33+33+33=100. In this respect the separateness of the first two cantos is underlined, since invocations occur in each of the first cantos of the succeeding *cantiche, Purgatorio* and *Paradiso*. At the same time, their structural similarity tends to make them a unit:

	Inferno I			*Inferno* II
1–27	Dante's peril		1–42	Dante's uncertainty
	simile (22–27)			*simile* (37–40)
28–60	three beasts		43–126	three blessed ladies
	simile (55–58)			*simile* (127–130)
61–136	Virgil's assurances		127–142	Dante's will firmed

The three segments of narrated action and reported speech, bounded by similes, are in evident parallel. And the last line of Canto II, *intrai per lo cammino alto e silvestro*, echoes, as many a commentator has seen, words that began I: *cammin* (1), *selva* (2), not to mention *intrai* (10), *alto* (16). Dante thus succeeds in giving Cantos I and II distinct purposes while combining them into a seamless introductory unit.

Since Homer, poets have troubled to establish their authority. What are Dante's qualifications as teller of this tale? His invocation does not make them immediately clear. It is one of the most vexed passages in the canto:

> O Muses, o high genius, help me now;
> o memory that set down what I saw,
> here shall your excellence reveal itself!
>
> (7–9)

From these three lines the commentary tradition has inherited three major problems, although only the first two are prominently recognized:

1. Why are pagan muses invoked in a Christian work?
2. What is (and to what power belongs) "high genius"?
3. Is the invocation double or triple? That is, are we to take memory as being invoked along with the first two entities or not?

My own responses are as follows:

1. Dante either invokes the pagan muses for aid in composing, by human art, the poetic artifact which makes his direct experience of God's universe available to mankind, or, he speaks of "Muses" as veiled metaphoric equivalences for the granting of inspiration by the Holy Spirit. Most commentators choose the former and certainly more comfortable alternative. Yet if *Muse* and *alto ingegno* are to be taken as synonymous, as many commentators believe (e.g., Mazzoni, 175–176), we are faced with a difficulty,

as the ensuing discussion of *alto ingegno* will attempt to show. In my view, the two powers invoked are probably of different orders, *Muse* representing what humans may learn of art, *ingegno,* on the other hand, the power of conceiving truth. Dante's four later couplings of the words *ingegno* and *arte* in the *Comedy* (*Purg.* IX, 125; XXVII, 130; *Par.* X, 43; XIV, 117) respect this significant difference, namely that between conceptualization and articulation. If this is the case, then *Muse* here represents the source that grants the human power of the poet—any poet, whether Christian or pagan—to express what he has conceived. Dante's own gloss on his invocation to Apollo (*Par.* I) in the letter to Cangrande (XIII, 18, 47) is of help here. Distinguishing between the proemial gestures made by rhetoricians and poets, he notes that, where both need to prepare their readers, only poets make invocation "since they must seek from higher entities [*superioribus substantiis*] that which resides not in the common human measure, something like a divine gift [*quasi divinum quoddam munus*]." If even in the *Epistola* Dante is careful not to make his claims for divine inspiration more than cautiously, his doubly hedged remark nonetheless points the way to a theological and Christian interpretation of the "good Apollo" invoked in *Paradiso* I, 13. The final invocations in the *Comedy* (*Par.* XXX, 97–99; XXXIII, 67–75) are overt appeals to God himself; they may lead us to suspect that others of the invocations are more veiled appeals to the same power (for recognition that there are nine invocations in the poem, see Hollander 1980, 31–38). In this first invocation a higher and veiled meaning seems far more likely to apply to *alto ingegno,* while the Muses retain their traditional role as overseers of more usual artistic abilities.

2. It is difficult to believe, given Dante's many high claims for the revealed truth of his *poema sacro,* that he would seek his ultimate inspiration from any other source than God. Yet few commentators have been open to this possibility (Castelvetro, Dionisi, Bennassuti; see Mazzoni, 176). The majority in the commentary tradition remains wedded to the unlikely view that the *ingegno* in question is Dante's own. For the poet to invoke his own "genius" would not only be in the poorest taste but would involve an error in logic. Can one *invoke* one's own genius? Whatever the agency invoked, it must be external to Dante. That much should be clear, as some commentators between Pietro di Dante and Mazzoni (173–177) have taught us, reminding us of the model to be found in *Aeneid* VI, 264–267. What remains at issue is whether *Muse* and *ingegno* are synonymous or, as I think is far more likely, differentiated. I would propose that Dante first seeks the human skills of poetic expression from traditional sources and then the power of the highest conceptualization from its sole and very source. The raw daring of such a claim understandably has kept our following wit at a nervous distance. (For circumstantial evidence that may help confirm the hypothesis, see *De vulgari eloquentia* II, iv, 10, where Dante quotes *Aeneid* VI, 125–131, to the effect that only those, like Aeneas, beloved of God [*dilectos Dei,* from

Virgil's *quos aequus amavit Iuppiter*], may be "raised to heaven" [*sublimatos ad aethera*]. Dante is here discussing the qualifications of the poet in a passage that represents the sole *locus* in the work in which he refers to *ingenium* and *ars*. It was likely to have been on his mind as he composed the first invocation of the *Comedy*.)

3. *Mente*, or "memory," is nearly universally understood as being the final element in a trinitarian invocation (cf. Pietro di Dante: "nam est in anima similitudo Trinitatis, scilicet mens, notitia et amor"). It is not. *Muse* and *alto ingegno* are sought outside the poet. *Mente* is put forward as the power within him that records what *alto ingegno* makes available to it. Surely it would have been a logical absurdity for Dante to invoke a capacity that he already possessed. *Alto ingegno* is invoked because it is exterior to him; *mente* is not, because it is within him. We should have understood these facts long ago.

With the conclusion of the proem of this prolusory canto, its dialogues begin. Excepting only two intervening similes, the first expressing Dante's lack of will to begin the journey and the second, his willingness (for discussion of the movement from fear to hope and from hope to fear in the chiastically related two pairs of similes in the first two cantos, see Lansing, 128–131), all between the invocation and the concluding two verses is direct discourse. The pattern of speakers is itself interesting:

1. Dante (10–36)
　2. Virgil (43–57)
　　3. Beatrice (58–74)
　　　4. Virgil (75–84)
　　5. Beatrice (85–114)
　6. Virgil (115–126)
7. Dante (137–140)

Through this extended and symmetrical series of speeches (exchanged between Dante and Virgil on earth, between Virgil and Beatrice in Limbo, and between Mary and Lucy, then Lucy and Beatrice, in heaven) we come to appreciate that the question of *auctoritas* is crucially at stake in *Inferno* II. To whom may it be said to belong? We must remember the opening six verses: Dante the pilgrim is alone despite the company of Virgil, as he thought Aeneas was alone despite the company of the Sibyl (*quando esso Enea sostenette solo con Sibilla a intrare ne lo Inferno* [*Convivio* IV, xxvi, 9]), and, as we recognize, he was alone in fact as he began to write the poem. We know that the activities of journeying and writing are one and the same except in the sense that the writing event is separate from the events written.

And we should remember that we have just read an invocation, the single poetic act that most directly confronts the question of *auctoritas*. Perhaps to our surprise, since we have been witness to the great enthusiasm that welcomes Virgil's first appearance in the poem, the entirety of what follows confirms Dante's—not Virgil's—poetic authority. And while it is undoubtedly true, on the testimony offered in the first canto, that the *Comedy* simply could not exist in anything like its actual form without the *Aeneid*, it is at the same time evident that the second canto has among its functions the desire to put Virgil, who is bathed in such effulgence in the first, in a less glorious light. It does so precisely by limiting his poetic authority.

Dante's First Speech (10–36)

While the Dante of the first canto is filled with humble enthusiasm in his initial response to Virgil (I, 79–87), by the second canto, the speaker of these lines has assumed the role of seasoned Christian commentator of the *Aeneid*: "You say that he who fathered Sylvius, / while he was still corruptible, had journeyed / into the deathless world with his live body." The reference to the *Aeneid* (VI, 763–766) is periphrastic with purpose, to remind us not only of the divine line of Roman kings to descend from Aeneas but also of the detailed knowledge possessed by Dante of his *auctor*'s text. And Aeneas's descent to the underworld, which will shortly be compared to Paul's ascent to heaven, is regarded as specifically sanctioned by God (16–21). In Dante's bold interpretation of *Aeneid* VI, God chose Aeneas to found Rome so that it might become seat of empire *and* church—a meaning decidedly absent from Virgil's poem. We shall never know whether Dante actually believed in the objective truth of this voluntaristic doctrine; we must grant that, within his poem, the fact is accorded every bit as much credence as those found in Scripture.

Virgil, however, is himself seen as a more questionable reporter of the event: *Tu dici* ("You say") that Aeneas went to the underworld, a journey later (25) referred to as the *andata onde li dai tu vanto* (literally, the journey over which you give him vaunt). These formulations do not withhold credence from Aeneas's journey so much as they hedge Virgil's account with a certain atmosphere of dubiety. (Here I strongly disagree with Padoan, who sees these phrases precisely as conferring *auctoritas* upon Virgil's words [45]; my position is in basic accord with Chimenz, 7–8; Mazzoni, 154 and 186; and Singleton 1970, 25.) *Per quest'andata onde li dai tu vanto* is rhetorically parallel to the opening line of the following tercet, which describes Paul's journey to heaven (but not to hell, despite Dante's nearly certain knowledge of the *Visio Pauli*—see Mazzoni, 223–231): *Andovvi poi lo Vas d'elezïone* ("Later the Chosen Vessel travelled there" [28]). The quotation of Acts 9:15, *vas electionis*, líke the phrase *di Silvïo il parente*, moves its reader to a source, this time to the Bible. But it does so without any similar questioning of authorial veracity. How can we fail to see that the comparison is to Virgil's disadvantage? The fictiveness of the *Aeneid* is what Dante calls to our attention. Yet such a tactic leaves Dante's own poem in jeopardy. He seems to seek out our challenge on the very ground we are to deny Virgil. Do we not wonder about the supposed veracity of the journey of this new Aeneas and new Paul, especially after Dante has made us aware of the relative fictiveness of the *Aeneid* when it is set against Scripture? Where shall we place Dante's poem, with Virgil's or with the Bible? It is a terrible chance to take with his readers; yet Dante will take it in still more breathtaking fashion when he swears that he saw the obviously fictive Geryon near the end of *Inferno* XVI. Allowing himself the claim of a Bible-like historicity, Dante treats Virgil's epic as truthful only at a second remove. And it is in this spirit that he will allow himself the various intentional misreadings of the *Aeneid* that have so long troubled his readers (e.g., *Inf.* XX, 52–102; *Purg.* XXII, 40–42; see Hollander 1980, 169–218).

Virgil's First Speech (43–57)

We understandably tend to see Virgil, since Dante's accolades are indeed enthusiastic, as possessing greater authority than the text in fact grants him. Just as Aeneas's mission is found to have been sanctioned in a Christian heaven, so is Virgil's mission to Dante. In this remarkable invention, Beatrice has descended to Limbo (for her resemblance to Christ harrowing hell see Iannucci, 23–45) in order to send Virgil to Dante on earth whence he will lead our protagonist back into the netherworld and eventually to Eden. Beatrice's descent gives Virgil motive and cause; without her intervention he would have known nothing (the damned, we learn in Canto X, do not know the present state of things on earth) and done nothing. Virgil's actions are so circumscribed that we can hardly miss Dante's point. It is Beatrice in heaven, not Virgil in Limbo, who is first aware of Dante's plight (50–53). And the burden of Virgil's words here is to give testimony to the power and glory of Beatrice, into whose charge he gives himself immediately (53–54). It is she, not he, who initiates the action of the *Comedy*, something we did not know a canto ago. (For an appreciation of Virgil's limited understanding of Beatrice see Singleton 1956, 32–33.)

Beatrice's First Speech (58–74)

Her utterance, which Daniello compared to Juno's words to Aeolus in *Aeneid* I, is described by Virgil as being *soave e piana* (56). She will in turn refer to Virgil's *parola ornata* (67). The two adjectives, *piana* and *ornata*, should remind us immediately of a major distinction, found in the medieval theory of styles, between the plain (*umile*) and the ornate (*alto*). Benvenuto da Imola was the first to say as much, glossing *soave e piana*: "Divine speech is

sweet and humble, not elevated and proud, as in that of Virgil and the poets" (Auerbach, 65–66; Hollander 1980, 217–218; Mazzotta, 157–158). Thus
Virgil's description of Beatrice's words corresponds antithetically to hers of
his; her speech, we may reflect, represents the sublimely humble style
championed by the *Comedy*, while his remembers the high style that marked
pagan eloquence. Dante's stylistic distinctions mirror his religious opinions,
which put Beatrice in heaven, and Virgil in hell. In this scene, it is Beatrice,
for all her humility and modesty, who is distinctly in charge: "I am Beatrice
who send you on" (70). Virgil, a posthumous Christian, is pleased to be so
commanded.

Virgil's Question (75–84)

His response (76–81) to Beatrice is as filled with awe as was Dante's to his
appearance in I (76–81). It precedes a question (82–84) that has met with
displeasure among the many commentators who find Virgil's wonderment
at Beatrice's being unafraid to enter Hell unnecessary and aesthetically
pallid. Yet, if we consider that Virgil owes his own presence in Hell precisely
to his lack of faith in Christ to come (he himself has told us in I, 125, that
he had been a rebel to God's law), we better understand the justice of his
condemnation. For even in his posthumous state Virgil, although he has
seen Christ harrow hell (*Inf.* IV, 52–63), does not understand that the
blessed fear no evil. The question is indeed an awkward one, emphasizing
once again Virgil's inadequacy in matters of faith. It leads to Beatrice's triumphant rejoinder; it is surely not a lapse on Dante's part.

Beatrice's Answer (85–114)

Since hell cannot harm the blessed, these do not remain absent from hell
because of fear (as Virgil assumes) but only because of the harsh law of
heaven (*duro giudicio*, 96): the blessed may not show the damned any form
of compassion, such as their very presence might seem to imply. It is mercy
for lost Dante, not pity for damned Virgil, that has initiated this heavenly
relay of intercession (which has a literary antecedent in the similar "relay"
in *Aeneid* I, 223–304; see Hollander 1969, 91–92). We have hitherto heard
the voices of Dante and Virgil, then Beatrice's voice in Virgil's, now Mary's
in Beatrice's as reported by Virgil. Mary, whom we shall see seated in glory
in *Paradiso* XXXII (after our first vision of her in *Paradiso* XXIII), is thus a presence in the second and penultimate cantos of the *Comedy*. *Inferno* II, 94–99,
attains, offstage as it were, the highest point of heaven that we as readers
shall confront before *Paradiso* XXXII, 1. Her *misericordia* is, chronologically
speaking, the first evidence of grace directed to Dante recorded in the
poem. Lucy and Beatrice are quickly enrolled in Mary's enterprise (the
modern commentary tradition tends, not accepting earlier formulations

that associate each lady with a separate category of divine grace, to take these three ladies as representing, respectively, charity, hope, and faith—see Giglio, 156–157, and Pasquazi, 40. The whole question of Dante's devotion to Lucy remains a problem; an important new contribution to our knowledge of Dante's likely awareness of Lucy is offered by Pasquazi, 40–60).

Lucy's question has greater relevance to the canto's concern for the truthfulness of poetry than is generally supposed. She describes Dante to Beatrice as one who "for your sake . . . left the vulgar crowd" (*uscì per te de la volgare schiera* [105]), a text that the early commentators glossed in various ways, but generally with the interpretation that Dante cut himself off from more usual human pursuits in order to study theology (a tradition that began with Guido da Pisa). I am in full accord with Mazzoni's interpretation (288–293) that the verse points to Dante's having left behind the herd of other poets in order to set off on his own to write poems in praise of Beatrice's true (and theologized) nature, a reading confirmed, in his eyes and mine, by *Purgatorio* xxiv, 49–51, where Bonagiunta marks the turning point in Dante's career as being the first poem to be written in the *dolce stil novo*, "Donne ch'avete intelletto d'amore." The Beatrice whom he praised then is now herself, in Lucy's words, "true praise of God" (*loda di Dio vera* [103]). She is asked to look down on Dante's piteous condition in the place where we saw him losing the battle against sin and that is now described as "that river ruthless as the sea" (108).

Perhaps no verse of the canto has had so tortured a history in the commentaries. Not only is there a continuing debate as to whether the river is to be construed as literal (see the Ottimo Commento and Pagliaro, 39–42) or taken figuratively (see Jacopo Alighieri and Mazzoni, 302–303), but there is no final consensus in either camp as to what the noun and its related clause mean (see Mazzoni, 296–303, for a detailed review of earlier interpretations). While it may seem that the very locution of the phrase tends to support those who find only a metaphorical sense operative here (Jacopo's "la viziosa e ignorante operazione del mondo" is still to the point), we should perhaps entertain the possibility that this river is Dante's "Jordan." If the actions of the first two cantos may be understood as linked to successive stages in the progress of salvation history (see Freccero), beginning with Adam's postlapsarian condition outside Eden (Villani, 99; Bernardo, 80; Mazzoni, 4; Hollander 1969, 80), have we come, in the poem's analogous record of event, to Jordan? Villani was the first to propose as much, for some of the same reasons given by Belloni (cited in Mazzoni, 297): the Jordan is not a tributary of a *mare*, but of the Dead Sea, a *lacus* according to him (perhaps reflecting Isidore of Seville's distinction, *Etymologiae* xiii, xix; see discussion in Hollander 1969, 262–263, also adverting to Freccero's arguments for Jordan, which develop an earlier interpretation of the verse by Singleton). Were this admittedly venturesome reading to find favor, Virgil would come as John the Baptist, a view of his role in the *Comedy* that I support (see Hollander 1980, 193n., for bibliography). Beatrice, hearing the *parole* of Lucy, departs for Limbo to seek the aid of Virgil's *parlare onesto* (113) in order to help Dante begin the process that will lead to his "baptism" (at the hands of Virgil in *Purg.* I, then under the supervision of the Christ-like Beatrice in *Purg.* XXXI and XXXIII).

Virgil's Questions (115–126)

Moved still further by Beatrice's tears of compassion, Virgil intercedes for Dante. He has completed his description (115–120) of the "prologue in heaven and hell," which occurred before the action that concludes the first canto. The rest of his final speech peppers Dante with four rapid questions (the word *perché* occurs four times in three lines, as Fallani observes, 44). One can sense the exasperation of the condemned pagan, wondering at the *viltà* of a Christian soul possessed of such potent friends and who yet lingers.

Dante's Response (133–140)

Virgil's message from heaven is the sun that, in simile, raises the sleeping flowers: Dante is finally ready to set out. The agency of his readiness is Virgil's voice: "your words" (136); yet these words are so significant because they contain verbatim reports of the words of his betters, those of Mary, Lucy, and Beatrice, which enfranchise his *parola ornata* (67). Virgil's role as guide in the *Comedy* is allowed by a favoring heaven that he is quick to obey (134). If Dante does not forget his debt to the greatest of the pagan poets, Virgil must pay a not inconsiderable entrance fee even to approach God's heaven.

In such ways, disturbing and surprising, Dante employs the seven symmetrically arranged speeches of *Inferno* II to explore the limitation and the power of the word. His *Comedy*, more than any other poem save possibly Milton's *Paradise Lost,* would have us believe that it purveys the Word.

NOTE

1. Inferno xx is the closest challenger: 103 of 130 (79 percent), followed by xxvii (104 of 136, 76 percent); xxxiii (117 of 157, 75 percent); xv (84 of 124, 68 percent); xiii (100 of 151, 66 percent); x (90 of 136, 66 percent); xxvi (88 of 142, 62 percent); v & xiv (83 of 142, 58 percent). As a control, we may consider xxv, so full of described action—only 17 of 125 verses (11 percent) are spoken, and by a total of six laconic speakers.

BIBLIOGRAPHY

An expanded version of this study appears in *Lectura Dantis Newberryana,* vol. 2, ed. Paolo Cherchi and Antonio C. Mastrobuono (Evanston, Ill., 1990). Since it was first written, in 1982, an important new study of the canto has been offered by Rachel Jacoff and William Stephany in the series *Lectura Dantis Americana* (Philadelphia, 1989).

The first six cantos of *Inferno* have been treated by Francesco Mazzoni, perhaps the finest commentator of Dante whom we shall ever know. His commentaries on *Inferno* i–iii are to be found in his *Saggio di un nuovo commento alla "Divina Commedia"* (Florence, 1967), with 149–313 devoted to the second canto. Ancient commentators are cited, whenever possible, from *La "Divina Commedia" nella figurazione artistica e nel secolare commento*, ed. Guido Biagi, vol. 1 (Turin, 1924). Other citations are from the following sources, a list that in no way pretends to offer a complete bibliography. For such instruction, see Mazzoni's 1967 work for the standard bibliography of the canto as a whole (158–159) and his individual glosses.

Auerbach, Erich. "Sermo Humilis." In *Literary Language and Its Public in Late Latin Antiquity and in the Middle Ages*. Trans. Ralph Manheim. Princeton, 1965.

Bernardo, Aldo S. "The Three Beasts and Perspective in the *Divine Comedy*." *PMLA* 78 (1963): 14–24.

Chimenz, Siro A. "Canto ii." In *Nuova Lectura Dantis*, ed. S. A. Chimenz. Rome, 1951.

Fallani, Giovanni. "Canto ii." In *Lectura Dantis Scaligera: Inferno*, ed. Mario Marcazzan, 25–45. Florence, 1967.

Freccero, John. "The River of Death: *Inferno* ii, 108." In *The World of Dante*, ed. S. B. Chandler and J. A. Molinaro. Toronto, 1966.

Giglio, Raffaele. "Il prologo alla *Divina Commedia*." *Critica letteraria* 1 (1973): 131–159.

Gmelin, Hermann. *Die göttliche Komödie, Kommentar*. Vol. 1. Stuttgart, 1966.

Guido da Pisa. *Expositiones et glose super Comediam Dantis*. Ed. Vincenzo Cioffari. Albany, N.Y., 1974.

Hollander, Robert. *Allegory in Dante's "Commedia."* Princeton, 1969.

———. *Studies in Dante*. Ravenna, 1980.

Iannucci, Amilcare A. "Beatrice in Limbo: A Metaphoric Harrowing of Hell." *Dante Studies* 97 (1979): 23–45.

Lansing, Richard H. *From Image to Idea: A Study of the Simile in Dante's "Commedia."* Ravenna, 1977.

Mazzotta, Giuseppe. *Dante, Poet of the Desert: History and Allegory in the "Divine Comedy."* Princeton, 1979.

Padoan, Giorgio. "Il Canto ii dell'*Inferno*." *Letture classensi* 5 (1976): 41–56.

Pagliaro, Antonino. *Ulisse: Ricerche semantiche sulla "Divina Commedia."* 2 vols. Messina-Florence, 1967.

Pasquazi, Silvio. "Il Canto ii dell'*Inferno*." In *"Inferno": Letture degli anni 1973–1976*, ed. Silvio Zennaro, 35–65. Rome, 1977.

Singleton, Charles S. "Sulla fiumana ove 'l mar non ha vanto." *Romanic Review* 39 (1948): 269–277.

———. "Virgil Recognizes Beatrice." *74th Annual Report of the Dante Society* (1956): 29–38.

———, trans. and ed. *The Divine Comedy: Inferno*. Vol. 2, *Commentary*. Princeton, 1970.

Villani, Filippo. *Comento al primo canto dell'"Inferno."* Ed. G. Cugnoni. Città di Castello, 1896.

CANTO III

The Gate of Hell

EUGENIO N. FRONGIA

Rhetoric is the art of persuasion. At the end of the second canto of *Inferno*, Virgil's rhetoric, wedded to his vatic stature, is instrumental in converting the pilgrim's "cowardice" of heart into "daring and . . . openness" (122–123). The journey, whose end is the salvific bonding of the free will of the creature with his Creator, must begin with the moral bonding of the guide and the pilgrim:

> "Now go: a single will fills both of us:
> you are my guide, my governor, my master."
> (II, 139–140)

The steep and savage path at the end of Canto II leads the travelers at sunset to the gates of Hell, which are, essentially, the gates of divine justice.

Canto III has three main episodes or sequences; the entry at the gate is the first episode; the second is the exhaustively developed narrative of the *ignavi* (the cowardly), occupying verses 31–69; and the third is the ferrying of the newly arrived souls across the river Acheron and the portraiture of the infernal boatman Charon. Let us begin with the first.

Hell's gate has been variously imagined as a Roman triumphal arch (Curfman, Hollander), a funerary inscription (Donato), and a low, wide medieval city gate, with a self-referential epigraph (G. Mazzoni). Whatever the shape of the gate, it certainly is a *monumentum* in the semantic implication of the word, namely, a poignant warning to the damned and to the travelers alike, and an eloquent reminder of the essence of Hell: a site of sempiternal, irrevocable justice, remote in its loneliness from a just God. Eugenio Donato remarks that "inscriptions on funerary monuments are the twice-removed representation of an empty center. Inscriptions on funerary monuments refer to the absence of absence in the present. Funerary monuments do not, simply, indicate absence; what they signify is that the irrevocable nature of absence is repeated by the inevitable mediation of graphic representations." Though the epigraph above the gate of Hell is "fatal text" (VIII, 127), because it is directed to dead souls, its "lapidary concision" (G. Mazzoni, 189) is one of the instances of "speech made visible" (*Purg.* X, 95) in Dante's poem, which Mazzotta calls "the synaesthesia which simulates the symbolic bond of words and vision and which organizes the triptych into a formal and sensory totality" (242).

This gate has the distinction of being one of a kind: a trinitarian gate bearing a trinitarian decree, wrought by Justice, Power, and Love. Those who enter it in ordinary circumstances, namely after death, are reminded of the nature and the scope of their final destiny: an eternity of Godlessness earned through a temporality of injustice. It is the reading of the final sentence on the scroll written by the supreme judge.

A tercet near the beginning of Canto XIX of *Inferno* instructs the reader in the ways God works in the universe:

> O Highest Wisdom, how much art you show
> in heaven, earth, and this sad world below,
> how just your power is when it allots!
>
> (XIX, 10–12)

God's participatory and distributive justice automatically implies retributive justice. Participation and distribution stamp on man, a rational and free agent, the *imago Dei.* "The damned" (*perduta gente*) are the permanent counterfeits of the *imago Dei.* Retributive justice either by analogy or contrast— the *contrapasso*—is, therefore, not only a punishment but also *ars Dei.* As God's creative rewards in *Paradiso* are *ars in bono,* so punishments befitting crimes in *Inferno* are *ars in malo.* In a recent study John Freccero explains that the representation of retribution in Hell follows the rule of rhetorical reification: "The punishments in Hell have little to do with moral theology and almost nothing with the physiology of pain. . . . Rather . . . the punishments are a clear example of what was later to be called 'poetical justice'. . . . Whatever the moral theology of *contrapasso,* at the level of representation it is above all ironic wit. . . . From God's perspective, therefore, Justice is an esthetic matter in the relationship of parts to the whole" (1983, 105).

Dante and Virgil realize that they have reached Hell proper when they enter at the gate. The gate is also the immediate entrance into the vestibule of

Hell, which is the setting for canto III. As Dante sees and reads ("I read / inscribed" [10–11]) the obscure text of the epigraph ("These words—their aspect was obscure" [10]), he gets, in the words of Francis Fergusson, "'the letter' with unparalleled impact, but not the meaning" (94–95). The impact is psychological, but not intellectual. Hence his instinctive turning to Virgil, "one who comprehends" (13), for both enlightenment and reassurance: "their meaning is difficult" (12). The qualifier *duro* can also signify hardness, not only the material hardness, but the intellectually repulsive message of hopelessness and eternal damnation. Some commentators make reference to John 6:61, "This saying is hard." Both in John and in Canto III of *Inferno,* the "hardness" of the message resides in its conceptual *newness,* and it indicates the psychological and intellectual limits of human nature when it is suddenly confronted with revelation, mystery, and grace.

Dante understands the relationship between justice and punishment in coldly logical scholastic terms, or as a fearful symmetry predicated upon the unity of the divine will. In Philip H. Wicksteed's view of the issue, the supreme excellence of God is revealed both as mercy and justice. The infliction of penalties is the manifestation of justice toward those who have withheld their love from divine goodness and have bestowed it on lower beings. As there is free will, there must be accountability and, therefore, retribution. The relationship is one of cause and effect. In *Summa theologica* I, 19, 3-3, Thomas Aquinas deals with the necessity and eternity of the will of God: "Apparently, whatever God wills, he must. For everything eternal is necessary. Yet whatever God wills, he wills from eternity, otherwise his will would be changeable. . . . Moreover God wills things other than himself inasmuch as he wills his own goodness. This he wills of necessity." God's will imposes necessity on some things, but not on all. He wills no *moral* evil, but he wills *physical* evil or suffering, by willing the good to which it is attached. This, in Aquinas's view, is the case with justice. In willing justice, God wills penalty, and in willing to maintain the balance of nature, he wills that some things should follow their course and die away. The eternal nature of Hell, physical and mental evil, is restated three times by the gate's "speech made visible" in order to hint at its trinitarian source: eternal pain, eternal things, and eternal endurance (ETTERNO DOLORE . . . COSE . . . IO ETTERNO DURO). The final verse of the inscription is the syllogistic capstone of Hell's existence and necessity: ABANDON EVERY HOPE, WHO ENTER HERE.

Dante's phrase JUSTICE URGED ON MY HIGH ARTIFICER (4; the Italian verb is *mosse,* and, in Thomist fashion, it refers to divine will moved of necessity) echoes Aquinas's thinking on "distributive justice." In *Summa* I, 21, 1, Aquinas compares this category of justice to "the rightness of a ruler or steward dispensing to each according to his worth. As this justice is displayed in a well-ordered family or community through its head, so the good order of the universe, manifested both in natural and moral beings, sets forth God's justice." Guilt and punishment form a necessary association in both Dante and Aquinas. The accountability of humans to others (God, society) and self brings about the concept of "merit" or "demerit." The decisive factors of guilt are the human act's "due order," and its reference to persons. Sin is "an action lacking due order" (*actus debito ordine privatus*). Order is a relationship of priorities and proportions. An act is said to have "due order" when it fits the exigencies of an end or a goal. Sin lacks "due order" because its act, in Aquinas's commentator, T. C. O'Brien's words, "lacks the totality exacted by the meaning of charity."

A notion of eternal damnation, formulated purely in terms of justice, simply cannot satisfy the mind. Dante's trinitarian epigraph at the top of the gate indicates recognition of this problem and provides an answer to it. If divine justice exacts "afflictive" punishment for the debt of sin (*malum poenae,* in Aquinas's words) and final impenitence, it is because the Power, the Wisdom, and the Love of God were all rejected by the free agency of the rational creature. Hence Dante's MY MAKER WAS DIVINE AUTHORITY, / THE HIGHEST WISDOM, AND THE PRIMAL LOVE (5–6). Most of us can understand that Hell was fashioned by the Power, the Justice, and the Wisdom of God. We are less easily reconciled to the association of Hell with God's "primal love." In Aristotelian terms, the human psyche moves toward its objects of desire. It is driven by love because it is created by a loving God. The souls in Hell, though they have lost "the good of the intellect" (18), still vividly retain the impulse of the "primal love" (6) that drives them, hopelessly, toward the object of desire. The last line of the epigraph, LASCIATE OGNI SPERANZA, means that the souls enter the fateful gate of no return stripped of the vestments of charity. The loss of the benefits of Christ's sacrifice places the dwellers in Hell beyond atonement and voids their pain of any possibility of redemption.

Lines 12–15 contain Dante's fearful reaction to the "speech made visible" (*Purg.* x, 95) and the master's stern warning against an overreaction. Virgil's reply does not explain the meaning of Hell, steering the reluctant and dismayed pilgrim in the direction of the *will* rather than the *intellect*. Fergusson points out that action is needed here more than speculation, faith more than reason. It is the humble and trusting acceptance of God's plan that will lead the lost wayfarer to enlightenment and salvation:

> "Here one must leave behind all hesitation;
> here every cowardice must meet its death."
> (14–15)

Hell is filled with "the miserable people, / those who have lost the good of the intellect" (17–18). In *Convivio* II, xiii Dante, echoing the *Nicomachean Ethics* of Aristotle (VI, 2), says that "truth is the good of the intellect." Hence the damned have a false and distorted view of reality. The pilgrim himself, in his experience of Hell, shares in the state of the damned by partially losing "the good of the intellect."

Once inside the gate, the pilgrim for the first time experiences the *sounds* of Hell. This cacophony corresponds to the loss of reason and intellect. These sounds alienate Dante from his surroundings. The language of the damned is appropriate to their status: it is corrupted, bestial. G. Mazzoni, Sapegno, and Padoan have pointed out the rich rhetorical texture and dynamic structure of verses 22–30 in their upward or downward progression (*sospiri, pianti e alti guai,* an *ascending* tonality in the Italian original, followed by *lingue, orribili favelle,* / *parole di dolore, accenti d'ira,* a *descending* pattern, degenerating into the spent echoes of physical violence, and fixed by the naturalistic simile "like sand that eddies when a whirlwind swirls" [30]).

As stated at the beginning, Canto III contains three main episodes: the entry at the gate, the narrative of cowardly souls, and the arrival on the shore of the river Acheron. The episode of cowards contains some of the most controversial tercets in the whole of Dante's poem, and some of the most semantically elusive utterances. The vestibule of Hell is inhabited by a commingling of cowardly angels and pusillanimous humans. Dante characterizes the former as "those who were not rebels / nor faithful to their God, but stood apart" (38–39). They are the so-called neutral angels. The theological problem posed by the neutrality of the angels was aggravated by the philological difficulty of the phrase *per sé fuoro,* frequently misread as "they were *for themselves.*" Freccero points the way toward a solution that respects Dante's text and the theological thinking of his day. Having observed the incongruities caused by the "for themselves" translation, Freccero offers another possibility: "The *per sé* angels represent the angelic nature depraved as surely as if it had sinned with Lucifer and his followers, for between love of God and love of self, there can be no middle ground. Some of the angels were for God, the others against Him and *for themselves.*" He goes on to say: "This is the *per sé* of the scholastic philosophers and the *da sé* of modern Italian" (1960, 5). Freccero's conclusion:

> [The neutral angels] simply did not act, but remained frozen in a state of aversion from God. . . . With the aversion from God, the bond of charity was smashed; with the abstention from action, they deprived themselves of the one positive element that could win them a place in the cosmos. They are as close to nothing as creatures can be and still exist, for by their double negation, they have all but totally removed themselves from the picture. To be deprived of action is to be deprived of love, and love is the law of Dante's cosmos, determining all classifications. There remains nothing for them but the vaguely defined vestibule of hell, and they merit not more than a glance from the pilgrim before he passes on to the realm of love perverted.
>
> (1960, 13)

The fate of the "neutral angels" is shared by the pusillanimous humans who "lived without disgrace and without praise" (36). Saint Thomas's *Summa* provides some useful insights into the theological problem of cowardice or pusillanimity (*viltà*) under the general heading *De Pusillanimitate* (II-II, 133, 1). "Just as presumption exceeds its capability by straining after what is greater than he can reach, so pusillanimity causes one to fall short of his capability when he refuses to extend himself to achieve an aim commensurate with his powers." Thus cowardice is a *recusatio tensionis,* a refusal to strive toward a goal set within the limits of one's natural capabilities. If intellectual ignorance and fear of failure are the root *causes* of cowardice, their *effect* is the privation of greatness of which a man is worthy. This premise explains the miserable state of these "sorry souls" (*anime triste* [35]) who live in eternal regret.

Both infamy and praise presuppose action of some magnitude; it is by their actions that human beings are usually judged. Infamy and praise are the echoes of either blameworthy or praiseworthy deeds. The "sorry souls" of the vestibule of Hell defy classification according to the moral categories of action or activity, and therefore they place themselves outside—the implication of the Italian *li sdegna*—the two divine options of *misericordia e giustizia,* mercy and justice (50). God's mercy is exercised on those who, having fallen away from Him, both originally and actually, repent and accept his saving grace through Christ. God's justice is brought to bear on those who, having sinned, remain frozen in a final denial of his mercy and grace, and therefore are subject to retribution. The morally uncommitted, to paraphrase the well-known passage of Revelation, are spewed forth from the mouth of God and the mouth of Satan, as they are unsavory to the one and the other. In lines 49–51:

> "The world will let no fame of theirs endure;
> both justice and compassion must disdain them;
> let us not talk of them, but look and pass."

These souls are "envious of every other fate" (48). Only they who have no fate can be envious of any fate. To have no fate means to be at the zero point in the scale of being and actuation; it means to be frozen *in potentia,* as a mere hypothesis of being, never to become, never to live ("These wretched ones, who never were alive" [64]). In Dante, the cowardly are characterized by a series of *negations.* They are nameless (36 and 49), spiritually deathless and hopeless (46), without pity and justice (50), without life (64). The uncommitted are, in fact, an ontological absurdity: they are the reification of nothingness. It is one of Hell's eternal ironies—and the *Inferno*'s first *contrapasso*—that the lifeless should undergo punishment by racing restlessly around what amounts to a zero:

> And I, looking more closely, saw a banner
> that, as it wheeled about, raced on—so quick
> that any respite seemed unsuited to it.
>
> (52–54)

Guido da Pisa, one of Dante's earliest commentators (1324), interpreted these lines as follows: "They abide between the gate of Hell and the river Acheron, and they race around the circle formed by the river" (58). The vagueness of the banner of Hell is appropriate to them. Guido Mazzoni comments: "The banner of these wretched ones, who, angels in heaven, men on earth, refused to follow either banner, flag, or insignia which took to the battlefield for whatever cause, good or bad, just or otherwise, has to be without discernible color or shape to themselves and to the readers." To this formless banner any respite seems unsuited. Mazzoni adds, "Unworthy of respite is he who does not commit himself, does not risk, does not struggle. After victory or defeat, one rests; or even after a journey; but these did not want to win, were afraid of losing, never made a move" (192).

In this amorphous crowd, Dante makes it a point to recognize someone who certainly is guilty of the Thomistic *recusatio tensionis,* a refusal to strive toward a great goal set within the limits of his natural capacity:

> After I had identified a few,
> I saw and recognized the shade of him
> who made, through cowardice, the great refusal.
>
> (58–60)

Commentators point out both the willing lack of historical specificity in the paraphrastic description of the one "who made, through cowardice the great refusal," and the personal, passionate, almost vengeful indictment of the unnamed coward. According to Francesco Mazzoni, here we have Dante the man who comes face to face with the one whom he blames for his recent troubles. The intensity and the scornful tone of the characterization following the recognition of the cowardly shade confirms the reading:

> At once I understood with certainty:
> this company contained the cowardly,
> hateful to God and to His enemies.
>
> (61–63)

According to some, Dante expunged Celestine V's name after he was canonized by the Church in 1312. Others emphasize the abstract exemplarity of the figure, which, in its historical namelessness and facelessness, embodies the very concept of the sin Dante is so harshly condemning. In the specific case of a supreme pontiff who, having put his hand to the plow, turned to look backwards and away from his task, the *recusatio officii* becomes *maxima recusatio;* it is *il gran rifiuto,* the unwillingness to exert himself to achieve aims commensurate with the power of the office and the grace pertaining to it. Celestine's office provided him with a unique historical opportunity for leadership. These are political and religious motivations for the presence of Celestine V in this particular place in Hell. Toward the end of the thirteenth century, especially among the spiritualist circles of Christianity, there were great expectations for a *papa angelicus* or *pastor angelicus,* who would profoundly renew the Church. The pusillanimity of him whom most readers indicate as Celestine V must be seen against this background of *renovatio temporis,* a revitalization of the evangelical vocation of the Church. Dante sees this "refusal" as the missed opportunity for the actuation of a reformation program. The personal and communitarian implications of Celestine's abdication are so serious as to warrant damnation in the poet's eyes. Instead of the *pastor angelicus,* upon the Church was bestowed, in his view, a *pontifex diabolus,* a satanic pontiff, in the person of Boniface VIII, a theme that Dante elaborates in *Paradiso* XXVII.

As is frequently the case in the *Divine Comedy,* where Dante often "mirrors" the characters he meets, there exists a significant existential and psychological contrast between Celestine V and Dante the pilgrim-prophet. In an era when concerned Christians and politicians such as Dante himself were hungering for a *renovatio temporis,* God raised the humble Pietro da Morrone to the role of prophet and anointed one and, against the counsel of the wise, placed in his hands the keys of the kingdom and the sword of the word. God sent him forth on a journey of renovation to redeem a corrupt Church. Likewise, the spirit of God called forth Dante, poet and pilgrim, humbled by the experience of sin and despair, to undergo "the battle / both of the journeying and of the pity" (II, 4–5), as a necessary exercise of salvation both for himself and for the *communitas fidelium.* In poetic and salvific terms, his call to the journey was a "fated path" (V, 22). The weakness of the spirit and the weariness of the flesh lead to the temptation of *viltà.* Both Dante and Celestine were subjected to this temptation, which was compounded by a misunderstanding of the larger scope of their mission. Dante's reluctance in Canto II reechoes the fearful wavering of the prophet in Jeremias 1:6, loosely translated as: "O Lord God . . . I can't do that!" In answer to Virgil, who argues for the necessity of the journey, Dante expresses doubt and feelings of unworthiness and inadequacy:

> But why should I go there? Who sanctions it?
> For I am not Aeneas, am not Paul;
> nor I nor others think myself so worthy.

> Therefore, if I consent to start this journey,
> I fear my venture may be wild and empty.
>
> (II, 31–35)

Virgil diagnoses Dante's doubts and fears as *viltà*: "Your soul has been assailed by cowardice" (II, 45). Dante emerges from temptation by giving willful assent to God's plan and grace. The same cannot be said of Celestine V. Willpower and trust in the sufficiency of God's grace, to paraphrase Saint Paul, were both wanting, and this led as a consequence to the notorious abandonment of the prophetic journey, "the great refusal."

Dante has his critics, chief among them Petrarch, for putting Celestine V in Hell. In *De vita solitaria*, the humanist makes of the life of solitude an absolute moral, personal, and cultural value and enlists Celestine among the great figures who chose solitude over all other conditions as a way of perfection. The abandonment of the pontificate by Celestine is interpreted by Petrarch as an act of courage and the liberation from a "deadly encumbrance" (232). Petrarch's own temperament differed substantially from Dante's, and this contributes to the disparity of points of view in the two poets. Petrarch sees Celestine's "refusal" as an act "advantageous both to himself and to the world" (233). Perhaps he also exhibits a modern conscience in the face of an inescapable moral dilemma and summons to his side strong existential arguments. While Dante's reprobation of moral cowardice and existential futility is objectively unassailable, one may venture to say, on the Petrarchan side of the argument, that the historical embodiment of cowardice and futility in the figure of Celestine V was conditioned both by Dante's preferential views of moral and political activism and by his still vivid recollection of the personal consequences of such "refusal." This is the view of several commentators, chief among them Guido Mazzoni (see his 1941 exposition of the canto, especially 194–196). In his reading of this canto, Sapegno criticizes the episode of the "cowardly," and, by implication, the presence of Pope Celestine among them, as "unconvincing and not justifiable from a rational and theological standpoint" (16). He hints that Dante's approach is a self-serving one, and faults him for confusing the cowardly with the mediocre, a category into which the majority of mankind may be fitted. Petrarch's sarcastic conclusion summarizes the difficulties with Dante's choice of Celestine as the chief coward of the vestibule of Hell: "But God be thanked, we have become so high-spirited that we may hope these two Peters [Peter Damian and Peter Celestine] are destined to be without rivals and that pusillanimity like theirs will be without an example in our time" (*De vita solitaria* II, 236).

The poetic language of the episode of the cowardly, particularly their bloody nakedness as a form of *contrapasso*, is worthy of detailed analysis. As is typical in Dante, here too, the punishment is simply the sin itself. The pusillanimous are appropriately—*contrapasso* by analogy—naked (65), divested of any merit as well as of any sin. They never "put on the new man," as Saint Paul exhorts all Christians to do. Their bodies are as futile as their souls. While it is said in the liturgical hymns to the Christian martyrs and confessors that their blood has made the garden of the Church bloom with new saints, the blood of the cowardly, spilled not by the instruments of torture and martyrdom, but by vile horseflies and wasps, feeds the basest of all creatures: worms. The souls are reified. Dante's language in Canto III is concrete and vividly pictorial in the elaboration of the *contrapasso*. It sets him apart from the Virgilian model, as commentators have pointed out. Giorgio Padoan observes that "rather than on abstract substantives," Dante relies on concrete dramatizations, whereby we see not "desperation" but "desperate souls," not "sorrow" but "the very souls conquered by pain" (54). Even the sound of slapping hands acquires a vividly realistic touch when the reader further on in the text realizes that it represents a spontaneous, if futile, effort to ward off unrelenting punishment and torture. The indecisive and sluggish herd, who apparently never suffered the pangs of conscience, are here goaded and stung by horseflies and wasps into pointless commitment and repetitive behavior.

Dante's glance beyond the intense entanglement with the cowardly, "And then, looking beyond them, I could see / a crowd along the bank of a great river" (70–71) signals an abrupt, and somewhat contrived transition to what can be considered the third *movement* of this canto. This "looking beyond" can be read literally as a specific moment in the pilgrim's onward movement, or symbolically as the mental contemplation of a new poetic matter. What the poet sees is the river Acheron, the river of death, on whose banks the great drama of the *massa damnata* unfolds. It is at this point also that Dante affixes his mimetic gaze upon *Aeneid* VI and Aeneas's descent to Hades, so that here Virgil is to Dante a double guide. While the primary resonance of these verses is distinctly Virgilian—"I could see / a crowd along the banks of a great river" (71)—this reader detects a more remote biblical echo, especially in verse 78 (*la trista riviera d'Acheronte*), the lament and the remembrance of the Hebrew slaves and exiles on the banks of the Babylonian rivers: "Upon the rivers of Babylon, there we sat and wept: when we remembered Sion" (Psalm 136:1). For the lost souls at the fateful crossing, this is a supreme moment of exile and the hopeless remembrance of freedom which can never be recovered.

From Guido da Pisa, Benvenuto da Imola, and Boccaccio to Charles Singleton, the poetic example of the *Aeneid*, especially book VI, is well established and faithfully glossed. More recently Giorgio Padoan has invited critics to focus more closely on the text that Dante might have used and on the poet's understanding of it. Sapegno devoted a sizable portion of his 1960 reading (18–23) to the positive and negative poetic results of Dante's closeness to Virgil's text. Dante, Sapegno maintains, does mimetically in

Canto III what he does psychologically in the uncertainty of the "dark forest": he relies on Virgil's *Aeneid* as a leading and reassuring guide. The tender, newly blossomed shoot of the *Comedy* leans heavily on and derives comfort from the Latin text. Sapegno's critique can be summarized as follows: Dante, working with unfamiliar subject matter and an uncertain technique, felt the need to "prop up his inexperience" and to adhere strictly to the Virgilian model, in the hope that the original would supply both narrative schemes and poetic language. Such exemplarity does not end in the episode of the infernal river and the boatman Charon who plies his trade on it but extends to the general conception of the canto and to its minutest details. We witness in this canto the transition of Dante's poetics from the lyrical to the epic. After a strictly allegorical and lyrical prelude in Cantos I and II, here is Dante's first attempt at narrative and the beginnings of poetic and aesthetic independence. The poet moves beyond "the descriptive and pictorial Virgilian modes" (21) through a vigorous dramatization of gestures and feelings. Sapegno attributes the different aesthetic results to the marked difference in personality between the Latin and the Romance poets. Dante's intense and polemic character leads him to dramatize rather than to describe, and to enrich the tone of the epic language. It is possible, in the transition from Virgil's to Dante's text, "to retrace the process by which *translatio* is resolved in *inventio*" (22). It is here that the contours of a new poetry of extraordinary power begin to emerge. Successful instances of the transition from translation to invention, according to Sapegno, include the similes of falling leaves and migratory birds, the dramatization of the figure of Charon, and the intense personification of the natural elements.

The dramatic appearance of the boatman is preceded by a meditative respite, whereby the new episode may be prepared and then introduced with suddenness and surprise: "I did not speak until we reached the river" (81). The transition, here and elsewhere, occurs rather casually, as Sapegno remarks, in a linguistic device that indicates both surprise and visual effect: "And here" (*Ed ecco* [82]). The critics have pointed out the differences between the Virgilian and the Dantean Charon. Dante makes the old ferryman into a dynamic, dramatic living person and marks the contours of his figure with vivid detail, for example, "his hair was white with years" (83), and "whose eyes were ringed about with wheels of flame" (99). Dante relies on qualifiers for both color and effect: "wooly cheeks," "livid marsh" (97–98). Charon impresses on the pilgrim and the reader alike a sense of urgency, loss, and irrevocability, perhaps best expressed in the curt "Woe to you, corrupted souls!" (84).

The interjection "Woe" (*Guai*) is akin to the Latin *Vae!*, which, in turn, recalls the expression *Vae victis!*, "Woe to the vanquished!" The expression announces a new condition of being (*vinti* and *pravi*), whereby the souls are totally and eternally at the mercy of others. As the episode unfolds, with Charon at the center of it, lines 91–93 allow the poet to predict his own salvation. The lines offer a foretaste of the beginning of *Purgatorio:* "Another way and other harbors" (91) and "a lighter craft will have to carry you" (93) foreshadow such expressions as "to course across more kindly waters" and "with boat so light, so quick / that nowhere did the water swallow it" of *Purgatorio* I, 1 and II, 41–42 respectively.

Virgil's formulaic retort to Charon in lines 94–96 ("our passage has been willed above, where One / can do what He has willed; and ask no more") "has a precise significance in the realm where God is known only for His power" (Padoan, 63). The formula, majestic and aloof in its impersonality, emphasizes the very divine attributes that Satan and his cohorts challenged. God's will and power hold all of Hell in awe. Satan was crushed in a power struggle, his will now subjugated once and for all. As the will of the enlightened and trusting angels lies eternally in the love and trust of their Creator, so the will of the unenlightened and rebellious angels was frozen forever in the fear and hatred of God. The episode parallels *Aeneid* VI, 507–549, and the present formula has on Charon the same becalming effect as the sudden showing of the "golden bough," which Apollo's priestess, the Sibyl, carries on the journey.

In the closing episode of the canto, attention shifts back to the souls. Their reaction to the sudden awareness of their damnation shows that there has been no change in their sense of moral values; they simply repeat the earthly pattern of sinfulness and recrimination. In Wicksteed's words, "It is not that their repentance is unavailing, but that they do not repent. They curse the parents who begot them, or accomplices that seduced or betrayed them, never their own inherently evil choice, for they still cling to it" (198). The curse of the damned seems to be a desperate and futile attempt radically to obliterate their very being, "the place and time / of their conception's seed and of their birth" (104–105). It is a curse according to the biblical pattern set forth in Job 3:3: "Let the day perish wherein I was born, and the night in which it was said: A man child is conceived."

The gathering of the souls "on the evil banks of Acheron" on their way to their final exile gives Dante another opportunity to lean on the classical model of the epic simile and to advance this rhetorical device to a stage of perfection that overshadows his Virgilian original.

> As, in the autumn, leaves detach themselves,
> first one and then the other, till the bough
> sees all its fallen garments on the ground.
>
> (112–114)

Robert Fitzgerald has retraced the classical and epic lineage of Dante's simile. From the sixth book of the *Iliad,* the powerful simile travels to book VI of the *Aeneid* and thence to Canto III of the *Inferno.* In the course of this literary journey, the simile undergoes aesthetic and psychological mutations. Homer's stance is "impartial," insofar as the lines are spoken by Glaukos in the context of a genealogical story. Virgil, abrogating the tenets of aesthetic distance, "personalizes" the simile by entering "into the leaf's point of view." The active verb of the Latin text, *cadunt,* refers to the leaves themselves (they fall). Thus in Virgil the figure has become "a descriptive simile in a narrative," or "a pictorial interlude," to use Sapegno's intuition, meant to emphasize the *multitude* of shadows, or souls, fallen into Hades. Fitzgerald insists on reading Dante's *si levan* as "they take off," or "they rise," not realizing that the reflexive verb *levarsi* in Italian means "to detach oneself" as well as "to take off" (as in *levarsi in volo*) or "to rise." Dante's text allows only for the *first* meaning, correctly rendered by Mandelbaum: "As, in the autumn, leaves detach themselves." The significance of Dante's departure from the classical models lies, as Sapegno states, "in a radical modification of tone," namely, in transforming narration into dramatization. This is accomplished mostly by the vivid personification of the living branch that "sees" its own leaves detaching themselves "one after another" in dramatic and inevitable sequence, and tragically realizes its own nakedness in the death of its own offspring. Thus both the spirit and the letter of the text allow Dante to intuit in the dramatic view of a branch the *planctus Ecclesiae* (the lament of the Church) as she realizes the final spiritual demise of her own children. This dramatic situation is strikingly similar to another famous episode of wounded parenthood in *Inferno* XXXIII, where Count Ugolino, narrating the slow, tragic death of his sons through starvation, tells the poet-pilgrim how he "saw [*Vid'io*] the other three fall one by one" (XXXIII, 71). The word *spoglie,* in its denotation of "garments" and its connotation of "mortal remains," occurs also in the Count Ugolino episode, but as a *verb,* when Ugolino's children beseech their father to feed on them: "for you *clothed* us in this / sad flesh— it is for you *to strip* it off" (*tu ne vestisti / queste misere carni, e tu le spoglia* [62–63; emphasis mine]). Thus Dante, through the simile of the leaves once again confirms his habit of injecting classical, pagan literary *topoi* with theological and Christian contents.

The canto comes to an abrupt and somewhat awkward close. Mandelbaum comments (155) that the end of this canto like that of Canto V is "crude," "abrupt," "medieval," and "miraculistic," the last two qualifiers referring to the quake and the sleep that overcomes the poet. He echoes the sentiment of critics who have made the point that in Canto III, the poetics of Dante are still engaged in the search for identity, continuity, and expressive efficacy. This is, after all, the canto that sets Dante's style beyond Hell's gate, in a narrative journey without return. Dante's poetics in this canto have been characterized as *in fieri* and "experimental." It is important to keep in mind that the stylistic reservations expressed by Sapegno, Padoan, and Mandelbaum in particular, are *not absolute,* but *relative* to Dante's mature and unsurpassed accomplishments in the *Comedy.*

BIBLIOGRAPHICAL NOTES

Robert Hollander's *Allegory in Dante's "Commedia"* (Princeton, 1969) deals with the shape of the Gate of Hell in appendix 2, "God's 'visible speech'" (297–300). The Roman triumphal arch reminds both the damned and the pilgrim passing through its archway "of the perfection of justice" (300). Power at the service of justice, imperial Rome's interpretation of her legal responsibilities, is the firm message engraved on the archway. Eugenio Donato's reference to the words above the gateway as a "funerary inscription" is contained in "The Mnemonics of History: Notes for a contextual reading of Foscolo's *Dei Sepolcri,*" *Yale Italian Studies* 1, no. 4 (1977): 1–23. John Freccero refers to Donato's essay in his own "Infernal Irony: The Gate of Hell," *Modern Language Notes* 98 (1983): 769–786 (reprinted in *Dante: The Poetics of Conversion,* ed. Rachel Jacoff [Cambridge, Mass., 1986]). Guido Mazzoni's allusion to the architecture of the gate of Hell as a medieval city gate is in *Almae luces: Malae cruces,* ed. Nicola Zanichelli (Bologna, 1941), 186–202. Giuseppe Mazzotta updates the discussion on the *visibile parlare* with his own insights in *Dante, Poet of the Desert,* 242 ff. Philip H. Wicksteed's work, *Dante and Aquinas* (London, 1913), deals with substantive theological issues relevant to Dante's *Commedia,* particularly the first canto. The edition of Thomas Aquinas's *Summa Theologiae*—Latin text and English translation—referred to here is the Blackfriars edition (New York, 1964); especially useful are T. C. O'Brien's discussion of justice (27:99–109, and appendix 1), and the remarks on cowardice (42:160–167). Francis Fergusson's insightful reading of Canto III is in *Dante* (New York, 1966), 99–104. The passage quoted from Cioffari's ed. of Guido da Pisa's *Expositiones* is in the *cantus tertius,* 58. Freccero's discussion of "Dante and the Neutral Angels" (1960) is reprinted in *The Poetics of Conversion,* ed. Jacoff.

The bibliography on the central episode of the "cowardly" is abundant. The opinions on Dante's mass condemnation of the "mediocre" range from Natalino Sapegno's dissatisfaction—most of mankind would have to be placed in this category and, therefore, in Hell (*Il Canto iii dell'"Inferno"* [Florence, 1960])—to Francesco Mazzoni's justification of the episode on the basis that "it fulfills a profound and organic structural need, and responds to a highly poetic concept" (*Saggio,* 365). The identification of the Great Coward has, likewise, elicited a vast range of opinions, but the overwhelming circumstantial evidence seems to unify the readers around the name of Pope Celestine V. Useful background information on the reformist expectations of the age of Celestine can be found in Angelo Marchese's *Guida alla "Divina Commedia: Inferno,"* and full discussions in the already cited texts of Guido Mazzoni and Natalino Sapegno. Francesco Mazzoni dedicates to this controversy a sizable portion of his *Saggio,* especially 390–415, as does Giorgio Padoan in *Il pio Enea, l'empio Ulisse,* 64–102. See also Giorgio Petrocchi's "Dante e Celestino V," *Studi Romani* 3 (1955): 273–285. For Petrarch's sarcastic jab at Dante's "I saw and recognized," see *De vita solitaria* II, trans. Jacob Zeitlin (Urbana, 1924), 236. On Dante's indebtedness to the Virgilian epic poem, the bibliography is copious. Recent useful discussions can be found in Sapegno's cited *lectura* and G. Padoan's *lectura* (in *Nuove letture dantesche* [Florence, 1968], 1:47–71); in Robert Hollander's *Il Virgilio dantesco: tragedia nella "Commedia"* (Florence, 1983); in E. Moore's *Studies in Dante, First Series* (1896; reprint New York, 1968), 166–197 and 344–348; and in the *Enciclopedia dantesca* (Rome, 1976), 5:1030b to 1049b. The stylistics of Canto III have received mixed reviews by various critics, among them Sapegno, Padoan, and Mandelbaum ("Ruminando e mirando: La capra di Dante," *Lettere italiane* 2 [1983]: 145–156). Sapegno's occasionally sharp criticism has caused several commentators to rally to Dante's defense, as, for instance, Steno Vazzana (*Canto iii dell'"Inferno"* [Turin, 1965]), Enzo Noè Girardi (*Nuovi studi su Dante* [Milan, 1987], 7–32), and Letterio Cassata (see his essay on Canto I in this work). Robert Fitzgerald's "Generations of Leaves: The Poet in the Classical Tradition" was published in *Perspectives USA* 8 (summer 1954): 68–85.

CANTO IV

A Melancholy Elysium

MANLIO PASTORE STOCCHI

Translated by Charles Ross

Dante arrives on the banks of Acheron after a fearful passage through tur-
bid, timeless air that quivers from the whirlwind tumult of cowardly and despairing souls. He has seen tormented crowds cry against their fate. He has
heard the threatening address of the demon Charon. There follows a moment of respite from terror, as brief as the interval between the red flash
that menacingly illuminates the close of the third canto and the "enormous
thunderclap" (IV, 2) that opens the fourth canto of the *Inferno,* awakening the
poet. Coming to his senses, he hesitates—along the margins where he finds
himself—before the shadows and dark clouds of the immense infernal abyss
that spews and exhales the deep and mighty rumbling, the "thundering, un-
ending wailings" (9) of all the damned. Finally, encouraged by Virgil, whose
"deathly pale" face shows his own distress for the loss of so many souls
(16–22), he ventures forward into the first circle of "the blind world" (13).

And here, suddenly, the atmosphere completely changes. In the quiet and
still air only sighs are heard. A vast gathering dwells in the joyless calm,
made more mysterious by faint sounds that issue forth:

> Here, for as much as hearing could discover,
> there was no outcry louder than the sighs
> that caused the everlasting air to tremble.
> The sighs arose from sorrow without torments,
> out of the crowds—the many multitudes—
> of infants and of women and of men.
>
> (25–30)

50

Throughout the canto there arise no more than the echoes of feeble, soft voices and traces of grave but placid movements. Soon a serene radiance overcomes the shadows (68–69), and a homogeneous luminosity reveals a "meadow of green flowering plants" (111), an "enameled green" (118) contrasting to the "bloodred light" that closes the previous canto and the world stained with blood conjured up by the one that follows (v, 90).

Dante's poetic strategy, which resists its Virgilian model (cf. *Aeneid* IV, 411–416), leaves undescribed the passage of Acheron so that no narrative will mediate and blunt the contrast between the two atmospheres, letting their opposition strike the reader suddenly with all its disorienting significance. Why is the uproar that leaps from the depths of the pit and immediately before evoked such terror, now—as if the sound somehow skips over this circle—not audible? Obviously the noise of the depths that travels across all of Hell is not only the product but also the instrument of the common suffering of the damned. If for the most part neither the poet nor the reader has occasion consciously to remark it, in no other circumstance does its absence become explicit, as it is here, where Dante's narrative underscores the sudden transition from sound to silence.

The transition affects not only the senses; its function is more than impressionistic. This anomalous break in the plausibility of a physical phenomenon signals to the reader the existence of an intellectual problem that confounds his or her reason. An analogous infraction occurs when flakes of fire fall in the seventh circle in the third ring of the violent (XIV, 28–30), contradicting the medieval physical principle that fire tends to drift freely upward toward its own sphere, not fall toward the center of the earth. In this case, the "right reason" of the law of physics is violated to inflict heavier torment in the form of a rain of fire on the wicked. In the first circle, however, the constant stream of sound (or better, of *certain* sounds) stops, certainly not as a reward, but to spare the souls that dwell there—as an active expression of indulgence or at least of respect—the burden of a torment diffused throughout the infernal regions. Such a benign purpose links this strange circumstance to another that occurs later in the circle, when Dante and the famous poets who escort him cross the "fair stream" by walking on water "as if upon hard ground" (IV, 108–109), where the prodigy, apart from a probable allegorical significance otherwise not easily decoded, succeeds above all as a means to facilitate the passage of the illustrious literary fraternity.

In Dante's literary scheme, similarly problematic physical aspects attributed by the poet to the structure of the Otherworld are generally offered not as whims of poetic license but as manifestations of God's dominion over nature. Their miraculous character is explained by frequent references to the power and providential scheme of the divine artificer. Dante obviously knows that he himself invents the otherworld that he describes in his *Comedy* and that every miracle or anomaly of reason in the story derives from his own mind and pen. Nonetheless, the invention inspired by, intended to confirm, doctrinal orthodoxy has in general no autonomy in the face of the law of God that Dante's learning recognizes and interprets. The flakes of flame in the circle of the violent, which violate the Aristotelian physics of the Scholastics (just as the vertical flames of the fraudulent counselors respect that law), even if prompted by Dante's fantasy, logically result from a divine cause. They reaffirm Dante's belief in the institution of a higher moral law in doctrinal sympathy with a Christian and medieval definition and condemnation of sin. The poet allows himself only the freedom of selecting, for his literary convenience, what characters to associate with what punishment (or, later, what penitence or heavenly joy); but where pity must be vanquished, the reason for and the mode of punishment, dictated by each sin, strictly conform to ethical rules and absolutely objective judgments.

As long as Dante realizes his own intentions—as he does almost everywhere in the *Comedy*—there are no relevant exceptions to this rule of composition. In particular, there are no characters in the *Inferno* dear to the poet or for some reason notable to his eyes (from Farinata to Brunetto Latini to Ulysses) who are spared by some special dispensation from the horror of their position and protected by some expedient from the torture of the punishment they have merited. Even had Dante wished to exercise poetic intercession, God would not allow it; and it is *his* law that governs Dante's decisions.

But is this the case in the first circle? Is there not a sympathy, a poetic deference, that governs the instances of doctrine and justice? Are the impressionable but illogical features of the atmosphere that first strike us to be considered miracles woven into the divine scheme or, just this once, the unconscious or involuntary slips of a Dante dazzled by the structure of his own story? These questions are relevant for a canto that even from the beginning, as we have seen, is subtly contradictory in its immediate context in terms of the entire poem, and even in relation to itself.

Virgil explains the place and conditions that govern it to Dante even before the pilgrim can ask (and this failure to question serves to highlight the recurring formula of "you want to know" that introduces so many responses to Dante's interrogatories in the poem):

> The kindly master said: "Do you not ask
> who are these spirits whom you see before you?
> I'd have you know, before you go ahead,
>
>   they did not sin; and yet, though they have merits,
> that's not enough, because they lacked baptism,
> the portal of the faith that you embrace.
>
>   And if they lived before Christianity,
> they did not worship God in fitting ways;

and of such spirits I myself am one.
  For their defects, and for no other evil,
  we now are lost and punished just with this:
  we have no hope and yet we live in longing."
                                          (31–42)

Virgil's long measure describes the inhabitants of the circle at first by using the third person of verbs: "they did not sin," "they have," "they lacked,"
"they lived," following the general principle of the canticle governing objective alterity (not to mention the moral distinctions) in similar situations.
The first person enters Virgil's grammar unexpectedly: "and of such spirits I myself am one." The apparent neutrality of this reference is torn by the
emotion that soon precipitates from the desolate, collective "we now are
lost." Virgil's later words reproduce the heavy and heartfelt mood of the
circle and, at the same time, of his character. We could even call the speech
melancholy if the pathetic overtone of this word were not inadequate to
the calm dignity of the souls in Limbo.

The state of the unbaptized is defined by Dante as *desire,* and whatever
the meaning of the word may be, it is at once clear that it designates a sad
but devout and respectful feeling that has God for its object and that maintains a distance from the area of blasphemy and foul gestures of scorn that
the other "lost souls" hurl at Heaven (cf. III, 103; xxv, 1–3). Once again the
logic imposed by the topography of Hell receives a jolt, for the placement
of the episode *within* the cruel abyss is negated by atmosphere and com-
posure that ought not to belong to that circle.

What, in itself, is this *desire?* The ancient commentators interpreted the
word in a banal, slightly abstract way. All gloss line 42 more or less as does
Buti: "We live in desire of the blessed state, without hope of reaching it."
Not even the modern commentators seem to doubt that at issue is an
"eternal desire for God, without hope of ever fulfilling it" (Chiavacci
Leonardi), as if the "desire" were an active attraction of will toward an object that the inhabitants of the first circle of hell aspire to obtain but one forever denied them. I do not believe, however, that this interpretation grasps
the meaning of the passage. A desire for God is, in Christian thinking, only
the premise to grace and eternal salvation; and as such, it allows no delu-
sive hope. (How could God deny eternally someone who calls to him?) Nor
can this desire be conceded to anyone already "lost" and confined to the inferno. Instead, the word here signifies, as elsewhere in Dante (cf. the "longings" of the "seafarers" in the famous passage in *Purgatorio* VIII, 1–2), the
Latin *desiderium,* which expresses the awareness of an unrestored loss, a deprivation of feelings. The "great-hearted souls" (119) in the first circle are
not "punished" by a foolish anxiety for what they desire, but by a recurrent
mourning for what they have lost. We might try to imagine their situation
as an eternal prolonging of sadness that the disappearance of someone

dear leaves at the deepest part of ourselves. Rather than frustration and anxiety, they manifest in faces "neither sad nor joyous" (84) a solemn decorum and above all a noble and balanced consciousness of who they are, the *megalopsychia* or *magnanimatas* described by Aristotle in his *Nicomachean Ethics,* by which the highest intellects accept the fate of not being happy.

For those who died without baptism and without recognizing Christ, even though guiltless, the most ancient Latin Christian thought conceded no significant release from the common otherworldly destiny of sinners. Saint Augustine, indeed, combated the belief that at least unbaptized infants might be saved, asserting that "for this they will be condemned, since they added nothing to the original sin by living wickedly themselves, it is rightfully able to be said [of them] that there is little penalty in that damnation, but some nevertheless" (*Epist.* CLXXXIV A).

Later a tradition inspired by a sense of pious moderation, rather than true and proper scriptural authority and theological rigor, succeeded in tempering the harshness of the condemnation to hell of the innocent whose original sin before the Redemption closed to them the gates of heaven. Saint Gregory the Great believed the unbaptized were not sent to the depths of the inferno to be tortured but were to live peacefully in one of the upper reaches of the underworld: "Yet we say such souls have not descended to the lower region, so that they would be held in punitive places, but that there are superior places of the lower region and that other lower places must be believed, so that the just take repose in the higher regions and the unjust are tormented in the lower regions" (*Moralia in Iob* XII, ix). Saint Gregory elsewhere insisted on the tranquillity and freedom from torment of these souls, noting that "even in the very places of the lower region the souls of the just are held, so that they descend to that place for the original sin and nevertheless they are not held guilty for their own actions, as if to have made ready a little couch in the shades and have prepared themselves with the sleep of death in the lower regions" (ibid., XIII, xliv).

The upshot of this debate was the reservation of the upper and most external portion, or *lembo* (whence the late Latin *limbus* and the vernacular *limbo*), of hell for the patriarchs of the Old Testament (the *limbus Patrum* merged with the scriptural "bosom of Abraham") and for those babies who died before receiving baptism (called the *limbus puerorum*), on the supposition not that they were stained by original sin, but that for various reasons they could not have committed the actual sins that would have irredeemably condemned them in the absence of salutary sacraments. In fact, as Dante himself recalls when he questions Virgil and gives evidence of learning from him in verses 46–63 of the canto, the just people of the ancient law were carried to Paradise by Christ crucified and resurrected, so that after a time only babies would remain in limbo. In fact, the Christian imagination represents the place as populated essentially by the souls of infants. But many exceptions, at the insistence of the pious faithful, conceded celestial beatitude, even to these infants. It suffices to recall, for example, the infants massacred by the decree of Herod, positioned in Paradise and venerated by the Church as the Holy Innocents. All this makes Limbo seem an otherworldly location whose population waned after the Redemption, whether because, as Saint Gregory adds, the Redeemer "does not allow us to go there, whence he has already set free others from descending" (ibid., XIII, xliii); or because the absence of baptism by water might be mitigated by the baptism of desire or the baptism of blood, both able to wash away original sin; or because, finally (in contrast to the case of the patriarchs), it was not considered a matter of verisimilitude that an adult deprived of baptism and the truth of faith should be confined in the absence of actual sin. Whatever the outcome, the discussion turned on whether a soul achieved immediate entry to Paradise, as Dante admits only in the case of the Trojan Ripheus (*Par.* xx, 67–72). The prevalent belief nonetheless consigned the ancient pagans and infidels of the Christian era to eternal death in hell proper, so much so that, for example, not even the fame for perfect justice that the emperor Trajan enjoyed in the middle ages was judged sufficient to exempt him. To award his soul salvation, the well-known legend of his life had to invent a complicated procedure whereby a miracle allowed him a brief resurrection to permit his baptism.

The limbo of Dante is, in contrast, thick with "the crowds—the many multitudes— / of infants and of women and of men" (IV, 29–30), who form a "wood . . . where many spirits thronged" (66), among whom there will be identified individually, in long catalogues, men and women who belong almost universally to myth, civil history, and the ancient cultures of Greece and Rome, with the notable exceptions of the Islamic Saladin—whose isolation is underlined ("solitary, set apart," 129)—and Avicenna and Averroës. The last two form part of the "philosophic family" presided over by Aristotle, "the master of the men who know" (131–132). The elect company of the *magni auctores* Homer, Horace, Ovid, and Lucan emerges from a noble castle to encounter and honor Dante and Virgil. Dante is led inside an allegorical edifice representing ancient culture, which without any reference to the possibility that limbo might host spirits from different human and moral persuasions, provides only for its own learned or heroic guests.

The theological justification for the presence in Limbo of these famous authors is that all were famous for their sublime virtue and unstained by any guilt, a condition that Dante concedes to classical antiquity and, in part, to the non-Christian world, in infinitely greater and more trusting measure than medieval thought was accustomed to do. In a passage in the *Purgatorio* that we will refer to later, Dante explains that the inhabitants of Limbo knew all the virtues except the three theological ones.

Even this argument would not seem to account sufficiently for Dante's leniency with non-Christians if it did not consider a singular, humanistic

nostalgia, the memory of the classical Elysian fields, that sacrifices ideological and formal coherence for something more just and gentle. Any de-
cent commentary will signal the congruencies between the fourth canto of
the *Inferno* and Virgil's description in the *Aeneid* that inspired the Otherworld of the blessed, where the chosen spirits dwell in felicity. Besides the
purely rhetorical aspect of his literary imitation, there is in Dante an understanding that *Elysium* and its inhabitants might be conflated with a
Christian version of the Otherworld, considering it as the true Limbo,
originally destined by God for the mass placement of the virtuous from
every culture and Testament, but now a place only for pagans. In his commentary on IV, 163, the friar Guido da Pisa makes conceit explicit when he
observes that *Elysium* is only the name that the poets give to that which
Christians call Limbo, but the place is the same: "The old poets call this circle Elysium. We Christians, however, call it Limbo. The Bible refers to the
place as 'the bosom of Abraham.' It is Elysium, according to the poets, because it is separate from the place of punishment. In it the souls of the righteous abide. And it is called Elysium because it is outside (*extra*) the *lision*,
which means misery. Thus *Elysium*, the place adjacent to the habitation of
the wretched."

Apparently, therefore, Dante forgives these souls the most severe punishment. It was certainly natural that the seat destined for the eternal
bearers of original sin should be associated with the dwelling of guilty
souls, considering, as Saint Thomas says in his *Summa theologica*, that "if
one considers the nature of the place, it is likely that the location is one
and continuous between Hell and Limbo. And therefore a certain upper
portion of Hell is called the Limbo of the Fathers" (*Summa* III, 69, 5). But
obviously Saint Thomas suggests the possibility that the site of Limbo
(here restricted to only the *limbus Patrum* and therefore to be considered as
emptied) might be either integrated with or adjacent to Hell, "idem locus
vel quasi continuum." Dante has already, in Canto III, considered the plau-
sibility of a place contiguous with hell but not contained within its ethical
and material dimensions—the vestibule or ante-inferno—he designs as an
ignoble and cruel locus for the "wretched ones, who never were alive" (III,
64). This construction differs little from the other, crueler circles of the
abyss with regard to the horror of the torments and the squalid nudity of
those whose moral inertia disqualifies them both from heaven and hell.
Dante offers, perhaps, a sort of negative Limbo, which condemns cowardice as a foul caricature of infant candor and innocence. It is strange that
Dante does not exploit the opportunity to image the ante-inferno positively
and to locate here, beyond the misery of the truly damned, the decorous
and melancholy ranks of lost souls whom he assigns to the first circle. He
prefers to give these a decidedly infernal identity, which their solemn nobility soon contradicts, although nothing obligated him to do so.

We can explain Dante's paradoxical decision by reconciling the difficulty of according salvation to pagans with Dante's impulse to love and defer to venerable antiquity, even though antiquity conflicts with Dante's own Christian convictions. The resulting compromise produces an inevitable series of contradictions and ambiguities. For example, as we have already suggested, the exceptions and privileges accorded to the souls in Limbo, which would be perfectly acceptable and reasonable if they defined a marginal site not subject to the harsh laws of hell, instead appear as irrational distortions to the ideological structure. Dante surrenders to a fascination for antiquity, aware of the temptation to make a religion of a culture that gently but insidiously lures a Christian.

Strikingly, some of the inhabitants of the circle retain intensely significant attributes of their worldly state. This privilege is not generally conceded to the damned of hell, who almost all appear naked. Traces of their terrestrial identity, such as heraldic insignia or the inscriptions on the tombs of the heretics (XI, 7–9), produce in hell only a terrible sense of ridicule and refine and increase the torment of the wicked. One thinks of the family heraldic emblems that the usurers wear around their necks (XVII, 54–65). By contrast, in the first circle Homer, "the consummate poet," brandishing a sword (86–88) and Caesar "in his armor, falcon-eyed" (123) both exhibit in honorable fashion the direct or symbolic emblems of what gave them dignity as men—the former as the founding poet of the epic tradition fit to celebrate in high style the battles and bravery of heroes; the latter, by means of the military dress and rapacious, noble eyes that identify him with the sacred sign of the imperial eagle, expressing the majestic and providential character that the Roman Empire has for Dante. Even here, therefore, the laws of the blind world fail as Dante superimposes, so to speak, his own poetic and scholarly purposes over divine justice.

The most categorically subtle infraction of Divine Law is that exposed by another singularity of the first circle. The subject of Limbo is renewed at least three times in the *Comedy,* always in the *Purgatorio.* In the first canto (*Purg.* I, 76–80), Virgil recalls Limbo when he presents himself to Cato and asks him to be kind in the name of Marcia, his dear wife, developing the brief reference to her given in *Inferno* IV, 128. Once again explaining himself, this time to Dante's contemporary Sordello, Virgil resumes in the seventh canto a theme from the distant *Inferno,* giving an exact account:

> There is a place below that only shadows—
> not torments—have assigned to sadness; there,
> lament is not an outcry, but a sigh.
>   There I am with the infant innocents,
> those whom the teeth of death had seized before
> they were set free from human sinfulness;

there I am with those souls who were not clothed
in the three holy virtues—but who knew
and followed after all the other virtues.

(*Purg.* VII, 28–36)

More ample still is the reference in the twenty-second canto, where the
poet Statius, after being introduced and having revealed that he had secretly
become a Christian through the influence of Virgil's verse, asks Virgil for
news of the underworld fate of other Latin poets. Virgil responds at length,
numbering in a series that includes Greek authors, those found in Limbo
who were not mentioned in the preceding catalog of spirits. Going beyond
what Statius asks regarding only writers, he adds the names of female characters from Statius's own work (*Purg.* XXII, 13–15, 97–114). Neither structure, tone, nor subject matter would prevent the transfer of this list to the
fourth canto of the *Inferno,* with no other effect but to enlarge the roll call
of names, a fact that has led some Dante scholars to regard the *Purgatorio*
passage as a mere appendix to what has already been said.

The key to the lists lies elsewhere. Dante's itinerary across the three regions of the Otherworld is relentlessly forward. It admits no returns, recalls,
or movement backwards. The poet proceeds on his journey as if his road
disappeared as soon as he passed over it, or as if the world he visits dissolves
behind his back as soon as he takes his eyes away from it. It suffices to recall that in a poem of such mass and dizzying bravura as the *Comedy* presents, there is not (with one exception that we will consider) a single flashback of substance except for those brief, practical ones needed to explain
circumstances that depend on anterior episodes. Their function is to anticipate what lies ahead. The reader perceives this aspect at first as the technical character of Dante's narrative, tempered by dense and rapid rhythms.
In this context even the frequency and duration of the recollection of
Limbo may be explained as tied to the continuity over two canticles of the
presence of Virgil, who naturally carries with him, as part of his allegorical meaning as well as his literal humanity, the memory of that otherworldly position from which he comes, and with it the evocation of its
other inhabitants and mood.

There remains nonetheless a necessity to Dante's itinerary that does
not depend on literary motives. At every stage of the voyage across hell and
purgatory, Dante concludes and eliminates an involvement with sin. Bit by
bit he renounces, after trekking across its tortures, a part of the evil rooted
in human nature. Every margin, every ledge, every bridge, every cliff he
overcomes in his walk across those two kingdoms makes impossible any return even in memory to what remains after he crosses, because otherwise
the voyage of discovery would be rendered vain by the retention of evil in
his mind, and the pilgrim would suddenly be transported to the dark wood
from which he departed while burdened by human infirmity. He cannot

proceed beyond each episode except by canceling it with the testimony of his own cure, just as in the transit from one level to the next of purgatory an angel cancels one of the seven P's inscribed on his forehead. The narrative thrust of the *Comedy* that makes improbable and inimical to literary taste the resumption in the poem of situations already confronted is only the reflection of a profound moral obligation. This obligation is suspended in the case of Limbo, just as the sound of the thunder of the abyss is transmuted. The first circle of hell is the only place in the whole otherworld that, at the moment of exiting ("beyond the quiet, into trembling air," as is so well said at 150, at the close of the canto), Dante leaves not with express relief but with a bitterness that echoes in the sound of the verse. The exception to this feeling—the ability to look back as well as forward—will be legitimated on the poetic level as well as on the doctrinal level by the coherence of Virgil's persona, characterized by the sad sweetness of Limbo. To think of the circle where Virgil dwells eternally does not depress Dante but rather confirms goodness and truth. The souls of Limbo who were unaware of the truth now know how to recognize it and their signs testify to its power.

In a poet's homage to poetry, Dante gives the other inhabitants of Limbo the same prerogative he takes, a prerogative not individualized as in the case of Virgil, but displayed in a categorical representation of a superior and honored order of humanity, from which the imperfections of the world cannot detract. Dante's God has adopted the inhabitants of Limbo as noble instruments in the execution of his providential design. They are the founders of empires (Caesar, Saladin), the authors of doctrines that Dante knew from scholastic theology (the "philosophical family" of Aristotle, his followers, and commentators), and poets.

In verses 85–90 and 121–144, Dante chooses to offer long lists of these personalities. Some he briefly individualizes with rapid though incisive strokes, but most are merely names, occurring a little mechanically and not without a monotonous repetition of the phrase "I saw." This schematic catalogue that organizes the poet's vision by categories of characters brought together by events or choice will be copied and varied by Petrarch in his *Trionfi,* but it remains rare in Dante's poem. Even in Canto v of the *Inferno,* which allows to the lustful a role similar to that in Canto IV of the unbaptized (cf. v, 52–69), yielding precedence to Paolo and Francesca, Dante prefers to set a few figures in strong relief against a background of anonymity. He usually focuses on one character, which assumes universal exemplarity. We might be tempted to attribute the mood of Limbo to the uncertainty of an art that has not yet fully decided on its own appropriate objectives and on the means best suited to achieve them, groping down the blind alley of a formal attempt that will be abandoned. Still, when after many years and a wider experience as a writer Dante renews the story of Limbo in Canto xxii of the *Purgatorio,* he will offer his original model once again intact, giving a new, long register of names. This renewal demonstrates beyond doubt that such lists should be associated not with a stiff and still uncertain technique of a poet, but with the nature and significance of the episode.

Considered as a unit, the catalog of *Inferno* IV and that of *Purgatorio* XXII strike us because of two extraordinary peculiarities of their interrelationship. The first is the harmonious division between the presence of Greek and Roman poets and philosophers and the express recognition that Homer holds the first place among poets (88 and 96; cf. *Purg.* XXII, 101–102) and Aristotle among philosophers. The Western medieval tradition did not clearly admit the superiority of Greek culture in comparison to Latin suggested by the population of Limbo. If we recall that over fifty years later Boccaccio would seek to clear himself of the charge of using Greek sources for his *Genealogia deorum gentilium* and that as late as the middle of the fifteenth century a few humanists sustained that studying Greek was useless, we must admit (and admire the more as we consider the many gaps in Dante's knowledge of individual writers) the genial independence and acute judgment with which the poet conceives of classical antiquity. This is perhaps the first time in the Middle Ages (but are we still in the Middle Ages?) that a synthesis of poetry and Greek and Roman culture so elaborate, so impassioned, and so far-flung succeeds in forming a universal history.

In his crowded Limbo from which the patriarchs have emigrated, Dante does more than name just writers, philosophers, and figures from secular history. The poets appear not just in themselves, but also with their poetic characters—this is the second great singularity of the first circle. From here on this model governs the population of Dante's otherworld, where by the same laws of reality characters from ancient and contemporary history, from Julius Caesar to Ugolino della Gherardesca, live with the heroes of poetry and myth such as Capaneus or Myrrha or Ulysses. Perhaps the protagonists of poetic fiction are no less real for Dante than people who actually existed simply because his thought lacks historical perspective and the critical acumen to distinguish them. This hypothesis finds support from the *Aeneid,* which Dante read as the witness to remote historical events prompted by a divine providence whose purpose was to prepare the future of imperial and papal Rome (cf., for example, *Inf.* II, 13–24). Lucan's *Pharsalia* also reflects this view, since the exegetical and critical tradition emphasized the ambiguous overlay of poetry and history. Ovid's *Metamorphoses* was a less obvious case from the moment that medieval culture insisted on allegorical interpretations of it, separating the fictional outer rind of myth from the hidden core of moral or scientific truth. Nonetheless, a different interpretive criterion, called *historialis,* covered the traces of the blurring of antiquities and real people. All this means little for Dante. The happy innovation of Dante lies essentially in the fact that he first imagines a narrative situation in which an author encounters on the same temporal and spatial plane beings from an earlier time of whom an author speaks in his text. Whether these beings are real or imaginary becomes now a secondary issue. When we learn that Virgil dwells with Aeneas in Limbo (and with Camilla, Latinus, and Lavinia), and Lucan with Julius Caesar; when Statius receives news in purgatory of his heroines; when Virgil and Dante meet Cacus and Ulysses, we cannot doubt that Dante has discovered and celebrates here in his Limbo the intrinsic poeticality that transforms (or retransforms) people into characters and abolishes any division between writing and reality.

I am aware at this point, as I draw together the disparate threads of my discourse, that I have neglected to pause in my task to clarify the effects of these characters. By what criteria are they grouped? What does the poet know about each one, and how does he know it? What meanings should be attached to presence or omission? These are arguments critics have pursued through countless articles and that are still fair game for further research. But even had I space enough, I would pursue a different path. Of the many philosophers and poets mentioned in the fourth canto of the *Inferno* and the twenty-second of the *Purgatorio,* especially of the Greeks (including Homer), it is unlikely that Dante knew more than their names. And so our first question is, how could he possibly base so much on so little, paying such high regard and as a passionate reader defying, in the warm welcome of his Limbo, the divine will, on the basis of mere names, empty of content, of poets and philosophers whom he had not read and could never (and he knew it) read.

Dante himself answers our questions in those pages of the *Convivio* where he speaks of the means he embraced to console himself for the loss of Beatrice. He turned for comfort to the great consolatory works of antiquity, to the *Consolation of Philosophy* by Boethius, and to *Laelius: On Friendship* of Cicero:

> Although it was difficult for me at first to penetrate their meaning, I finally penetrated it as deeply as my command of Latin and the small measure of my intellect enabled me to do, by which intellect I had perceived many things before, as in a dream . . . . I who sought to console myself found not only a remedy for my tears but also the words of authors, sciences, and books. Pondering these, I quickly determined that Philosophy, who was the lady of these authors, sciences, and books, was a great thing.
>
> (*Convivio* II, xii, 2–5)

Not just the pages he read, but the *words*—a vocabulary consisting of the bare names of writers, the bare titles of books, the bare titles of disciplines, sustain him. Those ancient words, those spoils, suffice of themselves. Nothing else remains, because the great voice of antiquity itself is total. It continues to echo, to fascinate, to satisfy even by desire—yes, by the *longing* or *desiderium* of Limbo that leaves its trace in one who knows and grieves that he or she has hopelessly lost it. In the courage of his Limbo, Dante, I believe, wishes to render homage and signal his debt to this voice.

BIBLIOGRAPHICAL NOTE

Although the text of this canto is relatively plain and offers no special difficulties for the interpretation of any particular passage, it involves complex ideological and cultural issues. A clear and informed introduction to the historical and theological problem raised by Limbo, as documented by patristic and Scholastic writers, is that of A. Gaudel, "Limbes," *Dictionnaire de théologie catholique,* IX, I (Paris, 1926), coll. 760–772. On the question of the otherworld fate of non-Christians, see L. Capéran, *Le problème des infidèles: Essai historique* (Paris, 1912); L. Capéran, *Le problème du salut des infidèles: Essai théologique* (Paris, 1912); S. Harent, "Infidèles (salut des)," *Dictionnaire de théologie catholique,* VII, II (Paris, 1928), coll. 1726–1930. On Dante's attitude toward the Greek and Roman world, a first orientation is given by Manlio Pastore Stocchi, "Classica, cultura," *Enciclopedia dantesca* (Rome, 1970), 2:30–36. Fundamental for the moral features of the classical names mentioned in *Inferno* IV are F. Forti, *Magnanimitade: Studi su un tema dantesco* (Bologna, 1977), and more generally, R.-A. Gauthier, *Magnanimité: L'idéal de la grandeur dans la philosophie païenne et dans la théologie chrétienne* (Paris, 1951). On some of the other doctrinale issues raised in this essay, see Manlio Pastore Stocchi, "Giulio Cesare," *Enciclopedia dantesca* (Rome, 1976), 5:685–686 (for the legend of his salvation). For all the other historical figures and writers mentioned there are exhaustive notes in the *Enciclopedia dantesca.*

My citations of the commentators on the *Comedy* come from: *Commento di Francesca da Buti sopra la "Divina Commedia" di Dante Allighieri,* ed. C. Giannini (Pisa, 1858), 120; Dante Alighieri, *Commedia,* with the commentary of Anna Maria Chiavacci Leonardi on *Inferno* (Milan, 1991), 1:112; Guido da Pisa, *Expositiones et glose super Comediam Dantis,* ed. Vincenzo Cioffari (Albany, N.Y., 1974), 67–68.

Essays and readings dedicated to this canto are naturally most numerous. I will cite only Giorgio Padoan, *Il pio Enea, l'empio Ulisse: Tradizione classica e intendimento medievale in Dante* (Ravenna, 1977)—"Il Limbo dantesco," 102–124, is fundamental and rich in further bibliography; Amilcare A. Iannucci, "Limbo: The Emptiness of Time," *Studi danteschi* 52 (1979–80): 69–128; F. Montanari, "Limbo," *Enciclopedia dantesca* (Rome, 1971), 3:651–654 (with ample bibliography).

CANTO V

The Fierce Dove

PAOLO VALESIO

L'enfer vient d'être complètement restauré; il n'avait plus ces derniers siècles qu'une valeur d'application: intellectuellement c'était parfait, au point de vue de la douleur morale, cela laissait à désirer.

(Satan is speaking, in André Breton, *Poisson soluble*)

The ritualistic apologetic references at the beginning of so many Dante essays about the gigantic Dantean industry, and the heavy bibliographical stratifications accumulated on every word written (or perhaps written) by the poet, are becoming by now rather tiresome. Such caveats, already topical in the times of Francesco De Sanctis, could remain meaningful when they were expressions of creative modernistic impatience, for instance from Gabriele d'Annunzio, Giovanni Papini, and, most virulently, from Filippo Tommaso Marinetti when he wrote: "Who can deny that the *Divine Comedy* today is nothing but a filthy verminous heap crawling with compilers of footnotes? What is the good of venturing out on the battlefields of thought when the fight is over, just in order to count the dead, examine the most exquisite wounds, collect the broken weapons and the remnants of plunder—and all this, while learned crows heavily fly overhead flapping their papery wings?"(267).

These warnings or disclaimers about the obfuscating filters of erudition were still functional when they reflected a gentle poetic attention (as from Eliot), or a carefully thought anti-intellectualistic position (as by Croce, whose 1921 book on Dante remains one of the most brilliant, and least understood, contributions to modern Dante criticism—see Gennaro Sasso's recent essay). But today such musings tend to be simply depressive. On the contrary, any critic engaging once again with Dante should feel at once the pleasure of rediscovering continuities of critical tradition and the excitement of making new interpretative explorations in areas of inexhaustible semantic richness. Otherwise, why bother?

Dante's poetry, like all great poetry, survives every critical onslaught and reemerges always fresh and ready for new challenges. Take the case of *Inferno* v, the most traditional and best known metonymy for the *Comedy*'s whole text and the most popular among its several popular episodes—in June 1992, Italian newspapers were describing a "retrial" of Paolo and Francesca in Ravenna, involving lawyers and literary critics. More seriously, what I propose to do here is to look at this fifth canto as a metonymy of the whole poem, not an isolated niche. Building on the foundations of a vast critical tradition, summarized in detailed essays such as those by Mario Marcazzan, Dante Della Terza, Enrico Malato, and Francesco Mazzoni, I probe areas in which the critical reading of the canto is still open to new explorations.

If it is true that these 142 lines have been read and reread, annotated and reannotated, their engagement with contemporary critical methodologies remains open, although such an exploration has definitely begun: witness the pages by Mark Musa, and essays like those by Carlos López Cortezo, who undertakes a semantic revision; Ray Fleming, who oscillates between contemporary ideological categories and traditional moralism; René Girard, who quickly turns from a look at the fifth canto to a general theoretical statement; Franco Masciandaro, who analyzes the cluster of desire and of nostalgia for a locus of innocence; Susan Noakes, who studies the subtle temporal relationship at work here; Barbara Vinken, who experiments with rhetorical concepts, although unconcerned with systematic developments on the rhetoric of antirhetoric; Mary J. Carruthers and Jerome Mazzaro, who investigate some key terms and concepts; Michelangelo Picone, who focuses on the intertextual dimension. It is an engagement that in a certain sense begins in the late 1950s, with the simultaneously appearing essays by Gianfranco Contini and Charles Singleton, is temporarily and bibliographically assessed in the pages of Antonio Enzo Quaglio and Teodolinda Barolini, and sanctioned by the *haute divulgation* of Vittorio Sermonti's collection of broadcast presentations.

As it usually happens (or should happen) such an engagement will take the form of a fuller recovery of the tradition, not of some naive search for novelty at all costs. But we should also avoid the defensive critical function of a watchdog, growling against anyone who dares approach the ancient sacred grounds with some new proposals. In fact what these two attitudes (the overturning and the reactionary) have in common, beyond their apparent opposition, is a polemical strain—what I have called elsewhere an *ablative* attitude. (Criticism as a way of producing divisions, excisions of matter, vindications of territory, goes back along a genealogical line to Risorgimento ideologies and religious-social debates in tracts like the 1857 work of Eugène Aroux, *L'hérésie de Dante démontrée par Francesca de Rimini, devenue un moyen de propagande vaudoise. . . .*) What I will be practicing here in contrast is an *oblative* kind of criticism: a criticism that offers itself up as a way of listening to the inexhaustible production of sense that every great literary text accomplishes. For instance, in treading once again the much frequented ground of Dantean numerology I do not search out polemical-technical points but rather try to reconstruct the full archetypal force of the number under whose rubric the story takes place: the number five (typical of what Jung calls "disturbed mandalas" [192, 213]); and I try to keep an open-minded sense of the relevant analyses—not only the ancient ones, that is, but also the ones reflecting contemporary methods.

The number five, which in the rationalistic strain of classical rhetoric (as in the *Rhetorica ad Herennium*) was a reference to the human hand with a mnemotechnical potential, also enjoys deeper and more intense associations in esoteric and in Christian lore as the number emblematic of the organic human being (the four limbs of the body plus the controlling head) and especially of the marriage relationship in its cosmic aspect (Heaven = 3 and the Great Mother Earth = 2) or in its human dimension (male odd + female even number), down to erotic lore both ancient and modern (as in one of Freud's case histories: "The patient remarked that the opening and shutting of the butterfly's wings while it was settled on the flower had given him an uncanny feeling. It had looked, so he said, like a woman opening her legs, and the legs then made the shape of a Roman V" [569]). Thus the development of a sensitivity to archetypes is no erudite exercise sufficient unto itself: it helps us to understand why a text like this is (to repeat) popular—but in the strong sense of this term (referring to the deep roots of certain symbols, configurations, situations in life, hence pertinent to folklore in its serious aspect), rather than in the weak one, having to do with mundane anecdotes like the above quoted new "trial" in Ravenna, which concerns folklore in its debased and cheapened sense. But the archetype of the pentad turns out (as we will see presently) to have a specific significance for the literary hermeneutics of Canto v.

In fact, moving from the semiotic frame of the canto to its central story, we find another archetypal image, that of the dove: "Even as doves when summoned by desire, / borne forward by their will, move through the air / with wings uplifted, still, to their sweet nest" (82–84). We are all familiar with the symbolic value of the dove as a sign of purity, simplicity, mildness, and peacefulness, and Dante orchestrates this sweet connotation in other places in the *Comedy* (for instance, in *Par.* xxv, 19–21). The poet is also aware, of course, of the deeper spiritual allegorization that makes of the dove a favorite Christian symbol of the soul and of spirituality in general, as he shows for instance when he explicitly quotes from the Canticle of Canticles 6:8, "One is my dove, my perfect one is but one," and thematizes this as the emblem of the "Divine Science" (i.e., theology) because, as Dante (always the poet, even when he writes in prose) says in a beautiful phrase (that at the same time embodies a wishful thinking), this science *è sanza macula di lite* (has no stain of contention [*Convivio* II, xiv]).

But Dante is also aware of the strutting, arrogantly and erotically exhibitionistic, aspect of the dove as the venereal bird par excellence—as for instance when he evokes Venus's chariot drawn by five doves (*Il Fiore* CCXVII, 11), or when he describes doves in a quiet situation that is unusual because they are "forgetful of their customary strut" (*Purg.* II, 126—and of course the Italian term used to describe them has moral implication: *sanza mostrar l'usato orgoglio*). If the turtledove symbolizes *charitas,* Venus's white dove stands for *cupiditas* (see Iannucci, 353). We can thus understand why the dove-as-soul is not associated only with righteously pure beings: there is a tradition according to which, when the legendary and lascivious Assyrian queen Semíramis died, she was transformed into a dove (this detail, together with many other relevant elements for the dove archetype, is to be found in Ernest Jones's essay [333]); and Semíramis (as we will see later), although a secondary character in this canto, is one of its most telling signifiers.

The apparent simplicity of the just-quoted simile, then, is misleading. For if we read it (as, up to a point, we must) in the context of a courtly, and specifically stilnovistic, rhetoric whose presence in Francesca's discourse has been abundantly analyzed, then it is important to point out that this simile echoes the opening of one of the most important poems in the whole history of Italian lyric poetry, a *canzone* by the Bolognese poet Guido Guinizzelli that is also a poetical manifesto explicitly acknowledged elsewhere by Dante: "Love always flees toward a gentle heart / like a bird in the wood flies to green things" (*Al cor gentil rempaira sempre amore / come l'ausello in selva a la verdura*). Such a connection is confirmed by Francesca's own words: "Love, that can quickly seize the gentle heart" (*Amor, ch'al cor gentil ratto s'apprende* [100]). This genealogy has already been analyzed in past criticism on the canto, but some additional remarks are in order. In the immediately quoted line Dante reprises the tenor of Guinizzelli's metaphor (the intrinsic link between love and a gentle heart), while in the dove simile he concentrates instead on the vehicle of that same metaphor (the link between the bird and the natural world). But actually he eschews what is too symmetrical in this intellectual dissection of the mechanism of metaphor, and (with the leap typical of great poetry) he blends elements of the vehicle with elements of the tenor in a chiasmuslike combination; thus he extracts and holds up to the light what was hidden in Guinizzelli's metaphor: a connection between the animal (the bird) that most vividly synthesizes the soulful with the bodily (especially after the poetical preachings of Saint Francis of Assisi), and with desire.

This is but one example—a systematic analysis would require a book— of one of the basic strategies that generate Dante's poetry as such (and of which we will see other crucial instances presently): its power of *refrac-*

tion—a term preferable to diffraction, because the latter has acquired a specialized meaning in the technique of textual criticism, especially (see Contini's work) in Italian usage. (If this term should appear at first sight to be too arid and harsh, let me point to this Proustian sentence from *Le temps retrouvé:* "soit qu'il n'y eût plus rien en lui de ces *sentiments,* soit qu'ils fussent obligés pour arriver jusqu'à nous de passer par des *réfracteurs physiques si déformants* qu'ils changeaient en route absolument de sens" [emphasis mine].)

But we have barely began to appreciate this simile—for its real challenge lies in spiritual and ethical evaluation rather than in formal intertextuality (such a differentiation being crucial to the critical understanding of this canto as a whole). These doves are flying through the darkness of Hell ("dark air" [51], or reddish-dark—"who through the darkened [*perso*] air have come to visit / our souls that stained the world with blood" [89–90]— *perso,* as Dante himself explains, is a color mixing deep red with black). Thus they evoke Venus's doves that Dante's master poet Virgil describes as guiding Aeneas to Avernus (see *Aeneid* VI, 190–205). But the strategic evocation here is the one that touches one of the nuclei of the Christian faith: these doves are a reversed and degraded image of the Holy Spirit or, as I prefer to say in this context, of the Holy Ghost (as has already been hinted by Anthony Cassell [10]). The fact that Dante strongly implants this connection, I might add, emerges in his poetic refraction of two distinct Gospel scenes, which he links subtextually by the apparition of the Holy Ghost: Jesus' baptism ("he saw the heavens opened, and the Spirit as a dove descending, and remaining on him" [Mark 1: 10]), and the Pentecost scene ("And suddenly there came a sound from heaven, as of a mighty wind coming, and it filled the whole house where they were sitting" [Acts 2:2]), the latter description being evoked in the canto by lines like "which bellows like the sea beneath a tempest, / when it is battered by opposing winds. / The hellish hurricane, which never rests . . . " (29–31). I also add that the degradation of the Holy Ghost symbolism is subtly implicit in the fact (which leads us back to numerological archetypes) that the doves are two: two, the number of antithesis and division, which splits the fundamental unity of the third person of the Trinity; and I finally add that all this connection is confirmed by the stately movements of the two dovelike figures ("with wings uplifted, still" [84]), which appear like a parody of the Holy Ghost in its processional aspect (*qui ex Patre Filioque procedit*).

Finally, apropos of the punitive hurricanelike wind in this canto: this description has roots, not only in theological narratives and classic literature, but also in the more "middlebrow" devotional literature (further confirming the popular character of this canto). An instance of this is constituted by a couple of stanzas from a traditional hymn of the *Missale Romanum:* "So that when the tribunal of the Judge / will condemn the guilty ones to the fire / and a friendly voice will call / the pious ones to the heaven which is owed to them, / we will not be twisted around through black eddies / as bait to the flames."

But it is not my intention to compile anything like a map of the literary phenomenology of this canto. Rather, I note in what sense even this intensely cultivated spot of Dante studies is still waiting for new efforts. What is needed at this point is a truly interdisciplinary analysis. The preceding phenomenology has already raised some hermeneutic questions; and it is to this aspect that I now turn.

Synchronically, the Paolo and Francesca story offers four concentric circles. At the center is the intricate complex of Old French prose romances concentrating on the figure of Lancelot (see the Sommer ed., 3:257–266), some of which were early translated into Italian (see the Polidori ed., and its Old French appendix, 2:260–264). I will refer to this complex as the Lancelot vulgate. Around this, the story of Paolo and Francesca unrolls. Around it, the Dante and Virgil story takes place; and around all this, the stratification of modern critical readings proliferates. But the actual situation is more complex. Between the version of the Lancelot vulgate that Paolo and Francesca read and Dante's account of it stands the most famous poetic account of illicit love in medieval Europe: the story of Tristan and Iseult. (The Pio Rajna article on this point is to my mind the single most important contribution in the history of the modern hermeneutics of *Inferno* v, more important than the critical literature on who kissed whom first that flourished in the years of that Rajna essay—a literature Hatcher and Musa summarize; and as I show elsewhere, one of the poetic narratives in the Tristan vulgate is the *direct* genealogy of the peculiar poetic narrative rhythm in *Inferno* v.)

Hence the iconic and ironic nature of this canto: Dante quotes the Lancelot story as the *literary* source of Paolo and Francesca's *existential* predicament (one of the earliest and more powerful manifestations of the modernistic topos of life imitating literature); but the poet is aware that by this very gesture he is evoking in the reader's mind the Tristan story as one of the crucial *literary* genealogies of his own *literary* account. It gives a peculiar twist to the hurried mention of Tristan in the first part of the canto: "'See Paris, Tristan . . .'—and he pointed out / and named to me more than a thousand shades" (67–68 [the ellipses belong to the English text]). Confirming this wink to the reader, the name whose standard Italian form is *Pàride* (a proparoxytonic word) appears here in the French oxytonic form *Parìs* (thus, 'Vedi Parìs, Tristano'; e più di mille). Of course, this form is "necessary" for the line to scan; but Dante is never slave to the meter. Thus, this variant form is an allusion to the Old French "matter of Troy" as a narrative strain parallel to the Arthurian vulgate (of which the Lancelot vulgate is a component).

But let us look a bit more closely at Dante's semiotic game—a very serious game indeed, which problematizes the by-now traditional dichotomy between the role of the pilgrim and that of the poet, and is crucial for determining the poetic value of the text. What Dante's first fully poetical canto in the *Comedy* realizes is the passage from a source relationship to a genealogical relationship. Instead of presenting to us a love story—that of Paolo and Francesca—in terms that allusively echo a more ancient text left in the background (the essential object of source criticism), Dante quotes the source explicitly, thus laying bare the literary genealogy of a "real" story. (That this story has at best a dubious historical status is culturally interesting but semiotically irrelevant: the Paolo and Francesca story is "true" in the "real world" posited as the alternative side and constant point of reference of Dante's voyage in the otherworld.) The poet shows us literature-becoming-history-becoming-literature; this is what I meant when I spoke of irony. Clarity requires here a minimum of schematization:

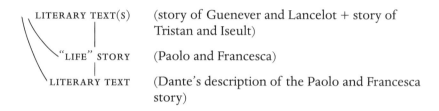

LITERARY TEXT(S)   (story of Guenever and Lancelot + story of
                    Tristan and Iseult)

"LIFE" STORY   (Paolo and Francesca)

LITERARY TEXT   (Dante's description of the Paolo and Francesca
                    story)

If the connecting lines were all straight, we would have a direct relationship of source to later text. But their curves define a genealogical relationship (one that unsettles the connection between straight source and later text). Dante enters twice (the curved lines are accordingly two) into the Lancelot vulgate: first indirectly (through Francesca's exposition), then directly with his own way of structuring Francesca's story as a literary discourse, *including* the transfer (refraction effect) of some elements of this story to the *Paradiso* (as we will see presently).

The strain that the poet must have felt in developing this brilliant narratologic operation leaves a trace in the line marking the basic dramatic transition in the whole canto—a line whose essential meaning seems to be clear but whose actual ambiguity is still being discussed by critics: "A Gallehault indeed, that book and he / who wrote it, too" (*Galeotto fu 'l libro e chi lo scrisse* [137]).

What the poet clearly wants to suggest—and this is the basic way in which he has always been interpreted—is a parallel between the level of the real world and that of literary fiction. He is saying something like, The book one of whose main characters is Gallehault fulfills, in the real world of Paolo and Francesca, the same role that Gallehault realizes in the fictional world of that book (I apologize for the pedantic paraphrase, but it clarifies the poetic structure; incidentally, when I directly mention this character I follow the spelling "Galehot," as in the Old French text edited by Sommer).

But in the actual structure of this verse, the (so to speak) horizontal metonymy of Galehot = romance of Lancelot is oddly enclosed in a vertical (or genetic) metonymy that makes the perception of the rhetorical figure particularly difficult, in that it contains, not two terms (as it is usual in this figure) but *three*: Galehot = romance of Lancelot = author of that romance. The inevitable question (which however no one seems to have asked until now) is "What is this semantically unneeded and rhetorically strained reference to the author doing here?" The question might be answered, in strictly rhetorical terms, as "Nothing, really." We would thus have a further reassuring proof that Dante is merely a human being (a fact that seems to be sometimes overlooked), and as such he is no more free from an occasional less than absolutely perfect line than the other great poets are. Sometimes Dante nods, just as Homer does: especially in what several critics have already noted as a slow and difficult beginning of the great narrative sweep of the poem.

There are some contextual elements that might reinforce this hypothesis. I remarked elsewhere on the pleonastic shadow hovering above the "with what and in what way" *repetitio* in 119: "with what and in what way did Love allow you / to recognize your still uncertain longings?" (*a che e come concedette amore / che conosceste i dubbiosi disiri?* [119–120]). Whether or not he is thinking of this specific Dantean locus, Andrea Zanzotto appropriately identifies the codified aspect of this rhetorical transition that is almost a space filler when, in one of his parodic, neo-neo-Petrarchist sonnets, he writes a line like "A che e per chi di nota in nota illinguo." An analogous (I will not say flaw, but) less-than-total perfection is to be found in the transition from Francesca's direct words: "how that was done still wounds me" (*e 'l modo ancor m'offende* [102]) to the poet's metawords in his narrative: "When I had listened to those injured souls" (*Quand'io intesi quell'anime offense* [109]), where the *repetitio* of the verb *offendere* seems to run counter to Dante's almost preternatural skill in *variatio* (considering also the fact that an alternative form, from another verb, had been used before: "I urged on my voice: 'O battered souls'" [*mossi la voce: "O anime affannate"*], 80). But such an analysis would, in this case, be insufficient—in fact, it would be deaf to the peculiar poetic effect that here emerges dramatically. Line 137 is indeed effective: but in the psychological-hermeneutic dimension, rather than in the strictly rhetorical one.

Dante abruptly introduces the image of the anonymous author of the Lancelot romance (*chi lo scrisse*), thereby dangerously stretching the metonymic texture of this line, because—with one of his usual bold moves of foregrounding—he wants to put himself as an author into the picture: both in the general sense (author of a previous large and ideologically polyvalent opus that bears a difficult relationship to the *Comedy*) and in the local sense (the author of this specific canto).

The former authorial perspective has long been recognized by Dante criticism, whereas the latter is still waiting for a full development—a development all the more urgent because these two perspectives are conflictual (and it is such a conflict that ultimately determines the poetic value and drama of this canto). What has long been recognized is the aspect of repentance, or self-criticism, or at least painful recollection and stock-taking of his own intellectual past—let us call it the palinodic dimension—that lies behind Dante's upset and perturbation in front of the lovers. A perturbation that is strongly dramatized by its prolongation over the boundaries of this canto (a kind of macroscopic, psychological enjambment), because the description of the poet's state, whose physical aspect is poignantly underscored, closes the canto ("And then I fell as a dead body falls" [142]) and also opens the following one ("Upon my mind's reviving—it had closed / on hearing the lament of those two kindred, / since sorrow had confounded me completely . . . —" [VI, 1–3]).

This interpretation confirms the above-noted metonymic value of Canto V with respect to the whole of the *Comedy*. The theme of revision of the past is sounded right from the beginning, and most explicitly in the words of Beatrice as quoted by Virgil (*Inf.* II, 61–69). Here, however, for the first time in the epic narration such revision enters deeply into the structure of poetic diction, not only of philosophical and theological statements. But this very move creates the conflict mentioned above and casts a shadow over the whole palinode, threatening to reverse that reversal.

Once again, the role of line 137 is crucial: this verse implies a subtle but cogent reasoning that—if not amenable to the rigorous requirements of a syllogism—has however the persuasive force of its rhetorical brother, the enthymeme. The strange message of this line (we recall) is that, in the wake of the "real" (i.e., institutionally fictional) Galehot as a character in an Old French romance, *two* metonymic "Galehots" are added, whereas we would expect only one. This intensification or apparent overdetermination can be justified only in one way: Dante wants to draw attention to the contagion of literature not only on the two readers Paolo and Francesca, but also on the vast community (both synchronic and diachronic) of readers—what rhetoricians call the universal audience. Traditional criticism on the canto has indeed pointed out such a lesson; what I am underscoring here is the link between this general moral (or moralistic) lesson and the rhetorical figure of *congeries* or "heaping up" (two "Galehots" instead of one). And I do this, not out of some pedantic desire to magnify a minor detail, but in order to show the full extent of the conflict at work here; for the "Galehots" involved are not two, really, but three: the third "Galehot" is Dante. With the prescience of the poet (the esthetic equivalent of his general prophetic tendency) Dante intuits that the very description he is writing will act through the centuries as a "Galehot" with successive generations of readers: not, of course, in the banally direct sense of making successive couples of readers fall into each other's arms, but in the subtle sense (of interest for esthetic theory in general, over and beyond the case of the *Comedy*) to make successive generations of readers empathize with the psychological node here evoked. The consequence is that the relationship between this *exemplum* and the moral-theological frame that supposedly explains it away becomes problematic. Thus, the concentration on Francesca's pathos at the (relative) expense of the context of her condemnation is not an anachronistic error of Romantic criticism; on the contrary, it is something that is built into the text by its author.

The proof of this is furnished by Dante's first great creative critic, Boccaccio, whose decisive contribution to *Inferno* v criticism is to be found, rather than in his professional *Esposizioni* (which are of hermeneutic interest for this canto, as shown by Gertz), in his own creative writings. What should we make of the Boccaccio phrase that constitutes one of the most famous "titles" in world literature? "Here begins the book called *The Decameron*, also known as 'Prince Galeotto.'" The almost scholastic obviousness of the Dante reference seems to have discouraged speculation on the full import of such allusion. What matters here is the implicit interpretative gesture toward Canto v, because it is *Dante's* irony there that Boccaccio has identified: a text (*Inferno* v) that refers to another text (the Lancelot romance) with the distancing, if not condemnatory, epithet of "Galehot" as it comes to play that very role.

The central axis of *Inferno* v has thus emerged: the esthetico-ethical reevaluation of a love story as instancing the problematic connection between the autonomy of passion and the heteronomy of sin. (If this metalinguistic synthesis of the canto sounds too philosophical, the answer is that nothing less can do justice to the complexity of Dante's poetical and religious thinking here.)

The early modern tradition of criticism on this canto has concentrated on the autonomy of passion (Romantic criticism's important, and unjustly underestimated, contribution), while the modern tradition has focused on the aspect having to do with the heteronomy of sin. Important and revealing as these two lines of investigation have been, the mere insistence on them would perpetuate an ultimately fruitless polarization. The exploration of the liminal areas between autonomous passion and heteronomous sin is the task of contemporary criticism; only thus can contemporary thought best respond to the polyvalence that makes of Dante such an excellent representative of the complexities of medieval *sensitivity*.

The nondichotomous (i.e., not moralistic) way of thinking that Canto v exemplifies appears most clearly at the beginning and the end of this narration (neither point coincides with the Francesca story). The beginning is a double-edged pun, and, as noted, the end takes place (with one of the most daring among the many bold refractions of the *Comedy*) in Paradise.

The pun that underlies the reading of the Paolo and Francesca story is one that Dante actually takes from the prose of a Latin historian, and it concerns the already-quoted legendary queen Semíramis: "Her vice of lust became so customary / that she made license licit in her laws / to free her from the scandal she had caused" (55–57 [*libito fé licito in sua legge* (56)]). We get an inkling of the structural importance of the figure of Semíramis in this narration when we notice that she rates nine lines (52–60), versus the two allotted to Dido (61–62) and the single (and undistinguished) one for Cleopatra (63): a detail not without interest, in the tight economy of Dante's narrative throughout the poem—what John Keats calls, with one of the best definitions ever offered of Dante's poetry, "brief pathos." We saw above the significance of the Semíramis legend within the general archetype of the dove. But what is hermeneutically significant here is the double valence of the paronomastic relationship between what is sensually desired (*libito*) and what is properly allowed (*licito*), in the quoted line 56: a duplicity in which, strangely, criticism on this canto has shown little interest. The obvious surface function of this paronomasia is that of underscoring the shocking transgression sanctioned and indeed institutionalized by Semíramis, a transgression that perversely blurs the distinction between two radically different modes of being: the realm of anarchic, unchained desire and the domain of legal-moral order. This is of course the "official" meaning of the verse. But the poet is, at one and the same time, saying that the difference between sensual disorder and moral order is minimal—just one phoneme! (*b* versus *c*).

This, then, is no frivolous pun but a deeply and critically ironic gesture, as proved also by the fact that its narrative logic is the same as the narrative logic at the culminating point of the Paolo and Francesca episode: poetic form makes all the drama of the *kairós* felt; it marks the rapid and apparently hair-thin discrimination between two radically different spiritual states: "and yet one point alone defeated us" (132), "that day we read no more" (138). And, apropos once again of Dante's brilliant poetic refractions, this key term *punto* returns in the culminating moments of the mystical vision: "around the Point that overcame me" (*sempre dintorno al punto che mi vinse* [*Par.* xxx, 11]; not only the noun *punto* but the same verb form *vinse* refract with *Inf.* v, 132), and "That one moment / brings more forgetfulness to me" (*un punto solo m'è maggior letargo* [*Par.* xxxiii, 94]). In Dante's astonishingly economical poetic diction, paronomastic clashes like *libito / licito* go always more deeply than the merry lore of "mere" puns.

The (open) end of the canto, which does not come at the end of it nor in the course of the following one, reveals the same radical questioning. But in order to understand this it is necessary to summarize the oft-invoked but rarely analyzed episode from the old romance. The point to underscore is that it is a scene with *four* characters, and *two* different moments. Galehot arranges a meeting between Queen Guenever accompanied by two of her ladies in waiting (one of whom is the lady of Malohaut) and Lancelot

(Sommer ed., 3:258). Guenever draws an avowal of love out of the reluctant and shy Lancelot with a series of aggressive and rather indiscreet questions; in order to mark her critical awareness of such indiscretion the lady of Malohaut pointedly coughs *and* reveals her face that until now she had kept veiled, so that Lancelot recognizes her and is upset (3:261; oddly enough, criticism has not dwelled on these strategic details). The most likely explanation for Lancelot's perturbation, in the reticent but revealing narrative context of this episode, is that the lady of Malohaut had been his mistress for a short time. As for the lady's coughing, it has at least two functions, only one of which is currently recognized: to signal her disapproval of the queen's verbal behavior (at this point in the narration, no kiss has been exchanged) *and* to make Lancelot aware that she is present, as a way of shaming him for his fickle behavior (this latter is the point that still awaits critical notice). Galehot comes to the help of Lancelot, who is on the verge of fainting, and asks the queen to have mercy on him. Guenever is more than willing but coquettishly remarks that Lancelot still has not asked anything of her. Then Galehot acts as an interpreter of Lancelot's unspoken wishes and asks *first* for her eternal love of Lancelot, *then* for a kiss to sanction this love (the progression is psychologically and ethically significant, and it is another neglected element of this important and beautiful romance); and Guenever grants these requests, with a verbal commitment as well as a kiss (3:263).

Canto v alludes of course to the *second* part of this episode, where the poetical roles or equivalences are: Lancelot = Paolo, Guenever = Francesca, Galehot = book (the Lancelot vulgate + the *Comedy*) and author (the anonymous Old French writer + Dante). But in order to find a reflex of the *first* part of the quoted episode we have to wait until *Paradiso* XVI (refraction effect, plus a sophisticated reversal of the narratologic succession with a wide-ranging implementation of the rhetorical figure of *hysteron proteron,* or putting first what comes last). There, the ironic-cautionary smile of Beatrice at (probably) a linguistic faux pas by Dante is compared with the lady of Malohaut's warning cough: "at this word, Beatrice, somewhat apart, / smiling, seemed like the woman who had coughed—/ so goes the tale—at Guinevere's first fault" (*onde Beatrice, ch'era un poco scevra, / ridendo, parve quella che tossio / al primo fallo scritto di Ginevra* [*Par.* XVI, 13–15]).

The criticism of Canto v has still to deal with the implications of this paradisial integration (or disintegration, or refraction) of the infernal story. Such a comparative analysis is urgently needed, because it marks a kind of esthetic solidarity between the first full-fledged female character in the *Comedy* and the woman whom Harold Bloom has called "the poet's most spectacular invention." But there are also cogent hermeneutic reasons for this connection. First of all, Francesca is evoked in the *Paradiso* passage when her metaphorical parallel, *Ginevra,* is explicitly named. (With an economically refractive effect that is typical of Dante's poetry, and which could be considered as a form of negative *variatio,* only one name from the Lancelot vulgate occurs in Canto v, and this is *Galeotto,* and only one other name occurs in the just-quoted *Paradiso* passage: *Ginevra.*) But at this point the connection is triple, because now it is Dante who is compared to Guenever who used to be compared to Francesca (refraction, once again). And the language, in this coin of Paradise, is remarkably similar to the language spoken in that coin of Hell: a courtly, mundane, literarily self-conscious language. The epistemological implication is important and goes beyond our episode.

If the story of Dante the pilgrim (adopting for a moment this too sharp dichotomy) is one of progression—of successive unveilings that make his spiritual sight keener and keener—the story of Dante the poet is much more static, in the sense that certain basic moves recur essentially unchanged canto after canto, canticle after canticle. What this particular refraction symbolizes is that, *at one level,* the story of Beatrice continues the story of Francesca. But, once again, to imagine a straightforward linear progression would be misleading; the interchange is more complicated. Certain aspects of the image of Beatrice as elaborated before the writing of the *Comedy* become refracted into the image of Francesca, which in its turn is later refracted (as we just saw) into the image of Beatrice. Thus, Francesca is not simply the antitype of Beatrice (Nolan, 178), and Beatrice is not monolithic perfection (Singleton).

This refraction begins with one of the great *canzoni* that define Dante's poetic itinerary, "Ladies that have intelligence in love" (*Donne ch'avete intelletto d'amore*): "Whatever her sweet eyes are turn'd upon, / Spirits of love do issue thence in flame, / Which through their eyes who then may look on them / Pierce to the heart's deep chamber every one. / And in her eyes Love's image you may see; / Whence none can gaze upon her steadfastly" (*Vita nuova* XIX, 51–56). This is a two-step succession of thematizations or focalizations that can be defined as metonymic: first the focus is on the eyes, then on the whole face. Of course, in the Italian of Dante's times, *viso* (*Voi le vedete Amor pinto nel viso* [55]) may mean not only "face" but also "look, gaze." However, we should not hasten (as an authoritative modern edition does) to read *viso* as "look" here, because Dante explicitly tells us that he reads the passage in a different way: "'Whatever her sweet eyes' (*De li occhi suoi*). This second part is divided into two; for, in the one, I speak of the eyes, which are the beginning of love; in the second, I speak of the mouth, which is the end of love" (*Vita nuova* XIX, 20). The complete text of the commentary does not strictly fit the poetic text, but whatever the cause of this Dantean shifting, one thing is clear: if the poet, reading *viso* in this passage, is led to think of *bocca,* this confirms the general metonymic move and specifically the "objective" sense of *viso* (face) rather than its "subjective" sense (look, gaze).

But what is relevant to the Canto v refraction is the immediate continuation of Dante's self-commentary: "And, that every vicious thought may be discarded therefrom, let the reader remember that it is above written that the greeting of this lady, which was an act of her mouth, was the goal of my desires, while I could receive it." *Excusatio non petita, accusatio manifesta* . . . the *vizioso pensiero* would not enter the reader's mind if Dante had not planted it there—as clear evidence as we are ever going to reach in literary matters of the author's mental processes as he is writing and rewriting, reading and rereading, his own text.

Dante's reasoning develops further when he comments upon his sonnet "My lady carries love within her eyes" (*Ne li occhi porta la mia donna Amore*)—which says, among other things, "He whom she greeteth feels his heart to rise" (4), and "The look she hath when she a little smiles" (12)— noting that in the second part "I say that same which is said in the first part, regarding two acts of her mouth, one whereof is her most sweet speech, and the other her marvellous smile" (*Vita nuova* XXI, 8).

The picture is essentially complete—but there is something that the poet leaves unsaid while clearly implying it, and that we must make explicit in order to understand the full import of the poetic discourse in Canto v. The "acts of the mouth" in a woman, both as a self-asserting subject and as the object of an admiring gaze, are three: the enunciation of words (the *saluto*), the smile ([*sor*]*riso*), the kiss.

The first two thematic elements are explicit in Dante's version of the stilnovistic poetic code, while the third is not but is clearly present in Dante's rhetorical strategy of *anticipatio* (in the quoted passage of *Vita nuova* XIX, 20), where by specifying what he does "not" mean, Dante is in fact telling the reader what he wants to suggest.

Now, Francesca recapitulates all these elements: "When we *had read* how the desired *smile* / was *kissed* by one who was so true a lover, / this one, who never shall be parted from me, / while all his body trembled, *kissed* my mouth" (133–136; emphasis mine). Here we see the protocol of the "acts of the mouth." Reading, especially when done together, as in this case (whether aloud or mentally), is a form of communication, a way of conversing, especially when such reading concerns a scene explicitly describing a delicate problem of communication; in short, this recognition-through-reading-about-speaking evokes that small drama of communication one of whose basic codifications is the *saluto* of the lady. Also, by merging the subjective element of desire with the objective perspective on the smile as a metonymy of the whole face (*il disiato riso* of line 133), the poet powerfully thematizes the smile. Finally, the act of kissing (twice mentioned, as we saw, in the space of four lines) is now out in the open; and it confirms the connecting link between Francesca and Beatrice.

The intuition of Romantic criticism was right: insofar as it foregrounds Francesca, *Inferno* v concerns the articulated assertion of a woman. What remained to be done, after the Romantic tendency to isolate Francesca too

much, was to recontextualize her. In so doing, contemporary criticism re-
discovers (as we just saw) the delicate poetic thinking that keeps meditating on a woman's smile and its implications—a poetic thinking that, in the
Vita nuova as in *Inferno* as in *Purgatorio* as in *Paradiso,* has to do with an on-
tic description of the worldly dimension more than with a metaphysical on-
tology. We observe here a consistent (almost obsessive) insistence on a certain refracted image that stubbornly persists as a locus of poetry, remaining
stable through the vagaries of the pilgrim's career.

It is difficult to underestimate the importance of this poetic insistence or
obsession. The woman's mouth is for Dante the locus of a complex and
tense synesthetic reflection—and, once again, the story of this synesthesia
(a story that can only be briefly sketched here) begins before the *Comedy,*
thus constituting the genealogy of the *Inferno / Paradiso* refraction that I
have been discussing. Of strategic importance here is the *Convivio* passage
(re-presented to my attention by Davide Stimilli, who is not responsible for
my analysis of it) where Dante notes that the human soul "reveals herself
in the mouth, almost like a color behind glass. What is laughter if not a cor-
uscation of the soul's delight—that is, a light appearing outwardly just as
it is within? It is therefore fitting that to show one's soul to be of moderate
cheer one should laugh in moderation, with proper reserve and little movement of the lips (*de le sue [l]a[bb]ia*), so that the lady who then reveals herself, as has been said, may appear modest and not wanton . . . . Ah, won-
derful smile of my lady of whom I speak, which has never been perceived
except by the eye!" (*Convivio* III, viii, 11–12).

This passage clearly shows that defining Dante's synesthetic analysis as
tense and complex is no exaggeration. Assimilating the soul to a color and
the mouth to a plate of glass is a jarring and creative metaphor: it assimilates something abstract and invisible (the soul) to the concrete vivacity of
the world of colors, and, by comparing the mouth to a pane or plate of
glass, it foregrounds the image of a row of dazzling white teeth. This image (whose cadence is that of an endecasyllable: *quasi come colore dopo vetro*)
anticipates some of the most delicately suggestive images of the *Paradiso.*
(This whole passage is characterized by a particular verbal elaboration;
note, for instance, the chiasmus of moderate merriment: *ne l'allegrezza
moderata, moderatamente ridere.*) The quoted passage and the following ones
show Dante synesthetically emphasizing three elements in the (*sor*)*riso* or
"laughing smile" (my spelling attempts to render the untranslatable ambiguity, in verbs like *ridere,* between "to laugh" and "to smile"). These elements are (1) the visual component of general luminosity or gleaming
(*corruscazione*—both spiritual and physical—is a *corruscazione de la dilet-
tazione de l'anima,* but it is also, as noted, a row of scintillating teeth); (2) the
component, visual and kinetic, of facial movements; (3) the auditory component (the noise of laughter).

Here I only sketch what will have to be a detailed phenomenology of the discourse of the smile in Dante's work—its imagery and metaphorizations, its subtle sensualization of intellectual data (as, for instance, at the end of this same treatise, the passage where the "persuasions" [*persuasioni*] of Philosophy allegorized as a woman are assimilated to her smile, while her "demonstrations" [*dimostrazioni*] are compared to her gaze [*Convivio* III, xv, 19]). But what matters for our research here is that, in the just-quoted description, Dante takes a somewhat puritanical stance (which is, among other things, a genealogy of Giovanni Della Casa's attitude in his *Galateo*), by advocating a stern control of the kinetic and auditory component of the *(sor)riso,* and privileging in their stead the visual component: the silent smile.

This control makes the Beatrice scene in *Paradiso* XVI all the more striking, for there Beatrice's smile is assimilated, with an almost brutal synesthetic juxtaposition, to a noise, and a prosaic one at that: a coughing spell (never mind how stylized and semiotically codified). This physical foregrounding underscores the persistence of Dante's fascination with the interplay of body and soul—especially in the face, and especially in the woman's face. The imagery he employs has, to be sure, deep roots in Old French and Provençal poetry as well as in the literature of Biblical exegesis, but the persistence and the refractive energy is the peculiar contribution of Dante as a poet. Furthermore, Beatrice's smile in the *Paradiso* scene has a more dense and tense dimension, which we perceive only if we go back to the source (the *libro Galeotto* maintains its hermeneutic importance even in Paradise). As I already recalled, the lady of Malohaut, besides coughing in an allusive way, suddenly uncovers the face that she had kept unveiled until then (hence Lancelot's shock of recognition).

Thus what Dante is describing is nothing less than a minuscule (or minimalist) epiphany—where the substantive (epiphany) is as important as the qualifying adjectives. In short: what we have here is a woman dramatically making her presence felt qua woman, and critically interrupting the solemn colloquy of two men. (Apparently no one has noticed until now that Beatrice's silent visual interruption of that verbal intercourse is a gentle criticism *of Cacciaguida* as well as of Dante.)

I noted above that Romantic criticism was sensitive to the movement of Dante's poetic thinking. Let me briefly go back to the genealogy of critical and poetic responses to Dante. The first and most creative critic of Canto v is, as already remarked, Giovanni Boccaccio, who addresses this poetic node in, among others, four interesting instances, in every one of which literary creation realizes itself at the same time as a hermeneutic gesture (for other Paolo and Francesca echoes in Boccaccio, see Usher). One of them is Boccaccio's free retelling of the Paolo and Francesca story in his commentaries to the poem, while the other three interpretative moves all belong to the *Decameron:* (1) the already commented reprise of the Galehot irony in the nicknaming subtitle of the book; (2) the allusion to the matrimonial symbol of the pentad implicit in devoting the *fifth* day to stories about lovers "who, after unhappy or misfortunate happenings, obtained happiness" (see Victoria Kirkham's article, with other materials on the symbolism of number five); and above all (3) the development of the character of Ghismonda, in *Decameron* IV, I.

It is very difficult to imagine how Ghismonda might have come into existence without recognizing Francesca da Rimini as one of her crucial genealogies. Ghismonda's great speech (integrating the silence of Guiscardo, as Francesca integrates the silence of Paolo) is a reprise of Francesca's ("I loved and still do love Guiscardo, and as long as I shall live, which will not be long, I shall love him") and develops Francesca's tortured reflection on sin in a way that is apparently its opposite yet has much in common with it. We should not underestimate Ghismonda's proud vindication, but beneath it runs a subterranean current of uneasiness, expressed by the *repetitio* of the idea of sin ("I had made up my mind to commit this natural sin," "having sinned in loving," "it is Fortune you should blame and not my sin," "I am the true cause of this sin, if it be a sin").

The second great creative critic of *Inferno* v is Ludovico Ariosto, who tells a perversely complex love story in the *fifth* canto of the *Orlando furioso*. What makes it not only one of the richest novellas in the poem but also a hermeneutic gesture is Ariosto's identification of the Dantean refraction. In his text Ariosto does not refer directly to *Inferno* v but to the continuation of the story in *Paradiso* XVI, as he makes clear through the interplay of the rhymes in the crucial speech by Dalinda: "and I, my wits dispersed, / My mind and heart distraught, did not perceive / In all the strategy he thus rehearsed / The obvious deceit he planned to weave. / So, putting on Ginevra's clothing first" (*Io che divisa e sevra / e lungi era da me, non posi mente / che questo in che pregando egli persevra, / era una fraude pur troppo evidente; / e dal verron, coi panni di Ginevra* . . . [*Orlando furioso* v, 26; emphasis mine]).

The strategic rhyme-words in this octave reproduce the rhyme-words in the tercets of *Paradiso* XVI already referred to: *persevra* (11), *scevra* (13), *Ginevra* (15); with a particular emphasis, in the Ariosto text, on the *s(c)evra* (devoid, exempt, apart) form, which is here part of a *trittologia synonymica* (in the quoted *divisa e sevra / e lungi*). Of course it is no coincidence, and others have noted this connection. But, if we limit ourselves to stating the allusion without further comment, all we do is identify a gratuitous and formalistic play. What we have instead, on the part of the poet-critic Ariosto, is a creative esthetic move that is at the same time a hermeneutic contribution. By incorporating in Dalinda's speech, as part of her self-description of erotic errancy and passion, Dante's mundane simile concerning Beatrice (which, in the quoted context of the *Paradiso* passage, does not overtly have to do with eros), Ariosto clearly shows that his real target is not *Paradiso* XVI, but *Inferno* v. Thus all three strategic rhyme words in the *Paradiso* passage recover their full meaning as they are refracted onto Canto v: *Ginevra* is the *figura* of Francesca; *persevra* describes Francesca's desperate persistence in her love for Paolo; and finally, the attribute *scevra* regains its full force, describing Francesca's passionate state of alienation from herself. Thus Ariosto—as a poetic interpreter of Dante's poetic thinking—identifies and confirms the startling refraction between Francesca and Beatrice. (Notice that the process of refraction is radically different from that of allegory.)

To capture the basic meaning or sense of this canto, however, requires an interpretation that is not only esthetic but also ethical. The canto is (to repeat) the esthetico-ethical reevaluation of a story of love as an *exemplum* of the intersection of the autonomy of passion with the heteronomy of sin. What we need to develop, in order to reveal this peculiar balance, is a spiritual meditation; what we do *not* need is yet another instance of derivative theology applied from outside and from above as some kind of sanction. The theology of Canto v must be a theology of Paolo and Francesca— something that develops from the inside of the story they represent, growing out of the daily phenomenology of existence.

The first to sketch out (in poetic and allusive terms, of course) this inner theology of passion is (as I have synthetically shown) Boccaccio. The genealogical line of Boccaccio's intuition continues in the Romantic criticism of this canto (first with poets like Ugo Foscolo and John Keats, then with critics like Francesco De Sanctis). But these brilliant readers couched their vindication in a resolutely secular language that obliterated what was spiritual (albeit not moralistic) in Boccaccio's intuition. It is to such a spiritual criticism or critique that we must now return.

The basic spiritual challenge offered by a poem like *Inferno* v goes beyond marriage regulations and kissing etiquette (significant as these phenomena are for a literary anthropology). It is a challenge that cannot be solved by moralistic assertions; it can be addressed by actual theological thinking, but not by a theological *system*. (Consider, for instance, Karl Rahner's idea of "a new and fresher autoreinterpretation of theology. . . . This theology will not lead to a synthesis of the pluralistic experience of existence, but rather to a form of humility, and hope" [86–87].)

The crucial spiritual node here is the paradoxical balance between two apparently opposite attitudes: passionate love, the love of lovers, is basically hell—whether or not they land in Hell (as Dante unforgettably synthesizes here seven centuries before Jean-Paul Sartre's phenomenological analysis and dramatic work, which Mark Musa appropriately recalls [1974, 32])— and yet every act of passionate love has something redemptive in it.

When Dante faints, his perturbation has a deeper root than the one that causes Lancelot to swoon in front of Guenever. Dante has come face to face with a great philosophical and spiritual problem: the lack of a complete "fit" between the basic theological categories he uses (for reasons of esthetic efficiency and of moral clarification alike) and what he himself properly identifies as his basic subject: "the state of souls."

The creaking rhetorical machinery of Francesca's condemnation cannot but evoke in the mind of Dante (and, it is to be hoped, in that of his readers) Jesus' words apropos of the "woman that was in the city, a sinner," when he says: "Wherefore I say to thee: Many sins are forgiven her, because she hath loved much. But to whom less is forgiven, he loveth less" (Luke 7:37, 47).

What I am *not* proposing (lest it be misunderstood by moralistic exegetes) is to reopen the dossier of Francesca's trial and condemnation. And I am not proposing it for the simple reason that such a trial and condemnation *never took place*. Dante is first and foremost a poet. (As Glauco Cambon well understands, when he speaks of Dante dwelling "with Francesca in that deceptive Elysium of a moment which was really the eye of the cyclone" [66].) He presents to us in *Inferno* v not a moralistic apologue to which we might anxiously subscribe but a poetic hypothesis on which we continue to meditate critically.

NOTE

A slightly different version of the present essay has appeared in *Lectura Dantis* 14–15 (spring–fall 1994): 3–25. I am grateful to George Trone for some bibliographical suggestions.

BIBLIOGRAPHY

Selected Contemporary Works on the Canto

Barolini, Teodolinda. *Dante's Poets: Textuality and Truth in the "Comedy,"* 4–5. Princeton, 1984.

Bergin, Thomas G. "*Inferno* v." In *Dante's "Divine Comedy," Introductory Readings: Inferno,* ed. Tibor Wlassics, 54–69. Charlottesville, Va., 1990.

Cambon, Glauco. "Francesca and the Tactics of Language." In *Dante's Craft: Studies in Language and Style.* Minneapolis, 1969.

Carruthers, Mary J. *The Book of Memory: A Study of Memory in Medieval Culture.* Cambridge, 1990.

Contini, Gianfranco. "Dante come personaggio-poeta della Commedia" (1957). In *Un'idea di Dante: Saggi danteschi,* 33–62. Turin, 1976.

Della Terza, Dante. "*Inferno* v: Tradition and Exegesis." *Dante Studies* 99 (1981): 49–66.

Fleming, Ray. "Francesca's New Subversive Style." *Lectura Dantis* 3 (1988): 11–22.

Gertz, Sunhee Kim. "The Readerly Imagination: Boccaccio's Commentary on Dante's *Inferno* v." *Romanische Forschungen* 105, nos. 1–2 (1993): 1–29.

Girard, René. "The Mimetic Desire of Paolo and Francesca." In *"To Double Business Bound": Essays on Literature, Mimesis, and Anthropology,* 1–8. Baltimore, 1978.

Hatcher, Anna Granville, and Mark Musa. "The Kiss: *Inferno* v and the Old French Prose Lancelot." *Comparative Literature* 20 (1968): 97–109.

Iannucci, Amilcare A. "Forbidden Love: Metaphor and History." *Annali della Facoltà di lettere e filosofia dell'Università di Siena* 11 (1990): 341–358.

López Cortezo, Carlos. "Bases para una restauración del Canto v del *Inferno*." *Cuadernos de filología italiana* 1 (1994): 49–62.

Malato, Enrico. "Dottrina e poesia nel canto di Francesca: Lettura del canto v dell'*Inferno*." In *Lo fedele consiglio della ragione: Studi e ricerche di letteratura italiana*, 66–125. Rome, 1989.

Marcazzan, Mario. *Il canto v dell'"Inferno."* Florence, 1968.

Masciandaro, Franco. *Dante as Dramatist: The Myth of the Earthly Paradise and Tragic Vision in the "Divine Comedy,"* 62–109. Philadelphia, 1991.

Mazzaro, Jerome. "From *Fin Amour* to Friendship: Dante's Transformation." In *"The Olde Daunce": Love, Friendship, Sex, and Marriage in the Medieval World*, ed. Robert R. Edwards and Stephen Spector, 121–137, 270–272. Albany, N.Y., 1991.

Mazzoni, Francesco. "Il canto v dell'*Inferno*." In *"Inferno": Letture degli anni 1973–1976*, 97–143. Rome, 1977.

Musa, Mark. *Advent at the Gates: Dante's Comedy*, 1–35. Bloomington, Ind., 1974.

———. "*Inferno* v: Text and Commentary." *Lectura Dantis* 8 (1991): 108–133.

Noakes, Susan. "The Double Misreading of Paolo and Francesca." *Philological Quarterly* 62, no. 2 (spring 1983): 221–239.

Nolan, Edward Peter. "The Descending Dove: Dante's Francesca as the Anti-Beatrice." In *Now Through a Glass Darkly: Specular Images of Being and Knowing from Virgil to Chaucer*. Ann Arbor, 1990.

Picone, Michelangelo. "Poetic Discourse and Courtly Love: An Intertextual Analysis of Inferno 5." In *Lectura Dantis Newberryana*, ed. Paolo Cherchi and Antonio C. Mastrobuono, 2:173–186. Evanston, Ill., 1990.

Quaglio, Antonio Enzo. "Francesca da Rimini." *Enciclopedia dantesca* 3:1–13. Rome, 1971.

Sermonti, Vittorio, ed. *L'"Inferno" di Dante*, 65–74. Milan, 1988.

Singleton, Charles. "The Irreducible Dove." *Comparative Literature* 9 (1957): 129–135.

Usher, Jonathan. "Paolo and Francesca in the *Filocolo* and the *Esposizioni*." *Lectura Dantis* 10 (spring 1992): 22–33.

Valesio, Paolo. "*Regretter*: Genealogia della ripetizione nell'episodio di Paolo e Francesca." *Yearbook of Italian Studies* 4 (1980): 87–104. Reprinted in *From Linguistics to Literature: Romance Studies offered to Francis M. Rogers*, ed. Bernard H. Bichakjian (Amsterdam, 1981), 121–135.

Vinken, Barbara. "*Encore*: Francesca da Rimini. Rhetoric of Seduction—Seduction of Rhetoric." *Deutsche Vierteljahrsschrift für Literaturwissenschaft und Geistesgeschichte* 62, no. 3 (1988): 395–415.

Works Cited

Alighieri, Dante. *Il Convivio*. Ed. Maria Simonelli. Bologna, 1966.

———. *Vita nuova*. Ed. Domenico De Robertis. Milan, 1980.

———. *Vita Nuova*. In *The Early Italian Poets from Ciullo d'Alcamo to Dante Alighieri (1100—1200—1300) in the Original Metres together with Dante's Vita Nuova*, trans. D. G. Rossetti. London, 1861.

———. *Il Fiore*. In *Il Fiore e detto d'amore* [attributed to Dante Alighieri], ed. Gianfranco Contini. Milan-Naples, 1995.

Ariosto, Ludovico. *Orlando furioso*. Ed. Cesare Segre. Milan, 1979.

———. *Orlando Furioso*. Trans. Barbara Reynolds. 2 vols. Harmondsworth, 1981.

Aroux, Eugène. *L'hérésie de Dante démontrée par Francesca de Rimini, devenue un moyen de propagande vaudoise, et coup d'oeil sur les romans du Saint-Graal, notamment sur le Tristan de Léonnois*. Paris, 1857.

Bloom, Harold. *The Western Canon: The Books and School of the Ages*. New York, 1994.

Boccaccio, Giovanni. *The Decameron*. Trans. Mark Musa and Peter Bondanella. New York, 1982.

———. *Esposizioni sopra la "Commedia" di Dante*, ed. Giorgio Padoan. Milan, 1965.

Cassell, Anthony K. *Dante's Fearful Art of Justice*. Toronto, 1984.

Contini, Gianfranco. *Breviario di ecdotica*. Milan-Naples, 1986.

Croce, Benedetto. *La poesia di Dante* (1921). 11th ed. Bari, 1959.

De Sanctis, Francesco. "Francesca da Rimini secondo i critici e secondo l'arte" (1869). In *Lezioni e saggi su Dante*, ed. Sergio Romagnoli. Turin, 1955.

Eliot, T. S. "Dante" (1929). In *Selected Essays*. New edition. New York, 1950.

Freud, Sigmund. "From the History of an Infantile Neurosis" (1918). In *Case Histories*, trans. Alix and James Strachey. London, 1925.

Jones, Ernest. "The Madonna's Conception Through the Ear." In *Essays in Applied Psychoanalysis*, 2:266–357. London, 1951.

Jung, C. G. *Psychology and Alchemy*. Vol. 1. Trans. R. F. C. Hull. 2d ed. Princeton, 1968.

Keats, John. "A Dream, After Reading Dante's Episode of Paolo and Francesca." In *The Complete Poems*, ed. John Barnard, 334, 636 n. Harmondsworth, 1979.

Kirkham, Victoria. "'Chiuso parlare' in Boccaccio's *Teseida*." In *Dante, Petrarch, and Boccaccio: Studies in the Italian Trecento in Honor of Charles S. Singleton*, ed. A. S. Bernardo and A. L. Pellegrini, 305–351. Binghamton, N.Y., 1983.

Marinetti, Filippo Tommaso. "La *Divina Commedia* è un verminaio di glossatori" (1915). In *Teoria e invenzione futurista*, by F. T. Marinetti, ed. Luciano De Maria. Milan, 1968.

Polidori, Filippo-Luigi, ed. *La Tavola Ritonda o l'Istoria di Tristano*. 2 vols. Bologna, 1864–1865.

Rahner, Karl. "Filosofia e procedimento filosofico in teologia." In *Nuovi saggi*, 3:73–97. Rome, 1969.

Rajna, Pio. "Dante e i romanzi della Tavola Rotonda." *Nuova Antologia* 55, no. 1157 (June 1920): 223–247.

Sasso, Gennaro. "Croce e Dante: Considerazioni filosofiche su *struttura* e *poesia*." *La Cultura* 31, no. 2 (August 1993): 191–261.

Sommer, H. Oskar, ed. *Le livre de Lancelot du Lac*. Part 1. Washington, D.C., 1910.

Zanzotto, Andrea. "Sonetto del che fare e che pensare (xi)." In *Il Galateo in bosco*, 70. Milan, 1979.

CANTO VI

Florence, Ciacco, and the Gluttons

MARIA PICCHIO SIMONELLI

It is well known that political issues mark the sixth canto of all three parts of Dante's *Divine Comedy*. This sequence gradually unfolds his denunciation of the ruin that threatens the political universe. Dante, the new Aeneas, aims to restore the *bonum mundi*.

In *Inferno* VI Florence offers the first example of misgovernment. Very few righteous people live in this city. In truth, only two righteous men (*giusti*) can be found, yet nobody listens to them (73). The fire of "envy, pride, and avariciousness" burns in the citizens' hearts (74–75). The counsel offered by the two *giusti* fades away like a voice crying in the wilderness, while dishonesty and special interests hold sway. All sense of justice is lost. The "divided city" (61) is presented as the kernel of a wider system of collapsing political institutions. Its image is part of a particular infernal landscape, but its didactic message is intended to spread everywhere.

In *Purgatorio* VI Dante's denunciation extends to the whole of the *regnum Italiae*. Partisan hatred, contempt of law, greed for wealth and power prevail throughout the cities. The emperor is at fault. Who will act as the rider of human reason, "when the saddle's empty?" (89). Because he is so ensnared in German wrangles, he neglects the "garden of the Empire" (105). The greatest blame, however, falls upon the Roman Curia. Its pious duty should be to let Caesar sit "in the saddle" (92). Instead, the Curia acts against the designs of Divine Providence by usurping imperial prerogatives, by depriving humankind of the guidance through which God wants to lead it toward happiness, and by turning the human race into a "fierce" beast, "recalcitrant and savage" (94, 98).

In *Paradiso* VI, Justinian's words are meant, even more than to praise the Roman Empire, to condemn its false servants. Dante stigmatizes as fatally wrong the attitude of those who, like the Ghibellines, misuse the "sacred standard" (32) by making of it a partisan banner, and those who, like the Guelphs, want to replace the imperial eagle with the French fleur-de-lis.

These cantos contain the fullest poetical expression of the *visio pacis* that Dante had previously outlined in *Convivio* IV, IV, 1–4. Such a greatly desired peace, however, is unattainable as long as neighbors fight within the walls of the same city, as long as quarrels among the cities bring ruin to the kingdoms, and kingdoms destroy one another because they lack that sole ruler who "would keep the kings content within the boundaries of their kingdoms and preserve among them the peace in which the cities might rest. Through this peace the communities would come to love one another, and by this love all households would provide for their needs, which when provided would bring man happiness, for this is the end for which he is born" (*Convivio* IV, iv, 4).

Thus, we can only agree with those critics who, for almost thirty years, have succeeded in demonstrating that there are thematic connections that make each of these sixth cantos a marked compositional unit. There is, however, another semantic and structural feature that helps us understand Dante's code and requires careful investigation.

In *Inferno* XVI we again find, besides Farinata and Mosca, those "worthy" Florentines (VI, 79) "whose minds bent toward the good" (81). These are the men about whose fate Dante had also asked Ciacco in Canto VI, and Ciacco gave the moral explanation for the problem of the *città partita* (61). When Dante again takes up what happened to the city in Canto XVI, he presents its historical dimension:

> "Newcomers to the city and quick gains
> have brought excess and arrogance to you,
> o Florence, and you weep for it already!"
> (*Inf.* XVI, 73–75)

It is the "newcomers" who, by corrupting civic life, have driven off "courtesy and valor" (67), virtues that still flourished in Florence at the time of Jacopo Rusticucci.

Purgatorio VI and XVI show the same thematic connection described above, even though the terms of the scheme are now inverted. The historical description comes first, and the moral justification follows. In the sixth canto Dante himself, speaking in the first person, vituperates the evil men of Italy who, by yielding to partisan grudges, subvert the common peace. Nevertheless, the true responsibility for this state of affairs rests with the

Church and the empire. These two authorities, by fighting each other, shirk their duty to provide spiritual and temporal leadership. In the sixteenth canto Marco Lombardo makes this point:

> For Rome, which made the world good, used to have
> two suns; and they made visible two paths—
> the world's path and the pathway that is God's.
>   Each has eclipsed the other; now the sword
> has joined the shepherd's crook; the two together
> must of necessity result in evil.
>
> (*Purg.* xvi, 106–111)

The sixth and the sixteenth cantos of *Paradiso* also display compositional similarities. Both cantos have as their focal point direct speeches uttered by outstanding characters: Justinian and Cacciaguida. Just as the sixth and the sixteenth cantos of *Inferno* and *Purgatorio* are linked to each other through mirror references to moral-historical and historical-moral motives respectively, in *Paradiso* vi Justinian praises the justice of the Roman Empire by saying that it was founded on the righteousness of its citizens. His words illustrate the moral foundations of Roman universal peace. Justinian also reasserts the providential nature of the Roman Empire: "God gave Rome not only a special birth but a special evolution" (*Convivio* iv, v, 10) in accordance with God's will, so that a world at peace might be ready to receive the miracle of the Christ's incarnation. Only the Roman Empire could vindicate the old sin—that is Jesus' sacrifice on the Cross—and provide a revenge for the revenge: Titus's destruction of the Temple at Jerusalem in A.D. 69.

Whereas in *Paradiso* vi the last embodiment of Roman power referred to by Justinian is Charlemagne, what Dante had previously written in the *Convivio* indicates that he was willing to extend the continuity of the empire at least to the age of Frederick, whom he calls the "the last of the Roman emperors" (*Convivio* iv, iii, 6). What is truly significant is the idea that, as long as the world listened to an emperor's voice, peace and happiness reigned on earth. It behooves Cacciaguida to provide the historical demonstration of this truth, and Cacciaguida again comes up with the example of Florence.

In Cacciaguida's day, Florence, "sober and chaste, lived in tranquillity" (*Par.* xv, 99). Later on, new kinds of people with "sharp eyes" (xvi, 57) arrived to subvert that peaceful life. Who is to blame for such a disaster? The Church should be blamed, and "those who, in the world, go most astray" (58). The Church did not behave "like a mother to her son" (60), but as the emperor's stepmother, as his *noverca* (59).

At this point the thematically marked connection between the sixth and the sixteenth cantos emerges with sufficient clarity. In *Paradiso* vi Justinian concentrates on political morals, stating that the reproachable misuse of the imperial insignia as partisan banners marks the moral decay of the world. In *Paradiso* XVI, Cacciaguida deals with the historical dimension of the same problem. He points out that the world's decadence takes root in the Church's illegitimate attempts to establish its temporal dominion.

Cacciaguida's praise of old Florence echoes and reflects Justinian's extolment of the providential nature of the empire. Florence, too, was part of a good and happy world when the "two suns," that is, the Church and the Holy Roman Empire, performed their duties each within its own sphere of competence, according to God's instructions. Florence was then "acclaimed and just" (*Par.* XVI, 152), living "in such repose / that there was nothing to have caused her sorrow" (149–150). Now the city is divided; *la città partita* resembles a sick woman "who finds no rest upon her featherbed, / but, turning, tossing, tries to ease her pain" (*Purg.* VI, 150–151). The circular sequence of images first introduced in the Ciacco scene finds its conclusion here. *Paradiso* XVI responds not only to *Paradiso* VI but to the sixth and the sixteenth cantos of *Inferno* and *Purgatorio* as well. Line 150 of *Paradiso* XVI—"there was nothing to have caused her sorrow"—sounds like a response of the good old days to the weeping of the present (see Avalle, 88–95); that is, the weeping of the oppressed Whites (*Inf.* VI, 72: "they weep indignantly"), and the weeping of the whole city (*Inf.* XVI, 75: "o Florence, and you weep for it already!").

Dante was confronted with particularly complex structural problems when composing *Inferno* VI: He was about to introduce the political question for the first time in direct terms. He did not want to break the continuity of his narrative from the fifth to the sixth canto; at the same time he wanted to call the reader's attention to Ciacco and his prophecies.

Dante chose a very apt structure, which reminds us of scholastic schemes. The first tercet establishes a connection with the preceding canto. The following thirty lines describe "new sufferings, new sufferers" (4). Sixty lines are then devoted to the poet's meeting with Ciacco. The last twenty-two lines contain the dialogue between Dante and Virgil, except that the very last line—"Here we found Plutus, the enemy"—links this canto to the next one. The Ciacco episode, which occupies a central position, is framed by the opening description and the concluding dialogue. Cerberus and Plutus, the two infernal monsters at the beginning and the end of the canto, also play a framing role.

This particular type of framing, which gives prominence to central themes and subjects, occurs consistently in our canto. Let us consider the thirty lines that open the description of the third circle (4–33). The first nine lines illustrate the kind of punishment used in this portion of hell. The next twelve lines depict Cerberus, while nine concluding lines, where Cerberus faces Virgil, complete the framing structure with numerical precision.

We should also note that if compared to the sparse style of the fifth canto and the sober rhetorical adornment of the seventh canto, these thirty lines of *Inferno* VI display an unusually rich apparel of formal devices (see Beccaria, 91–101, and Wheelock, 373–404). The sound effect of the anaphoric cluster *come ch'io . . . e ch'io . . . e come che io* (5–6) is emphasized and enriched by the contiguous assonance that immediately suggests a particular link between the end of line 5 and the marked pre-caesura word of line 6 (*mova . . . volga*). The latter sound figure occurs again at lines 11–12 (*riversa . . . terra*). There are, furthermore, alliterative signals (line 10: *grandine grossa;* line 26: *prese la terra, e con piene le pugna*), adjectival series marked by assonance (line 8: *etterna, maledetta, fredda*), and caesurae (/ /) marked by assonance (line 13: *Cerbero, fiera* / / *crudele e diversa;* line 24: *non avea membro* / / *che tenesse fermo*).

Ciacco's message emerges as the pillar of this complex structure. At the levels of meaning and of meaning-enhancing adornment as well, a frame of cross-references creates an emotional setting upon which Ciacco's image emerges. At the beginning and at the end of his speech Ciacco begs Dante to free him from the darkness of oblivion, to recognize him, to "recall me to men's memory" (89). This particular type of emotional framing humanizes Ciacco's political message, so that the reader can perceive Ciacco and Dante not only as conceptual symbols but as real characters. Nevertheless, the political message stands out precisely in the middle of a masterfully framed narrative scene.

The opening three lines of Canto VI provide a narrative link to the preceding canto. Dante faints because of his "pity" (*pietà*) and "compassion" toward Francesca, as Chiavacci Leonardi points out, overwhelmed by the distortion and destruction of that "human figure" (see Chiavacci Leonardi, 164–169). The word *pietà* occurs again at the beginning of this canto and is followed by a line that sounds like a gloss. It was because of pity, Dante says, that "sorrow had confounded me completely" (3).

After this introductory reminder, Dante calls his readers' attention to the new scene, that is, to the third circle, its sinners, and their punishments. The "new sufferers" (4), the gluttons are sunk in a fierce rain, mixed with hail and snow. By saying "new," Dante lays stress on his own experience and personal adventure. What is subjectively new to him cannot be new to the infernal world, where no change is possible. In fact, Dante had already warned his readers of this in Canto III when, among other words whose "aspect was obscure," written "above a gateway" (III, 10–11), he had cited the following sentence:

> BEFORE ME NOTHING BUT ETERNAL THINGS
> WERE MADE, AND I ENDURE ETERNALLY.
> (*Inf.* III, 7–8)

In light of this explanation, we should see the rain of the third circle as a tormenting movement deprived of any change. That rain is always the same, forever, and "its measure and its kind are never changed" (VI, 9). The adjective *novo,* preceded by *non,* is repeated intentionally. Subjective perception and objective reality are equally true, though they contrast with each other. Dante the pilgrim sees as new the eternal immobility that he knows is not and cannot be new. Aware that Dante never leaves a motif without further elaboration or a framing response, we perceive this first semantic signal as a foreshadow of the dialogue with Virgil at the end of this canto, which will deal with the condition of the damned souls after the Final Judgment.

Then Cerberus appears. In that foul atmosphere filled with rain, hail, and snow, he stands out as the first jailer of Hell. I call him "the first" jailer because Minos, despite his horrible growling, is a judge, not a ward or executioner. Cerberus, instead, whose barking precedes his image, is undoubtedly an executioner: "His talons tear and flay and rend the shades" (18). He deafens them with the howling of his three throats (as in Virgil's *Aeneid* VI, 417 ff.). What should be noted in this connection is that Dante did not deny the existence but the identity of the old false gods of antiquity who inhabited Mount Olympus and the underworld. Dante follows Saint Augustine who, in *The City of God* II, xxix, wrote: "Do not pursue false and fallacious gods. . . . They are not gods, they are malignant spirits for whom your [i.e., humankind's] happiness is their punishment." Saint Augustine, moreover, relied on the authority of Psalm 95:5: "For all the gods of the Gentiles are devils." Dante, too, considers the old gods "evil spirits fearing the eternal bliss" of man. In this way, classical mythology was allowed to become part of Christian thought. Such an attitude is detectable, for example, in the canto of *Inferno* devoted to the suicides (XIII, 143–150) and also in *Paradiso* XVI (145–147), when Cacciaguida speaks of the internecine strife that afflicts his city. Cacciaguida explains the misfortune of Florence by referring to a curse by Mars, who was consumed with jealousy when the Christianized city abandoned him and placed its trust in Saint John the Baptist. On the other hand, Charon too is a demon. All ancient gods are included in the Augustinian category of evil spirits.

Virgil had used words to explain Dante's "fated path" (*Inf.* v, 22) to Charon and Minos. No communication is possible with Cerberus, whose only perceptible stimulus is that of swallowing. To quiet the monster, Virgil fills his three throats with dirt. Swallowing it, Cerberus embodies the sin of gluttony. His behavior stands for that of those who "live to eat, and do not eat to live." If we were to believe Benvenuto da Imola, who used it in his comment on this episode (I, 224), this dictum should be attributed to Petrarch, Benvenuto's most revered inspirer.

The canto's central episode begins at line 34, where the shadow that stands up is the soul of Ciacco. But who was Ciacco? Although Dante lets Cac-

ciaguida tell him that the souls that appear before him in the three realms
are "only those souls that unto fame are known" (*Par.* XVII, 138), Ciacco remains for us a name "without family and family name, without profession,
with no history whatsoever" (Pézard, 1:982).

The first commentators of the *Divine Comedy* were unable to identify
Ciacco with any historical figure. It was after the mid-fourteenth century,
I would say—after the diffusion of novella IX, 8 of the *Decameron*—that
Ciacco, as a character, acquired a new identity. He became a "court gentle-
man," a "banker," a "witty speaker," and so on. All these features, however,
belong to fictional imagination.

The only historical Ciacco, who was a Florentine and became known in
the second half of the thirteenth century, seems to be Ciacco dell'Anguillara. Two poems written by him have come down to us in the Codex *Vat.
Lat.* 3793. Toward the end of the nineteenth century, Casini tried to prove
that Ciacco dell'Anguillara and our Ciacco of *Inferno* VI were one and the
same person (see his edition of the *Divine Comedy*, 197). More recent criticism, however, has rejected the hypothesis for lack of solid evidence.

Thus, the only Ciacco that Dante's readers can take into consideration
remains the sinner worn down by the infernal rain because of his "damning sin of gluttony" (53). He reveals a certain magnanimity, even if the
somewhat noble features of his personality may result from his feeling *ad
excessum*. Such people can begin "to despise and maltreat others" (Aristotle as cited by Saint Thomas, *Summa theologica* II-II, 130, 2). Ciacco does not
hold Hell in "tremendous scorn" (X, 36), as Farinata does, and his loquacity
is certainly more moderate than that of Farinata. Ciacco, according to
Sapegno, seems to speak almost by force.

What moves Ciacco to initiate a dialogue is his desire to be recognized
by a fellow Florentine and remembered by him "to the sweet world"
(88). To survive in the memory of other people is the only semblance of
life left to him. Such a feeling moves several damned souls. In spite of the
burden of their disfiguring sins, they still rely on whatever good they
might have accomplished through their ambition to bend "toward the
good" (81). This is the way Farinata, Pier delle Vigne, Brunetto Latini, Jacopo Rusticucci, Tegghiaio, and Mosca all feel. Ciacco feels the same way.
What kind of merits he could claim, we don't know. It seems, however,
that Dante was aware of some of them. Perhaps the importance of the information conveyed by line 42—"for you, before I was unmade, were
made"—has been overemphasized. These balanced, alliterative words
may reflect nothing more than what Francesco Mazzoni calls "well de-
finable traits of a lofty style that do not aim to define character and that
belong to the sophisticated patrimony of Dante's rhetoric" (159). Nevertheless, we should consider the whole structure of the dialogue, which in
many ways seems to contribute to the characterization of Ciacco. Ciacco
is not eager to talk, but what he says is extremely precise. There is noth-

ing vague or superfluous in his words. He gives the proper answer to each question.

After telling Ciacco that he is unable to locate him in his memory, Dante submits the first set of questions:

> "But tell me who you are, you who are set
> in such a dismal place, such punishment—
> if other pains are more, none's more disgusting."
> (46–48)

Apart from its juridical accuracy, Dante's language here betrays a vernacular tone. In the phrase *s'altra è maggio,* the form *maggio* is typically Florentine. It is taken from the nominative *major* instead of being patterned (as occurs in standard vernacular forms) after the oblique Latin stem. Even in the toponymy of today's Florence this form is extant in the name of an old street, *via Maggio,* which means "Main Street."

And this is Ciacco's answer:

> And he to me: "Your city—one so full
> of envy that its sack has always spilled—
> that city held me in the sunlit life.
>   The name you citizens gave me was Ciacco;
> and for the damning sin of gluttony,
> as you can see, I languish in the rain.
>   And I, a wretched soul, am not alone
> for all of these have this same penalty
> for this same sin." And he said nothing more.
> (49–57)

In very concise but exhaustive terms, Ciacco answers all the questions. Now Dante knows where this damned soul comes from, what name he bore, what Ciacco is damned for, and what kind of sin is being punished in this particular region of Hell. Dante's closing comment, "And he said nothing more," suggests that, given the completeness of his answer, Ciacco need not speak further. It is he, Dante, who wants to elaborate on Ciacco's initial words, even though those words have perfectly conveyed the essence of the political and moral message that the poet wants to hear. Ciacco says "your city" because, now and forever, *his* city can only be Hell. His language is marked by extreme precision. We have good reasons to believe that the term "envy" (*invidia*), which he emphasizes by placing it right at the beginning of his statement, has been also carefully chosen.

The extensive discussion of *invidia* by Saint Thomas in *Summa theologica* II-II, 36 can certainly help us figure out what the sociopolitical and moral

sense of this term might be for people like Dante and his infernal hero
Ciacco. Let us concentrate on those passages of the *Summa* that seem to
summarize general Christian ideas in scholastic language. Saint Thomas
personifies envy (*discordia*), saying that envy "is disconsolate over the good
of those who deserve it" (*Summa* II-II, 36, 3). Elsewhere he defines it as "despondency over our neighbor's good," which "gives rise to pleasure over his
evil" (II-II, 36, 4). The subsequent *questio* (II-II, 37, 2), which is devoted to *discordia,* states that envy comes from spite (*ex livore*) "rather than vainglory."
Not only is envy the cause of discord, but it also represents the negation of
wisdom, as we read in Wisdom 6:25–26: "Neither will I go with consuming envy: for such a man shall not be partaker of wisdom. Now the multitude of the wise is the welfare of the whole world: and a wise king is the
upholding of the people." This means that a city dominated by envy is
doomed to misgovernment, injustice, and internecine strife.

Thus, when he first hears the word *invidia,* Dante perceives it as a loaded
signal. We do not know who the historical Ciacco was. There is no doubt,
however, that Dante's Ciacco is depicted as a cultivated, sharp man, an expert in politics. The fact that Dante chose him as the main speaker in the
first of his sixth cantos suggests that Ciacco was to be viewed by the readers of the *Divine Comedy* as an authoritative figure. We may assume that his
historical prototype was a man well known in Florence during its most
troubled years, perhaps at the time when peace was made between the
Guelphs and the Ghibellines (1280) or in the immediately subsequent period, when the magnates and the people continuously fought until the battle of Campaldino (1290).

The pilgrim Dante does not seem to grasp entirely the tragic sense of
Ciacco's first words. He asks for more explicit explanations. To induce
Ciacco to talk further, as Guido da Pisa explains (128), Dante *benevolentiam
eius captat,* in this way:

> . . . . "Ciacco, your suffering
> so weights on me that I am forced to weep;"
> (58–59)

The pilgrim then asks more specific questions:

> "but tell me, if you know, what end awaits
>   the citizens of that divided city;
> is any just man there? Tell me the reason
> why it has been assailed by so much schism."
>   (60–63)

Dante wants to know what the Florentine feuds will eventually lead to;

whether there are any righteous citizens in Florence; and the cause for such great strife. Ciacco's three answers are right to the point. Question, "What end awaits?" Answer, "They'll come to blood" (65). Question, "Is any just man there?" (62). Answer, "Two men are just, but no one listens to them" (73). Question, "Tell me the reason" (62). Answer, "Envy, pride and avariciousness" (75). This is the core of the message. All other words provide an explanatory commentary for the author himself, that is for Dante's readers.

But let us analyze Ciacco's three points in detail. The first point reads:

> And he to me: "After long controversy
> they'll come to blood; the party of the woods
> will chase the other out with much offense.
> But then, within three suns, they too must fall;
> at which the other party will prevail,
> using the power of one who tacks his sails.
> This party will hold high its head for long
> and heap great weights upon its enemies,
> however much they weep indignantly.
>
> (64–72)

This prophetic style makes sense if we consider that Dante's trip was fictionally placed in the Holy Week of 1300; in that year Easter fell on April 10. In reality, the "future" events, which Ciacco announces, were largely known to any reader. The Whites and the Blacks, that is, the two factions into which the Florentine Guelph party had been split since 1293, engaged in bloody altercations on May 1, 1300. Vieri de' Cerchi was the leader of the Whites, while Corso Donati leader of the Blacks. Dino Compagni, an eyewitness and a White who belonged to the same faction as Dante, summarizes those events as follows: "The city was divided anew; the great, middling and little men and even the clergy could not help but give themselves wholeheartedly to the factions, this man to one and that to the other. All the Ghibellines sided with the Cerchi" (*Chronicle of Florence,* 25–26). On the side of the Donati family stood most of the Guelph magnates and some leaders of the *arti minori* such as "Pecora il beccaio." These leaders relied on the populace who, like the magnates, were deprived of political rights. The Cerchi, called the "wild party" because they came from the countryside, controlled the city through the Priorate of the guilds. In June 1300 the Priori decided to banish the leading figures of both parties. At the beginning of 1301 the Whites managed to have the Blacks exiled. Their success, however, did not last very long. Toward the end of the summer, the Blacks took over, with the help of Charles of Valois, the envoy of Pope Boniface VIII ("using the power of one who tacks his sails" [69]).

Although he was sent to Florence on a "peacekeeping" mission, Charles of Valois openly supported the Blacks. The Whites were banished in the fall of 1301. Dante was then in Rome, as their representative at the pope's court. Boniface VIII did not dismiss him until the first days of January 1302. He was officially banished from Florence on January 27, when he was traveling home from Rome. He did not reach Florence at that time, nor did he return to his city in his later years. He was to remain an exile forever.

It is not surprising that some Dante scholars have been tempted by the possibility of establishing "real" connections between the events fictionally alluded to in *Inferno* vi and Dante's concrete life experience. This canto contains no reference to Dante's exile even though Ciacco's "prophecies" reach the year 1302. Some years ago, this circumstance prompted Ferretti to assume that the *Divine Comedy* was composed in two successive stages. Sapegno seems to agree. "This episode provides the strongest argument to support the thesis according to which the composition of the first cantos of the *Inferno* should be dated to the pre-exile years" (77). This thesis is not convincing for at least two reasons.

First, it is hard to believe that, even before learning that he had been banished from Florence, Dante was ready to accept, as definitive or long-lasting, the takeover of the Blacks. Ciacco says: "This party will hold high for long" (vi, 70). Sapegno's comment reads: "The fact that the power of the Blacks was to last for a long time was then so evident that one could easily anticipate it." The opposite seems to be true if we consider how fluid and uncertain the situation might appear to a person like Dante, who was not a direct participant in events taking place within the walls of Florence. Dante was far away, still waiting for papal permission to leave. The Whites themselves had been the dominant party for only a few months. Why not think that new events could reverse the political balance once more?

Second, Sapegno writes: "If one considers that, in his prophecy, Ciacco does not refer to the banishment of the Whites, including Dante's banishment, which one would expect to be mentioned here, one is led to believe that the poet may have written this canto before being sentenced, that is, in January 1302, when all the events mentioned in the prophecy had already taken place but the situation had not reached its fatal conclusion." Apart from the unlikely hypothesis that Dante could write this canto in the tense atmosphere of the Roman Curia—when he alone, among the three Florentine envoys, was not allowed to leave—the argument of Ciacco's silence on Dante's exile seems extremely questionable.

Throughout Dante's poem the exile motive exists by allusion and oblique mention until it reaches its climax in Cacciaguida's words in *Paradiso* xvii. Even if they seem to be closely interrelated, the themes of Florentine corruption and Dante's exile do not necessarily go together. Not even in the sixteenth canto of *Inferno*—so closely connected with *Inferno* vi—do we find the slightest allusion to Dante's exile. The latter fact is of particular interest, especially if we recall that Dante had already referred to his own exile more than once before Canto xvi. Farinata had told him:

> And yet the Lady who is ruler here
> will not have her face kindled fifty times
> before you learn how heavy is that art.
>
> (*Inf.* x, 79–81)

And Brunetto Latini too, in even more explicit and friendly terms, had touched upon this subject.

Furthermore, a vague reference or allusion to Dante's exile may be seen in lines 71–72 of Canto vi, when Ciacco says that the Blacks' faction will "heap great weights upon its enemies, / however much they weep indignantly." What are "great weights"? Disqualification from holding public office? Pecuniary penalties? These are things of which one can "weep indignantly" (72). Should we not think of something even more disgraceful? Something like the pain of exile, which implied the loss of civil rights and of property at the same time?

Ciacco's second point reads, "Two men are just, but no one listens to them" (73). Mazzoni (169–173) is willing to consider *giusti* as the plural form of an abstract noun, in accordance with the interpretation first submitted by Jacopo della Lana and Pietro Alighieri. According to Jacopo, the form *giusti* is meant to signify "Justice and Reason." Pietro, on the other hand, refers to *jus naturale* and *jus gentium*. Though Mazzoni's defense of such an interpretation is conducted with remarkable critical acumen, it is not entirely convincing.

Dante's question to Ciacco was, "is any just man there?" If it were true that Ciacco's answer is that there are two types of law, the natural and civil, and that both have been abandoned by the Florentines, we should conclude that on this occasion Ciacco's answer is rather vague and general, certainly not to the point.

If, on the other hand, we fully rely on the text's features—which do emphasize Ciacco's right-to-the-point precision—the main question that still remains to be answered is why "two." Let us pass over, at this point, the various and doubtful hypotheses concerning the personal identity of "the two." In the Bible "two or three" are requested to witness the truth (cf. Deut. 14:29, 17:6; 1 Cor. 14.29; 1 Tim. 5:19). The tradition, according to which "two" trustworthy witnesses are needed, is still in the Florentine statutes, as Gaetano Salvemini documented many years ago (111). I believe, however, that we should concentrate above all on the eleventh chapter of the Apocalypse, where, concerning the *duo testes Dei* we read: "And I will give unto my two witnesses, and they shall prophesy a thousand and two hundred sixty days, clothed in sackcloth. These are the two olive trees, and the two candlesticks, that stand before the Lord of the earth . . . . And when they shall have finished their testimony, the beast, that ascendeth out of the abyss, shall make war against them and shall overcome them, and kill them." This biblical text explains "the two" and why they are not listened to (*intesi*) and why they are defeated on this earth. If we detect here an implicit biblical reference, Ciacco's words are meant to say that the city of Florence is apocalyptically doomed because "the beast" will make war upon God's "two witnesses" and will "overcome them."

Ciacco's third and last point is that "three sparks that set on fire every heart / are envy, pride, and avariciousness" (74–75). Ciacco now explains what he had only alluded to at the beginning of his speech. Where there is envy, there also must be pride and avarice. These are the three essential characteristics of the "beast that ascendeth out of the abyss." According to Saint Gregory, as cited by Saint Thomas (*Summa* ii-ii, 163, 8), pride is the "queen and mother of all vices" who gives birth to the "presumption of prevailing over others," which is the essence of envy. Saint Thomas cites Saint Augustine as well, who wrote "that pride begets envy, nor is it ever without this companion" (ii-ii, 162, 8). Envy engenders lack of charity toward one's neighbors—that is a lack of liberality, which is avarice in its essence. "Avarice means having more than is right in justice" (ii-ii, 118, 4). And the common condemnation of pride together with avarice goes back to the biblical tradition, in particular to Proverbs and Ecclesiastes (for example, Prov. 15:25, 27: "The Lord will destroy the house of the proud. . . . He that is greedy of gain troubleth his own house").

"With this, his words, inciting tears, were done" (76). Once again Ciacco, having made everything clear, does not want to add a word to his speech. And here again, it is Dante who is literally begging for the "gift" of more words:"I ask you for a gift of further speech" (78). Both the *captatio benevolentiae,* to which he had recourse before, and this humble request by the pilgrim to tell confirm the impression that, even though we don't know who Ciacco was, Dante held him in high esteem. We must give due consideration to this particular way of characterizing the central figure in the first of the great political cantos of the *Divine Comedy.*

Dante now wants to know the whereabouts of prominent Florentines of the elder generation such as Farinata, Tegghiaio, Jacopo Rusticucci, Arrigo, Mosca:

> "and all the rest whose minds bent toward the good,
>   do tell me where they are and let me meet them;
> for my great longing drives me on to learn
> if Heaven sweetens or Hell poisons them."
>
> (81–84)

Ciacco's last answer is no less precise than his preceding ones. Once again—even too cruelly, we may note—his response is right to the point:

> And he: "They are among the blackest souls;
> a different sin has dragged them to the bottom;
> if you descend so low, there you can see them."
>
> (85–87)

Dante will meet Farinata degli Uberti among the heretics (*Inf.* x), Tegghiaio Aldobrandi and Jacopo Rusticucci among the sodomites (*Inf.* xvi), Mosca de' Lamberti among the sowers of discord (*Inf.* xxviii).

The concluding tercet of Ciacco's speech brings us back to the personal grief of a damned soul, to its desire to be remembered in the "sweet world." In a well-arranged musical composition, he picks up the opening motive:

> "But when you have returned to the sweet world,
> I pray, recall me to men's memory:
> I say no more to you, answer no more."
>
> (88–90)

Ciacco will not speak again. The same spurring force of divine justice that goads the wicked souls toward Acheron pushes him back into the eternal mire ("as low as all his blind companions" [93]). The last sign of his lost humanity is his gaze set on Dante: "his straight gaze grew twisted and awry" (91).

Then Virgil speaks. His words confirm that Ciacco's ephemeral back-to-life interval is over. Ciacco speaks to Dante so that he and all men may profit from it. At the same time, Virgil's words open a new, mildly phrased, and largely suggestive dialogue with the poet-*viator* so that he might learn about future life.

There is no doubt about the biblical intonation of the next section, starting at line 94. Yet we should not look too closely for direct textual sources. Mazzoni (177) refers to Luke 21:7, Matthew 24:30, and Mark 23:26. It seems advisable to add to these references another quote from the Apocalypse (19:11–16), which can help us understand the "hostile Judge" as a figure of Christ the judge: "And I saw heaven opened, and behold a white horse; and he that sat upon him was called faithful and true, and with justice doth he judge and fight. And on his eyes were as a flame of fire, and on his head were many diadems, and he had a name written, which no man knoweth but himself. And he was clothed with a garment sprinkled with blood; and his name is called, THE WORD OF GOD. And the armies that are in heaven followed him on white horses, clothed in fine linen, white and clean. And out of his mouth proceedeth a sharp two-edged sword; that with it he may strike the nations. And he shall rule them with a rod of iron; and he treadeth the winepress of the fierceness of the wrath of God the Almighty. And he hath on his garment, and on his thigh written: KING OF KINGS, AND LORD OF LORDS." The judging authority, that is, the "Judge" is certainly "hostile" (nimica) in that it rides against the sinners in dreadful sights. The powerful Judge cannot be "benevolent"—as André Pézard, who insists on interpreting nimica podesta as "the second death" (1963, 1965), would like to see him.

> So did we pass across that squalid mixture
> of shadows and of rain, our steps slowed down,
> talking awhile about the life to come.
>   At which I said: "And after the great sentence—
> o master—will these torments grow, or else
> be less, or will they be just as intense?"
>
> (100–105)

Dante has just completed his immersion in the world of damnation of the third circle. The two poets walk away. They leave behind the "squalid mixture / of shadows and of rain" and proceed, their "steps slowed down" (100–101). They walk slowly—not, as Mazzoni (177) believes, because they do not want to dirty themselves with mud nor because Dante needs time to expiate in his mind his own sin of gluttony, as was once submitted by Pietrobono (whose words Mazzoni quotes [177 n.3])—because they are about to engage in common meditation concerning the life to come. It was not the right time to hurry. Dante was about to phrase "the first philosophical questio of the Divine Comedy," as Mazzoni rightly points out (177). It is clear that haste, which "denies all acts their dignity" (ogn' atto dismaga [Purg. III, 11]), would not be proper in such a grave atmosphere.

Dante's questio picks up a motif neatly alluded to at the beginning of this canto. If it is true that the infernal rain's "measure and its kind" (9) were established from eternity to eternity, how could the condition of the damned souls undergo any change? Once again, we should take note of the perfect consistency of Dante's use of circular schemes. Virgil answers this question in a calm, detached tone. He now plays the role of the good teacher. He reminds his pupil of what he already knows so that the pupil can use that knowledge to solve his problems by himself:

> And he to me: "Remember now your science,
> which says that when a thing has more perfection,
> so much the greater is its pain or pleasure.
>   Though these accursed sinners never shall

> attain the true perfection, yet they can
> expect to be more perfect then than now."
>
> (106–111)

Mazzoni explains Virgil's allusion to Dante's knowledge, locating the key reference in Saint Thomas's comment to Aristotle's *On the Soul*. There is no doubt that Dante took for granted that his readers were familiar with *lectio* xiv of Book I, which reads, *quanto anima est perfectior, tanto exercet plures perfectas operationes et diversas* (the more perfect a soul is, the more perfect and diverse are its workings; see Mazzoni, 177–178). The damned souls never reach true perfection. After the Last Judgment, however, their lack of being will be truly perfect. This perfection in the negative sense implies the possibility of increased suffering.

Inferno vi ends when Dante and Virgil walk from the third to the fourth circle:

> We took the circling way traced by that road;
> we said much more than I can here recount;
> we reached the point that marks the downward slope.
> Here we found Plutus, the great enemy.
>
> (112–115)

The encounter with Plutus, a new infernal monster, indicates that the pilgrim and his guide have left the territory under Cerberus's jurisdiction. As we noted above, another circular structure—which spans from monster to monster—reveals here its concluding weld.

BIBLIOGRAPHICAL NOTES

Among the many commentaries on the *Comedy,* in addition to consulting Chiavacci Leonardi, I have relied mostly on Sapegno's and Pézard's eds. See also André Pézard, "Le chant vi de l'*Enfer:* Ciacco et Florence," *Bulletin de la Société d'études dantesques—Annales du Centre universitaire méditerranéen* 12 (1963): 7–34; and his article "Ciacco" in *Enciclopedia dantesca,* 1: 982–985.

For the connections among the sixth cantos, see P. Conte, "Il canto vi del *Paradiso,*" in *Lectura Dantis Romana* (Turin, 1956). Conte's observations were first included in Daniele Mattalia's commentary on the *Divina Commedia* (Milan, 1960) and later discussed by Ettore Paratore in "Il canto vi del *Paradiso,*" in *Nuovi saggi danteschi* (Rome, 1973), 165 ff., as well as by F. Mazzoni in "Il canto vi dell'*Inferno,*" in *Nuove letture dantesche* (Florence, 1966), 1:133–181. Mazzoni's article is a fundamental study, not only for this particular argument.

On Dante's political universe, see R. Picchio and M. Picchio Simonelli, "I confini orientali del mondo di Dante" in *Dante e il mondo slavo,* Proceedings of the International Convention in Dubrovnik, October 26–29, 1981.

D. S. Avalle, "L'età dell'oro in Dante," in *Modelli semiologici nella Commedia di Dante* (Milan, 1975), 77–95, explains in a very convincing way the opposition of past and present in the sixteenth canto of *Paradiso* (esp. 88–95). For Dante's use of formal devices, see G. L. Beccaria, *L'Autonomia del significante: Figure del ritmo e della sintassi: Dante, Pascoli, D'Annunzio* (Turin, 1975), 91–101. J. T. S. Wheelock, "Alliterative Function in the *Divine Comedy,*" *Lingua e Stile* 13 (1978): 373–404.

On the infernal monsters, see C. Grabner, "Mostri e simboli dell'*Inferno* dantesco," *Annali della Facoltà di lettere e filosofia e di magistero dell'Università di Cagliari* 21 (1953): 47–66; Christopher Kleinhenz, "Infernal Guardians Revisited: *Cerbero, il gran vermo* (*Inf.* VI, 22)," *Dante Studies* 93 (1975): 185–199 (see esp. 197 n.3).

On the political situation in Florence at the end of the thirteenth and the beginning of the fourteenth century, see Dino Compagni, *Chronicle of Florence*, ed. and trans. Daniel E. Bornstein (1930; Philadelphia, 1986); and G. Salvemini, *Magnati et Popolani in Firenze dal 1280 al 1295*, ed. E. Sestan (Milan, 1966).

Among the older commentaries on *Inferno* VI, I have found particularly useful those of Benvenuto da Imola and Guido da Pisa.

For the interpretation of the two just men, Sapegno's comments on line 73—based on a gloss of Del Lungo—are not very convincing. His reference to Ezechiel 14:14–25 is inappropriate. The *tres viri isti* (not *iusti*, as Sapegno seems to have read) quoted by Ezechiel are three highly individualized examples of justice: Noah, David, and Job. The biblical concept, expressed by Ezechiel, that the few wise men "shall deliver their own souls by their justice," in contrast to others who will be doomed, does not seem very adequate to explain this canto; it would be more useful for interpreting the canzone "Tre donne intorno al cor," in which Dante extols his exile as proof of his righteousness. The quotation of Matthew 18:19–20, proposed by Pézard ("Ciacco"), is more appropriate.

CANTO VII

The Weal of Fortune

PHILIP R. BERK

> Is happiness one thing and fortune another?
> (Saint Augustine, *City of God* IV, 18)

Canto VI closes portentously on the prospect of encountering "Plutus, the great enemy," a note of melodramatic suspense commensurate with the radical primacy given to greed by 1 Timothy 6:10, which warns that "the desire of money is the root of all evils" (cf. *Purg.* XX, 43). But in the *Convivio* (IV, x–xii) Dante had reflected less on the consuming power of avarice than on the base "imperfection" of riches, incomprehensible in their origins and growth. The anticlimactic nature of the encounter with Plutus in this canto, his unintelligibility, vagueness of form, and quick deflation are more in keeping with the analysis of wealth in the *Convivio* than with the preceding canto; indeed, the fourth circle and *Inferno* VII as a whole are attended by an inherent obscurity and ambiguity that may be profoundly mimetic of human reason's inability to comprehend the displacement of love onto material goods and its condensation into wealth. Canto VII represents, then, the attempt to cope with "imperfection," to grapple with the unknowable, an effort that produces less a body of doctrine than a sequence of images, abstract forms and figures, themselves opaque, that challenge certainty in these matters.

Deflationary, abstract, fragmented, the seventh canto lacks the drama of a tormented protagonist. The sheer quantity of sinners and the effacement of their individuality had for De Sanctis a "modern" cast, but the initial confrontation with Plutus, the concluding description of the Stygian marsh, the symmetrical groups of paired sinners in circles four and five, the central discourse on Fortune, and Virgil's assured mastery throughout the canto, might suggest, on the other hand, a deliberate classicizing effort on Dante's part. Even so, the canto is dynamically innovative in that, for the first time in the *Comedy*, the canto's formal boundaries do not coincide with one discrete moral area but straddle two circles of Hell. Yet this transitional structure cannot be considered merely as a formal breakthrough, for it has thematic implications as well. Insofar as the canto is an imaginative unity, its dual subject solicits us to understand avarice and anger in terms of one another and to contrast these vices against Virgil's representation of Fortune within a providential framework. But throughout the canto it is the foregrounding of the incomprehensibility, inadequacy, deprivation, ambiguity of language itself, with the effacement of human identity, which constitute more disturbing indices of its modernity. Plutus's fearsome clucking—*Pape Satàn, pape Satàn, aleppe!*—is more grotesque than formidable. If his cry to or for Satan sends a deep taproot into the nethermost reaches of Hell, the rest of his strange bark—desperately interpreted by scholars as allusions to the papacy, or as elemental Greek and Hebrew exclamations of surprise and pain (i.e., *aleph*)—carries little semantic bite but exposes at the outset greed's corruption of rationality.

Dante counterbalances the vague, ungraspable disjointedness of Plutus, who has only a shadowy role in the *Aeneid* (VII, 327), by his sharp delineation of Virgil, "the gentle sage, aware of everything." If Virgil does understand Plutus's language, he omits an explanation to address more relevant matters. Seeking to reassure the pilgrim before he expeditiously reduces Plutus to silence, Virgil mediates between the pilgrim and his fear by virtue of his mansuetude, which "denotes a calm temper, not led by emotion but only becoming angry in such a manner, for such causes and for such a length of time as principle may ordain" (Aristotle, *Nicomachean Ethics* IV, 5). Nor does Virgil refer to Plutus's role as the deity of wealth, but only to the demon's rage that he commands him to stifle here: "Be quiet, cursed wolf! / Let your vindictiveness (*rabbia*) feed on yourself" (8–9). Plutus's nature and function retrospectively clarify the far more fearsome, but unexplained, she-wolf encountered in *Inferno* I (and for another clarification, see *Purg.* XX, 10). We may infer that an angry, thrusting attack and inward consumption, which harks back to the circle of gluttony, are the two gestures characteristic of greed; the same verb describes the wrathful two times—"they struck against each other" (*percotëansi* [28] and *questi si percotean* [112]).

Although he watches over the circle of avarice, Plutus is explicitly characterized by his anger and the pride, shared with the usurping angels, routed by the archangel Michael (Apocalypse 12:7–9), as Virgil reminds him in the first of his appeals to broader perspectives and higher authority in the canto. The demon's "swollen face" may possibly allude to the "angry Chremes" who "with swollen mouth" (*tumido ore*) was allowed by Horace (*Art of Poetry*, v. 94; cf. Dante, *Epistola* X, 16) to the upper range of comedy. Plutus's sudden arousal and rapid deflation would suggest his kinship with the short-tempered among the irascible temperaments distinguished by Aristotle (*Ethics* IV, 5); his erratic fitfulness runs counter to the firmness of the stoic sage "who is neither puffed up, nor crushed, by the happenings of chance" (Seneca, *On the Happy Life* IV, 2). Saint Augustine chided pagans for revering good Fortune as a goddess, while bad Fortune "is suddenly changed into a malignant demon" (*City of God* IV, 18). May not Plutus, characterized as a "child of Fortune" by Phaedrus (*Fable* IV, 12), display the pagan goddess's other semblance? In a vivid nautical simile, which may amplify the Boethian conceit of "noxious care swollen by earthbound winds [that] grows beyond measure" (*Consolation of Philosophy* I, m. 2), Plutus collapses like the sails of a ship whose mast has snapped, an image that plays on the iconographically fecund, semantic ambiguity of *fortuna,* which also denotes a "tempest," as in Dante's well-known sonnet to Guido Cavalcanti.

The descent into the fourth circle is told in a homely idiom that corresponds to the baseness of avarice. Such words as *pigliare* (to take), *insaccare* (to put into a sack), *stipare* (to pile up; cf. constipate), and *scipare* (to waste) portray a sordid Hell more greedy than any errant soul, but Dante has other means of exposing the sin. Consider the unsuspected rhetorical cunning of the following tercet:

> Justice of God! Who has amassed as many
> strange tortures and travails as I have seen?
> Why do we let our guilt consume us so?
> (19–21)

While its double interrogation adumbrates the impoverished questions of the sinners, the apostrophe to divine justice, countering Plutus's invocation to Satan, ironically answers the rhetorical questions posed by evoking the transcendent principle that governs the revenge of the archangels, the norm that the sinners violated and by which they are punished, as well as the unfathomable ground of Fortune's activity.

Dante introduces the punishment of the fourth circle with a second seascape, a condensation of Virgil's more elaborate description of Charybdis in *Aeneid* III, 420–423:

> Even as waves that break above Charybdis,
> each shattering the other when they meet,
> so must the spirits here dance their round dance.
> (22–24)

The analogy reduces human activity to the futile, inanimate fluctuations of the sea, but its force is itself subverted by the subsequent deflation of the sublime clash of waves to a prosaic "round dance" (24). These metaphoric waters will further congeal in the canto into the metonymic heaviness of the sluggish Stygian marsh.

Rather than foregrounding a pathetic hero, Dante describes the punishment of the avaricious and prodigal with redundant choreographic precision, faintly comical in its mechanical, grunting gymnastics. The "multitudes" (25) of sinners push weights with their chests in two semicircular files that collide, then turn around to repeat the process in the opposite direction. This ponderous "joust" (35)—and jousting was often attacked as an example of conspicuous waste—borrows motifs from the *Aeneid:* the sheer number of brooding misers and neglectful spendthrifts (VI, 610–611), and rolling heavy stones as punishment (VI, 616), a Sisyphean task made horizontally banal. The spendthrifts, seemingly unaware that their punishment is identical, taunt the miserly with "Why do you hoard?" to which the latter reply, "Why do you squander?" (30). (Cf. the terse interrogative rebuke of both prodigal waste and anger in Seneca, *On Anger* III, 42: "Your fortunes admit no squandering, and you have no spare time to waste. Why do we rush into the fray? Why do we invite trouble for ourselves? Why do we, forgetting our weakness, take up the huge burden of hate, and easily broken as we are, rise up to break?" Dante would seem tacitly to have choreographed most of Seneca's images and rhetorical moves.) The brief, sharp physical and verbal encounters, like the scenes between Molière's Harpagon and his spendthrift son, lie between comedy and drama; they offer a bleak parody of the chief systems of symbolic exchange, money and language. Language here serves only minimally as a medium of reproachful incrimination, although, ironically, the brief taunts raise valid but unanswered questions about motive and purpose. The punishment precisely corresponds to the sin; for their "undiscerning life," Virgil observes, the avaricious and prodigal have become individually "unrecognizable" (54). Wealth is disclosed as a burden; its pursuit, a repetitive and wearying dance; its price, the erosion of humanity, rationality, and language. The dehumanized formalism of the punishment provokes a qualified sympathy in the pilgrim, whose heart was "almost pierced through" (36), and dulls his capacity to make any sense of the spectacle, other than to wonder whether all the tonsured heads he sees on his left belong to clerics.

Recognition itself becomes problematic here when, in response to the pilgrim's questions, Virgil explains that the accusatory barking is more telling than the tonsure, the visual sign of earthly office, since the verbal signs clearly announce a lack of measure with respect to spending. However, the confusion between moral and professional categories is not entirely dispelled by Virgil's explanation that at the Last Judgment some will rise up "with fists clenched tight," others "with hair cropped close" (57). A critical consensus holds that the clerics on the left must belong to the miserly, since avarice is a graver condition than prodigality for both Aristotle and Aquinas. Yet it is puzzling that "hair cropped close," the definitive sign of prodigality, should so closely resemble, and perhaps derive from, the tonsure that distinguishes the clerics, who are supposedly burdened with the contrary sin. Aquinas himself blames clerics not for hoarding but for squandering the Church's goods, which properly belong to the poor (*Summa theologica* II-II, 119, 3). Are we then to understand baldness in the fourth circle as marking clerics or prodigals, or have we some inductive riddle whereby the sign of the one ironically metamorphoses at the Last Trumpet into the sign of the other? The difficulty in discerning prodigality from avarice informs as well the fifth terrace of Purgatory.

The peculiar foulness of avarice, which is conveyed by such bristling rhymes as *sozzi, cozzi, mozzi* (53–57), flies in the face not only of right knowledge, but of the world's beauty; nor does Virgil wish to "embellish" its sordidness. At the canto's unsteady fulcrum, Virgil draws the lesson about the brief "sport" (61) or instability, for *la corta buffa* could mean either "farce" or "puff of wind," and both readings accord with the canto's imagery, of goods placed "in Fortune's care," another amphibology that could mean "risked [by men]," or, less obvious immediately but subsequently confirmed, "assigned [by providence]." The ambiguous central tercet may be construed to signify the endlessly displaced, pyramiding desire of avarice (Lat. *avere* "to desire"), never to be sated on earth, or else the impossibility of ever ransoming the punished sinners for any sum of money: "For all the gold that is or ever was / beneath the moon could never offer rest / to even one of these exhausted spirits" (64–66). The intensification of indeterminate meaning here seems to mimic the unstable world of "empty goods" subject to Fortune. The pilgrim's question, "what's she, who clutches so all the world's goods?" (69) by its naive presupposition of Fortune as a grasping, malevolent nemesis, triggers Virgil's indignation at human ignorance. Virgil's request to the pilgrim to "digest" his words plays nicely against the canto's other, less nourishing reverberations of the third circle: Plutus's "feeding" on his rage (9), the angry biting of flesh (114), "the swallowers of slime" (129).

Virgil's presentation of Fortune, with its vast perspectives and elegant command of theological cosmology, may tempt us to believe that he speaks for Dante himself, rather than in character as a nobly minded pagan. It is significant that the subsequent canticles dispense with Fortune as an explanatory principle, while in the *Monarchia* (II, ix) a pagan's invocation of Fortune is subjected to the correction, "whereas we may more properly and justly call such judgment that of divine providence." The church fathers, most notably Saint Augustine, attempted to ridicule or legislate pagan notions of fortune, chance, and fate out of existence, since their function was assumed by God's will (*City of God* IV, 18, 33; V, 1). As a poet, Dante is more conciliatory and syncretistic, although he does not indulge in the proliferation of realistic detail with which many vernacular medieval poets amplified the figure of Fortune and her habitation.

In the first of his extended theoretical discourses, Virgil sets forth a succinct image of the Christian-Ptolemaic universe: the divine mind, "whose wisdom transcends everything" (74), created the heavens over which it sets intelligences who distribute the light equally, while the external goods—wealth, honors, power—of the sublunar realm are similarly in the possession of an intelligence who distributes them not just among individuals, but from one people to another (cf. Ecclesiasticus 10:8). Fortune is none other than this active intelligence; the changes she effects are unpreventable; her judgment is impenetrable. In an often misunderstood passage, she is subject to "necessity" (89) only in the sense that the enormity of her task, that is, the goods to be distributed, and the numbers who must be served, entails that she work quickly so as to be fair. Fortune is neither blind nor chastising, as she appears in Boethius, but she is deaf to the unjust blame of men who should rightly praise her as the efficient executrix of the divine will. Above chance herself, she is blessedly subservient, happily self-contained, a moral equilibrium masterfully conveyed in Italian by an overarching chiasmus, *ma ella s'è beata . . . e beata si gode* (94, 96), which exceptionally makes repeated use of pleonastic reflexive verbs, and which culminates in the sustained dactylic rhythm of *volve sua spera e beata si gode* (96).

Although shorn of most of her traditional attributes, Fortune is no abstract principle but is subtly personified. First characterized austerely in hierarchical administrative language (78), then neutrally in terms of her faculties and operations (86–90), then sympathetically as a victim of men's calumny (91–93), Fortune is at last depicted in her active and serene joyousness. A vestige of her wheel appears as the sublunar sphere itself. These few traits suffice to form a rounded literary figure, and a case might even be made for her as "the other woman" of the *Inferno*—the buoyant, bustling comic soubrette in juxtaposition to the tragically passionate Francesca—yet she rarely figures among "the ladies of the *Comedy*." It is to Dante's credit, however, that Virgil's prosopopoeia runs counter to the image of the blind, cruel, fickle female, born of the ambiguous alterity of gender, sought after and despised from antiquity to Machiavelli and beyond, among whose later avatars may be counted the feckless Manon Lescaut.

For Virgil, Fortune is praiseworthy but otherwise remote and inscrutable, even though he initially took humans to task for ignoring her true nature. While Virgil's lesson constitutes itself as orthodox discourse, the objects of this discourse—the divine mind, Fortune's dispensation—defy human understanding. Augustine observes: "God, therefore, the author and giver of happiness, because he is the only true God, himself gives earthly kingdoms to the good and the bad. This is not done rashly or at random, for he is God, not Fortuna, the goddess of luck. He does this in accordance with an order of things and of times which is hidden from us but very well known to him" (*City of God* IV, 33). What the avaricious and prodigal are through their punishment, Fortune is in essence, knowable only with respect to her role within the divine economy. At the center of Virgil's speech appears the word "hidden" (*occulto*), qualified with an authentically Virgilian simile, "like a serpent in the grass" (84; cf. Virgil, *Eclogues,* III, 93), an intertextual reminiscence whose recognition may compensate for the deeper ignorance he imposes upon us.

Yet Fortune, in her joyous play of difference and dissemination, functions not simply as a mediating figure of the unfathomability of divine providence with regard to the distribution of worldly goods, but as a pivotal counterexample to Plutus's boom and bust and the dark Stygian marsh, to "all these telegrams and anger," in E. M. Forster's memorable hendiadys. In her detachment, she exemplifies a comic, felicitous, and temperate mean between the burdensome, angry farce of avarice and the rending pathos of anger: "The distinctive and natural property of virtue is to rejoice and be glad; it no more comports with her dignity to be angry than to be sad" (Seneca, *On Anger* II, 6). But if Fortune paradoxically embodies the rational and virtuous ideal established by pagan philosophers to remedy her traditional caprice, she is constituted by the noble eloquence of Virgil, whose breadth and clarity of vision can be understood as a proper antidote to Plutus's incomprehensible language, the "squint-eyed" (41) barking of the avaricious, the blind self-destructiveness of the angry, and the tormented speechlessness of the sullen.

Virgil's discourse brooks no response on the part of the pilgrim; it concludes with an urgent imperative to progress to the next circle of "greater sorrow" (97). The master's intuitive sense of stellar motion—for the sinking stars indicate that it is past midnight—dictates the descent. The reference to a more remote, yet more reliable movement than Fortune's abruptly announces the further goals of the journey, easily forgotten in the noble pleasure of contemplation. The reminder of time's passing echoes, but also reverses, the sentiment of *Aeneid* VI, 539: "The night is near, Aeneas; we waste our time with tears." The ponderous, semicircular dance of the avaricious and the swift revolutions of Fortune's sphere are recapitulated and subverted by the incisive linear movement of the travelers: "We crossed (*ricidemmo*) the circle to the other shore" (100).

Virgil and the pilgrim now come to a spring that flows downward to become the Stygian marsh (cf. *Aen.* VI, 323), the second of Hell's four rivers. Here anger is punished. The "melancholy stream" that is the source of the Styx plays on the presumed etymology of Styx as *tristitia* or "sorrow," the passion seen by Aquinas (*Summa* II-II, 35–36) to be the psychological "source" of anger, sloth and envy, and hence, for Dante, the appropriate condition of punishment. We have come, once again, to a deeper root than "desire of money." Unlike the avaricious, the wrathful, "those whom anger has defeated" (116), naked on the surface of the mire, bear their condition on their faces, but the darkness of the marsh itself is insistently recalled.

In the murky vertical organization of the Styx, two kinds of anger are punished, for submerged within, as Virgil explains, are the souls of those whose sighs cause bubbles to form on the surface, souls commonly, but not with complete assurance, glossed in Aristotelian terms as the sullen. The sullen too are punished in their speech, for the slime prevents them from making an intelligible utterance. They are forced to gurgle their "hymn" (*inno*), inwardly, a pun no less cruel than its counterpart in v. 33, the *metro* or "measure" meted out by the immoderate spenders. Theirs would be the most tragic chorus in the *Inferno* were it not that their communal threnody must be given voice by Virgil:

> . . . "We had been sullen
> in the sweet air that's gladdened by the sun;
> we bore the mist of sluggishness in us;
> now we are bitter in the blackened mud."
>   (121–124)

The very beauty of these richly assonanced verses—what translation could do justice to *Tristi fummo / ne l'aere dolce che dal sol s'allegra* (121–122)?—their nostalgic representation of a *paysage moralisé* intensifies the poignant irony of the punishment. These embittered souls ignored the implicit lesson of the beauty of the world and the word, a fault they share with the avaricious, and so they are doubly denied sight and speech in Hell. Sullenness as the poisonous repression of anger was well understood by Aristotle (*Ethics* IV, 5), but the text muddies the conceptual waters, as it were, of the Aristotelian vice, by associating with it the sinful disposition to sloth or *acedia*, the besetting sin of the monastic life, in the ambiguous reference to *accidïoso fummo*, the "mist of sluggishness." Since ecclesiastics are the only group identified among the avaricious, one wonders whether the choir of the sullen should not be *sous-entendu* as monastic. It would be all the more galling that a pagan should voice their claustral sorrow. A striking passage in Horace's *Art of Poetry* (108–111) on the necessary and natural fittingness of speech to the emotions offers a precedent for Virgil's curious role as an interpreter, faithfully transcribing the grief of the sinners, but unnaturally disjoined from their passionate intention.

The concluding narrative tercet subverts the lyric pathos of the sullen "in the blackened mud" by a return to the plain style of "that disgusting pond" and by a releasing arc of movement, rhythmically conveyed by an enjambment (127), a circling that subtends the pilgrim's intent gaze upon the "swallowers of slime." The canto's final verse abruptly arrives at a terminus that recalls the illusory relation between tower (nobility) and river (riches) in "Le dolce rime d'amor" (*Conv.* IV, x): "We came at last upon a tower's base" (130). However, this apparently decisive ending—the *omega* of *al da sezzo* (at last) answering the opening *aleph-alpha* of *aleppe*—will be undermined by the problematic backtracking at the outset of *Inferno* VIII. Boccaccio reported that Dante had suspended the composition of the canticle at this point, and this may be the case, but there is possibly something deeper at stake in this retraction, a questioning of the sustained rational mastery manifested by Virgil and witnessed by his attentive pupil in the classical fullness of *Inferno* VII.

The calling of rational discourse into question is already implied within the seventh canto by an overarching structure built on an easily overlooked numerical symmetry, a mysterious, transcendent spatial pattern that reveals itself only in retrospect but silently asks to be pondered and interpreted. The canto's last ten tercets (100–130) are given to the Styx, sullenness, and anger, while Virgil's discourse on Fortune exactly occupies the ten previous tercets (70–99). If ten is the canto's unit of measurement, we can now see that it is precisely ten tercets from Plutus's opening bark to the hemistich shouts of the avaricious and prodigal: "Why do you hoard?" "Why do you squander?" (30), a verse that dramatically marks the turning point of the fourth circle's punishments, whose description continues for another ten tercets (31–60). That leaves three tercets at the canto's center, surrounded on either side by two units of ten tercets. These three tercets are thematically transitional in that they relate avarice to fortune; indeed, the word *fortuna* occurs twice here (62, 68) and nowhere else in the canto, three verses on either side of the numerically central verse (65), which speaks of the avaricious as "these exhausted spirits." How are we to interpret this subtle articulation and insistent symmetry: 10–10–(1–F–2–C–2–F–1)–10–10? I am reminded of a ring or sphere revolving around a center, say, a model of the Ptolemaic universe, with Fortune's sublunary sphere comprehended within more perfect celestial spheres, an inversion of Boethius's figure of the wheel of which the supernal mind is the center and fate is the rim (*Consolation* IV, pr. 6). Are these proportions merely fortuitous or does this quantitative irony represent the provident mind of the Creator "whose wisdom transcends everything; / that every part may shine unto the other" (74–75)? And does not the play of this abstract but orderly totality promise a greater joy than that illusory material totality that appears ten lines earlier: "all the gold that is or ever was / beneath the moon"?

BIBLIOGRAPHY

Translations, with the exception of Allen Mandelbaum's of the *Comedy* and the *Aeneid* and Herbert W. Schneider's of *Monarchia*, are taken from the respective Loeb Classical Library editions. I am grateful to A. Benston, C. Caramello, R. Hollander, and D. Kelley for their advice.
    Among the works that offer perceptive readings of the canto are

Achity, Kenneth John. "*Inferno* VII: The Idea of Order." *Italian Quarterly* 12 (1969): 5–62.
Bacci, Orazio. [Lectura in] *Lectura Dantis*. Florence, 1906.
Bernardini, Giovanni. [Lectura in] *Dialoghi* 5 (1957): 27–38.
Bignone, S. F. [Lectura in] *Lectura Dantis Genovese*, 263–293. Florence, 1904.

Carroll, John S. *Exiles of Eternity,* 110–125. London, 1903.

Figurelli, Fernando. [Lectura in] *Nuove letture dantesche,* 1:183–208. Florence, 1968.

Getto, Giovanni. (1947). [Lectura in] *Letture dantesche,* ed. Giovanni Getto, 115–131. Florence, 1965.

Kirkpatrick, Robin. [Lectura in] *Dante Soundings,* ed. David Nolan, 4–27. Dublin, 1981.

Looney, Dennis. *"Inferno* VII." In *Dante's "Divine Comedy," Introductory Readings: Inferno,* ed. Tibor Wlassics, 82–92. Charlottesville, Va., 1990.

Marti, Mario. *Realismo dantesco e altri studi,* 45–62. Milan, 1961.

Torraca, Francesco. [Reading in] *Nuovi studi danteschi,* 309–334. Naples, 1921.

Ulivi, Ferrucio. [Reading in] *"Inferno": Letture degli anni 1973–1976,* ed. Silvio Zennaro, 175–196. Rome, 1977.

Vallone, Aldo. *Studi su Dante medievale,* 143–159. Florence, 1965.

On the opening crux, see

Enciclopedia dantesca, 4:280–282, s.v. "Pape Satàn, pape Satàn aleppe." Rome, 1973.

Guerri, Domenico. "Papé Satan, Papé Satan Aleppe!" *Giornale dantesco* 12 (1904): 138–142.

Marti, Berthe M. "A Crux in Dante's *Inferno." Speculum* 27 (1952): 67–70.

Rheinfelder, Hans. "Dante und die Hebraïsche Sprache." *Miscellanea medievale* 4 (1965): 442–457.

Staedler, E. "Das rhetorische Element in Dantes *Divina Commedia." Deutsches Dante Jahrbuch* 13 (1940): 107–151.

On Fortune, see

Bommarito, Domenico. "Boezio e la fortuna di Dante in *Inf.* VII, 61–96." *L'Alighieri* 20 (1979): 42–56.

Busetto, N. "Origine e natura della fortuna dantesca." *Giornale dantesco* 12 (1904): 129–138.

Cioffari, Vincenzo. *The Conception of Fortune and Fate in the Works of Dante.* Cambridge, Mass., 1940.

Doren, A. "Fortuna im Mittelalter und in der Renaissance." *Vorträge der Bibliothek Warburg* 1 (1924): 71–144.

Enciclopedia dantesca, 2:983–986, s.v. "fortuna." Rome, 1970.

Falorsi, Guido "La fortuna nel VII dell' *Inferno." Giornale dantesco* 35 (1932): 155–183.

Mancini, A. "Il crin mozzo dei prodighi." *Giornale dantesco* 10 (1902): 134–135.

Mazzotta, Giuseppe. *Dante, Poet of the Desert: History and Allegory in the "Divine Comedy,"* 319–328. Princeton, 1979.

Murari, R. *Dante e Boezio,* 271–297. Bologna, 1905.

Patch, Howard Rollin. "The Goddess Fortuna in the *Divine Comedy." Thirty-Third Annual Report of the Dante Society* (1914): 13–28.

———. *The Goddess Fortuna in Medieval Literature.* Cambridge, Mass., 1927.

Toja, Gianluigi. "Due noterelle dantesche." *Studi danteschi* 42 (1965): 235–260.

On the much debated identity of those submerged in the Styx, see

Filomusi-Guelfi, Lorenzo. "Gli accidiosi e gl' invidiosi nell' *Inferno* di Dante." *L'Alighieri* 1 (1890): 168–183.

Klostermann, Wolf-Gunther. "Acedia und Schwarze Galle." *Romanische Forschungen* 76 (1964): 183–193.

Wenzel, Siegfried. *The Sin of Sloth: Acedia in Medieval Thought and Literature,* esp. 200–202. Chapel Hill, N.C., 1967.

CANTO VIII

Fifth Circle: Wrathful and Sullen

CARON ANN CIOFFI

In Canto VIII of the *Inferno,* Dante and Virgil cross the dark marsh of the Stygian fifth circle and arrive at the gates of the City of Dis. The canto thus marks the important transition between upper Hell, occupied by those whose sins were due to incontinence of desire or temper, and lower Hell, occupied by those whose sins were due to the graver evil dispositions of bestiality and malice. The incontinent of temper are divided into two groups: the wrathful, who attack each other on the surface of the Styx, and the sullen, who are sunk beneath the muddy swamp.

The symbolic embodiment of anger is the boatman of the Styx, Phlegyas. In classical mythology, Phlegyas was a tyrannical king of the Lapithae, whose daughter Coronis was raped by Apollo. In revenge, Phlegyas set fire to Apollo's temple at Delphi, whereupon the god killed him and condemned him to Tartarus, lower Hell. He is mentioned, without specific punishment, in the *Aeneid* (VI, 618–620): "And Phlegyas, most unblest, gives warning to all and with loud voice bears witness amid the gloom: 'Be warned; learn justice and do not scorn the gods.'" Statius's *Thebaid* supplies a more explicit account of Phlegyas's torture: "To avenge [Apollo] grim Megera holds fast the starving Phlegyas, who lies ever pressed beneath the cavernous rocks, and torments him with the unholy feast" (I, 712–715).

In the mythographic tradition, Phlegyas is a figure of impiety and sacrilege against the gods (*Mythographus Vaticanus* I, 205). Similarly, early Dante commentators like Boccaccio, Pietro di Dante, and Benvenuto da Imola characterize Phlegyas as proud and vexatious. Benvenuto goes on to say that the boatman's function—to carry souls to Dis, where violence and fraud are punished—is an allegory of pride leading men to great evil. Etymologically, the name Phlegyas is said to be derived from the Greek root *phleg-*, which, as Dante knew from Servius's commentary on the *Aeneid,* refers to fire (as in Phlegethon, the boiling river in *Inferno* XII).

In the canto, Phlegyas manifests both types of wrath punished in the Styx. He first speeds like an arrow toward Dante and Virgil, shouting "Now you are caught, foul soul!" (18). His response corresponds to the quickness of anger represented by the damned on the marsh's surface. After Virgil's rebuke, Phlegyas's active rage turns to the sullen anger of "one who hears some great deception / was done to him, and then resents it" (22–23). It corresponds to the melancholy resentment demonstrated by the damned beneath the muddy surface.

Although critics have debated whether Phlegyas's duty is to ferry over all the souls destined for Dis or merely to unload the wrathful spirits in Styx, they agree that he symbolizes the psychological progress from pride to wrath. Dante would have known from medieval theological treatises (especially Saint Thomas Aquinas, *Summa theologica* I-II, 47, 3) that kings and all proud people are particularly susceptible to anger. Virgil alludes to this notion when he states that many arrogant rulers on earth will lie with the wrathful in Hell (49–51). Phlegyas's presumption led to the wrathful and impious act of vengeance against a god. Similarly, at the canto's end appear the rebel angels, whose pride led to the irreverent attempt to overthrow God and ultimately to impotent fury in Dis. The other major figure in the canto—Filippo Argenti—is also both "presumptuous" on earth and "hot with fury" in Hell (46–48).

The main drama of Canto VIII begins when the pilgrim is confronted by this shade, who was his former Florentine neighbor and political enemy. Dante insults Argenti, who in turn reaches toward him, presumably to grab Dante from the boat in which he and his guide are riding. Virgil intercedes to protect the pilgrim and praises Dante's rigorous severity toward the sinner. This episode ends with Dante thanking God for having allowed him the pleasure of seeing Argenti punished.

The second focal point of the canto is the actual arrival at the vast wall that encircles Dis. Hosts of devils suddenly appear upon the ramparts to oppose Dante's entrance. Virgil, whose authority over the guardians of previous circles was unchallenged, is powerless against the fallen angels. The demoralized guide and his terror-stricken follower experience a veritable impasse, alleviated only by the descent of a heavenly messenger at the end of the following canto.

Current critics are swift to note that both Dante and Virgil behave differently in the canto of wrath than they had in the preceding circles of Hell. Up to this point, the pilgrim has reacted with pity, regret, or, at worst, indifference to the plight of the souls he encountered. Now Dante manifests a vindictiveness toward Argenti that comes dangerously close to wrath it-self. Likewise, Virgil had been confident, at times even disdainful, toward the classical figures who had threatened to impede the providentially willed journey. But here, in his first battle with explicitly Christian denizens of Hell, he appears confused and humiliated. The incident undermines Virgil's privileged status as invulnerable guide and forces the pilgrim into a tem-porary state of despair. Not surprisingly, the majority of Dante's inter-preters have found these reversals of character difficult to explain.

In fact, many commentators have condemned the pilgrim's reaction to Argenti as an instance of savagery unbefitting a man on the road to salva-tion. Parodi calls Dante "brutal, insulting, and implacable." To Rossi, the pilgrim is bestial on account of his cruelty. Borgese speaks of Dante's fe-rocity, and Momigliano of the satanic quality of Dante's hate. Sapegno refers to the poet's perverse pleasure in his growing brutality, while Bosco views the Argenti episode as a rare example of a personal vendetta against one of the damned. Even Pietrobono, who tries to vindicate Dante's be-havior on the grounds that Argenti doesn't represent an individual but rather a political allegory (i.e., Black Guelphism, as opposed to Dante's White Guelphism), is forced to admit that the pilgrim appears to be exces-sively harsh. Likewise, Romagnoli claims that, while Dante is not guilty of injustice, he nevertheless manifests extreme inhumanity.

Having accepted the premise that Dante is unduly severe toward Argenti, these critics seek recourse in biographical information about the latter. Drawing upon Boccaccio and other early sources, they remind the reader that Argenti's actual name was Filippo Cavicciuli degli Adimari, that he ac-quired the nickname Argenti from shoeing his horse with silver rather than iron, that he enjoyed riding through the narrow streets of Florence with legs outstretched in order to wipe his boots on pedestrians, that he had once struck Dante in a quarrel, that a relative (possibly Argenti's brother) had come into possession of the exiled poet's property and that consequently the Cavicciuli family strongly opposed a revocation of Dante's banishment. In the *Decameron* (IX, 8), Boccaccio characterizes Argenti as "sinewy and strong, scornful, prone to anger, and eccentric." Sacchetti (*Trecentonovelle* CXIV) recounts the story of a certain haughty member of the Adimari fam-ily whose reckless behavior was reported by Dante to a magistrate and pun-ished by a heavy fine. In revenge, the family sought and attained Dante's ex-ile from Florence.

As early as the fourteenth century, Dante commentators began to rely on these characterizations as a way of justifying the harsh manner in which Ar-genti is treated. Benvenuto da Imola, for example, repeats the condemna-tion of Filippo as proud, wrathful, and lacking all civility. He adds that Fi-lippo hated his fellow citizens so much that, as a nasty joke, he offered a horse for use to any Florentine in need of one. Of course, he could only lend it on a "first come, first serve" basis, and would laugh insultingly at any

latecomers. Pietro di Dante also emphasizes Filippo's arrogance by glossing the adjective that Dante applies to him, *bizarro* (62), as *bis errantem,* that
is, twice wandering, in both interior and exterior pride. Such revelations are
useful in illuminating the possible relationship between Dante and Argenti
in life, and there can be no doubt that the poet had contempt for the Adimari. In *Paradiso* XVI they are referred to as "the breed—so arrogant and
dragonlike / in chasing him who flees, but lamblike, meek / to him who
shows his teeth or else his purse" (115–117).

Modern critics have generally accepted the suggestion that the Adimari
played a large role in securing Dante's exile. Toffanin in particular uses this
information to forge a symbolic parallel between Florence and Dis, and to
relate the drama of Argenti to that of the devils. In his reading, the devils'
barring of the pilgrim from Dis, the infernal city devoid of justice, is intentionally juxtaposed with the memory of the Adimari's barring of the
poet from Florence, the earthly city devoid of justice.

Besides the attempt to establish a record of Argenti's criminal behavior,
there exists the critical effort to view Dante's actions as an example of so-
called just anger. Proponents of this view, among them Porena and Torraca,
believe that the treatment of Argenti is intended to dramatize the philosophical distinction between good anger (*ira bona*) and bad anger (*ira mala*).
This interpretation appears in the early commentaries as well. Benvenuto
da Imola speaks of Dante's noble indignation against the pride of Argenti,
and Boccaccio refers to a type of anger that is not a sin but rather a virtue,
named "mansuetude" by Aristotle. In the *Nicomachean Ethics* (II, 7), Aristotle mentions a moderate kind of anger called meekness (rendered as mansuetude by medieval translators). He later glosses the notion as "being im-
perturbable, and not of being led away by passion, but of being angry in
that manner, and at those things, and for that length of time, which reason
may direct" (IV, 5).

This concept of a reasonable and managed anger was developed by
Thomas Aquinas in the *Summa,* an authoritative source of Dante's theological knowledge. In an important passage (II-II, 158, 1–8), Aquinas asserts
"if one is angry according to right reason, then to get angry is praiseworthy. . . . The absence of the passion of anger is as much a vice as is the failure of the movement of the will to punish according to the judgment of
reason." However, Aquinas goes on to say that anger—inward or outward—
can become a sin if it grows excessively and is a mortal sin whenever it is
contrary to charity.

With Aristotle and Aquinas in mind, several critics acquit Dante of the
charge of bad anger. D'Ovidio admits that anger appears everywhere in the
canto—Phlegyas, Argenti, Dante, Virgil, and the rebel angels all manifest
this passion. But in Dante's case, wrath results rather from his high moral
sense than from personal resentment of Argenti. According to D'Ovidio
and Pietrobono, the pilgrim's anger is primarily a reaction to Argenti's ar-

rogance, and is applauded by Virgil, the symbol of right reason. Likewise, Casagrande believes that the wrath of Dante stems from the attempt by Argenti to impede both the will of the pilgrim and the will of God as reflected in the pilgrim.

The difficulty with this approach centers on the actual verbal exchange between Dante and Argenti. When the mud-covered sinner rises from the marsh to ask the identity of the pilgrim, Dante avoids answering the question and inquires instead, "who are you, who have become so ugly?" (35). Argenti's response is indeed ambiguous. He replies, "You can see—I'm one who weeps" (36). As Bosco and Sapegno claim, the verb *piango* can also mean "I pay the price for my sins." If the lines are read according to this more technical usage, then Argenti is acknowledging that he is, deservedly, one of the damned. If the former interpretation is applied, Argenti's statement acquires a more sorrowful tone and becomes a plea for sympathy directed to the pilgrim and the reader.

However, Dante rejects a compassionate stance and wishes instead that Argenti remain in his state of suffering. Dante's lack of pity goes even further. After Virgil praises Dante's reaction, the pilgrim expresses his desire to see the arrogant soul "soused within this broth" (53) of the boiling marsh. This willingness to view a sinner's torture strikes an odd note with the reader, who has grown accustomed in the preceding seven cantos to the pilgrim's tears at the plight of damned souls like the glutton Ciacco (*Inf.* vi) and the love heroine Francesca (*Inf.* v). Indeed, Borgese speaks of "a decisive crisis of the personality" in which Dante abandons the psychic attitudes associated with the sweet new style of love poetry (attitudes bordering on the sentimental) and adopts instead the prophetic strain of a justiciar of God's wrath.

How can we explain Dante's very different reaction to Argenti? The likely answer is that Dante finally begins to understand, in *Inferno* viii, that pity for the damned is wickedness before God. As Donno succinctly states, "The pilgrim shifts away from those entirely human attitudes that are so much in evidence in most of his encounters with the damned, and . . . shunning all human sentiment, he reacts to [Argenti] as God has done." Donno goes on to claim that the Argenti episode intentionally creates a dichotomy between reason and feeling in the reader, who is compelled (by Virgil's words and God's compliance with Dante's wish) to accept the pilgrim's conduct as a reflection of divine justice despite its falling short of earthly standards of humane behavior. Virgil's praise of Dante—"Indignant soul, / blessèd is she who bore you in her womb!" (44–45)—was originally addressed to Christ (Luke 11:27), and the Christ-Dante equation lends support to Donno's argument that the pilgrim's lack of pity is harmonious with the divine will.

The biblical context of this allusion has been reexamined by Hawkins and Kleinhenz, who conclude that the compliment, dismissed by Jesus as inappropriate to the occasion, is likewise misapplied to Dante by a well-intentioned but misguided Virgil. In the scriptural passage, Christ humbly defers the praise to those who hear and keep the word of God. But the actions that lead to this pronouncement support Boccaccio's exemplary view that Virgil is correct in his benediction, which clears Dante of the charge that all anger is sinful. The Christological story centers on Jesus' exorcism of a demon (an act that, like the harrowing of Hell, requires aggressive tactics), and his self-defense against those witnesses who wrongly attribute his power to Beelzebub rather than God. In a striking rebuttal, Christ uses the analogy of a household that falls because of internal division to show that Satan's kingdom could not exist "if Satan also be divided against himself" (Luke 11:18). By extension, the kingdom of God depends on unequivocal unity: "He that is not with me, is against me; and he that gathereth not with me, scattereth" (Luke 11:23). The relevance to *Inferno* VIII is clear. Argenti is literally in the devil's camp; Dante knows it and chooses to side with God and against evil. In so doing, the pilgrim does keep the word of God.

Regarding the words of Argenti, several critics refuse to accept that they connote pathos at all. Rather, they assign hostile and base implications to the lines he utters. Argenti's tone and manner are said to convey insolence (D'Ovidio), vanity (Szombathely), derision (Montano), aggression (Mattalia), and insult (Momigliano). Sanguineti believes that Argenti's response is a futile attempt to remain an anonymous damned soul. Bosco adds his opinion that Argenti, owing to his arrogance, hopes not to be recognized so that his humiliating position will remain unknown to Dante.

Donno is the most extreme advocate of this view. Beginning with Argenti's question, "Who are you, come before your time?" (33), Donno asserts that the insolent sinner takes it for granted that Dante will be damned after death. In so doing, Argenti seeks to erase the spiritual distinction between himself and the pilgrim. Dante's reply, "I've come, but I don't stay" (34), purposefully reinforces the difference between his fate and that of the eternally unregenerate Argenti. About himself, all Argenti will reveal is that he is damned, which Dante already knew. Donno sees this as a refusal to admit Dante's superior destiny, which results in the pilgrim's contemptuous revelation that neither the muddy disguise nor the evasive answer has prevented him from recognizing his old adversary: "Though you're disguised by filth, I know your name" (39). Finally, Apollonio mentions the "diabolic action with which Filippo Argenti attempts to impede the fated journey of Dante" and applauds Dante's "righteous zeal" in contemning him.

Triolo interprets Argenti's speech and actions in light of what he terms "bad indignation." Triolo finds that medieval theologians like Aquinas and Saint Bernard viewed indignation in a negative sense, as the offspring of both wrath and pride, triggered by a feeling of superiority that desires homage from one's peers and that envies those peers if they advance in eminence. Viewed positively, however, indignation can refer to the just anger of God as well as to the virtue by which one can assail sin—either one's own or another's—out of zeal. Dante's disdain falls under this latter definition, while Argenti's pride (46) brands him with the sinful type of indignation. Likewise, the "great disdain" (88) of the rebel angels is played off its dialectic opposite, the disdain of the heavenly messenger in the next canto (IX, 88). In Triolo's reading, Canto VIII revolves around Dante's defense of justified human and divine anger and his condemnation of the chaotic anger of Argenti and the vitriolic anger of the devils.

When they reach the end of the area of the wrathful, Dante and Virgil are deposited at the entrance of Dis, the city of infidels, and can glimpse the fiery red mosques within the ramparts. The walls themselves appear to be forged of iron, and the architectural description, as Boccaccio and Moore have noted, follows the portrayal of Tartarus in the *Aeneid* (VI, 548–558). Indeed, Acciani speaks of Dante's desire to create a "new Tartarus" in which he functions as another "pious Aeneas," threatened not only by pagan monsters (the Furies and Medusa of Canto IX) but also by the fallen angels of Christian mythology. In so doing, Dante transforms the Virgilian model, in which the gateway of Tartarus remained impenetrable to Aeneas, who stood listening to the Sibyl's account of the sinners inside. Instead, the pilgrim must cross the horrid threshold, thus conquering his fears. Aeneas's awe is replaced by Dante's dynamic struggle, both with his own emotions and with the force of evil concretized in the devils.

The army of rebel angels immediately congregates above the gates, creating a picture of a military world besieged by enemies. They will allow Virgil alone to pass; they oppose Dante's entrance because he has dared to travel through the kingdom of the dead while still alive (84–85). For the first time in the *Inferno,* the pilgrim is threatened with the loss of his guide, who will remain with the devils while Dante returns alone on "his mad road" (91). The demonic implication that Dante's journey may indeed be a crazy undertaking so unnerves the pilgrim that he begs Virgil not to abandon him. Virgil reassures Dante, then speaks to the devils in private. Their response is to shut the gates in his face. Virgil appears confused, vexed, and humiliated at this resistance, although he is aware of the devils' futile attempt, during the harrowing of Hell, to oppose Christ "at a gate / less secret" (125), that is, the outer portal of Hell (*Inf.* III). The canto ends with Virgil's prophecy of the advent of a heavenly agent who will open the gates of Dis for the wayfarers.

The episode of the rebel angels presents a number of interpretive cruxes. First, there is Virgil's failure to influence the devils with his normally effective rhetoric. He had controlled the previous guardians of Hell—Charon, Minos, Cerberus, and Plutus—by verbally asserting the divine will that moves him. He subdues Phlegyas with less linguistic fanfare: Virgil merely tells the boatman that he will have the pilgrim and his guide only during the crossing of the Styx (VIII, 19–21). Virgil repeats the formula about a beneficent providence to Dante (104–105) near the canto's end, and while this assertion gives Dante renewed hope, it accomplishes nothing against the diabolic insolence.

Most critics view this defeat as an allegorical demonstration of the inadequacy of human reason (Virgil) in the face of radical evil. Special grace (the heavenly messenger) must descend from God to aid the despairing spirit (Dante). Bacchelli mentions Virgil's limited knowledge of the mysteries of grace, revelation, and redemption, a limitation he shares with the other virtuous pagans of Limbo who, lacking baptism, lack "the portal of the faith" (IV, 36). He also points out that Virgil fails to distinguish the pagan figures, who have no personal interest in hating God, from the Christian devils, "who once had rained from Heaven" (83), who vent their resentment against the divine by thwarting his disciple. In fact, Bacchelli suggests, Virgil's strategy with the devils backfires by increasing their rancor toward one privileged by God to see Hell without having been damned, as they were. Furthermore, Virgil's lack of the theological virtues—faith, hope, and charity—prevents him both from conquering the fallen angels and expelling all Dante's despair. Similarly, Apollonio concludes that Virgil's problem is the error of an intellect cut off from grace in a realm actively antagonistic to that very grace. Acciani notes the absurdity of Virgil's attempt to persuade the devils to obey God's decrees, when primal disobedience to his will is the very sin for which they are punished.

Pequigney and Dreyfus go a step further and indict Virgil's entire ethical theory. They claim that Virgil views the wall of Dis merely as a dividing point between two different categories of sin, but not as an obstruction designed to repel divine influence. He understands that the sins punished within Dis are characterized by injuriousness but is unaware that they also involve a willing rejection of God. According to Pequigney and Dreyfus, Virgil's superficial grasp of the moral scheme of Hell, the result of his reliance on pagan ethical philosophy (Aristotle and Cicero), leads him to underestimate his diabolic adversaries.

Another problem is that of Virgil's shifting psychological reactions to the obstinacy of the devils. He at first expresses confidence that none can hinder the journey (104–105), but after the gates are shut he appears dejected, with eyes lowered and "his brows deprived / of every confidence" (118–119). He sighs, then questions the audacity of his opponents in a tone that conveys either scorn or perplexity. Finally, he recovers with the prediction of rescue through divine intervention, only to suffer an acute relapse in the next canto, when the Furies appear on top of the tower of Dis and invoke Medusa.

Musa explains the psychodrama in view of Virgil's status as one of the damned. Just as he could not believe during his lifetime in the coming of Christ, so now he cannot quite believe in the coming of the heavenly messenger. Musa goes on to read Virgil's disequilibrium as part of Dante's artistic agenda—it adds suspense to the narration and allows for a symbolic reenactment of the harrowing of Hell. Triolo rejects the common view that Virgil loses hope after his interview with the devils and claims instead that the guide moves emotionally from a state of repose to one of angry impatience. This is a necessary transition, for entry into Dis is not to be achieved "without anger" (IX, 33). Similarly, Toffanin notes that Virgil becomes much more aggressive in the fight with the devils than in previous confrontations.

In concluding this synopsis of critical readings of Canto VIII, I would argue that the actions of Dante and Virgil should be viewed in light of the Virgilian concept of *pietas* (piety) which the pilgrim, as an alter-Aeneas, must master as part of the lesson of his infernal descent. It is Virgil's task to program his disciple along the lines dictated by piety. Although the Middle Ages (especially the tradition of twelfth- and thirteenth-century love poetry) assigned to this term the meaning "pity" or "compassion," in religious and political contexts piety retained its classical sense of justice before God, a justice that also embraced duty to one's parents and one's country.

In the *Aeneid, pietas* essentially denotes the fulfillment of one's destiny decreed by the gods. Thus, Aeneas is *pius* (pious) not only because he fought to save his father, Anchises, and fellow citizens from Troy's flames, but also because he abandoned Dido and killed Turnus in order to accomplish the divinely sanctioned mission of founding the Roman Empire. Piety demands the removal of all obstacles that impede the providential plan, for acquiescence to such impediments constitutes injustice to the gods. This Virgilian doctrine is capsulized in the lines spoken to Aeneas by Anchises in the Elysian Fields: "Remember, Roman, to rule the people under law, to teach the ways of peace to the conquered, to spare the humble and subdue the proud" (VI, 851–853). Forgiveness is only part of the injunction; the proud must be destroyed, not in a spirit of vengeance but one of justice.

Dante himself is careful to distinguish true piety (*pietà*), a noble disposition of mind apt to receive "charitable emotions," from the mere passion of *pietà,* which consists of a potentially debilitating sorrow for the ills of others (*Convivio* II, x, 6). Perhaps the most famous example of this destructive form of *pietà* occurs in *Inferno* V when the pilgrim hears the tragic story of Paolo and Francesca and so identifies with their feelings that he lapses into unconsciousness. Dante's vicarious sympathy with Francesca and her language of courtly love blinds him to the larger meaning of the episode, which actually indicts lust and shows it to be essentially narcissistic. The pilgrim must progressively rid himself of compassion for the damned, a false piety that is a violation of God's justice. Virgil makes this clear when he rebukes Dante for weeping at the twisted forms of the diviners: "Here pity only lives when it is dead: / for who can be more impious than he / who links God's judgment to passivity?" (XX, 28–30).

The eighth canto, with its echoes of the sixth book of the *Aeneid,* contains the first display of Virgilian *pietas* exhibited by Dante. It thus reinforces the typological comparison of his journey with that of Virgil's epic hero, "the righteous son of Anchises" (*Inf.* I, 73–74), which Acciani and others have made. The descent to the underworld teaches Aeneas that true piety is a virtue belonging to the realm of justice. He discovers this through the words of Phlegyas, the impious ruler who, having abandoned justice, suffers in Tartarus, and through the words of Anchises, the pious soul who, having lived justly, rejoices in Elysium. Similarly, Dante learns the incompatibility of justice and false piety in the encounters with Argenti and the rebel angels.

Dante's supposed cruelty in wishing to witness Argenti's immersion is part of the code of *pietas*—the necessary vanquishment of the proud. In fact, divine justice immediately wreaks a worse revenge than what Dante had hoped. Argenti is not only dunked in the marsh but also rent by the other souls even as he sinks his teeth into his own flesh. Anger is thus shown to be self-defeating and self-destructive. Dante's praise of God for this sight (60) should be read as a pious response to a divine judgment of sin, rather than as the odious fulfillment of a personal vendetta.

Virgil's blessing of his pupil's newfound *pietas* is consistent with his own views. After all, Virgil himself had condemned the passion of *furor* (wrath) in the *Aeneid*. Its two most poignant examples are the deaths of Amata and Turnus. The former is the mother of Lavinia who, infected with madness by the Fury Allecto (VII, 341–405), kills herself out of rage at her daughter's impending union with Aeneas (XII, 593–607). Turnus, the Rutulian prince who had been promised Lavinia in marriage, is likewise maddened by Allecto (VII, 413–474). He foments the war between the Trojans and the Italians and is dominated, not by *pietas,* but by violence, barbarism, and *cupido* (the relentless pursuit of individual desires and goals, with no regard for the welfare of one's people or the will of the gods). At the poem's end, Aeneas's piety prompts him to kill Turnus (XII, 938–952). Virgil thus shows the annihilating nature of wrath and the folly of resisting divine providence. Dante was aware of these ethical themes, for he makes Amata an example of wrath (*Purg.* XVII, 31–39) and views the fallen Turnus as a victim sacrificed to the higher claim of Rome's destiny (*Inf.* I, 106–108).

In Virgil's poetic world, impiety never triumphs. This fact may account for his confusion at the devils' resistance, a confusion that seems rooted in his inability to understand the ontological status of the first nonpagan custodians he meets in Hell. "See who has kept me from the house of sorrow!" he exclaims (120). In the following canto, Virgil is at least familiar with the threat of Medusa and can physically shield the pilgrim from the danger she represents. Against the rebel angels, however, he must rely on the "holy words" (IX, 105) of the divine messenger, who rebukes them for kicking against the unalterable will of providence (IX, 91–97).

Although Virgil can foretell ultimate victory over the devils, his spiritual beliefs nevertheless remain circumscribed by his limited pagan vision. Like the Sibyl in *Aeneid* VI, Virgil functions as a medium who has prophetic powers, but only when possessed by the godhead. In Canto VIII, and indeed throughout most of Hell, Virgil can articulate and comprehend things primarily in terms of his own value system. He knows that Dante's actions with Argenti comply with the doctrine of *pietas,* and that the wrathful have merited their torments. But against the impious actions and "abominable words" (95) of the devils, Virgil can only respond with language that, like Limbo, is lofty and noble, but unsanctified by faith.

BIBLIOGRAPHY

Canto VIII has generated much debate. Of the early commentators, the ones I found most useful are Boccaccio, *Esposizioni,* 6:446–470; Pietro di Dante, *Commentarium,* 110–116; and da Imola, *Comentum,* 1:273–301. Of the modern annotated editions, those by C. H. Grandgent (Cambridge, 1972); Mattalia; Momigliano; Vittorio Rossi (Naples, 1923); Sapegno; Singleton; and Torraca.

Specific studies of problems raised in this canto abound, and these readings often focus on either the first half (lines 1–66) or second half (lines 67–130) of Inferno VIII. On the identification of Phlegyas, see

Caretti, Lanfranco. "Una interpretazione dantesca." *Studi e ricerche di letteratura italiana,* 3–14. Florence, 1951.
D'Ovidio, Francesco. "Flegias." In *Nuovo volume di studi danteschi,* 193–228. Rome, 1926.
Scherillo, Michele. "Il 'Flegias' di Dante e il 'Phlegyas' di Virgilio." *Rendiconti: Reale Istituto lombardo di scienze e lettere,* 2d ser., 42 (1909): 327–365.
Stocchi, Manlio. "Flegias." *Enciclopedia dantesca,* 2:945–946. Rome, 1970.

On Dante's struggle with Filippo (autobiographical and moral aspects), see

Bigi, Emilio. "Moralità e retorica nel canto VIII dell'*Inferno.*" *Giornale storico della letteratura italiana* 154 (1977): 346–367.
Borgese, G. A. "The Wrath of Dante." *Speculum* 13 (1938): 183–193.
Casagrande, Gino. "Dante e Filippo Argenti: Riscontri patristici e note di critica semantica." *Studi danteschi* 51 (1978): 221–254.
Donno, Daniel. "Dante's Argenti: Episode and Function." *Speculum* 40 (1965): 611–625.
D'Ovidio, Francesco. "Filippo Argenti e gli altri cani." In *Nuovo volume di studi danteschi,* 229–271. Rome, 1926.
Forti, Fiorenzo. "Filippe Argenti." *Enciclopedia dantesca,* 2:873–876. Rome, 1970.
Nicosia, Paolo. "Il più calunniato dei personaggi danteschi ovvero il canto della vendetta." In *Alla ricerca della coerenza: Saggi d'esegesi dantesca,* 135–167. Florence, 1967.
Parodi, E. G. *Poesia e storia nella "Divina Commedia,"* 74. Vicenza, 1965.
Piemontese, Filippo. "Filippo Argenti fra storia e poesia." In *Studi sul Manzoni e altri saggi,* 169–185. Milan, 1952.
Pietrobono, Luigi. "Il canto VIII dell'*Inferno.*" *L'Alighieri* 1 (1960): 3–14.
Pischedda, Giovanni. "Motivi provinciali nel canto VIII dell'*Inferno.*" In *Dante e la tematica medioevale,* 35–40. L'Aquila, 1967
Porena, Manfredi. "Atti della R. Accademia d'Italia." *Rendiconti di scienze morali,* 7th s., 2 (1941): 539–540.

On the entry into Dis, see

Acciani, Giuseppe. "L'ingresso di Dante nella città di Dite." *L'Alighieri* 19 (1978): 45–58.

Apollonio, Mario. "Il canto VIII dell'*Inferno.*" In *Nuove letture dantesche,* 1:209–235. Florence, 1966.

Bacchelli, Riccardo. "Canto IX: Davanti alla città di Dite." In *Saggi critici,* 853–861. Milan, 1962.

Moore, Edward. *Studies in Dante, First Series: Scripture and Classical Authors in Dante* (1896), 360–361. Reprint; New York, 1968.

Musa, Mark. *Advent at the Gates: Dante's "Comedy,"* 65–84. Bloomington, Ind., 1974.

Pequigney, Joseph, and Hubert Dreyfus. "Landscape and Guide: Dante's Modifying of Meaning in the *Inferno.*" *Italian Quarterly* 5 (1961): 51–83.

Russo, Vittorio. "Dite." *Enciclopedia dantesca,* 2:518–519. Rome, 1970.

Triolo, Alfred. "Ira, Cupiditas, Libido: The Dynamics of Human Passion in the *Inferno.*" *Dante Studies* 95 (1977): 1–37.

For general *letture* on punishment, poetic unity, and techniques see

Bosco, Umberto. *Il canto viii dell'"Inferno,"* 7–20. Rome, 1951.

Kleinhenz, Christopher. "*Inferno* VIII." In *Dante's "Divine Comedy," Introductory Readings: Inferno,* ed. Tibor Wlassics, 93–109. Charlottesville, Va., 1990.

Montano, Rocco. "I modi della narrazione in Dante." *Convivium* 26 (1958): 546–567.

Novara, A. "Canto ottavo." In *Lectura Dantis Genovese,* 299–326. Florence, 1904.

Romagnoli, Ettore. "Il canto VIII dell'*Inferno.*" In *Letture dantesche: Inferno,* ed. Giovanni Getto, 133–150. Florence, 1955.

Sanguineti, Edoardo. "Dante, *Inferno* VIII." In *Il Realismo di Dante,* 31–63. Florence, 1966.

Szombathely, Marino. "Il canto VIII dell'*Inferno.*" *Lectura Dantis Romana,* ed. Giovanni Fallani. Turin, 1959.

Toffanin, Giuseppe. "Il Canto VIII dell'*Inferno.*" In *Lectura Dantis Scaligera: Inferno.* Florence, 1967.

As a final note on the culpability of Dante and Virgil, I should like to add that the most current scholarship on *Inferno* VIII views the actions of Dante and Virgil in an unfavorable light: Dante is wrong to succumb to personal revenge, and Virgil is also at fault for his lavish praise of the pilgrim. The limitations of both characters are addressed by Victor Castellani, "Vergilius Ultor: Revenge and Pagan Morality in the *Inferno,*" *Lectura Dantis* 9 (1991): 3–10; Peter Hawkins, "Virgilio cita le Scritture," in *Dante e la bibbia,* Atti del Convegno internazionale promosso da "Bibbia," ed. Giovanni Barblan (Florence, 1986), 351–359; and Kleinhenz, "*Inferno* VIII," 101–104.

Other useful studies include Uberto Limentani, "*Inferno* VIII," in *Dante's Comedy: Introductory Readings of Selected Cantos* (Cambridge, 1985), 34–47; John Freccero, "Infernal Irony: The Gates of Hell," *Modern Language Notes* 99 (1984): 769–786; and the excellent line-by-line notes by Mark Musa in *Dante's Inferno: Commentary* (Bloomington, Ill., 1996), 2:108–123; and by Robert Durling and Ronald Martinez, eds., *Inferno,* 1:134–139.

CANTO IX

The Harrowing of Dante from Upper Hell

AMILCARE A. IANNUCCI

Just before the celestial messenger arrives and scatters the infernal forces impeding Dante's and Virgil's entry into the City of Dis, the poet interrupts the narrative and invites his readers to observe the doctrine hidden "beneath the veil of verses so obscure" (*Inf.* IX, 63). Dante's hermeneutic imperative has certainly not gone unheeded. Indeed, in their eagerness to interpret, the commentators have thoroughly allegorized the episode. I shall not attempt to summarize the various interpretations here. Suffice it to say that there is no general agreement as to what the episode and its main images mean. By way of example, let me just mention a few of the glosses on the principal actors in the drama before Dis. The Furies may signify, among other things, guilty conscience, remorse, envy, malice, the three major divisions of lower Hell, evil thoughts (Allecto), words (Tisiphone), and deeds (Megaera) that lead to heresy, and simply, along with Medusa, "vices to overcome." The Medusa herself has an equally tormented exegetical history. She may represent, depending on the commentator, despair of salvation, the consciousness of sin, obliviousness of one's spiritual well-being, worldly pursuits, lust, astuteness, the demon of heresy, obstinacy, religious doubt, and idolatry. And the majority view of the messenger (*messo*) is as just a plain ordinary angel—or else as the Archangel Michael, the angel of Limbo, Moses, Christ, Hercules, Mercury, Aeneas, Caesar, or Henry VII.

Despite the obvious differences, what virtually all interpretations have in common is that they apply to the episode the exegetical procedure that Dante used in the *Convivio* to interpret his *canzoni,* that is, the allegory of the poets. In other words, the episode is interpreted primarily in abstract moral terms as the struggle between the forces of good and evil in which even the figures of Dante and Virgil lose, to a large extent, their historical identity to assume their exemplary roles as personifications of Everyman and Reason. At this critical point in the journey Reason (i.e., Virgil) is revealed to be inadequate; Divine Grace, through the mediation of the *messo*, must intervene in order to assure that the Christian soul (Dante the wayfarer) may continue the pilgrimage toward salvation. In this interpretative frame the doctrine, if not entirely lost, is certainly somewhat diminished.

I attempt to retrieve the episode's typological significance by reading it in the light of the *Descensus Christi ad inferos*. The harrowing of Hell is, in my opinion, the underlying structural model for the little *sacra rappresentazione* that unfolds before the City of Dis, and also the key to understanding its doctrine or meaning.

Dante himself, of course, invites us to read the episode in these terms. At the end of *Inferno* VIII Virgil, who had just been rebuffed by the fallen angels (turned devils), recalls a similar scene of misplaced defiance when Christ descended into Hell:

> This insolence of theirs is nothing new;
> they used it once before and at a gate
> less secret—it is still without its bolts—
> the place where you made out the fatal text;
> (VIII, 124–127)

Immediately following these words he announces the arrival of one (*tal*) who will unlock the door of Dis:

> and now, already well within that gate,
> across the circles—and alone—descends
> the one who will unlock this realm for us.
> (VIII, 128–130)

Then, at the end of the episode itself the *messo*, already triumphant, chastises the would-be hell-stoppers for their insolence and compares his victory to that of Hercules, who overpowered Cerberus when he rescued Theseus from Hades (IX, 91–99). Thus, the poet himself points to the parameters within which his recreation of the harrowing will take place. It will take the form of a radical synthesis of pagan and Christian images, in which Hercules' descent is seen, through an appropriation typical of Dante's theological allegory, to prefigure Christ's more determining, final gesture of salvation. The celestial *messo* as an analogue of Christ, early in the morning of Holy Saturday, A.D. 1300, reenacts these two previous descents inscribed in the book of the universe and Dante's cultural consciousness; one page is profane, the other sacred.

To be sure, commentators note the allusions but, surprisingly, do not pursue the subject in any systematic way. Not even Mark Musa, who analyzes the episode in terms of the first of Christ's three advents described by Saint Bernard in his *Sermons on the Advents,* makes much of the paradigm of the harrowing and certainly no one that I am aware of explicitly links the harrowing that encodes the episode to Dante's allegory and doctrine.

Perhaps one of the impediments to this kind of analysis is the episode's strong Virgilian substratum, which has deflected the commentators' attention. Its presence is thoroughly documented and I shall, therefore, not linger over it, except to restate the obvious. Dante plundered Book VI of the *Aeneid,* the episode's other major subtext, to erect his own Tartarus and, to a certain extent, to populate its fiery fortifications. The setting, therefore, is decidedly Virgilian. Also, Virgil provides Dante with the opportunity to restage the harrowing. The struggle before Dis is dictated more by a literary than a theological imperative, although it ultimately takes a theological form. In Book VI of the *Aeneid* the Sibyl had warned Aeneas that "it is forbidden that any man who is pure in heart should set foot on the threshold of wrong" (562–563). For the two pilgrims to venture beyond the threshold of Dis would mean to defy the Sibyl's interdiction and undermine Virgil's poetic authority. That pagan law, however, must be shattered or else Dante's journey will end in the swampy waters of the river Styx.

But how is this to be done? Not through Virgil, despite his previous pagan experience of Tartarus. Early in Canto IX (16–33), we learn, to our surprise, that Virgil had gone to the very bottom of Hell before, thanks to the incantations of the Thessalian sorceress Erichtho of Lucan fame (*Pharsalia* VI, 508–827). His present failure indicates the uselessness of that experience. After Christ, the Sibyl's interdiction cannot be broken through magic or other pagan devices. Only through Christ and in imitation of him can the door of Tartarus be unlocked.

In fine, Virgil's text provides the pretext for the episode, as well as descriptive and stylistic elements, but not its defining structure and meaning. Indeed, the meaning of Virgil's text is being, if not completely rejected, reevaluated and assimilated into a new Christian context where Aeneas's descent prefigures Dante's, just as Hercules' prefigures Christ's.

The dramatic aspect of the episode derives therefore not from Virgil but from the harrowing story. The primary source of Christ's descent into Limbo was not so much the sparse accounts of the event in the New Testament as the apocryphal fifth-century *Gospel of Nicodemus,* which soon acquired almost canonical status. Indeed, early on the harrowing made its way into the Apostles' Creed and quickly affirmed itself as a favorite theme in the Middle Ages. Its immense popularity stemmed from the fact that it was associated with and became the most concrete and powerful symbol of the redemption, which especially in the West was conceived of as the victory of Christ over Satan, who with the fall had acquired jurisdiction over man. Further, in some accounts Christ's death and descent into Hell were seen as the ransom price man had to pay in order to reacquire his freedom. The harrowing therefore dramatized Christ's release of man from the bondage of sin, and in particular his liberation of the Hebrew patriarchs from Hell.

The nature of the story was inherently dramatic, and already in the *Gospel of Nicodemus* the material was distributed in a series of almost theatrical scenes. Later, of course, the harrowing was dramatized and staged. One of the earliest Italian representations of the harrowing is a Franciscan *lauda* that, as far as we can tell, dates from about Dante's time. It is the Perugian Disciplinati's *devozione* for Holy Saturday. (Note that the drama before Dis takes place early on Holy Saturday morning.) Closely modeled on the *Gospel of Nicodemus,* the Franciscan *lauda* contains all the stock images that had become part of the theme: a dark infernal prison, a boastful Satan, an apprehensive personified Hell, a troop of demons, a struggle in front of Hell's gates, and finally a victorious Christ, crowned in glory and bearing the cross. He scatters the forces of darkness, smashes Hell's gates, and releases the just of the Old Testament, starting with Adam, from the infernal dungeon.

Dante was thoroughly familiar with the story, if not directly from the *Gospel of Nicodemus* and later representations such as the one cited above, then from Vincent of Beauvais's paraphrase of it in the *Speculum maius* and certainly from the "visual" representations of the harrowing to be found everywhere, in mosaics, manuscript illuminations, ivory carvings, enamel, stained glass, painting.

Dante evokes the harrowing in *Inferno* IV, and I should like to discuss, if only briefly, his novel treatment of it there. This discussion may help us understand better his equally bold manipulation of the theme later on, before the City of Dis. By introducing virtuous pagans into his Limbo, Dante breaks abruptly with Western theological tradition that had evolved from the New Testament through Saint Augustine and Gregory the Great to Saint Thomas; by shifting the emphasis from the *limbus patrum* and the harrowing of Hell to the plight of the virtuous pagans, Dante completely revolutionizes the typical depiction of Limbo. All previous representations had focused exclusively on the *Descensus Christi ad inferos,* which had come to symbolize, as I have already mentioned, the redemption itself, because it dramatized Christ's victory over Satan and his release of man from sin. Dante changes all this. He pushes the harrowing into the background, as a remarkable illumination from *Inferno* IV in a mid-fifteenth-century Italian manuscript beautifully illustrates (Madrid, Biblioteca Nacional MS 10057, f. 9^r), and populates the foreground with Virgil and other illustrious and virtuous representatives of pagan civilization (ibid., f. 10^r). The thematic and structural implications of this shift are vast.

In Canto IV the harrowing of Hell is undisplaced—Virgil recounts in the preterite the event that he witnessed—but it is radically redefined in terms of the preceding tradition. First the account is reduced to its essential details— twelve lines in all, 52–63—and inserted into a Limbo that has been completely overhauled both theologically and poetically. Its very structure and meaning are altered. In Dante's Limbo, the harrowing announces not so much victory as defeat in that the episode focuses not on those who were released from Hell by Christ (the Hebrew fathers) but on those who were left behind (the virtuous pagans). In Dante's unique vision of Limbo, the high epic style dominates, the imagery is stark, the tone solemn and melancholic, the structure "tragic," not "comic."

Yet Dante was too alert to the dramatic possibilities of the imagery traditionally associated with the harrowing to abandon it altogether. The Sibyl's interdiction concerning Tartarus gave him an opportunity that he could not resist. The episode is often referred to as a *sacra rappresentazione,* and some commentators even divide it into acts. But for chronological reasons, it is perhaps more accurate, as Bosco suggests, to refer to those acts as *momenti dell'azione.* But no one (not even Bosco, an astute critic) sees in the dramatic unfolding of the scene before Dis its striking similarities with the harrowing of Hell, not only in content but also in tone and in rhythm.

The first moment is characterized by defiant resistance and tension that quickly build to a crescendo. In the Perugian *lauda,* which faithfully follows the *Gospel of Nicodemus,* Satan orders his troops of devils to station themselves for combat:

> O my beloved legions,
> block the entrance to this pass;
> everyone take their positions,
> some up high, some below.
> (115–118)

The Hebrew fathers demand repeatedly that Hell open its gates:

> Open quick and do not close,
> for soon you will see him arrive!
> (119–120)

An angel's voice reinforces their imperative:

> O you, prince of evil,
> open these gates of yours!
> (157–158)

Satan, however, stubbornly refuses.

The second moment is dominated by a sense of waiting and expectation, which becomes urgent as Christ approaches. Suddenly Christ appears, smashes the door, and crushes his enemy beneath his feet. Then he ties him up and banishes him to the furthest reaches of Hell:

> Satan, you have caused
> mortal man much pain.
> I will tie you with my chain
> so you can hurt him no longer!
> (229–232)

Finally, Christ extends his hand to Adam and the other Hebrew fathers and takes them out of Hell.

In Dante's text the first moment covers the latter part of Canto VIII (67–130). Devils, bent on impeding Dante's entry into the city, rush menacingly about the fiery walls of Dis:

> About the gates I saw more than a thousand—
> who once had rained from Heaven—and they cried
> in anger: "Who is this who, without death,
>   can journey through the kingdom of the dead?"
> (VIII, 82–85)

An infernal council is summoned and Virgil attempts to negotiate Dante's safe passage into Dis (VIII, 103–117), but negotiations soon break off and the door is slammed in Virgil's face: "And these, our adversaries, slammed the gates / in my lord's face" (115–116). Virgil is perplexed: "See who has kept me from the house of sorrow!" (120). Dante is struck with fear and ready to abandon the enterprise: "if they will not let us pass beyond, / let us retrace our steps together, quickly" (101–102). This first moment, characterized by feverish action and quick dialogue, ends with Virgil's announcement of the imminent arrival of one who will, in a gesture like Christ's at the harrowing, force the door open.

The end of the canto serves to heighten the sense of expectation that prevails until the middle of Canto IX (1–60). This is the second moment, which culminates in the Furies' threat to summon the Medusa (34–60). At this climactic point Dante interrupts the narrative and addresses the reader. Then the *messo* arrives to complete the pattern (64–105). He scatters the devils, overcomes the Furies and the Medusa, and with a touch of his scepter opens the door (88–90). Finally, like Christ at that "less secret gate" (VIII, 124–127), he chastises the infernal powers for their useless defiance:

> "O you cast out of Heaven, hated crowd,"
> were his first words upon that horrid threshold,

"why do you harbor this presumptuousness?
　Why are you so reluctant to endure
that Will whose aim can never be cut short,
and which so often added to your hurts?
　What good is it to thrust against the fates?
Your Cerberus, if you remember well,
for that, had both his throat and chin stripped clean."
(IX, 91–99)

Dante and Virgil are now free to enter into Dis: "We made our way inside without a struggle" (106). The rest of the canto describes the vast necropolis immediately within the walls and belongs therefore to the next episode, that of the heretics.

Although the harrowing is displaced in Cantos VIII and IX, the essence of the theme, which Dante had largely forsaken in Canto IV, is recovered, and so are the structure, tone, and dramatic rhythm of traditional accounts. In short, the whole episode is an original and powerful stylistic reworking of the harrowing of Hell, governed by the laws of Dante's cultural syncretism.

One other point supports this claim. I have stated that the setting in which the drama unfolds is essentially Virgilian:

. . . "I can already see distinctly—
master—the mosques that gleam within the valley,
as crimson as if they had just been drawn
　　out of the fire."
(VIII, 70–73)

The city that Dante the pilgrim sees looming in the distance is strongly reminiscent of Tartarus (*Aen.* VI, 548–550). Moreover, like Tartarus's iron tower (555–556), Dante's fiery walls are made of iron: "the ramparts seemed to me to be of iron" (VIII, 78). And they too are protected by bloody Tisiphone. This time, however, she is assisted in this chore by her sisters, Megaera and Allecto (IX, 34–51), and a band of demons (VIII, 82–84). Indeed, the presence of Virgil's text is so overwhelming that another obvious source for the episode has been to a large extent overlooked, namely, the traditional medieval representations of Hell as *civitas diaboli*. But there is more. In the thirteenth century there emerged a particular iconographic type of the harrowing in which the struggle between Christ and Satan was depicted precisely in front of a *civitas diaboli*, a fortified city guarded by devils. For example, in an English miniature of the first third of the fourteenth century (London, British Library Add. 47682, f. 34), Christ carrying a cross is shown breaking down the gates of the infernal city and rescuing the patriarchs of the Old Testament. Horned demons guard the battlements. Inside, fire from Hell's mouth heats a blast furnace in which the damned are punished. The shape of the furnace both recalls Dante's iron towers and suggests the open burning tombs of the heretics. The thirteenth-century bronze relief of the harrowing on the main door of the church of Saint Zeno in Verona also uses the fortresslike setting, characteristic of this iconographic type of the descent into Hell, which may have influenced Dante's daring use of the theme in *Inferno* VIII and IX.

The illuminations to *Inferno* IX that most faithfully reproduce Dante's text highlight the correspondences between the iconographic tradition of the harrowing described above and the drama before Dis. The illumination in an early fifteenth-century Bolognese manuscript captures the action exactly at the instant when the angel sweeps forward and forces the gates open with his *verghetta,* which, like Christ's cross, is a sign of his authority and power (Rome, Angelica 1102, f. 8ʳ). The devils, prominent in the illustration to the previous canto, have already dropped out of sight. However, the three Furies, naked and crowned with snakes, appear menacingly on a tower. A similar, if somewhat more static, picture of the scene adorns a late fourteenth-century Florentine manuscript (Vatican, lat. 4776, 32ᵛ). The master of the *Vitae imperatorum* does not paint the Furies but shows the devils retreating into the city with the arrival of the *messo* (Imola, Com. 32, f. 7ʳ). All three illustrations recall that particular "urban" type of the harrowing of Hell, popular in the thirteenth century and later. Indeed, with a few minor modifications they could easily be mistaken for a harrowing. It is difficult to determine whether the illustrators were aware of the connection and, therefore, were consciously following a model. But surely this is irrelevant: Dante's text describes the action so clearly that the illustrators did not need to look for sources.

In Tuscan art, especially after Dante, another iconographic type seems to prevail, the one in which Limbo is depicted as a cavern, from which Christ draws the Hebrew patriarchs, magnificently clad (ready to be redeemed and glorified). In these representations, such as the one by Andrea di Bonaiuto in the Cappella degli Spagnoli in Santa Maria Novella, the action is frozen at a slightly later moment in the drama. Here the battle is shown as already won, but the idea of struggle and victory is still very much present. Christ has Satan trapped under the fallen door of Hell and reaches for the patriarchs. The devils, defeated but still threatening, lurk in the background.

Regardless of iconographic details, the substance of the harrowing story remains the same for all accounts. They all dramatize the shattering of Satan's hold over man. From this perspective, there should be little doubt that the paradigm of the descent into Hell informs *Inferno* VIII–IX. Dante's imaginative adaptation of the theme in this episode manages to preserve the original story's inner meaning. Like the earlier account, Dante's re-creation (which skillfully plots pagan myth over Christian truth) celebrates the victory of the forces of good over those of evil, and man's release from the slavery of sin. And it does this in no abstract way. Here it is Dante who is being "harrowed" from Hell. Actually, the divine *messo* intervenes to make it possible for Dante to descend from upper to lower Hell, into the mosqued City of Dis, as he must do if he is to ascend Mount Purgatory and rise into Paradise.

We are now in a position to discuss the doctrine hidden "beneath the veil of verses so obscure" (*Inf.* IX, 63). Where does the doctrine lie? In what precedes (the threat of the Furies and Medusa) or in what follows (the arrival of the *messo*)? Or is it to be found in the whole episode? I express it in these terms because it is a much debated question in the exegesis of the episode. I would agree with those who argue that Dante's aside points us to what is to come—the *messo*. But inasmuch as the *messo*'s action fulfills the pattern and *telos* of the episode, the doctrine is to be found in the whole elaborate drama and what it stands for. The drama, as I have argued, is a displaced postfiguration of the harrowing of Hell. In his aside to the reader, Dante is therefore pointing to this pattern and inviting us to read the episode within its terms. In effect, what Dante the poet is saying is that the descent into lower Hell can take place only within the context of and in imitation of Christ's determining gesture of salvation. In other words, only through Christ can the Sibyl's interdiction be broken.

If this is the case, and I believe it is, then the defining mode of signifying in the episode is that of the theologians, not that of the poets—typology not personification, which, of course, does not exclude a tropological significance. Rather the moral import of the episode lies within the broader allegorical pattern.

In this light, Dante the pilgrim is not merely a representative of Everyman; Virgil is not just Reason vanquished; the Furies are not simply "vices to overcome"; the Medusa is not solely an image of despair, oblivion, heresy, idolatry, or whatever; the *messo* is not generically Divine Grace. They are first and foremost themselves, players in the drama of providential history, caught at a moment when the most significant event in the drama is being reenacted: the redemption, signified in the *Descensus Christi ad inferos*. The specific roles the various actors assume in the drama are largely dictated by what they were in life (as is the case for the mythological characters, who are inexorably drawn into the logic of Dante's typological scheme). Despite his wisdom, Virgil fails primarily because he is locked into a pagan mode of thought; the Christian Dante is again seized by cowardice (*viltate*) because at this stage in his otherworldly journey he is still metaphorically burdened by Adam's sin and his own transgressions. The only way to overcome the resistance of Satan (Dis) and company is through divine intervention, and it comes in the form of a descent into Hell. In this context, the celestial *messo* clearly postfigures Christ and his actions therefore occur within the typological frame of the *Descensus Christi ad inferos*.

The doctrine comes into sharper focus if we situate the episode within the structure of the poem, and especially that of the *Inferno*. The drama before Dis is often compared to the little *sacra rappresentazione* in the Valley of the Princes, where a similar address to the reader (*Purg.* VIII, 19–21) precedes a miraculous descent that permits the pilgrim to enter yet another gate—this time that of Purgatory. But its link with an episode in Canto II of the *Inferno*—where Dante was also beset by fear and cowardice, ready to abandon the enterprise—has not, in my opinion, been sufficiently clarified. In order to persuade the hesitant Dante that his mission is willed in heaven, Virgil recounts to him Beatrice's descent into Limbo. Dante's renewed willingness to undertake the journey and his subsequent passage at the beginning of the next canto into that "less secret gate" are a direct result of Beatrice's intervention. As I have shown elsewhere, there is a complete spatial and temporal correspondence (within the liturgical time frame of the poem) between Christ's descent into Hell and Beatrice's. In *Inferno* II Beatrice completes the analogy to Christ in his first coming established in the *Vita nuova*. Her first appearance in the poem is thus delicately modeled on the harrowing—stripped of its traditional agonistic imagery but preserved in its full theological significance. In other words, both the passage into the main door of the infernal city (*Inf.* III) and the passage into the lower City of Dis (*Inf.* IX) follow a divine intervention that takes the form of a bold and imaginative reworking of the *Descensus Christi ad inferos*. These heavenly intrusions resolve the pilgrim's fearful dilemma and allow the journey to begin and to continue. In both cases, the doctrine is essentially the same: this miraculous journey is possible only because of Christ's redemptive act and must take place within a pattern that typologically reenacts that event.

In addition to Dante's innovative treatment of the harrowing in these two episodes and in Limbo, there are several other allusions to it in the *Inferno*. For instance, the landslide—*ruina*—caused by the earthquake at the moment of Christ's death on the cross and descent into Limbo (XII, 31–45), is mentioned in each of the *Inferno*'s three major structural subdivisions (v, 28–36; XII, 4–10, 31–45; XXI, 106–114; and XXIII, 133–138). The references in the lowest zone are especially intriguing since they occur in an episode—that of the barrators (XXI–XXIII)—that in many respects recalls Cantos VIII–IX. In the *bolgia* (ditch, or pouch) of the boiling pitch, we are again confronted with a troop of mischievous devils determined to thwart the pilgrim's progress, with a fear-stricken Dante, and with a Virgil incapable of dealing with the situation. Indeed, Malacoda, the devil-in-chief, hoodwinks Virgil into believing that one of the bridges over the sixth *bolgia* is still standing (XXI, 106–114), when they were all destroyed by the earthquake (XXIII, 127–148). Here no divine intervention assures the pilgrim's safe passage to the next level, but the pattern reasserts itself forcefully yet unobtrusively through a subtle allusion charged with significance. After a series of comic misadventures, Dante and Virgil elude the ill-intentioned demons, climb to safety by means of the *ruina* (XXIII, 131–138), and thus continue on their way. Malacoda's earlier time-telling with reference to the shattering event ("Five hours from this hour yesterday, / one thousand and two hundred sixty-six / years passed since that roadway was shattered here" [XXI, 112–114]) also reminds us that the pilgrim's own descent into Hell takes place between Christ's death and resurrection.

In fine, these strategically placed references to the harrowing would seem to suggest that Dante considered the second part of the *Gospel of Nicodemus,* along with *Aeneid* VI and the Exodus story, a major narrative model, within which he cast his own pilgrim's journey, especially the first phase. Much has been written about Dante's use of Book VI of the *Aeneid* and of the Exodus story. And yet the harrowing paradigm has been almost completely neglected by Dante critics, perhaps because, of Dante's three models, the *Descensus* is the least authoritative (despite its immense popularity in the Middle Ages and its early inclusion in the creed). Certainly it is the most wanting from a narrative point of view. However, it was also the closest thing to a Christian epic narrative that Dante could find. The canonic Gospels offered no clear narrative pattern for him to follow in constructing his *poema sacro.* Thus Dante appropriated the harrowing story and its powerful dramatic imagery, extended it beyond Limbo, artfully combined it with his other narrative models, and generally infused the theme with new life and vigor. In this fashion, he hoped to create the great Christian narrative epic that, in his view, was missing. This much we can gather from his encounter with the great poets of antiquity in *Inferno* IV, 80–102. In this ambitious enterprise, the drama before Dis represents a significant moment. It offers the poet an opportunity to reveal—through a bold but calculated manipulation of his sources—both the nature of his allegory and the doctrine that underlies it.

BIBLIOGRAPHY

The critical focus of the episode is Dante's aside to the reader in *Inferno* IX, 61–63, which should be considered in the light of his other asides to the reader, on which see E. Auerbach, "Dante's Addresses to the Reader," *Romance Philology* 7 (1954): 268–278; L. Spitzer, "The Addresses to the Reader in the *Commedia,*" *Italica* 32 (1955): 143–165; and more recently, V. Russo, "Appello al lettore," *Enciclopedia dantesca* (Rome, 1970), 1:324–326. Although Dante's aside here touches explicitly on his signifying system, few critics link the episode to the vexed question of allegory in the *Comedy,* on which the bibliography is enormous (R. Hollander, *Allegory in Dante's "Commedia"* [Princeton, 1969]; and J. Pépin, *Dante et la tradition de l'allégorie* [Montreal, 1970] provide useful summaries of the debates on the subject, which have subsided recently). Most commentators have been content to interpret the episode within its local context and largely in abstract tropological terms as a struggle of the Christian soul to overcome evil. Within this general, stabilizing interpretative framework, there is little or no agreement on the significance of the principal actors in the little mystery play that unfolds before the City of Dis.

For a review of the various meanings attributed to the Furies, see G. Padoan, "Furie," *Enciclopedia dantesca* (Rome, 1971), 3:78–79. Ultimately, the infernal sisters are reduced to emblems of vice itself—*vizi da combattere,* according to A. Vallone, "Il canto IX dell'*Inferno,*" in *Nuove letture dantesche* (Florence, 1966), 1:237–260. On the equally tormented exegetical history of the Medusa, see again G. Padoan, "Medusa," *Enciclopedia dantesca* (Rome, 1971), 3:883–884. In North America the Medusa has been given undue prominence: Freccero's view that she represents idolatry, and more specifically, that she is a figure of literalism, of the "letter that kills," has largely prevailed (cf. Mazzotta and Shoaf).

On the *messo,* see S. Pasquazi, "Messo celeste," *Enciclopedia dantesca* (Rome, 1971), 3:919–921, and, for a more extensive treatment of the subject, in *All'eterno dal tempo* (Florence, 1972), 59–159. E. Auerbach, in *Literary Language and Its Public in Late Latin Antiquity and in the Middle Ages* (New York, 1965), 231 n.43, states that the *messo* "represents the figure of Christ and symbolizes Christ's descent into hell," but unfortunately he does not pursue the subject. For a detailed treatment of Dante's unorthodox use of the *Descensus Christi ad inferos* in *Inferno* IV and elsewhere in the *Commedia,* see A. A. Iannucci, "Limbo: The Emptiness of Time," *Studi danteschi* 52 (1979–80): 69–128. This study also includes a brief section in which the struggle before Dis is already interpreted in terms of the harrowing of Hell.

Most commentators deal in varying degrees with the Virgilian substratum of the episode: most recently, see Quint and especially Acciani on this aspect. For Dante's recourse to the "sublime style of antiquity" in this stylistically complex episode (especially with reference to the arrival of the *messo, Inf.* IX, 64–81), see Auerbach, *Literary Language,* 225–233. Virtually all commentators compare the events before Dis to the little *sacra rappresentazione* in the Valley of the Princes, where a similar address to the reader (*Purg.* VIII, 19–21) precedes the resolution of the drama, but the relationship is perhaps explored most fully by Musa, followed by Heilbronn. On the dramatic structure of the episode and its relation to *Purgatorio* VIII as well as the episode of the barrators (*Inf.* XXI–XXIII), see especially Bosco. On the relationship between *Inferno* II and *Inferno* VIII and IX in terms of the harrowing paradigm, see A. A. Iannucci, "Beatrice in Limbo: A Metaphoric Harrowing of Hell," *Dante Studies* 97 (1979): 23–45, revised Italian version in *Forma ed evento nella "Divina Commedia"* (Rome, 1984), 51–81. For the illuminations on *Inferno* IV and *Inferno* VIII–IX, see P. Brieger, M. Meiss, and C. S. Singleton, *Illuminated Manuscripts of the "Divine Comedy,"* 2 vols. (London, 1969). The fourteenth-century English miniature of the harrowing mentioned in the text is from the *Holkham Picture Bible,* and is reproduced in L. Freeman Sandler, *A Survey of Manuscripts Illuminated in the British Isles,* vol. 5, *Gothic Manuscripts [I] 1285–1385* (Oxford, 1986), fig. 247. For a more detailed analysis (with illustrations) of the iconographic similarities between the harrowing of Hell and the drama before Dis, see A. A. Iannucci, "Dottrina e allegoria in *Inferno* VIII, 67—IX, 105," in *Dante e le forme dell'allegoresi,* ed. M. Picone (Ravenna, 1987), 99–124. The text of the Perugian *lauda* is from *Laude drammatiche e rappresentazioni sacre,* ed. V. De Bartholomaeis (Florence, 1943), 1:243–258. The translations are mine.

Since Canto IX concludes an episode that begins in the middle of the previous canto (at *Inf.* VIII, 67, to be precise), most *lecturae* of *Inferno* VIII are pertinent to a discussion of *Inferno* IX and should be consulted—and, up to about 1970, the "Appendice bibliografica" on both cantos in Francesco Mazzoni, ed., *La Divina Commedia: Inferno* (Florence, 1972)—along with the following works, as a supplement to Mazzoni's bibliography:

Acciani, G. "L'ingresso di Dante nella città di Dite." *L'Alighieri* 19, no. 2 (1978): 45–58.

Barber, J. A. "*Inferno* IX." In *Dante's "Divine Comedy," Introductory Readings: Inferno,* ed. Tibor Wlassics, 110–123. Charlottesville, Va., 1990.

Bárberi Squarotti, Giorgio. *L'artificio dell'eternità,* 431–446. Verona, 1972.

Bosco, Umberto. "Dante e il teatro medievale." In *Studi filologici letterari e storici in memoria di Guido Favati,* ed. G. Varanini and P. Pinagli, 135–147. Padua, 1977.

Freccero, John. "Medusa: The Letter and the Spirit." *Yearbook of Italian Studies* 2 (1972): 1–18. Reprinted in *Dante: The Poetics of Conversion,* ed. Rachel Jacoff, 119–135. Cambridge, Mass., 1986.

Greco, A. "Canto IX." In *Lectura Dantis Neapolitana: Inferno,* ed. Pompeo Giannantonio, 127–139. Naples, 1980.

Heilbronn, Denise. "Dante's Gate of Dis and the Heavenly Jerusalem." *Studies in Philology* 72 (1975): 167–192.

Kleinhenz, C. *"Inferno* VIII." In *Dante's "Divine Comedy," Introductory Readings: Inferno,* ed. Tibor Wlassics, 93–109. Charlottesville, Va., 1990.

Mansfield, M. N. "Dante and the Gorgon Within." *Italica* 47, no. 2 (1970): 143–160.

Mazzotta, Giuseppe. *Dante, Poet of the Desert: History and Allegory in the "Divine Comedy,"* 275–318. Princeton, 1979.

Musa, Mark. *Advent at the Gates: Dante's Comedy,* 65–84. Bloomington, Ind., 1974

Pisanti, T. "Canto VIII." In *Lectura Dantis Neapolitana: Inferno,* ed. Pompeo Giannantonio, 115–126. Naples, 1980.

Quint, D. "Epic Tradition and *Inferno* IX." *Dante Studies* 93 (1975): 201–207.

Ruggieri, R. M. "Il canto IX dell' *Inferno.*" In *"Inferno": Letture degli anni 1973–1976,* ed. Silvio Zennaro, 219–240. Rome, 1977.

Shoaf, R. A. "The Franklin's Tale: Chaucer and Medusa." *The Chaucer Review* 21, no. 2 (1986): 274–290.

Tartaro, A. "Il canto VIII dell' *Inferno.*" In *"Inferno": letture degli anni 1973–1976,* ed. Silvio Zennaro, 197–218. Rome, 1977.

CANTO X

Farinata and Cavalcante

ROBERT M. DURLING

This canto has always been recognized as one of the summits of Dante's art. Full of human drama, it touches on Dante's exile and the fate of his friend Guido Cavalcanti; it is also, as recent scholarship demonstrates, theologically precise and rich in iconographic allusions. After the suspense-filled events of the two previous cantos—when Dante and Virgil are barred by "more than a thousand" (VIII, 82) devils from entering the city of Dis and are menaced by the Medusa, and after "Heaven's messenger" (IX, 85) has unlocked the gates with his "wand" (IX, 89)—the poets enter, to see no one, and nothing but a plain filled with sarcophagi that, Virgil explains, house the leaders of heresies and their followers. At the very end of Canto IX, the poets make an unusual turn to the right (in hell the poets turn always to the left, except here and in Canto XVII). This departure from tradition adds to the high pitch of anticipation with which we begin, and the canto's richness and drama amply reward us.

Canto X is part of a series of cantos of the *Inferno* that presents souls from Dante's native city and develops the closely related themes of the present corruption of Florence, as Dante views it, its bitter history of faction and civil strife, and Dante's own involvement, which will lead to his permanent exile. The first of these cantos is *Inferno* VI, where we meet the glutton Ciacco, whom the pilgrim questions about the political future of Florence and the fate, in the afterlife, of prominent leaders. Ciacco's first answer predicts the temporary victory of the White party (to which Dante belonged) and the Black coup that followed it (an armed coup d'état by

Charles of Valois and the Blacks in 1302), but Ciacco does not mention the repercussions this coup will have in Dante's life. Dante next inquires about five Florentines of the previous generation, all of whom, Ciacco replies, are even lower in hell. We meet the most important of them, Farinata degli Uberti, in this canto, and it is he who predicts Dante's exile.

The historical Manente degli Uberti, called Farinata (ca. 1205–1264), was from 1239 until his death the leader of the Florentine Ghibellines. In 1248 they drove out the Guelphs, only to be driven out, in turn, three years later. Farinata then led a Tuscan coalition of Ghibellines against the Florentine Guelphs, slaughtering them in a particularly bloody battle at Montaperti, near Siena, in 1260. A subsequent council in Empoli would have decided to raze Florence itself, if not for Farinata's singlehanded opposition. After another Ghibelline defeat at Benevento in 1266, a popular uprising in Florence drove the Ghibellines out of the city and destroyed a number of their houses (the Piazza della Signoria results from the destruction of the Uberti, Foraboschi, and other Ghibelline houses). Peace was established in 1280, from which Farinata's descendants were specifically excluded, as they were from later amnesties.

A minor problem presented by the canto concerns the charge for which Farinata and his wife were condemned in 1283 (when Dante was eighteen years old, and nineteen years after Farinata's death) by the Franciscan inquisitor for Florence, Fra Salomone da Lucca. The posthumous charge labeled them "Paterini," that is, adherents to the heresy of the Cathars, or Albigensians. Reconciling the charge in *Inferno* of epicureanism with Fra Salomone's claim is difficult, for the Cathars accepted the New Testament as inspired and held firmly to the immortality of the soul. Since the iconography of the canto involves the Eucharist, it is possible that the Cathars' rejection of the Lord's Supper (as a sacrament) is partly Dante's target. Or he may simply have decided to disregard the facts here, as in other parts of the poem.

We meet one other Florentine in this canto. Cavalcante dei Cavalcanti was also a member of the high nobility. He was a prominent Guelph, so prominent that in 1266, in one of the efforts to make peace in the city, his son Guido was betrothed to Farinata's daughter. That the two former political enemies share a single sarcophagus is a statement both about the intimacy of factional division within the walls of the city and about an essential identity of worldliness in the opposing leaders, who are now the prisoners of their shared pessimism. Cavalcante probably did not live beyond 1280, several years before the beginning of Dante's friendship with his son, dated by the *Vita nuova* as 1283.

In Farinata and Cavalcante, then, Dante encounters fathers: literally the father and father-in-law of his closest friend, but also fathers of his city, past leaders of Florence, where they were partly responsible for the heritage of civil strife that plagues it. Behind this encounter, as behind the meetings with his teacher Brunetto Latini (*Inf.* xv) and his ancestor Cacciaguida (*Par.*

xv–xvii), lies the encounter in *Aeneid* vi of Aeneas and his father, Anchises. Anchises prophesies the difficult struggle Aeneas will undergo in Italy, shows him the spirits of his descendants (future heroes of Rome), and explains to him the workings of the universe, especially the cycles of incarnation and purification that immortal souls undergo. *Paradiso* xv–xvii correct and outdo this major model of eschatological poetry, and the encounter in *Inferno* x is in many ways its antitype. Farinata and Cavalcante are shown to lack Anchises' most striking traits, particularly his devotion to the gods and to his people. Also, both fathers here challenge or reproach Dante, rather than certify him for his mission, as Anchises encourages Aeneas and Cacciaguida certifies Dante.

As Dante and Virgil walk with the walls of Dis on their right and the tombs on their left, Dante asks if the inmates of the tombs can be seen, pointing out that "the lids—in fact—have all been lifted; / no guardian is watching over them" (8–9). This observation picks up and renews the original description of the tombs at the end of Canto ix: "The lid of every tomb was lifted up" (121). Exactly what position is imagined for the covers of the tombs is not stated clearly, but the question is probably resolved by lines 6–7, which imply that they are leaning against the sarcophagi. Expectation is further whetted by Virgil's assurance that the wish Dante has expressed to see the souls will be fulfilled, as well as the one he has not stated ("the longing you have hid from me" [18] is almost certainly a reference to Dante's desire to see Florentines). Virgil's identification of the Epicureans as those "who say (*fanno*) the soul dies with the body" (15) provides a provisional understanding of the *contrapasso* of this canto—these souls will be eternally buried with their bodies. The phrase includes a telling ambiguity. They *make* (*fanno*, 15) the soul die with the body. In so believing, these heretics literally *cause* their souls to die.

Within this context, then, the intense drama of the canto begins with the introduction of the main personage, Farinata, in stages carefully graded to set off the episode. First is the abrupt appearance in the text of Farinata's unannounced and unlocated words; only at their end are we told that the sound came "out of one sepulcher" (29). Dante is startled and frightened. Virgil explains that Farinata has stood and is visible "from the waist up" (33). There are several implicit stage-directions here. Since Farinata was not visible when the poets turned to the right, he was lying in his tomb. He has overheard the talk between Dante and Virgil, has identified Dante as a Florentine, and therefore has stood up to speak; since Dante must turn in order to see him, he is behind Dante and Virgil and to their left. Dante and Virgil still do not see Farinata directly, but his voice arrests them.

> "O Tuscan, you who pass alive across
> the fiery city with such seemly words,
> be kind enough to stay your journey here.

> Your accent makes it clear that you belong
> among the natives of the noble city
> I may have dealt with too vindictively."
>   This sound had burst so unexpectedly
> out of one sepulcher that, trembling, I
> then drew a little closer to my guide.
>   But he told me: "Turn round! What are you doing?
> That's Farinata who has risen there—
> you will see all of him from the waist up."
>
> (22–33)

Finally we see Farinata directly through the pilgrim's eyes:

> My eyes already were intent on his;
> and up he rose—his forehead and his chest—
> as if he had tremendous scorn for Hell.
>
> (34–36)

All generations of readers have been struck by the indomitable pride and courage conveyed by Farinata's monumental figure, perhaps the most impressive in the entire *Inferno*. Especially the expression "up he rose" (*s'ergea*) conveys a sense of power and size. Later on Farinata is called "great-hearted" (*magnanimo* [73]), and, although in the last analysis Farinata is judged negatively (and as John A. Scott showed, the term *magnanimo* itself had both a positive sense and the negative sense of "ambitious, overweening"), still the initial impression is of a powerful personality, and we are forced to entertain, if only for the moment, the possibility of such a soul's actually being superior to the sufferings of hell. This accounts for the Romantic misreading of Farinata, from Francesco De Sanctis through Benedetto Croce and Erich Auerbach, which supposed that the theological "structure" of the poem was a kind of ex post facto encrustation, obscuring Dante's true subject, human individuality and force of character. Actually, Dante's emphasis on Farinata's breast is directly related to the fact that heresy sins against faith, wisdom, and love, all of which traditionally have their seat in the heart. But at this point the sense of respect inspired by Farinata's commanding figure is reinforced by the tone of Virgil's lines, his pushing of Dante toward Farinata, and his advice that Dante's words be *conte,* that is, "appropriate" (39), and possibly also "counted," "few."

The first part of the interview with Farinata is tense and hostile. The old nobility and family pride speak as Farinata asks, "Who were your ancestors?" (42), but it should be noted that Dante is not embarrassed by his own family's social status. Farinata identifies Dante's ancestors in a way that suggests they were of comparable social status with his own. He raises his eye-

brows not in scorn at their social obscurity, but at their presumption in opposing him, his family, and his party. He is so caught up in the old strife that
he clearly still takes satisfaction in having twice dispersed the Guelphs, and
it is entirely characteristic that he speaks of the victories of his party and
his armies as if they belonged to himself exclusively. Because the word for
"occasion" (*fiata*) resembles that for "breath" (*fiato*)—Dante often associates them—Farinata's phrase *per due fiate* (48) conveys a suggestion that he
dispersed his enemies with a mere breath each time.

The pilgrim has been instantly caught up in this confrontation of Guelph
and Ghibelline, and he, too, acts out the old enmity, giving blow for blow
and claiming that the ultimate victory belongs to his side. It is the pilgrim
who introduces the terminology of art in connection with exile and return:

> "If they were driven out," I answered him,
> "they still returned, both times, from every quarter;
> but yours were never quick to learn that art."
>
> (X, 49–51)

Farinata had used the familiar *tu* form when scornfully inquiring of Dante's
antecedents, but we find Dante answering him with the respectful *voi* form.
(Only to three individual inhabitants of hell does Dante use the polite
form: to Farinata and Cavalcante here and to his teacher Brunetto Latini in
Canto xv; all are Florentines of the older generation.) It is a token of
Dante's complexity of nuance that it is precisely in his assertion of Guelph
superiority over the defeated Ghibelline that the respectful form occurs (as
it does in line 63, a parallel context).

The exchange is interrupted now by another abrupt surprise, the appearance of the excited Cavalcante. He, too, has listened to Dante's voice
while lying in the tomb; he has heard him identify his family. Now he appears as far as the chin; Dante infers that he is kneeling. Dante tells us in
lines 64–65 that he also infers the identity of this new personage; he is evidently not able to recognize him. Thus Cavalcante's recognition of Dante
as an intimate of Guido's seems to be a result of the strange foreknowledge
of the damned, soon to be introduced as a major focus of the canto.

Everything about Cavalcante contrasts with Farinata. Farinata is heard
before he is seen; we see Cavalcante look anxiously about before speaking.
Farinata's erect bearing is the result of deliberate intention; Cavalcante
rises only to his knees because he is so intent on seeing his son, and he
stands erect only as a result of panic. Farinata speaks gravely and ceremoniously; Cavalcante speaks entirely without ceremony. Finally, Farinata
must inquire into Dante's family, whereas Cavalcante knows Dante's connection with his son. Throughout, Cavalcante is excited, in motion, and
without dignity; Farinata is calm, immobile, and self-contained.

The contrast has iconographic significance. Dante with his fertile sense of analogy is establishing a parallel between Saint Paul's confrontation of two pagan philosophers (identified by Augustine as a Stoic and an Epicurean, philosophers of human self-sufficiency) in Acts 17:18, and the pilgrim's meeting with the two heretics, one subject to every wind of fleshly impulse, and thus particularly Epicurean, according to the traditional view, and the other utterly in command of himself and confident of his *virtus animi* and thus, in this respect, particularly Stoic.

Cavalcante's actions derive from a series of misunderstandings. His hope of seeing Guido springs from a misconception of the nature of Dante's journey, as he supposes Dante has undertaken it on his own, because of his natural gifts. If so, why hasn't his son accompanied him? He misinterprets Dante's reply, and finally he leaps to a mistaken conclusion about Dante's hesitation. The misunderstandings occur in rapid succession:

> He looked around me, just as if he longed
> to see if I had come with someone else;
> but then, his expectation spent, he said
>   in tears: "If it is your high intellect
> that lets you journey here, through this blind prison,
> where is my son? Why is he not with you?"
>
>   (55–60)

The first part of Dante's reply corrects Cavalcante's first misunderstanding. He is not led by his "high intellect," but by Virgil:

> I answered: "My own powers have not brought me;
> he who awaits me there, leads me through here."
>
>   (61–62)

Of course this beginning is already evasive. It does not explicitly state that his being led by Virgil (whom he does not identify) is the result of divine intervention, though the implication is perhaps clear enough. But the rest of the reply is so obscure as to have become the most famous crux in the entire poem, when Dante refers to "one your Guido did disdain" (*forse cui Guido vostro ebbe a disdegno* [64]). Cavalcante interprets *ebbe* (the ambiguous *passato remoto*) as meaning that Guido is dead:

> Then suddenly erect, he cried: "What's that:
> He 'did disdain'? [*dicesti 'elli ebbe'?*] He is not still alive?
> The sweet light does not strike against his eyes?"
>
>   (67–69)

and when the puzzled Dante hesitates, Cavalcante despairs and falls backward into the tomb.

Cavalcante can be forgiven for misunderstanding Dante's reply; its obscurity has elicited much debate (see Chimenz and Mazzoni for accounts of the controversy up to 1972). The disagreements have focused on *cui* and *ebbe*. Does *cui* refer to Virgil, to Beatrice, or to God? Is the grammatical subject of *ebbe* Guido, or whoever is referred to by *cui*? If it is Guido (the usual view), what aspect of the verb is implied? Is it an aorist, denoting a definitive action? a perfect, denoting an action that has ceased (either because Guido is dead, as Cavalcante assumes, or for some other reason)? a present perfect, denoting an action that just now took place (like Cavalcante's own *dicesti* in line 68, as Charles Singleton pointed out)? Most critics have assumed that the line has a single, ascertainable meaning, and since the pilgrim's remark is not favorable to Guido they have assumed that when writing the *Comedy* Dante was willing to consign his friend to damnation.

But we simply do not know to what extent the two poets had become estranged. No doubt the *Vita nuova,* in spite of its dedication to Guido and signs of his influence throughout, is in part an elaborate refutation of the naturalistic and pessimistic view of love taken in Cavalcanti's great canzone "Donna mi prega," and it may have contributed to the cooling of their relations. There exists also a sonnet, addressed to Dante by name, in which Cavalcanti reproaches him with "low life" and wishing to please the many. A possible reading interprets the sonnet as condemning Dante's entrance into elective politics in the wake of the new Ordinamenti di Giustizia of 1295, which barred magnates like Guido, but not lesser nobles like Dante (Marti). After the outbreak of bloody rioting Dante, as a *priore* of the city, voted in June 1300 to banish the turbulent Guido along with other White and Black leaders. We have no direct evidence of the degree of conflict this decision evoked in Dante. A last piece of evidence from outside the *Comedy* is furnished by Dante's fifteenth-century biographer Leonardo Bruni, who relates that after the Black coup Dante was accused of having favored Guido's return to Florence (he was allowed to return because of the illness of which he died in August), and that Dante wrote an epistle, now lost, pointing out that by the time the decision was made, Dante was no longer a prior and had no voice in the matter. Again, the evidence is ambiguous.

Along with *Purgatorio* xi and *Paradiso* xiii, *Inferno* x gives much insight into Dante's attitude toward Guido. In Canto x Guido's fate is still a source of turbulence for Dante. The elder Cavalcante's anxiety about his son's death, with the pilgrim's ambiguous reply, is partly a projected version of Dante's own anxieties and ambivalences. They can be stated as a series of questions. To what extent was Dante responsible for causing or hastening Guido's death (by voting for his exile)? To what degree did he desire Guido's death? Did Guido die unrepentant, and if so, did his early death prevent his repentance? Most serious, to what extent did Dante take satisfaction from his friend's (or former friend's) early death and possible damnation? The presence of such questions in Dante's spirit, their burden of guilt and anxiety, has left its mark on all three canticles of the poem, in each case in or near the gateway cantos, the entry into the city of Dis, the entry into Purgatory proper, and the cantos of the Sun.

We see the intensity of Dante's anxiety in the dialogue with Cavalcante, which parallels God's questioning of Cain about Abel. Both feature the agonizing question: "Where is [he]?" (*Ubi est Abel frater tuus?* [Gen. 4:9]/*Mio figlio ov'è?* [61]), followed by an evasive reply, emphasizing custodianship: "Am I my brother's keeper?" (Gen. 4:9)/"He [Virgil] . . . leads me through here" (62)—Cain denies that he is a leader, Dante asserts that his own leader is another. There follows a further question, referring to the death of the brother/son: "What hast thou done? (*Quid fecisti?*) the voice of thy brother's blood crieth to me from the earth" (Genesis 4:11)/"What's that? (*Come dicesti?*) . . . He is not still alive?" (68). Finally, both passages predict the exile of the protagonist.

These striking parallels show that Dante was deeply troubled over his connection with Guido's death and possible damnation. They show that he felt he was in a sense answerable to Guido's father, though he evidently had not known him. The parallel with Cain, like the couching of the supposedly candid confession of poetic pride in *Purgatorio* XI in terms of a desire to exile Guido, shows that there was a fratricidal ingredient in Dante's rivalry with Guido. Thus both Dante's poetic and—a fortiori—his theological victories over Guido are charged with their degree of guilt. Currently the most widely held reading of line 63 is that offered by Pagliaro: "he who is waiting there is leading me to one (Beatrice) to whom your Guido disdained to be led." John Freccero suggested that Dante's *ebbe a disdegno* draws on Augustine's phrase *dedignantur ab eo discere* ("they disdain to learn from him" [*Confessions* VII, 21, 27]) and therefore contains an implicit reference to Christ. Dante's most severe criticism of Guido—or fear for him—would thus be that Guido's pride of intellect barred him from a true understanding of the Gospels and therefore from conversion.

But the search for a single unambiguous sense of the line not only disregards the pilgrim's hesitation and evasiveness (for example, in the context of the *Comedy* as a whole, Dante does represent himself as chosen for the journey because of his poetic genius, *per altezza d'ingegno*). It has also distracted attention from the deeper significance of Cavalcante's mistake, which springs from the Epicureans' systematic tendency to interpret the data of experience in a negative way, to see everything in terms of death. The text features the ambiguous *ebbe* and shows that it does not mean that Guido is dead; in the context of Dante's demonstration of the futility of negative misinterpretation, it seems clear that the text requires us to inquire into the possible positive meanings of Dante's *ebbe*.

Dante's "perhaps" is the key word in the line. It shows that he is unwilling to be definite. He dare not represent himself as certain of Guido's ultimate fate, but he is free to express his misgivings, which in themselves do him no discredit. His "perhaps" casts doubt on all definite meanings and requires the entire line to be spoken hesitatingly. Perhaps Guido's disdain bars him from this journey; on the other hand, perhaps there is hope for Guido. In fact when Dante later sends word to Cavalcante that his son "is still among the living ones" (111), he uses terms directly related, *per antithesin,* to heresy and its punishment. Heretics are not "among the living." They, unlike Guido, separate themselves from those alive in the faith.

Bruno Nardi was one of the few scholars who have been reluctant to believe that *Inferno* x damns Guido. He went so far as to suggest that the fictitious date of the journey, April 1300, was chosen partly, perhaps even mainly, in order to situate the journey before Dante's priorate and Guido's exile and death, so that Dante could avoid representing Guido's fate. Dante's famous *ebbe,* in any case, functions to keep open the possibility of Guido's salvation; Dante will give no unambiguous sign that he considers him damned. In a context filled with mystifying events, the pilgrim is contrasted sharply with the hasty Cavalcante. He is shown to be careful and accurate in his inferences (e.g., 64–66), and he inquires carefully into misunderstandings. Thus the poet's own refusal to draw a conclusion about Guido is part and parcel of his attack on the hasty pessimism of the Epicureans (cf., in a context closely related to *Inferno* x, Saint Thomas Aquinas's warnings against supposing one can know who is damned, who saved, *Par.* XIII, 112–142).

After Cavalcante has disappeared, attention reverts to Farinata, who has remained utterly immobile:

> But that great-hearted one, the other shade
> at whose request I'd stayed, did not change aspect
> or turn aside his head or lean or bend;
>   and taking up his words where he'd left off,
> "If they were slow," he said, "to learn that art,
> that is more torment to me than this bed."
>
>   (x, 73–78)

He has been pondering Dante's last words to him. They seem to have brought him new knowledge of the fate of his descendants (Gramsci suggested that his immobility results from his being transfixed by his new knowledge), and he confesses that he is tortured by it. This constitutes some softening of the rigidly hostile tone that governed the earlier conversation. That the unhappiness of his descendants "is more torment to me than this bed" rests, it would seem, on the distinction between physical suffering, to which, as great-hearted, he holds himself superior, and spiritual suffering, to which he must now confess he is not immune. There is even some shade of altruism in his concern for others.

> "And yet the Lady who is ruler here
> will not have her face kindled fifty times
> before you learn how heavy is that art."
>
> (79–81)

Fifty months would take Dante to June 1304, a few weeks before the abortive attempt of the Florentine Whites based at Arezzo to force their way back into Florence, when Dante himself will have learned how difficult it is to return from exile. This is the first and the most explicit prediction of Dante's exile in the *Inferno*. The pilgrim himself had introduced the metaphor of art, in his taunt at line 51 ("Yours were never quick to learn that art"). There is a particular pathos and irony here, for not even Dante's poetic genius will win him readmission to Florence. As Mario Sansone suggests, Farinata seems in some sense to have accepted Dante as a fellow-sufferer.

In his initial greeting to Dante, Farinata had said that "perhaps" he had been too harmful to Florence (27). Now he reveals that he does not understand at all why he is hated there. Why, he asks, do the Florentines persecute his descendants? Dante explains that the cause is their memory of Montaperti:

> To which I said: "The carnage, the great bloodshed
> that stained the waters of the Arbia red
> have led us to such prayers in our temple."
> He sighed and shook his head, then said: "In that,
> I did not act alone, but certainly
> I'd not have joined the others without cause.
> But where I was alone was there where all
> the rest would have annihilated Florence,
> had I not interceded forcefully."
>
> (85–93)

There is considerable complexity here. On the one hand, Dante wishes to pay a certain tribute to Farinata's saving of Florence and to suggest that the persecution of his descendants is excessive. On the other hand, if the Ghibellines had not attacked the city under Farinata's leadership, there would have been no opportunity to destroy it: Farinata should not be surprised that he is not regarded as a benefactor. His question shows a reluctance to condemn himself (27), which contrasts sharply with Dante's reluctance to judge Guido (63). Farinata's failure to understand is a further instance of the heretics' blindness.

That Farinata's impassivity may be crumbling points to one of the larger ironies that govern the canto. Dante's visit to the heretics contributes substantially to their sufferings by bringing knowledge of the fates of their descendants and their own reputations (secular versions of immortality). These human concerns are of course universal, so much so that, according to Cicero's widely read *Tusculan Disputations,* their universality is the most important single proof of the soul's immortality. In a whole range of matters, then—from their reliance on exclusively worldly values, to their mistaking the evidence in their own natures for the immortality of the soul, to Cavalcante's misparsing of Dante's *ebbe*—the Epicureans' pessimism betrays their systematic, willfully negative misinterpretation of experience.

A further important mistake of the heretics' comes into focus when Dante questions Farinata about the foreknowledge of the damned:

> "Ah, as I hope your seed may yet find peace,"
> I asked, "so may you help me to undo
> the knot that here has snarled my course of thought.
>
> It seems, if I hear right, that you can see
> beforehand that which time is carrying,
> but you're denied the sight of present things."
>
> "We see, even as men who are farsighted [*c'ha mala luce*],
> those things," he said, "that are remote from us;
> the Highest Lord allots us that much light.
>
> But when events draw near or are, our minds
> are useless; were we not informed by others,
> we should know nothing of your human state.
>
> So you can understand how our awareness
> will die completely at the moment when
> the portal of the future has been shut."
>
> (94–108)

Farinata's explanation involves an inversion of the natural pattern of memory (distant things are indistinct, closer ones clear). The metaphor of bad light (*mala luce,* 100), along with the reference to God as the intellectual sun, makes it clear that what Farinata is describing is like evening twilight, in which distant things, outlined against the bright horizon, are more easily visible than closer things, already enveloped in darkness. The metaphor of the end of time as like the closing of a door focuses a parallel with the future closing of the tombs. Until the Last Judgment, the damned will enjoy some vestige of the "good of the intellect," but afterwards hell will be as devoid of "light" as midnight. It has been debated whether the knowledge Farinata describes is shared by all the damned (more likely) or limited to the heretics; in either case the epistemological theme is central to this canto because those who denied the immortality of the soul necessarily mistook also the intellectual nature of the soul's supernatural goal (the Beatific Vision), implicit for Dante in the very gift of intellect.

That Dante's visit increases the punishment of Farinata and Cavalcante, as Sapegno observed, is one of the ways in which it prefigures the Last Judgment, when they will see Christ, their judge, face to face (cf. line 34: "My eyes already were intent on his," and Farinata's initial position to Dante's left). The canto is permeated with allusions to it, as we have in part already seen. Since the Epicureans denied the immortality of the soul, they denied the resurrection of the dead: "What doth it profit me, if the dead rise not again? *Let us eat and drink; for to morrow we shall die,*" wrote Saint Paul (1 Corinthians 15:32), lines widely understood as referring to the Epicureans. As Augustine wrote, "Some Christians are Epicureans. What else are those one hears every day saying, 'Let us eat and drink, for tomorrow we die'? and that other saying, 'There is nothing after death, our life is the passage of a shadow'?" (*Sermo de scripturis* CL, 6). And so the Epicureans must act out an abortive resurrection, including its occasion in an act of hearing, for "the trumpet shall sound, and the dead shall rise again" (visual representations of the Last Judgment, like Dante's depiction of Farinata and Cavalcante, regularly show the dead as *harkening*). Their incomplete resurrection prefigures their final burial. And the denial of the general resurrection involves also the denial of the resurrection of Christ, to the iconography of which there are many allusions, such as the mention of the open tombs and the absence of guards in lines 8–9, and the fact that Dante's visit to a tomb recalls the visit of the Marys to Christ's (empty) tomb. In the *Convivio* (IV, xxii) Dante allegorized this visit as figuring the primacy of the contemplative life over the active life. Moreover, he identified epicureanism, stoicism, and Aristotelianism as "the three schools of the active life."

The impact of the allusions to Christ's death and resurrection (including Farinata's unintended echo in line 25—"Your accent makes it clear" [*La tua loquela ti fa manifesto*]—of those who accused Peter when he denied Christ for the third time, "For even thy speech [in the Vulgate, *loquela*] doth discover thee" [Matthew 26:73]) is intensified by the image of Farinata erect and visible from the waist up, an allusion to a particularly famous iconographic motif known as the *imago pietatis,* which represents the dead Christ from the waist up, with his head bent and his hands crossed in front of him. As numerous commentators have shown, most conclusively Ewald Vetter, this figure is a Eucharistic symbol; that is, it is a representation, not of the dead Christ at any particular historical moment (such as the descent from the Cross), but rather of the Body of Christ as it was believed to be present in the consecrated host of the Mass, the substance which, according to the doctrine of transubstantiation, is hidden under the appearance of the bread.

To deny Christ resurrected, then, is also to deny him in his Passion (as Peter denied him), to deny him in the Mass, and—in late medieval terms—to deny the Real Presence of the Body of Christ in the consecrated host. The doctrine of transubstantiation promulgated in 1215 and its somewhat later appendage, the Feast of Corpus Christi (dedicated to the consecrated host), were considered major weapons in the fight against heresy, since the heretic's proud adherence to his own errors sets him against the Eucharistic bond of love that unites the Church (see my article listed below). As Anthony Cassell notes also, with reference to the sacrament of baptism (the "portal of the faith that you embrace," Virgil calls it in *Inferno* IV, 36), the heretics' being visible to the waist alludes to the iconography of baptism, and their very tombs (*arche* [29]), allude to Noah's ark, the first great figure of baptism and of the Church.

The interview with Farinata ends with Farinata's revealing that his tomb contains more than a thousand souls, including the emperor Frederick II and Cardinal Ottaviano degli Ubaldini, another famous Ghibelline; we are not told the manner of Farinata's disappearance. Now it is Dante's turn to ponder what Farinata has said about his exile. Virgil admonishes him:

> And then that sage exhorted me: "Remember
> the words that have been spoken here against you.
> Now pay attention," and he raised his finger;
>   "when you shall stand before the gentle splendor
> of one whose gracious eyes see everything,
> then you shall learn—from her—your lifetime's journey."
>
> (127–132)

Like Cavalcante, Dante has heard words he finds threatening; he is to store them up in memory, assured that his doubts will be answered. Virgil says that Beatrice will tell him of his future life, but in fact it is Cacciaguida who will do so, and Dante will cite Farinata's and Brunetto's prophecies when questioning him (*Par.* XVII). Thus the pilgrim's carefulness in not jumping to conclusions but inquiring until he has reached an accurate understanding, behavior that so markedly contrasts with Cavalcante's, is shown to be a model of what his attitude should be toward the central tragedy of his life, his exile. He must have faith that at the appropriate moment its meaning will be made clear.

In admonishing Dante, Virgil adopts a traditional and, for Dante, very emphatic gesture: he raises his finger (129) in the timeless gesture of instruction. This signal is the second of two references to Virgil's hands in the canto. The first occurred when "my guide—his hands encouraging and quick—/ thrust me between the sepulchers toward him" (37–38). Virgil's hands are "encouraging (*animose*) and quick," it would seem, because he used them to write his poems, thus to instruct and delight and to convey his spirit. (Allegorically, this is one of the indications that Dante's reading of Virgil, perhaps of *Aeneid* VI, had much to do with his interest in the Florentine past.) All references to the body and its gestures in this canto—as elsewhere in the poem—have turned out to be richly significant (for a discussion of the overall parallel between Hell and the human body, see my essay on Canto xxx in this volume). It is striking, and doubtless intended to be noticed, especially in connection with the crossed, wounded hands of the *imago pietatis,* that in the entire detailed representation of the gestures of Farinata and Cavalcante there is not a single reference to either's hands or arms. It would seem that in spite of their pride in intellect, power, and worldly success, and in spite of their dedication to the active life, in the last analysis they accomplished nothing.

BIBLIOGRAPHY

Bambeck, Manfred. *Göttliche Komödie und Exegese,* 1–59. Berlin, 1971.

Browe, Petrus. *Die Verehrung der Eucharistie im Mittelalter.* Munich, 1933.

———. *Textus antiqui de festo corporis Christi.* Münster, 1934.

Bruni, Leonardo. "Vita di Dante." In *Le vite di Dante, Petrarca, e Boccaccio scritte fino al secolo decimosesto,* ed. Angelo Solerti. Milan, n.d.

Cassell, Anthony K. "Dante's Farinata and the Image of the Arca." *Yale Italian Studies* 1 (1977): 335–370.

———. "Farinata." In *Dante's Fearful Art of Justice,* 15–31. Toronto, 1984.

Chimenz, Siro A. "Il 'disdegno' di Guido e i suoi interpreti." *Orientamenti culturali* 1 (1945):179–188.

Contini, Gianfranco. "Cavalcanti in Dante." In *Un'idea di Dante: Saggi danteschi,* 143–157. Turin, 1976.

Croce, Benedetto. *La poesia di Dante.* Bari, 1920.

De Sanctis, Francesco. *De Sanctis on Dante: Essays.* Trans. and ed. Joseph Rossi and Alfred Galpin. Madison, Wis., 1957.

Durling, Robert M. "Farinata and the Body of Christ." *Stanford Italian Review* 2 (1981): 1–34.

Freccero, John. "Ironia e mimesi: il disdegno di Guido." In *Dante e la Bibbia,* ed. Giovanni Barblan, 41–54. Atti del Convegno Internazionale promosso da "Bibbia." Florence, 26–28 September 1986. Florence, 1988.

Frugoni, Arsenio. "Il canto x dell'*Inferno.*" In *Nuove letture dantesche,* 1:261–283. Florence, 1966.

Marti, Mario. "Cavalcanti, Guido." *Enciclopedia dantesca,* 1:891–896. Rome, 1970.

Nardi, Bruno. "Dante e Guido Cavalcanti." In *Saggi e note di critica dantesca,* 190–219. Milan, 1966.

Ottokar, N. "La condanna postuma di Farinata degli Uberti." In *Studi comunali e fiorentini,* 115–123. Florence, 1948.

Pagliaro, Antonino. "Il disdegno di Guido." In *Saggi di critica semantica,* 359–380. Messina, 1953. Reprinted in *Ulisse: Ricerche semantiche sulla "Divina Commedia"* (Messina-Florence, 1967), 1:198–210.

Paratore, Ettore. "Il Canto x dell' *Inferno.*" *Letture classensi* 5 (1976): 215–255.

Sansone, Mario. "Cavalcanti, Cavalcante de'." *Enciclopedia dantesca,* 1:891. Rome, 1970.

———. "Farinata." *Enciclopedia dantesca,* 2:804–809. Rome, 1970.

Schiller, Gertrud. *Ikonographie der christlichen Kunst.* Vol. 3, *Die Auferstehung und Erhöhung Christi.* Gutersloh, 1971.

Scott, John A. *Dante magnanimo: Studi sulla "Commedia."* Florence, 1977.

Singleton, Charles S. "*Inferno* x: Guido's Disdain." *MLN* 77 (1962): 49–65.

Vetter, Ewald M. "Iconografía del *Varón de dolores:* Su significado y orígen." *Archivo español de arte* 36 (1963): 197–231.

CANTO XI

Malice and Mad Bestiality

ALFRED A. TRIOLO

At the end of Canto x Dante and Virgil have traversed the entire fiery circle of the heretics without incident, when they arrive at the brink of the seventh circle. Their initial perception is olfactory, of a wall of stench thrown up by the abyss. The ensuing description of what they see is brief and stark: a rim that is an isolating barrier of massive boulders. There is no indication at this point that they perceive the rock slide leading downward into the seventh circle. At the end of this canto we are given one of the *Inferno*'s rare time markings, which establishes arrival at between 3 and 4 A.M. of Holy Saturday morning.

In order to adjust to "the outrageous stench" (4), symbolizing the heinous sin below, the poets draw back until they come upon the slanting open lid of a great tomb and read what is written there. This is incidentally the only such inscription alluded to in the circle of heresy: "I hold Pope Anastasius, / enticed to leave the true path by Photinus" (8–9). Pope Anastasius II (496–498) was the victim of a double historical misunderstanding. First, the Middle Ages believed erroneously that he had espoused the variety of Monophysite heresy influential in the eastern Church of his time, which denied that Christ was true God and true man, affirming that the human nature had been absorbed into the divine. Secondly, Anastasius II was mistakenly supposed to have been corrupted by Photinus, deacon of Thessalonica, whom the pope had in fact simply received cordially in the hope of mending the schism between Orient and Occident (the Photinus in question was perhaps confused with an earlier heretic, Photinus of Sirmium).

A false assessment of Anastasius II entered the *Liber pontificalis* and ultimately the influential *Decretum* of Gratian in the twelfth century, and Dante
shares this mistaken opinion. What is significant in all this is that after total concentration on the broad naturalist epicureanism of Canto x, for
which pagans and Christians alike can be held responsible, Dante now
strikes at a specific traditional Christological heresy. The charge also places
a pope in the circle, perhaps to offset the presence of an emperor in x, 119.

When Dante asks Virgil for some means to benefit from the time required for adjustment to the odor, Virgil readily outlines the structure of
the rest of hell. In six lines (16–21) he states that the three remaining circles, smaller in circumference than those already negotiated, punish sins of
violence and sins of fraud. He efficiently sets forth their substance in terms
of a "malice" that is coterminous with "injustice."

> Of every malice that earns hate in Heaven
> injustice (*ingiuria*) is the end; and each such end
> by force or fraud brings harm to other men.
>   However, fraud is man's peculiar vice;
> God finds it more displeasing—and therefore,
> the fraudulent are lower, suffering more.
>
>   (22–27)

Thus, according to Virgil, while malicious injustice includes both violence
and fraud (which he soon subdivides), fraud is more repugnant to God than
violence because it is specifically characteristic of humans. And thus the entire lower hell is accounted for in its broadest lines. We need to measure the
malice Virgil mentions here against the malice in line 82, when Virgil seems
to divide all hell into three parts, now under the dispositions of "incontinence / and malice and mad bestiality" (81–82). Since there is no scholarly
agreement on the applicability of the last two terms, and specifically on
how or whether the malice of line 22 correlates with that of line 82 in terms
of the violence-fraud subdivisions, each of the terms demands our attention if we are to understand the structure of Dante's hell. Having anticipated this central problem, let us begin with the sources for Dante's conceptions of injustice and malice.

The most often cited source for Dante's placing lower hell under the
rubric of injustice, and the latter's division into force and fraud, as well as
the idea that fraud is worse than force is Cicero's *De officiis* (a text Dante
echoes in *Inf.* xxvii, 75): "wrong" (*ingiuria*) may be done in two ways, that
is, by force or by fraud. Fraud seems to belong to the cunning fox, force to
the lion; both are wholly unworthy of man, but fraud is the more contemptible (*odio digna maiore* [1, 13]). Cicero does not use the term "malice"
in connection with injustice and we will have to find the former's subtext

elsewhere. As for fraud and not force being distinctively characteristic of human wrongdoing, Cicero tells us in *De officiis* 1, 11 that the resolution of disputes by means of rational discussion is specifically human (*proprium . . . hominis*) whereas the use of force is characteristic of beasts. Cicero's *proprium* resurfaces in Dante's designation of fraud, by way of the perversion of rationality, as "man's peculiar vice" (*proprio male,* 25).

Now in addition to this Ciceronian definition, Virgil inserts a Judeo-Christian corollary, that malice "earns hate in Heaven" (22). This hate has strong biblical warrants. In Psalm 5:6–7, the psalmist addresses God's hatred of two kinds of evildoers whom he discriminates as violent and fraudulent: "Thou hatest all the workers of iniquity. Thou wilt destroy all that speak a lie. The bloody and the deceitful man [in the Vulgate, *virum sanguinum et dolosum*] the Lord will abhor." To this frequently cited passage we may add another from Proverbs 6:16–19: "Six things there are, which the Lord hateth, and the seventh his soul detesteth: Haughty eyes, a lying tongue, hands that shed innocent blood, a heart that deviseth wicked plots, feet that are swift to run into mischief, a deceitful witness that uttereth lies, and him that soweth discord among brethren." This seventh sin, of fomenting division, we shall pick up later.

Dante's conception of malicious injustice goes deeper still into the tradition of classical antiquity. The duality of force and fraud is also very prominent in Roman legal thought and practice. But the authentic matrix for Dante's conception of malice and injustice is the fifth book of Aristotle's *Nicomachean Ethics* (hereafter, *Ethics*), where "the Philosopher" discusses justice and virtue and their opposites malice and injustice. At the outset injustice is seen as the whole of malice (*tota malitia,* as the thirteenth-century Antiqua translatio puts it), and the unjust man is lawbreaking, unfair, and covetous. But Aristotle subdivides justice and injustice in a more complex way than does Cicero later. It seems clear that Dante in his initial statement in lines 22–24 simplified Aristotle by resort to Cicero. In his category of "particular justice" Aristotle discriminates the subtype he calls "involuntary transactions," deeds committed against an "unwilling" party, the victim; these unjust actions are perpetrated by violence and by fraud. Although no gradation of seriousness is stated between the two modes, Aristotle's listing of specific violations under each is very close to Dante's. We are now in a better position to understand why Virgil says that "Of every malice . . . injustice is the end." I shall treat the "malice" of line 82 later and in its proper context.

Here it is crucial to underscore that Dante's resort to the Ciceronian notion that fraud is more odious or contemptible than violence is by no means self-validating as an ethical absolute. Nowhere in the main traditional sources, Aristotle, Roman law, or the Christian moral tradition is it held that *all* fraud is more serious than *all* violence. Dante's choice is his own and in it we detect his aim to establish a new systematization (*ordo*) for his hell. Saint Thomas Aquinas saw it differently. For him violent robbery (*rapina*), for example, is more heinous than theft (*furtum*) because it adds bodily harm to the deprivation of property (*Summa theologica* II-II, 69, 9). He would never have dreamed of generalizing and stratifying the violence-fraud dyad in so radical a way as did Dante. However, in a specialized context in which Aquinas sets forth the "offspring" (*filiae*) of the capital or deadly sin avarice (*avaritia*) he provides a systematic structuring of that avarice "in action" (*in effectu*), this in *Summa* II-II, 118, 8. His set of distinctions may be schematically represented as follows:

force or violence (*vis*)
deceit (*dolus*):   A.   guile (*fallacia*), in word; fraud (*fraus*), in deed
                     B.   perjury (*periurium*), in word; treachery
                           (*proditio*), in deed (as in Judas's betrayal of
                           Christ)

Saint Thomas's patterning, whose source is surely Cicero, served Dante's project well. Deceit (the Roman legal form is *dolus malus*) is precisely the principle of judgment in Virgil's Tartarus (*Aen.* VI, 567). Dante simply reverted to the narrower term for deceit or cunning, fraud (*fraus*). We may clearly infer that avarice in its broadest expanse of meaning (*avaritia-cupiditas*), which Saint Thomas calls the chief adversary of justice (*Summa* II-II, 55, 8; and see Dante's *Monarchia* I, xi), lies at the root of the entire lower *Inferno* in its various nuances as the partner of malice.

Dante's text now outlines three categories of recipients of violence in terms of their persons and possessions: God, self, and neighbor. The source of this triad has been said to be Saint Thomas (e.g., *Summa* I-II, 72, 4). This gloss is partially misleading because Aquinas used the categories to rank *all* serious sins (*ex certa malitia;* it goes back at least to *Summa sententiarum* III, xvi of Hugh of St. Victor [died 1141]). The upshot is that Saint Thomas would locate all elective sins against God at the very bottom of a structure like Dante's. Instead Dante restricted the distinction to violence alone. This departure enables the poet to assign to violence an enormous semantic range moving from the physical to the highly metaphorical, including very serious sins indeed against the deity. Let us go back to the triadic division, to each of whose components Virgil's exposition devotes six taut lines, presenting each offense in the order in which he and Dante will encounter them as they descend.

1. Against neighbor: this is pure violent injustice, of which murderers and all sorts of perpetrators of harm against the persons and possessions of others (brigands, arsonists, pirates, and the like) are guilty. The vicious petty tyrant will be the object of special obloquy in Canto XII, 104–112.

2. Against self: suicide is premeditated violence, but can it strictly speak-

ing be called "injustice"? Aristotle (*Ethics* v, 11) allows the *metaphorical* injustice of suicide in that we may conceive a person to be divided against himself, one part of the soul (the lower) inflicting injustice on the other (the higher). Christian tradition easily accommodated the notion of injustice against the self along with its strict definition as against the other. Saint Bonaventura, for example, held that justice is not limited to respecting one's neighbor but also applies to one's actions toward the self (*Breviloquium* v, 4–5). Aquinas suggested that suicide can also be taken as an act of injustice against the community or state, as Aristotle speculated, or even against God (*Summa* ii-ii, 65, 1). Dante closely unites to this category of unjust suicides an analogous one of spendthrifts, wasters of their patrimony. Aristotle elucidates such a category in his discussion of liberality and its opposite in *Ethics* iv, 1. Line 44 is somewhat ambiguous (as commentaries and translations show). Dante uses the verb *biscazzare,* which signified gambling in his time, and the line seems to be limited to this form of wantonness if we take *biscazza e fonde* to mean "gambles and (thereby) destroys his patrimony." However, since Canto xiii brings in exemplars of other types of excessive expenditure, we may read it "gambling away, wasting his patrimony." Dante's positive Aristotelian evaluation of our proper material stake in life becomes "weeping where he should instead be happy" (45).

3. Against God and created nature: this is violence as willed violation, a psychological exercise of coercion against God (by definition immune to actual violence), and against nature. Violence against the divinity can only take the form of blasphemy for Dante, while sodomy and usury ("Sodom and Cahors" [50]) he takes to be sins against nature.

(a) Blasphemy: this sin is the rejection of God's power and majesty (not of his existence) and exteriorizes itself in language and gesture. The usual gloss is of two separate sins, a secret one of the heart and an external one of the mouth, in the tradition of Saint Thomas. However, Umberto Bosco may well be correct in his preference for Siro Chimenz's interpretation of line 47 as a univocal characterization, that of a sinner who having scorned God in his heart proceeds to blaspheme him (Bosco and Reggio, 168–169). The key verb is *spregiare,* denoting the psychological "violence" of contempt of the deity, the offender hubristically assuming that God is an equal and, therefore, the putative "involuntary" sufferer of the assault.

(b) Sodomy: the sodomite in practice vents his contempt on nature, presumably because his act is sterile. The various *schiere* or groups of sinners in Canto xv who run on the burning sand are hard to classify in situ; they may be taken to be either homosexuals belonging to different social or professional groups, or "unnatural" sexual offenders of various kinds.

(c) Usury: Dante also perceives usury as a form of contemptuous violence against nature seen as the tangible expression of the divine bounty (48). This perplexes the pilgrim, and Virgil's elucidation forms his second coda (94–111). Usury, defined as the charging of any interest whatever for money lent, had long been anathema in both classical and Judeo-Christian tradition. For Aquinas usury is contrary to nature, as it is for Aristotle (*Politics* I, 10). In his long treatment of usury in *De malo* (13, 4, ad 7), Saint Thomas suggests in passing that the usurer inflicts not absolute violence on the borrower but something tantamount to it (*quemdam violentiam mixtam*) because he imposes a heavy burden on a needy person. In treatises on sins and crimes, usury was seen as very close to theft. Dante thus had the materials at hand to structure usury as a sin against one's neighbor, but he was seeking something more grandiose, perhaps in order to single out for heightened condemnation a practice so widespread in the society of his time. Virgil's argument syllogistically fuses pagan and Judeo-Christian formulae. The Aristotelian commonplace (for example in *Physics* II, 8, 199) has it that human industry imitates nature, the letter being assumed to follow the divine intellect in its creative activity; human "art" is therefore, so to speak, God's grandchild. Genesis concurs—in God's original expectations for his creatures: "And the Lord God took man, and put him into the paradise of pleasure, to dress it, and to keep it" (2:15; this positive source is preferable to the oft-cited condemnation of Adam and his wife to "labour and toil," after the Fall [3:17]). The usurer pins his hope for sustenance and advancement on an unearned increment and thus aggressively deviates from the divine and natural precepts.

Concerning malicious violence in general, despite its location within the fully responsible operation of the human will, Dante posits an underlying emotional factor that limits all its manifestations, including usury, when set against fraud. But paradoxically the apparently colder, more guileful fraud is itself often inseparable from its own insidious and even more perverse subtending psychopathy (or moral illness), as will emerge.

Virgil begins his exposition of fraud by qualifying it as something "that eats away at every conscience" (52). The meaning of this specification is not fully clear. We may perhaps take it that Dante wishes to underscore the notion that those endowed with "right reason" will suffer most over the corruption of what is most inherent in the human being, the faculty of reason. The discussion proper opens with the key distinction that fraud can be perpetrated against those who place their trust in the defrauder and against those who do not (53–54). We are then told that the second mode severs the bond (*vinco*) that nature forges among all humankind (55–56), whereas the first signifies the loss of a profounder composite made up of that natural love and another more powerful love based on a relationship of special trust (61–63). It is convenient to call the latter "fraud complex" and it will occupy the ninth circle; "fraud simple" is practiced against those who have no special trust. It is important to define the positive face of this second group whom we meet in the eighth circle. Dante's term *vinco* stems from Cicero's *vinculum* in *De officiis* I, 16–17, where the Roman writer-statesman sets forth the principles of the universal human community created by nature. The chief binding link within humanity consists of reason and speech, since it is by dint of teaching, learning, communicating, discussing, and reasoning that we are unified in a natural society. Cicero goes on to articulate the degrees of human bonding, which give us first our general ties simply as humans, that is, those which oblige us universally. Dante's "one who has no trust" (54) designates precisely this relationship by means of a negative, but he soon expresses it affirmatively: "the bond of love that nature forges" (56).

Virgil devotes one tercet to the listing of the sins that make up fraud simple, and it is strangely helter-skelter.

> hypocrisy and flattery, sorcerers,
> and falsifiers, simony, and theft,
> and barrators and panders and like trash.
> (58–60)

There is no correspondence here to the order we encounter later in the journey, and two categories occupying complete divisions of the eighth circle are summed up in the phrase "like trash"; we shall soon see what they are, but it should be added here that those we call "seducers," who share the first of the ten *bolge* (ditches or pouches) with the panders, are also unnamed. It is curious that Dante should provide so little precision for the subspecies of fraud in this canto, considering the space occupied by the sins of fraud in his hell. And he says nothing whatever on the specific divisions of the remote four rounds that subdivide "treachery." We must deduce the nature of these areas from their names, Caïna, Antenora, Ptolomea, and Judecca, dropped as the poets pass through the dire zone of ice, Cocytus. The two categories omitted from the list cited above are (1) the damned of the ninth *bolgia*, recorded there as "sowers of dissension / and scandal" (XXVIII, 35–36; *seminator di scandalo e di scisma* [35]); and (2) those in the eighth *bolgia*, who have traditionally been labeled Fraudulent Counselors, extrapolating from the case of Guido da Montefeltro (XXVII, 116). I have been able to locate the source for these categories in the *Speculum morale* (*Speculum maius*, pt. 3) attributed to Vincent of Beauvais, but in fact a late thirteenth- or early fourteenth-century work heavily dependent on Aquinas. The section "On Discord" (bk. 3, 12, pt. 3, dist. 12) has a subsection entitled "Concerning the sowing of discord and other vices," which contains among other things "On the sin of wicked counseling" (cols. 1045–1046). The context provides solid grounding for both the naming of and the close rapport between the eighth and ninth *bolge*. And let us recall the biblical correlation here with the seventh type of sinner whom God detests in Proverbs 6:19: "him that soweth discord."

Given the plethora of sins and crimes treated by medieval moral and le-

gal literature, it is clear that Dante must exercise great selectivity. His criteria for choice are surely based on a balanced dosage of fraudulent actions
by word and deed, perpetrated against individuals and, more prominently,
against humanity's most basic institutions, church and community.

With line 61, Virgil's exposition of the structure of lower hell seems
complete—but not quite. A pair of perplexities mars the satisfaction of
Dante the pilgrim. Two codas are needed to illuminate them. I have already
discussed the second coda regarding usury. The first is broader: why are the
sinners of circles two through five not punished within the city of Dis, if
they have incurred God's anger—Dante designates the sinners according to
their punishment (what XXVIII, 142 will call the *contrapasso,* counter-
penalty)—or, if they have not incurred God's anger, why are they condemned at all? Virgil upbraids his ward severely, charging him with either
uncharacteristic distraction or the pursuit of some idée fixe. And indeed we
may wonder why the wayfarer failed to grasp that the malice-injustice
nexus rules out what has been encountered in the upper hell, and also why
he did not assume it to be incontinence in its several forms, since the Aristotelian work that Virgil calls "your *Ethics,*" (80) carefully analyzes incontinence, contrasting malice to it, as does Saint Thomas at length: classically
the incontinent are those who, overcome momentarily by weakness or
passion, soon recover their possession of the principles of right behavior,
so that even if they commit an objective sin of injustice they cannot be
called unjust. Virgil's careful coupling of malice and injustice in lines 22–23
should not lead to any assumption that God's special hatred of the malicious precludes his lesser but real anger against what is found in the upper
hell. It is scarcely credible that the pilgrim has drifted into the Stoic view
that all sins deserve equal punishment (as some heretics of his time apparently held), for the enormous weight of the orthodox tradition on a hierarchy of sin militates against it. Does the wayfarer purposely assume a
naive posture in order to elicit a fuller clarification of hell, braving Virgil's
disapproval? This is possible, but I shall advance a more hidden intention,
which has very significant implications for Dante's ultimate conception of
the *Inferno.*

The fact is that at various points throughout upper hell, theoretical
statements are made regarding the sins punished in the individual circles
about which Dante has now queried Virgil, but that material has not been
explicitly generalized. Lust (*lussuria*) characterized the carnal sinners in
the second circle (V, 55 and 63). Gluttony (VI, 53), avarice and prodigality
(VII, 48 and 42), wrath and despondency (VII, 116 and 121) were called
vices and *culpae* (the Italian words *vizio* and *colpa* are used). It may well be
assumed that the pilgrim takes them to be a partial but solid list of the
seven deadly sins. But by now, in Canto XI, the poet changes course, abandoning an earlier project to design his hell in accordance with the system
of the seven deadly sins, which he will follow in *Purgatorio.* I subscribe to no

hypothesis concerning the dating of this decisive turn in design, but the point of change is very probably marked in the narrative by the arrival of the poets at the Stygian marsh. It turns out that the first five of the seven deadly sins parallel the Aristotelian manifestations of incontinence in *Ethics* VII: the incontinence of lust, gluttony, avarice, wrath, and sloth. Dante's decision to bring his infernal structure into an Aristotelian ground plan could thus take in the original deadly sins by *appropriation*. A test case for this maneuver is the figure of the lustful queen Semíramis who, we are told, actually enshrined various forms of lust in law! That bespeaks a deliberation and corruption that cannot authentically be called incontinence. My suggestion is that the pilgrim's perplexity is inserted by the poet in order to cover the change in ground plan, and at the same time to affirm its now definitive Aristotelianism, indeed to round out that theory.

What has been said leads us back now to the second and third "dispositions" of lines 82–83 and their role in the structure of Dante's hell. The poet surely does not bring them in merely to introduce the useful term "incontinence," as some have held; he could do that far more simply. Our inquiry is concerned with how Dante used *Ethics* VII. Aristotle, at its beginning, sets forth three "undesirable states of character"; for these "states" he alternates three terms. The Antiqua translatio gives *mos* for *ethos*, *habitus* for *hexis*, and *dispositio* for *diathesis*. Thomas Aquinas adopted *dispositio* as the general term in his gloss on this work, which Dante clearly consulted, and he followed suit, hence "dispositions" (81). It is important to note what Dante could not have failed to grasp, namely that these dispositions describe certain ethico-psychological states that operate solely within the individual person, as contrasted to those affecting our relation to others. The incontinent human is one subject to temporary weakness or passion, as we have seen, and is far less corrupt than the intemperate one. "Intemperance" is now a weak, vague term but in classical ethics it denoted with precision a deliberate profligacy or "cold" sensualism. And intemperance fell under the description "malice" (*malitia*), as did general injustice. "Malice" thus has two uses or subdivisions with respect to chosen, fully responsible evil behavior. For Aristotle, it is clear that the malice of injustice enjoys preeminence over that of intemperance and even somehow encompasses it. Thus the aptness of the expression *tota malitia*, the whole breadth of malice that the Antiqua translatio yields in *Ethics* v for injustice most broadly conceived. This is the notion under whose aegis Dante places the entire lower hell. But it does not mean that he left out of account the malice of intemperance, which parallels that of the injustice from beneath, as heinous sensuality, anger, and greed.

Dante's ingenious theoretical weaving and patterning can now be analyzed as follows. *Ethics* v has an overall triadic pattern (which the Scholastics also perceived): (1) it mentions incontinence in order to show that a person characterized by it may commit an act of injustice without thereby

being unjust because he has not lost possession of the principles of right behavior, as stated earlier. This condition contrasts with (2) the corruption of
the unjust man, who carries out unjust acts by deliberate choice; (3) then
there is the person who violates the important principle of equity, which is
different in kind from and superior to justice and yet somehow broadly included within it; thus the one guilty of "inequity" is among the worst of the
unjust. We thus have a triple/dual pattern and its analogue in *Ethics* VII: (1)
incontinence, here in its proper context; (2) the malice of intemperance;
and (3) bestiality. The peculiarity of the term "bestiality" is that Aristotle
used it, on the one hand, to describe certain reprehensible behavioral traits
among the "barbarians," such uncivilized things as cannibalism, hair
pulling, eating earth and coal, and the like. At the same time, he states that
"bestiality" is used to denote an extremely low degree of "malice." The Antiqua translatio registered this second possibility as "a great increase in
malice" (*magnum augmentum malitiae*). In my critical analysis of the text and
its medieval reception (see reference in the bibliographical note) I have
shown that while Saint Thomas only entertained the first meaning (the
"morbid states," which can have little meaning in a Christian moral context), Dante and others saw it in the light of the second application. Thus
"bestiality," to which Dante prefixed the adjective "mad," is simultaneously
a disposition in its own right and an extreme form of the malice of intemperance. In this other triple/dual pattern the "mad bestial" person is afflicted
with the gravest intemperance. The manner in which Dante fused these patterns with the violence-fraud division can be schematized as follows:

Ethics V: Just and Unjust Action (and Modifications: Cicero and Aquinas)	*Ethics* VII: Psycho-moral Dispositions
[incontinence]	incontinence
malice-injustice	malice-intemperance:
violence—seventh circle	human scale (*malitia humana*)
fraud 1—eighth circle	
fraud 2—ninth circle	infrahuman scale
treachery against special obligations; includes inequity	(*malitia bestialis*)

This is a powerful interlocking structure in which violence and simple
fraud—distinct divisions—share the common designation of evil in ordinarily conceivable human dimensions, whereas the second degree of fraud
denotes a corruption somehow beyond the normal human pale, a very special "infrahuman" status. To the malice of violence and fraud simple Dante

will at times, down through hell, apply the word *bestiale,* and that is why he affixes "mad" to the lowest manifestation of a "process" of intemperance. It should be noted that the ninth circle is divided off from the eighth by a sheer cliff, thus heightening its special status.

The view that sees Dante maintaining the exact order of the Aristotelian dispositions is currently advocated by few scholars, chiefly by the present writer and Francesco Mazzoni. The prevailing interpretation upsets that order by seeing "mad bestiality" as "incarnate" in the violence of the seventh circle. This reading requires that the "malice" of xi, 82 be restricted to, indeed be another name for, fraudulent injustice alone. Advocates of this position cite in its support one occurrence of the term in Canto xxii: the black demons call a grotesque maneuver of the grafter Ciampolo *malizia* (xxii, 107). Here the term colloquially means "a trick." There is no reason whatever to read this meaning back into the "malice" of xi, 82. The majority interpretation is unpersuasive largely because it is highly unlikely that Dante, in a closely argued theoretical context, would use a key term in two ranges of meaning. There is far more explanatory power in the position that the two malices—one of injustice, the other of intemperance (its *Ethics* vii background now fully in view)—are wholly coextensive, while "mad bestiality" functions as I have described.

The interpretation just outlined is far from abstract or eccentric. Let us take some further steps to document it. There are strong underlying theoretical convergences between the moral and philosophical concept of "mad bestiality" and Dante's ninth circle, the nadir of hell. The reader will recall that we have already glimpsed some of them as we return to Cicero, this time the Cicero of the early rhetorical work *De inventione,* which contains some principles that may be placed beside those of the later *De officiis.* In *De inventione* ii, 53, 161 Cicero posits a category of virtues that the later Middle Ages will call the special natural virtues allied to justice. All of them embody certain deep moral obligations that we incur in the sphere of special relationships. The first is called *religio,* religion in the sense of reverence for and worship of a being humanity recognizes as divine. This is followed by *pietas,* the virtue of piety in terms of what we owe parents, kin, fellow citizens, country, and friends of our country (this is of course the great virtue of Virgil's *pius* Aeneas). Then come *observantia,* a sacred respect for people of preeminent dignity in the light of their renown and usefulness to the common good; *gratia* or *gratitudo,* the gratitude to be shown toward benefactors; *vindicatio,* the balanced sense of justice in meting out punishment; and *veritas,* full truthfulness in communication with our fellows.

Saint Thomas wholeheartedly appropriated these virtues and treated them at length (*Summa* ii-ii, 81–120), adding to them a significant seventh, the "equity" (*aequitas*) of Aristotle, the virtue that moderates the letter of the law for the sake of authentic justice and the common good. The opposites of these virtues lie solidly under the four zones of the ninth circle,

Cocytus. Obviously Dante singled out principal ones, *pietas,* which sub-tends Caïna and Antenora, *gratia* and *observantia* underlying Ptolomea and Judecca. The opposite of *religio* may be seen in the relationship between the giants and deity. The others, unjust punishment and inequity, as well as the perjurious violation of truth, are dramatized in the crucial encounters be-tween Ugolino and Ruggieri and with Fra Alberigo in Canto xxxiii. Now, Mazzoni holds that Dante's *Monarchia* furnishes the following clarifying principles underlying the zones of Cocytus: *domus, vicinia, civitas,* and *reg-num* (family, neighborhood, city, and kingdom). There is no conflict be-tween violation of these entities and the perversion of the special natural virtues, but I believe that the latter provide a richer and more amply ap-plicable set of features.

Finally I maintain that the reader will grasp the full meaning of the "bestiality" of *Ethics* vii and Dante's "mad bestiality" only through re-course to two Aristotelian works close in many ways to his *Nicomachean Ethics,* namely, the *Rhetoric* and the *Politics,* and their medieval commen-taries. The first locus is *Rhetoric* i, 14–15, where Aristotle examines the gravest injustices that an individual can commit: the breaking of solemn oaths and obligations, wrongs against benefactors, crimes that cause the greatest harm to humanity, and violation of the unwritten law. In the thir-teenth-century Latin paraphrase of the gloss on these chapters by Aver-roës, the great Arabic commentator who finds a place in Dante's Limbo, other such unjust acts are added: the infliction of excessive punishment, crimes against kin and close associates, perjury, and the betrayal of al-liances. The reader will immediately perceive the rapport between these maximal crimes, Cicero's and Aquinas's special natural virtues, and Dante's ninth circle. But there is more. Can these lowest of violations be associated with a metaphorically "mad bestial injustice," which is inher-ent in the denizens of Cocytus? Indeed they can, if we go on to examine the text and glosses of *Politics* i, 2, our second key locus. Here Aristotle's subject is man in general as a social and political animal. Most men fall somewhere between the two polar human types: the first is the utterly self-sufficient man, who is ordinarily outside the scope of the polis; he is com-pared to a god and is therefore the clear counterpart of the "divine man" mentioned at the beginning of *Ethics* vii and exemplified by Hector. At the other extreme, we find a man whom Aristotle calls "bestial"; totally anti-social, he is incapable of participation in the polis. Thus the ethical and po-litical conceptions of the lowest human condition coincide in Dante's "mad bestiality." For both the classical Virgil and Dante a central example of the "divine man" is Aeneas. And Dante's Brutus and Cassius, masticated in Sa-tan's mouth at the nadir, are the worst of the "mad bestials." On another level Saint Paul, coupled with Aeneas in Dante's disclaimer in *Inf.* ii, 32, con-trasts with Judas. More than incidentally, the concept of the "divine man" was a key concept in Augustan Rome, as Brooks Otis has demonstrated.

The picture is not yet complete. Aristotle, in *Politics* I, goes on to say that political man, when perfected, is the best of animals, but when unlawful and unjust he is the worst of all. From birth he possesses significant "weapons" for perpetrating injustice, which is the more reprehensible the more it is "armed." Now, one of the chief human weapons is language, which may be used to pervert the moral prudence and virtue it is intended to serve. Man may thus become a most unholy and savage being. The Scholastics used the words *saevus* (savage) and *bestialis* (bestial) to characterize the guileful intellect bent on doing evil. Albertus Magnus's gloss on this passage has it that human injustice can be most savage (*saevissima*) due to the special weapons it possesses. Saint Thomas Aquinas also states that injustice is the more savage (*saevior*) the more instruments for evildoing it has at its disposal. These glosses may be said to be crowned by the post-Thomistic commentary of Giles of Rome (*Aegidius Romanus*) on *Rhetoric* I, 14, to which we now return. Where the Latin translation of Aristotle's *Rhetoric* says that an act of injustice is greater the more brutish (*bestialior*) it is, Giles adds that this means that the crime is more "inordinate" (*illa est maior injustitia quia magis inordinata*). The terminus of the process is clearly the maximal injustices assembled in the ninth circle, as we have seen. It is hardly surprising then that the most dire combination of "weapons" for evil is found in the giant guardians of the final circle: intellectual excellence (perverted), evil will, and physical power, this (in *Inf.* XXXI, 55–57) in words uttered by Virgil in Cocytus itself as the two poets face the giants. Dante's giants in their mammoth but fully human form are fitting emblems for the "mad bestiality" of the abyss. We may generalize the conception thus: people classifiable as treacherous are prey to the worst psychoethical impulsion or disposition, and singly or in groups they can perpetrate far more damaging injustice and harm to our most sacred religious and communitarian bonds than any conceivable animal. This "mad bestiality" is thus a stark and ironic metaphor for such a dire human condition.

For the sake of completeness I add here that Virgil's exposition in *Inf.* XI says nothing regarding three of the zones of Dante's hell: the vestibule, Limbo, and the sixth circle, where, within the walls of the city of Dis, we encountered the heretics. It is not possible to speculate here on the reason for this omission. This writer is convinced, however, that some interesting Aristotelian notions contribute something to the theoretical composition of each of them.

In conclusion, I submit that Dante quite consciously set himself the task of constructing a mosaic synthesis of the following chronological-ideological strata: (1) the Aristotelian and biblical; (2) modified by the Ciceronian and Roman legal traditions; (3) after which the Patristic and Scholastic insights contributed significant features. Cicero, whose role I have shown to be far more substantial than traditional commentary has seen, was pivotal, in the light of his nearness to Virgil and to the opening of the Christian dispensation. Dante borrows from Aquinas (and others), but he also acts as an independent Scholastic. That the resulting system was not designed to be exclusively theological in a sense acceptable to an Augustine or a Thomas has been instantiated in one key trace, the Thomistic hierarchy "against neighbor, self, and God." While his predecessors, and Christian instinct, would have united all grave sins against God in a ninth circle, Dante redistributed the various transgressions through the circles of lower hell. The poet's structure is a political-communitarian as well as theological composite, into which all time enters *sub specie aeternitatis*, as the Trinity *might* have conceived and designed it; it may accommodate all sinners from just after the moment the "eternal things were made" (*Inf*. III, 7–8) through to the end of time.

BIBLIOGRAPHICAL NOTES

For the Antiqua translatio of the *Nicomachean Ethics* and the Aquinas commentary, see S. *Thomas Aquinatis in Decem libris Ethicorum Aristotelis ad Nicomachum Expositio,* ed. R. M. Spiazzi, (Rome, 1949). The easily available English translation is Thomas Aquinas, *Commentary on the Nicomachean Ethics,* trans. C. I. Litzinger (Chicago, 1964). For Aquinas's commentary on *Politics* I have consulted *In politicorum Aristotelis Expositio* I, 1, 41, ed. R. M. Spiazzi (Rome, 1951), and for that of Albertus Magnus, *In politicorum Aristotelis Expositio* I, 1, ed. Borgnet, vol. 8 (Paris, 1891). The Averroës paraphrase of the *Rhetoric* can be found in *Aristotelis, De rhetorica et poetica libri, cum Averrois Cordubensis in eosdem paraphrasibus* (Venice, 1550), fol. 44; and for Giles of Rome see *Rhetorica Aristotelis, cum Egidii de Roma luculentissimis commentariis* (Venice, 1515), fol. 45. For Pseudo-Vincent of Beauvais I have used *Speculum morale* (Graz, 1965), a reprint *of Speculi Maioris Vincentii Burgundi,* vol. 3 (Duaci, 1624).

The following outline includes some of the more important theoretically committed books, articles, and commentaries on the central problem of malice and mad bestiality in Canto XI, 81–82, grouped according to their views:
1. One interpretation sees "mad bestiality" expressed in the heresy of circle six. Its fountainhead was G. Ferretti, "La matta bestialità," in *Saggi danteschi* (Florence, 1950). It is held by very few, conspicuously by K. Foster in *God's Tree* (London, 1957), 50–66; and by G. G. Meersman, "Il canto XI dell'*Inferno*," in *Nuove letture dantesche,* vol. 2 (Florence, 1968). Its degree of textual support comes from Dante's labeling the denial of immortality as a deep "bestiality," in the *Convivio*.
2. Those who see "mad bestiality" manifested in the category of violence, with the restriction of the "malice" of line 82 to fraud, may be said to be subdivided into two groups:
(a) The great majority hold that there is a total convergence, such that "mad bestiality" is "incarnate" in violence. Apparently first formulated by Boccaccio—not clearly in his commentary on Canto XI, but rather in that of XII (*Esposizioni sopra la "Commedia" di Dante,* ed. Giorgio Padoan [Milan, 1965])—it has had a long history. In this century it was elaborated at length by G. Busnelli in his influential *L'Etica Nicomachea e l'ordinamento morale dell'"Inferno" di Dante* (Bologna, 1907) and by a series of now almost forgotten contemporaries and followers. In 1951 the great medievalist and Dante scholar Bruno Nardi lent it his authority, in his monographic *lectura* of Canto XI—see "Il Canto XI dell'*Inferno*," in *Nuova Lectura Dantis,* ed. S. A. Chimenz (Rome, 1955), partially reproduced in *Letture dantesche,* ed. Giovanni Getto (Florence, 1962). Nardi admitted some uncertainty concerning the interpretation, and a broad arc of critics and commentators, from his moment to the present day, accept it with varying degrees of conviction in their editions of the *Divine Comedy:* for example, M. Porena (rev. ed. 1966); G. Vandelli (16th ed., 1955); H. Gmelin (1954); S. A. Chimenz (1967); Bosco and Reggio (1979); Pasquini and Quaglio (1980) accept it but allow room for other views, including that of the present writer; J. Freccero espoused it in his "Dante's Firm Foot and the Journey without a Guide," in *Dante:*

The Poetics of Conversion, ed. Rachel Jacoff (Cambridge, Mass., 1986), 29–54 (originally in *Harvard Theological Review,* 52 [1959]); G. Petrocchi's agreement is clear in his *L'"Inferno" di Dante* (Milan, 1978). The list includes many distinguished Dante scholars.

(b) The variant position is that "mad bestiality" is visible in only one or two types of violence. In modern times this view of it was elaborated by W. V. Reade in his still-consulted *The Moral System of Dante's Inferno* (Oxford, 1909); Reade cites sodomy, and perhaps tyranny, as his limited examples. Charles Singleton does not give a clearly focused analytic opinion but cites Reade profusely in his well-known commentary (in his 1970 ed., 2:166–167, and 176–178).

3. There are those who refuse to see any exact area corresponding to "mad bestiality": prominently N. Sapegno, who strongly rejects the majority position above (see his ed., 13th reprint, 1980, 127–128); A. Pagliaro in his "Le tre disposizioni," *L'Alighieri* 5 (1965): 21–35, turgidly defends the view that "mad bestiality" either does not appear at all in Dante's hell or is dispersed through its circles indistinctly. For A. Hatcher and M. Musa, "Aristotle's Matta Bestialitade in Dante's *Inferno,*" *Italica* 47 (1970): 366–372, Dante brought the last two dispositions in for essentially no other purpose than to lay hold of the term "incontinence." But the most limpid version of this general view is that of Edward Moore; his considered interpretation was that the malice of line 82 is coextensive with that of line 22, such that together they account for circles seven through nine but he assigns no role to "mad bestiality." Moore went on to say that if the latter disposition had entered Dante's picture, it would have had to be located at its very bottom and nowhere else. I contend that we can find it there, and thus I deem the analysis outlined in the present reading to be heir to that of Moore in "The Classification of Sins in the Inferno and Purgatorio," in *Studies in Dante, Second Series* (Oxford, 1899), 157–162.

4. The position defended in this essay was briefly outlined in F. Mazzoni's review of B. Nardi's reading of Canto XI, *Studi Danteschi* 31 (1953): 209–214; and in his notes to his ed., *La Divina Commedia: Inferno* (Florence, 1972–1979), 219–220, 649, and 725–726; and a 1981 reading, "*Inferno* XI," in *Lectura Dantis Neapolitana* (Naples, 1986), 167–209. For its development in detail see A. A. Triolo, "Matta Bestialità in Dante's *Inferno:* Theory and Image," *Traditio* 24 (1968): 247–292; "*Inferno* XXXIII: Fra Alberigo in Context," *L'Alighieri* 11 (1970): 39–71; and "Ira, Cupiditas, Libido: The Dynamics of Human Passion in the Inferno," *Dante Studies* 95 (1977): 1–37. Cesare Vasoli, "Il canto XI dell'*Inferno,*" *L'Alighieri* 33 (1991): 3–22 is strongly inclined toward this interpretation. The core of my critique of other views is that they do not adequately see into how Dante used *Ethics* VII in tandem with key passages in Aristotle's *Rhetoric* and *Politics,* and how they correlate with crucial Ciceronian and Scholastic notions. However, I would add that the partial truth in most of these positions hinges on the simple term "bestial" in its "process" or continuum aspect as a metaphor: for Dante bestiality in descending seriousness underlies the whole *Inferno* and, categorically, the city of Dis, but its terminus in circle nine is "mad bestiality."

On the concept of the "divine man" (in Greek, *theios aner*) in Augustan Rome see Brooks Otis, *Virgil: A Study in Civilized Poetry* (Oxford, 1963), 219–222 ff.

Finally, with regard to the key role of the special natural virtues allied to justice, I submit that the clincher is to be found in a passage in *Paradiso* XVII: lines 61–69. In my "Matta Bestialità in Dante's *Inferno:* Theory and Image" (1968), I pointed out that the only other place in the entire *Comedy* in which Dante uses the adjective *matto* and *bestialità* in close proximity is this tightly woven passage: in delineating Dante's exile, Cacciaguida, Dante's ancestor, predicts that the group of Dante's fellow White Guelphs in exile will show itself to be *tutta ingrata, tutta matta ed empia* ("completely ungrateful, mad and impious" [64]) toward him, and just subsequently (67), that the *bestialitate* of the group will issue in disastrous results for its members. Thus, framing "mad" we have two of the opposites of the chief special natural virtues we have discussed, *gratitudo* and *pietas.* Here Dante refers to the "mad bestiality" of those White Guelphs, who are not merely stupid but also wicked: *la compagnia malvagia e scempia* (62), and he is asserting that they will commit treachery against their *socius.* This interpretation is far more precise than the usual gloss of this passage and makes very good sense once the theory of what underlies circle nine is clear.

CANTO XII

The Violent against Their Neighbors

VITTORIO RUSSO

Translated by Charles Ross

The exordium to Canto XII of the *Inferno* picks up the same narrative situation that occupied the entirety of Canto XI: that is, the pause by Dante the pilgrim and his guide Virgil on the edge of a "high bank" (XI, 1) "formed by a ring of massive broken boulders" (2) that divide the sixth circle from the "deep abyss" (5) of lower Hell from which rises a noxious smell (X, 136) so strong that the travelers draw back and pause on their way until they can accustom themselves to the "outrageous stench / thrown up in excess" (XI, 4–5):

> "It would be better to delay descent
> so that our senses may grow somewhat used
> to this foul stench; and then we can ignore it."
> (XI, 10–12)

Virgil employs the long pause to sketch the moral topography of Hell's interior for his disciple. What is important for the impending resumption of their travels is that Dante and the reader learn from Virgil that the seventh circle encloses those who sin by violence in ways that sort into "three divided rings" (XI, 30), and that the next to be encountered will be the violent against their neighbors and possessions (35).

The representation of the new and horrid scene between the "alpine" bank and the toppled boulders below, traversed by a stream of boiling blood, is central to the story of Canto XII. No direct encounter, no dialogue with the damned immersed in the "bloodred, boiling ditch" (101)—"more cruelly pent" (xi, 3), according to the seriousness of their sin—breaks the absorbed and fearful silence of the protagonist. At first the "high bank," the "cliff" (xi, 1 and 115), on which in the preceding canto Dante and Virgil had paused, comes into focus as they renew their descent and shows itself to be a steep and rocky declivity rendered more fearful by the presence of something or someone whose sight is horrible:

> The place that we had reached for our descent
> along the bank was alpine; what reclined
> upon that bank would, too, repel all eyes.
>
> (1–3)

As the story resumes, the lexical repetition of "bank" recalls the exordium of the preceding canto (the "high bank"), adding a new narrative tension in the announcement of a terrifying but imprecise presence. The reader remains suspended for two successive tercets in which the scene is compared to the geography between Trent and the right bank of the Adige, known for its rock slides:

> Just like the toppled mass of rock that struck—
> because of earthquake or eroded props—
> the Adige on its flank, this side of Trent,
>   where from the mountain top from which it thrust
> down to the plain, the rock is shattered so
> that it permits a path for those above:
>   such was the passage down to that ravine.
>
> (4–10)

Only at this point do we learn that "what reclined" to "repel all eyes" was the Minotaur, the mythical monster born of the union of Pasiphaë, wife of Minos, king of Crete, with a bull. But the seventh circle has not yet revealed its most sinister aspect. Finding a "pass" (26) among the rocks and descending "across that heap / of stones" (28–29), Dante finds himself among a mass of collapsed boulders and sees through the shadows before him a river of boiling blood curving along the plain. This stream is Phlegethon, but Dante will say its name only later (xiv, 130). The damned immersed in it raise a chorus of suffering cries, and along its banks gallop a thick band of Centaurs, more double monsters, whose features are human in the head and chest and equine below, armed with bows and arrows to shoot whoever tries to surface from the red and flaming liquid.

Virgil turns his disciple's attention to this infernal scene, which Dante describes in such calculated fashion, informing him that there dwell the violent against their neighbors:

> But fix your eyes below, upon the valley,
> for now we near the stream of blood, where those
> who injure others violently, boil."
>
> (46–48)

The following tercet reveals Dante's interior turmoil and ethical reaction to what he sees as the reader waits expectantly for a description of the new scene of torment:

> O blind cupidity and insane anger,
> which goad us on so much in our short life,
> then steep us in such grief eternally!
>
> (49–51)

This ethical reflection suggests the fundamental key for interpreting the whole canto—obtuse greed for wordly good, "blind cupidity," prompts people to mad violence, to "insane anger," which receives this punishment after death. At the root of the sins of tyranny, of which those Dante witnesses were guilty, lies avarice directed against those close by. Perfectly suited to the zone of the Inferno reserved for "mad bestiality" are the ancient monsters who guard the abyss and the first category of the damned of the seventh circle—the Minotaur and the Centaurs—because of their bestial and human nature, the principal features of their histories, and the way their animality overwhelms reason (here illustrated by the bestial "fury" of the Minotaur and the sadistic task assigned the Centaurs).

Finally the sinister landscape appears before the amazed eyes of the pilgrim:

> I saw a broad ditch bent into an arc
> so that it could embrace all of that plain,
> precisely as my guide had said before;
> between it and the base of the embankment
> raced files of Centaurs who were armed with arrows,
> as, in the world above, they used to hunt.
>
> (52–57)

As for the monsters, as Virgil soon explains,

> " . . . many thousands wheel around the moat,
> their arrows aimed at any soul that thrusts
> above the blood more than its guilt allots."
>
> (73–75)

The scene Dante has arranged for the ensuing narratives, then, occupies the shadows of hell, in the "dark and deep" "of an abyss, the melancholy valley" (IV, 10 and 8), at the foot of a rocky precipice on a curved plain through which runs a river of red blood whose banks are thronged by multitudes of Centaurs firing their arrows to keep the milling and screaming damned submerged.

The Minotaur lies impacted on the extremity of a "toppled mass" (4) that Dante describes as *rotta lacca* ("cracked abyss" [11]), a very rare rhyme (the other two instances in the *Comedy* are *Inf.* III, 16 and *Purg.* VII, 71) always found, as here, with *fiacca* ("devastates" [17]). Other odd words used to describe the landscape are *burrato* ("ravine" [10]), *scarco* ("heap" [28]), the hapax legomenon *vecchia roccia* ("ancient boulders" [44]) that are "toppled"— and Dante chooses a second word that occurs only here (*fece riverso* [45]). These lexical variations indicate that Dante was searching for rare rhymes and harsh sounds to express the degradation of what he was representing:

> And at the edge above the cracked abyss,
> there lay outstretched the infamy of Crete,
>   conceived within the counterfeited cow;
> and, catching sight of us, he bit himself
> like one whom fury devastates within.
>   (11–15)

The Minotaur of ancient tradition, not named until verse 25, is referred to by a periphrasis based on the nucleus of the mythical legend as Dante would have learned of it from Ovid's *Art of Love,* where Pasiphaë, longing to feel the embrace of a bull, constructs a wooden cow, which she enters to satisfy her perverse desire. Dante chose the gross word *vacca* for cow to suit the other rare and comic rhymes of the canto. It (*vacca*) occurs one other time in the *Comedy,* again in connection with Pasiphaë, in *Purg.* XXVI, 41–42 ("That the bull may hurry toward / her lust, Pasiphaë hides in the cow").

When Pasiphaë bears the Minotaur, the monster is confined to the Labyrinth, a network of inescapable corridors, where it feeds on human flesh, requiring an annual tribute of young men and maidens until Theseus, the son of Egeus of Athens, kills it. Theseus succeeds in entering and leaving the Labyrinth with the help of Ariadne, the daughter of Pasiphaë and Minos—and therefore the half sister of the Minotaur—who gives Theseus a clue of thread to string along the meandering passageways to guide his way out. Virgil alludes to the concluding events of the story when he faces the monster's "inhuman rage" (33):

> Turning to him, my sage cried out: "Perhaps
> you think this is the Duke of Athens here,
>   who, in the world above, brought you your death.

> Be off, you beast; this man who comes has not
> been tutored by your sister; all he wants
> in coming here is to observe your torments."
>
> (16–21)

It is difficult to know if Dante envisaged a man with a bull's head, following the ancient iconographic tradition, or whether he created a bull with a man's head, as the initial description of the creature with its body "outstretched" (12) suggests, a reading supported by its plunging back and forth (24), as if mortally wounded, when Virgil addresses it. Ovid speaks only of a creature half man, half bull (*semibovemque virum, semivirumque bovem*). It is also hard to decide whether the Minotaur should be considered as the guardian of the entire seventh circle or whether like the other mythical demons already encountered "such as Minos, and perhaps Pluto . . . the Minotaur is irreducible to an allegory of a single category of sin." The beast is "the guardian, not of a circle, but of that 'toppled mass' over which one descends to lower Hell" (Sapegno). The image of a "beast" "berserk" (19, 27) or of a being governed solely by "inhuman rage" (33), signals the passage to the deepest zones of Hell, which contain the sins caused by human bestiality that distorts reason and will and operates with "mad bestiality" and "malice."

The Minotaur shares and augments many traits of aggressivity and beastliness common to other infernal demons with classical roots. Like Minos on the edge of the second circle, he gnashes his teeth (v, 4); like Plutus, the "cursed wolf," on the margin of the fourth circle, his rage feeds on itself (vii, 8–9) as he hears the stern words of Virgil. But the Minotaur is more crudely, more realistically described. At the sight of the two intruders, he turns his fury inward: "He bit himself / like one whom fury devastates within" (xii, 14–15). His rage is impotent, as Virgil communicates his and Dante's inexorable progress. He "plunges back and forth" like a bull that has received a mortal stroke just as it "breaks loose from its halter" (*si slaccia*). Favati notes that Dante's verb translates the Latin *solvi,* which Ovid uses as an absolute, in place of the phrase *solvi morte.*

The poet's representation reaches a tone of grotesque tragedy:

> Just as a bull that breaks loose from its halter
> the moment it receives the fatal stroke,
> and cannot run but plunges back and forth,
> so did I see the Minotaur respond.
>
> (22–25)

The comparison has a strong representational function, but it also witnesses the way in which Dante translates and appropriates his classical sources to his own purposes and in his own personal way. The comparison harks back to Virgil's *Aeneid* (*qualis mugitus, fugit cum saucius aram / taurus et inertam excussit cervice securim* [II, 223–24]), "but it also echoes Seneca's *Oedipus*, 341, where it is said of a mortally wounded bull, *huc et huc dubius ruit*" (Russo).

Contini rightly questions the narrativity of the *Comedy* from the moment the outcome of Dante's travel is assured. But the outcome is not known, from the internal viewpoint of the voyages, and there are many moments of impediment caused by external obstacles of fear, weariness, or negligence that gradually give the reader a feeling of narrative tension that creates surprise, curiosity, and attentiveness. At this point, as on other occasions (as in Canto VIII, for example, before the obstacle created by the devils in front of the City of Dis), Virgil himself understands the danger of the circumstances and acutely alerts his disciple to seize the moment of the Minotaur's seizure to slip past and down the valley, even as Dante's weight further disturbs the rubble. This emotional sequence is characterized by a triad of rough rhymes, *varco, scarco, carco*, typical of the canto:

> and my alert guide cried: "Run toward the pass;
> it's better to descend while he's berserk."
>   And so we made our way across that heap
> of stones, which often moved beneath my feet
> because my weight was somewhat strange for them.
>   (26–27)

The apparently superfluous references to the stones that move under Dante's weight will find its purpose in the following narrative when Chiron, the captain of the Centaurs, noticing that Dante "moves what he touches" (81), concludes that he faces a prodigy and so assists Dante's forward voyage.

The difficulty of the passage and the height of the ravine impede progress. Dante is silent, but his mind returns to that other perilous circumstance before the City of Dis when Virgil, to quiet his pupil's fear, mentioned his previous trip to the depths of Hell, soon after his death: directed by the sorceress Erichtho, he had entered to "draw a spirit back from Judas's circle," from whence he can now say, "I know the pathway well" (IX, 22–30). But then, why such uncertainty and surprise before the rocky landslide? Virgil reads Dante's thoughts and explains that "the other time / that I descended into lower Hell, / this mass of boulders had not yet collapsed" (34–36). His entry had been "just before" Christ's descent to Limbo to take "from Dis," from Lucifer, "the highest circle's splendid spoils" (37–39), the soul of Adam and other Old Testament persons who have been gathered into Paradise (as Dante and the reader have already learned from Virgil in Canto IV, 52–56). That is to say, according to the Gospels, at the instant of Christ's death the earth and the "steep and filthy valley" of Hell "trembled" (40–41). *Feda* (filthy) is a hapax and a rare Latinism, "a refined word, which Dante nonetheless felt more accurately expressed crudeness than the corresponding vulgar term," according to Favati. So violent was the earthquake that many believed, as the philosopher Empedocles had held, that all the elements of the universe (fire, air, water, earth), formerly held apart by the power of discord and hatred, were fused together by concord and love, recreating the original Chaos. At that time, "these ancient boulders toppled, in this way" (45). "Here as well as elsewhere" (44), Virgil tells Dante—and we and Dante remember this later, in Cantos xxi–xxii, in the seventh pouch of the eighth circle, when a new impediment and danger (this time caused by the demonic Malebranche during an episode whose dynamic has close affinity to the encounter with the Centaurs) arises because all the bridges passing to the further ditches or pouches are revealed to have been destroyed by this same earthquake, causing the voyagers to "climb" "where its ruins slope along the bank / and heap up at the bottom" (xxiii, 137–138).

Critics have generally found Virgil's discourse excessively long and heavy. But in reality it inserts itself perfectly into the narrative logic of the action, since the descent too takes time, allowing for one of the exegetical moments woven through the poem where the pilgrim/pupil learns doctrine. Bosco believes that this expectant pause separates the Minotaur and his rocks from the ensuing Centaurs, who occupy a different landscape.

The new landscape is "the valley" toward which Virgil urges Dante to turn his eyes as they "near" the river "where those / who injure others violently, boil" (47–48). The passage to the second narrative portion of the canto is signaled by the sequence of scrannel rhymes (*roccia, s'approccia, noccia*) that prefigure motifs of the upcoming river of blood. These rhymes are rare and inevitably linked in the rest of the *Comedy* (*Inf.* vii, 2–6; *Inf.* xxiii, 44–48; *Purg.* xx, 5–9).

The larger more terrifying view that now opens to the sight of the travelers includes the sudden appearance of a multitude of biform monsters, the Centaurs, divided militarily into "files" and "armed with arrows" (56), galloping, as "many thousands wheel around the moat, / their arrows aimed at any soul that thrusts / above the blood more than its guilt allots" (73–75). Pietro Alighieri suggested that his father had in mind as the source for this image of guardians given to continual, cruel punishment those companies of adventurers and bands of mercenaries who infested the countryside of the entire peninsula at the service of various tyrants. Francesco da Buti finds it appropriate that they suffer the same violence they meted out in their lifetimes.

Like the Minotaur, the Centaurs are symbols of human beastliness, and their names are linked. Theseus, who killed the Minotaur, also fought the Centaurs, killing many: "Remember those with double chests, / the miserable ones, born of the clouds, / whom Theseus battled when they'd gorged themselves" (*Purg.* XXIV, 121–23), Dante recalls. On the other hand, as divinely appointed guardians of the violent who sinned against their neighbors, the Centaurs differ from the Minotaur in that they are not beasts dominated by brute fury, but beings possessing both force and intellect, although subject to innate anger and lust, inclined to cruelty and sudden violence, as Ovid portrays them in the *Metamorphoses* (Dante also may have been inspired by the *Achilleid* of Statius and the *Aeneid* of Virgil). Dante could have seen images of the Centaurs in the Florentine baptistery of San Giovanni or at San Miniato al Monte, but it should be recalled, as Fallani observes, that the Centaurs appeared in illustration of battle and fury to the point of madness, as in the medieval scenes in the Duomo of Piacenza and San Zeno in Verona.

Virgil alludes to these events of legend when Nessus, with two of his band, threatens the travelers with a taut bow and Virgil reminds him that his "hasty will has never served [him] well" (66). Once before, when Nessus was carrying Deianira, the wife of Hercules, on his back over a stream, he was seized by a sudden passion for the woman and tried to rape her (but Hercules wounded him with a poison arrow, and he, in revenge gave Deianira a cloak woven with blood and poison, saying that it would make whoever wore it fall in love; Deianira gave it to Hercules to win back his affection, causing his madness and his death):

> "That one is Nessus,
> who died because of lovely Deianira
> and of himself wrought vengeance for himself."
> (67–9)

There follows Pholus, "he who was so frenzied" (72). During the riot of the drunken Centaurs at the wedding of Perithous, he tried to seize the bride and the other women of the Lapiths.

The only one different is Chiron, whom tradition presents as a prestigious teacher, an expert in medicine and music, whose pupils included Achilles (71). He leans his solemn head in thought (70) while Virgil faces the aggression of Nessus, having already taken notice of a living being and realized he is witnessing an exceptional event. He "parted his beard back upon his jaws" (78) with the notch of an arrow, a habitual gesture, to signal his companions that one of the travelers "moves what he touches" (81). Dante makes Chiron less impulsive, more aware and thoughtful than the other Centaurs, traits appropriate to the captain of the bands. He alone merits Virgil's verbal attention: "We shall make reply / only to Chiron" (64–65). He is addressed in a calm and favorable, almost oratorical tone (but not necessarily deferential), when Virgil informs him of the "necessity" (87) of their voyage, explaining to him that a soul in Heaven (Beatrice, as the reader learned in Canto II, but here referred to only by the periphrasis "one / who had just come from singing halleluiah" [88–89]) had entrusted this "new task" (88) to him, prompting him to move his "steps / to journey on so wild a path" (91–92) and to ask Chiron, finally, for help in crossing the river.

Critics have too often made the Centaurs the fulcrum of the canto for aesthetic reasons, as when Momigliano reads their behavior as an illustration of Vico's heroic primitiveness, suited for a decorative fresco; or Pasquini, also inspired by Vico, finds a pride and nobility in these demonic figures; or G. Mazzoni detects a statuary grouping; Bosco finds a triptych with Chiron at the center. Goffis hears in Chiron a dim prefiguration of Statius, in the *Purgatorio,* and Figurelli responds to the episode as an unforeseeable parenthesis of serenity on the banks of the boiling river, so soothing that one may believe oneself no longer present in Hell.

But the intense plasticity is also a sign of realism that goes well beyond mere aesthetic or decorative values, according to Sapegno. The Centaurs, including Chiron, are nothing but "agile beasts" (76), beings with animal features and agile limbs. They are demons—though not grotesquely deformed and tragically ridiculous like the devils of Malebolge, but patterned on the idea of *deformis formositas ac formosa deformitas* (a formula of Romantic art), an ideal contrary to the principles of Bernard of Clairvaux, but in accord with the thought of Hugh of St. Victor and Saint Thomas Aquinas.

Their great physical bulk accentuates the impact of the Centaurs' monstrous animality. Nessus is called a "huge Centaur" (104), and Chiron has an "enormous mouth" and beard (79). Virgil reaches as high as his chest when he speaks to him ("my good guide—now near the Centaur's chest" [83]). That they form disciplined military ranks for the divine purpose of punishing sinners seems to complement their former inclination to blood and violence. Fallani says that they delight in seeing others suffer, a beastly trait, according to Saint Thomas (*Summa* II-II, 159, 2).

When Virgil requests help—not obsequiously, as some critics have claimed, but with the caution proper to the travelers' situation—Chiron turns to his right and orders Nessus (whom Ovid termed *scitus vadorum,* an expert in fords) to guide the pair and to carry Dante "upon his back" (95) over the river, avoiding other banks of Centaurs who might impede their progress:

> Then Chiron wheeled about and right and said
> to Nessus: "Then, return and be their guide;
> if other troops disturb you, fend them off."
> (97–99)

The wise Chiron expresses himself in the low and comic style of a semidemon of Hell. The second narrative portion of this canto concludes with a triad of puerile terms "on account of their simplicity" (*De vulgari elo-quentia* II, vii, 4), again in the rhyme position: *groppa, poppa, intoppa.*

The final portion of the canto opens with the image of a river of boiling blood, announced by Virgil and seen by Dante at a distance, but now here before him in all its horror, including the groans of the damned rising up from their agony:

> Now, with our faithful escort, we advanced
> along the bloodred, boiling ditch's banks,
> beside the piercing cries of those who boiled.
>
> (100–102)

The review (in the words of Nessus) of the violent against their neighbors that concludes the canto has been held to be too cursory and lacking in action for an encounter with dialogue between Dante and a sinner. But a larger narrative purpose justifies this treatment. The protagonist has been silent throughout the canto and now continues speechless, gripped by terror at the sight of the boiling river and the monstrous demons of the seventh circle, as well as intent to register with his eyes what confronts him. He does not even speak to Virgil to express a thought or question. Up to this point Virgil, the teacher, intuits Dante's thoughts and responds to his unexpressed doubts. Here even Virgil is silent. Dante listens to Nessus point out how Obizzo d'Este, lord of Ferrara—among the damned tyrants—was truly killed not, as was believed, by his legitimate son Azzo VIII, who succeeded him to power, but by a bastard son (*figliastro* [112]). Dante then turns an inquiring gaze toward Nessus, perhaps seeking more information, but Virgil cuts him off, signaling for him to listen in silence to what Nessus says ("Now let him be your first guide, me your second" [114]).

The river crossing is brief; the ford "grew always shallower" (124). Nessus explains that the boiling river has varying depths along its course and therefore offers diverse torments according to the category of violence waged against a neighbor by the souls immersed in it and the degree of gravity of their sin, which some have found a commonplace of medieval art (Gmelin, cited by Sapegno). Nessus then indicates a dozen of the damned, without specifying their classification beyond saying they include tyrants. This moral judgment includes past and recent names: Alexander is probably Alexander of Pherae, the tyrant of Thessaly (ca. 368 B.C.). Dionysius, the tyrant of Syracuse, "who brought such years of grief to Sicily" (108), is associated with the former in other medieval texts, including Brunetto Latini's *Livres dou trésor* (II, 119, 6). Ezzelino III da Romano (1194–1259), tyrant of the march of Treviso and leader of the Ghibelline party, made famous for his ferocity by Guelph historiography, appears with his contemporary Obizzo II d'Este, who according to the first book of Salimbene's *Chronicle* conquered his dominion of Ferrara by slaughter and destruction, raped daughters and wives, and had carnal relations with his own sisters and the sister of his wife before he was assassinated as a result of obscure court intrigues.

Among the homicides immersed "as far up as their throats" (117), the Centaur pauses before "one shade" (118) and indicates him by periphrasis: it is Guy de Montfort, viceroy of Charles of Anjou in Tuscany, who, in 1272, to avenge the death of his father (whom Edward I, king of England, had ordered murdered) stabbed with his own hands the king's cousin Henry, whose heart was preserved, according to Giovanni Villani's *Chronicle* (VII, 39), "in a goblet of gold . . . on a column at the foot of London Bridge over the Thames," where it was venerated (*si còla,* from Latin *colere,* the reading of most ancient commentators and the most accepted) or where it dripped blood (*sí cóla,* the suggestive reading of several modern commentators).

The final, rapid list of names of authors of ferocious violence from Attila the Hun to Rinieri da Corneto and Rinieri de'Pazzi, who terrorized the Maremma between Tuscany and the Roman territories, like the brief pause on the other bank, adds to the realism of the scene. What most interested Dante was the almost anonymous image of terrestrial violence, of a world blindly overwhelmed by crime. The river of blood is the tragic confluence where all the abuses and violence of the world disgorge. The list is rapid but sufficient for the pilgrim, who has already learned from his guide whom the first ring of the seventh circle punishes—murderers and plunderers and robbers (XI, 37–39).

Typical of Dante's extraordinary technique is the representation of Ezzelino and Obizzo by means of a contrast between the one's dark and the other's blonde hair, set against the river of red blood (109–111). The two tyrants are totally immersed in blood, just as they were in life. Their faces don't show, just their hair (Dante uses the term *pelo,* as if they were beasts) and foreheads, which suffice to identify them. Raimondi finds not just an antipathy on Dante's part for the Este, but for the whole region of the Po. Dante's vocabulary contributes to the violence of these souls, as when he identifies the Tuscan brigands: there, divine justice torments and "milks" (*munge,* an expressive and ironic word) them:

> it milks the tears that boiling brook unlocks
> from Rinier of Corneto, Rinier Pazzo,
> those two who waged such war upon the highroads.
> (136–138)

Boiling, cooking, immersion—these are the terms of violence that characterizes this zone and echo the contemporary chronicles and, more obliquely, the suffering of Dante due to the degradation of civil life during his lifetime.

The canto concludes with the image of Nessus retracing his steps along the river till he finds the ford ("Then he turned round and crossed the ford again" [139]). This last glimpse foregrounds the bestial, biform, equine nature of the Centaur. The term *guazzo* (ford) that ends the last verse also complements the comic hapax *Pazzo,* which occurs elsewhere only in *Inf.* XXI, 123, a canto with close ties and a similar narrative dynamic to this one, as analyzed by Sacchetto.

In the critical history of this canto there are those who appreciate its unity and style, but most are inclined to isolate the episode of the Centaurs as the single moment of artistic success. It seems impossible to call this a mere canto of transition, given the structure and expressive language this essay has revealed. One hesitates to yield to the voices that find a "disharmony of tone and inspiration," a "discontinuous narrative line" "unequal to the style and expression" (Figurelli), undermined by "numerous atonalities" (Favati), or even the soul of the poet in his representation of the Centaurs.

The silence of the central hero, the horror of the scene, the presence of inhuman monsters, the search for a more adequate mode of expression between harshness and comedy—these are the narrative instruments by which Dante happily represents the first anxious impact of lower Hell on the protagonist, at the same time introducing the reader to the more complex themes of the ensuing stories and their ethical significance.

BIBLIOGRAPHICAL NOTES

On Dante's appropriation of classical sources and the presence of the medieval romance element of surprise in the narrative plot of the poem, as well as the medieval aesthetic of *formosa deformitas,* see my "Virgilio autore di Dante," *Annali della Facoltà di lettere e filosofia dell'Università di Napoli,* n.s., 11 (1980–1981): 93–113, and *Il romanzo teologico: Sondaggi sulla "Commedia" di Dante* (Naples, 1984), 13–30, 102–104.

On the representation of the Minotaur and the Centaurs, see C. Grabher, "Mostri e simboli nell'*Inferno* dantesco," *Annali della Facoltà di lettere e filosofia dell'Università di Cagliari* 22 (1953): 2, 14–15; P. Renucci, *Dante disciple et juge du monde gréco-latin* (Paris, 1954), 225–228; A. Ronconi, "Per Dante interprete dei poeti latini," *Studi danteschi* 41 (1964): 19–20; and the articles by Manlio Pastore Stocchi and G. Izzi in *Enciclopedia dantesca.*

For the *slavini di Marco* (the landslides of Marco), see E. Lorenzi, *La "ruina" di qua da Trento* (Trent, 1896) and *La leggenda di Dante nel Trentino* (Trent, 1897).

For the identification of Alexander, see Umberto Bosco, "Particolari danteschi, *Inferno* XII, 107," *Annali della Scuola Normale Superiore di Pisa,* 2d s., 5–11 (1952): 131–147. For Ezzelino da Romano and Obizzo d'Este and their times, see V. Fainelli, "L'Azzolino dantesco," *Giornale dantesco* 16 (1908): 230–235; R. Manselli, "Ezzelino da Romano nella politica italiana del sec. XIII," in *Studi ezzeliniani* (Rome, 1963); G. Arnaldi, *Studi sui cronisti della Marca Trevigiana nell'età di Ezzelino da Romano* (Rome, 1963); J. K. Hyde, *Padua in the Age of Dante: A Social History of an Italian City State* (Manchester, 1966); G. De Leva, "Gli Estensi recordati dall'Alighieri," in *Dante e Padova* (Padua, 1865); I. Del Lungo, "Dante e gli Estensi," in *Dante ne' tempi di Dante* (Bologna, 1888); T. Sandonnini, "Dante e gli Estensi," *Atti e Memorie di storia patria per le province modenesi,* 4th s., 4, no. 4 (1893). Above all see E. Raimondi, "L'aquila e il fuoco di Ezzelino," in *Metafora e storia: Studi su Dante e Petrarca* (Turin, 1970), 123–130 (formerly titled "Dante e il mondo ezzeliniano," in *Dante e la cultura veneta* [Florence, 1966]).

For the debate on *sì cóla,* see Petrocchi's edition.

Useful readings of the entire canto include Guido Mazzoni's 1906 lectura published in *Lectura Dantis Sansoni* (Florence, 1925) and *Almae luces: Malae cruces,* ed. N. Zanichelli (Bologna, 1941); Umberto Bosco's lectura, included among his "Tre letture dantesche" (1942), in *Letture dantesche: Inferno,* ed. Giovanni Getto (Florence, 1955), 211–219 (reprinted also in *Dante vicino,* 237–254); A. Sacchetto, *Dieci letture dantesche* (Florence, 1960); F. Figurelli, in *Lectura Dantis Scaligera* (Florence, 1962) and in *Letture classensi* (Ravenna, 1967), 394–419; G. Favati, "Osservazioni sul canto XII dell'*Inferno* dantesco," in *Studi in onore di Italo Siciliano* (Florence, 1966), 423–436; and G. Fallani, in *Nuove letture dantesche* (Florence, 1968), 2:17–31. More recently, see C. F. Goffis, in *Lectura Dantis Neapolitana* (Naples, 1981), 5–24, and V. Sermonti's elegant exposition in *L'"Inferno" di Dante* (Milan, 1988), 171–180.

CANTO XIII

The Violent against Themselves

GIORGIO PETROCCHI

Translated by Charles Ross

"*Canto thirteen, which treats the second ring of the seventh circle, where the violent against themselves are punished, both those who kill themselves and those who squander their possessions.*" So says the ancient rubric of the so-called type *a*, found in Trivulziano 1080 and many other Florentine manuscripts.

In the transition from the boiling stream of blood in the preceding canto to an arid, smooth, and silent landscape in Canto XIII, there lies a countryside compared to the wild Maremma and echoing the robber baron of Corneto (*Inf.* XII, 137) and the wasteland bordered by Cécina and Corneto (XIII, 8). Dante uses his lexical and onomotopoetic skills to bring imitation to a new level. His "wood," "no path," "black" leaves, branches "knotted, gnarled," "briars bearing poison," and "holts so harsh and dense" reveal a radical determination to overcome the example of high tragedy in the third book of the *Aeneid*. The process of emulation (Virgil's *clangoribus* becomes Dante's laments and cries) permits a lowering of tone and, with regard to the figure of Virgil, the knowledge that reality is superior to its representation: "you'll see such things / as would deprive my speech of all belief" (XIII, 21). This canto's connection back to the boiling brook of blood and forward to the burning sands creates an extensive area of imitation, from evocations of Ovid's Daphne and Driope to Virgil's Polydorus, although it lacks reference to Celenus's prophecy of the protagonist's future sufferings, which already featured in Canto X, when Farinata tells Dante he will "learn how heavy is that art" of returning to Florence from exile (X, 81).

The displacement of prophecy has point, because the distance is short between Farinata's pronouncement and the affirmation of an exemplary case of heroic, valorous, but unrecognized loyalty shown by Pier delle Vigne. Foreseeing exile, Dante expresses its cause, ingratitude, and its effect, the abandonment of all friendships and the unbreakable bond between the personalities of men and political misfortune. Nonetheless he varies the ethical and psychological situation: Pier delle Vigne offers an *exemplum* of eternal condemnation, whereas Polydorus receives compensation for his violent murder by Polymnestor.

This variation is brought about by the attentuation of one of the peculiarities of the narrative voice, the first-person speaker, who does not parley with Virgil or with the shades until halfway through the canto, at line 82, and only in that tercet. The representation moves from the fantastic to the ambiguously symbolic, filling the Virgilian setting with a rich texture of allegorical figures. The mood of Virgil's episode is mysterious and prophetic, however broadened by its narrative character. Dante's offers the aesthetic experience of sin—rather, of two different and opposed sins. Dante also requires us to penetrate what Momigliano called the *chiaroscuro* of his "tragic scene," beyond the troublesome zone of silence in the incipit and into the moaning wood, in order to evaluate the nature of his undertaking. His purpose is to conjoin political and cultural history as he does by selecting an emblematic figure from the imperial court. Dante becomes another Virgil as he updates this classical borrowing. His task is to describe the journey not of a hero who must find a new homeland, but of a soul seeking to reach the heavenly kingdom that his Christian faith assures him is tangible and attainable.

Spitzer's 1942 essay, which did not appear until 1959 ("Speech and Language in *Inferno* XIII," in *Romanische Literaturstudien: 1936–1956*), marks a clear division in the critical history of the canto. We must remember that if a new wave of Dante exegesis began forty years ago, after the Florentine "readings" and the interpretation of Croce and Vossler in the wake of the celebrated pages of De Sanctis, the most recent studies have taken up the question of whether the words of Pier delle Vigne form the heart of the canto, or whether the canto has its own complete, organic, and unified structure. Certainly what Contini calls the technique of individual characterization by means of rhetorical style finds its prime example in the words of Pier delle Vigne, but it would be useless to make a clear distinction between his speech and that of his dialogic opponent Virgil. It matters little whether the other main speaker, the anonymous Florentine suicide, be Lotto degli Agli or Rocco de' Mozzi, since the purpose of the passage is to portray an "eloquent" Florentine living between 1280 and 1290, the generation before Dante. As we said, Dante speaks only one insignificant tercet in this canto. As a result the linguistic contract of the canto is struck between two literary men, first Virgil and Pier delle Vigne—from Capua, as Virgil was said to be of Naples because he died there—and then between a master of absolute linguistic coherence and a figure of minor importance in the Florence of the late thirteenth century.

The question of the sin of suicide maintains an ideological tension throughout the canto, but there are coordinates differentiated by the way the *viator* participates, brought out by variations in the fearful figures of the landscape that personifies and makes visual the sin; by attention to the rhetorical and stylistic bipolarity of the "briers bearing poison," the "holts so harsh and dense," the "foul Harpies," their "great bellies," and "strange trees"; by Pier's human cry, complaint, and commiseration for himself; by the fear of Dante (who himself stands for a being of fear and trembling); by his reexperiencing of Pier delle Vigne's loyalty and illusion; by the sudden onset of despair; by the gentility of Pier's almost courtly demeanor toward the guide of the man who has hurt him by breaking off a branch ("Your sweet speech draws me so" [55]); and by the inevitable arrival of catastrophe. We find at this stage of the *Inferno* a peculiar system of alternations in the emotional overtones among the violent. There are negative characters (Attila, Pyrrhus, Sextus, Rinieri da Corneto, Rinieri de'Pazzi) and positive ones (here, the chancellor of Frederick II). There are images of strong moral repulsion despite their titanic aspects (Capaneus). There are noble figures (Brunetto Latini, the three Florentine knights). The result is a type of grandiose hyperbole in the structure of the circle in which the sequence continually alters from disdain to respect, execration to piety. Each offers a different valence, the changing forms of *exemplaria,* based on a constant play of classical or scriptural, ancient or modern *auctores* (the symbolism of the tree of evil, a painful echo of the tree of Judas, the explicit reference to the Day of Judgment—in short, the complex figuration of a symbolic landscape counterposed or conjoined with the realism of a forest), in such a way as not to contradict theological coherence. Dante invents the idea that suicides will be excluded from the resurrection of the flesh and combines two moments of orthodoxy and singularity into a single circumstance of moral topography, drawing on the suicide of Judas, which Resta regarded as one of the foundations of Christian history, the "first suicide of a man who knew Christ's word and despaired, creating what was taken as an archetypal configuration of Christian suicide," and which filtered through medieval legends to create "an iconographic flowering that pictured a lifeless body hanging from a sterile, withered tree."[1]

The jurist Pier delle Vigne—judge, canon lawyer, and what today we would call "administrator"—interested Dante beyond his role in the imperial chancellery and as agent for the foreign affairs of Frederick II, which involved a series of diplomatic assignments certainly well known to Dante, especially as regarded the papal court and the court of Paris. Dante's Pier was *imperialis aulae protonotarius et regni Siciliae logotheta,* protonotary of the imperial court and orator of the kingdom of Sicily. He was subject to the burdens that directly touched the internal affairs of the emperor, a fiduciary responsibility that corresponded with terms of friendly solidarity, and was destined to be upset when his duties were stripped away while the court was in Cremona in February 1249. He was imprisoned and blinded. The orator's suffering under torture led him to suicide. Although Dante regarded his deed as a moral protest by one overwhelmed by injustice and ingratitude, the real cause of Pier's suicide was his resolution to spare himself the physical pain of bodily torments even worse than his blindness.

We do not know which of the various accounts of Pier delle Vigne's suicide Dante judged the most accurate, but the chancellor's strong moral discourse seems to privilege accounts of the public spectacle carried out as a bitter protest before Frederick II, in which Pier jumps from a window of his house in Capua just as Frederick and his retinue are passing in the street below. For Dante, influenced by the *vox publica* and written tradition (as registered by Salimbene and in the Ricordiano Malispini), Pier's action proclaimed his innocence. Modern historians from Hampe to Kantorowicz to Baethgen have not altered the fundamental picture of Dante's episode.

The chancellor and the man of letters are intertwined in the process of physical and linguistic creation. Pier delle Vigne marshaled all the skills of the *ars dictandi* in his letters. He was also a poet, although we have no certainty that Dante knew this. As a symbolic figure of eloquence in the first kingdom of the otherworld, Pier forgets the echoes of Latin songs and Sicilian lyrics, which in any case are not easily transferable to the level of comic and tragic discourse prevalent in Dante's Florentine poetry. Instead he evokes the memory of courtly prose. If the application of the *ars* of the chancery to the speech of Pier's character was made possible by effective citation (by appropriating some vocabulary to give a "voice" to the chancellor, just as Farinata has the "voice" of a politician and Brunetto that of a professor of rhetoric and philosophy), I do not see what part of the Latin or vulgate poetry of Pier might have been appropriated to testify to his taste for versification. There were too many other features for Dante to pack into his portrait, especially the political quality of his *pietà* (84). We will soon see if the sign of the "pity" reveals a partial autobiographical identification. Here we must underscore the valorization by De Sanctis of the "fantastic" and the "pathetic," unified by an urge to create a "great man" ("pity derives from a deeper source. It is an entirely human pity . . . . It is a pity that has its roots in the situation itself, whoever the man might be who speaks"). It is evident that the pronouncements of De Sanctis on the "single" humanity of Pier delle Vigne are insufficient, as when he suggests that the essence of his humanity is his memory. A noteworthy progression was identified by Novati and Parodi: "realism" is a precise element that imposes the necessity of recuperating the entire theological structure of the episode as a moral *exemplum* for Dante the pilgrim. This realism gives Dante the poet the extraordinary possibility of turning his admiring but inquisitorial scrutiny toward the imperial court where *Fredericus cesar* showed his *nobilitatem ac rectitudinem,* as Dante called it in his *De vulgari eloquentia.* He and Manfred, when both were alive, were *brutalia didignantes,* and they gathered together men worthy of them, *corde nobiles atque gratiarum dotati* (*De vulgari eloquentia* I, xii, 4). Dante remembered a fleeting impression of the difficult figure of the chancellor, outstanding among the *excellentes animi Latinorum* at the court among other philosophers, poets, and jurists.

Dante's undoubtedly negative judgment of the imperial court, his critical perspective of Frederick II's *modus agendi,* makes it possible to hypothesize the existence in Canto XIII of the same bipolarity that operates so effectively in Canto x. Here too the portrait of Dante is that of a Guelph, who *must* find fault with the imperial milieu in order to promote the superiority of the free life of a citizen of the Commune and to emphasize the scandalous intrigues of Frederick, "who was so worthy" (XIII, 75). But at that period (circa 1306) Dante was deep in a different political situation. He had been cordially received at the Scagliger court in Verona and had turned his back on that wicked company (*compagnia malvagia e scempia* [*Par.* XVII, 62]). He no longer saw the world through the eyes of a popular militant living in the spring of 1306. He had evolved the dream of a political situation that sought to reproduce the results of five years earlier, this time from the vantage (we know it was only illusory) of an aspect of human justice beyond universal peace, in which episodes of the kind suffered by Pier delle Vigne would not have been more than an exception, an unfortunate ransom for the happiness of the human race. Still, the guidelines of Dante's poetic fiction did not allow him to omit, in the necessary selection of possible protagonists, a case so worthy of being held up as a most eloquent counterpoint and motive for condemnation, with Farinata, of Frederick II. The emperor's heretical abandonment of the path of Christian virtue involved as much the vice of reason as a repudiation of the strict human instruction to love one's neighbor. Dante spares Frederick as a monarch at the moment he condemns him as a heretic. He makes him an observer but not the cause of his loyal follower's misfortune. If we consider the relative closeness of x, 119, and XIII, 64–69, it appears that Dante wished to make himself the historian but not the judge of the monarch and his chancellor, who for different but not opposed motives were both guilty before God, although neither was guilty toward the other.

The pity of Virgil—or if we prefer, of Aeneas—for Polydorus is perhaps upset by a severer feeling that results not from the bitter consequence of suicide as much as the prideful rejection of life in the name of personal dignity. It is disputable whether the ideals of Dante and Pier coincide, as a glint of that autobiographical projection throughout the poem so legitimately made evident by Olschki and by Bosco, who argues that Dante identified with Pier's loyalty. We might add that the figure sketched in the otherworld and profiled on earth shows loyalty—unfortunate and seriously sidetracked, but constant in life and in death, in youth and, at the last moment, publicly advertising his virtue and rendering it sacrosanct and elevated by the sacrifice of his own soul, whose damnation serves as a warning to others at the instant it becomes a personal holocaust to eradicate or proclaim the results of the calumny that hurt him and still hurts him. His suicide minimizes the good he did during thirty years of service to his lord. Bosco also reminds us of Romeo of Villeneuve (*Par.* VI, 127), who saved himself by voluntary exile: *alter Dante* in a more direct way, but in a sense anticipated by Pier delle Vigne, just as many of the damned prefigure, despite the different destinies of their souls, ethical-political situations exalted in the *Paradiso*.

The undoubted narrative jump in the second part of the canto is merely the result of the expository flow. It creates no break in the canto's unity (the unity of the moral system and literary function), substituting for laments a "roar" (111), for the immobility of trees the crashing as if of a boar chase (a third reference to the Maremma?), for the rotund rhetoric of the chancellor's discourse the fragmentation of a scene broken by the fury of beaters and dogs and enriched by the elision of the phrase touching the greyhounds ("he hears / the beasts" [113–114] rather than "hears the baying of the hounds"). Nonetheless the most significant narrative invention derives not from the direct and solitary colloquium with another shade—with a spendthrift after a suicide—but from the appearance of another suicide who comments on the savage pursuit of the spendthrifts and complains of being wracked as a shrub, when the shade vainly hides in him, and of being torn by those "black bitches . . . just as eager and swift / as greyhounds that have been let off their leash" (124–126). Suicides destined to immobility, spendthrifts to convulsions and laceration—in this contrast between stasis and flight lies all the picturesque inventiveness of a hunting scene: the surprise of the pilgrim-poet is equally distributed onto the identity of the two runners, Lano (da Siena) and Jacopo da Santo Andrea, and onto the shade, not directly identified, submerged in the shrub. The contrast between a tree and a bush perhaps emphasizes the importance of Pier delle Vigne with respect to the Florentine, as the public nature of the former's invitation to suicide compares to the private action of one considered as a man who either destroyed his potential or gave false counsel. If we consider the geographical provenance of the two pairs, a "southerner" and a Florentine, one from Siena and one from Padua, the representation strongly underscores the diverse origins and different characterization of the figures, even with regard to internal connections. Jacopo da Santo Andrea was also a follower of Frederick II, and Messer Lotto (if that's who it is) was captain of the guard at Cremona and Modena, podestà at Trento and at Cremona, and in command not far from the country of the dissipated victim of the fury of Ezzelino da Romano. Rocco de' Mozzi would provide a suggestive opening into the difficult life of Florentine bankers in France and England and would shift the suicide to Paris, accounting for the Gallicism of *gibetto* or *giubetto* (151). Nonetheless the Florentine nature of the last scene seemed indubitable to Boccaccio himself: "In that era, as if one city was cursed by God, many hung themselves." This perspective permits us to reevaluate the *explicit* to Canto XIII in terms of the strong patriotic emotion roused in Dante by such a bitter picture of the unfortunate customs and events of his city.

Dissipation is a sin different from prodigality, which is punished as we know in the fourth circle, where no one is named and where the watchword, "Why do you squander?" (VII, 30), is the prodigals' only sign of identification. The difference between the two sins is that the loss of the former is the loss of one's possessions, where that of the latter is the loss of oneself. This distinction might appear too subtle even to a contemporary of Dante, if he did not accept the suicidal aspect by drawing a reference from medieval legendaries. Even here Dante varies his stylistic method: classical in the first part, medieval in the hunt through hell.

The transition from the imperial court to Florence occurs almost spontaneously on the emotional level: the statue of Mars, the reference to the Ponte Vecchio, the anonymity of the speaker that seems to lead the exile's mind back to the land of his city, where he searches for someone whom he wants to be undetermined, for the "house" that he holds in his memory (XIII, 151). The reference to the Baptist does not omit to conjure the baptistery—"my handsome San Giovanni" (XIX, 17). The culmination is a glimpse of someone suspended in the heart of Florence—alone, tragic, horrible. The close of the canto holds up for a moment the silent specter of the scaffold, a perennial offense to Dante's city and an intolerable sight to the imagination. An instant before the incipit to Canto XIV evokes the silent emotion of Dante's love of his homeland, the stillness of the poet is released by a fraternal movement toward a despairing fellow citizen who desperately has asked that there be an end to the "outrageous laceration" (140)—inhuman, devastating, and unjust.

NOTE

1. G. Resta, "Il canto XIII dell'*Inferno*," in *"Inferno": Letture degli anni 1973–1976*, ed. Silvio Zennaro (Rome, 1977), 335–336.

CANTO XIV

Capaneus and the Old Man of Crete

JOHN A. SCOTT

The canto is an outstanding example of the importance of classical myth and its fusion with biblical elements and moral themes in Dante's poem. Before we consider the canto overall—in its main themes—a line-by-line analysis will highlight details of structural or linguistic interest.

1–3: like Cantos VI and IX, Canto XIV opens with a backward-glancing reference to the narrative: in this case, to the anonymous Florentine suicide who had entreated the pilgrims to gather the torn branches and place them at the foot of the bush in which his soul is imprisoned (XIII, 139–142). In an instinctive reaction foreshadowing Sordello's in the next canticle (*Purg.* VI, 71–75), Dante, fired by love of his native city, complies with the sinner's request—a gesture of compassion in clear contrast with the pilgrim's behavior in nether Hell (*Inf.* XXXIII, 148–150). The poet, however, specifies that he was moved not by pity for the individual but by his love for Florence. He uses the verb *stringere* (literally "to clasp"), part of the vocabulary of the courtly love lyric (cf. *Inf.* V, 128; *Rime* LXVIII, 33; XCI, 34; *Vita nuova* XIII, 5).

4–6: the significance of the number three, basic to the *Comedy*'s structure, alerts readers that we are entering the section where violence against God is punished. In the phrase "dread work that justice had devised" the poet creates a virtual oxymoron to make readers aware of the horrendous spectacle of God's justice at work. Leaving aside all aesthetic connotations, the word *arte* normally evokes wonder and satisfaction at the skill employed and the effects produced; here both wonder and horror are surely intended.

7–9: the epithet *nove* here means "unknown," possibly "horrific" in total contrast with its meaning in the title *Vita nuova* (cf. *Inf.* XIII, 73). Notice the rhetorical emphasis of *dico che* ("I declare unto you" [33]) and the utter sterility of this desert landscape reflecting the wasteland of the spirit after the unnatural vegetation in the wood of the suicides.

10–12: this tercet encapsulates three landmarks of Dante's underworld: the wood of the suicides, which is encircled by the river of blood of the tyrants and itself encircles the wasteland of the violent against God and nature. By this narrative flashback, the poet sets the scene ever more firmly in the reality described.

13–15: the wasteland is anchored to a precise historical and geographical context. It is an exact replica of the Libyan desert crossed by Cato and described with horrific details by Lucan in his *Pharsalia* (IX, 377–941). Notice the striking use of alliteration spaced out in the first line (*spazzo . . . spessa*) and interspersed with assonance (*era . . . rena . . . arida*), concentrated in the middle of the second line (*foggia fatta*), and leading up to the plosive force of *piè . . . soppressa*.

16–18: early commentators were quick to point out the theological absurdity of speaking of God's justice and punishments as his "revenge," thus attributing "passions" to the godhead. They ignored Deuteronomy 32:35 ("Revenge is mine, and I will repay them in *due* time" [cf. *Epistola* VI, 1]), as well as the essential link with Capaneus's boast in line 60. From the outset, the poet makes it clear that God's retribution has overcome these sinners. The apostrophe may be taken as a variant on the poet's addresses to the reader; *manifesto* emphasizes the reality of the revelation (cf. *Par.* XXX, 95–96).

19–30: all the sinners in the *Inferno* are naked (except the hypocrites), but the poet stresses their nudity whenever this makes them more vulnerable (III, 65; VII, 111; XIII, 116; XVIII, 25). First, the poet describes the blasphemers who lie supine gazing at the heavens toward which they had raised their faces in rebellion; the usurers are seated motionless, as they had remained at their counting desks, spurning labor and creative activity; the sodomites are driven into perpetual motion, reminiscent of the whirlwind of lust in *Inf.* v, 31–33. Moralists denounce the frequency of homosexuality, while the blasphemers' utterances reflect both their misuse of the faculty of speech ("granted to humanity alone" [*De vulgari eloquentia* I, ii–iii]) and their greater suffering. This is the only instance where the poet seems to have broken the rule that the sins and punishments in Hell intensify as the narrative proceeds. Here, those guilty of sinning directly against God are encountered *before* those who had sinned against God's offspring, nature. Dante extends to the blasphemers and usurers the punishment of fire meted out to the perverted inhabitants of Sodom and Gomorrha (Genesis 19:24). The surprise expressed by scholars that the poet did not work out a more specific form of *contrapasso* for each sin is in itself surprising, when one remembers the unifying concept painstakingly expressed in *Inf.* XI, 46–51. It is also possible that the poet was inspired by Jude 7–8: "As Sodom and Gomorrha . . . were made an example, suffering the punishment of eternal fire. In like manner these men also defile the flesh, and despise dominion, and blaspheme majesty." Dante emphasizes the unnatural element that characterizes blasphemy, sodomy, and usury, because the fire falls from heaven (28–29), whereas it is in its nature to rise upwards (cf. *Par.* XXIII, 40–42). The image in line 30 is found in Cavalcanti's sonnet "Biltà di donna" (*e bianca neve scender senza venti*) and Dante's own *Rime* (C, 20–21, *e cade in bianca falda / di fredda neve*); but here the chromatic element is gone, the *cader lento*, the inversion and rallentando vowel music of *di foco dilatate falde*, the predominance of disyllables in line 30, all convey the ineluctable silent descent of the torment.

31–39: Dante drew his (mis)information for this comparison from Albertus Magnus's *De meteoris* I, iv, 8, where he read that in India, Alexander the Great had ordered his men to stamp upon clouds of fire that fell from the skies like snow. The reinforcement of *sanza* by *mai* is made all the more effective by the inversion of the normal word order in line 40 and the enjambment between 40 and 41, the latter verse containing strong alliteration (*misere mani . . . quindi . . . quinci*) and leading to the cruel irony of *arsura fresca* in line 42. The *tresca* of line 40 was a dance, whose movements evoked the sinners' frenetic attempts to protect themselves from the fire.

43–48: Dante's reminder of Virgil's inability to overcome the hostility of the devils guarding the City of Dis (*Inf.* VIII, 82–126) may strike the reader as tactless pedantry on the pilgrim's part; his present question, however, is well within Virgil's competence. The great physical stature of the silent soul lying stretched out on the burning sand, and whom the rain of fire does not seem to touch, attracts Dante's attention.

49–60: the blasphemer is Capaneus (63), one of the seven kings who went to the aid of Polynices against Thebes. In the *Thebaid,* Statius describes his immense strength and physical courage. The first to scale the walls of Thebes, Capaneus challenges Bacchus, Hercules, and Jove to save their cherished city; the latter strikes him with a thunderbolt, as Capaneus continues to express defiance. Here, Capaneus fulfills his whole raison d'être in a final blasphemy, a senseless act of defiance against the supreme ruler of the universe. The oxymoron *vivo . . . morto* in line 51 condenses his whole spiritual drama in one act of rebellion that continues for all eternity.

52: Jove's smith is Vulcan, who with the help of the Cyclops (*li altri* [55]) forged the god's thunderbolts in the bowels of Mount Etna (Mongibello [56]) and thus helped Jove to defeat the Titans at the battle of Phlegra (similarly recalled by Statius at the moment of Capaneus's defeat, *Thebaid* XI, 7 ff.). Capaneus's boast that Jove will never be able to taste sweet vengeance reflects his anthropomorphic vision, which can only conceive God's justice in terms of human emotions and has already been contradicted in line 16. The complex period of nine verses (52–60) is skillfully structured to express Capaneus's ravings, with its crescendo leading to the egocentric climax; *e me saetti* (Jove, victor of the Titans, is now faced with a single opponent [59]), followed by the ninth line with its double consonants hammering out the damned soul's absurd boast.

61–75: Capaneus's violence brings out Virgil's moral strength (N.B., *forza . . . forte* [61–62]). The most deeply religious of the ancient poets gives a theological commentary on Capaneus's sin. The fact that pride still devours him is his greatest punishment. His madness can best be punished through its own rage, of which he is the only victim, while his condition illustrates the axiom that a soul possesses for all eternity whatever it chose at the moment of death. The reference to Capaneus's kingship in line 68 may alert the reader to Dante's pronouncements on the duties and responsibilities of his office (e.g., *Par.* xviii, 91–93) and to the fact that the other great sinner chosen from classical antiquity for the *Inferno* was also a king (Ulysses, *Inf.* xxvi). Virgil's reference to God in lines 69–70 is another, blinding example of Dante's syncretism. On the one hand, the Christian poet does not hesitate to denounce the "false and lying gods" of the ancient Romans (*Inf.* i, 72); on the other, he associates ancient divinities with the angelic intelligences that govern the various heavens (*Convivio* ii, iv, 1–7), as though the pagan Romans had glimpsed part of the Christians' truth. In fact, the Christian poet who was bold enough to refer to Christ as "supreme Jove" (*Purg.* vi, 118) judges a pagan by the laws and religious *numina* he knew and should have revered. Capaneus is therefore damned for his impious rebellion against God, known to him under the mask of Jove. In the *Comedy* he is the antithesis of Cato (*Purg.* i, 31–108; ii, 118–123), who (Lucan, *Pharsalia* ix, 580) had affirmed the ubiquity of God's presence (see *Epistola* x, 22). Ripheus, too, is saved because of his love of justice (*Par.* xx, 67–69; *Aeneid* ii, 426–427). Dante, who had described God as *segnore de la giustizia* in *Vita nuova* xxviii, 1 and who referred to himself as a "man preaching justice" in *Epistola* ix, 3, condemns the pagan king who had despised both religion and justice, according to Statius (*Thebaid* iii, 602: *Superum contemptor et aequi impatiens*). Readers will note the *adnominatio* in lines 71–72 (*dispetti . . . petto*), the use of the same rhymes as in *Inf.* vii, 5–7–9, and viii, 47–49–51, as well as the irony in the "ornaments" that should be part of a king's regalia (72).

The end of Virgil's speech pinpoints the halfway mark in a canto 142 lines long, in which the first half is devoted to the violent, the second to the problem of the origin and course of the rivers of Hell. Similar introductions to both halves affirm the canto's symmetry: the narrative tercets of lines 4–6 and 76–78, paralleled by Virgil's injunctions to the pilgrim in lines 73–75 and 139–142.

76–84: the red waters of the stream, reminiscent of the blood shed by tyrants and murderers, glow against the dark wood and the red of the burning desert. The Bulicame (79) is a hot spring near Viterbo (its name already used to describe the boiling waters in *Inf.* XII, 117 and 128). Fazio degli Uberti (*Il dittamondo* III, x, 61–66) claims that its waters were so hot that they could cook a sheep in less time than it takes a man to walk a quarter of a mile. The poet refers to the prostitutes' custom of sharing the sulfurous hot water by having it piped to their houses (80), while his narrative realism leads him to point out that the sides of the stream were made of stone—a detail that will allow Dante and Virgil to walk above the burning sands (*Inf.* XV, 1–3). An interesting linguistic detail is provided by Guido da Pisa, who points out that the form *lici* ("there" [84]) is peculiar to Florentine speech (*Expositiones*, 272).

85–93: Virgil's insistence on the stream's notability has provoked considerable debate. Some have taken it to refer to its ability to extinguish the flames, thus making possible the pilgrims' progress. However, Dante's eagerness to know more (91–93) is satisfied by Virgil's account of the common origin of all the infernal waters (and not of their effects). The poet draws the reader's attention to the grandiose myth illustrating the source—both literal and figurative—of the souls' suffering in Hell. This is to be found in the effects of original sin, which produce the mortal sins that lead souls to Hell and create the misery caused by such sins—a truth magnificently illustrated by the myth of the old Man of Crete, which now occupies one-third of the canto.

94–102: the island of Crete was, for the ancients and Dante, at the center of the earth, located in the "middle of the sea" (*Aen.* III, 104), "the sea" whose name—Mediterranean—reflected its central position in the known world. "Cradle of the human race" (*Aen.* III, 104), under Saturn, its first king, it knew total innocence, an age of gold celebrated especially by Ovid in his *Metamorphoses* (I, 89–112; cf. *Purg.* XXVIII, 139–144; *Par.* XXI, 25–27). It may be noted that the homonym of Crete in Italian (*creta*) denotes clay, indicative of that primal substance from which God created Adam (Genesis 2:7), yet another detail adding substance to classical myth for the Christian poet. The chiasmus (*fu già . . . già fu* [96–97]) emphasizes not only the opposition but also the remoteness of the Golden Age, contrasted with the present desolation (99). Rhea, wife of Saturn, hid her son Jove on Mount Ida, in order to save him from his father, who had learned that he would be supplanted by one of his children and had determined to devour each one as it was born. So that Saturn should not hear the infant's cries, Rhea ordered her priests, the Curetes, to clash their weapons (100–102).

103–120: these eighteen verses hold the core of Dante's great myth. Inside Mount Ida stands a tall old man (*grande* is used to describe both Capaneus and the Old Man), who turns his back on Damietta and looks toward Rome. Damietta (104) is situated on the eastern point of the Nile's delta. Many commentators have seen in this detail an indication of civilization's progress from east to west, the *translatio imperii* whereby supreme power and empire were transferred from the Assyrians to the Romans. The true destiny of Rome and its providential role in the salvation of mankind are also indicated by the statue's gaze directed toward the Eternal City.

The description of the statue's limbs is taken from Daniel 2:32–33, where the prophet recounts and explains Nebuchadnezzar's dream. There are differences. In the Bible, the statue's belly and thighs are all of bronze, whereas the Old Man's bronze stops at the groin; the former has both feet part iron and part clay, but the Old Man's clay is concentrated in his right foot, the other being of pure iron. 112–120: each section—except the gold—has a crack that weeps. The mass of tears produced by the statue perforates the rock of Mount Ida and works its way down through Hell, forming its rivers and, finally, Cocytus, which the pilgrim will behold as a frozen mass at the earth's center (*Inf.* XXXII, 22 ff.). The names for these watercourses are all found in Virgil (*quello stagno* [119] echoes *Aen.* VI, 323: *Cocyti stagna alta vides*).

121–129: the author's meticulous realism is again evident in the pilgrim's question: if the present stream descends from "our world," why has it not been encountered before? Virgil reminds his pupil that Hell is in the shape of an inverted cone and that, while always moving to the left, they have not yet traversed its whole circumference, so that it is not surprising if they come across something not seen before, but which descends from a point not yet reached on the circumference. Virgil conceals that they had moved to the right (*Inf.* IX, 132) on entering the City of Dis. Once more, in *Inf.* XVII, 31, the pilgrims will move in that direction. These two striking exceptions to the general rule may be a narrative device used to pinpoint the frontiers of two essential classes of sin (*Inf.* IX: heresy and violence; XVII: fraud and treachery). An allegorical intention may also be present, indicating that a different strategy is necessary to combat the distortion of faith, both human and divine, implicit in fraud and heresy (cf. Proverbs 4:27). For the present, lines 125–126 remind us that the general movement is a leftward one. The spiral of the pilgrims' descent turns in a clockwise direction, moving leftward when seen from the pilgrims' vantage point, looking downward toward Lucifer at the center of the abyss.

130–142: the pilgrim's question is prompted by Virgil's omission of Lethe from the list of infernal waters and the fact that Phlegethon is first named in line 116 of the present canto. Virgil replies that the boiling red waters of the river of the tyrants in *Inf.* XII, 47 ff. should have made Dante realize that he was in the presence of *tartareus Phlegethon,* which Virgil's poem describes as encircling a broad city with burning fire (*Aen.* VI, 549–551) and which was associated with fire in Statius's *Thebaid* (IV, 523). Lethe, the remaining river in the classical underworld (*Aen.* VI, 703–705), is one of the two rivers in Dante's Earthly Paradise (*Purg.* XXVIII, 25 ff.), that which brings oblivion to the purified souls, before the waters of Eunoe restore the memory of their good actions (*Purg.* XXVIII, 127–133). The close of the canto seems to bring some relief from the horrors and sufferings described, while drawing back the reader from the contemplation of fallen humanity in toto to the spectacle of the individual sinners described in canto xv.

Main Themes

After noting the canto's structural symmetry, the reader will be struck by the extraordinary influence of classical culture. Canto xiv is an outstanding example of Dante's determination to display the essential truths hidden beneath the dross of pagan superstition, in the works of the greatest poets known to him: Virgil, Ovid, Statius, and Lucan—only Horace is missing (*Inf.* iv, 89), but for good reason if Giorgio Brugnoli is right in claiming that Dante had little acquaintance with Horace (s.v. "Orazio," *E.D.*). The poet's syncretism is illustrated in exemplary fashion in the two figures that dominate the canto: Capaneus and the Old Man of Crete.

Capaneus

Dante's boldness in choosing a pagan as the only example of blasphemy has already been noted. It is all the more surprising if we recall that Christ highlighted the sin against the Holy Spirit as the worst—and unforgivable—form of blasphemy (Matthew 12:31–32). The poet's words in *Inf.* xi, 47—"one's heart denying"—cannot mean that the blasphemers deny God's existence (atheism, a sin of the intellect), but that in their hearts they deny his supreme power and sin against the supreme commandment, "Thou shalt love the Lord thy God with thy whole heart . . . " (Matthew 22:37–38).

In the pagan world, Capaneus stands in exemplary opposition to both Cato and Ripheus. Dante's portrayal of Capaneus is rooted in Statius's description of the *superum contemptor* whose faith lay solely in his own valor and in his sword and who claimed that God was a figment of man's fear (*Thebaid* iii, 615–616, 661). Struck down by Jove's thunderbolt, Capaneus is described as *magnanimus* in *Thebaid* xi, 1. This epithet seems to find an echo in Capaneus's appearance as "that giant" (46), constraining scholars to specify that an excess of *magnanimitas* leads to the sin of *praesumptio*—which would seem to be the hallmark of the pagan king. It is also important to remember that in the Latin tradition *magnanimus* could be used to describe the soul guilty of hubris (Ovid, *Metamorphoses* ii, 111; *Fasti* iv, 380), that in the medieval period Hugh of St. Cher wrote simply and to the point *magnanimus, id est superbus* (PL xxiii, 1388), and that Dante must have been well aware of "Franciscan" opposition to Aristotelian magnanimity with its connotations of pride and ambition (cf. Villani, *Chronicle* vii, 54, 58). It is therefore possible to see reflected in Dante's "that giant" two essential traits that define Capaneus: his immense physical stature and his pride (the latter inextricably linked with the *grandi* or *magnati* of Dante's native city). Regarding the former, it is significant that Virgil's words (64) give us the only example in the whole *Inferno* of the word *superbia* used to sum up a sinner's behavior. The only other reference to Capaneus—a flashback in *Inf.* XXV, 13–15—also associates the pagan king with overweening pride of hubris directed against God. It is of course a truism that the sin of pride is found everywhere in Hell. But the fact remains that Dante chooses here to emphasize the pride that marks man's rebellion against his Creator. As Augustine asks (*City of God* XIV, 13): "What then is pride if not the desire for sinful eminence (*perversae celsitudinis*)?" This fundamental trait in Capaneus is reflected in his physical size, which makes him—in the *Comedy*'s own system of cross-references—a prefiguration of the giants (*Inf.* XXXI) and of Satan himself (*Inf.* XXXIV). Indeed Virgil's comment on Ephialtes might equally well describe Capaneus's tragedy: "This giant in his arrogance had tested / his force against the force of highest Jove," / my guide said, "so he merits this reward" (*Inf.* XXXI, 91–93). "And you will be like gods": the promise held out to Adam and Eve by *il primo superbo* has been seized on once more by a mortal who thinks himself God's equal and who vainly refuses to acknowledge defeat. The poet's choice of Capaneus as the first great actor in the *Comedy* drawn from pagan antiquity warns us that man must respect the godhead in whatever form it is revealed to him and shun the sin of hubris.

The Old Man of Crete

Dante's syncretism is just as much in evidence in his construction of this myth (a good example of the "allegory of the poets"). While taking the Book of Daniel as his point of departure, Dante places his statue in Crete, thus adapting Pliny the Elder's *Natural History* (VII, xvi) and Augustine's *City of God* (XV, 9), both of which mention the discovery after an earthquake of a gigantic man inside a mountain in Crete. The coincidence that the statue's metals are listed in the same order in both the Bible and Ovid has led a majority of commentators to suppose that the statue represents the progressive corruption of mankind as described in *Metamorphoses* I, 89–150. Against this, however, must be set the fact that Dante's Christian view of man's history could hardly accommodate such a gradual downward progress. Man's fall was immediate and terrible. Moreover, even an allegory of the history of the human race must reflect its most important event, the Incarnation, while in *Convivio* II, xiv, 13 Dante clearly followed Augustine in dividing history into six chronological periods (and not four moral stages, as in Ovid).

Daniel's political interpretation of Nebuchadnezzar's dream has encouraged other commentators to claim that Dante's statue reflects the history of the Roman Empire—with the Augustan golden age clearly identified and the split into the western and eastern empires signified by the poet's innovation in extending the iron to the bifurcation in the groin. The tears represent the consequences of this political degeneration, the feet civil discord. Once again, it must be objected that there is no evidence to support the idea that Dante saw the history of the empire as one of constant degeneration.

Instead, the basic allegory of the Old Man must be understood along the broad lines of the interpretation first proposed by Busnelli, according to which the statue represents the Old Adam (1 Corinthians 15:22). The fact that this truth escaped the early commentators is not a major obstacle, if we remember the truism that Dante's poem is an encyclopedia of medieval culture. Some of the religious elements in that culture were quickly lost sight of, partly because of the impossibility of recreating the poet's own vast learning and partly because of the growing importance of the classics in the fourteenth century. Canto XIV is exemplary in this regard. Early commentators such as Guido da Pisa and Pietro Alighieri, spurred on by the beginnings of humanistic culture, immediately spotted the origins of Capaneus in Statius but, blinded by the seemingly obvious Ovidian reminiscence, were incapable of deciphering the religious significance of the Old Man of Crete. This significance may be deduced, as Busnelli has argued, from a work by Richard of St. Victor, *De eruditione hominis interioris libri tres.* Dante's statue is thus an allegorical portrayal of the state of man, corrupted by original sin. The head of gold represents man's free will, immune from Adam's sinful heritage. The silver limbs indicate the corruption of man's reason by *error;* the bronze, his will undermined by *malitia;* the iron, his *appetitus irascibilis* subject to *infirmitas;* and the terra-cotta, his *appetitus concupiscibilis* a prey to *cupiditas.* The tears that flow from all parts, except the head, signify the sufferings produced by the effects of man's original sin. By a dramatic stroke of genius, Dante gives strikingly concrete, visual expression to the theological idea that links Hell with humanity's sinful nature and acts in the form of the infernal waters nourished by the statue's tears— a detail possibly suggested by Statius's poem (*Thebaid* VIII, 26–27) but a concept far removed from the tendency to claim the devil as the root cause of humanity's sins and suffering. The greatest poet of the Christian Middle Ages asserts men and women's ultimate responsibility for their acts (cf. *Purg.* XVI, 58–10; XVII, 61–75). At the same time, as Silverstein points out (184), the antithesis of the weeping statue in the medieval universe is to be found in "the bruised figure of Christ crucified, from whose wounds flow the waters of salvation" (prefigured by Lethe in the Earthly Paradise [136–138]).

The political dimension may be glimpsed in the statue's feet. Most commentators have seen the papacy in the right foot of terra-cotta and the empire in the left foot of iron. Now, the polysemy of medieval allegory made possible alternative readings—as Albertus Magnus took splendidly for granted when he affirmed (*pace* Gertrude Stein): "And note that Christ is a rose, Mary is a rose, the Church is a rose, the soul of the faithful is a rose" (*De laudibus beatae Mariae Virginis* XII, iv, 33). In more modern terms, when interpreted diachronically, the statue shows the nourishment of Hell through man's sins; synchronically, it represents mankind in 1300, suffering the effects of original sin in this world (the *vulnerae naturae*) and the next (the waters of Hell). At this same synchronic level, the two feet may indicate the Church and the empire, regarded by Dante as remedies for man's sinful nature in *Monarchia* III, iv, 14. The notorious political role played by the papacy has destroyed the equilibrium (*Purg.* XVI, 106–114), so that the statue has been thrown off balance, resting most of its weight on its right foot.

The statue's orientation likewise combines religious and political elements. At one level, it signifies the Exodus from the land of sin, via Rome, the spiritual and political center of mankind (*Inf.* II, 22–24). Thus, Aeneas and his Trojans had obeyed God's will in abandoning Crete for their true goal, Rome (*Aen.* III, 161–190). Rome's providential mission was at the heart of Dante's poem and of his admiration for Virgil. At another level, the statue's gaze may provide further justification for the borrowing from Daniel (2:44), where the prophet declares "The God of heaven will set up a kingdom that shall never be destroyed, and his kingdom shall not be delivered up to another people," a belief dear to the poet's heart, in defiance of the theory of *translatio imperii* (*Convivio* IV, iv, 10). Synchronically, Rome mirrors the statue's corrupt state; diachronically, it reflects humanity's supreme goal and the means to achieve it.

Just as Capaneus prefigures the giants and Satan, so the Old Man, a mass of matter imprisoned in the mountainside, is a *figura diaboli,* prefiguring Satan held fast in the ice of Cocytus (itself originating in the Old Man's tears). Similarly, Hell—in a graphic illustration of the line describing it as the pit *che 'l mal de l'universo tutto insacca* (*Inf.* VII, 18)—is irrigated and delimited by the waters that flow from these tears: Acheron, the frontier crossed by all damned souls; Styx, gathering the tears of all the sins of incontinence; Phlegethon, those of violence; Cocytus, marking absolute evil, where water is turned to ice, utterly sterile and indicating a total absence of life-giving heat and the fire of love. In this grandiose vision of humanity's life on earth conditioned by original sin and feeding the rivers of punishment in the afterlife, Dante created perhaps the greatest myth of his poem.

Purgatorio will act as a corrective. There, Dante will see the reality of the Earthly Paradise, dimly perceived by the ancient poets through their myth of the Golden Age (*Purg.* XXVIII, 139–144), while Cato (mentioned here in line 15) appears as the antithesis to the Old Man. The word *veglio* is reserved for these two figures: *in malo,* in *Inf.* XIV, 103; *in bono, Purg.* I, 31 and II, 119; the first, *figura diaboli,* the second, *figura Dei* (*Conv.* IV, xxviii, 15). The first illustrates Adam's fall, the second his redemption (*Purg.* 1, 37–39) through the inscrutable workings of God's justice and mercy.

Through the diptych of Canto xiv—with the pagan Capaneus and the biblical Old Man—we gain a further insight into the fusion of pagan and Christian elements that went to make up the sacred poem *al quale ha posto mano e cielo e terra* ("this work so shared by heaven and by earth" [*Par.* xxv, 2]).

BIBLIOGRAPHICAL NOTES

An extensive bibliography may be compiled by consulting the following articles in the *Enciclopedia dantesca:* s.vv. "Capaneo," "Fiumi dell' *Inferno* e del *Purgatorio,*" "Orazio," "Veglio di Creta."

The best overall analysis of the canto is by E. Bigi, "Un caso concreto del rapporto di struttura e poesia: il canto xiv dell'*Inferno,*" in *Forme e significati nella "Divina Commedia"* (Bologna, 1981), 83–107 (originally published in *Cultura e scuola* 4 [1965]: 455–470).

Line 48: G. Petrocchi (introduction, 176–177) has chosen *marturi* as the *lectio difficilior,* while the traditional reading *maturi* is upheld by U. Bosco ("Il canto xiv dell'*Inferno,*" in *Nuove letture dantesche* [Florence, 1968], 2:47–73) and E. Paratore ("Il canto xiv dell'*Inferno,*" in *Tradizione e struttura in Dante* [Florence, 1968], 221–249).

Line 80: *le peccatrici* is in Petrocchi and most modern editions, but not in N. Sapegno's (*Divina Commedia* [Milan, 1955], 167), whose commentary remains an outstanding achievement; Sapegno prefers the conjectural *pectatrici* (workers who hackled the hemp) proposed by G. Mazzoni, *Almae luces: Malae cruces,* ed. N. Zanichelli (Bologna, 1941), 239–266—but, for the whole problem, see M. Barbi and A. Duro, "Peccatrici o pectatrici?" *Studi danteschi* 28 (1949): 11–43.

Lines 121–138: scholars have debated the question whether each of the rivers of Hell runs down separately from the Old Man or whether they issue from a single waterway originating in the statue's tears. The latter explanation now prevails, while Charles S. Singleton points out (*Divine Comedy: Inferno, Commentary* [Princeton, 1970], 2:248) that, between Acheron and Styx, the pilgrims have come across "a connecting canal," since "if the above named 'rivers' are actually *stagni* and as such do not flow down, then it follows that there must be connecting streams or canals between them."

See also

Apollonio, M. "Il canto xiv dell'*Inferno.*" In *Lectura Dantis Scaligera: Inferno,* 451–478. Florence, 1967.

Branca, V. *Boccaccio medievale.* Florence, 1956.

Busnelli, G. "La concezione dantesca del Veglio di Creta." Appendix to *L'Etica Nicomachea e l'ordinamento morale dell'"Inferno" di Dante.* Bologna, 1907.

———. *Il Virgilio dantesco e il gran Veglio di Creta.* 2d ed. Rome, 1919 (essential for an understanding of the allegory).

Cassell, A. K. *Dante's Fearful Art of Justice,* 57–65. Toronto, 1984.

Di Scipio, G. C. "*Inferno* xiv." In *Dante's "Divine Comedy": Introductory Readings: Inferno,* ed. Tibor Wlassics, 173–188. Charlottesville, Va., 1990.

Hardie, C. "The Mountain in *Inferno* 1 and 2, the Mount Ida in Crete, and the Mountain of Purgatory." *Deutsches Dante Jahrbuch* 46 (1970): 81–100 (suggests that the *colle* in *Inf.* 1, 13–18 is the Mount Ida of *Inf.* xiv, or in some way parallel to it).

Hein, J. *Enigmaticité et messianisme dans la "Divine Comédie."* Florence, 1992 (see esp. 441–442 and 525: the Old Man and his "Roman homologue" embody the two universal empires of Babylon and Rome, the latter destined to be replaced by a young, golden empire under the rule of Henry VII's son).

Hollander, R. "Dante's Pagan Past: Notes on *Inferno* xiv and xviii." *Stanford Italian Review* 5 (1985): 23–26.

Marti, M. "Canto xiv." In *Lectura Dantis Neapolitana: Inferno,* ed. Pompeo Giannantonio, 243–258. Naples, 1980.

Mazzotta, G. *Dante, Poet of the Desert*. Princeton, 1979 (makes some excellent points [14–65] regarding the opposition between the Old Man and Cato).

Nardi, B. *Saggi e note di critica dantesca*, 154–156. Milan, 1956.

Pagliaro, A. *Ulisse*, 2:513–525. Messina-Florence, 1967.

Santangelo, S. "Il Veglio di Creta." In *Studi letterari: Miscellanea in onore di E. Santini*, 13–23. Palermo, 1956 (a wholly "political" interpretation).

Silverstein, H. T. "The Weeping Statue and Dante's *Gran Veglio*." *Harvard Studies and Notes in Philology and Literature* 13 (1931): 165–184.

Tateo, H. T. "Il duplice *modus tractandi* di *Inferno* xiv e i canti della violenza." *L'Alighieri* 21 (1980): 3–25 (claims that "the circle of the violent figures a political world that has lost the principle of justice. . . . In that world Capaneo can rightly act as the central figure" [my translation]).

Varese, C. "*Inferno*–Canto xiv." In *Letture dantesche: Inferno,* ed. Giovanni Getto, 251–266. Florence, 1955.

CANTO XV

The Canto of Brunetto Latini

DANTE DELLA TERZA

Translated by Charles Ross

When the poet invites the reader to follow him over the sandy plain on which the blasphemers, sodomites, and usurers are punished, he has already passed through the complex narrative apprenticeship represented by the didactic opening of Canto XI, the violent iconography of the canto of the Centaurs, and the invention of the wood of the suicides. The architecture of the landscape, firm and peremptory in its contours, gains secure relief from the rich range of events and moods that precede its appearance. It is distinguished into a foreground dominated by groups of souls and a background fixed within the parameters of an immense natural prison: A river of blood encircles the forest, and the forest encircles the sand whose aridity is mitigated and at the same time underscored by the wooded terrain. The line of trees will be the constant point of reference—the horizon of the two pilgrims—while the vertical axis of their glance focuses on the slow spiral of a rain of fire that the reader perceives through the language of a line Dante borrowed from a *plazer* of Guido Cavalcanti. Implacably averse to the sinners of violence, Dante's canto twists the borrowed line from pleasure to punishment:

> Above the plain of sand, distended flakes
> of fire showered down; their fall was slow—
> as snow descends on alps when no wind blows.
>
> (XIV, 28–30)

The rivulet of water that threads its way through this prison constructed like a set of graduated boxes not only encloses the forest and represents an invisible border but reveals itself as both an instrument of punishment—a river of boiling water—and the source of a protective cloud of humidity that stretches like a unique vault of heaven over the pilgrims trudging along the riverbed:

> Now one of the hard borders bears us forward;
> the river mist forms shadows overhead
> and shields the shores and water from the fire.
>
> (1–3)

This ambiguous functionality reappears in the extended comparisons that follow immediately: that of the Flemings who hurry to construct "between Wissant and Bruges" a wall of dykes against the floods; and the simile of the Paduans who "along the Brenta, / build bulwarks" before the sun melts the snows of Carentana. Just as a cooling relief meets the vertical glance by means of a purely verbal antithesis between the flakes of fire and the snow falling undisturbed by breezes in the mountains, so these verbal comparisons offer a reinforcing and in some sense compensating image of a world besieged by water.

The first important movement of the canto takes place along the coordinates of the composite landscape when the forest disappears in the distance and a bank of human figures that emerges along the ridges of the margins substitutes for the formerly vegetal horizon:

> By now we were so distant from the wood
> that I should not have made out where it was—
> not even if I'd turned around to look—
>   when we came on a company of spirits
> who made their way along the bank.
>
> (13–17)

The landscape left behind is so clearly defined by the arboreal world of the forest of the suicides that it can only be described by the rhetorical figures of *privatio*—

> To make these strange things clear, I must explain
> that we had come upon an open plain
> that banishes all green things from its bed.
>
> (XIV, 7–9)

The landscape now entered derives its definition from the human figures who wend their way across it. The fixed horizon of the margins replaces the distant horizon of the wood: the new landscape is populated by characters who seem intent to decipher the physiognomies of the two travelers. They are as absorbed by their concern as old tailors whom a glance catches at work in their shops as they squint to thread a needle; a hand reaches out from their anonymous rank of staring souls to seize Dante by the hem, and a voice expresses surprise and wonder:

> And when that family looked harder, I
> was recognized by one, who took me by
> the hem and cried out: "This is marvelous!"
> 　　That spirit having stretched his arm toward me,
> I fixed my eyes upon his baked, brown features,
> so that the scorching of his face could not
> 　　prevent my mind from recognizing him;
> and lowering my face to meet his face,
> I answered him: "Are you here, Ser Brunetto?"
> 　　　　　　　　　　　　　　　　(22–30)

　　Of lesser importance in the drama of recognition that follows is the isolation of one of the pilgrims with respect to the other, so that Virgil soon assumes the vicarious role of one who discreetly accompanies—or, in Dante's phrase, "him with whom I go" (*costui che vo seco* [36]). A more decisive element makes the scene memorable. Dante's role as the omnipotent poet who has secretly organized the story as a monument of personal revelation sharply contrasts to the wonder of the character who is soon identified as Ser Brunetto, and to the astonishment of the pilgrim expressed by the adverb "here" (*qui* [30]), a single rapid monosyllable that nonetheless stands in bold relief because of the repercussions it provokes: it echoes the unmeasurable surprise that grips the pilgrim's mind and holds him in a state of anxious expectation. The character who prompts this expectation responds with a tentative, rhetorically controlled attempt to give a sense of normalcy to the event by resorting to a mode of address that draws on old habits of affection at the same time that it declares the speaker's own official position—boldly, but nonetheless sadly, resignedly confirming the truth of the earlier identification:

> And he: "My son, do not mind if Brunetto
> Latino lingers for a while with you
> and lets the file he's with pass on ahead."
> 　　　　　　　　　　　　　　　　(31–33)

The first thirty-three lines form a series of steps that converge decisively to create the scene where the pilgrim learns the troubling news of his own impending exile. We must not miss the theatricality of this encounter—the spectacle—as the topography of the infernal circle of the violent reverses the roles of teacher and pupil. The teacher called upon to further the story by means of his wise and urgent discourse imparts his lesson while gazing on his disciple from the base vantage of his unseemly position, while the pupil listens to him along the margin of the sandy wasteland. As he listens, the pupil progresses at a measured and dignified pace, while the teacher, who purveys wisdom, is constrained by the pace to withhold his flight. His race explodes ignominiously at the moment his lesson concludes:

> And then he turned and seemed like one of those
> who race across the fields to win the green
> cloth at Verona; of those runners, he
>   appeared to be the winner, not the loser.
>
>   (121–124)

In addition to the alienating effect of the reference to the countryside of Verona, the poet succeeds in giving an impressionistic picture of flight. We first follow Ser Brunetto visually to measure the distance intervening between him and the moving and remote group toward which he runs (the pronoun *coloro* refers to distant subjects). This distance is counterpointed by the faithful certainty that his race will end victoriously, as the soul of Ser Brunetto fuses with the homogeneous group to which it belongs (the demonstrative pronoun *costoro* implies nearness and identify). The central portion of the canto consists of the pilgrim's confrontation with the imminent reality of his exile that Brunetto reveals. This exile insinuates itself into the events of his life not as a mysterious threat or disgrace, but as an inalienable token of honor.

A rereading of Canto xv of the *Inferno* that takes account of both the surface events and the deeper revelations about Dante the poet finds its justification as early as the second tercet, where the word *fiotto* ("tide" [5])—a hapax legomenon (that is, occurring only here in Dante)—is a sign of the dramatic transplant into circles of violence of scientific notions and fictions dear to the heart of the master of the *Trésor*. It derives from Brunetto Latini's encyclopedic treasury, where he explains the influence of the moon on the seas: *car quant ele croist . . . cancres et escrevisses et tous animaux et poissons croissent en lor moolles; neis la mer croist et boute lors grandisme flos* ("for when it waxes . . . the marrow of crabs and crawfish and all animals and fish grows; even the sea swells and produces great waves").[1] Dante, who is a superb translator, renders Brunetto's *boute* with another word that explodes with energy: *s'avventa* ("floods" [5]), while with a deft touch he camouflages *flos* as *fiotto*, a word that Brunetto had already signaled as a neologism in his description of the ocean in the *Tesoretto*:

> *Or prende terra, or lassa,*
> *or monta, ed or dibassa,*
> *e la gente per motto*
> *dicon c'ha nome fiotto.*

Now it takes land, now it leaves it behind; now it surges, now it retreats;
and the people have a word for it: they call it the Tide.
                                                        (*Tesoretto,* lines 1039–1042)

Dante's transplanting of Brunetto's science, which produces such a powerful expressive synthesis, does not seem to me to be the only clue to the
dynamic of a palimpsest (new writing layered over old) destined to come
to the fore without delay in the words pronounced by Dante's old teacher
just before his hasty departure:

> Let my *Tesoro*, in which I still live,
> be precious to you, and I ask no more.
>   (119–120)

Brunetto describes the new moon: *Et quant ele vient en. i. signal u tout le
soleil est, ele est alumee de la partie deseure dont li solaus l'esgarde, a ce k'ele cort
desous lui, et por ce n'en poons nos point veoir* ("And when it reaches a sign with
the sun, it is illuminated on the other side where the sun looks upon it, as
it proceeds below [the sun], and for this reason we cannot see it" [*Trésor,* I,
cxv, 3]). Dante carefully positions this scientific fact, drawn from the vast sea
of the *Trésor,* to give drama to his characterization:

> By now we were so distant from the wood
> that I should not have made out where it was—
> not even if I'd turned around to look—
>   when we came on a company of spirits
> who made their way along the bank; and each
> stared steadily at us, as in the dusk,
>   beneath the new moon, men look at each other.
>   (13–19)

And in the same way the *intelletto* ("mind," or understanding) of line 28
is a probable reminiscence of *l'entendement est la plus haute partie de l'ame*
("understanding is the highest quality of the soul" [*Trésor* I, xv, 2]). Or, if you
prefer, of the *intelletto* of the *Tesoretto,* defined as "the power to learn / what
you can understand," while the iterative form of the verb *aguzzavan le
ciglia* ("they knit their brows" [20]) and the participial form *adocchiato*
("eyed" [22]) refer back from the powerfully realistic context of the canto

to the abstractive and ancillary operation of reason, the eye of the intellect *ki asoutille la veue de l'entendement et trie le voir dou faus* ("which heightens the awareness of understanding and separates truth from falsehood" [*Trésor* I, xv, 2]), a well-known passage from Brunetto's work. In a certain sense, Dante mobilizes Brunetto's encyclopedic notions, the very instruments of his teaching, and turns them against him, building around him a prison of well-known words. The words handed down by the master to the younger poet and absorbed by him only to be distributed through a decisive act of diffraction along the surface of this first part of the canto are called upon to punctuate the stages of an inexorable destiny. They become things themselves, one more element of a landscape that exists, so to speak, apart from the pilgrim's pious intentions. But these words, at once features of the intellectual portrait of Brunetto and component parts of his infernal destiny, are the product of a profound metamorphosis that removes them from their original encyclopedic function to plunge them into the crucible of a stunning and irreversible drama. They are the intellectual portrait of Brunetto as seen through his encyclopedic culture. They signal the limits of that type of culture, which Dante absorbs and renews in the rhythm of his infernal journey.

As often happens in Dante, the portrait overgoes the thing it portrays; its very execution demonstrates the superiority of Dante's polished and dramatic art over the less developed traditions of the figures he portrays. By dislocating, for different ends, Brunetto's archaic schemes, Dante demonstrates his ability to balance an appreciation that contains *in nuce* the history of his successful distancing against the certain attainment of his own autonomy.

It bears emphasizing that if we divert our attention from the scandalous figure of Brunetto traveling among the pilgrims and the souls in flight and concentrate instead on the incisive discourse that he gives on the theme of Dante's imminent exile, we should also recognize how much that discourse conditions how Dante uses the *Trésor* to construct Brunetto's prison of words. Simplifying as much as possible what Dante does, we can say that what assumes a marginal and parenthetic position in the *Trésor*—the insertion of the very personal theme of exile within an otherwise doctrinal articulation—becomes in Dante's episode a propulsive force, capable of echoing through the most distant branches of the canto. This repositioning, a radical affirmation of the Dantean personality that willingly assumes the privilege of revitalizing his reading of history according to his own purposes and perspective, does not occur without some obvious risks and complications. The stylistic cohesion pursued as the dramatic nucleus of the canto expands along the surface of events that compose it, and the consequent tendency to render homogeneous the choice of signifiers, does not exclude incoherence and rupture at the level of signification.

Within this extremely lucid and purposeful story, unmarred by any hesitations or changes in rhythm and tone, where events follow one from another in coherent progressions, the reader is continually aware of the difference between the meaning of words that, as they come from the "baked" features of Brunetto, underscore the pitiful misery of the deforming sin that dares not speak its name while at the same time registering the truths of a master whose incisive and passionate pronouncements impart a lesson to the disciple so unexpectedly encountered. An irreducible, consubstantial ambiguity results from the counterpoint of Brunetto's two personalities—the first arising from his discourse, the second from his sin; the one belonging to a far-sighted teacher, the other rooted in a humbling nearsightedness, the *mala luce* of the damned. Although Brunetto's infernal fate is ineluctable and poetically just—and it would be vain to attempt to explain Dante's filial piety with regard to it (a false path proposed by well-known romantic schemes of interpretation)—it is nonetheless plausible to credit that Dante as pilgrim and poet accepts the content of the lesson given to him by his old teacher, as part of the expansion of his powers of thought. Had Dante wanted to distance himself from the words of his teacher, he had at his disposal every rhetorical means to do so.

The fact that Dante privileges the more personal and hortatory aspects of the *Trésor*'s prose over the didactic and encyclopedic references that are the book's true purpose greatly increases the probability of an encounter between Dante's text and its model for the theme of exile common to them both. The verification for such a thematic encounter finds its first expression in the synoptic Italian *Tesoretto* where the verses—crude, but not void of a certain persuasive force and a distinct cadence—mirror the movement of Brunetto's doctrinal material in the direction of a Dantean canto.[2] The *Tesoretto* provides a distant justification for the choice of Brunetto as the one to make a case for the value of exile in the ontological formation of the pilgrim's character, in that the book offered Dante the stimulus of seeing an author intent on defending his city and fearful of the divisive forces provoked by the discords that afflicted her. It is precisely that character of proceeding with "head bent low" (*a capo chino* [*Tesoretto,* 187]) because torn by sorrow for the fall of his city that furnishes Dante, by an acute dissociation prompted by Brunetto himself, with the gesture of *capo chino* as a sign of respectful anticipation. The distant, interrogative consonance of the rhyme, moreover, conjures up Brunetto's theme of the great lost way (*cammino smarrito*):

> *ma 'l capo chino*
> *tenea com'uom che reverente vada.*
>   *El cominciò: "Qual fortuna o destino*
> *anzi l'ultimo dì qua giù ti mena?*
> *e chi è questi che mostra 'l cammino?"*

> but I walked with head bent low
> as does a man who goes in reverence.

And he began: "What destiny or chance
has led you here below before your last
day came, and who is he who shows the way?"

(44–48)

The theme of exile explodes suddenly and uncontrollably in the *Trésor* only at the culmination of those comprehensive chapters given over to the universal history of ages past, like the record of some remote geological epoch. After tracing the Italian and Trojan origins of the realm of Great Britain (I, xxxv) and having reviewed the shift in Rome from the old monarchy to the republic (I, xxxvi), Brunetto pauses to sketch the lively history of Florence (I, xxxvii). The master of the *Trésor* tells a story we find echoed and amplified and partially corrected in the words of the anonymous suicide at the end of Canto XIII of the *Inferno*. Brunetto asserts with a moving sense of fatality how the disgraceful civil discord of Florence derives from the bellicose influence of Mars, under whose aegis Florence had been founded. In contrast to the anonymous suicide who suddenly distances his own personal fate from his assessment of the struggle of Florence to survive, the Brunetto of the *Trésor* translates his awareness of the lethal influence on Florence of the planet of hate into his own autobiographical suffering: *De ce doit maistre Brunet Latin savoir le verité, car il en est nés, et si estoit en exil lors k'il compli cest livre por achoison de la guerre as florentins* ("Master Brunetto Latini should certainly know the truth about this, for he was born in that city and he was in exile when he compiled this book because of the wars among the Florentines" [I, xxxvii, 3]). But this experience of the flesh endured more at the level of the instincts than of the reason is mediated by the literary tradition of Seneca's *De remediis fortuitorum* and carried to a level of superior comprehension in the eighty-fourth chapter of the second book of the *Trésor*, the portion of Brunetto's work destined to impinge with greatest persuasive impact on the imagination of Dante, as he sought to construct a paradigm of his life in which exile would appear as the power that promotes his great poetic destiny. In this chapter, *Seurté* and *Paor* meet in a strange confrontation, following the tradition of the medieval psychomachia. *Seurté*, a somewhat idiosyncratic translation of the personification *Ratio* in the dialogue attributed to Seneca, is sureness of self and force of mind, the capacity to dispose of one's own destiny without disgrace or any show of temerity. *Paor*, which has the role assigned by the *De remediis* to the term *Sensus*, is the terror that afflicts one's consciousness, destroying its ability to operate and to project the future. *Paor* terrorizes men by presenting a squalid picture of a life that is deconstructed and made unreal by death. *Seurté* insists on the historical Christian triumph over any remnant of a life doomed to paralysis by the terror of impending death. Where *Paor* offers a dizzying descent to the abyss, *Seurté* reacts by proclaiming the calm consciousness that life is a pilgrimage and death an inevitable and necessary return to the eternal source of life. Every vision of terror held up by *Paor* is countered by a fervid statement of reason expressed in a language of high style and persuasive transparency that seems like a prelude to the more peremptory tones and the wisdom of Montaigne. What meaning can there be, for one who knows, in *Paor*'s allusions to threatening dangers and the sufferings that accompany sickness? Courage is the virtue, Brunetto tells us, that is shown not just on the battlefield but also in the closed space of a bed where a patient struggles with fever. Why bother to tell the wise man that he is exposed to the bites of detraction and calumny? Doesn't he know that the wicked hate praise and reward because they are dogs who howl at the wind not from love of truth, but force of habit?

It seems to be worth noticing that Brunetto uses the lashing accents of the *De remediis* in his attacks on wickedness. This virulence anticipates the rapid ending by the anonymous suicide as he finishes speaking against those Brunetto calls the "beasts of Fiesole" (xv, 73), responsible for Dante's exile. Even more noteworthy is the fact that the attack of reason on calumny in the *Trésor* introduces the moment of greatest tension in Brunetto's discourse on exile, a topic that touches the profoundest chords of his heart and prompts the most personal translation of the *De remediis* and the insertion of bizarre and capricious voices. This is how the debate sounds in Brunetto's translation of *De remediis* II, lxxxiv, 10:

> Fear says, "They will chase you into exile." Strength of mind answers: "They can take me from where I am, but they cannot move my native land. Wherever I go there will be cities, seas, and ports. All the world is a homeland for the strong, as the sea is for fish. Wherever I wander I will find my house. Any land may be strange to me, but none a place of exile. Man's task is goodness, not to live in one place."

A discourse tending toward a stoic victory over nostalgia captures, in its flux, the Ovidian sentence *omne solum forti patria est, ut piscibus aequor* (every land is to the brave his country, as to the fish the sea [Ovid, *Fasti* I, 493]). But the identification of the homeland (*la moie terre*) with nature contains an acute paradox, the price owed for his victory over despair by a writer who treats exile. On the one hand Bruno expands the boundaries of the *pais* until they are coterminous with those of the world; on the other, he confines boundless nature to within the limits of the known: the cities, ports, and seas of the world mirror the cities, ports, and seas one knows. Every discovery is a rediscovery, every corner of the globe reproduces the absent homeland. In *De vulgari eloquentia* I, vi, 2–3, Dante reproduces the sentence of Ovid and Brunetto that underscores how rationality overcomes the passions. While justifying this solution, however, Dante chooses a syntax fragmented by the insertion of a large concessive parenthesis, better suited to the contrasting emotions stirred up by exile: exile understood both as a good to accomplish a fuller understanding of the world and as a mental return to things previously known. By this means, the seas become the fresh water of the Arno that the exile drank in his infancy, and the cities of the world assume the name of Florence, the place where he was born, and for this the object of his love. But Florence also condemned him to an unjust exile, and for this reason has become the object of his hatred. In the fifteenth canto of the *Inferno,* the debate between *Paor* and *Seurté* transforms into an assertive and didactic lesson. The canto contrasts to the first-person declaration of the proverbial and universal Everyman of the *Trésor* who summons up the language given to him by "force of mind" and contrasts it as well to the secret, autobiographical points of reference of the *De vulgari eloquentia.* The fourth canto devoted to the violent sorts itself out more rigorously and more lucidly. It falls to Brunetto to explain that exile constitutes shame for those who impose it, not for those who submit to it— for the Florentines, not for Dante. Dante's role is to absorb instantly the lesson directed toward him:

> "One thing alone I'd have you plainly see:
> So long as I am not rebuked by conscience,
> I stand prepared for Fortune, come what may.
> My ears find no new pledge in that prediction;
> therefore, let Fortune turn her wheel as she
> may please, and let the peasant turn his mattock."
>
> (91–96)

The final two verses contain a striking echo of Brunetto's phrasing: *fortune est avuglee, et . . . tournoie tousjours sa roe en non veant* ("fortune is blind, and always turns its wheel without seeing" [*Trésor* II, cxv]). The dramatic situation of the pilgrim demonstrates the truth of this thought, even as the homage overgoes its source.

As critics have shown, the debate about exile spills over the borders of the canto in order to propose, to the reader of the *Comedy,* the problem of a life transformed by destiny. But because we may verify that Brunetto's discourse to Dante is amplified and clarified, by means of a startling symmetry, in the warning of Cacciaguida, and because this discourse may be perceived as a token to accompany the pilgrim on his progress toward the edifying spaces of Paradise, it is necessary that it also fulfill a determinant local function. It is above all a point of convergence for the themes that operate in the canto. Only by understanding the rhetorical double effect of Brunetto's discourse—at once a clarification of the mechanism of evil and a way station on the path to enlightenment that the poet trusts with some trepidation as an augury of future certainty—can we be prepared to overcome the paradox of the dialogue that assumes an absolute validity throughout the context of the poem, even though it unfolds irredeemably in hell. The critical alternative to the position that makes a single long wave of Canto xv of the *Inferno* and Cantos xv and following in the *Paradiso* can do no more than declare a lack of complementarity between episodes that we believe are connected, an affirmation of polarity—anti-episode and episode—that provides the only link between the words of Brunetto and those of Cacciaguida. If we concede, as we must, a positive interpretation to Brunetto's discourse, we must also accept the concomitant principle of the existence of a periphery and a center to the canto, a poetic strategy that, while it conducts all the elements of the episode toward the high declarative moment of the lesson, yet refuses to concede to it more than the presence of an outward shell.

There are, in short, shadowy words understood as hints of mystery, words intentionally chosen by the poet *not* to clarify, as well as explicit, exhaustive words that attract these other and give them a rhythmic function somehow alien to their content. To make these words the center of critical interest means overturning the rhythm of the canto, to prefer what we might call a structure of reticence to the explicit discourse of Brunetto in his canto. Whatever might reveal this structure to us remains open to debate. But all our attempts to penetrate what Dante conceals under the veil of reticence will fail of their purpose if we discount Dante's initial freedom to throw his message of hope into relief by setting it in contrast to the depth of desperation and sin that so dramatically confirm it.

It is well known that André Pézard has dedicated a study of unmatched learning to the most shadowy zone of the canto—the sin of Brunetto. Even today, twenty-eight years after this study's publication, it does not cease to represent the largest obstacle to the traditional interpretation of the condemnation that overwhelms the ancient professor of rhetoric. Pézard has acceded to the calls of those critics who, interpreting as erroneous all of the declarations that pass the lips of the cleric, read the canto as an anti-episode, seeking in it their natural allies at least as far as their insistence on the intellectual understanding of Brunetto's sinful deviance. But as Pézard remains a firm supporter of the position that accepts Dante's affectionate agreement with the message of his teacher, he winds up occupying an exegetical position exposed not only to the opposition of those who, trusting in the arrogant "vain eloquence" of Brunetto, find Pézard too inclined to sympathize with the content of the discourse directed at the pilgrim, but also to the objections of those who, while accepting the idea of a rapport between Brunetto and Dante, differ in their view of the nature of the sin for which he is condemned to the circle of the violent. It is not sufficient merely to indicate Pézard's isolated position on this issue. Because he structures and interprets Dante's entire culture by focusing on the canto of Brunetto, any reading of it must not conclude without examining the findings he has set forth.

We must accept some of Pézard's questions: if the hypothesis is admissible that Dante knew of Brunetto's sodomy and that of Bishop Andrea dei Mozzi or the Florentine jurist who emigrated to Bologna, Francesco d'Accorso, from what mysterious and undiscovered writing could he have obtained the notion that the grammarian Priscian, who lived eight hundred years earlier, was inclined to this unnatural sin? Moreover, why are all the documents known to us boldly silent about the sodomy of Accorso and Brunetto himself? As for Bishop dei Mozzi, is it really necessary to interpret the verse applied to him ("he left his tendons strained by sin" [114]) in the traditional way that insists he was guilty of sodomy? Beginning with these not implausible inquiries, Pézard searched for a sin that might more plausibly provide a common denominator for the "sorry crowd" (109) of these transgressors of God's law, and he found it inscribed in their thought and their words rather than in their lascivious deeds. Priscian, a radical defender of Grecian innovations to Latin phraseology, supported a refined and various culture, favoring tropes that eroded the Latin tradition. His disciples in this struggle between artificiality and naturalness stretched their arrogance so far as to censure the simple syntax of the Holy Scripture. Brunetto Latini, the professor of rhetoric, renounced his maternal tongue and, by writing his *Trésor* in the *langue d'oïl,* offended the art of writing, the only art defined as "rational" in the *Convivio.* Abandoning the verses of his *Tesoretto* to write the *Trésor* in prose on the pretext that only prose is capable of handling the encyclopedic scope of all knowledge, he overvalued prose, to which Dante in the *Convivio* attributes only an ancillary function, and he insulted poetry, whose greater nobility of conceit presented Dante with far greater problems of composition. As an unyielding follower of Cicero (the Cicero of the *De natura deorum* I, viii, 18, who railed against the *delirantium somnia* of the allegorists), Brunetto shows little interest in the polyvalent function of the figure of Virgil or the allegorical dimension of poetry in general. Accorso, the author of the *Glossa magna* to the *Pandects* of Justinian, attributes greater value to the *Decretals* than to the writings of the church fathers; he attributed virtue to the civil law and their own appropriate powers to the moral and theological sciences. Andrea dei Mozzi, whom Benvenuto appropriately called *magnus bestionis,* aimed his rhetorical bow at unusual targets, grounding the arc of his discourse in definitions of squalid countertruths. Brunetto, Accorso, Priscian, and Andrea dei Mozzi are by this line of reasoning all violent sinners against the Holy Spirit.

After this summary of Pézard's thesis, a question must arise in the mind of the discriminating reader. Are the majority correct in believing that Brunetto endures the purifying fires that destroyed Sodom and Gomorrha, or must consideration be paid to the French critic's opinion that the fire in question is that mentioned in Acts 2:1–2, although in this case the fire falls not to illuminate but to consume? In answering, I would praise the unmatched richness of Pézard's portrait of Dante's culture. His exegetical un-dertaking sharpens the critical tools even of those who disagree with him. I would also acknowledge the contours he outlines of the doctrinal frontier that separates Dante from Brunetto and the clerics whom he proclaims ac-company him in his punishment. But insofar as his hypothesis applies to the events Dante asks us to judge, everyone must make his own decision, for his cultural critique is only tangentially related to the poetry of the canto. The terrifying fate of the intransigent Decretalist Accorso, consumed by his long struggle against the hierarchy of knowledge; the exotic grammatical theories of Priscian, who broke with Latinity; the denigration of vulgate Italian by Brunetto himself even as Dante defended it against the subtle ar-guments of the most articulate neolatinists and the expansive force of the grammatical tongue, are facts unrelated to the events of the canto. We might say with Aristotle that the truth is not coextensive with the verisimil-itude of poetry.

I would see in the condemnation of Brunetto not an image of his sins of intellectual pride—that is, not a *contrapasso* corresponding to a similar type of sin—but rather a conscious realization of the degradation and humilia-tion imposed on his worldly existence as dictated by a society as structurally complex as that of Florence. There exists a type of dissociation or onto-logical separation between the reality of a great cleric, who earns a sus-taining and reverent judgment on the part of the poet who observes him, and the vilifying nature of the sin he has committed, which Dante registers in the unyielding verdict given as a warning by divine justice. The sin, in short, and the representation of it in the canto offer a sort of moment of neutralizing suture between the glitter of a dominant historical personal-ity and the shameful anonymity of his companions about whom, in the words of Dante's Brunetto, "silence is to be praised" (104). As for the plau-sibility that Priscian, Accorso, and Andrea dei Mozzi, whom Brunetto names, were guilty of sodomy, it must be said that what we see on the sur-face is the Dantean representation of a peremptory gesture whose affir-mative force is inversely proportional to the quality of the historical proof that sustains it. But this is not surprising. Doesn't the power of conviction, the compulsive force of Dante's reality, always depend more on the irre-versible flash of an action rather than on historical correctness for justifi-cation? Dante spares Bonconte, but he did not have to. His Manfred repents at the moment of dying when Dante could have made him share, without obvious injustice, his father's infernal destiny. He sends Ulysses across the ocean to die, when he might have devised another death. Do we mean to say that Dante delights in inventing charges of sodomy in order to distrib-ute them more or less creditably along the arc of a millennium to de-fenseless clerics? Let us say only that there are circumstances in which the *source* of Dante's basis for condemnation escapes our comprehension. If we have an obligation to search for implied reasons, it also remains true that an excessive attempt to rationalize that rapport between poetic representation and the historical facts on which it is based can distort our perspective of literature and make us lose our way.

If we exclude as circumstantial and tautological that Dante condemned his old professor of rhetoric because of his personal knowledge of Brunetto's dubious reputation in Florence, of which we have no other indication, we may imagine that he weighed in the tribunal of his own judgment the evidence that Brunetto left in his writings. There is above all the indication seized on by Giovanni Villani (*Chronicle* VIII, 10) of an earthiness that justifies the contribution of the repentant author of the *Tesoretto*. His desire "to travel with the holy brothers" (*di gire ai frati santi* [*Tesoretto*, 2563]) indicates a certain unidentified guilt that jars with the heavy condemnation of sodomy found both in the *Tesoretto* (2852–2855) and in the *Trésor*, where the pleasure derived from sensual gratification is deemed worthy of condemnation unless chaste—that is, done for the purpose of generating children—and performed *selonc la humaine nature* (*Trésor* II, lxxvii). Nonetheless the interest shown in the sexual behavior of animals by this inveterate exploiter of the encyclopedic tidbits found in Giulio Solino's *Collectanea rerum memorabilium* reveal what Dante may have considered a hidden but excessive delight: *Perdrix . . . a le fois oublient la cognoissance de nature, en tel maniere que li malles gist avec le malle* (partridges sometimes "forget natural intercourse, and the male lies with the male" [*Trésor* I, clxvii]). Of revealing interest is the anecdote Brunetto tells in *Trésor* II, lxxv, about Pericles, a straitlaced defender of the public good, who reproves Sophocles, as they work together, for allowing his gaze to linger over a young boy passing by instead of concentrating on the *haute besoigne* of their mutual burden. The moral of the story seems not so much a condemnation of Sophocles' desire as the assertion of the idea that everything has its time and place: *vicieuse chose est es hautes besoignes dire noz de solaz* ("it is a vice to say words of frivolity in solemn circumstances"). As Brunetto says elsewhere (*Trésor* II, lxxvi), *se ta oevre n'est chaste, si soit privee*—that is, *nisi caste, saltem caute* ("if what you do is not temperate, let it be concealed"). We must admit that reading these texts offers no conclusive proof in one direction of the other, nor do they offer a sure source of Dante's condemnation.

As readers of the canto, however, we may learn something from this investigation of the structural articulation between the reticence that veils Dante's text in order to concentrate on the discourse of Dante and Brunetto. We should perhaps explore a little more deeply the semantic range of *adocchiato da cotal famiglia* ("and when that family looked harder" [22]), where the image of the tailor serves vicariously to illustrate how the souls stared. The unusual and oppressive gaze *may* allude to their former earthly habit of sad and weary staring—the bleary gaze of the sodomites.[3] I would not, however, hesitate to identify in the *tigna* ("scurf"

[111]) of the bishop the homosexuality that history has assigned him and that encompasses the other members of his group, including Brunetto. That the tendons strained by sin, left by the bishop on the banks of the Bacchiglione, allude to his vocal cords is not impossible, but the image of a strained voice seems somewhat forced, more fit for the infernal punishment of one who sings scurvy or salacious songs than to Dante's *Inferno*. Certainly—partially to justify the thesis of Pézard—it must be said that critics wedded to the ancient interpretation of those punished in the canto have presumably let themselves remember the crudely naturalistic, Priapean image at Pompeii in the Aula Vetto Conviva and the Aula Vettio Restituto that guides show to tourists with some hesitation after having invited the ladies present to withdraw. The concise expressiveness of Dante's verse indicates, both forcefully and discretely, the pathology of a vulnerable nervous system; a body tensed for the search for (or expectation of) sensual contact; the stream of onrushing and devouring sensuality that swallows and sweeps away its victims in the world, making a grouping for eternity of Andrea dei Mozzi, Priscian, Francesco d'Accorso, and Maestro Brunetto Latini. In their way, by means of Dante's careful deliberations, the world that signifies the sin of the most insignificant of the souls named by Brunetto is called upon emblematically to reduce the once fervid existence of thought and action to the degrading level of anonymity and silence; to seal in the humble declaration of opprobrious guilt of one soul the destiny of all the souls that travel through the space of the canto.

NOTES

1. *Li Livres dou Tresor de Brunetto Latini,* ed. Francis J. Carmody (Berkeley, 1948), I, cxvii, 2; with English wording (here and throughout) from Brunetto Latini, *The Book of the Treasure,* trans. Paul Barrette and Spurgeon Baldwin (New York, 1993).

2. *Ond'io non so nessuno / ch'io volesse vedere / la mia cittade avere / di tutto ala sua guisa, / né che fosse divisa, / ma tutti per comune / tirassero una fune / di pace e di ben fare; / ché già no può scampare / terra rotta di parte. / Certo lo cor mi parte / di cotanto dolore, / pensando 'l grande onore / e la ricca potenza / che suole aver Fiorenza / quasi nel mondo tutto. / Ond'io, in tal corrotto / pensando, a capo chine, / perdei lo gran cammino, / a tenni ala traversa / d'una selva diversa* (So that I know none / Whom I would wish to see / Have my city / Entirely in his control, / Or that it be divided; / But all in common / Should pull together on a rope / Of peace and of welfare, / Because a land torn apart / Cannot survive. / Truly my heart broke / With so much sorrow, / Thinking on the great honor / And the rich power / That Florence is used to having / Almost through the whole world; / And I, in such anguish, / Thinking, with head downcast, / Lost the great highway, / And took the crossroad / Through a strange wood [*Tesoretto,* 170–190; ed. and trans. Julia Bolton Holloway (New York, 1981)]).

3. How much of the inviting wink is present in Dante's *adocchiare?* The poetic tradition posterior to Dante constantly refers *adocchiare* to amorous games (Politian, *Rime* 233; Ariosto, *Orlando furioso,* xxv, 28). I insert the conditional because Dante also uses the verb to indicate an insistent but disdainful gaze in his encounter with Alessio Interminelli (*Inf.* xviii, 123). As is typical in the articulation of reticence, we begin with a valence of degree zero in which "that family" (22) signifies only "such a group of souls" without any allusion to the strange-

ness of their behavior, and *adocchiato* means only "stare attentively," and the semantic space expands as in retrospect we consider the phrase within the context of Brunetto's sin. The same thing occurs, although the evidence of metaphoricity is much stronger, with the *mal protesi nervi* ("tendons strained by sin" [114]) left by Bishop Andrea dei Mozzi in Vicenza; here the phrase loses its neutrality and its character as a written source of information to assume a more complex ambiguity and valence as soon as we opt for *one* of the meanings of the sin punished in the canto.

CANTO XVI

From Other Sodomites to Fraud

SUSAN NOAKES

Any reader who encounters *Inferno* XVI for the first time is likely to be haunted by the canto's concluding episode (106–136); the atmosphere Dante creates there, when he depicts Virgil throwing the pilgrim's "cord" into the abyss and then the emergence from that abyss of "a figure swimming" through the air, inevitably fascinates with its mystery. Moreover, if this final, puzzling incident transfixes the attention of novice readers, it has become a veritable obsession for numerous scholarly readers, who have proposed a plethora of symbolic interpretations of the "cord" and the "figure," none of which has attained wide acceptance. To allow ourselves to be distracted by only the closing episode, however, is to overlook that the canto is made up of three principal episodes of equal interest and significance, and of roughly equal length (about 45 lines each). The first is the pilgrim's interview with the so-called three Florentines; the second, the poet's first diatribe *in propria persona* against the city he loved and hated, Florence. The first of these episodes is mysterious in its own way, in that it requires for its understanding some knowledge of long-forgotten details in the history of thirteenth-century Florentine politics, together with reflection on the significance such details came to have for Dante. Dante was a man of political action (even serving for a time as one of the ruling priors of Florence), who came in his long exile to abandon all the political parties of his day. He instead turned his attention to meditating and writing ever more assiduously on political theory during all the years of exile, even as the possibilities of political action came to seem to him more and more remote.

He mulled over political events and personalities already half forgotten even by his contemporaries, those early commentators on his poem whose literary lives did not give them cause, as Dante had, to interrogate obsessively past political events. Dante was driven, like no other Florentine of his day, to find some explanation for the events that shaped the last two bitter decades of his life.

In Canto xvi Dante reflects yet again on the history of Florentine politics and makes a step toward answering the question (and thus consoling the questioner): "What went wrong with the city, my home, which I loved and served to the best of my ability?" His answer arises from consideration of two topics that concerned him throughout his adult life: first, the effort to discover the *natural* model of human community, the way that people should organize themselves on earth so as to live in closest conformity with God's plan; and, second, the role of rhetoric in serving human community, which is to say, the role of language in politics.

From beginning to end, the canto is thoroughly political, although it may not appear to be so from the viewpoint of a twentieth-century concept of what politics is. For Dante, politics is not essentially a struggle between parties, classes, or nations. He understood politics fundamentally as Aristotle had described it in the *Ethics* and *Politics*: an art of moving, organizing, and motivating groups of people to understand and collaboratively seek their own highest good, rather than some distracting and thus ultimately destructive lesser good. In the art of politics so conceived, rhetoric, applied to both writing and speech, played a central role, a role with which Dante was personally deeply involved, since he had been perhaps the principal rhetorician of the White Guelph party for an extended period. (For example, for his skill as *arengador*, master of spoken rhetoric or orator, he was chosen to go on the all-important embassy to the pope, to persuade him to prevent Florence from being invaded on behalf of the Black Guelphs, and the failure of this mission led directly to Dante's exile. For his skill as *dettator*, master of written rhetoric, he was chosen by the banished White Guelphs in the early and still hopeful first days of exile to compose appeals on their behalf.)

When Dante tried to understand his own role—past, present, and to come—in that artful seeking after the communal good that was politics, he necessarily thought of his role not as a dispenser of blows (a soldier) or of florins (a power buyer), but as a dispenser of words (a rhetorician), whether in speeches, or epistles, or poems. In the canto that precedes the one discussed here, the poet confronts, with great ambivalence, the man he sees as his teacher in civic rhetoric: the man from whom he learned not only *what* tools of rhetoric to use but also, and more important, *when* to use them and *why*. Brunetto Latini was the translator-author of an important treatise on rhetoric, as well as a practitioner of rhetoric, both written and oral, in the service of the Guelph party and the Florentine state. Moreover, his *Trésor* was the source of much of Dante's rhetoric on the nature of political virtue in the latter's first draft of his mature political doctrine (in *Convivio* IV). The Brunetto presented in Canto XV is thus not merely an example of sodomy or some other more metaphorical form of violence against nature; nor is he simply the old schoolteacher whom the mature Dante regards with sentimental reverence. Brunetto represents also the rhetorician who has used his literary training to serve the city-state and who has taught Dante to do the same.

The role of rhetoric in the city-state, thus suggested in Canto XV, will remain the most prominent theme throughout Canto XVI. To show how this is so, I should like first to deal with the canto's three principal episodes in turn (leaving the introductory and interstitial passages to be considered later, after their historical and intellectual context has been reconstructed). The first of these episodes begins in line 4 with a description of the departure of a group of three souls from the larger group with which they suffer. As he describes the general nature of their crime and punishment in Canto XV, Brunetto distinguishes two subgroups in this zone of Hell: the "file" of the professionally lettered whom he allows temporarily to "pass on ahead" (XV, 33) and the other subgroup, which almost catches up with him and from which he emphatically wishes to keep himself separate: "with whom I must not be" (XV, 118). Brunetto thus forms a bridge that almost links the two subgroups but, for an important reason, does not completely do so. The second subgroup includes those who have, like Brunetto, served the Florentine city-state, at precisely the same period in its history as Brunetto did, and from within the same political party: All are prominent Guelphs of the third quarter of the thirteenth century. All three may be said to have been rhetoricians, in the sense that they provided political counsel for or against certain actions or served as political negotiators; they were unlike Brunetto in that they were not professional men of letters, and their rhetorical contributions were entirely oral, oratorical, while his was also written. When Brunetto discriminates between this group and himself (XV, 118), he goes on to mention his encyclopedia as the basis of his hope for a kind of immortality (for his name and ideas) that his soul can never attain. The canto's last line further discriminates Brunetto from the group that runs up to the pilgrim in his wake: Brunetto (at least) "appeared to be the winner, not the loser" (XV, 124), in that he left a book to live on when his own soul perished. The three Florentines of Canto XVI are thus cast metaphorically as "losers," in that they do not belong to the subgroup of men of letters: They spent their rhetorical skills on political deliberation, an activity of necessarily transitory value; in fact, by the time Dante writes this canto, all that their deliberative rhetoric achieved has been destroyed.

These three, usually lumped together as the "three Florentines" by those who devise the canto headings in editions of the *Comedy,* might indeed be more specifically and tellingly described as the "three Guelphs" or "three heroes of the Golden Age of the Guelph party." The names of all three would be known to the very oldest among the early Florentine readers of the canto simply because of all their civic fame in the third quarter of the thirteenth century; moreover, the pilgrim, in *Inferno* VI, 79–80, specifically names two of the three (the relatively less renowned ones) when asking Ciacco whether he would find these "men so worthy . . . whose minds bent toward good" in Heaven or Hell. This moving question, and the mere fact that their names appear twice in *Inferno,* show that Tegghiaio Aldobrandi and Jacopo Rusticucci were much on Dante's mind. The reader is thus virtually obliged to share Dante's acute interest in them. Ciacco's statement that "They are among the blackest souls" (VI, 85) implies that the pilgrim's assessment of their worth, and of their notion of the good, is somehow defective: His evaluation is not in harmony with God's judgment, meaning that the pilgrim requires moral instruction in this matter. Indeed, the pilgrim's eventual encounter with these Florentines and their companion, Guido Guerra, constitutes a step in the pilgrim's education as to the error of his own earlier political values and especially his earlier activities as a rhetorician in the service of the Florentine city-state.

The (initially unnamed) spokesman of this group, Jacopo Rusticucci, first identifies his very eminent compatriot Guido Guerra (38) through an allusion (37) to his grandmother Gualdrada dei Ravignani. Precisely what basis Dante might have for calling her "good" is impossible to say, although by shortly after Dante's time (and perhaps even as a result of Dante's allusion) a charming and quite impossible legend had grown up about her proud defense of her chastity. Gualdrada's virtue, whatever its nature, stands in contrast to the destructive savagery of the only other woman mentioned in the canto, Rusticucci's wife (45), the two female figures thus providing a kind of frame for what is said of the three men. By means of metonymy, Gualdrada's goodness certainly casts favorable light on her grandson, who is thus presented as coming from "good" stock even before any of his own deeds, virtuous or otherwise, are mentioned. In the heavily Florentine context of this and the preceding canto, it seems likely that the goodness Dante had in mind when mentioning Gualdrada was more civic than moral: her marriage to a Guidi count had been extremely important to Florence politically, bringing to an end the lengthy hostilities between the city and the Guidi family, which had previously harassed the city and its commerce from its many fortified holdings in the surrounding countryside. In fact, Guido Guerra's grandmother and grandfather had established their family for periods of time within the city walls, in a house that was part of Gualdrada's inheritance, thereby contributing much to the "Florentinization" of the powerful Guidi clan.

Guido's second name, *Guerra* (war), was a nickname traditionally assigned to him, as to certain of his ancestors, because of his military prowess.

Dante, however, stresses equally with Guido Guerra's military achieve-ments ("his sword") the high quality of his political counsel ("his good sense accomplished much" [39]). Indeed, Guido Guerra represents much more than just an important general. To White Guelphs of Dante's gener-ation, he was a major symbol of their cause, an example of one who put the ideal of the independent city-state above old aristocratic alliances and self-interest.

The family to which Guido Guerra belonged, the Palatine counts Guidi, had probably originated with an ancestor who had come south into Italy with Otto I in the tenth century, and the family had long been affiliated with the Ghibelline or imperial party; by Dante's day, however, many of the Guidi had, on various occasions, given their allegiance to the Guelph cause, at least temporarily. Guido Guerra, offspring of a branch of the family with more than one Guelph connection by way of marriage, indeed became the chief leader of the Tuscan Guelph party. He fought at the head of the Flor-entine (Guelph) troops against the (Ghibelline) Aretines in 1255 and played a leading role on the Guelph side at the notorious battle of Montaperti (1260), where the Guelph government of the Primo Popolo of Florence was humiliated. Though family connections probably would have allowed him to reconcile with the new Ghibelline government (headed by another Guidi count) and return to Florence, Guido Guerra remained faithful to the exiled party and, by contributing his efforts to the defeat at Benevento of Emperor Frederick II's natural son, Manfred, had the honor of playing a leading role in restoring Florence to Guelph rule in 1267.

The second of the Florentines depicted here, Tegghiaio Aldobrandi, a member of the Adimari family, was also active in Guelph politics. He was a participant in the negotiation of peace treaties among various Tuscan city-states in 1236–37 and served as *podestà* of four of them between 1238 and 1259. In 1260 Tegghiaio was one of the chiefs of the ill-fated Florentine army at Montaperti, although, as Rusticucci suggests (41–42), he had ad-vised that Florence not engage the Sienese and Ghibelline troops on that disastrous occasion, famed as having "stained the waters of the Arbia red" (x, 86) with the blood of between twenty-five hundred to ten thousand Florentines, according to contemporary accounts. Tegghiaio's lengthy ca-reer as negotiator and *podestà* suggests that his powers as a rhetorician were well respected by his party, even though it did not heed his words on the eve of Montaperti: His prescience on that occasion must have consid-erably embellished his reputation as a counselor.

Jacopo Rusticucci's name frequently appears in historical documents alongside Tegghiaio's; indeed, the two owned contiguous houses in the area of Porta San Piero, one of the older sections of Florence. He too was a leading Guelph, assisting in the negotiation of Tuscan peace treaties in 1237. His rhetorical skills are further attested by the gifts he received in 1238 from the commune of San Gimignano for his effectiveness in defending it in the council of Florence. In 1254, he was charged by Florence to negotiate peace with other Tuscan cities.

Indeed, the very structure of the speech that Dante has Rusticucci deliver suggests that he is a practiced orator. He opens with a display of deference toward his hearer (28–30) calculated to win the pilgrim's goodwill. He then introduces his two companions in the most favorable light possible (36–42) and names himself while excusing his sin (43–45). After being assured that the pilgrim has been won over by his words (52–60), Rusticucci goes on to put forward his request, having effectively, as an experienced orator, prepared the way for a favorable response.

Because these three Guelph heroes are assigned by Dante to suffer damnation with the sodomites, they present the reader with a genuine problem, the kind of problem Dante sets up again and again for the reader to puzzle out. The problem is this: why does the poet show such great respect for Guido Guerra, Tegghiaio Aldobrandi, and Jacopo Rusticucci when he is at the same time assigning them to public ignominy by placing them not just in Hell but in a part of Hell associated with a sin regarded by his society as particularly undignified and repugnant? The contrast between the explicit and implicit treatment accorded the three is highlighted by the comments the pilgrim's guide, Virgil, makes about them (15–18): He is emphatic about the necessity for the pilgrim to "show courtesy" to them, despite their nakedness, their wounds, and their sin. (The puzzle is as great as if an American writer known for patriotic values and public service were to depict the founding fathers of the American republic as sodomists. Only a radical change in spirit, and a crisis that had swept away the writer's patriotism, would explain such a conversion.)

Whatever the sexual practices of the three Guelph heroes, Dante's placement of them here is not easy to explain, given the great respect his narrative evidences for their character and achievements. Dante could show his respect for these heroes by passing over their sin in silence, choosing as his example of sodomy someone he hated or even creating an anonymous soul, as he does on other occasions. But here, as in the case of Brunetto Latini, Dante writes ambivalently: He brings the names of the three Guelph patriots before all eyes and at the same time besmirches the names for all eternity.

The solution to this problem is to be sought in an understanding of Dante's changing attitude toward his own White Guelph past in the light of his banishment from Florence. Passerin d'Entrèves has shown that we cannot understand Dante's political thought wholly by reference to the long-accepted notion of his later, so-called Ghibellinism: if in any sense Dante comes to hope for a revival of the Holy Roman Empire, it is in reaction to and within confines created by his earlier Guelphism, that is, support of the concept of the autonomous city-state owing a degree of allegiance only to the pope. The concept that the city is the ideal form of government is the very beginning of Dante's political thought. This early idea of his is based on the concept that legitimate government is not the result of mere human need or hunger for power but rather an expression of what is most human in human nature, the impulse to live happily, which no one can do in isolation. This Aristotelian notion, that friendship is the natural extension of the quest for the happy life, lay at the foundation of Guelph thought. Guelphism was based on the notion that the city is the most natural form of government because the bonds of friendship can extend only where citizens live in proximity: fellow citizens share interests and needs with one another in a way they cannot do with those in a faraway imperial court. Guelphism was but one manifestation of a notion that swept through Europe during Dante's lifetime and only centuries later took on its present-day form in the doctrine of national sovereignty. This notion, that there could be such a thing as a free state, recognizing no authority higher than its own, had been claimed already by France. In Italy, its earliest influential champion was Florence.

In Canto XVI Dante calls into question the acts by the political heroes of his youth to promote the Guelph ideal of state sovereignty free from the authority of the Holy Roman emperor. In so doing, Dante also implicitly criticizes his own youthful political ideals. He comes to believe that there is innate to humans a desire for aggrandizement that implies that the autonomous state will never be adequate to maintain for its citizens the "good life." In his treatise *Monarchia* (argued by Nardi to have been complete before Dante began work on the *Comedy*), Dante looks back on his earlier allegiance to Guelph political doctrine and describes it in a way that bears directly on this canto: "I admit that once I wondered not a little how anyone could think that the Roman people had come to dominate the world without meeting any effective resistance; for, *looking only on the surface* of things, I thought they had achieved this dominance through force alone, with no basis in law. But when later I came to *look into things deeply* with the eyes of my mind and saw from *indisputable signs* that this [the Roman Empire] was the work of divine providence, my earlier wonder was replaced by disdain as I thought about other peoples who rebelled against the supremacy of the people of Rome, for I saw other peoples *acting* as *vainly* today as I had in the past . . . " (*Monarchia* II, i; translation and emphasis mine).

The political conversion Dante describes in this passage is one he conceives of as a change in viewpoint: a movement from insight that is superficial to one that is more profound. Thus, the Guelph ideal of civic autonomy is attractive on the surface, but ultimately unsatisfying to one who reflects on politics deeply. The notion that fellow citizens can, through deliberative rhetoric, create an autonomous state that will make possible earthly happiness is definitively rejected. What Brunetto Latini and the other three Guelph rhetoricians represent is a beautiful but ultimately superficial political ideal. Dante's placement of these counselors of civic autonomy with those who have done violence to nature has meaning not only in the erotic but also in the political domain. Dante comes to see the Guelph doctrine that the city is the most *natural* fulfillment of human political needs as based on a superficial and thus deceptive notion of human nature, one that thus does violence to nature.

Canto XVI thus commemorates Dante's turn away from his earlier hope that, by using his skill with words at the service of his city, that is, by being a deliberative rhetorician, a *dettator* and *arengador,* he could make an important contribution to the world's happiness. Abandoning deliberative rhetoric, he returns to use his linguistic skills once again primarily in the creation of poetry, but poetry that differs from that of his youth because its ends are not simply esthetic or moral but also in the highest sense political. The concluding portion of the canto, the episode of the cord, brings us to the principal problem of poetry with political ambitions.

But before this final episode begins, Dante concludes this highly ambivalent homage to the old Guelph party with one last display of the art of oratory, which had been of supreme importance to the champions of a free Florence. The pilgrim's brief speech (73–75) forms the canto's center. It blames the expulsion of "courtesy and valor" from Florence and the city's current tears on recent immigrants from the countryside and excessive commercial growth. The pilgrim thus echoes the bitter words of Ciacco (VI, 64–75) and Brunetto (XV, 61–78). His position seems to confirm the Aristotelian notion (later taken to be typical of Ghibellinism) that one can be virtuous only if one comes from old stock and possesses the kind of old wealth that presumably offers protection against greed.

What is interesting here is not so much what the pilgrim says as how he says it, as is clear from the way the three Guelphs respond (lines 79–81). Their question (66–72) arises from concern for the city they had long served. Yet, after hearing the pilgrim's answer, they do not comment on the civic plight he describes, that is, on the content of *what* he says; their attention instead shifts to *how* he says it. The pilgrim's style in these three lines differs markedly from the one both he and Jacopo use earlier. It is not courteous. It does nothing to prepare the pilgrim's hearers for what is to come. Clearly, if the words of Guglielmo Borsiere cause them "much affliction" (72), to the point that they even begin to doubt his veracity, they will be even more vexed by what the pilgrim says; yet he does nothing to mitigate the abruptness and violence of what he has to say. The three accept as truth (78) from the pilgrim what they have been unwilling to believe in the words of Guglielmo Borsiere, and they praise the pilgrim for the readiness of his reply. Yet there is ambivalence and irony in their response that the pilgrim will be happy if he is always able to answer so readily, for he will certainly not always be able to do so, as the final third of this very canto demonstrates. His first political speech *in propria persona,* almost too righteous, "cried out with face upraised" (76), will indeed not set a pattern for what the pilgrim (or his alter ego, the poet) will say.

The difficulty Dante comes to have in speaking clearly and directly about the problems the *Comedy* treats will in fact be dramatized in the canto's concluding episode, the mysterious scene dominated by the throwing of the cord. This scene is central to the *Inferno* in that it initiates the transition from Hell's second realm (bestiality) to the third and final one (fraud). Dante devotes fully half of Hell to the fraudulent, suggesting that fraud is not only the worst category of sin but is also more important to the development of the poet's overall intention in the *Comedy* than are incontinence and bestiality. The initial allegorical representation of fraud thus takes on particular importance.

Dante in this episode creates a metamorphosis, following a tradition in which he is preceded, among others, by Ovid and Lucan. The cord that Virgil throws down into the abyss is "knotted and coiled" (111); it returns as a serpent whose flanks are "adorned with twining knots and circlets" (xvii, 15). It is singularly appropriate that the character Virgil should be the poet Dante's tool for the accomplishment of this metamorphosis, for the episode is based on a passage from Virgil's *Aeneid* (bk. ii, esp. 203–227). The Virgilian metamorphosis in question takes as its point of departure and of culmination the Trojan priest Laocoön, who, in the famous episode of the Trojan horse, is the only one to speak the truth about the horse's character. Laocoön is, at this moment, in a position not unlike that of Tegghiaio Aldobrandi on the eve of the battle of Montaperti: He speaks against a particular course of action in wartime, culminating his plea with the famous line: "I fear Greeks, even when they bear gifts." He even suggests that there may be Greeks hidden inside the horse. But his fellow Trojans do not believe his words, despite their truth. Instead, the Trojans believe the false words of the traitor Sinon. Laocoön indeed, after finishing his unsuccessful speech, hurls against the horse a spear that poetically changes into dragonlike serpents, which rise from the deep to destroy Laocoön and his sons. At the end of his account of Laocoön's truthful but unsuccessful speech, Aeneas emphasizes its archetypal political context. He interjects that Troy would still be standing if the Trojans had believed Laocoön, thus implying to the reader who knows Aeneas's destiny that, if the Trojans had believed the truth when Laocoön spoke it, Rome, seat of Church and empire, would never have been founded.

To write a metamorphosis, to imagine a symmetrical relation between two disparate forms and then describe the transformation of one into another, is a rhetorical feat to be accomplished only by a virtuoso of poetry. Dante was greatly interested in accomplishing such feats with his words, as is clear from *Inferno* xxv, 94–99, where he challenges both Lucan and Ovid, vaunting the metamorphosis he creates in the episode of the Florentine thieves as superior to any created by his classical predecessors. The details

Dante employs to achieve the metamorphosis here are, indeed, ingenious. The pilgrim's knotted and coiled *corda* emerges fron the abyss as a knotted and circled *coda* (the tail, of the serpent-monster). The spelling of these two Italian words connects them by punning word play, paronomasia. Still another instance of paronomasia connects not the cord but, indeed, its wearer to the monster of fraud: it links the *note* (127) to *notando* (131). *Note*, translated as "lines," indicates specifically the sounds, letters, or words that Dante writes and upon which he swears to the veracity of his vision of the monster. *Notando* is from another etymological root entirely and simply means "swimming." The similarity in form of these two words gives Dante a rhetorical opportunity that he exploits to the fullest to accomplish a kind of parabasis, creating an interlude that breaks the fiction of his poem by commenting upon it.

The vertex of this rupture in Dante's fiction is the paradox stated at lines 124–127: Dante asserts that his true words will seem false. The poet's situation here is very different from that of the pilgrim in lines 73–81, when the others commend him for the clarity of his speech; the correspondence between lines 78 (*com' al ver*) and 124 (*a quel ver*) emphasizes this contrast. Dante thus characterizes his rhetoric in the canto's concluding episode as anything but clear and ready: It seems to lie. His language in describing "this strange sign" will seem to be an example of the category of sin that he is about to introduce: fraud.

Why should Dante at the beginning of his treatment of fraud accuse himself of such a vice? At the simplest level, it is easy to understand why Dante must apologize for what he is about to do. Fourteenth-century readers were no more likely than readers today to believe that Dante, or anyone else, had seen "through the dense and darkened air . . . a figure swimming." The reader who granted a kind of assent to the fiction of a journey through Hell will nonetheless at least momentarily balk at this episode. Knowing that such a withdrawal of the reader's assent is inevitable, Dante uses this rupture in the relation between reader and text to make a point about the new direction his poem is about to take.

Through the rhetorical devices of metamorphosis and paranomasia the poet suggests a symmetrical relation between himself and the monster of fraud. The introductory lines (127–129) of his apostrophe to the reader allude to Dante's entire undertaking in writing his otherworldly fiction while naming it *comedìa*. (Medieval books did not have title pages; we call Dante's poem *Comedy* because he does—here in line 128 and only once again, in Canto XXI, 2. To a learned person of Dante's time the word would promise a work of humble style, set off from tragedy's elevated style. And, according to the lights of its day, this work is humble because it is written in the vernacular rather than in Latin and because it treats "low" people and themes as well as "high" ones. A *comedy* in the fourteenth century was not a humorous work.) Dante's comment on his *Comedy* here was prepared earlier in the canto (61–63) when Dante summarized its plot while introducing himself to the three Guelph heroes. Thus, Dante implicates his whole poem in preparing the cord episode.

Dante links himself rhetorically to the "figure" of fraud to confess that he is, as a poet, a perpetrator of fraud. That fiction works by persuading its readers to accept as true something that is false may seem to some twentieth-century readers so obvious and acceptable as to be scarcely worthy of comment; but in the early fourteenth century, when works of literature could have value only if they served ethical ends, and vernacular works were generally expected not to have ethical value, the possibility that a charge of falsehood might be leveled against his *Comedy* was something Dante had to take seriously.

He meets this issue of poetic ethics squarely as he readies himself for the Malebolge ("evil-pouches"), the eighth circle, a section of *Inferno* where figures from classical myth and history appear much more frequently than they do in other parts of this canticle. Dante enters into a struggle to equal (and surpass, as a Christian poet must) his classical forebears from the moment he begins the metamorphosis of the cord, so similar in context to that of Laocoön's spear. He thus emphasizes in this canto his turn away from a primary focus on his activity as a *political* rhetorician (*dettator* and *arengador*) to one on his activity as a *poetic* rhetorician. The "knots" that characterize both the pilgrim's cord and the monster's body are well known in the Middle Ages as symbols of poetic language. Their appearance points the reader to the rhetorical issues that lie at the heart of this canto. The word "figure" (131), too, points to rhetorical concerns. Dante's use of it, rather than of some more specific word indicating a "monster," "dragon," or "beast," might seem to leave him open to the charge of vagueness. In fact, however, "figure" suggests another common image: the "rhetorical figure." The thing into which Dante's own cord has been transformed is indeed a rhetorical figure, a "figure of speech"; it is also, more fundamentally, a figure that represents rhetoric, in all its ethical ambivalence.

Inferno XVI is thus a complex canto. Its unity, though not immediately apparent, emerges from the issues Dante raises in the canto's three sections. At the surface level, the canto is integrated by the continuing description of water. It opens with an indication of the distant murmur of the infernal river falling into the eighth circle (1–3). It continues (91–105) with the description of the deafening roar as the two poets draw closer to the water. And it concludes with the emergence of a "figure swimming . . . like one returning from the waves" (lines 131–136). This surface motif, however, is mere topographic detail that derives interest only from the resonance it sets up with the canto's most prominent theme: words. When first mentioned, the water is cited not for its appearance but for its sound. The second time Dante writes about it, he conceives it as creating a sound so loud as nearly to wipe out speech (93); a bit later, it is something that will eliminate the capacity to hear speech (105). The final allusion to water moves from this emphasis on water's sound to point to its capacity to hide things (135), to snag (134), and, above all, to disgorge the horrifying. More than water, this canto returns obsessively to the theme of words, as its many references to words, voices, and telling make clear.

If water is but a surface motif, then, it nonetheless points the way to the canto's central concern with language. Dante, in the relation he creates between water and words here, illustrates once again the relation between surface and center, a problem posed in this canto both explicitly and implicitly. Dante asserts (124–125) that his words are true although their surface lies. He implies (and states in the *Monarchia*) that the Guelph ideal, a trust in the power of deliberative rhetoric—words—to ensure peace, is a superficial notion. Perhaps the lesson of this canto is that words which on the surface seem honest (like the pilgrim's diatribe placing blame on the "new people" for corrupting Florence) may hide falsehood (in that Florence's problems are to be solved only by a restructuring of world government, rather than by a change in immigration patterns, or even in civic morals), while a surface of falsehood (poetry that uses all the false techniques of pagan rhetoric to evoke "figures" like those of pagan literature) holds truth. In any case, such are the words that Dante chooses to employ as he moves into the deepest part of his *Inferno*.

BIBLIOGRAPHY

A version of this essay appeared in *Lectura Dantis Virginiana* 1, a special issue of *Lectura Dantis* 6 (1990 suppl.): 209–221.

Baransky, Zygmunt. "The 'Marvellous' and the 'Comic': Toward a Reading of *Inferno* xvi." *Lectura Dantis* 7 (1990): 72–95.
Becker, Christopher. "Dante's Motley Cord: Art and Apocalypse in *Inferno* xvi." *MLN* 106, no. 1 (1991): 179–183.
Caretti, Lanfranco. "Storia e poesia in Dante (il canto xvi dell'*Inferno*)." *Cultura e scuola* 4, nos. 13–14 (1965): 476–488.
Friedman, John B. "L'allegoria della corda nel canto xvi dell'*Inferno*." *Rassegna della letteratura italiana* 84, nos. 1–2 (1980): 97–100.
Marti, Mario. "Tematica e dimensione verticale del xvi dell'*Inferno* (dai 'campioni' alla 'corda')." *L'Alighieri* 8, no. 1 (1967): 3–24.
Mercuri, Roberto. *Semantica di Gerione: il motivo del viaggio nella "Commedia" di Dante.* Rome, 1984.
Pasquazi, Silvio. "Il canto dei tre fiorentini." In *All'eterno dal tempo*, 13–48. Florence, 1966.
———. "Sul 'getto della corda' e su Gerione." In *All'eterno dal tempo*, 49–98. Florence, 1966.
———. *Il canto xvi dell'"Inferno."* Florence, 1968.
Pézard, André. *Dante sous la pluie de feu.* Paris, 1950.
Pietrobono, Luigi. "Tre fiorentini: Guido Guerra, Tegghiaio Aldobrandi e Jacopo Rusticucci." *L'Alighieri* 3, no. 2 (1962): 17–24.
Sacchetto, Aleardo. "Il canto dei tre fiorentini." In *Due letture dantesche*, 5–37. Rome, 1953.
Salsano, Fernando. *La coda di Minosse e altri saggi danteschi.* Milan, 1968.
Santini, P. "Sui Fiorentini 'che fur sì degni.'" *Studi danteschi* 6 (1923): 25–40.
Vallone, Aldo. *Il canto xvi dell'"Inferno."* Turin, 1959.

CANTO XVII

Geryon's Downward Flight; the Usurers

PAOLO CHERCHI

Canto XVII is like a busy railroad station, where a number of tracks end and new ones originate. These tracks are themes, motives, and narrative segments. Geryon owes his appearance to a magic stratagem recounted in the previous canto. The roaring of the Phlegethon waterfall, an important landmark for Dante's trip, also sounds first in Canto XVI. The episode of the usurers begins thematically with the invective against *i sùbiti guadagni* ("quick gains" [XVI 73]), and the explanation of their sin comes in Canto XI, 94–111. Among the themes that meet in Canto XVII, the most obvious is that of the monstrous combination of different natures. The Minotaur, the Centaurs, the Harpies, and the souls of the suicides had combined human, animal, and vegetable natures; Geryon, who incorporates two natures and three animal species, brings to a climax the theme of monstrosity. Another conspicuous and related theme pervading the seventh circle is the presence of outlandish phenomena, known to rhetoricians as *adynata:* the talking plants of the suicides, the fire that falls like rain, and a weeping composite statue. These *impossibilia* seem to culminate in the horrific "downward" flight of Geryon. Several themes that will be developed in the eighth and ninth circles are introduced in this canto. One of them is explicitly mentioned by Virgil when, ready to board Geryon, he says *omai si scende per sì fatte scale* ("for [now] our descent is by this kind of stairs" [82]), alluding to the "lifts" to be provided by Geryon, Antaeus, and Lucifer. In all three cases the pilgrim Dante experiences physical contact with his "means of transportation." Geryon's triune nature reminds us of Cerberus's three heads, but it also looks forward to the three giants who guard Cocytus, and the three-headed Lucifer. Dante's flight on Geryon's back may even foreshadow Ulysses' *folle volo* ("wild flight" [xxvi, 125]). Finally, Geryon's fraudulent image introduces us to the stealthy world of Malebolge.

Do we have here, therefore, a "transitional" canto? This tends to be the traditional perception, which is also based on the fact that a good third of the canto actually describes a trip between two circles. Moreover, the canto's narrative is discontinuous, giving the impression of a loose structure. It also lacks an outstanding character (a Francesca, a Farinata, a Brunetto, a Ulysses, a Ugolino), of the type whose story often determines a canto's unity. Yet, despite all the ties to previous and subsequent cantos and despite the peculiar organization of its materials, Canto xvii does not represent a mere "transitional" moment in Dante's journey. It has in fact a strong poetic unity of its own, and its remarkable features make it one of the most memorable cantos in the entire *Comedy*. Its exceptionality is confirmed by the fact that the author, in announcing the extraordinary event that is about to take place in this canto, uses for the first time in the text the title of his work (*comedìa* [xvi, 128]; he does so only once again, in xx, 2).

The first and the last line of the canto correspond to each other in an almost specular way, as if to mark the autonomy of its narrative space and its poetical unity. In both lines the image of the "tail" appears, *coda* and *cocca* combining synonymy with alliteration. More interesting, however, than the acoustic echo and the similarity of meaning is the fact that both times this image appears as a synecdoche, a rhetorical figure by which the part indicates the whole. This could be taken as a mere coincidence, but it also happens to be a major stylistic feature in a canto that teems with tropes indicating a dislocation from the abstract to the concrete, from the whole to the detail. These figures are mostly synecdoches, metonymies, catachreses, and periphrases. They are all found in the first tercet (1–3):

> "Behold the beast who bears the pointed tail,
> who crosses mountains, shatters weapons, walls!
> Behold the one whose stench fills all the world!"

Coda ("tail") in line 1 could be taken as the part for the whole (synecdoche); *monti, muri,* and *armi* (mountains, walls, weapons [2]) stand for "obstacles": the concrete substitutes for the abstract—thus we have metonymy; *appuzza* (fills with stench) stands for "destroys," "ruins," which constitutes a catachresis or *abusio* because the word is used improperly; finally the whole tercet is a periphrasis because it indicates Geryon without mentioning him directly.

In order to appreciate how pervasive this stylistic feature is, let us look at a few examples of each of these figures, bearing in mind that the difference between them is often tenuous and that at times they are interchangeable.

Among the synecdoches we may consider *lo dosso e 'l petto e ambedue le coste* ("his back and chest as well as both his flanks" [14]), an enumeration of parts that stands for the whole (the trunk); *la fiammella* ("fire" [33]), and *lo bivero* ("beaver" [22]), both singular for plural; *tele* ("webs" [18]) and *marmi* ("marbles" [6]), where the material is given for the product; *omeri* ("shoulders" [42]) and *reni* (kidneys, "sides" [109]), meaning "back," where the part stands for the whole.

Examples of metonymy are *pelle* ("skin" [11]), which stands for "outer semblance"; *i passeggiati marmi* ("the walked-on marbles" [6]) for "stone causeway"; *la destra mammella* ("right breast" [31]) for the "right side"; *sinistro fianco* ("left flank" [69]) for "left side"; *al piè al piè* ("at the very foot" [134]) for "at the bottom"—all these metonymies substitute the concrete for the abstract; *doloroso foco* ("the painful fire" [53]), meaning "the fire that causes pain"; *tra li Tedeschi lurchi* ("among the guzzling Germans" [20]) for "in Germany."

Examples of catachresis are *a proda* ("ashore" [5])—but there is no real sea, lake, or river; *guerra* ("war" [22]) for "hunting"; *testa* (head [43]) for "outer margin"; *si cosse* (was cooked [108]) for "scorched"; *notando* ("swimming" [115]) for "flying." An interesting series of catachreses is used to indicate Geryon's back: the first term used is *omeri,* appropriate for a man; then *groppa* (croup, hindquarters; "back" [78]), more appropriate for a donkey or other pack animal; then *spallacce* (big ugly shoulders, "enormous shoulders" [91]), again tilting toward the brute. Indeed the composite nature of Geryon seems to make it difficult to find the exact words to describe him.

The cases of periphrasis are frequent and quite interesting. Many of them refer to Geryon. He is mentioned by name only twice, at the very beginning and at the end of the flight, otherwise he is always presented only through periphrasis—*quella sozza imagine di froda* (7 ["that filthy effigy / of fraud" (6–7)]); *la fiera pessima* ("that squalid beast" [23])—in which periphrasis and antonomasia coincide. Another set of periphrases will be seen in the episode of the usurers, identified simply as "Paduans" and "Florentines"; while we also find the expressions '*l cavalier sovrano* ("the sovereign cavalier" [72]) and *la gente mesta* ("the melancholy people" [45]). Virgil too is presented through periphrasis: *lui che di poco star m'avea 'mmonito* ("him who'd warned me to be brief" [77]).

The high frequency of these figures of speech gives us a clue to the way in which Dante the pilgrim lives through the experience of this canto. On the one hand, he sees things in the most concrete way, while on the other, he is unable or unwilling to define them. Synedoche, metonymy, and catachresis are figures that aim at concrete, material representation, whereas periphrasis exists in order to avoid precise definition or identification. The presence of both tendencies reveals a situation in which fascination and repulsion go hand in hand. It is a situation dominated by horror and disgust, the main themes of the canto. Things speak to the senses with their strong physical evidence; the mind, almost paralyzed by the horror they evoke, refuses to comment upon them. Thus the canto is eminently descriptive. Another rhetorical feature that corroborates this finding is the unusually high number of similes. There are fifteen in all, mostly taken from the animal world. Not only do they belong to the same class of tropes as the periphrases, but they also serve to heighten the physical texture of the canto as a whole.

The stylistic homogeneity of the canto seems to be in contrast to the nonlinear organization of its materials. This, too, is a fallacious impression. The canto is built on a mortise technique. Its parts balance one another in length, not in order to achieve a mere external sense of proportion, but to create instead suspenseful increments of fear, repulsion, and horror. The canto may be divided as follows: lines 1–42 contain the description of and the encounter with Geryon; 43–78, the meeting with the usurers; 79–136, the flight. Each one of these three sections could be further subdivided: (a) 1–27, description of Geryon; 28–42, closer view of Geryon and Virgil's advice on visiting with the usurers; (b) 43–75, description of the usurers; 76–84, return of Dante to Virgil; (c) 85–99, the climb onto Geryon's back, and 100–126, the actual flight. The three major parts—all of them descriptive—balance in rhythmic units that range in length from 27 to 32 lines. On the whole, however, Geryon dominates the canto, for he is present in two of the three major parts. The usurers play a lesser, almost incidental, role; but it is precisely in this treatment that Dante's indifference and scorn for these sinners makes itself fully manifest. At this point it is worth noting that the episode of the usurers not only interrupts the main narration but also results in a lacuna of information. While Dante visits the usurers, Virgil parleys with Geryon. We know nothing about what they say to each other and consequently we do not see how Reason succeeds in overcoming Fraud. The function of this lacuna may be better understood if we recall that what we know about the usurers' sin is explained in an earlier canto rather than here where it would seem most appropriate. These two forms of lacuna have a similar function—one operating through absence and the other through distance—to remove from our canto any intellectual complication, so that the "descriptive" nature of the canto can be sustained throughout. Style and content work together. The warp of the canto is clearly set. It is now time to see how Dante weaves his narration into it, to see how our observations so far become meaningful in the poetical discourse. We are ready now for a detailed reading of this canto that, as these preliminary considerations have shown, is quite closely knit.

The opening of the canto is abrupt and dramatic. In the initial anaphora *ecco . . . ecco* ("behold . . . behold" [1–3]), the tension created by the hurling down of the knotted and coiled cord to conjure up Geryon explodes in the deictic presentation. The spell has worked, and the beast is now within sight of the two wayfarers, having surfaced from darkness. Virgil immediately calls Dante's attention to Geryon's tail: this recurring motif (the "tail" will be mentioned no less than five times, in lines 1, 9, 25, 84, 103) is introduced from the first line and will continue to underline Dante's fear and horror. Virgil signals Geryon to come a riva, which literally means "ashore" (catachresis). The word riva introduces the motif of the "edge" that dominates the first part of the canto. It is taken up in the synonymic paradigm proda (5) and fin ("end" [6]), riva (9, 19), orlo ("margin" [24]), le stremo ("brink" [32]), and strema testa (lit., outer margin [43]). This "edge" is the boundary between the solid terrain and the emptiness beyond (loco scemo [36]). The sense of that limit, which makes it necessary to replace walking with flying, is constantly present as an obsession in the mind of the wayfarer even when the episode of the usurers seems to remove it temporarily from his concerns. It has been marked in such a firm way that it cannot be erased: in fact, the temporary distraction increases the expectation and tension brought on by the dreaded experience of aerial navigation.

This "edge" is also the point where Geryon comes to rest, occupying— as is proper for his ambiguous nature—both spaces. Geryon "docks" the upper part of his body (the verb arrivò [8], which normally means "arrived," is used here etymologically to mean "brought to shore": another catachresis). The upper part of Geryon remains perfectly immobile, or so it appears in the poet's detailed and composite description, which follows a classical pattern, beginning from the head and ending at the equivalent of the feet. Geryon's face appears to be that of a just man. When we get to his chest, however, he unexpectedly changes nature: he has the midsection of a snake with the paws of a lion. What Dante notices about his paws is not, as we might expect, their claws but their hairiness, almost an extension of Geryon's human nature; and Dante's eyes follow it up to the armpits (catachresis) where the several natures—man, quadruped, and reptile—meet. The sequence of vignettes continues, describing now the serpentine part: not its length and width, but the pattern of circlets and knots on the skin. They constitute the visualization of an idea; they allegorize the entanglements of Fraud; yet the intensity of the vision is such that no reflective faculty seems to be engaged. Reason, however, cannot be totally absent; it functions with its weakest and yet most imaginative tool, namely analogy. The colors and the immobility of Geryon awaken visual and literary memories. A chain of no less than four similes seems to convey the sense of Dante's tardy awakening to an intellectual perception. The first two comparisons affirm that neither Turks nor Tartars ever fashioned fabric more colorful than Geryon's snakelike skin, nor did Arachne ever spin a comparable web. Humanity, historical or mythological, cannot match this demonic craft. We should note that these two comparisons, along with those of Icarus and Phaethon, which we will examine later, are the only ones to involve persons, and they are all expressed in the negative. Essentially these comparisons are hyperboles that emphasize the exceptionality of what is seen and experienced in this canto.

The mode of analogy is also used to describe Geryon's position. Two similes stress his amphibious nature, which well befits his symbolic ambiguity. The first comparison, taken from the realm of inanimate things, suggests the perfect immobility of the beast. The second, taken from the animal world, implies the tension of a snare, suggesting the presence of a hidden tail lying in wait to entrap fish. Then, announced by these final two comparisons, the extreme part of Geryon's body appears at last (25–27):

> And all his tail was quivering in the void
> while twisting upward its envenomed fork,
> which had a tip just like a scorpion's.

The four foregoing comparisons have delayed the description of Geryon's tail; they have severed, as it were, this tremendous part from the rest of his body. This delay is a narrative strategy that creates a powerful effect of estrangement. Not only does the tail quiver in contrast to the immobility of the rest of the body: it also grafts onto Geryon's composite nature yet another animal species: we were expecting the tail of a serpent, and we now see the tail of a scorpion. The reptile turns into an arachnid. Poised in the void, ready to sting, this bifurcated tail completes and epitomizes the presentation of Geryon.

Who was the "historical" Geryon? This mythological character was a giant, perhaps a legendary king of the Balearic Islands. He fed his flock of sheep with the human flesh of his guests whom he treacherously killed until Hercules killed him. Geryon was said to have three bodies in one, but, as far as we know, all these bodies were of the same nature. Dante used this mythological detail and conflated it with others drawn from medieval zoology. Medieval bestiaries tell of monsters having three natures; they may be variations of the locusts found in Apocalypse 9:7–10. Many paintings and miniatures also provide instances of such kinds of hybrids. Scholars have repeatedly pointed out models for Dante's Geryon, but none of them coincide exactly with Dante's creature. This original demonic figure is clearly a figment of Dante's imagination.

Geryon's triune nature symbolizes Fraud. He is, however, a living emblem, and Dante responds physically to his presence: he is fascinated by this monster just as a rabbit is fascinated by the hypnotic charm of the snake. A sign of this mental paralysis is the total lack of any comment on the vision of the tail. Only the voice of Virgil breaks in upon Dante's horrified attention, and Dante follows him mechanically. Master and pupil must turn to the right in order to reach the beast, and in so doing they are deviating for the second and last time (the first deviation occurred in Canto IX, 132) from the normal leftward pattern followed in Hell. Undoubtedly there is an allegorical meaning in this change of direction, and its sense is quite clear: "one cannot go straight toward fraud; one must approach it askew" (Ottimo Commento). However, there is no insistence on this second meaning in the text; Dante proceeds mesmerized, automatically counting his ten steps toward the beast. This is the first time we have encountered such a precise spatial measurement: it is actually a psychological measurement, since it indicates the distance from the dread beast and from the edge of the precipice as well as the need to test at each step the solidity of the soil.

Reaching Geryon should represent the climax of the narration. But the dramatic encounter is artfully postponed. Dante's attention is distracted by a group of sinners whom he sees sitting on the burning sand next to the outer edge. Virgil encourages his pupil to go and talk to them so that his knowledge of the sins punished in this seventh circle will be complete. Virgil stays to parley with Geryon, while Dante goes all alone toward the group of sinners. The separation is exceptional; it has happened only once before (in Canto VIII outside the gates of Dis) and in a similar situation, when, that is, Virgil had to overcome diabolic resistance or forestall a diabolic danger. The separation from Virgil, the symbol of Reason, accentuates the lack of "mental" participation on Dante's part. Indeed the episode that follows presents an extreme case of mental indifference and noncommitment, foreshadowed by Virgil's warning not to waste any time.

The sinners in the group are the usurers. Since they are in this circle, we must assume that they sinned against nature. Why usury is a sin against nature is not easy to explain. Dante's explanation in Canto XI calls for further clarification, among other things because it might help us understand the *contrapasso* they suffer. Without repeating what has already been said apropos of Canto XI, it should be observed that Dante's explanation is philosophical in nature. This is quite unusual, because usury—a widespread practice with vast social implications—is a sin studied above all by canonists and by theologians. But the first thinker to give a detailed philosophical explanation of its negativity is Saint Thomas, and Dante follows the gist of his argument. Usury is not just a sin against charity, but against nature. In order to see how, we must understand that money is different from any other commodity in that its very essence coincides with its use. Consider, for instance, a house or a horse or a bottle of wine. Their nature is different from the use we make of them: they may or may not be consumed; money, on the other hand, *is* meant to be consumed, spent, that is its very essence. Usury is a sin because it gives away the substance and charges for its use, as if these were two separable things: we would never sell a house and then continue to charge for its use. Usury is a sin against the very nature of money, and it is, consequently, a sin against commutative justice and against humanity. Perhaps the behavior of the one usurer who talks to

Dante only to slander his fellow usurers reflects his sinning against "commutative justice."

No attempt is made in the text to explain the *contrapasso* suffered by the usurers. Their punishment has no self-evident reason, and Dante gives us no clue as to why they are sitting immobile under the rain of fire and brimstone. An explanation I would venture is provided by the literature on usury. Usurers are often depicted, in medieval collections of *exempla* or in sermons, as wanderers who go from city to city, from nation to nation, in pursuit of their ill-gotten gains. They never rest: time for them is precious (remember Virgil's admonition). This typical portrait is even found in philosophical works, such as the *De peccato usure* by Remigio de' Girolami, a Florentine Dominican who died just two years before Dante (1319) and whose work Dante probably knew. At a certain point in his treatise, Remigio says that usurers operate in ways opposed to those of the four natural elements. The usurer, going counter to the element of fire that has a natural tendency to rise,

> always goes downwards, toward the earth and Hell, not resting at any time on his travels either by day or night, on working days or on holidays; eating or drinking, awake or asleep, he is constantly on the move. Therefore in the Psalm [16:11] we read: "They have set their eyes bowing down to the earth."
>
> (*De peccato usure*, 629)

Stereotypical images such as these perhaps prompted Dante to condemn the usurers to sit motionless gazing down at their purses. It remains, however, to be explained why, like the sodomites, they submit to the rain of fire. What do these two sins have in common? Parodoxically, what they have in common is what opposes one to the other. Sodomites make sterile the act of copulation that is supposed to be productive; usurers instead make productive a substance like money that by its nature is unproductive or sterile. Both groups of sinners are thus punished for their sterile lives, and their punishment is a rain of fire that consumes life rather than fecundating it as natural rain is supposed to do.

This explanation is no more than a hypothesis, which may or may not be proven correct by further study. For the time being, the only alternative thesis is that of André Pézard according to whom the rain of fire symbolizes the fire of the Holy Ghost—the Pentecostal gift of tongues—which sinners like Brunetto (not a sodomite, according to Pézard) perverted in their writings by exalting a language other than their native tongue. The usurers, having sinned against "art" (in Dante's terminology), are, it is claimed, punished in the same way. Pézard's thesis has not won universal acceptance.

The episode of the usurers may be compared to a sequence of cinematic frames. The congestion of *verba videndi* and words semantically related to sight—*li occhi porsi* ("I had set my eyes" [52]); *riguardando* ("looking about" [58]); and the crude metonymy of line 61, *di mio squardo il curro* (lit., the dolly of my sight)—underlines once again the merely visual engagement on the pilgrim's part. The first frame presents the eyes of the sinners, eyes that show pain and see only the cause of their condemnation. The second frame catches the movement of the usurers' hands as they ward off the flakes of fire and the burning sand. This motion prompts an analogy (another frame) from the animal world: dogs who with their muzzles or paws defend themselves against insects. This degrading simile introduces a series of animal images. Dante looks intently at several individuals, trying without success to recognize someone. He then realizes that each sinner carries a pouch or moneybag hanging from his neck. Every sinner's eye (singular for plural) is fixed on his pouch, and the intensity of his glance seems to the poet (but the observation is sarcastic) to reflect the fact that the usurer derives pleasure from this contemplation. On each pouch is a family crest representing an heraldic animal. Dante sequentially observes and describes three of them, one per tercet; a fourth, belonging to a future inmate of Hell, is described by one of the usurers. We have therefore no family names, only visual emblems of their identity. Technically these emblems cannot be considered periphrases even though that is what they appear to be. They could be considered metonymies, since each family name (the abstract) is indicated through a picture (the concrete). The only person mentioned by name (Vitaliano) has no coat of arms. The poet's (and the pilgrim's) disdain for these sinners is shown in the (partial) anonymity in which they are kept, like the "neutrals" and the avaricious and the prodigal; the poet's (and the pilgrim's) sarcasm expresses itself in the presentation of aristocratic families through animal imagery. The only usurer who cries out plays into Dante's observer's technique: he betrays through periphrasis (Paduan, Florentines) and by means of another emblem (a purse with three goats) the identity of his companions. When he has done talking, he twists his mouth and sticks out his tongue like an ox licking its nose, becoming himself a degraded emblem.

With this perfect identification of sign and referent (it is hard to say whether a man has become a grotesque emblem of himself or whether an emblem has taken on life), the review of the usurers is concluded. Because the visual survey brings in so many animals, we are hardly aware that the pilgrim has moved away from Geryon: indeed Dante's gaze moves away from the beast to a series of bestial emblems. There are, naturally, differences: Geryon is one individual with three natures; the usurers have one nature but are identified by means of another. Thus the sight of Geryon produces horror, while that of the usurers causes physical disgust. The lack of mental engagement remains constant; but in the case of Geryon the cause is paralysis of the mind; in the case of the usurers the cause is disdain. In neither case does Dante say a word. The manner of transition to the last part of the canto (*E io* . . . ["And I . . . " (76)]) shows the narrator's superior detachment from the usurers' moral world. The delayed journey must now be resumed.

The crescendo of disgust and horror built up by the insistent vision of animality reaches a higher level when Dante is compelled to come into actual physical contact with it. Upon leaving the usurers he finds Virgil already seated on Geryon's rump. Virgil's encouragement only serves to increase Dante's tension and fear because he makes the trip sound unusual and dangerous. He asks Dante to sit in front so he can shield him against Geryon's tail. The allegorical meaning of this seating arrangement (Reason prevents Fraud from stinging) does not in the least diminish the drama of the situation. The theme of Geryon's tail, and with it the theme of Dante's terror, come again to the fore; this time, however, the terror is greater because Geryon's tail is closer and still quivering. Dante's physical and mental paralysis is almost complete, as the comparison with a man seized with the chills of malaria suggests. But, fearing Virgil's reproach (a dim sign of moral awareness), Dante forces himself to climb onto the monster's back. He would like to ask Virgil to hold him; but his attempt at speech (his only attempt in the whole canto) is choked by fear. It is worth noticing that this is one of the very few cantos in the whole *Comedy* in which the pilgrim utters not a word. In this instance, his silence confirms the complete removal of Reason in order to emphasize the crude physicality of Dante's whole experience. Virgil—just as an omniscient author knows all the needs of his characters—understands his pupil's fears and embraces him. He finally gives orders to Geryon (this is the first time the monster is called by name) to take off and proceed slowly, bearing in mind that he is carrying a real body.

Geryon moves back from the edge like a boat undocking. Making an about-face, he puts his tail where his chest was before. He moves his tail—the obsessive motif of this canto—as if he were an eel. The attention paid to the tiniest detail of this aquatic operation spells out fear and suspense. The beast is gradually transformed as its functions seem to change. At first, it is a boat, then it becomes a fish, then a bird; or a bird that propels itself like a fish, moving its claws as if they were fins. The slowness of Geryon's motion renders irrevocable and even more suspenseful their detachment from solid ground. Dante and Virgil travel now through a new medium; they have left the earth (the burning sand) behind, along with the rain of fire (the two dominant elements in the first part of the canto) and they move through air palpable as water (the other two elements, which pervade this second part).

The psychological suspense has become physical. Dante is now in a vacuum. He needs some point of reference if he is to assess, however approximately, his exceptional experience. Literature provides two analogues for his predicament: the myths of Phaethon and Icarus. Dante could have chosen other literary examples: the aerial journey of Alexander the Great, for example, or that of Cleomedes; but these journeys were successful. He needed examples of failure because they would explain his fear. There may however be a further contrastive motivation for the choice of the Ovidian examples. Both represent cases of *folle volo* ("wild flight"), whereas Dante's flight is merely a moment in his journey to Beatrice. On the literal level, then, the two similes convey a sense of hyperbole; on the allegorical level, they justify Dante's flight. This justification makes the flight necessary but no less fearful. We should also bear in mind that Dante's flight, contrary to any model he may have had in mind, is retold in the first person. In announcing the arrival of Geryon (Canto XVI), he reminds his readers that his trip is real; its dangers are no less so.

Introduced by the evocation of the greatest imaginable terror, the description of the actual trip begins. It is one of the most memorable episodes of the entire *Comedy.* The sense of sight, so acute in the first part of the canto, is now impeded. In that vast and empty darkness Dante can see only the untrustworthy beast; Dante and Geryon are for a time the only presences, Virgil being completely forgotten. It is a blind flight with no perception of space and time. Only through the reaction of his skin is Dante aware of the downward movement of Geryon. The beast swims *lenta lenta* ("slowly, slowly" [115]). This is a notation of speed and of time: on the one hand the slow speed makes the trip safer; on the other it prolongs their suspension in the air. It takes the power of a unique genius to create such a dramatic situation simply through the perception of the breeze against the protagonist's skin. In this blind, silent, and lonely suspension in an unknown part of Hell, the tactile sense—if we may call it that—supplies the coordinates of space and time so necessary to the journey. But this sense yields only the feeling of movement; so that the traveler's psychology is free to magnify those coordinates to an ineffable degree. Indeed the intensity of the drama is sustained precisely by the lack of any attempt to explain it further. In line with the rest of the canto, things and situations are allowed to speak for themselves.

After an indefinable time and distance, another sense provides a new element of orientation. Dante hears the noise of the water falling to the bottom of the pit. The sound gives a vague indication of distance. Dante now wants to see. He cranes his neck to glimpse the bottom. He sees fires and hears laments. His fear increases and he holds on tight to Geryon's coat. His recovery of vision confirms the perception that the descent has been performed in a series of circlings. Now it is finally coming to an end. As it was at the beginning of the trip, Geryon's movement is described in great detail by means of an elaborate comparison. Geryon is now compared to a falcon unsuccessful in the hunt. He unloads his two passengers at the very foot of the wall of rock (which retrospectively appears to be perpendicular) and settles like the thwarted hawk, "embittered and enraged" (132). The two adjectives are revealing: Geryon's "face of a just man," mentioned at the beginning of the canto, has shown its true nature, epitomized in his bifurcated tail, and the canto cannot end without underscoring it. Geryon, who glided down so slowly, now leaves with the speed of an arrow. The last image that Dante gives us of him, in a final simile, again draws attention to the monster's forked tail: "he vanished like [the nock of] an arrow from a bow" (136). Fortunately the tail is now departing. With its departure the canto closes on a note of liberation.

BIBLIOGRAPHICAL NOTES

A version of this essay appeared in *Lectura Dantis Virginiana* 1, a special issue of *Lectura Dantis* 6 (1990 suppl.): 222–234.

Canto xvii has been unevenly studied. Few of the traditional *lecturae* are worth mentioning, whereas the bibliography on some aspects of the canto, especially those considered symbolic or allegorical, is luxuriant. Much of this exegesis, however, deals with the meaning of Dante's "cord" and Virgil's casting it into the depths.

For the scriptural and iconographic models of Geryon, see the bibliographical references in A. R. Chisholm, "The Prototype of Dante's Geryon," *Modern Language Review* 4 (1929): 451–454; J. Block-Friedman, "Anti-Christ and the Iconography of Dante's Geryon," *Journal of the Warburg and Courtauld Institute* 35 (1972): 108–122; M. Bregoli-Russo, "Per la figura di Gerione," *L'Alighieri* 17 (1977): 51–52. On Geryon's triune nature in relation to Cerberus, Lucifer, and the Holy Trinity, see G. Pascoli, *Minerva oscura*, in *Prose*, ed. A. Vicinelli (Milan 1971), 401 (Pascoli sees in the three natures an allegory of intellect, evil will, and sensible appetite); and P. Priest, *Dante's Incarnation of the Trinity* (Ravenna, 1982), 29 ff. On the myths of Icarus and Phaethon, and their figural rapport with Ulysses and Dante, see P. Renucci, *Dante juge et disciple du monde gréco-latin* (Paris, 1954), 208 ff; R. Hollander, *Allegory in Dante's "Commedia"* (Princeton, 1969), 249. On all of the above, as well as on many other details viewed as allegorical (the animals on the usurers' moneybags; the simile of the falcon; the flight of Geryon; the designs on Geryon's skin; the ten steps of Dante and Virgil, etc.), exhaustive bibliographical information is provided by R. Mercuri, *Semantica di Gerione: Il motivo del viaggio nella "Divina Commedia" di Dante* (Rome, 1984). This very well informed book typifies the subtlety (with what is often, alas, off-the-wall speculation) that inspires the hermeneutics of this canto.

Other problems, many of them important, are left practically untapped. One such problem is the nature of the usurers' *contrapasso*. André Pézard, who has written extensively on the fiery rain (*Dante sous la pluie de feu* [Paris, 1950]), hardly touches upon this issue, nor does R. Kay (*Dante's Swift and Strong: Essays on "Inferno" xv* [Lawrence, Kans., 1978]). For an ample survey of the literature on usury, see John T. Noonan, *The Scholastic Analysis of Usury* (Cambridge, Mass., 1957). Remigio de' Girolami's treatise (*De peccato usure*, in *Studi medievali*, ed. O. Capitani, 629)—translated in the discussion above—describes the usurer, who does not rise but *semper vadit deorsum versus terram et infernum, nullo tempore quiescens in itinere, nec die nec nocte, nec in feris nec in festis et comendo et bibendo et vigilando et dormiendo continue vadit. Unde in Psalmis* [16:11] *Oculos suos statuerunt declinare in terram.*

Another neglected problem is that of the canto's language. The only valuable observations are those of G. Cambon, "Examples of Movement in the *Divine Comedy*: An Experiment in Reading," *Italica* 40 (1963): 108–131, where the imagery and the language of Geryon's moving away from the edge are studied with great finesse. On the specific technique of periphrasis in Dante there are two important studies: one by E. R. Curtius in his *Gesammelte Aufsätze zur Romanischen Philologie* (Bern, 1960), 321–333; the other by E. N. Girardi, "La perifrasi nella *Divina*

Commedia," *Quaderni d'Italianistica* 8 (1979): 514–538 (neither of these studies, however, quotes a single example from Canto XVII).

As for the *lecturae* of the entire canto as a poetic unit, there is much still to be done. The readings of G. Getto (in *Letture dantesche,* ed. Giovanni Getto [Florence, 1965], 335–352), P. Soldati (in *Lectura Dantis Scaligera: Inferno,* ed. Mario Marcazzan [Florence, 1967], 565–577), and F. Lanza (in *Nuove letture dantesche* [Florence, 1970], 3:117–135), to mention only the most recent, are impressionistic and of little help. The best interpretation of the canto's overall construction is provided by E. Pasquini, "Il canto di Gerione," *Atti e Memorie dell'Accademia dell'Arcadia* (1967): 346–368. An interesting attempt at examining the Geryon episode from a narratological and psychoanalytic point of view is that of F. Gabrieli, "Gerione tra mito et favola: Dante attraverso Propp," in *Psicoanalisi e strutturalismo di fronte a Dante* (Florence, 1972), 65–89.

CANTO XVIII

Introduction to Malebolge

JAMES NOHRNBERG

"What brings you to sauces so piquant?," Dante asks the pander he meets in Canto XVIII, the pungent *salse* apparently naming what was once a criminals' unhallowed burial pit near Bologna.[1] How did the poet's old acquaintance get into such a pickle? Or come under such a sentence? The trembling of the earthquake in the third canto, the threatened onset of the dreadful Gorgon in the ninth, the gyres of the Leviathan fished up in the sixteenth, and the icy blast from Satan's wings in the last canto of the *Inferno* are all effects in the guise of causes, veiling sin's origins by externalizing motions otherwise internal to the sinner himself. The sinner's personal assent to transgression hides itself in distracting epiphenomena that beg the larger questions: what surprised Francesca's senses, hardened Farinata's heart, twisted and buried Venèdico's judgment, and froze Ugolino's pity?

Perhaps Venèdico got here as Dante did, via the Geryon of Fraud: he was seduced into pandering by the marquis d'Este, his employer. But we also hear the frauder's own inclination, in the evil pride he takes in all the children being taught to say yes in his own region's distinctive way. Once we cross a major threshold of infernal assent, however, any disclosure of hell's design on the sinful will is made cartographically, taxonomically, or categorically. Self-destructive impulses appear only elliptically, as if sinners were what they often claim: caught in webs not of their own devising.

After the marvels of Geryon and his flight in the preceding cantos, the account of the physical structure of the fraud zone, which begins Canto XVIII, is deliberately quotidian and anticlimactic. "There is a place" (*Luogo è*) the narrator relates matter-of-factly, locating us in Malebolge by means of a topos from Latin poetry that may introduce a description of a precinct of enhanced allegoricalness (cf. *Est locus* in Statius, *Thebaid* II, 23: the grove of Sleep). But *Luogo è* is used at the end of the *Inferno* (XXXIV, 127) to introduce the antiallegorical numb-space of the tunnel leading from the apex of Beelzebub's tomb up to the shores of the mount of Purgatory, at the pilgrim's exodus from earthbound locales as a whole. The descent to Malebolge on Geryon's flanks anticipates the reascent to earth's surface on Satan's. As early as the sodomites' reference to Dante's return to the stars (XVI, 82–84), just before the emergence of Geryon at the *Inferno*'s textual midpoint, the way in has begun to be the way out.

The images of Phaethon and Icarus, introduced in Canto XVII for Dante's airborne descent on Geryon, are especially relevant here, because Icarus was escaping from a labyrinth, and because the solar charioteer's wrong-way visit to the heavens recurs in *Purgatory* IV, in Dante's account of the co-ordinates on which the sun's relation to the hemispheric midpoints is inscribed: the zodiacal band or ecliptic is "that same path which Phaethon drove so poorly" (73). Another mythological allusion suggests Dante's cosmic repositioning more dimly: "nor had Arachne ever loomed such webs" (*Inf.* XVII, 18). These webs refer to designs tattooed on the sides of the beast bearing Dante down to Malebolge, because the plan of nether hell, top view, resembles one of the cobweblike diagrams in the texts of Chalcidius on Plato's *Timaeus* and Macrobius's *Commentary on the Dream of Scipio*. Imagery for a cosmic dance of intellect also determines the periphery of the subterranean maze of fraud, because the circles in Canto XVIII map onto those in the solar heaven of *Paradiso* X–XIV. Arachne's web veils Ariadne's labyrinthine dance floor; the latter appears in *Paradiso* XIII, 1–21, and XIV, 19–23, there transfigured into Ariadne's stellar crown.

The analogy between celestial and chthonic milieux emerges from Dante's oblique account of two opposed motions in the first of ten ditches, where the pilgrim sees crowds of people moving round in a ring and hears how many have been undone by being taught to just say yes to their own undoing.

> Upon the right I saw new misery,
> I saw new tortures and new torturers,
> filling the first of Malebolge's moats.
> Along its bottom, naked sinners moved,
> to the outside of the middle, facing us;
> beyond that, they moved with us, but more quickly—
> (22–27)

One group files toward the pilgrims; their faces oppose Dante's and Virgil's. The other group moves around the circle with the travelers, toward a bridge over which they will cross to the farther side of the ditch—the side nearer Satan. Only on top of the bridge do they turn and face the file they have been accompanying. But which is the more "outside" file: the one nearer Dante (farther from hell's center), or the one further beyond him (nearer hell's center)? Which "middle" is the approaching file said to be beyond: the middle of the ditch, or of the earth? Which file moves more quickly? Is the faster one the one beside Dante, traveling a greater circumference in the same time interval as the file inside it? Faster than what: the dallying pilgrims, or the opposed file?

We naturally assume, even though the text is silent on this point, that the first conversation at the first ditch, with the pander Venèdico, takes place between Dante and the originally nearer, "outside" file. The subsequent sighting, from the middle of the bridge, of the seducer Jason, would pertain to the coordinated "inside" file. But there are objections to this well-nigh universal reading. At the outset the narrator says the sinners moving with the pilgrims are traveling *with greater steps* (*con passi maggiori* [27]). To preserve a "uniform motion" around the circle, so that the pander and seducer can be scourged equally, the inner file must needs take *smaller* steps. The *outer* file should move with the greater steps—to cover its track's greater circumference in the same time as smaller steps cover the lesser circumference of the inner file. The coordination is quasi-cosmological: the sun goes around the sky in the same time the fixed stars go around the pole—in the contrary direction.

A reversal of the narrative order by the geographic one helps explain Virgil's subsequent instruction to Dante on the bridge:

> When we had reached the point where that ridge opens
> below to leave a passage for the lashed,
>   my guide said: "Stay, and make sure that the sight
>   of still more [=further, other] ill-born spirits strikes your eyes,
> for you have not yet seen their faces, since
> they have been moving in our own direction."
>
> (73–78)

Here it is simpler to assume that the file traveling with the pilgrims has indeed been the outer one, to which they were closer, before crossing over it. But does it matter which file has the inside track, nearer the ditch holding the flatterers? Why would Dante have the pilgrims initially travel with the outer file, while talking to the inner one? Why reverse the temporal order of interviews from the moral order of sinners, and put panders half a ring closer to Satan than seducers? Is this exception to structural clarity itself the point, a sign that pandering and seduction are virtually interchangeable? The pander seduces a girl to do the will of one who, could he solicit for himself, would be a seducer; the seducer gains by flattering persuasions and false promises what is otherwise procured by the harlot's client's money, or the pander's false counsel—by the girl's "coiner," in place of her "con-er" (*da conio* [66]).[2]

Like a divided path cycling visitors through the stations of an oversubscribed tourist attraction, this ditch solves a problem in crowd control:

> as, in the year of Jubilee, the Romans,
> confronted by great crowds, contrived a plan
> that let the people pass across the bridge,
>   for to one side went all who had their eyes
> upon the Castle, heading toward St. Peter's,
> and to the other, those who faced the Mount.
>
> (28–33)

Indeed, the poet's vision and the pope's jubilee intersect each other. For while pilgrims to Rome flowed to and fro over the bridge on the Tiber, Dante crossed the bridge in Malebolge over the flow of panders and seducers. Each kind moves toward the other, for on the pontiff's bridge any given visitor would have passed in both directions. A pilgrimage and its sites caused a two-way traffic: promises of salvation for visiting the churches of Peter and Paul seduced the crowds to Rome, where the pope pandered indulgences. But an earthly journey for remitting the pains of Purgatory produces only an earthly circuit, at right angles to the axis traversed by Dante—he crosses over to that Rome where Christ is a Roman.

Canto xviii announces the artful design of Malebolge overtly, in the narrator's exposition of the terrain, and covertly, in an extended allusion to the love that moves the sun and other stars. For the "eternal circlings" of the sexual frauders imitate "the eternal circles" of the heavens (*cerchie etterne* [72]; *l'etterne rote* [*Par.* 1, 64]). As per Dante's prescription in Canto xi, 97–105, the "art" of the first ditch "would follow nature," that is, the revolution of the spheres. Thus the files of seducers and panders, like the sun and fixed stars, move in two opposed directions. Moreover, the two rings encircle the nine remaining ditches of Malebolge, as the ecliptic and celestial equator circumscribe the nine remaining heavens—which in turn enclose the four layers of air, or the four sublunary elements, as Malebolge hems in a fourfold ring of ice. At the motionless dead center of either of these configurations, Satan finds his natural place.

The *Timaeus* is the ultimate source for the coordination of the "desire and will" of the *Comedy*'s last tercet, for it is Plato who first divided the stellar and planetary rotations dialectically so that, according to a famous *metrum* of Boethius (*Consolation of Philosophy* iii, metrum 9), the divided World-Soul "pursues its revolving course in two circles" (*duos motem glomeravit orbe*):

[The artifex] took the whole fabric and cut it down the middle into two strips . . . which he . . . fastened . . . to each other . . . to make two circles, one inner and one outer. And he endowed them with uniform motion in the same place, and named the movement of the outer circle after the nature of the Same, [and the movement] of the inner after the nature of the Different. The circle of the same he caused to revolve from left to right, and the circle of the Different from right to left . . . and made the master revolution that of the Same. For he left the circle of the Same whole and undivided, but slit the inner circle six times to make seven unequal circles . . . and he made these circles revolve in contrary senses relative to each other.

(Timaeus 36b–c, trans. H. D. P. Lee)

For Macrobius, the proportionalized stellar motions argue for the existence of the music of the spheres: Plato says that a siren sits upon each of the spheres, cosmogonists make the Muses the song of these planetary spheres, and Apollo leads the Muses as the sun does the planets. Moreover:

In the hymns to the gods . . . the verses of the strophe and antistrophe used to be set to music, so that the strophe might represent the forward motion of the celestial sphere and the antistrophe the reverse motion of the planetary spheres; these two motions produced nature's first hymn in honor of the Supreme God.

(Commentary on the Dream of Scipio II, 3, 5,
trans. W. H. Stahl)

Such ideas give new meaning to the book of Job's "When the morning stars praised me together, and all the sons of God made a joyful melody" (38:7), and they may explain three phenomena found in Dante's heaven of the sun, at *Paradiso* XIII, 20–26: namely, "the double dance" gotten by doubling an image of Ariadne's crown, the replication of the stellar motion's speed by that of the coronal motion, and the paean not of Bacchus but of the Trinity.

But why apply the great Timaeic emblem of the cosmic rotation of the Same and Different to the motions of seducers and panders? The motion of the two files in Canto XVIII is propelled by the *frustatori* (tormentors) with horns and whips. The goads function like the winds on which the lustful suspire in Canto V, or the rain of fire that urges the sodomites' race in Canto XV. But the "eternal circlings" of this canto are understood as a fetter, and thus a parody of the timepiece of the cosmos as found, for example, in the note of an alleged pre-Socratic Pythagorean, pseudo-Archytas: "For some of the ancient philosophers defined time as a kind of choral dance of the Now."[3] The dancing-masters are the demons, who parody the angelic intelligences causing—urging—the motion of the planetary spheres.

The point made by the agitation in the vicious circle devoted to sexual frauds is that of Robert Burton: "A true saying it is, 'Desire hath no rest'; is infinite in itself, endless; and as one calls it, a perpetual rack, or horsemill, according to [Augustine], still going round as in a ring."[4] The *molam asinarium,* if it were Augustine's, might also be the *mole asinaria* of Matthew 18:6, the millstone tied around the neck of the offender cast into the sea. The second chapter of Gregory's *Pastoral Rule* domesticates this punishment: "By the millstone is expressed the round and labor of worldly life, and by the depth of the sea is denoted final damnation." Origen's explanation, of a scriptural mill as "the mill of the cosmos," finds its counterpart in Dante's heaven of the sun, where the pilgrim describes the zodiacal or horological circle after Saint Thomas has finished speaking: "the millstone / of holy lights began to turn, but it / was not yet done with one full revolution / before another ring surrounded it, / and motion matched with motion, song with song" (*Par.* XII, 2–6).[5] Like the cosmic music in Macrobius, this song is produced as if by a siren. Sirens are singing tops, tops are propelled by whips.

If the two files of Canto XVIII are engaged in the cosmic contradance, it is significant that the motions of this dance were psychologized. An example is the following textbook case from the widely disseminated *Tractatus de sphaera* of Sacrobosco (John Holywood), writing before 1250:

> Be it understood that the "first movement" means the movement of the *primum mobile,* that is, of the ninth sphere or last heaven, which movement is from east through west back to east again, which is also called "rational motion" from resemblance to the rational motion in the microcosm, that is, in man, when thought goes from the Creator through creatures to the Creator and there rests.
>
> The second movement is of the firmament and planets contrary to this, from west through east back to west again, which movement is called "irrational" or "sensual" from resemblance to the movement of the microcosm from things corruptible to the Creator and back again to things corruptible.[6]

If pandering and seduction correspond to the contemplation and love—the cherubim and seraphim—that communicate the first motion from God to the heavens, this reading glosses the two circles of Malebolge's first ditch.

Dante implies there were two schools of thought about the mode in which the mind experiences God. The Franciscan-Victorine emphasis was on the informing of the charitable will; for the Franciscans, *love* of God was knowledge of him. The Thomist-Dominican emphasis was on intellectual comprehension per se. The two circles of the Church's intellectuals divide along these lines. Francis, in one circle, is "all seraphic in his ardor"; Dominic, in the other, "for his wisdom, had possessed / the splendor of cherubic light on earth" (*Par.* XI, 37–39). But where love and contemplation energize the dance of the cosmos, cupidity and malice (or lust and greed) provide the motor power of Malebolge, or Hell's ardor and intellectual capacity—for fraud. If the correspondence were to hold, the seducers as lovers would be the outer file: the primum mobile, and / or seraphim. The panders as spectators would be the inner file: the crystalline sphere or fixed stars, and / or cherubim. In Sacrobosco, however, the rational motion is outside, the appetitive inside. Perhaps, apropos the beatific vision, we must have it both ways: the soul loves what, as mind, it contemplates; and it contemplates what, as will, it loves.

If the characters in Canto XVIII are not so very strong individually, an infernal policy of strong characterization nonetheless remains in force collectively. Subsequent observations will show that the intercalation of the sins of fraud extends beyond the boundaries of the first ditch. False counsel and coining, found later in Malebolge, both apply to the sinners here, but an early connection between the two sexual evils and flattery is also indicated: by their being treated in the same canto and adjacent ditches. The pattern locking the first three frauds together is clear. The pander is an articulate modern Italian from Bologna, the seducer a famous and unspeaking hero from ancient Greek epic; the first flatterer is a garrulous modern Italian from Lucca, the second a famous and unspeaking courtesan from ancient Roman drama. The distribution is complementary:

	[Actually Speaking] Modern Christian Italy	[Reported Speaking] Pagan Antiquity and Literature
pander / seducer:	Venèdico Caccianemico	Jason
flatterer:	Alessio Interminei	Thaïs

The paired characters of the second ditch parallel the divided ones of the first: the haughty, silent classical womanizer Jason counterbalances the shrewish classical B-girl Thaïs; the scandal-mongering and sister-procuring Venèdico counterbalances the ingratiating, soft-soap artist Alessio. Thus the personnel of the second ditch reveal sins comparable to those in the first, in a chiasmic mirror. Where concupiscence compelled Jason to cozen women for his advantage, cupidity compelled Venèdico to solicit for both his sister and employer. A similar character stamps the flatterers. The classical flatterer Thaïs, like the contemporary pander Venèdico, was driven to pander; the contemporary flatterer Alessio, like the classical seducer Jason, was driven to seduce. But the flatterers do not circle in a double ring; rather, they muck about in a deep ditch of their own.

The panders and seducers raise love's tent next to the excremental place where flattery collapses it. Nonetheless, given that the motions of pander and seducer mime the circlings of the wheels in the solar heaven, we may ask how flattery, like the third ring of "spirituals" in *Paradiso* XIV, proceeds from the preceding rotation—or rather from Saint Thomas's discourse, in the same heaven, about the imperfection of that matter upon which the divine ideas are imposed (*Par.* XIII, 52–81). Plutarch once likens the flatterer to prime matter, on account of his endlessly resourceful adaptability (*Moralia* I, 5, 51b–c). Though the sycophantic Alessio and parasitic Thaïs are stuccoed in this stuff permanently, the second ditch may still represent the third fold in that bond of threefold nature—as Boethius describes it in the famous *metrum* cited earlier[7]—from which the first two folds are made, as pandering and seduction are made from flattery. For the *tertium quid* of the Same and the Different is the existence common to both; the fabric from which the artifex cuts the two "eternal circles" of the ecliptic and celestial equator is the *prima materia*. In Chalcidius's medieval version of the *Timaeus,* this unformed and inchoate material has only a lowly existence; like the flatterers' mire, the ur-stuff is radically indigent.

Alessio Interminei's speech is short and acute, but there was no end of his former flatteries: "If name makes meaning, as 'tis said to make" (*Par.* XII, 80), they were interminable. His tongue never tired of his vanities or felt a surfeit (XVIII, 125). Flattery this gross implies "laid on with a trowel"— *stucca*. It may please the ear, yet a rising stench offends the nose; on the walls of its ditch the breath of hell itself has condensed. Flattery is hellmouth's halitosis, but it burns the eyes as well—that is, it offends common sense. On the bridge, Dante is mounted over a sewer, but the sewage in which the sinners are sunk "seemed / as if it had been poured from human privies" (113–114). The pilgrims, having seen more than enough, quit both ditch and canto. Nothing flattering remains to be said—the visit to the privy is over.

Benvenuto sounds equally fed up, and his note sounds the ditch's depths:

> Well, this Alessio had a terrible habit: he was so given to flattery, that he was unable to say anything at all without seasoning it with the oil of adulation. He greased everyone, he licked everyone, even the most vile and venal servants. In short, he completely dripped with flattery and stank of it.[8]

Where once Alessio stroked and soft-soaped others, he now dirties and beats his own pate. Like an Old Testament breast-beater, he accedes to his just deserts—foul abasement—for debasing any faculty for fair appraisal. Alessio was so given to schmaltz that it well-nigh drowns him.

Thaïs squats in this ditch not as a harlot, but as an abuser of speech that was *venal;* like propaganda and advertising, she prostituted words for gain and advantage. "If [the speaker intending to please does] it with the intention of making some gain out of it, he is called a *flatterer* or *adulator,*" says Aquinas, noting "the false praise of the flatterer softens the mind by depriving it of the rigidity of truth and renders it susceptive of vice" to be "a gloss on [Psalm 140:5], 'Let not the oil of the sinner fatten my head'" (*Summa theologica* II-II, 115, 2-2). Doubtless Alessio's hair was once dry, and Thaïs's kempt—slovenly moral habits can turn a physical habitus into a pigsty. The self-torment of the besmirched wench—she "scratches at herself with shit-filled nails, / and now she crouches, now she stands upright"—repeats the scratching of the violent against art, like "dogs in summer—now / with muzzle, now with paw" (XVIII, 131–32; XVII, 49–50). The reflex may retain traces of a fading courtesan's anxious and excessive toilette. The visit to Thaïs ends when Thaïs is reported to have said the climactic *maravigliose,* but the beauty school dropout does not look marvelous. The diviner whom Virgil takes to be Manto is disheveled too: in Malebolge a woman's hair is not her glory or covering.

Thaïs's hellish uglification might refer to heavenly beatification, all the same. Hers is a name legendary for harlotry, and a special instance occurs in Jacobus de Voragine's *Golden Legend.* Before her conversion, the future Saint Thaïs worked in a brothel. One day she led a particularly squeamish customer to an inner closet, so they could consummate their bargain in complete secrecy: only God, she protested, could possibly see them. Thus awakened to her own condition, she undertook a lifelong penance, at the order of the local abbot—her erstwhile visitor, now acting in his proper person. Before her final glorification she lived incarcerated in a virtual privy, the mirror image of her former brothel's closet:

> He closed her in a cell, and sealed the door with lead. And the cell was little and straight, and but one little window open, by which was ministered . . . her poor living. For the abbot commanded that they should give her a little bread and water. And when the abbot should depart, Thaisis said to him: Father, where shall I shed the water, and that which shall come from the conduits of nature? And he said to her: In thy cell, as thou art worthy. And then she demanded how she should pray, and he answered: Thou art not worthy to name God . . . [nor] stretch thy hands to heaven, because thy lips be full of iniquities, and thine hands full of evil attouchings, and foul ordures.
>
> (*The Golden Legend, or Lives of the Saints as Englished by William Caxton,* ed. F. S. Ellis [London, 1900], 5:242–243)

Like the abbot, Dante imposes a long-term penalty on a harlot called Thaïs and indicts her hands as "full of evil attouchings, and foul ordures."

The company Thaïs keeps is significant. She, Potiphar's wife, and Myrrha are the only women correctly named in nether hell, if Manto is a case of mistaken identity. Thaïs is in the same canto as the seducers and *galeotti,* as Potiphar's wife and Myrrha are in the same berth as the liar Sinon. The flatterer exaggerates a sentiment that may not have been a true one in the first place: a harlot's affirmation of affection is hardly to be trusted except insofar as her salesmanship is itself part of the purchase. Virgil quotes Thaïs while subtextually silencing her original go-between in Terence's *Eunuchus,* with the result that she pandered for herself.

Venèdico, on the other hand, not only pandered for his sister, but also panders to the prurient interests of his present audience: he caters to a fascination with the scandal of widespread seduction of the innocent. Seduced, perhaps, by his own hyperbole, the tale-teller claims there are more procurers in his region than children being taught to say the Bolognese form of yes: all members of such a society are destined to be corrupted, and there exists an even larger number to corrupt them!

If Venèdico's exploitation of his sister does him no credit, neither can it do any for his employer. Venèdico hardly flatters the memory of the d'Este family, if his reluctance to be recognized in hell implies he brought his sister to do the Marquis's will shamefully or unwillingly. But telling tales correctively, he also reveals how gossip, lacking better sources, improves information about what really happened mainly through surreptitious and intimate exchanges about money, sex, and crime. A scandal sheet set in stone, the *Inferno* elides any sharp antithesis of contemporary conjecture and historical consensus and thus collapses Kierkegaard's antinomy of true and false talk:

> If we could suppose for a moment that there was a law which did not forbid people talking, but simply ordered that everything that was spoken about should be treated as though it had happened fifty years ago, the gossips would be done for, they would be in despair. On the other hand, it would not really interfere with any one who could really talk.
>
> (*The Present Age,* trans. Alexander Dru, 1962)[9]

But the *Inferno's* gossips can all really talk—and in particular Venèdico.

Indeed, Venèdico vindicates Kierkegaard's suggested time requirement in a unique (if roundabout) way. Venèdico might well have a special place in history, in Malebolge, and in the choral dance of the now, if Dante has been at pains to tell us in the pander's canto—and no place else—that there was a papal jubilee within living memory. Biblical jubilees occur every fifty years, and the event in question took place in 1300: the fictive date of Dante's own visionary *astronautica.* Three cantos after Venèdico's, Malacoda— "Evil-Tail"—dates his mendacious speech from hypocrisy's landmark victory in A.D. 33: he speaks 1,266 years after the Crucifixion (XXI, 112–114). But it is Canto XVIII that cites the great public event of 1300. Because the pope had granted a plenary indulgence to all repentant and confessed sinners who in the course of this year visited the churches of the Apostles Peter and Paul, Christians were drawn to Rome by the thousands. Dante alludes to their pilgrimage by means of the large number of souls allowed to cross directly into Purgatory from the first month of the year of the poet's journey (*Purg.* II, 98–99). In this same year the pope also adopted the triple tiara, giving him lordship over heaven, earth, and hell. Boniface's affirmation of his own apostolic succession is resoundingly answered at the critical juncture of Dante's journey: Rome's greatest poet, Virgil, crowns and miters Dante over himself (*Purg.* XXVII, 142).

While the pilgrims crossed the pontiff's bridge over the Tiber, the poet of Canto XVIII crossed the first two bridges over Malebolge. In the next canto, he re-begins by conscripting the pope's absolutist and universal claims in order to pass his own final sentence on simony and papal venality; Boniface is not dead, but the time for judgment is *now*. The chastisement and castigation of Venèdico also go together; he is scourged even as he is condemned (64–66): "a demon cudgeled him / with his horsewhip and cried: 'Be off, you pimp, / there are no women here for you to trick'"—or *coin*. Speaking allegorically about cleansing the soul, Meister Eckhart explains why Jesus whipped the money changers out of the temple: "when the truth is known, the merchants must be gone—for truth wants no merchandising!"

But even as Dante offers the first fruits of the Last Judgment, he refers to the Roman bridge retrospectively—as if the jubilee were well in the past. Venèdico's sudden recovery of his own past, at the sound of an Italian accent from the world of living, also implies a remove from the present; moreover, Dante has made some fuss about taking a few steps back to interview this sinner, who had moved these same steps beyond Dante, and against his direction. This quasi-planetary accommodation of retrograde and recovered forward motion creates an epicyclic loop, and perhaps for a good allegorical reason: in 1300 Venèdico was apparently *still alive*.[10]

In Canto XXXIII two hosts who treacherously murdered their guests only seem to remain on earth. Their bodies actually host two animating demons, while their souls are already permanent guests in hell. *Vengeance is mine*, their sin might say, meaning *now*. But why is Venèdico's case analogous? Like Hell's early-admitted traitors, *this* "Pandaro" is guilty of an internecine betrayal of trust: he should have *guarded* a kinswoman, not sold her. For seduction pertains to violating a virgin "in the care of her father or her guardians," Aquinas says (*Summa* II-II, 154, 6: obj. 3; reply to obj. 1). (Hypsipyle is an inverse case, if she *evilly counseled* with her sisterhood to kill its men but *hypocritically* exempted her own father.) A host who violates his guest is a traitor; so is a brother who corrupts his sister. Venèdico, correcting bad stories about an earthly life before he can have gotten into hell to tell them, does advance publicity for the Marquis—yet only to slander himself as a predead Branca Doria or Fra Alberigo.

Venèdico's evil genius appears to have gotten quite ahead of itself. His predated disposal in hell, in relation to the grand chronometer constituted by the poem's whole universe, presents only a slightly slipped cog; but if a *very* contemporary pander draws attention to the poem's alignment with the jubilee year, so does the ancient seducer he circles against—and with whom his steps are synchronized. The first sinner recognized in Canto XVIII taught his sister to say *sipa*—for *si*. The second one deceived the deceiving woman whom Dante calls *Isifile*—for Hyp*si*pyle. Their times also index each other. For the poem's last classical allusion refers Dante's apotheosis at the end of the thirteenth century A.D., to Jason's voyage at the end of the same century B.C., twenty-five hundred years before: Neptune was amazed by the Argo's shadow on the ocean floor (*Par.* XXX, 96), Dante by his arrival at a vision of God. In Canto XVIII Jason took the "greater steps"; in *Paradiso* XXXIII he has the deeper date. The concluding retroversion to an origin for voyaging signals the fulfilling of a virtual great year of jubilees—*fifty* fifty-year periods—at the journey's completion. The pander and seducer defrauded women, it appears, with purposes that looked quite beyond them.

Urged on by whips, the still regal Jason manages to impose on Virgil by means of an impressive dignity of carriage—its maintenance must be a tour de force, under the circumstances. It may also be a kind of plausible lie: the seducer knows that there is no chance of "bringing them in," if the objects of your solicitude think you have given up on yourself. In a speech Churchill made to a secret session of the House of Commons in June 1940, before the United States joined the allies, his text says, "No good suggesting we are down and out": *to them,* adds the prime minister's inked-in superscript.[11] His calculation makes a Ulysses-like point about survival, the need to put on a good front. Jason maintains his pose in adversity, but his pretensions already lead toward the false counselors. Virgil's own *polished words* (91, as in II, 67 they are *persuasive*) will seduce the giant Antaeus, beyond the last ditch, into abetting the pilgrims' final descent into hell.

The seducer accomplishes an evil persuasion that corrupts another will by way of a darkened understanding. A habitual sinner in this regard, Jason seduced Hypsipyle "with polished words and love signs"; she was "the girl whose own deception / had earlier deceived the other women" (91, 92–93). And he cheated Medea, whom hell now avenges (96). Jason "with heart and head / deprived the men of Colchis of their ram" (86–87); he won by courage and craft the cunning Hypsipyle, the aid of the witch Medea, and the golden fleece. Again and again the Don Juan figure has gotten his way. Lives reported in hell often have a destructive repetition in them; Virgil's life of Jason shows this is especially true of a prize-winning careerist who leaves other people smarting after cunningly and thanklessly using up their persons and their resources. Hypsipyle, Medea, and the Colchians are all owed *vendetta,* if in fact they were treated not only artfully, but also vindictively.

Art, however, is an issue. Usury's site borders on Geryon's—violence *against* art verges on perversion *of* art. Being crafty, fraud is artful; the counterfeiter Master Adam, technically speaking, is a Master of Arts. Seduction, flattery, divination, hypocrisy, false counsel, and falsifying can all be rationally called arts. Augustine lists flattery as a kind of lying (*De mendacio* xxv), and each of these practices makes lying into an art. Usury's bags also signal the *venality* of several Evil-Pouches (or *Malebolge*): pander, simonist, barrator, and thief are all venal, virtually by definition.

The inversity of pander and seducer in the first ditch can also lead us to distinguish venal crime from verbal sin through the rest of Malebolge. Moreover, if we put the seducer first and the pander second—that is, in the order indicated by the seducers' "greater steps"—and if they are types of lust and greed, extroverted and introverted cupidity—then the frauds divide evenly and successively between craftiness effected by guileful words, and craftiness effected by guileful deeds: an inexact distinction, but one found in Aquinas.[12] The contrast between mendacities in even-numbered ditches and violations in odd-numbered ones produces a ripple-like alternation across the whole of the eighth circle. Crimes desecrating the social contract sort themselves out from sins vitiating honest self-representations:

Sins against the Truth of Representations	Crimes against the Integrity of Covenants and Bonds
Geryon / usurers (violence against art)	
(–) seduction (persuasive lies)	
	1. pandering (sale of the marriage-relation)
2. flattery (pleasing lies)	
	3. simony (sale of church offices)
4. divination (prophetic lies)	
	5. barratry (sale of state offices)
6. hypocrisy (lies about appearance)	
	7. theft (covert violence against property)
8. false counsel (lies about wise action)	
	9. schism (violence against one church or state)
10. falsifying (lies about identities)	
Nimrod / giants (violence against heaven)	

This binary model for Malebolge shows us that every crime against the public interest is only one remove from a sin against the use of reason.

In the right column, the pander sells his sister (Ghisolabella), or her marriage; the simonist sells the Church as bride, or the mystical body (Beatrice); the barrator sells the state, or the Holy Roman Empire (Virgil). The remaining invasions of communal institutions pertain to thievery, schism, and primeval rebellion from God. The thief violates a person's legal body; the schismatic violates the body of Christendom or empire ("monarchy"); and the rebellious giants divide from divine society. Socially alienating and internecine, these violations go back to the pander who betrayed his own flesh—his sister. In the left column, the somber movement common to the ditches of the sorcerers and hypocrites and false counselors ranks them together, but their evil begins from the seducers' polished words and the flatterers' whining—these end in the falsifiers' counterfeiting and perjury, and Master Adam and Sinon's backbiting.

While sinfully fraudulent minds tend to desolation and dementia, criminally fraudulent institutions tend to violence, riot, and chaos. Frauds against *ratio* (reason) and *oratio* (speech) are punished in the depressive and claustral recesses of introversion and masochistic self-infliction, but frauds against society are punished more outrageously, by a fierce and manic cadre of demons and externalized sadistic tormentors: horns and whips for pandering, Dante's lay-sermon and sodomization for simony, hooks and pitchforks for barratry, reptilian possession for theft, and sword-inflicted mutilation or dismemberment for discord-sowing. In the last two ditches society collapses into mere heaps of disfigured bodies, yet even in the afterlife an emergency room and a ward for incurable diseases will still differ: the schismatics are a battlefield, the falsifiers a malarial swamp.

The inclusion of three sins within the single canto of *Inferno* XVIII might also argue for organizing Malebolge triadically, if this canto's three circles sandwich the venal sin of pandering between the verbal sins of seduction and flattery. Combining the dialectical rhythm with our former classification will show Malebolge as organized by four tercet-like triads:

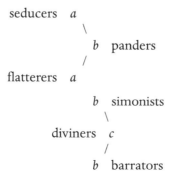

```
hypocrites   c
              \
               d   thieves
              /
false counselors   c
                    d   schismatics
                     \
falsifiers   e
            /
        [d   giants]
```

The pattern of enclosing a new kind of sin between two varieties of a kind already introduced implies the poem's whole mystery of advance, retardation, and recapitulation, as exemplified in the *terza rima:* two steps forward and one step *back, aba;* or, one back and two *forward, abc*—one step back into hell, two steps forward into the lower and upper paradises.

Canto XVIII contains the first triad, in which seduction and flattery make the verbal sin of evil persuasion *habitual.* Simony and barratry contain the second triad, in which the merchandising of church and state make venality *official.* This evil commerce carries over to the third and fifth ditches from the coining of women in the first. Simony owes its name to Simon *Magus,* and the medieval character of Virgil, as a prophet to the Gentiles, also made him a prognosticator—like his own character Manto—and a magician. Characterized by Dante as his faithful mentor, Virgil must nonetheless emend his own *Aeneid*'s former prophecy of Mantua. Thus divination, in the fourth ditch, forms the antithetical interpolant between Simon Magus, punished in the third, and Mantuan Virgil, jeopardized in the fifth. Menaced by the *diaboloi* (accusers) and demons of barratry, the prophet of empire and defender of world-monarchy escape into hypocrisy—concurrent with their removal from the entanglements of the second triad. Hypocrisy and false counsel, which frame thievery in the third triad, are linked because they pervert understanding, as it were complicitously. Aquinas says a hypocrite steals a reputation among men.[13] False counsel also qualifies as theft; Dante punishes it in the "thieving fire" (XXVII, 127), for it steals a victim's judgment. To make a final triad, the falsifiers are set between the schismatics and giants; these last are a step beyond Malebolge itself, to a *primeval* kind of schism. Nimrod, a giant or mighty hunter *against God,* divided the original unity of language.[14]

Near the face worn by Geryon, Dante's early illustrator inscribes *ipocresia.*[15] Geryon represents Malebolge's great evil, namely, split representations; his face "was that of a just man, / so gracious was his features' outer semblance," yet all the trunk was the body of a serpent (XVII, 10–12). The gross, eel-like body dissimulates a divided tongue, like the one—based on James 3:4–10—in which the false counselor Ulysses burns:

Behold also ships, whereas they are great, and are driven by strong winds, yet are they turned about with a small helm, whithersoever the force of the governor willeth. Even so the tongue is indeed a little member, and boasteth great things. Behold how small a fire kindleth a great wood. And the tongue is a fire, a world of iniquity. The tongue is placed among our members, which defileth the whole body, and inflameth the wheel of our nativity, being set on fire by hell. For every nature of beasts, and of birds, and of serpents, and of the rest, is tamed, and hath been tamed, by the nature of man: But the tongue no man can tame, an unquiet evil, full of deadly poison. By it we bless God and the Father: and by it we curse men, who are made after the likeness of God. Out of the same mouth proceedeth blessing and cursing. My brethren, these things ought not so to be.

So Guido da Montefeltro wills and—"out of the same mouth"—repents his will. The demon seizing on Guido's soul implies that he and saintly Francis cannot both have it—*the law of contradiction will not consent* (*Inf.* XXVII, 120).

Virgil's own deceitful speech will bring the pilgrims—via the flattered Antaeus—down to the sides of the pit. But the sinner speaking last in Malebolge proper is Virgil's Sinon. The suave and specious words of the seducers, the ingratiating and manipulative words of the flatterers, the future-twisting projections of the diviners, the insidious dissimulations of the hypocrites, and the malicious and disastrous promises of the false counselors, all find their way into Sinon's speeches in *Aeneid* II, where he is master of the plausible, pleasing, distorting, misleading, ill-advising, and perjurious representations that brought the wooden horse into Troy—and the pilgrims down to the sides of the pit.

The dropsical Master Adam, as drum-bodied as Sinon's gift, is also as exemplary of its hollowness. Malebolge is given to craftiness, and "it belongs to craftiness to adopt ways that are not true but counterfeit" (Aquinas, *Summa* II-II, 55, 4: per contra). A corrupter of the proud florin, the medium of exchange, the counterfeiter has the most telling of names, if the original Adam was stamped with the image of God in the same motion he was given speech. Endowed with the language of appraisal and the mastery of nomenclature, such an Adam bore the image of us all, for we all speak and sign. Malebolge begins with the seducer who conned Hypsipyle out of her *sipa,* a pander who turned his sister into coin, and flatterers whose verbal matter had the zero-value of scum and waste; it ends with a mastery of fraudulent arts almost being a mastery of representation itself.

Malebolge's sequence of self-contradictory representations began at Geryon; it ends at Nimrod. Like Geryon's face, Nimrod's speech hides a tongue. As if he too were a master coiner, Dante invents the words but at the same time debases *Eli, Eli, lamma sabacthanì,* Jesus' cry of dereliction from the Cross. Nimrod unsays what the Gospel took from Psalm 21; thus the rhyme-word *salmi* (XXXI, 69). The loud cry, like Jesus', is unintelligible to its hearers. Forsaken by his liege-lord, as Roland was by Charlemagne, the giant rebukes a giant-god (Hebrew *Raph-el*) that can only be hell's own Geryonic prince: the fallen angel whose advancing standard—the *vexilla* of *Inferno* XXXIV—Nimrod so witlessly trumpets, even while he divides the tongue of the Son of God against itself.[16]

Nimrod's five words finalize that erosion of intelligibility which all the frauds of Malebolge stealthily promote. "The execution of craftiness with the purpose of deceiving," Aquinas says, "is effected first and foremost by words, which hold the chief place among those signs whereby a man signifies something to another man, as Augustine states (*De Doctr. Christ.* ii.3), hence guile is ascribed chiefly to speech" (*Summa* II-II, 55, 4: reply to obj. 2). In the apocryphal Gospel of Peter, Jesus' words from the cross form a declaration: "My *power,* my *power,* thou hast forsaken me." Nimrod, "through whose wicked thought / one single language cannot serve the world" (*Inf.* XXXI, 77–78), thus asks, by the very incoherence of his idiolect, why the power of speech has forsaken him. Virgil's response, "He is his own accuser" (76), implies that the giant's garbled tongue and internecine self-division are all that remain to him of God's image as stamped on the original Adamic coin.[17] Worn off its matter by fraudulent sinners' repeated abuse of the endowment that marked them as human in the first place, this image was discourse of reason, *libero arbitrio* (deliberating judgment: *Purg.* XVIII, 74) and "the good of the intellect" (*Inf.* III, 18).

If he understands others as poorly as they understand him, then Nimrod is his own accuser where no one else can be. In his *De vulgari eloquentia* (I, iv) Dante says that the first man's first word must have been "El," *either as a question or an answer.* Nimrod commences with *Raphèl*—but he is no longer an answerable moral subject, or convocable as one. Dante also says that men differ so much in their intellects "that each man seems almost to constitute a species by himself" (ibid., I, iii, I); common language is the means whereby men have avoided an isolation like Nimrod's.[18] But according to Malebolge, it is the deception wrought by the intellect's abuse of language that divides the sinner from his neighbor, as from himself. A single tongue is not used in the world through the Nimrod of an ignorant mind, but also through the Geryon of a cunning fraud.

Midway through Malebolge's "evil field" (XVIII, 4), Virgil awakens to the fact that the demon Malacoda, who has provided the pilgrims with an untrustworthy escort around the fifth ditch, has also misled Virgil about a highway across Malebolge. The collapsed bridges show the limits of Malacoda's reliability—and the damage to Virgil's innocence. Hereupon a hypocrite slyly remarks that he once heard the devil called a liar and the father of lies (XXIII, 143–144). The appearance of Geryon and the sound of Nimrod astonish Dante on Malebolge's thresholds and are thus signs for whatever catches up the pilgrims in between. Malacoda's deceits, in particular, are marked by a sign that the poet greets as prodigious. Charged to take the pilgrims on their supposedly direct way, Evil-Tail's gang of demons alerts its appointed leader, and "Curly-Beard" goes bugling off responsively and uniquely:

> They turned around along the left hand bank:
> but first each pressed his tongue between his teeth
> as signal for their leader, Barbariccia.
> And he had made a trumpet of his ass.
>
> (XXI, 136–139)

Geryon hides the evil of the tongue behind an honest-looking face; Barbariccia divulges it at the venomous fork of a treacherous tail—or tale.

NOTES

1. Singleton (*Inferno: Commentary,* 2:317–319) reports Benvenuto's note: *salse* denominated "a certain, sloping concave place" near Bologna. "The bodies of desperate criminals, usurers, and other unspeakable persons used to be thrown there." Thus Dante might ask Venèdico, "Are you indeed already dead and disposed of?" According to our essay, this is the right question. Also cf. the English proverb, "to be served with the same sauce."

2. We might conclude that "conning" and "coining" occur in the same word from reading scholars' explanations and parallel citations as collected and summarized in Singleton (ibid., 2:321–322). With the district of Italy where *sipa* is the word all the young are taught for *yes* should be compared "that land" in *Inf.* XXI, 40–42, where (ironically) "everyone's a grafter but Bonturo; / and there—for cash—they'll change a *no* to *yes* [*ita* (so)]." The buying and selling of consent classifies pandering with barratry in ways consistent with binary and triadic schemes developed in the present essay.

3. Pseudo-Archytas, as in Simplicium, *In Physicorum libros* 786.29–33, quoted in James Miller, *Measures of Wisdom: The Cosmic Dance in Classical and Christian Antiquity* (Toronto, 1986), 438.

4. *Anatomy of Melancholy,* pt.1, sec. 2, Mem. 3, Subs. 11 (1st para.), 1:280, noting the source's Latin for horsemill—but the passage is not in Augustine.

5. Origen, *Commentary on Matthew,* 10:409–512. In the original (*Origines in Matthaeum commentariorum series:* "Ser. 57, p. 132, 6," in *Patrologia Graeca,* ed. Migne, vol. 13, col. 1169 [lacks Gr.]), *de animabus molentibus in gravi mole mundi vel corporis* (from souls being milled in the heavy mill of the world or body); *Thesaurus linguae latinae,* s.v. "mola" adds "(Ser. 58, p. 132, 33 [*gr. utrobique ἐν τῷ μυλῶνι τοῦ κόσμου*)." For the millstone as the laborious round of terrene activity see Gregory I, *Morals on Job,* 5.26; Rabanus Maurus, *Allegories in Holy Writ,* at *mola* (*Patrologia Latina,* ed. Migne, vol. 112, col. 1000: "the millstone on his neck" = *circuitus laborum in necessitate eius*); *Glossa ordinaria* (*Pat. Lat.,* vol. 114, col. 1734); Aquinas, *Catena Aurea* in Matthew 18:6 (citing Hilary—Jews punished major crimes by casting the stone-laden offender in the sea). The youth on Homer's dance floor—like the one Daedalus made Ariadne—"run round with cunning feet . . . as when a potter sits at his wheel . . . and tries if it runs; in rows they run toward each other again" (*Iliad* XVIII, 599–602).

6. John Holywood is quoted in *The Sphere of Sacrobosco and Its Commentators,* ed. and trans. Lynn Thorndike (Chicago, 1949), ch. 2, "Of the Circles and Their Names." The notion that the circles of the Same and Different correspond to two motions in the soul or Soul is "Middle Platonic"; it may derive from Aristotle, *On Generation and Corruption* II,10, 336a6-6 (cf. also *On the Cosmos* III, 392a12). Freccero, "Dante's Pilgrim in a Gyre," in *Poetics of Conversion* (Cambridge, Mass., 1986), 77, quotes Chalcidius: "The sphere of the fixed stars in the soul is reason; of the

planets, *iracundia* and *cupiditas* and other movements of this sort" (*In Platonis Timaeum comment.*, 95). Dante refers to the two circles in *Paradiso* x moving "obliquely"—recalling Aristotle's name for the zodiacal band, "the oblique circle" (*On Generation and Corruption, loc. cit., ton loxon kyklon*), found in Sacrobosco's second chapter: "Then, reader, lift your eyes with me to see / the high wheels; gaze directly at that part / where the one motion strikes against the other; / . . . See there the circle branching from that cross-point / obliquely: zodiac to bear the planets / that satisfy the world in need of them" (*Par.* x, 7–15; cf. *l'oblico cerchio* che i pianeti porta [14]).

7. *Consolation of Philosophy* III, metrum 9: "Entwining all-moving Soul throughout the cosmos' concordant members, you release it as medium of threefold nature." Guido delle Colonne, *Historia destructionis Troiae* II, 244–254, likens Medea's womanly inconstancy to matter's appetite for various forms; but Chaucer, *Legend of Good Women*, 1582–1588, will offer the same likeness for Jason's promiscuity. (Guido delle Colonne, *Historia destructionis Troiae*, trans. Mary Elizabeth Meek [Bloomington, Ind., 1974], 15; Geoffrey Chaucer, *Works of Geoffrey Chaucer*, ed. F. N. Robinson, 2d ed. [Boston, 1957], 506).

8. Benvenuto, as quoted in Singleton, *Inferno: Commentary*, 2:326

9. Cited in Patricia Meyer Spacks, *Gossip* (New York, 1985), 18.

10. Cf. Singleton, *Inferno: Commentary*, 2:317, for the record on Venèdico's death, in 1303.

11. So the typescript reproduced in *Winston Churchill's Secret Session Speeches*, ed. Charles Eade (New York, 1946), 11.

12. *Summa theologica* II-II, 55, 3–5; Augustine, *To Consentius: Against Lying*, 17, says evil words, like evil deeds, are done by a member—the tongue. *Inferno* XI, 58–60, lists frauds in even-numbered ditches (6, 2, 4, 10) before those in odd-numbered (7, 3, 1, 5). (It holds back frauds in ditches 8 and 9.)

13. Aquinas, as cited by Grandgent (ed., *Dante's "Divina Commedia"* [Boston, 1933], 204), where the reference should be *Summa theologica* II-II, 111, 3: "A hypocrite, or as the Latin has it, a *dissimulator*, is a covetous thief: for . . . he steals praise for a life which is not his" (a gloss from Gregory, *Morals on Job*, XVIII, on the hypocrite in Job 27:8, who may "through covetousness . . . take by violence").

14. Nimrod checks pride in *Purg.* XII, 34–36; cf. Augustine, *City of God*, bk. XVI. ch. 4: "The safe and true highway to heaven is built by humility, which lifts up the heart to the Lord, not against Him, like this giant who is called 'a hunter against the Lord.'"

15. *Ipocresia*, in Peter Brieger, Millard Meiss, and Charles S. Singleton, *Illuminated Manuscripts of The Divine Comedy*, vol. 2, *Plates* (Princeton, 1969), 199, *a*. "Oxford, Bodleian Can. it. 108, 15ᵛ (Mid XIV cent.)."

16. *Raph-el* is formed like *Bab-el* (gate of God [Akkadian]). Dante's *Raph-* = Hebrew *rapha*, giant, 1 Chron. 20:4, 6, 8; 2 Sam. 21:16–22; Deut. 2:11, 20, 3:11, 13; and Josue 12:4 (Septuagint *gigas*), 13:12, 15:8, 17:15, 18:16. Heb. *gibbor* (mighty man) is translated *gigas* (giant) by the Septuagint at Gen. 6:4 and 10:8–9 (= Nimrod). For Jesus' cry, cf. Matt. 27:46, Mark 15:34–39, Heb. 5:7, Psalm 21:1–2 (and AV Psalm 22:1–2); and Dante, *Par.* XI, 32–33, *Purg.* XXIII, 73–74, *Inf.* XXXIII, 69 (Father, why do you not help me?) with 87 (*a tal croce* [on such a cross]). For God's original name according to Dante's Adam, cf. *Par.* XXVI, 134–37.

17. God's image refers to Augustine's *De Trinitate*, especially bk. XV, ch. 16 (sec. 26), "at that time [when we are re-formed in the divine likeness] our word will not indeed be false, because we shall neither lie nor be deceived," with bk. XIV, ch. 16 (sec. 22): "That which is meant by 'created after God,' is expressed in another place by 'after the image of God.' But it lost righteousness and true holiness by sinning, through which that image became defaced and tarnished; and thus it recovers when it is formed again and renewed." Cf. Aquinas, *The Disputed Questions: On Truth*, art. 10, "Whether Anything Is False," *contra* 1: "the false is *that which is accommodated to the likeness of any thing and does not pertain to that whose likeness it bears*. But every creature bears the likeness of God. Since, therefore, no creature pertains to God himself by the mode of identity, it seems that every creature is false." Geryon, if he is the truth of fraud, might be a falser one than most.

18. Cf. Augustine, *City of God*, bk. XVI, ch. 4, on Nimrod and the people of Babel: "and justly was their evil intent punished by God, even when not successfully effected. But what kind of punishment was imposed? As the tongue is the organ of domination, so in that organ was [their]

pride sentenced: in order that the one [Nimrod] who would not understand God, when He gave His commands, should not be understood himself, when he gave orders to men . . . each man separated from those he could not understand, and associated with those whose speech was intelligible."

BIBLIOGRAPHICAL NOTES

It may be thought that the present essay presents several—as it were—*frauds:* the panders' and seducers' order (right church, wrong pew), Venèdico's early report of his mortal sin (right fate, wrong date), and Thaïs's legendary persona (early sinner, late saint). The critical literature seems to have neglected these anomalies (if they are noted at all), and it has not translated Nimrod's idiolect (counterfeit tongue, true language or sign). Here I argue that the anomalies are all part of the plan and dissimulate Malebolge's invention or poetics. On these ideas see my studies in other edited volumes: "The Descent of Geryon: The Moral System of *Inferno* xix–xxxi," *Dante Studies* 114 (1996); "The Love That Moves the Sun and Other Stars in *Inferno* xviii," *Sewanee Mediaeval Colloquium Studies* for 1995, ed. Susan Ridyard (forthcoming); and "The *Inferno*," in *Homer to Brecht: The European Epic and Dramatic Tradition*, ed. Michael Seidel and Edward Mendelson (New Haven, 1977), 76–104. Below are studies grouped according to the topic order of the foregoing commentary.

Architecture and Topography of Malebolge

Many critics note Malebolge's resemblance to a moated castle of fortification; fewer note the comparison to the regularized, circular-style labyrinth. Some have doubted there is more than one bridge across the eighth circle. Allan Gilbert, in notes to his translation, *Dante Alighieri: Inferno* (Chapel Hill, N.C., 1969), 320, discusses the bridge through Malebolge as singular. But the word "gathers in" (*raccoglie* [re-collects], at *Inf.* xviii, 18) implies more than one bridge. Cf. Charon reaping the harvest of the damned—"beckoning to them, [he] *gathers them all in*" (*Inf.* iii, 110: *tutte le raccoglie*)—and note that the souls respond to Charon's signal "as a falcon—called—will come" (117). Geryon is also a falcon under human mastery (xvi, 127–132, *Come 'l falcon* . . .). Gilbert discounts Malacoda's indications (*Inf.* xxi, 111; xxiii, 140–144), and the rhyming plural *castelli* (*Inf.* xviii, 11), and magnifies "a rock" at *Inf.* xxiii, 134–135 ("a rock [*sasso*] that . . . crosses all the wild valleys"). But the other bridges exist conjecturally—like the twelve, invisible spokelike lines astronomers draw to divide the circles of the ten (or fewer) heavenly spheres. For "Who ever discovered or established twelve divisions of the sky when there are no demarcations for any of them apparent to our eyes?," asks Macrobius's naive student (*Commentary on the Dream of Scipio* i, 21, trans. W. H. Stahl [New York, 1952], 176). The postulate of several bridges is standard: Edward Moore, "Geography of Dante," *Studies in Dante: Third Series* (1903; reprint, Westport, Conn., 1968), 109–143; Pietro Mazzamuto, "Malebolge," *Enciclopedia dantesca* (Rome, 1971), 3:787–789.

Mythography of Geryon and Malebolge

For Arachne in relation to the whole poem, see Pamela Royston Macfie, "Ovid, Arachne, and the Poetics of Paradise," in *The Poetry of Allusion: Virgil and Ovid in Dante's "Commedia,"* ed. Rachel Jacoff and Jeffrey T. Schnapp (Stanford, 1992), 158–72, esp. 164–67 for Geryon and Arachne. Also linking Arachne to the creation of Dantean texts as Daedalean artifacts is Teodolinda Barolini, *The Undivine "Comedy": Detheologizing Dante* (Princeton, 1992), 130–132. On imagery for Geryon with cosmic implications, see Kevin Brownlee, "Phaeton's Fall and Dante's Ascent," *Dante Studies* 102 (1984): 133–144. On Geryon's relation to the midpoint of the *Inferno*, see John Kleiner, *Mismapping the Underworld: Daring and Error in Dante's "Comedy"* (Stanford, 1994); on the place of Canto xviii at the start of the *Inferno*'s second half, see Lanfranco Caretti, "Canto xviii," in *Lectura Dantis Scaligeri: Inferno*, ed. Mario Marcazzan (Florence, 1967), 583–611; esp. 606–609. John Ruskin describes the Minotaur as "the creature who, in the midst of his labyrinth, lived as a spider in the centre of his web" (*Fors Clavigera*, in *Works* [New York, ca. 1902], 1:310, letter 23)—which applies, topographically, to Satan, but also to Geryon, in the middle of the *Inferno*'s text. On cobweblike diagrams in Chalcidius and Macrobius, see James Miller, *Measures of Wisdom: The Cosmic Dance in Classical and Christian Antiquity* (Toronto, 1986), 453. For Arachnean designs as Ariadnean, cf. Shakespeare's "Ariachne" in *Troilus and Cressida*, ed. S. Wells and G. Taylor (Oxford, 1988), v, ii, 154–155.

Pope Boniface and 1300

The accounts I rely on are Giovanni Villani, *Chronicle* VIII, 36, in Singleton, *Inferno: Commentary*, 2:314–315; Guglielmo Ventura's chronicle of Asti, and Charles Eliot Norton, "Notes of Travel and Study in Italy," both in *The Divine Comedy*, ed. Henry Wadsworth Longfellow (Boston, 1913), 160–161; Lonsdale Ragg, *Dante and His Italy* (New York, 1907); Friedrich Heer, *The Medieval World: Europe 1100–1350*, trans. Janet Sonheimer (New York, 1963), 332; E. R. Chamberlin, *The Bad Popes* (1969; reprint, New York, 1986), 74–123; R. W. Southern, *Western Society and the Church in the Middle Ages* (Harmondsworth, 1970), 4–7, 16–21; Charles T. Wood, "Vita: Boniface VIII," *Harvard Magazine*, July–August, 1980, 54–55.

Heavenly Patterns in Nether Hell

John Freccero describes the relevant cosmic milieu, in "Dante's Pilgrim in a Gyre," and "*Paradiso* x: The Dance of the Stars," both in *Dante: The Poetics of Conversion*, ed. Rachel Jacoff (Cambridge, Mass., 1986): Freccero's second essay shows how *Timaeus* 36 applies to the X—or Chi— in *Paradiso* x, as formed by the two circles' equinotical intersection. See also Edward Grant, "Cosmology," which is ch. 8 in *Science in the Middle Ages*, ed. David C. Lindberg (Chicago, 1978), 265–302. On the fictive time of the poem, see Philip Wicksteed, "The Chronology of the *Divina Commedia*," in *Aids to the Study of Dante*, ed. Charles Allen Dinsmore (Boston, 1903), 253–261. For more on the relation between cosmic themes and schemes for sin, see Morton Bloomfield, *The Seven Deadly Sins* (East Lansing, Mich., 1952); and my essay, "The Love That Moves the Sun and Other Stars," mentioned above (forthcoming).

Imagery in Inferno *XVIII*

F. T. Gallarati Scotti, "Il canto XVIII dell'*Inferno*," in *Letture dantesche*, ed. Giovanni Getto (Florence, 1962), 333–344, at 343 quotes Christoforo Landino on vital vs. dead words as an analogy for vital food vs. dead matter in the flatterers' ditch. Tibor Wlassics, "The *Villanello* (*Inferno* XXIV, 1–15)," *Lectura Dantis* 1 (1987): 61–72, at 62–63, reflects on the flatterers' ditch as a sewer or septic tank and notes the critique of flattery as relying on a universal language of imagery for unctiousness—sucking up, smearing over, etc. But this canto's *rhetoric* and *diction* are often grating and abusive: quite the opposite of ingratiating.

Rhetorical or Lexical Analysis of Inferno *XVIII*

Such analysis is not a subject of the present essay, but melopoeia belongs with both this canto's phanopoeia and its *lexis*, as in Robin Kirkpatrick's treatment, *Dante's "Inferno": Difficulty and Dead Poetry* (Cambridge, 1987), 236–248. Guilio Bertoni, "Il canto dei lenoni e degli adulatori," *Archivum Romanicum* 12 (1928): 288–302, contains interesting notes on the text, such as words like the teutonic-sounding *berza* in line 37 (295). Marino Barchiesi, "Arte del prologo e arte della transizione," *Studi danteschi* 44 (1967): 115–207 (esp. 142–155) is relevant to this canto, and to the poetics of the threshold throughout the *Comedy*. Many commentators note the divided diction of *Inf.* XVIII, elevated for Jason, and base, crude, demotic, barbarous, or obscure, at several points, for the others. H. Wayne Storey, "Mapping Out the New Poetic Terrain: Malebolge and *Inferno* XVIII," *Lectura Dantis* 4 (1989): 3–41, pays particular attention to the new harshness and vulgarity of language ("so strong and offensive that later in the canticle Dante will declare himself, quite falsely, incapable of achieving such a taxing and aberrant style" [*Inf.* XXXII, 1–12]). Storey notes the new relation of topography to proto-cinematic viewpoints here (beginning from Geryon—Dante is now in a superior position in relation to the sinners sunk in the various ditches). He also compares Alessio's self-epigramaticization to the public destruction of family reputations in Florence by wall paintings of malefactors, identified by brief rhyming captions ("bubbles," we'd call them). For the canto as a whole, Storey gives a fine bibliography, to which I am indebted.

Personnel of the First Two Ditches

Barolini, *The Undivine "Comedy,"* 76–77, cites commentators and describes character-pairs in Malebolge in ways parallel to those of the present essay. See also my article, "The Descent of Geryon" (esp. on Ulysses/Diomede = Guido/Sylvester), and my projected study, "Dante's Adam's Dropsy: A Case Study in the Literary Etiology of the Sickness of Sin" (on Sinon / Master Adam). Rhetoric, genre, and ethical stance figure heavily in Caretti, but the study also observes the symmetries of *Inf.* xviii's four sinners (586).

   Since one of the denizens of flattery's ditch is a harlot (Thaïs), her punishment tends to illustrate the allegedly Aquinine thesis that society needs the stews in the way a human dwelling needs a sewer. As suggested by the legend of the saint, the flatterers' situation derives from the absence of normal amenities: "Remove the sewer and you will fill the palace with ordure"—to which is added, "similarly with the bilge from a ship; remove whores from the world and you will fill it with sodomy" (*De Regimine Principium,* iv, xiv, in Thomas Aquinas, *Opera Omnia* [Parma, 1864], 16:281).

Time Schemes Relating to Personae

An overall treatment of *foundations* for this subject is A. C. Charity's *Events and Their Afterlife: The Dialectics of Christian Typology in the Bible and Dante* (Cambridge, 1966). On our theme, see Bernard Knox, "Author, author" [="The Shock of the Old"], *New York Review of Books,* November 16, 1995, 16–20; and cf. Longfellow's citation in his translation (*Divine Comedy* [Boston, 1913], 161), at *Inf.* xviii, 36, of "Landor, *Pentameron,* 15": "The filthiness of some passages would disgrace the drunkenest horse-dealer; and the names of such criminals are recorded by the poet, as would be forgotten by the hangman in six months."

Schematizations of Malebolge

The generic considerations that cause Caretti to contrast "epic" with "comic" emphases in *Inferno* xviii, when merged with our manic vs. depressive classification, lead to a contrast of ironic modes with satiric ones (cf., e.g., the death of Ulysses vs. that of Guido da Montefeltro). Joan Ferrante, in "Malebolge (*Inf.* xviii–xxx) as the Key to the Structure of Dante's *Inferno,*" *Romance Philology* 20, no. 4 (May 1967): 456–466, suggests the existence of poem-wide patterns in Malebolge according to a scheme of virtues. Cf. also Robert Hollander, *Allegory in Dante's "Commedia"* (Princeton, 1969), 301–307 (appendix 3), for another analysis; Hollander depends on an Aristotelian theory of tragic responses to sin, from empathy to repudiation. Neither a system of virtues nor a theory about the progressive educating of Dante's reactions supplies the scaffolding for an internal and objective order in Malebolge; that requires plotting out a systematic and progressive *erosion* of objective values by lying, and community values by venality or divisiveness. Ferrante's reference to prudence and wisdom wants re-applying to Malebolge, where fraud disguises itself as worldly wisdom: cf. esp. Aquinas, *Summa theologica* ii-ii, 47, 49, and 55. Space has not permitted much exposition of the *relation* of crimes against institutions to sins against other minds, beyond the alternation in the first two ditches; the idea is to apply Eckhart's theme—"Truth is not merchandise"—beyond the judgment the demon makes on Venèdico's coining of his sister's integrity.

   The problem of our binary scheme—the objection that it reverses the order of presentation at the outset—may be met my way, by proposing a reversal of the inner and outer lanes of the first bolgia; or one may consider seduction and flattery as belonging together, and thus as occupying the second position à deux, following on pandering in the first position.

Speech Motifs in Inferno *XVIII*

Giuseppe Mazzotta, *Dante, Poet of the Desert* (Princeton, 1979), 158–159, reflects on the recurrence of Virgil's "ornate speech" in Jason's history: the contrast between morally opposed uses of rhetorical blandishment, he says, "cannot hide the sense of the inevitable duplicity of poetical language." Cf. Robert Hollander, "Dante's Pagan Past: Notes on *Inferno* XIV and XVIII," *Stanford Italian Review* 5 (spring 1985): 23–36, esp. 29–33.

Thaïs's characterization, after her speech in Cicero, *De amicitia* XXVI, 98, after Terence, *Eunuchus* III, i (Lat. *ingentes* = Ital. *maravigliosi*), has been traced to John of Salisbury's enmity to flattery in *Policraticus* III, iv, by André Pézard, "Du Policraticus à la *Divina Commedia*," *Romania* (Paris) 70 (1948): 1–36, 136–191; cf. 3–13. Cf. *Patrologia Latina*, ed. Migne, vol. 199, col. 281–283 ("What is more unfaithful than to circumvent him to whom you owe faith with blandishing words . . . and, having blinded him by pandering to all of his vanities, to push him into the squalor of vice [*sordes vitiorum*] and depth of perdition?" [281C]; Thaïs added *ingentes* "because of the adulator's *fraud*" [282D]). Kirkpatrick, *Dante's "Inferno,"* 248, contrasts Thaïs's gracious words with Beatrice's marvellous grace: correctly, if the two women construct the Dantean eternal feminine's polar opposites.

For Nimrod's speech, cf. Robert Hollander, "Babytalk in Dante's *Commedia*," in *Studies in Dante* (Ravenna, 1977), 115–129, and his *Dante and Paul's "Five Words with Understanding"* (Binghamton, N.Y., 1992).

On the Canto as a Whole

For running commentaries, headnotes, summaries, and so forth, especially within editions of the canticle or *Comedy*—besides Grandgent's, and Charles Sinclair, *Dante's Inferno* (New York, 1939), 234–235—see William Warren Vernon, *Readings on the Inferno of Dante,* 2d ed. (London, 1906), 2:32–65; Natalino Sapegno, ed., *La Divina Commedia* (Florence, 1968), 1:200–208; Attilio Momigliano, ed., *La Divina Commedia* (Florence, 1972), 132–139; Umberto Bosco and Giovanni Reggio, eds., *La Divina Commedia* (Florence, 1979), 1:261–275; Giuseppe Giacalone, ed., *La Divina Commedia: Inferno* (Rome, 1987), 268–283; Emilio Pasquini and Antonio Quaglio, eds., *La Divina Commedia* (Milan, 1988), 195–203.

Works Cited

The following texts are used or adapted in the present essay but are incompletely cited in situ or in the notes.

Aquinas, Thomas. *Catena Aurea in quatuor Evangelia,* ed. Angelico Guariento. 2 vols. Taurini, 1953.
———. "The Disputed Questions on Truth." In *Selections from Medieval Philosphers,* ed. Richard McKeon, 2:159–234. New York, 1958.
———. *Summa theologica.* Trans. Fathers of the English Dominican Province. 5 vols. 1948. Reprint, Westminster, Md., 1981.
Aristotle. *On the Cosmos.* Trans. D. J. Furley. In *On Sophistical Refutations et alia,* ed. and trans. E. S. Forster and D. J. Furley. Loeb Classical Library. Cambridge, Mass., 1978.
———. *On Generation and Corruption.* Trans. E. S. Forster. In *On Sophistical Refutations et alia,* ed. and trans. E. S. Forster and D. J. Furley. Loeb Classical Library. Cambridge, Mass., 1978.
Augustine. *Concerning the City of God against the Pagans.* Trans. Henry Betenson. Baltimore, Md., 1977.
———. *To Consentius: Against Lying.* Trans. H. Browne. In *A Select Library of Nicene and Post-Nicene Fathers, 1st Series.* Vol. 3, *St. Augustin,* ed. Philip Schaff, 457–477, 481–500. Grand Rapids, Mich., 1988 [= *Contra Mendacium ad Consentium* in *Patrologia Latina,* ed. Migne, vol. 40, cols. 517–48].
———. *De Mendacio,* in *Parologia Latina,* ed. Migne, vol. 40, cols. 487–518 (trans. as *On Lying,* in *NPNF, 1st Series,* 3:457–477).

————. *On the Trinity.* Trans. H. W. Haddan, rev. W. G. T. Shedd. In *A Select Library of the Nicene and Post-Nicene Fathers, 1st Series.* Vol. 3: *St. Augustin,* ed. Philip Schaff, 15–276. Grand Rapids, Mich., 1988 [in *Patrologia Latina,* ed. Migne, vol. 42, cols. 819–1098].

Boethius. *The Consolation of Philosophy.* Trans. S. J. Tester. In *Philosophical Tracts* and *The Consolation of Philosophy,* ed. and trans. H. F. Stewart, E. K. Rand, and S. J. Tester, Loeb Classical Library. Cambridge, Mass., 1973.

Burton, Robert. *The Anatomy of Melancholy.* 1621. 3 vols. London, 1932.

Chalcidius [Calcidius]. *Platonis Timaeus, interprete Chalcidio, cum eiusdem commentario.* Ed. Johann Wrobel. Leipzig, 1876.

Dante Alighieri. *Literature in the Vernacular* [*De vulgari eloquentia*]. Trans. Sally Purcell. Manchester, 1981.

Meister Eckhart. "Truth is not merchandise," Sermon 13. In *Meister Eckhart: A Modern Translation,* trans. Raymond Bernard Blakney, 156–160. New York, 1941.

Grandgent, Charles, ed. Introduction to *Dante's "Divina Commedia."* Boston, 1933.

Gregory I [the Great]. *Moralium Libri, sive Espositio in Librum B. Job.* In *Patrologia Latina,* ed. Migne, vol. 75, cols. 509–1162.

————. *Regulae Pastoralis.* In *Patrologia Latina,* ed. Migne, vol. 77, cols. 13–128.

Hilary of Poitiers. *In Evangelium Matthaei Commentarius.* In *Patrologia Latina,* ed. Migne, vol. 9, cols. 917–1078.

Macrobius, Ambrosius Theodosius. *Commentary on the Dream of Scipio.* Trans. W. H. Stahl. New York, 1952.

Miller, James. *Measures of Wisdom: The Cosmic Dance in Classical and Christian Antiquity.* Toronto, 1986.

Origen of Alexandria. *Commentary on Matthew,* Books I, II, and X–XVI. Trans. John Patrick. In *The Ante-Nicene Fathers, Original Supplement to the American Edition,* ed. Allen Mezies, 10:409–512. 5th ed. Grand Rapids, Mich., 1990 [= *Patrologia Graeca,* ed. Migne, vol. 13, cols. 835–1600].

Plato. *Timaeus.* Trans. H. D. P. Lee. Baltimore, 1965.

Plutarch. "To Discern a Friend from a Flatterer." Trans. Philemon Holland (1603). In *Plutarch's Moralia: Twenty Essays,* 36–101. London, n.d. [ca. 1912].

Singleton, Charles. *Dante Alighieri: The Divine Comedy: Inferno.* Vol. 2, *Commentary.* Princeton, 1970.

Thesaurus linguae latinae 8, no. 9, s.v. "mola." Leipzig, 1960.

CANTO XIX

Simoniacs

CHARLES T. DAVIS

Inf. xviii, canto of panders, seducers, and flatterers, ends with the sight of the whore Thaïs standing in filth; Virgil points her out in a tone of contemptuous mockery. The theme of seduction persists in Canto xix, where a greater and more abstract whore is invoked, and so does the tone of mockery, this time in a more mordant key. The canto begins (1–21) with an apostrophe from Dante the poet denouncing simony, and exalting the divine art for creating the hideous hellscape of livid rock full of round, fiery openings that Dante the pilgrim now beholds. It ends (88–133) with a sermon from the pilgrim about the wickedness of the contemporary papacy and warm approval for his pupil from Virgil, who then picks him up and carries him toward the next valley. In between the canto recounts the punishment by fire of the simoniacs and the conversation the pilgrim has with one of them, Pope Nicholas III. This pontiff, upside down in his hole, mistakes Dante for Pope Boniface VIII and condemns himself, Boniface, and their successor Clement V for having deceived and dishonored the "Lovely Lady" (57), the Church. Such self-accusation wins no sympathy from the pilgrim, who rapidly loses all his shyness and, even at this early stage in his journey, assumes his full role as reformer-prophet. Musa (1964) points out that the learning process the pilgrim undergoes through the whole poem is here telescoped into one canto. At its end the pilgrim denounces the wicked popes in tones as ringing as those that will be used by Saint Peter in *Par.* xxvii for his very similar denunciation, saying that it was these popes the evangelist saw when he beheld the great harlot fornicating with the kings. As Herzman and Stephany observe, the pilgrim's words recorded by the poet here fulfill the command of Saint Peter in *Par.* XXVII not to conceal the truth about papal corruption. At the conclusion of his tirade the pilgrim also condemns the Donation of Constantine, the alleged gift of the western part of the empire that the Middle Ages believed he made to Sylvester I in gratitude for having been cured of leprosy by baptism. Dante says the donation was the mother of later ecclesiastical evil.

In this canto Dante takes center stage both as poet and pilgrim. The poet speaks first, and later the voice of the pilgrim develops and reinforces his opening apostrophe. Differences between their outlooks, often discerned by critics in other passages of the poem, here seem nonexistent. This close union of the two voices is also apparent in their use of sarcasm. Implicit in the description by the poet of the simoniacs' grotesquely appropriate punishment, it becomes explicit in the words of the pilgrim (and even in those of the tormented pope, Nicholas III). Dante's contempt for simony is thus triply underscored. Nowhere in the poem is he more personally involved. Nowhere does he seem to regard his message as more important to his purpose, described by the author of the letter to Cangrande (probably Dante) as the intention "to remove those living in this life from the state of misery and bring them to the state of happiness." For Dante the main cause of this state of misery was the prevalence of cupidity, of which he believed simony was by far the most perverted and virulent result, since it produced a clergy that poisoned not only the clerical church but also the whole world. In Canto XIX he expresses this theme dramatically by applying to curial rather than pagan Rome the image of the great harlot of the Apocalypse fornicating with kings. In *Purg.* XIX he deals again with the subject of the cupidity of rulers; there the pilgrim, after his dream of the siren woman with the stinking belly, somewhat reminiscent of John's vision of the harlot, meets Hadrian V, who is represented as having barely saved himself by repenting his sins just after becoming pope. The next canto, *Purg.* XX, continues this theme with an apostrophe by the poet against the wolf, symbol of cupidity, and with Hugh Capet's violent invective against the greedy members of his house.

The subject reappears at roughly the same point in *Paradiso.* At the end of Canto XVIII after the pilgrim sees the words DILIGITE IUSTITIAM . . . QUI IUDICATIS TERRAM (love justice, you who judge the earth [91–93]) spelled out by the souls in the heaven of Jove, the poet condemns the pope for having his desire so fixed on the image of John the Baptist imprinted on the gold florin of Florence that he no longer remembers either Peter or Paul. In *Par.* XIX the eagle of justice speaks to the pilgrim and assures him that many of those who cry, "Christ! Christ!" will stand further from Christ on the day of judgment than many pagans. The eagle goes on to describe the cupidity and other vices of contemporary kings. Thus near the middle of all three canticles, as well as in many other places in the poem, are found condemnation of what is for Dante the most fundamental and destructive kind of human wickedness, and also close coordination between the views of the pilgrim and the poet.

Medieval moral theologians regarded simony as a particularly disgusting form of cupidity, since it perverted the Holy Spirit's gift of sacred orders by buying, selling, and otherwise befouling them in a selfish struggle for power and gain. The name itself comes from that of Simon Magus, the magician of Samaria who, according to Acts 8:9–20, tried to buy from the apostles Peter and John their gift of imparting the Holy Spirit to the faithful and was in consequence cursed by Peter. By Dante's time the sin of simony was often interpreted broadly to include any worldly and selfish use of ecclesiastical authority. Dante shared this view, and simony aroused in him not only anger but the deepest contempt, a contempt he expressed in the imagery as well as in the words of Canto xix. In the account in Acts Simon Magus is also scorned by Simon Peter and cursed for his temerity.

Legend enlarged upon this modest episode and turned Simon Magus into a sort of anti-Peter, indeed an Antichrist, picturing him as contending with Peter in Rome and showing his powers by flying with the aid of the devil over the city. The saint prayed to Christ that he would make the evil Simon fall, and fall he did, headfirst. (This story was well enough known in the Middle Ages to be frequently represented in art and to be repeated by a number of Dante's early commentators, among them the Ottimo, the Anonimo Fiorentino, and Francesco da Buti.) Simon's ignominious end, as Singleton observed, may have suggested to Dante the headfirst position of the simoniacs in Hell. Perhaps it also suggested the headfirst position of Satan, fixed in ice at the center of the world after an even greater fall (*Inf.* xxxiv). There is certainly a similarity between the position of the simoniacs and that of Satan, as many commentators have pointed out.

In any case, the predicament of the simoniacs is an image of the way in which they have betrayed the heavenly purpose of their office. Planted upside down in the holes of the rock as if still seeking only earthly things (the rock itself, according to Scott, is a parody of that solid foundation on which Christ told the other Simon he would build his church), they frantically kick their feet, which are licked by flames that issue from those holes. (Do these flames, as some of the early commentators suggest, represent cupidinous desire, in contrast to the warmth of charity by which these feet should have been moved to do good works? Or do the flames parody, as Kenelm Foster says, the tongues of fire that accompanied the first imposition of holy orders at Pentecost? or both?) The fact that the fire is playing over their soles as if over an oily surface is perhaps a reminder of the holy oil applied to the head in ordination.

The pilgrim timidly asks Virgil about one who kicks more than the others, and whose feet are sucked at by a redder flame. Virgil carries him down to stand near the sufferer's hole, which turns out to be that of Nicholas III. The fact that the fire is particularly red in this hole, which we learn is reserved for simoniac popes, may be intended not only to show the greater severity of Nicholas's punishment but also, Gmelin suggests, as a sarcastic reference to the fact that the Roman pontiff wore red boots (see the comment of Charles of Anjou about Nicholas III in Giovanni Villani, *Chronicle* VIII, 54). Described by the poet as that sinner who lamented with his legs (45) (Singleton notes that Simon Magus was said to have suffered a triple fracture in that part of his anatomy when he fell), Nicholas is interrogated by the pilgrim in a pitiless and almost flippant way. Translated literally, the pilgrim's words to him are approximately the following: "O whoever you are who hold your top to the bottom, poor soul stuck down like a pole, say something if you can." The poet thereupon describes the pilgrim as being in a position similar to that of a friar confessing the "foul assassin" already with his head in the hole (and about to suffer the judicial punishment called "planting"); before the hole is filled and he is buried alive upside down, he calls the friar back again in order to delay death. Dante the layman stands in the place of the friar and Pope Nicholas in the place of the assassin. The simoniac is comparable to an assassin, observes Francesco da Buti ingeniously: the assassin sells the bond of natural love for money, and the simoniac sells likewise the bond of grace or divine love.

So Dante the pilgrim "confesses" Nicholas, though he has neither the power nor the desire to give him absolution. The only release the pope can hope for is to sink down deeper into the fiery hole, when his successor in simony arrives to take his turn, as Nicholas puts it, at being "planted here with scarlet feet" (81). Thinking Dante is that successor he cries out, sarcastic even in his agony, "Are you already standing, / already standing there, o Boniface? / The book has lied to me by several years. / Are you so quickly sated with the riches / for which you did not fear to take by guile / the Lovely Lady, then to violate her?" (52–56). The simoniac, remarks Pietro di Dante appropriately, dishonors the church, the spouse of Christ, by making her produce and bring up children who are illegitimate and adulterine. As for the "book" to which Nicholas refers (54), Grundmann has suggested that it may be a text like that of the *Vaticinia de summis pontificibus,* which he observes converted Byzantine imperial prophecies to papal ones condemning all the popes from Nicholas III through Boniface VIII except for Celestine V, and which he thinks can be traced to a group of Spiritual Franciscans in Perugia in 1304.

When told by Dante that he is not Boniface, Nicholas answers with an especially violent kick. He thereupon describes himself as the bear (a play on the name of his family Orsini) who was so eager to advance the little bears (the *Vaticinia* speaks of "the bear feeding her cubs") that "I / pursed wealth above while here I purse myself." Boniface, who died in 1303, will not have to occupy his position as long as Nicholas, already dead in 1280; soon another even worse pastor will come: Clement V, who died in 1314. Nicholas says that the king of France (Philip IV) will be as "soft" to Clement as the king Antiochus IV was to the high priest Jason, who secured his office by promising to pay the king 440 talents. Clement was supposed to have promised Philip future payments for helping him attain the papal throne. The adjective *molle* suggests the fornication of the harlot with the kings in Apocalypse 17, and the pilgrim seems to allude to the image for his own tirade against the popes.

"Your avarice," he says, "afflicts the world: / it tramples on the good, lifts up the wicked. / You, shepherds, the Evangelist had noticed / when he saw her who sits upon the waters / and realized she fornicates with kings, / she who was born with seven heads and had / the power and support of the ten horns, / as long as virtue was her husband's pleasure." For John, the great harlot represented the new Christian-persecuting Babylon of pagan Rome drinking the blood of the saints; for Dante, she represents the newer Babylon that he thought was curial Rome, still persecuting true Christians. Similar imagery appears in *Purg.* xxxii, when the chariot of the Church suddenly grows seven heads and ten horns, and in *Par.* xxvii when Saint Peter speaks of Gascons and Cahorsines (Pope Clement V and Pope John XXII) preparing to drink his blood and that of his virtuous successors. The theme of the poisoning of both world and church is strongest, however, in *Inf.* xix, with its emphasis on the harmful effects of the donation. The mordant note comes again during the pilgrim's oration. Nicholas is told that he should guard well the money "that made him so audacious against Charles" (Charles I of Anjou; perhaps this is a reference to the rumor that Nicholas was bribed to participate in the conspiracy of the Sicilian Vespers). On hearing this indictment Nicholas again kicks hard with his feet.

Most commentators are in agreement about the nature and importance of Dante's message in this canto and about its extraordinarily bitter and caustic tone. The task of interpreting it in more detail, however, is complicated, for it presents the reader with a number of problems to which varying, and often contradictory, solutions have been proposed.

A first major difficulty is constituted by a curious autobiographical episode. Dante says (15–18) that the round holes in the stone were the same size as those in the baptistery of Florence made to serve *per loco* (lit., as the place) of the *battezzatori* (baptizers; baptismal fonts [or, as Varanini suggests, "baptizings"]). The poet remarks (19–21) that he broke one hole open "not many years ago" to save someone who *v'annegava* (was drowning in it; was suffocating in it). The poet says this should be a "seal (*suggel*) to set men straight." Most of the ancient commentators (for example, Jacopo di Dante, Jacopo della Lana, Pietro di Dante, Guido da Pisa, Benvenuto da Imola, Francesco da Buti, and the Anonimo Fiorentino) and many modern ones interpret *battezzatori* as priests standing in the outside fonts around the central one in which they baptized the children, in order to shelter themselves against the crowds on Holy Saturday. Bambaglioli and the author of the Ottimo Commento (probably Andrea Lancia) take the opposite view and say these fonts were used for baptizing. Their view is preferable, for the Ottimo was not only a contemporary and acquaintance of Dante but a native Florentine who had actually seen the fonts. He said, moreover (in a passage printed by Vandelli from MS Vat. Barb. Lat. 4103), that it was still possible to see where Dante had broken one of the fonts to save a boy caught inside it. Measurements of these fonts were made by Gelli before Buontalenti destroyed them in 1557, and since they were only 0.58 m in diameter and 0.725 m in depth they would have been very constricting for baptizers (though one resourceful commentator speculates that perhaps only the smallest priests were used for this function). Garzelli observes that the recently restored baptismal font of Pistoia is very similar in size and shape to the old one in the Florentine baptistery; at both four priests could baptize, one at each of the outside fonts, all standing behind a screen.

The point is not without importance for an understanding of the imagery of the canto. If the outside fonts were actually filled with water and used for baptisms, then the imprisoned child who was in danger of drowning would have been undergoing a parody of his real baptism. In that case, it is likely that the poet intends the prelates in the fiery holes of stone to enact a similar, if more dreadful, parody of this sacrament.

Why, however, does the poet tell the story at all, thereby breaking the medieval convention against speaking of oneself? Some of the earliest commentators say that the story was a "seal" documenting Dante's authorship of the *Comedy;* other early, and most later, commentators maintain that the poet wanted to justify his action, using the truth as a "seal" to undeceive past or future critics. Spitzer denies that self-exoneration is involved and says Dante means that the exemplary punishment of the simoniacs should be a "seal" to open man's eyes to the fate of sinners. Scott suggests that the account of breaking the font is intended to encourage men to break the "stone of cupidity" in which the simoniacs and many others are imprisoned. Nolan believes the story is an image of the breaking of the "corrupt and undermined rock of the papacy," which Dante actually performs by writing this canto. Dante obviously has no wish to save the wicked popes, but since a major purpose of the *Comedy* is to extricate the Church from the imprisonment in cupidity that it inevitably shares with its avaricious and simoniac heads, it seems likely that "seal" here means "figure" and that Dante is telling the story to indicate that his attack on simony is also an attempt at rescue.

Another point in the canto that has caused controversy is the prophecy of Clement's death. Nicholas says that he has already spent more time "with scarlet feet" (twenty years by 1300, since he died in 1280) than Boniface will have to spend before the arrival of Clement V. This means that Clement's death will have to occur before 1323, which would be twenty years after Boniface's death in 1303. How could Dante, if he was writing this canto before Clement's actual death in 1314, be sure that he would die by this date? It is true that Clement was sickly, but would it not have been irresponsible of Dante (particularly in view of the punishment that he meted out to the diviners in the very next canto) to have turned even a probability into so definite a prediction? Can we therefore say that *Inf.* xix was written after Clement V's death?

This would seem a natural conclusion, but many commentators are unwilling to accept it. One of their major arguments is that in an autograph gloss to Francesco da Barberino's transcription of his *Documenti d'Amore* there is a reference to "a certain work" by Dante "that is called the *Comedy* and that treats of Hell among many other things." Petrocchi thinks this gloss was composed no later than March 1315; some other commentators date its completion as early as 1313. It refers, in a garbled fashion, to Dante's words in the first canto of *Inferno* about his study of and devotion to the *Aeneid;* Hardie observes that this lack of accuracy makes it doubtful that Francesco had more than hearsay knowledge even of this first canto. We do not know whether any more of the *Inferno* had been completed before he wrote this gloss, though it is perhaps worth noting that Dante's first reference to his poem as a comedy occurs in Canto xvi. Petrocchi thinks that both the *Inferno* and the *Purgatorio* were in existence before Francesco's gloss, but that they underwent minor revisions by Dante between 1313 and 1315 and were only published in the latter year. One of these minor revisions, he believes, was the introduction of the mention of Clement V into Canto xix. But since Dante builds the dialogue between Dante and Nicholas around the question of when first one and then the other of Nicholas's evil successors will arrive in Hell (and around the successive accretions of evil that they are supposed to represent), it is hard to see how such a revision, if it ever took place, could have avoided a major recasting of the canto.

In any case, such an argument from silence is not necessary. There is no need to assume that Dante wrote the cantos of the *Comedy* in the order in which they are presently arranged. Even if he did, there is no need to assume that he had finished *Inf.* xix by the time Francesco wrote his gloss. Moreover, as Berardi has pointed out in his thorough and judicious commentary on the canto, another work of Dante's that was certainly composed in 1314 has numerous and striking similarities to Canto xix in theme and phraseology, suggesting that they may have been written close together, stimulated by the same historical situation. This is *Epistola* xi, which also condemns the greed and simony of modern popes, which also places Dante the layman in a prophetic role vis-à-vis the rulers of the Church, and which denounces Clement in similar terms for his submissive relationship to Philip IV, also comparing him to one of the false pontiffs of Israel. (In the poem he is Jason [2 Machabees 4:7] who bribed Antiochus to become high priest; in the letter he is Alcimus [1 Mach. 7:9] who intrigued against Judas Machabeus in order to be appointed by Demetrius to the same office.) Indeed, without Clement the use of the image of the great harlot fornicating with the kings of the earth loses much of its point. To Dante the pope who accommodated Philip but resisted the emperor must have seemed, more than Nicholas, who attacked Charles of Anjou, or Boniface, who resisted Philip IV, the prostitutor of his office par excellence.

It is Dante's use of the image of the whore to which we must now turn. The great harlot comes from Apocalypse 17, and there her symbolism is explained in the biblical text itself. She is the new Babylon, Rome, who has fornicated with the kings of the earth. She sits above many waters and upon a red beast having seven heads and ten horns; she holds a gold cup in her hand filled with the abomination and filth of her fornication; and she is drunk with the blood of the saints and the martyrs. The angel says to John that the seven heads are seven mountains and seven kings. The ten horns are ten kings who have not yet attained power but will take it together after the beast. The waters are peoples and races and languages. The ten horns and the beast will hate the whore and destroy her. She is the great city who has dominion over the kings of the earth. Many things in the Apocalypse text are obscure; indeed it is not always grammatically clear whether the heads and the horns are the woman's or the beast's, whether the woman and the beast are to be regarded as separate or as one flesh, or whether the whore is sitting on the waters, the beast, and the heads simultaneously or at different times. This ambiguity is reflected in medieval commentaries; sometimes the woman and the beast are interpreted separately, sometimes together. But certain things in the gloss (Apoc. 17:9–18) that follows the vision are less obscure: the gloss says that the woman is the great city, that the heads are seven mountains and seven kings, that the horns are ten kings, and that the waters are the peoples of the earth. Obviously one meaning of the heads is the seven hills of Rome. Dante eliminates the beast and gives the seven heads to the woman, thereby identifying her firmly with Rome, the papal as well as the imperial city: "She who was born with seven heads and had / the power and support (*argomento*) of the ten horns, / as long as virtue was her husband's pleasure" (109–111).

To interpret the great harlot of Canto xix as Rome has the merit of keeping Dante's reading as close to the Apocalypse text as possible, and we know from *Monarchia* that he did not like gratuitous altering of the literal sense of Scripture. The Apocalypse had clearly identified the woman with Rome; Dante's exegesis therefore can be called literal. It was also radical, however, in extending the meaning of the symbol to include the papal as well as the pagan city and in connecting the image of the woman with her new governors the popes. A very similar thing had been done a few years before by the Franciscan theologian and reformer Petrus Johannis Olivi. In his commentary on the Apocalypse, Olivi also adopted the literal meaning of Rome for the woman of Revelation and extended it to the Christian city, applying it to what he regarded as a new Roman persecution by avaricious and simoniac prelates. He, like Dante, merged the woman and the beast, explaining that the woman could be called a beast inasmuch as she was carnal and bestial; inasmuch, however, as she formerly ruled over the bestial races of the world and still ruled over much bestiality, she could be said to sit upon the beast. One of Olivi's followers, Ubertino da Casale, in the *Arbor vite crucifixe Jesu* (finished 1305), a work with which Dante was acquainted, went further and made a specific application of similar apocalyptic imagery to Boniface VIII and his immediate successor, Benedict XI. Probably it was from Olivi and Ubertino as well as from the Apocalypse that Dante derived the inspiration for his use of the image of the great whore. As to the strong involvement of Virgil in the canto and his apparently warm approval of the pilgrim's sermon, this (as Renucci has noted) is natural in view of the fact that for Dante he is preeminently the poet of Rome and therefore can be expected to deplore the papal degradation of her divinely ordained mission.

Dante could not have derived his Roman and papal interpretation of the great harlot from the traditional exegesis of Apocalypse 17, which tended to be moral and allegorical rather than historical, and which identified the whore with the reprobates of all times and all places. Dante commentators have followed the same exegetical path. Some (for example, Bambaglioli and the Anonimo Fiorentino) call the seven heads the seven vices and the ten horns the ten transgressions against the commandments. Most (for example, the Ottimo, Jacopo and Pietro Alighieri, Lana, and Buti) interpret the heads *in bono* as the seven gifts of the Holy Spirit or sacraments or virtues, and the horns as the ten commandments; only after the Church was corrupted did they become seven vices and ten transgressions. This last reading has been followed by practically all the modern students of Canto XIX. I have been unable to find a precedent for such a gloss in any medieval commentator on the Apocalypse that I have consulted; in them the heads and horns never signify virtues but usually past, present, and future evil kings or kingdoms. What has driven most students of the canto to adopt so idiosyncratic an interpretation?

They have apparently felt that it is necessary to do so in order to account for the statement that the woman had argomento from the ten horns "as long as virtue was her husband's pleasure." According to them, Dante is saying that the government of the Church was virtuous until Constantine's gift created "the first rich father." If the woman of Canto XIX is the Church, then her husband must be the pope (who can also be said to represent prelacy in general). If she was born with seven heads and drew strength from ten horns as long as virtue pleased him, then the heads and horns have to be interpreted *in bono* at least for the period before the donation.

But there is an even more puzzling complication. As Kay observes, the whore of this canto, though originally a wife and apparently an honest woman, was born with seven heads. But the very similar whore of *Purg.*

XXXII, who replaces Beatrice on the chariot of the Church, first appears after the Donation of Constantine, and only then does the chariot acquire its seven heads and ten horns, as a result of receiving the eagle's feathers. In this case the heads and horns have to be interpreted *in malo* from the moment they appear, since they obviously mark the monstrous transformation of the chariot. Thus they signify the absolute reverse of their original meaning here. So opposite interpretations have to be applied to two obviously similar allegorical images. This is a rather drastic way of solving the problem presented by the words "as long as virtue was her husband's pleasure."

The difficulty disappears if we take the two appearances of the woman to be complementary rather than identical. In *Inf.* XIX the woman with seven heads and ten horns represents not the Church but Rome, the honest wife who becomes a whore after Constantine entrusts her to Sylvester and after his successors prostitute her to the kings. In *Purg.* XXXII this whore, representing now only corrupted papal Rome, replaces Beatrice on the chariot of the Church at the time in history when the evil effects of the donation become manifest and the chariot after receiving the eagle's feathers sprouts heads and horns, as a sign of its usurpation of Roman rule and temporal power and its abandonment of the poverty and asceticism of Christ and his apostles.

The images are very closely related, but the first emphasizes the papalizing of part of the empire and the second the consequent Romanizing, in a secular sense, of the Church. Both developments pervert the true functions of the temporal and ecclesiastical powers and become the joint cause of the misery of the human race. The Roman Empire's vocation was to govern mankind, just as that of the Roman Church was to lead mankind to heaven. Long before the birth of Christ, whose life was to be the Church's foundation, the woman of Canto XIX started her existence on seven hills and under seven kings and came to rule the world with the "argomento" or support (for this interpretation see the entry "argomento" of the *Enciclopedia dantesca*) of subordinate kings, represented by the ten horns (ten being the number of universality). They then helped rather than harmed her. She lived in this fashion as long as *virtù* (which should be interpreted as strength, power, uprightness) pleased her husband.

But this husband was not, as is usually surmised, the pope. Rome's first, and for a long time her sole, spouse was the emperor. At length the exercise of virtue (in his case the exercise of universal dominion) ceased to please him. Constantine "made himself Greek" (*Par.* XX, 57). Probably Dante thought that he only intended to give the pope a *patrocinium* over Rome and other western possessions, while retaining ultimate *dominium* over them, for in *Par.* XX, 55–60 and in the political treatise *Monarchia* II, x, 2–3 and II, xi, 8 Dante is willing to grant his good intentions, while remarking that they destroyed the world. Constantine therefore entrusted to Rome's new husband, the pope, a portion of the imperial patrimony so that its fruits might be distributed to Christ's poor. It was Constantine's innocence rather than his guilt that led to the subsequent disaster: to the popes' treating this dowry as a gift rather than a trust. Even after granting it, the emperor remained Rome's ultimate ruler and temporal spouse. According to Dante, Constantine could not legally transfer ownership of imperial property to the pope, since he had no right to alienate any part of his universal jurisdiction, and since the clerical church, whose foundation was the poor and unworldly life of Christ, had no right to accept it. The pope had his ordained place in Rome, but only to point the way to the other world and not to govern this one. Many later emperors, however, accepted a perverted interpretation of Constantine's blunder, and his generous if imprudent act kept them from entering and ruling from their capital. Therefore Dante pictured Rome in *Purg.* vi as complaining like a widow because of Caesar's neglect. In *Epistola* xi, written after the departure of her other husband to Avignon, he said she was widowed in a double sense, "deprived of both her lights."

The poet believed that the cause of her degradation was papal cunning taking advantage of imperial folly. The combination of imperial fecklessness and papal cupidity permitted the pope to usurp an alien jurisdiction and thereby poison the Church and ruin the world. Of this moral and ecclesiological message so central to the *Comedy, Inf.* xix gives a vivid and compelling exposition.

BIBLIOGRAPHY

Many of the items listed in this bibliography are referred to in the essay above. Most limit themselves to particular aspects of the canto. Of these, Berardi's article (1975) is particularly useful. I am grateful to Nicholas Havely for helpful suggestions and further bibliography on the prophetic book to which Pope Nicholas refers in line 54. For commentary on Herbert Grundmann's views about the date and provenance of the *Vaticinia de summis pontificibus,* which he set forth most fully in his article "Die Papstprophetien des Mittelalters," *Archiv für Kulturgeschichte* 19 (1929): 77–138 (reprinted in *Ausgewählte Aufsätze,* Schriften, Monumenta Germiniæ Historica no. 25 [Stuttgart, 1977], 2:1–57), see especially Robert Lerner "On the origins of the earliest Latin Pope Prophecies: A reconsideration," in *Fälschungen im Mittelalter* [Hanover, 1988], 5:611–635 (Schriften, MGH 33). Lerner does not contradict but rather seeks to reinforce Grundmann's thesis suggesting a link between the *Vaticinia* and Dante.

Berardi, Gianluigi. "Dante, *Inferno* xix." In *Studi in onore di Natalino Sapegno,* ed. Walter Binni et al., 2:93–143. Rome, 1975.
Bertoldi, A. *Il canto xix dell'"Inferno."* Florence, 1900.
Borzi, Italo. "La cupidigia dei pontefici: Canto xix dell'*Inferno.*" *L'Alighieri* 32, no. 2 (1991): 28–51.
Brezzi, P. "Il canto xix dell' *Inferno.*" In *Nuove letture dantesche,* vol. 2. Florence, 1970.
———. "Il Giubileo di 1300: Boniface e Dante." *L'Alighieri* 25, no. 1 (1984): 3–22.
Bufano, Antoinette. "Il canto xix dell'*Inferno.*" *Critica letteraria* 13, no. 47 (1985): 211–232.
Chiari, Alberto. "Il canto dei Simoniaci." In *Nove canti danteschi,* 31–68. Varese, 1966.

Davis, Charles T. *Dante and the Idea of Rome,* 195–235. Oxford, 1957.

———. "Rome and Babylon in Dante." In *Rome in the Renaissance: The City and the Myth,* ed. P. A. Ramsy, 19–49. Binghamton, N.Y., 1982.

Della Terza, Dante. "*Inferno* XIX." In *Dante's "Divine Comedy," Introductory Readings: Inferno,* ed. Tibor Wlassics, 247–261. Charlottesville, Va., 1990.

D'Ovidio, Francesco. "Il canto dei Simoniaci." *Nuovi studi danteschi,* 335–443. Milan, 1907.

Emmerson, Richard K., and Ronald B. Herzman. "Antichrist, Simon Magus, and Dante's *Inferno* XIX." *Traditio* 36 (1980): 373–398.

Fallani, Giovanni. "Il Canto XIX dell'*Inferno*." In *Poesia e teologia nella "Divina Commedia,"* 1:77–93. Milan, 1959.

Ferrante, Joan M. "Malebolge (*Inf.* XVIII–XXX) as the Key to the Structure of Dante's *Inferno.*" *Romance Philology* 20, no. 4 (May 1967): 456–466.

Foster, Kenelm. "The Canto of the Damned Popes, *Inferno* XIX." In *The Two Dantes,* 86–106. Berkeley, 1977.

Garzelli, Annarosa. *Sculture toscane nel Dugento e nel Trecento,* esp. 15–36. Florence, 1969.

Grundmann, Herbert. "Bonifaz VIII und Dante." *Hochland* 52 (1960): 201–220.

Hardie, Colin. "The Date of the *Comedy* and the *Argomento barberiniano.*" *Dante Studies* 86 (1968): 1–16.

Hatcher, Anna Granville, and Mark Musa. "Lucifer's Legs." *PMLA* 79 (1964): 191–199.

Havely, Nicholas. "'Standing Like a Friar': The Franciscanism of *Inferno* XIX." *Dante Studies* 110 (1992): 95–106.

Herzman, Ronald B., and W. A. Stephany. "*O miseri seguaci:* Sacramental Inversion in *Inferno* XIX." *Dante Studies* 96 (1978): 39–65.

Holmes, George. "Dante and the Popes." In *The World of Dante,* ed. Cecil Grayson, 18–43. Oxford, 1980.

Kaulbach, E. "*Inferno* XIX, 45: The *Zanca* of Temporal Power." *Dante Studies* 86 (1968): 127–136.

Kay, Richard. "The Pope's Wife: Allegory as Allegation in *Inferno* 19, 106–111." *Studies in Medieval Culture* 12 (1978): 105–111.

Kirkpatrick, Robin. *Dante's "Inferno": Difficulty and Dead Poetry,* 248–257. Cambridge, 1987.

Musa, Mark. "Aesthetic Structure in the *Inferno,* Canto XIX." In *Essays on Dante,* ed. M. Musa, 145–171. Bloomington, Ind., 1964.

———. "From Measurement to Meaning: Simony." In *Advent at the Gates: Dante's Comedy,* 37–64. Bloomington, Ind., 1974.

Nardi, Bruno. "La *Donatio Constantini* e Dante." In *Nel mondo di Dante,* 109–159. Rome, 1944.

Noakes, Susan. "Dino Compagni and the Vow in San Giovanni: *Inferno* XIX, 16–21." *Dante Studies* 86 (1968): 41–63.

Nolan, David. "*Inferno* XIX." In *Dante Commentaries,* ed. D. Nolan. Dublin, 1977.

Pagliaro, Antonino. "Il canto XIX dell'*Inferno.*" In *Lectura Dantis Scaligera: Inferno,* ed. Mario Marcazzan, 617–668. Florence, 1961. Revised and reprinted as "Ahi, Costantin" in *Ulisse* (Messina-Florence, 1967), 253–291, with app. "per luogo de' battezzatori," 292–309.

Petrocchi, Giorgi. "Il canto XIX." In *"Inferno": Letture degli anni 1973–1976,* ed. Silvio Zennaro, 461–476. Rome, 1977. Reprinted as "La prosapia del mago Simone di Samaria," *Studi danteschi* 51 (1978): 255–269.

———. "Intorno alla pubblicazione dell'*Inferno* e del *Purgatorio.*" *Convivium* 6 (1957): 652–659. Reprinted in *Itinerari danteschi* (Bari, 1969), 83–116.

Petrucci, E. "Costantino." *Enciclopedia dantesca,* 2:236–239. Rome, 1970.

Pietrobono, L. "Il canto XIX dell'*Inferno.*" In *Lectura Dantis Genovese.* Florence, 1904.

Proto, Enrico. *L'Apocalisse nella "Divina Commedia."* Naples, 1905.

Renucci, P. "Le chant XIX de l'*Enfer.*" In *Letture dell'"Inferno,"* ed. Vittorio Vettori, 155–181. Milan, 1963.

Ricci, P. G. "La donazione di Costantino." *Enciclopedia dantesca* 5:569–570. Rome, 1976.

Sanguineti, E. *Interpretazione di Malebolge.* Florence, 1961.

Sarolli, Gian Roberto. "Simon Mago." *Enciclopedia dantesca,* 5:259–260. Rome, 1976.

Scott, John A. "The Rock of Peter and *Inferno* XIX." *Romance Philology* 23 (1970): 462–479.

Reprinted as "La presenza antitetica di Simone Pietro in *Inferno* XIX," in *Dante magnanimo* (Florence, 1977), 75–115.

Singleton, Charles S. "*Inferno* XIX: 'O Simon Mago!'" *MLN* 80 (1965): 92–99.

Spitzer, Leo. "Two Dante Notes." *Romanic Review* 34 (1943): 248–256.

Tocco, Felice. *Lectura Dantis: Il canto XXXIII del "Purgatorio."* Florence, 1903.

Vandelli, G. "I fori del 'bel San Giovanni.'" *Studi danteschi* 15 (1931): 55–66.

Varanini, Giorgio. *L'acceso strale*, 197–227. Naples, 1984.

———. *Canto XIX dell'"Inferno,"* 29–46. Naples, 1982.

CANTO XX

True and False See-ers

TEODOLINDA BAROLINI

This canto, devoted to the seers and diviners, elicits disproportionate reactions from its readers. Streams of critical ink have been spilled on a canto routinely omitted from their syllabi by harried pedagogues, who, at the very least, pass over the digression on the founding of Mantua that takes up 42 of the canto's 130 lines. This same digression is an integral factor in the fascination the canto exerts on its professional interpreters, since it is a key feature in the aberrant behavior that overcomes Dante's guide at this point of the journey, signaling an intertextual node of particular bumpiness in the *Comedy*'s never smooth texture. That Virgil behaves in an odd and noteworthy fashion in Canto xx is indisputable: He displays unprecedented anger toward the pilgrim, harshly rebuking him for the tears called forth by the twisted shapes of the diviners, and he dominates the discourse in a way he has not done before and will not do again. Beginning to speak in line 27, Virgil does not give up the floor—but for a six-line break in which Dante asks him a question—until the canto's penultimate verse; he takes it upon himself to present and describe each of the sinners, whom Hell has rendered speechless, as well as to initiate the lengthy digression on the founding of his natal city with an unusual assertion of his own desires: "I'd have you hear me now a while" (57). Virgil's comportment has been connected by critics with his medieval reputation as a sorcerer and magician; indeed, exegetes from D'Ovidio on have claimed that, by allowing Virgil vociferously to condemn and thus disassociate himself from the diviners he sees here, Dante intends to rescue his *magister* from any guilt by association.

Canto xx falls into four narrative segments. Lines 1–30 present the sin of divination in general terms; lines 31–57 introduce famous diviners of antiquity, each of whom figures in and represents a major classical text: Amphiaraus from the *Thebaid,* Tiresias from the *Metamorphoses,* Aruns from the *Pharsalia,* and Manto from the *Aeneid;* lines 58–99 encompass the digression on Mantua; lines 100–130 contain Dante's query regarding further diviners, and Virgil's response, in which he names Eurypylus from the *Aeneid* and various contemporary practitioners. We note the canto's symmetry; the general opening and closing sections, each of thirty lines, frame the more particularized interior sequences. The seemingly extraneous section on Mantua is thus entirely surrounded and informed by the commanding issue of prophecy, an issue that is directly related to the canto's highlighting of poets and poetry, to its evocation of the classical *auctores,* and to the arresting behavior of Virgil. For prophecy is in fact a textual issue; a *profeta* for Dante is one who foretells, who reads in the *magno volume* of God's mind (*Par.* xv, 50) and deciphers the book of the future. Because prophecy is therefore essentially a matter of correct and incorrect reading, the canto's emphasis on textuality is insistent: from the initial tercet, which proclaims in deliberately technical language the author's need to make verse and give form to his twentieth canto, to the equally technical reference to the *Aeneid* as an *alta mia tragedia* in line 113. If this is the only locus in the poem in which Dante affixes a numerical tag to a canto, it is also a unique definition of Virgil's poem as a text belonging to a specific genre. Moreover, the textual awareness of the canto's opening lines—"I must make verses of new punishment / and offer matter now for Canto Twenty / of this first canticle"—is shared by its final verse: "These were his words to me; meanwhile we journeyed"—*Si me parlava, e andavamo introcque.* Here the presence of a word, *introcque,* whose use by the Florentines is caricatured in the *De vulgari eloquentia,* raises a host of questions about writing and genre and serves to close the canto on the same textual key with which it began.

Inferno xx deals with the validity and legitimacy of the acts of writing and reading. As Hollander has shown, Dante evokes his classical *auctores* in order to correct them, misreading their texts in such a way as to damn diviners, like Amphiaraus and Tiresias, whom the ancients considered noble practitioners of the art, tellers of truth. By placing these diviners in the fourth *bolgia,* Dante establishes their falsity, and his disagreement on this score with his classical predecessors. One of the classical predecessors so invoked is Virgil, the *Comedy*'s resident *poeta,* and it is as his new self that Virgil retells the story of Manto, altering the earlier account found in the tenth book of the *Aeneid.* The Latin poem relates that the prophetess bears a child, Ocnus, who founds the city and gives it his mother's name: *qui muros matrisque dedit tibi, Mantua, nomen* ("who gave you walls and the name of his mother, O Mantua" [*Aen.* x, 200]). The *Comedy,* on the other hand, relates that Manto, "the savage virgin" (82), settled and died in a spot later chosen by men from the surrounding regions as suitable for a city: "They built a city over her dead bones" (91). Most interesting about Virgil's speech is his closing injunction to the pilgrim to disregard all other accounts of Mantua's founding; since the only true story is the one he has just heard, the pilgrim must "let no lie defraud the truth"—*la verità nulla menzogna frodi*—that is, he must reject all other accounts as false:

> "*Però t'assenno che, se tu mai odi*
> *originar la mia terra altrimenti,*
> *la verità nulla menzogna frodi.*"

> "Therefore, I charge you, if you ever hear
> a different tale of my town's origin,
> do not let any falsehood gull the truth."
> (97–99)

But in what source could Dante find the story of *mia terra* told *altrimenti* if not in the *Aeneid?* According to Virgil's own statement, then, the *Aeneid* is a text that—like the false prophets of this *bolgia*—is capable of defrauding the truth.

The language of line 99, with its harsh juxtaposition of the two absolutes *verità* and *menzogna,* is emblematic of the chief concern of this canto, which is precisely the truth or falsity of a statement, reading, or text. It is no accident that in both places in the poem where Dante employs traditional expressions denoting genre he also uses the terms *ver / verità* vs. *menzogna,* just as it is no accident that the question of textual truth or falsity should arise in the canto of the diviners, those who claim to divine the truth. Fourteen lines after Virgil's extraordinary self-indictment—*la verità nulla menzogna frodi*—the *Aeneid* is defined as an *alta tragedìa;* as Ferrucci points out, this is a passage that recalls the end of Canto XVI, where Dante first names his poem *questa comedìa* (128). When the monster Geryon swims up through the murky air at the end of Canto XVI, the poet tells us that he is in the position of a man who must recount an unbelievable truth and for whom it would be easier to keep silent, since his story will only bring him the reproaches of his listeners; although he does not expect us to believe him, we must, for his story is *quel ver c'ha faccia di menzogna:* "that truth which seems a lie" (124). The terms *ver* and *menzogna* are analogous to *verità* and *menzogna* here; most important is the different alignment vis-à-vis these terms accorded to the two texts in question. Virgil's poem, a *tragedìa,* is implicitly defined in Canto XX as a lie that defrauds the truth, while Dante's poem, a *comedìa,* is implicitly defined in Canto XVI as a truth that has the appearance of a lie. The disjunction between the two genres and the two representative texts—Virgil's and Dante's—is deepened at the outset of Canto xxi, where Dante refers to his poem for the last time as *la mia comedìa* (2), thus confirming that it is the opposite of the *Aeneid,* which has just been defined a *tragedìa,* and therefore also the opposite of *menzogna.*

If Virgil's text is capable of falsehood, Dante, by revising it, restores truth to it. The process of disassociating Virgil from the inhabitants of this *bolgia* begins with the first words he speaks, the lacerating question addressed to the pilgrim: "Are you as foolish as the rest?" (27). Up to Virgil's intervention, *Inferno* xx consists primarily of description, first of the sinners and then of the pilgrim's reaction to them; Dante sees the souls approach in a slow procession, "mute and weeping" (8), with their faces twisted around in the direction of their loins so that they have to move backwards, "because they could not see ahead of them" (15). Thus, their status postmortem consists of silence, fittingly imposed on those who once spoke excessively and falsely, compounded by an inability to look ahead in even the simplest physical sense, let alone in an attempt to read the future. In the following address to the reader, we learn that the pilgrim had been unable to refrain from tears at the sight of "our image so distorted":

> when I beheld our image so nearby
> and so awry that tears, down from the eyes,
> bathed the buttocks, running down the cleft.
>
> (22–24)

"Of course I wept," resumes the narrator, and it is as a result of his weeping that Virgil explodes with "Are you as foolish as the rest?," implying that he, unlike the pilgrim, is completely unmoved by the vision that has so shaken his charge. Indeed, Virgil appends one of his strongest indictments on the impossibility of pity in Hell—"here pity only lives when it is dead" (28)—and concludes his rebuke with another fierce question, impugning those who, like the diviners, attempt to render the divine will inactive: "For who can be more impious than he / who links God's judgment to passivity?" (29–30).

Thus, Virgil's first four lines in Canto xx consist of a reproof that, for greatest effect, is articulated as two questions separated by an apparently paradoxical injunction of enormous vigor; he passes directly from his final condemnation, on the wickedness of viewing God's judgment as an extension of our own, into his presentation of Amphiaraus, who appears on the narrative horizon as a concrete exemplum of the indeterminate *scellerato* ("impious") of the preceding lines. (There has been much debate as to whether Virgil's second question refers to the pilgrim or to the diviners: Who is impious in line 29? This issue is linked to the interpretation of line 30, *che al giudicio divin passion comporta,* for which the variants *passion porta* and *compassion porta* exist. The variant *compassion porta* is undoubtedly the *lectio facilior;* if we were to read thus, the question would follow from "Are you as foolish as the rest?" and refer to the pilgrim's compassion. The interpretation offered here is based on Petrocchi's text and Parodi's gloss, which takes "passion" as "passivity"; in this reading, the second question refers forward to the diviners, whom Virgil begins to present in the following verse, rather than backward to the pilgrim.) Virgil's presentation of the canto's first seer is marked by the same agitated style that has characterized his speech thus far in this *bolgia;* he begins with a series of imperatives— "Lift, lift your head and see the one for whom / the earth was opened while the Thebans watched" (31–32)—and continues with the insertion of a brief vignette of Amphiaraus's final moments, complete with dialogue between the seer and the gloating Thebans ("so that they all cried: 'Amphiaraus, / where are you rushing? Have you quit the fight?'" [33–34]), to culminate finally in a relatively calm and straightforward rendering of Amphiaraus's destruction and arrival in front of Minos, followed by a reiteration of the *contrapasso:*

> See how he's made a chest out of his shoulders;
> and since he wanted so to see ahead,
> he looks behind and walks a backward path.
> (37–39)

After the nine lines devoted to Amphiaraus, Virgil presents Tiresias and Aruns in six lines each; the presentation of Manto, beginning in line 52, seems to conform to the same pattern until, rather than ending at the end of the second tercet as we expect, Virgil uses the sixth line to request Dante's further attention and launches into his speech on Mantua. One striking feature of the language Virgil employs to introduce the diviners is the preponderance of imperatives and verbs of sight: "Lift, lift your head and see" (31); "See how he's made a chest out of his shoulders" (37); "see Tiresias" (40). This is the language of prophecy, which the *Comedy's* author hands his character deliberately as part of his strategy of disassociation; because what Virgil sees is the truth, such language—illegitimate in the mouths of the diviners—is now fully justified. Virgil's legitimacy is conferred by Dante, who as God's secretary, the writer of "that matter of which I am made / the scribe" (*Par.* x, 27), cannot err. In that he speaks for Dante here, Virgil too speaks as a "scribe," whose words are guaranteed true by the highest authority. In this context, it is noteworthy that Dante omits from the *Comedy* a term that he uses for Virgil in the *Monarchia,* and that is particularly relevant to *Inferno* xx, namely *vates.* In the second book of the political treatise, where his attempt to legitimize Roman rule is buttressed by quotations from Latin authors, Dante calls Virgil *divinus poeta noster* (II, iii, 6) and *noster Vates* (II, iii, 12), both expressions that relate to Virgil's prophetic powers, his divine gifts of divination. The word *vates* is directly linked to the thematic material of our canto, in that it historically embraces and conflates the two realms of prophecy and poetry. Originally signifying "foreteller, seer, soothsayer, prophet," it came to mean "poet" (interestingly, Lewis and Short point out that *vates* was the oldest name for poet but fell into disfavor, until it was restored to honor by Virgil). As Mineo notes, Isidore of Seville, who in his *Etymologies* treats the terms *propheta* and *vates* as synonymous, explained that a Latin *poeta* was also called *vates*, thus firmly connecting prophecy with poetry.

Dante's avoidance of *vate* in the *Comedy* seems related to the term's prophetic and divinatory connotations. One of the medieval legends attached to Virgil regards a bronze fly, allegedly fabricated by the Roman poet, which had the power to keep all other flies out of Naples. Dante's friend and confidant, Cino da Pistoia, refers to this legend in his satiric *canzone* on Naples, "Deh, quando rivedrò 'l dolce paese":

> O supreme seer, what evil you did (was it not better for you to die in
> Pietola, where you were born?) when you put in such a place the fly, in
> order to drive the others away.
>
> (13–17)

The fact that Cino here rebukes Virgil for the evil he committed in creating the fly, while simultaneously addressing him as *O sommo vate,* is suggestive; perhaps Dante felt that in the popular mind *vate* was associated more with witchcraft than with the providential calling it describes in the *Monarchia.* Dante's position, however, is ambivalent. If he strives on the one hand to disassociate Virgil from divination and witchcraft, avoiding terms like *vates* and dramatizing Virgil's disgust at the diviners of his fellow poets, on the other hand he goes out of his way to link his guide with Lucan's witch Erichtho, inventing the story whereby Virgil was once sent to lower Hell by the hateful sorceress of the *Pharsalia* (*Inf.* IX, 22–27). Such behavior suggests that Dante wants to distinguish between the utterly false prophets housed in the fourth *bolgia,* and Virgil, the *propheta nescius* as he was known in the Middle Ages, who is unknowingly a carrier of both truth and falsehood. As I sought to demonstrate in *Dante's Poets,* Dante both accepts and corrects Virgil, according to his perception of whether he is dealing with *verità* or with *menzogna.*

Dante's characterization of Virgil as an unwitting prophet provides an ideological framework for Dante's ambivalent treatment of his *magister*'s text in the *Comedy,* and for the running critique of the *alta tragedia* that in *Inferno* XX invests not only its content but also the crucial issue of its style. We have noted two stylistic features of the canto that have dismayed or startled critics, strategically situated at its beginning and end: the first, an allegedly tired and useless opening tercet, which at least one scholar wanted to delete from future editions of the *Comedy;* the second, its ostentatious ending on *introcque,* carefully planted in a canto that invokes the authority of the *De vulgari eloquentia* at its outset, in its use of the word *canzone* in line 3. I would suggest that both the canto's opening tercet and its last line are part of a unified commentary on style that runs through Canto xx, and that the critical reactions are not only justified but deliberately induced. The *prosaicità* of the initial tercet, as Barchiesi puts it, is indisputable; equally incontrovertible is the *De vulgari eloquentia*'s judgment of *introcque,* used only this once in all of Dante's verse, as a word unfit for poetic discourse (i, xiii, 2). When Machiavelli, in the *Discorso o dialogo intorno alla nostra lingua,* points to the last verse of *Inferno* xx as an example of a line from the *Comedy* that does not succeed in avoiding *il goffo,* he is reacting precisely as Dante would have wished: The line's prosaic clumsiness is intentional, as is that of the first tercet. Such *prosaicità* signals the presence of the comedic style.

The comedic style is one that is not shy of using clumsy or ugly language if such language is called for, because it is devoted more to the truth than to the *parola ornata.* While the comedic style need not be prosaic or low, since it is characterized by the ability to exploit whatever register it needs, Dante goes out of his way in this canto to display it at its humblest, even humbling himself to use a word that he mocks in his treatise. The fact that *introcque* appears at the end of the canto, immediately preceding the reference to *la mia comedìa* at the beginning of Canto xxi, is significant; the mark of a *comedìa,* a poem that tells the truth, is its freedom from stylistic restrictions. And it defines Virgil's text precisely in terms of the genre's stylistic restrictions, as an *alta tragedìa,* that is, a poem written exclusively in the high style. *Inferno* xx seeks to correct the *Aeneid* not only with respect to its content, regarding the founding of Mantua, but also with respect to its unremittingly high style. It corrects this last "flaw" by way of the digression on Mantua, which deliberately takes up the same unexciting prosaic manner that characterizes the canto's opening verses. In other words, I am suggesting that the tedium of the digression, experienced by so many naive readers, is intentional: Dante not only makes Virgil rewrite the story of Mantua, but he has him write it in a style that is distinctively not his own.

The simplest and most orthodox type of tercet in the *Comedy* is, as Valerio Lucchesi demonstrates, the type he calls "closed," in which the metrical unit corresponds to the syntactic unit. As the poem progresses, however, Dante has ever more frequent recourse to techniques such as enjambment, resulting in more "open" tercets. Longer periods that overflow the bounds of the metrical unit are, as Lucchesi points out, "often used to impart variety, to raise the tone of the narration, or to confer solemnity, eloquence, or pathos on the speeches of his protagonists" (187). We might expect that Virgil's discourse on Mantua, his most personal speech in the poem, coming in the canto where his epic is singled out for its loftiness, would possess a particularly elevated style. Instead, we find that the opposite is true. The digression consists of an unusually long series of unrelievedly basic tercets, in which the end of the tercet is consistently the end of the sentence. The prosaic simplicity of the digression is the more noticeable because the section just before it, devoted to introducing the diviners, is characterized by syntactic units that regularly overflow the metrical unit; the presentations of Amphiaraus, Tiresias, Aruns, and Manto are all accomplished in sentences that require two tercets. We recall the convoluted verses on Amphiaraus, where the transition from one tercet to the next coincides with the interpolated comments of the Thebans witnessing his downfall: *per ch'ei gridavan tutti: 'Dove rui, / Anfiarao? perché lasci la guerra?'* "So that they all cried: 'Amphiaraus, / where are you rushing? Have you quit the fight?'" (33–34). Following the digression, we find the equally complex description of Eurypylus in lines 106–111; here the sentence is interrupted by a parenthetical remark inserted at the tercet break: *fu—quando Grecia fu di maschi vòta, / sì ch'a pena rimaser per le cune—/ augure* "when Greece had been so emptied of its males / that hardly any cradle held a son, / he was an augur" (108–110). Both passages are strikingly different from the perfect closed tercet, in which each line constitutes a complete syntactic unit, with which Virgil begins his discussion of his native city:

> *Poscia che 'l padre suo di vita uscìo*
> *e venne serva la città di Baco,*
> *questa gran tempo per lo mondo giò.*

> When Manto's father took his leave of life,
> and Bacchus' city found itself enslaved,
> she wandered through the world for many years.
>
> (58–60)

Virgil continues in this way for fourteen tercets, if we add the tercet in which Dante reacts to Virgil's account, and the tercet in which he asks about other diviners, we accumulate sixteen tercets of one sentence each (or 48 lines) before arriving at the syntactic relief of lines 106–111. In itself such an accumulation does not seem so unusual; looking at the cantos on either side of Canto xx, we find that the preceding one contains a spate of fifteen end-stopped tercets in a row (22–66), while the following contains thirteen (97–135). The similarities, however, are only apparent, for in cantos xix and xxi the chains of closed tercets belong to passages of fast-paced dialogue and action, in one case involving Pope Nicholas and in the other the Malebranche, where the dramatic content disguises the metrical regularity. And here in Canto xx we find no action or dialogue but an account rendered graceless and choppy by the short and symmetrical units in which it is composed, units that parse out the syllables of Manto's story with a deadeningly equal emphasis: the location of Lake Garda, Manto's death, Mantua's medieval vicissitudes are all related with the same impartial detachment. Indeed, the quantitative emphasis placed on geography serves to further distance the narrator from the object of his narration, insofar as this is Manto; of the 42 lines required for her story, fully half are devoted to the course of the river Mincio as it leaves Lake Garda, heading for the Po and the swamps around Mantua.

The story of Mantua is told in a style that is remarkably non-Virgilian, one we might easily define as a parody of the seamless classical line for which Virgil is renowned. Such stylistic inversion befits the revisionism of the account. In the passage of *Aeneid* x that Dante is revising, Ocnus is a hero sailing to the aid of Aeneas; his ship's prow is emblazoned with the figure of the river god Mincius, referred to as the son of the lake from which the river flows, Benacus (205–206). Dante omits the man, the hero of the Virgilian account, in order to dwell at length on Benaco, otherwise known as Lake Garda, and the lake's "son," the river Mincio. After twenty-one verses dedicated to the river's course, Manto, the "savage virgin," is reintroduced into the story. Dante's redistribution of emphasis is in fact a reordering of Virgilian priorities, as is indicated by the stream of anachronisms that flood the new Virgilian account. The Latin Benacus is now the place where the bishoprics of Trent, Brescia, and Verona converge. Dante has redesigned the founding of Virgil's heroic birthplace in such a way that geographical genealogy takes precedence over heroic genealogy (which is suppressed to the degree of making Manto a virgin), the quotidian realities of landscape over the exalted exploits of heroes.

Extrapolating from the passages on Mantua to the larger narratives in which they are situated, *Inferno* xx becomes a commentary on *Aeneid* x, one of whose themes is mankind's tragic ignorance: *Aeneas ignarus abest* ("Aeneas is unknowing and away" [25]), complains Venus at the council of the gods with which Book x opens, and her adversary Juno repeats *Aeneas ignarus abest: ignarus et absit* ("Aeneas is unknowing and away; let him be unknowing and away!" [85]). Two-thirds of the way through the book, Turnus too will be called *ignarus* (666); even more telling is the commentary on the "unknowing mind of man" that follows Turnus's exaltation at the death of Pallas, whose baldric will later seal his fate: *nescia mens hominum fati sortisque futurae* ("O mind of man, ignorant of the end and future fate" [501]). So speaks Virgil, the poet of *fati nescia Dido* (1, 299), himself the *propheta nescius*, the unknowing prophet.

For Dante, the issue entails no tragic ignorance, but our ability to read. He, for one, is quite sure of his ability to read correctly in his letter to the Florentines, where he warns his former citizens of the destruction that will attend their erring ways; indeed, how can he fail to read correctly, when the very signs he must decipher are labeled *veridici,* "truth-telling": *Et si presaga mens mea non fallitur, sic signis veridicis sicut inexpugnabilibus argumentis instructa prenuntians* ("And if my prophetic mind does not err, that announces the future instructed both by truth-telling signs and by unassailable arguments" [*Epistola* VI, 17]). Thus, if Virgil is a *propheta nescius,* an unwitting prophet capable of error (like the "tragic error and mistaken prophecies of Troy," to which Jupiter refers in X, 110), Dante is an unconditionally true prophet, the bearer of a *presaga mens,* a prophetic mind instructed by truth-telling signs. It seems only fitting that the commentaries to Dante's letters should point to a passage from none other than the tenth book of the *Aeneid* as the source for Dante's *presaga mens.* The passage in question follows the death of Lausus, in itself a kind of tragic balancing of the death of Pallas; Lausus's father, Mezentius, as yet ignorant of his son's death, interprets all too keenly the wails he hears, deciphering them with his *praesaga mali mens: adgnovit longe gemitum praesaga mali mens* ("his ill-boding mind knew their moans from afar" [843]). Thus the passage from the *Aeneid,* which stands as one more testament to tragic human ignorance, to knowledge acquired only when it is too late, is translated—with the significant omission of *mali*—into the ringingly confident clairvoyance of Dante's *epistola.*

Mezentius's dark knowledge is transformed into Dante's bright knowledge, the same knowledge that underlies *Inferno* XX and that ultimately condemns Virgil. The disjunction between Dante and the inhabitants of the fourth *bolgia* is established even before the canto begins, in the last line of the preceding one, where he tells us that *Indi un altro vallon mi fu scoperto,* thus insinuating revelation into the discourse: *mi fu scoperto* (it was revealed to me) will be immediately echoed by *scoperto fondo* of XX, 5. Dante appropriates for himself as scribe the *contrapasso* of describing the prophets in their own language. Thus, we find not only the repetition of *scoperto,* but the adverb *mirabilmente,* with its etymological undertones relating to miraculous revelation, used in the opening description of the diviners. Perhaps most suggestive in this regard is the canto's first line: "I must make verses of new punishment." The diviners wanted to be like God, who is defined in *Purgatorio* X as "One / within whose sight no thing is new" (94). God never saw a new thing because nothing is new to him; nothing is new to him because he sees everything before it happens, before it becomes "new." For God, who knows the future, there are no surprises in store, no new things ever on the horizon. The diviners aspired to precisely this condition; they divine in order to become divine, see in order to reach a vantage from which there will be nothing left to see. They desired to know all the "new things," to achieve a state in which such things would no longer be new: God's own state. Thus, there is a particular irony in Dante's making of their appearance a "new punishment"; they appear to the pilgrim as one of those very marvels of the future, those new things that they were dedicated to making "un-new," to obliterating by foretelling.

We are left with a final problem, the problem on which my book *The Undivine "Comedy"* is centered: the problem of an author who is himself dedicated to obliterating the new things that await us upon our deaths. Dante would say that he foretells what we may expect to find after death in order that we may choose more wisely in life. He is distinguished from his colleagues in the fourth *bolgia* only by his ability to persuade us that he alone is a teller of truth; indeed, the only way to distinguish one *presaga mens* from another is to distinguish between those that are truthfully inspired and those that are not. Although the seers of Canto xx were not instructed by *signis veridicis,* they are nonetheless Dante's colleagues, differentiated from him by the outcome of their experiments but similar to him in their desire to see. There is a Ulyssean dimension to the diviners, as there is to the poet himself. The diviners' "backward path" will be evoked by the "backward steps" of the prideful Christians condemned in *Purgatorio* x; the *trapassar del segno*—the prideful transgressing of the limits set for humans—is the common denominator that unites Ulysses, the diviners, and Dante himself. Thus, Benvenuto was undoubtedly right when he wrote of Canto xx that "the present matter touches the author himself, who to some degree took pleasure in astrology, and wanted to predict some future things, as appears in this book" (II, 67). I take issue only with Benvenuto's qualification "some future things," by which he most likely intends the *Comedy*'s specific prophecies regarding the *veltro,* the DXV, and so forth. More to the point is the fact that the entire poem is a prophecy, a revelation concerning matters hidden to ordinary mortals, matters not given to us to see. In Canto xx Dante is dealing, as nowhere else, with versions of himself, immeasurably distanced because of their potential proximity; the uneasy surface of *Inferno* xx conceals the outermost limits of its author's textual daring.

BIBLIOGRAPHICAL NOTE

A version of this essay appeared in *Lectura Dantis Virginiana* 1, a special issue of *Lectura Dantis* 6 (1990 suppl.): 262–274.

Baldelli, Ignazio. "Il segno del demonio sui maghi e sugli indovini." *L'Alighieri* 17 (1976): 14–26.
Bárberi Squarotti, Giorgio. "*Inferno* xx." In *L'artificio dell'eternità*, 235–281. Verona, 1972.
Barchiesi, Marino. "Catarsi classica e *medicina* dantesca (del canto xx dell'*Inferno*)." *Letture classensi* 4 (1973): 11–124.
Barolini, Teodolinda. *Dante's Poets: Textuality and Truth in the "Comedy."* Princeton, 1984.
———. *The Undivine "Comedy": Detheologizing Dante.* Princeton, 1992.
Benvenuto da Imola [Benvenuti de Rambaldis de Imola]. *Comentum super Dantis Comoediam.* Ed. J. P. Lacaita. 5 vols. Florence, 1887.
D'Ovidio, Francesco. "Dante e la magìa," and "Ancora Dante e la magìa." In *Studi sulla "Divina Commedia,"* 76–112 and 113–149. Milan, 1901.
———. "Esposizione del canto xx dell'*Inferno*." In *Nuovo volume di studi danteschi,* 313–355. Rome, 1926.

Ferrucci, Franco. "Comedìa." In *Il poema del desiderio: Poetica e passione in Dante*, 91–124. Milan, 1990.

Hollander, Robert. "The Tragedy of Divination in *Inferno* xx." In *Studies in Dante*, 131–218. Ravenna, 1980.

Lucchesi, Valerio. "The Dantean Stamp." In *The World of Dante: Essays on Dante and his Times*, ed. Cecil Grayson, 166–197. Oxford, 1980.

Mineo, Nicolò. *Profetismo e apocalittica in Dante*. Catania, 1968.

Paratore, Ettore. "Il canto xx dell'*Inferno*." *Studi danteschi* 52 (1979–80): 149–169.

Parodi, Ernesto Giacomo. "Il canto xx dell'*Inferno*." In *Lectura Dantis*. Florence, 1907.

———. "La critica della poesia classica nel ventesimo canto dell' *Inferno*." *Atene e Roma* 11 (1908): 183–195, 237–250.

CANTO XXI

Controversial Comedy

STEVE ELLIS

Many commentators point out that Canto XXI might be said to take its tone from the final word of Canto XX, *introcque* ("meanwhile"), a Florentine dialect word recorded in *De vulgari eloquentia* I, xiii, 2. Canto XXI is the *bolgia* of the barrators, those who buy or sell public office, or exploit such office for private gain through crimes like embezzlement or bribery (42); and the sense of a municipal corruption that is widespread and almost, so to speak, everyday, leads Dante here to a portrayal of hell far less "elevated" than elsewhere in the canticle. In Canto XXI, in fact, we have an approximation to the hell of popular fantasy and tradition, "even down to its clownish elements" in Sapegno's words, the medieval pageant of black devils with pitchforks, and the language of the canto is accordingly full of colloquialisms, slang, and crudity: the "highly-spiced, scurrilous language of the Florentine 'underworld,'" as Boyde puts it. The devils' satirical use of slang expressions in their interchange, for example, at 100–102—*groppone* ("rump" [i.e., of an animal]), *fa che gliel' accocchi* ("let him have it!")—is characteristic of Dante's employment throughout of a rough, grating *terza rima* exploiting the force of doubled consonants: *graffi, raffi, accaffi* (50–54); *occhi, tocchi, accocchi* (98–102); *scheggio, veggio, cheggio* (125–129). This is precisely the type of diction, as Montano amongst others points out, that Dante in the *De vulgari eloquentia* declares inappropriate to the "grand style" to be used by "tragic" poets (II, vii), where inadmissible words include those with z *vel* x *duplicibus* (double z or x) or those rejected *propter hausteritatem* (because of harshness) such as *greggia*. This vocabulary Dante describes as *silvestria* (uncouth), and the uncouth level of diction we have in Canto XXI reaches a climax with the names of the devils themselves, Draghignazzo, Cagnazzo, Graffiacane, Libicocco, and so on (118–123). It is clear then that Dante's reference to his "Comedy" in line 2 of this canto, coming so soon after Virgil's reference to his "high tragedy" at Canto XX, 113, indicates succinctly the contrast between the *bolgia* of the magicians, with its personages from classical literature and its discourse on the founding of Mantua, and this thoroughly unclassical scene of "low" language and crude actions culminating in the famous last line.

Roncaglia talks about the poetic "tonality" of this canto having occasioned an amount of debate and perplexity that few other episodes in the *Comedy* can match. Amongst the abundance of critical literature we can isolate two main areas of concern. The first considers precisely the status and nature of the "comedy" that is here presented, a comedy that continues through the *nuovo ludo* ("new sport") of Canto XXII (118) and on into the undignified escape of Dante and Virgil from the Malebranche in Canto XXIII (37–45). Many critics have felt that Dante's poetry throughout the fifth *bolgia* expresses a "loathing and contempt" (Scolari) that severely qualifies any comic intention; in other words the moralist in Dante is still uppermost despite the "comic" situation the protagonist has found himself in. Such a view seems unobjectionable and the majority of commentators espouse some version of it; it has however been criticized quite recently by Bosco, who seems to find in it a resurgence of the Romanticism prevalent in De Sanctis's (and, we might add, T. S. Eliot's) dismissal of Dante's attempts at comedy as in some way lapses from the sublime and passionate emotion the "true" Dante is held to display. The case for the comic Dante was first proposed fully by Sannia, and first answered by Parodi, for whom Dante's moral earnestness would not allow "that accentuation or deformation or stylization of reality that is necessary for it to appear comic." Bosco, however, regards Dante the moralist as temporarily off-duty, or at least relaxed in the *bolgia* of the barrators, his feelings somewhat "slackened": the barrators are sinners "against whom any deep religious or political resentment would be out of proportion to the triviality of the crime." Such relaxation therefore permits Dante, as author, to enjoy the comic discourse of this canto, to portray his own fears with a light and jocular exaggeration (as when he pictures himself *quatto quatto* at line 89, the doubling of the adjective emphasizing his undignified crouched position), and to borrow devils from popular fantasy "who are not too frightening."

A similar thesis had already been taken to excessive lengths by Salinari, who even found a certain sympathy in Dante's portrayal of the devils, akin to that we feel when watching animals and children "in their instinctive manifestations of vitality." Critics like Sanguineti oppose this view by insisting that Dante's portrayal of his own fear is not only devoid of any jocularity but is the main focus and structuring element of the entire episode with the Malebranche that stretches over this canto and the succeeding ones. Emphasis on the genuineness of Dante's fear is also a feature of a rather severe reading of the canto by Conrieri. Bosco, however, takes issue with such critical sobriety, attacks readers like Montano who see the Dante of Canto XXI as invested with "horror and dismay," and quotes approvingly from the famous study of Croce that here "Dante laughs" at his creation. This reaction against the nineteenth-century Dante of the furrowed brow seems today, however, curiously outdated itself; what Bosco objects to, as the concluding lines of his essay indicate, is the multitude of contemporary critics "who only see the *Comedy* as a treatise of moral theology," and who are thus unable to laugh at it when necessary. Such a comment has again a Crocean ring to it, recalling his devaluing of the philosophical and ethical elements in Dante's poem and his presentation of it as a series of brilliant "poetic" scenes and vignettes.

We may share Bosco's worries about approaches that see the *Comedy* as only "a treatise of moral theology," but the fact remains that a more balanced and convincing view of this canto is presented by critics who do keep in mind the fundamental ethical and political concerns of the poem, and who see the episode of the fifth *bolgia* in the context of the entire canticle. They reject the notion of Canto XXI and its successors as in any way an intermezzo or comic interlude. Spitzer, for example, though giving the label "farce" to Cantos XXI–XXIII, insists that the comic presentation of Dante's fears is not incompatible with the "real terror" the protagonist experiences not so much of violence but of "the defiling contact of vulgarity." The trivialization that is the essence of farce gives here a picture of man "wallowing in the pitch and mire of his infrahuman nature," and the "comically" self-abased Dante crouching behind rocks is himself a victim of this trivialization. This type of dualistic interpretation is also put forward by Sapegno and Montano: Whatever the jokes, irony, and buffoonery of this canto "one cannot laugh," in the latter's words, "about the drama of souls faced with eternal perdition." Scolari (who in my view provides just about the most comprehensive single essay on this canto) rejects the Crocean position: Dante "does not laugh, notwithstanding the comic qualities of the action"; and Scolari also reminds us that in spite of the folk elements here in Dante's portrayal of hell as "the devils' kitchen" (referring particularly to lines 52–57), the seriousness of the representation "admits nothing of that crude and infantile banality we find in [contemporary medieval] works of popular culture."

Pirandello's reading of this canto also alerts us by its title—"The comedy of the devils and the tragedy of Dante"—to Dante's essential nonparticipation in the buffoonery around him: "Not only does he not laugh, he cannot laugh; and we cannot laugh either, because we come to understand that what we have here is sarcasm, and sarcasm is never comedy." The comment introduces us to the other main area of controversy aroused by this canto, its autobiographical implications. Pirandello interprets the enigmatic reference to "things my Comedy is not / concerned to sing" at the opening of the canto by connecting it with Virgil's reminder of the "deep wood" and Dante's escape from it at the end of Canto xx; these "things" that are not repeated are then understood as referring to Dante's political entanglements and in particular to the very charge of barratry that afforded the pretext for his being exiled from Florence in 1302. This interpretation of the opening lines has also been put forward, at greater length, by Guerri, but it should be noted that there has always been much disagreement concerning these "things my Comedy is not / concerned to sing": other suggestions include the continuation of Dante's and Virgil's remarks on false diviners, a discussion of the craft of poetry, or, giving the lines their face-value, things that are truly negligible and irrelevant and that emphasize by contrast the frenetic action of the *bolgia* the travelers are just coming into. For Pirandello, the entire canto has a latent dimension of personal tragedy that occasions Dante's sarcasm and scorn in presenting this fifth *bolgia:* a scorn that amounts to a symbolic rebuttal of the charges against him. This idea had already reached an extreme in Rossetti's allegorical "key" to the poem, in which this canto figured as a portrayal of the political events surrounding Dante's exile and in which the diabolic names like Malebranche and Graffiacane were held to refer to a certain Manno Branca and Raffacani respectively, who both held office in Florence in 1303. In fact several of the devils' names do occur in documents as Tuscan patronymics of the time. Critics such as Bosco and Principato who wish to maintain the suggestion of a "laughing" Dante naturally deprecate this idea of Dante's personal resentment: The charge of barratry was such a common political weapon that no one, including the person charged, would be liable to get very worked up about it; it was little more than a formula in the to-and-fro of faction. "Antiautobiographical" critics further note that there are no direct charges against Florence itself in this canto. Scolari however, in his examination of the historical context of the canto, labels it firmly as the vendetta of a "man of party," though when Dante wrote it his anger was directed specifically at Lucca, which in the early years of the fourteenth century was hostile to the white Guelph exiles and was a "tenacious adversary of the imperial party" in the years following the death of Henry VII. Bonturo Dati, referred to with cutting sarcasm at line 41, had seized power in Lucca in 1308 and headed the demagogic government that Dante castigates to a man in that same line. Dante's party prejudices are even more apparent if we accept the contention in Rossi's reading of this canto that in the thirteenth century, "and for several centuries to come," Lucca was "the best governed city in Tuscany and perhaps in all Italy," noted for the fairness of its commercial dealings and the fact that its political squabbles did not lead, as elsewhere, to civil war and the exile of its citizens. Other recent readings, whilst not going as far as Rossetti, maintain that there is a definite

Florentine "subtext" to this canto despite Dante's silence over the charges against him. Favati sees Dante's references to his military service at Caprona (94–96) and Campaldino (XXII, 1–12) as quiet reminders of Florence's injustice, whilst the rather confused reading of Baglivi and Mc-Cutchan tries to relate Dante's exile and ruined career to the death of Christ and the ruined bridges that were occasioned by it, as Malacoda explains (106–114).

We can, I think, agree with the "dualistic" interpretation of this canto that any humor that does exist here is one underlain by the seriousness of Dante's deepest moral and political commitments, by his ideal of civic freedom and honesty under imperial rule. Critics who see a relaxation in Dante's moral tone in this fifth *bolgia* because of the widespread and relatively trivial nature of barratry underestimate the dismay that proceeds from endemic pettiness as much as from the *Inferno's* more spectacular horrors. There is an atmosphere throughout of low, futile cunning, of almost infantile trickery: the deceit practiced on Virgil and Dante that sends them off in search of a nonexistent bridge (109–111); the would-be treachery of Ciampolo in the next canto and the trick he plays on the devils; the brawl amongst them that results from it. The fifth *bolgia,* with its black pitch sticking to devils and sinners alike, is a scene in miniature of the anti-state, a community of internecine intrigue and malevolence. Having said that, we still find lighter moments; for example, whether the ultimate line is intended to amuse or disgust, Dante's reflections upon it at the beginning of Canto XXII sound a rather elaborate note of irony that is rare in the *Inferno.*

The conspicuous contrast in the behavior between Dante and Virgil in this canto has been widely discussed, receiving particular attention from Sayers, Bacchelli, and Ryan. Malacoda tricks Virgil into believing that by taking a detour he can continue his journey (106–114); in fact Virgil later learns that *all* the bridges over the sixth *bolgia* were smashed when "the earth quaked, and the rocks were rent" at Christ's death (Matthew 27:51). He also learns in Canto XXIII that the guiding party of devils do have vicious designs on him and Dante, so that Dante's fear at the end of XXI, rather than his own confidence, turns out to be the correct response. Bacchelli therefore sees the canto as an exposé of the limitations of classical humanism, in that all Virgil's "philosophical wisdom" falls short of Dante's "Christian reluctance"; the unbaptized Virgil, proudly relying on the experience of his previous descent into hell—"I've had to face such fracases before" (63), a statement referring, I think, to the episode described in *Inferno* IX, 22–30 rather than to the confrontation at the gates of Dis in the same canto—has no access to any conception of diabolic evil nor to "the lesson of Christian humility, which is however there in every line of Dante's confession of fear." Ryan's subtle development of this idea sees Virgil's speech in this canto (as in his reference to Dante's *quatto quatto* position again at line 89) ominously taking on the sarcastic tones of the devils' language, a sure indication that "comedy, like barratry, can be all too catching." Chiari had also suggested that the devils' ability to fool even Virgil, "the gentle sage, aware of everything" (*Inferno* VII, 3), should be read as symbolic of the all-enveloping nature of barratry, that no one is safe from it and that no one can know "where, when, and how much he might be irrecoverably ensnared." An interesting recent reading by Hollander suggests that Virgil's gullibility in the Malebranche episode is part of the unresolved, "liminal" ambiguity toward the classical poet embodied in the *Comedy* as a whole, with Dante's fervent tributes to his master coexisting with just such "cruel" devaluations of him.

Other studies worthy of note include that by Roncaglia, whose stylistic analysis of this canto highlights its verbal intricacy in extraordinary detail. Indeed Roncaglia concludes that Dante shows "an excessive concern with technique" in *Inferno* XXI and suggests that this indicates a deliberate attempt on Dante's part to repress his emotional response to the charges against him and the exile that resulted. Favati's detailed study of the theatrical elements in the canto claims that Dante responds to past accusations by comic dramatization, in the tradition of the northern European mystery plays, with the protagonist and Florentine-speaking devils (representing his political enemies) acting out what Favati terms a "*jeu* di Dante." The bridge over the fifth *bolgia,* with the Malebranche underneath it, is related to the medieval stage below which devils would wait to enter the action through a trapdoor, whilst those of them like Alichino (118)—the ancestor of the modern Harlequin—were already known as stage personages. Similarly the final gesture of Barbariccia (139) was a traditional part of a devil's theatrical language.

It seems fitting to conclude this general summary of criticism with a word on the writings of Chiari, who has returned to Canto XXI intermittently over a period of forty years, maintaining its central importance to the canticle. The fifth *bolgia* is in the middle of the eighth circle of fraud; it is the darkest place in the *Inferno* (6) and gets the most attention, in terms of the number of cantos, of any of the infernal settings. These factors are testimony to the "centrality" of its corrupt workings on earth and the difficulty of escaping from them, a difficulty that even Virgil, as noted above, only just avoids. It is hardly then surprising, to return to the start of our discussion, that Chiari sees no humor in this canto; rather the *bolgia* of the barrators, even more than the gate of the city of Dis, is the point in which Hell stages its major attempt to "cut off the road of salvation." Whether or not we can regard the ruse of the devils with quite this gravity, it should be noted that *Inferno* XXI has a centrality in one respect: it contains, in Singleton's words, "the *one* explicit reference and the *one* fixed point of reference by which the time of the journey through Hell is disclosed." This lies in Malacoda's words at lines 112–114; yesterday, five hours later than this, 1,266 years were completed since the bridges over the sixth *bolgia* were smashed, a reference that dates Dante's journey for most commentators to the year 1300 in relating it to the death of Christ, which Malacoda cannot mention directly, and to Christ's descent to harrow hell. The passage has, however, long been the object of critical ingenuity from scholars who propose an alternative dating; readers are directed to the article by Edward Moore.

We may turn to further passages that have aroused particular discussion, noting first the famous comparison of the *bolgia* with the shipyard at Venice, described in lines 7–18. For Croce this was another instance of Dante's producing self-contained lyrical passages, inserted into the narrative with dubious reference to the immediate context and to be enjoyed in their own right, given that the actual point of comparison is restricted to the pitch mentioned in line 8. Many commentators suggest however that the picture of busy activity in the Venetian scene acts as an introduction to the atmosphere of lively drama and interchange in the *bolgia* itself. But surely the primary function of the shipyard scene is one of contrast, as Favati and in particular Applewhite have maintained. The latter reminds us that the picture of cooperative civic activity at Venice stands in ironic relation to the scene of civic corruption that follows it; he also notes that the refitting of ships emphasizes the eternal "wreckage" of souls for whom the pitch cannot act as a restorative, especially since the *Comedy* repeatedly uses "the imagery of the sea and boats to suggest man and the voyage of life." An interesting insight into the thoroughgoing allegorical interpretation of the *Comedy* characteristic of medieval critical practice is provided by Benvenuto da Imola's gloss on this simile in his *Comentum*. For Benvenuto each of the various activities in the arsenal is to be read as a reference to a different type of governmental malpractice, the whole to be seen as an illustration of corruption in the papal curia. Thus those who make new boats are scheming to enter the curia, whilst those who repair the old are using gifts and bribes to appease the envy and slander that have already damaged them, the bubbles of the pitch itself representing the rumors and whispers that circulate in such a situation.

The anonymous sinner who appears slung over the devil's shoulder at line 35, before his immersion in the pitch, is probably unnamed to emphasize not only the ignominy of being carted along like a piece of butcher's meat, in Benvenuto's phrase, but also to indicate his representative nature as one of the many administrators of Lucca under attack. In fact early commentators identified him with one Martino Bottaio who died on the night between Good Friday and Easter Saturday in 1300, an identification documented in the twentieth century by Luiso. Dante may have suggested that this sinner was snatched straight from earth to the fifth *bolgia* without going through the tribunal of Minos (v, 4–15) to emphasize the contrast between this "black" descent and the holy Easter descents of Christ and

Dante himself, especially as in the scene that follows the other devils make ironic comparisons between the sinner and the "Sacred Face." Kleinhenz suggests that a play on Christian iconography is a pervasive feature of the canto, the devil shouldering the sinner being a parody of the traditional representation of the Good Shepherd carrying his sheep, with the substitution of the devils' hooks for the pastoral staff later enforcing the point. Lines 46–54 have again been the subject of much differing interpretation; all critics agree, however, that they show on the part of the Malebranche a certain talent for pointed wit. The first devil, in referring to Lucca by the name of "Saint Zita" at line 38, probably conveys some of Dante's own antipopulist feelings about the cult of this thirteenth-century Lucchese infant whose saintly status had not been officially ratified but who, it appears, was the object of fanatic veneration in the city; according to Luiso, one Lucchese critic of the cult was tied in a sack on the council's orders and thrown into the river Serchio, so that the devils' sarcasm in line 49 has an extra dimension with its nuance of another type of *contrapasso*. The sinner reappears, after sinking into the pitch, *convolto* (46), which is sometimes taken to mean huddled up in the "dolphin" posture described in the following canto (19–24); this would suggest that the sarcasm of line 48—"The Sacred Face has no place here"—is prompted by the attitude of prayer such a position suggests to the devils. A more trenchant sarcasm is permitted however by the present translation, which aligns itself with those who interpret *convolto* as "smeared" (with the pitch); the black appearance of the sinner's features now afford the devils the chance of a mock comparison with the famous crucifix of black wood displayed in Lucca in the church of San Martino.

Many of the details of the rest of the canto have already been touched on above, but we might note the contrast toward the end between the rather gentlemanly speech of Malacoda (106–117)—almost the only time the language of the canto assumes any measure of formality—and the speech immediately following (118–126), when on Malacoda's turning back to the Malebranche the language resumes its more characteristic notes of asperity in the names and epithets of the devils. The courtesy is instantly undercut, just as the name *Malacoda* ("Evil-Tail") suggests that at the rear of these compliant appearances lurks danger, as Virgil and Dante later discover. As for the other names, modern commentators in general avoid trying to pin them down to specific meanings, preferring to regard them as exhibiting a "phonic grotesqueness" (Cattaneo's words) that echoes the teeth-grinding and other grotesque noises of the devils' behavior. Elements of meaning are however present: *Malebranche* can be directly translated as "Evil-Claws," *Barbariccia* as "Curly-Beard," and *Graffiacane* as "Scratch-Dog"; *Scarmiglione* comes from the verb *scarmigliare*, to dishevel, or to ruffle someone's hair (an obvious euphemism; compare line 100, *Vuo' che 'l tocchi* [Shall I give him a touch ...]); while *Calcabrina* is composed from *calcare*, to trample, and *brina,* frost. *Ciriatto* is held to derive from the Greek word for boar, and *Rubicante* from the Latin *ruber,* red. *Cagnazzo* and *Draghignazzo* are grotesque intensifications of *cane,* dog, and *drago,* dragon. *Alichino* is conspicuous by his *ali,* wings (see his role in the following canto, line 115) and *Farfarello* may derive from *folletto,* sprite or goblin. The most problematic name seems to be *Libicocco;* the sources suggested include *libeccio,* the southwest wind, or the country of Libya whose deserts were the legendary habitation of demons. A more ingenious speculation was put forward by Spitzer, who sees it as a reference to earlier forms of the word for apricot, *albicocca,* "which via an obscene sense" (the comparison of the fruit to the female pudenda) came to mean "fool" or "rash person" (for an Anglicized version, see Edgar's "Pillicock sat on Pillicock hill" [*King Lear* III, iv, 75]).

BIBLIOGRAPHICAL NOTES

Applewhite, James. "Dante's Use of the Extended Simile in the *Inferno.*" *Italica* 41 (1964): 294–309.

Bacchelli, Riccardo. "Da Dite a Malebolge: la tragedia delle porte chiuse e la farsa dei ponti rotti." *Giornale storico della letteratura italiana* 131 (1954): 1–32. Reprinted in *Saggi critici* (Milan, 1962), 845–878.

Baglivi, Giuseppe, and Garrett McCutchan. "Dante, Christ, and the Fallen Bridges." *Italica* 54 (1977): 250–262.

Bosco, Umberto. "Il ludo dantesco dei barattieri." In *Essays in Honour of John Humphreys Whitfield,* ed. H. C. Davis, J. M. Hatwell, D. G. Rees, and G. W. Slowey, 30–40. London, 1975. Reprinted with minor alterations in his and Giovanni Reggio's edition of the *Divina Commedia: Inferno* (Florence, 1979), 307–314.

Boyde, Patrick. *Philomythes and Philosopher,* 189. Cambridge, 1981.

Cattaneo, Giulio. *Bisbetici e bizzarri nella letteratura italiana.* Milan, 1957. Extract reprinted as "Canto XXI: Diavoli e barattieri," in *Lettura critica della "Divina Commedia": Inferno,* ed. Tommaso Di Salvo (Florence, 1969), 265–268.

Chiari, Alberto. "Il canto XXI dell'*Inferno*" (1934). In *Lectura Dantis Romana.* Turin, 1966.

———. "Nota su la baratteria." *L'Alighieri* 16 (1975): 85–88.

Conrieri, Davide. "Lettura del canto XXI dell'*Inferno.*" *Giornale storico della letteratura italiana* 158 (1981): 1–43.

Croce, Benedetto. *La poesia di Dante,* 90–93. 11th ed. Bari, 1966.

Falvo, J. "The Irony of Deception in *Malebolge: Inferno* XXI–XXIII." *Lectura Dantis* 2 (1987): 55–72.

Favati, Guido. "Il *jeu* di Dante: (Interpretazione del canto XXI dell' *Inferno*)." *Cultura neolatina* 25 (1965): 34–52.

Guerri, Domenico. "Il canto XXI dell' *Inferno.*" Florence, 1929.

Hollander, Robert. "Virgil and Dante as Mind-Readers (*Inferno* XXI and XXIII)." *Medioevo romanzo* 9 (1984): 85–100.

Kleinhenz, Christopher. "Deceivers Deceived: Devilish Doubletalk in *Inferno* 21–23." *Quaderni d'Italianistica* 10 (1989): 133–156.

———. "Iconographic Parody in *Inferno* 21." *Res Publica Litterarum: Studies in the Classical Tradition* 5 (1982): 125–137.

Luiso, F. P. "L'Anziano di Santa Zita." In *Miscellanea lucchese di studi storici e letterari in memoria di Salvatore Bongi.* Lucca, 1931.

Montano, Rocco. "L'episodio dei barattieri e lo stile comico." In *Storia della poesia di Dante,* 1:488–501. Naples, 1962.

Moore, Edward. "The Date Assumed by Dante for the Vision of the *Divina Commedia.*" In *Studies in Dante, Third Series,* 144–177. 1903. Reprint, New York, 1968.

Parodi, E. G. "Il comico nella *Divina Commedia.*" In *Opere: Poesia e storia nella "Divina Comme-dia,"* ed. G. Folena and P. V. Mengaldo, 2:69–134. Vicenza, 1965.

Pirandello, Luigi. "La commedia dei diavoli e la tragedia di Dante." In *Opere: Saggi, poesie, scritti varii,* ed. Manlio Lo Vecchio-Musti, 6:343–361. Verona, 1960.

Principato, Mario. "Il canto xxi dell' *Inferno.*" In *Nuova Lectura Dantis,* ed. S. A. Chimenz. Rome, 1951.

Roncaglia, Aurelio. "Lectura Dantis: *Inferno* xxi." *Yearbook of Italian Studies* 1 (1971): 3–28.

Rossetti, Gabriele. La *"Divina Commedia" di Dante Alighieri con comento analitico di Gabriele Rossetti,* 2:161–162. London, 1827.

Rossi, Paolo. "Il canto xxi." In *"Inferno": Letture degli anni 1973–1976,* ed. Silvio Zennaro, 495–508. Rome, 1977.

Ryan, C. J. *"Inferno* xxi: Virgil and Dante: A Study in Contrasts." *Italica* 59 (1982): 16–31.

Salinari, Giambattista. "Il comico nella *Commedia.*" In *Dante e altri saggi,* ed. Achille Tartaro, 25–48. Rome: 1975.

Sanguineti, Edoardo. *Interpretazione di Malebolge,* 97–124. Florence, 1961.

Sannia, E. *Il comico, l'umorismo e la satira nella "Divina Commedia."* Milan, 1909.

Sayers, Dorothy L. "The Comedy of the *Comedy.*" In *Introductory Papers on Dante,* 151–178. London, 1954.

Scolari, Antonio. "Canto xxi." In *Lectura Dantis Scaligera: Inferno,* ed. Mario Marcazzan, 727–760. Florence, 1967.

Singleton, Charles S. "The Vistas in Retrospect." *MLN* 81 (1966): 55–80.

Spitzer, Leo. "The Farcical Element in *Inferno,* Cantos xxi–xxiii." *MLN* 59 (1944): 83–88.

———. *"Libicocco* in Two Dante Notes." *Romanic Review* 34 (1943): 256–262.

CANTO XXII

Poets as Scoundrels

GIULIANA CARUGATI

The entrance to Malebolge marks a new stage within Dante's hell. Terminological correspondences can be detected between the outset of the infernal voyage and the descent into the pouches of fraud: *cammin(o) silvestro* (II, 142; XXI, 84), *selva* (I, 2; XX, 129), *oscura* (I, 2; XXI, 6). Domenico De Robertis observes that the episode of the barrators, which spans cantos XXI–XXIII, represents Dante's "longest stay, at least as regards number of lines, in the same place of punishment," calling it "a representation, in a minor key, of the general voyage" (De Robertis, 1–2). This structure, like an intricate puzzle box, opens up to reveal the secret of fraud, "man's peculiar vice" (*Inf.* XI, 24), and would be sufficient to exclude, even without other interpretive signals, the possibility that these cantos concerning the demons' play are merely a comic interlude interjected to provide a welcome break in the moralistic gloom and unrelieved grimness of the *Inferno*. In the textual itinerary that opens with Geryon's flight and unfolds within the metaphorical cluster of "fraud," reaching its emblematic climax with the episode of Ulysses, the interlude of the devils functions as the narrative articulation of the question of truth, which is of course the question that underlies and structures the *Comedy* as a whole.

Let us consider—from a metaphorical as well as from a narrative point of view—the links between Canto XXII and the cantos that precede and follow it. Dante's own textual strategy underlines such unity, when he amplifies the endings of both Cantos XXI and XXII with the authorial interventions that strongly mark the beginning of Cantos XXII and XXIII. In this unity, the privileged locus where the reflection on truth is made explicit is the figure of Virgil.

As several commentators have observed (in reaction against the traditional interpretation that sees Virgil as the allegory of reason, the unfailing guide to human wisdom), the *maestro*—a title, along with that of *duca*, especially frequent in Malebolge—appears in these cantos to be pathetically naive and incompetent, altogether unprepared to face the resourceful malice of the devils (Bacchelli, Montano, Guyler, Bosco, Ryan, Hollander). The whole of Canto XXII unfolds under the shadow of Malacoda's successful deceit, a dramatic development that even the pilgrim Dante had foreseen and to which he had tried to alert Virgil:

> "If you are just as keen as usual,
> can't you see how those demons grind their teeth?
> Their brows are menacing, they promise trouble."
> (XXI, 130–132)

In the course of this canto Virgil speaks, prompted both by Dante ("My master, if you can find out / what is the name of that unfortunate" [42–44]) and by the demons ("Ask on, if you would learn some more from him" [62]), and ends up acting as foil to the unreliable Navarrese—or even authorizing the spinning of the episode's fictional cloth. His unteacherly behavior, following closely on the lack of perspicacity underlined at the end of Canto XXI ("Just let them gnash away as they may wish; / they do it for the wretches boiled in pitch" [134–135]), can be seen as a dramatic variation on and confirmation of the self-correction in Canto XX:

> "Therefore, I charge you, if you ever hear
> a different tale of my town's origin,
> do not let any falsehood gull the truth."
> (97–99)

This acknowledgment of "past" error, or forgery, is followed by Dante's ironical, unctuous comment:

> "O master, that which you have spoken
> convinces me and so compels my trust
> that others' words would only be spent coals."
> (100–102)

In this emblematic core of the whole *Inferno,* Virgil's guidance emerges in its infernal, diabolical character. What Virgil teaches Dante is something that neither the *dolce stil nuovo* school of lyric poetry nor philosophy could teach him, something that a centuries-old theological tradition placed beyond the pale of orthodoxy—the poet's sinful lies. He who "seemed faint because of the long silence"—as Virgil is first introduced (*Inf.* I, 63)—is the wise man who taught Dante to "descend," in order to be "saved," into the blasphemous fiction of a poetic narrative. Of course Virgil is an unknowing guide, since the problem of truth and falsity, as Dante formulates, or rather orchestrates it, is something "new," something that Christianity has adapted from Plato. Dante's Virgil unwittingly accuses himself of lying even as he haughtily proclaims his devotion to the truth, as he does in Canto xx. At the conclusion of the episode that occupies Canto xxiii, Virgil listens shamefacedly to the not exactly abstruse characterization of the devil that the friar of Bologna offers for his benefit:

> "In Bologna, I
> once heard the devil's many vices—
> they said he was a liar and father of lies."
> (xxiii, 142–144)

Virgil stands accused not simply of lying—Dante is also guilty of this sin—but of being blind to it, "as he who goes by night and carries / the lamp behind him—he is of no help / to his own self" (*Purg.* xxii, 67–69).

Do *tragedìa* and "falsity"—Virgil's peculiar *ante litteram* falsity, so to speak—go together? It cannot be denied that the widening of stylistic register to include "low" words and expressions, and therefore a "low" subject matter, is the correlative, or one of the correlatives, of a new vision, at once poetic and spiritual. Mario Marti has identified in the *tenzone,* the exchange of scurrilous sonnets with Forese Donati, and its "low" realism, "the most resonating element of Dante's crisis, after the conclusion of the first organic cycle of his life, experience, and literary activity" (499). The *dettato d'Amore,* however, a mode of writing based on the poet's inner experience, is, in this crisis, not repudiated in its revolutionary implications, in its claim to open up a new epistemological and ethical path to salvation. Rather, what is stressed is its transitional value, as a passage or opening to what lies beyond. According to Marti's analysis, the language of the *Comedy,* particularly of the *Inferno*—and within it of Malebolge, its fraud-centered core—a language "born from the mixture of styles" is "the only one which . . . could satisfy Dante's poetic intransigence, insofar as it constituted the specular, linguistic epiphany of his human intransigence" (528). Now, while it is certain that the *Comedy* is situated well beyond the *dolce stil nuovo* poetically and represents the final outcome of a process that had started with the *tenzone* and continued with the *rime petrose,* we cannot say that it is the inclusion of "low style" alone that characterizes Dante's outlook in his last work. Marti speaks of "years of crisis and of radical investigation, of adventures of the spirit and of stylistic technique, during which

what was at work was more the spirit of 'Virgil' than that of 'Beatrice'—
of a Virgil, indeed, who seems, at times, to have forgotten the luminous
Beatrice" (532). How could Virgil, the tragedian, have become the master
of "low" style, on the side of the *tenzone*'s possibly lewd allusion to the *cop-
ertoio . . . cortonese* and, perhaps, of the "ass trumpet"(xxi, 139)? The answer does not reside in questions of style. When Dante follows Virgil
and, at the same time, distances himself from him, it is not a style that he
imitates, and it is not a style that he renounces. If following Virgil means
descending into the realm of *ragione,* or language, explored even down to
its potentiality for fraud, then overcoming Virgil does not mean leaving
him behind because he is too refined or insufficiently realistic in his approach to narrative poetry. Virgil's "falsity" is not linked to the "tragic"
quality of his style; rather, it is closely connected to that poetic, fictional
capability that long centuries of Christian orthodoxy had excluded from
the realm of legitimate writing. Conversely, the introduction of the "low
style" in Dante is but one indication of the blasphemous freedom in which
Dante's writing produces itself. "Virgil" is what opens up for Dante's the
horizons of narrative fiction, closed from Plato to Thomas Aquinas. It may
well be that in some preliminary approximation (perhaps never totally
abandoned) the value of Virgil's poetry appears allegoric and "prophetic."
But when Dante rolls up his sleeves and begins to mold—*fingere*—the clay
of his narrative, he realizes, without illusion, that his work as a poet is precisely what Saint Thomas condemns, as indeed he himself does elsewhere.
It is the *bella menzogna,* the *favola de li poeti* (*Convivio* ii, i, 3), characterized
by a *modus tractandi* that is *poeticus* and *fictivus* (*Epistola* xiii, 27) and that can
be redeemed only by being denounced. When we speak of the "devalua-
tion" of Virgil that Dante's text performs—a "devaluation" that reaches its
climax in the dismissal of the master in the last cantos of the *Purgatorio,*
we must not forget that this is not a definitive operation, with Dante
emerging as the pure champion of Christian orthodoxy. Fictiveness—self-
conscious, overtly recognized—lasts as long as the text of the *Comedy,*
whose paganism, derived from Virgil, persists until the final line of the *Paradiso.* What Virgil stands for is the last shore of "reason"—or in other
words, paradoxically, of "folly."

It is no coincidence that the problem of fiction, and Virgil's role in it,
should take center stage in Malebolge, and in the cantos of the barrators,
where the historicity of the characters and their political significance, normally so important, are temporarily eclipsed by the coarse materiality of
the feisty devils. The cantos of the barrators should be seen, in Riccardo
Bacchelli's words, "as a singular moment, extremely consistent in its specificity, with the descent to hell of Dante led by Virgil, of the mystical voyage in the other world" (846). Its consistency stems, not from a depiction
by the ultra-Christian and ultraorthodox Dante of divine grace overcoming
human reason and human culture, as Bacchelli suggests, nor, as Kirkpatrick

claims, from a Christian poet's staging of his own narrative perversity, but from the cantos' subtle infratextual play, in which the opposition *factual truth–narrative lie* structures and guides the unfolding text as a lasting monument to human "folly."

The opening simile of the cavalry in Canto xxii—numerically the central canto of Malebolge, as well as the central canto of the ones devoted to the barrators—has been given many different interpretations. For Sapegno it helps "to relieve and ennoble, by an artistic device, a coarse and vulgar subject matter, to clear up and air out the close and sultry atmosphere." For Chiappelli it is a "moment of irony," an "antiphon in which the discord of the two voices introduces the strange tone of the canto" (Getto, 347). Favati observes that "this simile and that of the *fanti di Caprona* in the preceding canto (vv. 94–96) are the only citations in the whole of the *Commedia* of the two battles in which Dante is known—by his own acknowledgement—to have taken part" (49). As I see it, Dante is being neither spiritual, nor ironical, and certainly not self-righteous; instead he places vividly before our eyes the indisputable factuality of an autobiographical event: "I've seen horsemen start to march . . . I've seen / rangers and raiding parties" (1, 4–5). Dante suggests that these episodes of war, these military exercises, can be documented. Compared with the ascertainability of history, the "bugle" is "strange" (12). It is a diabolical event, but not because there is anything evil in anal sonorities per se, or in their use as strategic signals, or in their artistic representation. Dante stresses that here we are not *coi santi* (15), practicing safe theological jargon; we are, instead, *coi ghiottoni* (15), engaging, that is, in the practice of fabling, which the Christian Dante perceives in all its sinful potential. This contrasting of the real and the fabulous is pursued through the use of a rapid succession of similes drawn from the observation of animals. These images are not so much the tools of realistic rhetoric, as intrusions of factuality meant to persuade the reader that the proffered terms of comparison—the sinners, the demons, the poets—exist only on the level of "pagan" fictionality. The stakes are infinitely higher, for Dante and for the reader, than those involved in a "representation" of moral rectitude and a plan to obtain salvation. Salvation is what is at stake right now, in the erecting of this monument of words, which becomes—for all of Dante's intended orthodoxy—truth itself. Dante wants to be able to "show the base of all the universe" (*Inf.* xxxii, 8), to bring forth a volume that, he suspects, could stand side by side with all the other volumes—including the "sacred" volume itself, on which the shadow of human fragility also falls.

The same function of distancing is performed by the famous "O you who read, hear now of this new sport" (xxii, 118), when the line is seen in the context of other similar interruptions of the narrative flow. All the appeals to the reader interspersed in the first canticle are situated in a context strongly characterized by an opposition between truth and lying fiction. As an example, we might recall the appeal that interrupts, thereby highlighting, the fantastic, fabulous quality of the Geryon episode:

> "Faced with that truth which seems a lie, a man
> should always close his lips as long as he can—
> to tell it shames him, even though he's blameless;
>   but here I can't be still; and by the lines
> of this my Comedy, reader, I swear—"
>
> (XVI, 124–128)

Dante leaves us in no doubt as to the "shameful" character of his fiction, or his diabolical, almost desperate determination to reach its ever-deferred truth. By directly addressing the reader, Dante produces a distancing effect, permitting the question of the legitimacy of his work to arise and to shape the text itself, as well as the reader's perception of it.

In addition to the autobiographical reference, the similes, and the dramatic interruption of the unfolding of his farce / fable, it is the very "personnel" of the canto—the nature and quality of its main protagonists—that signals where exactly the narrative lie is taking us. The devils take center stage here. With the Malebranche Dante does not simply display a more or less good-natured vulgarity or, as other interpreters would have it, a vulgarity geared to the moralistic intent of the episode. Rather, he stages a radical emancipation from any model of narrative legitimacy. Throughout the voyage in the afterlife, Dante generally backs his creative arrogance either with incursions into history, which give a structure to the episodes of the famous "characters," or with invectives, which lift the narrative out of its fictionality and thrust it dramatically into the contemporary world. Unlike them, the cantos of the barrators do not altogether abandon the support of history and factuality and yet seem to lay aside all scruples of veracity, in order to plunge into a realm of pure imagination, however realistically rendered. The only nondiabolical character to emerge from the pitch is left without a name—which cannot be by chance, even though the commentators have hastened to supply him with one (Ciampolo, 44).

The centrality of the devils in Canto XXII suggests that Dante is freeing himself not just from the history of the real world—the warriors of Caprona and Campaldino, for example, himself included—but also from literary history, from the authority of those who "gave" him the mythical figures of Cerberus and Minos, Plutus and Charon, Phlegyas and Geryon. Once these figures, these products of his master's teachings, have been introduced into Dante's poetic universe, the very logic of his construction, the implacable laws of fantastic invention, compel him to conjure up and fashion his own personal devils:

"By now I knew the names of all those demons—
I'd paid attention when the fiends were chosen;
I'd watched as they stepped forward one by one."
(37–39)

Dante knows all their names: this time he is not bound to respect either history or someone else's poetry—which does not mean that Virgil does not remain, now more than ever, *maestro* and *duca*. If these are Dante's "personal" devils, they do not, however, spring, original and intact, from his private imagination. The Malebranche, as many commentators have underlined, are devils who have their origin in medieval folklore; their description and behavior matches those found in the figurative arts and in popular legends, where, for example, the intestinal "wind"—often believed to be identical with the soul—is a frequent theme. Piero Camporesi has shown that in popular medieval culture—the "low" culture never totally ousted by Christianity—the devil is basically a figure personifying the vital forces inherent in the cycles of nutrition and reproduction. Surviving within an officially Christian society with all the eschatological rigor of its values, this figure is both celebrated and exorcised as the pagan primal force that presides over life. This is not to say that the Malebranche should be seen as standing for repressed tendencies of a pagan kind in Dante's nature, however sensual and passionate we know that nature to have been. Rather, they have the function of dramatizing the "paganism" of the text itself, the freedom of its inventiveness, limited only by the poet's awareness of its blasphemous character. The distance between the text and its own fiction—a distance particularly noticeable here and an inextricable component of the text in its entirety—might explain why a keen commentator like Francesco De Sanctis was able to speak of "false poetics" that "hamper the spontaneity of his genius" and "give it a vacillation, a something of unsureness and incompleteness, a crudeness and confusion of colour" (183). This distance also explains why Dante does not make us laugh. His "comical" inventions lie at the extreme possibility of language—a possibility that must be abandoned in an itinerary that tends toward its own consummation. No laughter can accompany a quest for salvation from words, through words, a journey toward salvation that ends in shipwreck.

The cantos of the barrators take us to the core of an exploration that goes far beyond the inclusion of the low style (Barolini), and far beyond the narrative fraudulence of cheating the reader (Kirkpatrick). Dante's irredeemable sin is rather the sin of the tongue, which "inflameth the wheel of our nativity, being set on fire by hell" (James 3:6)—the "sin" by which man, endlessly repeating the enterprise of Babel, erects monuments of words, in perpetual defiance, and deferral, of God's silence. The devils of Malebolge, known by Dante in their ancient essence, though with newly

forged names, are both the product of Dante's fiction and its metaphor—
the metaphor of Dante's writing at its lying core. In this book—but what
book is without lies?—no "truth" exists that does not "seem a lie." But precisely because for Dante that which "appears" in this language is not simply "fiction" but a lie (menzogna), no "truth" exists that does not hope to free
itself from these manmade veils. The truth is therefore an itinerary, a voyage, a leaving-behind. In the course of the Comedy Dante will try relentlessly to free himself from Virgil's ragione, from his parola ornata, in order
to take refuge in the philosophical theology of Beatrice. That refuge will
also prove illusory. No way out will be found except in silence. The "teaching . . . hidden . . . beneath the veil of verses" (Inf. IX, 62–63) has been unveiled anyway, in ways no doubt beyond the intentions of Dante the medieval
poet and thinker, but not outside the text itself, the text as blasphemous,
partial, and perennial "unveiling." "What is" can only emerge in the words
that utter "it"—words irredeemably caught in their own web of fiction.
Malebolge, the locus of fraud, like the Comedy as a whole (could Dante have
found a better title?), is the cammino silvestro (the savage path), through the
selva selvaggia (the wild forest). And disentanglement from it brings about
the shipwrecked, Ulyssean salvation that is the scriptural itinerary itself.
Like every other text, human and "divine," Dante's Comedy bears witness
only to itself.

BIBLIOGRAPHICAL NOTE

For an exhaustive bibliography of the studies on this canto, the Casini-Barbi-Momigliano edition remains an indispensable tool (La Divina Commedia, ed. Francesco Mazzoni [Florence,
1972–79]). The chiose a luoghi puntuali following canto XXI offers an accurate status questionis,
centering as it does upon the problems of "the comic" and "the autobiographic." These problems have not been totally abandoned, as is testified by Vittorio Russo (Il romanzo teologico:
Sondaggi sulla "Commedia" di Dante [Naples, 1984]), who explains Malebolge in the abstract
terms of the "grotesque." Among the less recent studies quoted in my text are Francesco De
Sanctis, History of Italian Literature, trans. Joan Redfern (1931; reprint, New York, 1959); Guido
Favati, "Il 'jeu di Dante' (Interpretazione del canto XXI dell'Inferno)," Cultura neolatina 25 (1965);
Giovanni Getto, ed., Letture scelte sulla "Divina Commedia" (Florence, 1970); Natalino Sapegno,
ed., La Divina Commedia (Florence, 1955).

More recent studies have shifted the ground on which this canto—and the whole of Malebolge—is situated. Already, studies on style and genre had begun shaping new questions about
Dante's "realism" and the value of the term comedia. Alfredo Schiaffini (Momenti di storia della
lingua italiana [Rome, 1953]) had discussed the treatment of "high" vs. "low" style in Dante's
theoretical works and concluded that the comedia admires both styles. Mario Marti ("Sulla genesi del realismo dantesco," Giornale storico della letteratura italiana 137, no. 4 [1960]: 497–432) had
traced Dante's "realism" and "low" style back to the tenzone and the rime petrose. Anna Maria
Chiavacci-Leonardi ("La guerra de la pietate," in Saggio per un'interpretazione dell'"Inferno" di
Dante [Naples, 1979]) stresses the "comic" realism of Malebolge, while traditionally relating it
to the Christian poet's lack of sympathy in the face of human debasement. For Domenico De
Robertis ("In viaggio coi demoni," Studi danteschi 53 [1981]: 1–29), Dante's mixed style is meant
to portray the confusion of human reality. Lucia Battaglia Ricci (Dante e la tradizione letteraria
medievale: Una proposta per la "Commedia" [Pisa, 1983]) uses the concept of "contamination" of
styles and genres to determine that the Comedy should be defined as an epic poem.

In the wake of a few forerunners (Riccardo Bacchelli, "Da Dite a Malebolge: la tragedia delle porte chiuse e la farsa dei ponti rotti" [1954], in *Saggi critici* [Milan, 1962]; Rocco Montano, "Lo stile comico di Dante e il canto dei barattieri," in *Suggerimenti per una lettura di Dante* [Naples, 1956]), a recent spurt of American studies on Virgil's "limitations" has begun to establish this figure as central in text structured around the problem of truth vs. falsehood. Sam Guyler, "Virgil the Hypocrite—Almost: A Re-interpretation of *Inferno* XXIII," *Dante Studies* 90 (1972): 25–40, sees Virgil as blinded by overconfidence in his authority as a guide to the underworld. For C. J. Ryan ("Inferno XXI: Virgil and Dante. A Study in Contrasts," *Italica* 59 [1982]: 16–31) evil escapes full comprehension by Virgil. Robert Hollander stresses Virgil's lies and his failure as a prophet in the eyes of Dante (*Studies in Dante* [Ravenna, 1980]; *Il Virgilio dantesco: tragedia nella "Commedia"* [Florence, 1983]; "Virgil and Dante as Mind-Readers [*Inferno* XXI and XXIII]," *Medioevo romanzo* 9 [1984]: 85–100; "Dante's Virgil: A Light That Failed," *Lectura Dantis* 4 [1989]: 3–9). Teodolinda Barolini ("True and False See-ers in *Inferno* XX," *Lectura Dantis* 4 [1989]: 42–53) dwells on Virgil's *tragedìa* as a lie, and on the *comedìa* as Christian truth.

We finally come to the studies in which textuality is foregrounded. Robin Kirkpatrick (*Dante's "Inferno": Difficulty and Dead Poetry* [Cambridge, 1987]) explores the "lying" component of the *Comedy* but fails to point out the full implications of the question of fictivity, falling back on a traditional interpretation of Dante as a staunchly orthodox moralist. Fredi Chiappelli ("Il colore della menzogna nell'*Inferno* dantesco," *Letture classensi* 18 [1989]: 115–128), in a more limited perspective, suggests that the individual lie is "the cohesive fiber of the rhetorical fiber of the *Inferno*." Giuseppe Mazzotta (*"Theologia ludens: Angels and Devils in the Divine Comedy,"* in *Discourses of Authority in Medieval and Renaissance Literature,* ed. Kevin Brownlee and Walter Stephens [Hanover, N.H., 1989]) points to the theological/rhetorical dimensions of "fraud." Teodolinda Barolini ("Stile e narrativa nel basso inferno dantesco," *Lettere italiane* 2 [1990]: 173–207) stresses the fraudulent aspect of Dante's Christian realism. My own work, *Dalla menzogna al silenzio: La scrittura mistica della "Commedia" di Dante* (Bologna, 1991), deals with the relationship between "fraud" and fiction. In an unrelated area of research, Piero Camporesi (*Il paese della fame* [Bologna, 1978]) provides useful information on the medieval conception of the devil.

CANTO XXIII

The Painted People

TIBOR WLASSICS

The single file in which the wayfarers enter and leave this narrative segment functions like a top and bottom frieze: it delimits the space of Canto XXIII, separating its vast and varied subject matter from that of the canto preceding and following it. The key words are *dinanzi* (before) and *dopo* (after) in the first lines of the canto: "Silent, alone, no one escorting us, / we made our way—one went before, one after—" (1–2). The canto closes with *dietro* (behind; following): "at this I left those overburdened spirits, / while following the prints of his dear feet" (147–148). This frame of before and after emphasizes the unity of Dante's tableau, which depicts a complex group of sinners, a spectacular chase, obsessive fear, suspenseful flights, a vivid treatment of thirteenth-century Florentine politics, and ends with a subtle farce at the guide's expense.

These elements of the narrative are inscribed in a largely unseen ecclesiastical blueprint, which surfaces here and there. Dante and the medieval *vox populi* associate hypocrisy with the clergy. Most commentators point out the clerical atmosphere of the canto, which suits the two protagonists among the damned—they are lay monks, "Jovial Friars" (103). The monasterial setting surfaces in the precise, sartorial details of the sinners' garments: "And they were dressed in cloaks with cowls so low / they fell before their eyes, of that same cut / that's used to make the clothes for Cluny's monks" (61–63). Some commentators also see a monkish ogle in their gestures and attitudes—"when they came up, they looked askance at me / a long while, and they uttered not a word" (85–86)—and in their vocabulary:

They call their "heavy mantle" a *stola* (90) and invite the pilgrim to identify himself to "this *assembly* (*collegio* [or 'synod']) of sad hypocrites" (92). Their style of speech is rich in scriptural information (such as the New Testament references of Brother Catalano, 114–123), as well as clerical unction and deviousness (e.g., the convent corridor aside, 87–90, and the gloat in Catalano's final sermon, 142–144).

The atmosphere of the cloister transforms the two wayfarers even *before* the main subject matter unfolds, suggesting a central image that will pull into its orbit the unrelated elements of the canto. From the outset, Dante and Virgil, "when they walk together" (3), seem to imitate the "painted people" (58), that is, the Friars Minor. They model their gait on that of the Franciscan friars, and the image of the single file survives the flight of Dante and Virgil from the Malebranche, their meeting with the Jovial Friars, their conversation with the crucified Caiaphas, and Virgil's impatience with the demons' lies, which surfaces at the end to complete the framing of the canto.

There are other smaller (but not weaker) sequences of imagery in this canto, reinforced by visible or invisible threads. For instance, nowhere in the *Comedy* does the word *pensier* occur as insistently as in the exordial segment of this canto (5, 10, 28), as Dante sets about to study a series of puzzling phenomena: the spontaneous birth of thought; the mechanics of the stream of consciousness or free association of ideas (see 10–12); the psychosomatic reaction to one's own mental creations (19–20 and 24); the relation between memory and imagination; and the transmittal of thought through emotion (25–30).

Dante's dramatic instinct transforms even the most abstract and impalpable happenings into concrete scenes. Here, Virgil's mind reading is represented as a social call between two groups of thoughts, those of Virgil and the pilgrim, who to their own surprise and contentment discover themselves to be doubles of each other—and thus amenable to be united by a common denominator, the guide's resolve (25–30):

> "Were I a leaded mirror,
> I could not gather in your outer image
> more quickly than I have received your inner.
>   For even now your thoughts have joined my own;
> in both our acts and aspects we are kin—
> with both our minds I've come to one decision."

Moreover, the text attributes to the pilgrim Dante's own capacity of recalling events—in our case imaginary events—with such vividness as physically to relive them, a faculty that made the existence of the *Comedy* possible. This inner compulsion occurs in nearly every canto of the poem. The

simplest instance is at the very beginning: "that savage forest, dense and difficult, / which even in recall renews my fear" (I, 5–6), and the *Comedy* is
indeed the outcome of that initial horror. In Canto xxiii the same idea is
developed to a maximum efficacy; the last line of the following quote
(19–24) could indeed be an epigraph or motto to the whole *Comedy*—a
poetics *in nuce:*

> I could already feel my hair curl up
> from fear, and I looked back attentively,
> while saying: "Master, if you don't conceal
>   yourself and me at once—they terrify me,
> those Malebranche; they are after us;
> I so imagine them, I hear them now."

The first thirty lines of Canto xxiii are an on-and-off essay on mental activity in the broadest sense. Observe the sketch of his source treatment (4–
7), his attention to homonymy and synonymy (7), and the sample he gives
of his ever-present syllogistic precision (13–18). Note also the comparatist
(of folklore and fable-lore) at work (4–9):

> The present fracas made me think of Aesop—
> that fable where he tells about the mouse
> and frog; for "near" and "nigh" are not more close
>   than are that fable and this incident,
> if you compare with care how each begins and
> then compare the endings that they share.

Commentators note, however, that the parallelism between the brawl
and the pseudo-Aesopian *fabula* is far from being as precise as Dante insistently claims. These lines of Canto xxiii have in fact a sizable literature of
their own, owing to the debates between two schools: the interpreters
who refer the frog-mouse-kite adventures to the feuding of the fiends
among themselves and their final fall into the pitch, and the interpreters
who find a place in the comparison for the pilgrim or Virgil or both. I note
that the condition ("if . . . " [8]) Dante so carefully specifies is just that—a
proviso. It is a warning to the reader about the *limits* of the parallelism and
of the subtle ("with care" [8]) mental operation that is required. Do not
simply compare the two stories, Dante seems to say; the similarity is strictly
limited to the initial intentions ("how each begins") and to the sorry outcome ("endings"). But even those two—or rather four—points jibe only if
you *force* your mind to see the moral parallel (the original text prescribes *la
mente fissa* [9; my emphasis]), just as a man under extreme duress and beset
by great anxiety might see things where there are none. So the old allegory

is misread by the pilgrim's fear; and I suspect that the frog and mouse tale functions best if we see it as an *illustration* of the wayfarer's funk.

Virgil, the mind reader, is like a mirror reflecting thought. The mirror, however, is not simply a mirror but a *recipe* for making a "leaded" mirror. The metal-backed glass mirror was a technological innovation of Dante's own age, which at last managed to produce plate glass, replacing the polished silver plate used as a mirror during the preceding millennia. The ingenious novelty interested Dante, the pre-Renaissance *aficionado* of machines, contraptions, gizmos. He describes them in his poem with transparent enjoyment—both as they existed in fact or as Dante himself invented them for the special technological needs of his Hell, Purgatory, and Paradise. The jumbo jet of Geryon and the early public-address system of Ulysses and Guy of Montefeltro exemplify the latter; we see the former in Dante's essay on ways and means in military communications (at the outset of Canto XXII) and in the minute, technical description of the Venetian shipyard at the outset of Canto XXI.

The text provides a snapshot of a millrace (46–49):

> No water ever ran so fast along
> a sluice to turn the wheels of a land mill,
> not even when its flow approached the paddles,
>   as did my master race down that embankment
> while bearing me with him upon his chest.

Galileo and his scientific revolution are three centuries in the future, but Dante's attention seems to have, *mutatis mutandis,* a scientific bent in the modern sense. He is able to see not only the phenomenon as a monolithic whole, but as the sum of separately perceived parts or phases. His careful measuring of the speed of the current as it approaches the paddles reminds us of a host of similarly punctual observation of minute detail. My favorites are his experiments with fire: the investigation, for instance, of "a sapling log that catches fire / along one of its ends, while at the other / it drips and hisses with escaping vapor" (*Inf.* XIII, 40–42); the punctual researcher's report, for another, on the burning of parchment, with the observations on its several layers or zones—the intact white of the paper, its gradual discoloration and graying and blackening at the approach of the flame, the flame itself—all moving in unison, all described with an almost scientific precision by Dante the technician of Hell.

In Dante's rambling similes, the ramble is more important than the simile. The affectionate lingering over the figure of the *villanello,* or farm boy, who mistakes frost for snow (XXIV, 1–15), the sketch of the *villano* who at sunset takes a breather on the hilltop above his fields (XXVI, 25–33), the vast Flemish fresco of the Venetian arsenal are among the memorable passages of the *Inferno*. Dante, past master of the foreshortened lightning-speed analogy and of the stenographed telegram of a metaphor (see his cruelly enjoyed brevity, very much a part of the show, on "Frederick's capes" [66]), at times is seduced into developing an analogic idea close to his heart well beyond its narrative usefulness.

One such case is our canto's picture of Virgil as the mother who is wakened by flames around her bed and rushes to save her child. One commentator wondered just what corresponds to the nakedness of this medieval young woman in Virgil's tobogganing down the ditchside. Nothing, evidently. Dante enjoys the evoked scene for itself; he chooses to forget its role in the narrative. He stops short in his storytelling in order to take in and report on the frightening night scene, varied by the sight of a fleeing nakedness lit up by the burning house.

There is a common denominator to the presentation of the hypocrites in this canto and the presentation of the soothsayers three cantos earlier:

> Below that point we found a painted people,
> who moved about with lagging steps, in circles,
> weeping, with features tired and defeated.
>
> (58–60)

Like these, the figures in Canto xx enter in a procession:

> I was already well prepared to stare
> below, into the depth that was disclosed,
> where tears of anguished sorrow bathed the ground;
> and in the valley's circle I saw souls
> advancing, mute and weeping, at the pace
> that, in our world, holy processions take.
>
> (xx, 4–10)

First, both passages have, directly or indirectly, the same correlative: a religious procession. Second, as some readers have noticed, the two segments sound alike. Both are musical compositions set to the nasal drone of *nt*, *nd*:

> *Là giù trovammo une gente dipinta*
> *che giva intorno assai con lenti passi,*
> *piangendo e nel sembiante stanca e vinta.*
> (58–60)

> *Io er già disposto tutto quanto*
> *a riguardar ne lo scoperto fondo,*
> *che si bagnava d'angoscioso pianto;*

e vidi g<u>en</u>te per lo vallo<u>n to</u>n<u>do</u>
venir, tac<u>en</u>do e lagrima<u>ndo</u>, al passo
che fanno le letane in questo mo<u>ndo</u>.
(XX, 4–10)

Hieratic ponderous slowness of gait, especially of a multitude, seems to be
musically connected in the poet's mind with a murmuring roll of the lines.

Sound symbolism is perhaps best left to the individual impressions of the
reader (no two readers will react to onomatopoeia alike); the exegete with
ears may, however, go as far as to allude to its ubiquitousness in Dante's
text. The *Comedy* is like an immense libretto (of lyric opera). What we read
with our eyes is the mere plot. To *hear* the recitatives, the arias, the duos,
the *tutti's*, you must auricularly decipher the score Dante has indelibly but
invisibly engraved above and into each verse. This *partitura* of the *Comedy*,
while ever present, is never obtrusive. To the happy few who are in the
know, the verse without its melodic line is like a silent film. You do *see*
Caiaphas crucified, twisting wormlike on the ground; but his irate puffing
into his beard, his hoarse wheeze of exasperation is inscribed in the hidden
soundtrack of the verses: *tutto si distorse / soffiando ne la barba con sospiri*
("the sinner writhed all over / and he breathed hard into his beard with
sighs" [112–113]).

The actual *sounds* of Hell are wondrously amplified by Dante's hen-
decasyllable, but sometimes an insistent vowel or consonant may give us
even physical shape, size, or movement. The arch-hypocrite Caiaphas is
stretched out naked across the path of the lead-coated hypocrites, *ed è
mestier ch'el senta / qualqunque passa, come pesa, pria* ("and he must feel the
weight / of anyone who passes over him" [119–120]). The alliteration
paints the heavy trampling tread of the "painted people."

Inferno XXIII is an acoustically privileged canto, an infernal fugue where
the rhyme-words, the acoustical part of the text, that run down the right-
hand side of the page, create both hypometric and hypermetric lines. Line
145 ends on the accent (*Appresso il duca a gran passi sen gì, / turbato un poco*
["And then my guide moved on with giant strides, / somewhat disturbed"]),
giving us a sudden jolt. A sliding rhyme (*rima sdrucciola*) produces an effect
different from the truncated rhyme. It seems to linger on and destabilize
the context, as when the wayfarers move cautiously on the dike of the
sodomites, between two sheets of fiery rain (XV, 1–3), or when the traveler
must negotiate "jagged, narrow, difficult" crags (XXIV, 62).

Rhymes in *-éndere*, for example, give a slippery quality to the line that describes Dante's descent in this canto.

"S'elli è che sì la destra costa giaccia,
che noi possiam ne l'altra bolgia scendere,
noi fuggirem l'imaginata caccia."

Già non compié di tal consiglio rendere,
ch'io li vidi venir con l'ali tese
non molto lungi, per volerne prendere.

"If that right bank is not extremely steep,
we can descend into the other moat
and so escape from the imagined chase."
He'd hardly finished telling me his plan
when I saw them approach with outstretched wings,
not too far off, and keen on taking us.

(31–36)

The canto's acoustic variety goes from the anxious andante adagio of the incipit to the crescendo agitato of the flight; from the leaden dirge of the hypocrites' procession to the obbligato and moderato of the exchange between the pilgrim and the Jovial Friars; from the sforzando of the Caiaphas episode to the pizzicato mode in the scherzo of Catalano's lesson in demonology, and the staccato of the coda finale.

Dante's *contrapasso* (Shakespeare called it "measure for measure") is named rather late, appropriately, through the words of a colleague, the *trouvère* Bertran de Born (end of *Inferno* xxviii). Sometimes correspondence of an eye for an eye is strictly applied and evident to all readers (once or twice the poet himself points it out). Sometimes *contrapasso* is not self-evident, nor is it eminently fitting. Sometimes there is no correspondence between crime and punishment, although a vast number of interpreters (especially of the American denominations) do take pains to find it in obscure hints, overcomplicated etymologies, and *calembours* ("crime and pun," to apply Nabokov's formula). Our canto belongs to the first category: The sin relates to its punishment. The cloaks, golden on the outside and of lead within, as well as the crucifixion of Caiaphas (but this more in the manner of figural representation), are fit images of hypocrisy. Dante the storyteller knows that a visual evidencing of the abstract concept of sin cannot but help his transcendental travelogue. *Contrapasso* does function time and again as an aid in visualizing the hellish funnel. There *is* coherence in Dante's route for himself and the reader. Left and right indicate actual directions. Dante the storyteller seems to be interested not in the elementary symbolism of right and left, up and down, forward and backward, but in the lively *gesticulating* implied in the indications. The *Comedy* is a vast choreographic production—a ballet of steps, gestures, countenances by the pilgrim himself, by Virgil, and by the damned. There is admirable casualness in the thumb-over-the-shoulder motion with which Virgil accompanies his vexed words: "He who hooks sinners *over there [di qua]* / gave us a false account" (140–141; my emphasis). In *Inferno* xx the pilgrim sets an example for the reader: he himself points out this kind of reading. The urge of the jolly brothers to catch up with the hurried visitors shows on their faces (82–84). Dante choreographs the exit of Virgil mocked by the unctuous Catalano: "And then my guide moved on with giant strides, / somewhat disturbed, with anger in his eyes" (145–146). Minimal changes (in a gesture), sometimes only rhythmic or positional, account for a subtle nuancing in the emotion behind it. Hearing, for instance, of the deceit he was made a victim of, Virgil "stood awhile with his head bent" (139). His actions are explained by exegetes as "a thinking back"; and the movements are expressive of the feelings of the guide taken aback by the treachery of his informants.

My favorite instances of Dantean choreography are the movements that go beyond momentary emotion to bring out character. The two seasoned politicians in Canto XXIII, former co-ombudsmen in Florence, Catalano and Loderingo, spectacularly dance out their personalities in hell:

> When they came up, they looked askance at me
> a long while, and they uttered not a word
> until they turned to one another, saying:
>   "The throbbing of his throat makes this one seem
> alive; and if they're dead, what privilege
> lets them appear without the heavy mantle?"
>
> (85–90)

The actions of Caiaphas are readily seen. Less prompt is our identification of the emotion (and its causes) or the character trait the actions represent: anger, resentment, pique ("that sinner writhed all over, / and he breathed hard into his beard with sighs" [112–113]).

I am surprised at the number of commentators who explain Dante's reference to his birthplace as the *gran villa* by noting that Florence is the largest urban development along the course of the Arno river. The topographic information is certainly there:

> "Tuscan, you who come
> to this assembly of sad hypocrites,
> do not disdain to tell us who you are."
>   I answered: "Where the lovely Arno flows,
> there I was born and raised, in the great city."
>
> (91–95)

I find unmistakable, in the tone of the reply, the pride this ill-treated son of a great town takes in his being a Florentine. Dante's hatred for the traitor city and its inhabitants is expressed vigorously by the exiled poet on a number of occasions. Yet his love for the renegade place shows through in expressions not less vigorous.

A more difficult crux than the *gran villa* is Virgil's reaction to the sight of Caiaphas:

> Then I saw Virgil stand amazed above
> that one who lay stretched out upon a cross
> so squalidly in his eternal exile.
>
> (124–126)

There is great disagreement among the interpreters. Most of them seek coherence in Dante's dream tale of a dream voyage. There is no wholly satisfactory source for Virgil's *maraviglia* here.

Most probably, the trick known to every storyteller (and every good liar) is at play here: the habit of anchoring one's *fiction* into some preexistent (and accepted) *reality*. When Aeneas, the refugee from Troy, disembarks for a sort of olympiad in Sicily (Book v), he meets, lo and behold, a blind giant—Polyphemus who, and here is the wonder of it, has been blinded quite recently by another chance visitor to the island and another actor in the Trojan tragedy. The reader's shock of recognition confers the strength of the familiar upon the unfamiliar. Virgil seems to know something of Christian history and dogma. But his creator limits the guide's awareness for excellent *narrative* reasons. He witnessed the harrowing of hell:

> "I was new-entered on this state
> when I beheld a Great Lord enter here;
> the crown he wore, a sign of victory."
>
> (IV, 52–54)

The ancient poet's marvel at Caiaphas is both a surprise at seeing the hallowed sign of victory debased this way and at the blasphemous *imitatio*, by this wretch, of the mighty lord whom Virgil once, long ago, saw descend into his own infernal dwelling place.

BIBLIOGRAPHY

Bertoni, G. "Il canto degli ipocriti" (1927). In *Letture dantesche: Inferno,* ed. Giovanni Getto (Florence, 1955), 431–445.

Bonora, E. *Gli ipocriti di Malebolge,* 3–29. Milan, 1953.

Camilli, A. "La meraviglia di Virgilio." *Lettere italiane* 4 (1952): 127–129.

Croce, B. *La poesia di Dante,* 93–94. Bari, 1920.

Della Giovanna, I. *Lectura Dantis: Il canto XXIII dell'"Inferno" letto nella sala di Dante in Orsanmichele.* Florence, 1901.

Di Pino, G. "Il canto XXIII dell'*Inferno*." *Quaderni d'Italianistica* 8 (1979): 499–513.

Di Salvo, Tommaso, ed. *Lettura critica della "Divina Commedia: Inferno."* Florence, 1969.

Fubini, M. "Dai Malebranche agli ipocriti." *Convivum* 34 (1966): 210–233.

Guyler, S. "Virgil the Hypocrite—Almost: A Re-Interpretation of *Inferno* XXIII." *Dante Studies* 90 (1972): 25–42.

Hamilton, G. L. "The Gilded Leaden Cloaks of the Hypocrites (*Inferno* xxiii, 58–66)." *Romanic Review* 12 (1921): 335–352.

Larkin, N. "Another Look at Dante's Frog and Mouse." *MLN* 77 (1962): 94–99.

———. "Inferno xxiii, 4–9 Again." *MLN* 81 (1966): 85–88.

Maggini, F. "Lettura del canto xxiii dell'*Inferno*." In *Due Letture inedite*, 1–22. Florence, 1965.

Mandruzzato, E. "L'apologo 'della rana e del topo' e Dante (*Inf.* xxiii, 4–9)." *Studi danteschi* 33, no. 2 (1955): 147–165.

Padoan, G. "Il liber Esopi." *Studi danteschi* 41 (1964): 75–102.

Pagliaro, A. *Ulisse: ricerche semantiche sulla "Divina Commedia,"* 655–656. Florence, 1966.

Pietrobono, L. "Il canto degli ipocriti (xxiii dell'*Inferno*)." In *Lectura Dantis Romana*. Turin, 1961.

Raimondi, E. "I canti bolognesi." In *Dante e Bologna nei tempi di Dante*, 239–248. Bologna, 1967.

Russo, V. "*Inf.* xxiii." In *Nuove letture dantesche*, 2:225–256. Florence, 1968. Reprinted in *Esperienze dantesche* (Naples, 1971), 9–52.

Sacchetto, A. "*Inferno* xxiii." In *Lectura Dantis Scaligera: Inferno*, ed. Mario Marcazzan, 799–826. Florence, 1967.

Sanguineti, E. *Interpretazione di Malebolge*. Florence, 1961.

CANTO XXIV

Thieves and Metamorphoses

JOAN M. FERRANTE

The formal category of sin presented in Canto xxiv is theft, the fraudulent appropriation of others' property, which is the seventh division of fraud. That this section has a particular importance for Dante is indicated by his devotion to it of two cantos (xxiv and xxv), and by his display of literary virtuosity through both, culminating in the assertion that he has surpassed two of his major classical models, Ovid and Lucan (xxv, 94 and 97). Obviously, Dante is concerned with much more here than the simple stealing of material objects. Theft may involve material goods or money (it includes embezzlement and other illicit business practices and may be practiced by cities as well as by individuals), but it may also involve words. That is, a poet may steal from other poets, openly as Dante does from Ovid and Lucan— which he acknowledges in Canto xxv—or more subtly, as he frequently does from Virgil. Dante, in other words and in others' words, is concerned both with the wrongful acquisition of material goods, which is disruptive to society, and also with the justifiable acquisition of intellectual goods, which enriches society. He glorifies his own use of his sources, even as he condemns the thieves' relation to theirs.

Deception, a key factor in theft, and the link among all the sins of the eighth circle, may be unintentional, as in nature's action at the beginning of the canto, but even when intentional, it need not always harm the victim, as in the thieves' actions and the devils' treatment of Virgil; it may help, as when Dante pretends to greater strength than he feels in order to carry on, and when poets deceive their audiences in order to encourage and persuade them to good action, as Dante, Virgil, Ovid, and Lucan do. Lucan, in a passage from Book IX of the *De bello civili,* which Dante draws on for other purposes in this canto, complains of those who demand superficial "truth" from poets: *Invidus . . . qui vates ad vera vocat* (IX, 359–360). Theft, in contrast to violent robbery, is based on deceptive action that intentionally misleads the victim; in that sense, it is the essence of fraud, which is why the souls of this section (and of no other in the ten *bolge* of the eighth circle) recall Geryon, the monster of fraud. Geryon has a human face with the body of a serpent; the souls in this *bolgia* alternate between the bodies of men and the bodies of serpents. Geryon is the static symbol of deception; the souls and serpents are its dynamic representation.

Deception involves the alternation between the posture that inspires confidence and the act that harms, between the surface appearance and the hidden purpose. By presenting the two in continual flux, Dante reveals the reality of fraud, and in this sense goes beyond the metamorphoses of his sources that, once accomplished, remain fixed in the new condition. His thieves can never attain a state of rest, of permanent identity, either as individuals or as political entities. Their cities, Pistoia and Florence, thieves on a greater scale, also undergo continual flux, destruction, and renewal to no purpose. Of course, change, flux, is natural, and even in nature it can be either violent, as in the storms of the simile that ends the canto, or peaceful, as in the change of seasons that opens it. But nature's change is always moving toward a stable goal, following the providential plan to the end of time, when eternal life will conquer death and change in nature. The single but permanent rebirth in human existence, the resurrection of the body, which conquers time and death, is implied by the description of the phoenix, periodically reborn out of its own remains, a traditional symbol of the resurrection.

Fame is another means of overcoming time and death, not so absolute as resurrection but effective in human terms. In *Paradiso* IX, 39–40, Cunizza tells Dante that Folco's fame will last five hundred years, the life span of the phoenix, suggesting the relation Dante sees between literary fame and eternal life. Dante contrasts the recurring and futile changes of the souls and their cities both with the permanence of eternal life and with the enduring nature of literary fame. Virgil encourages Dante with the reminder that fame can only be won by continual striving, which in this canto is translated into the difficult climb up the moat, a foreshadowing of later and longer climbs, in Purgatory and in life (XXIV, 55). The climb is not direct or easy—in Hell it is possible only because it is ultimately leading downward—but Dante must descend through Hell in order to reach the full knowledge of evil before he can begin to climb the mountain of Purgatory or rise through heaven, the ascent that will win him fame through poetry. Ovid claims the same fame "for as long as Rome's power lives" at the end of the last book of the *Metamorphoses,* in which he describes change and flux in human life and in all nature, as well as the periodic rebirth of the phoenix. Lucan comments toward the end of Book ix (980–981) that the poet's task is great and sacred, conquering fate and bestowing immortality. As the poet's labor wins true fame and conquers death, so the thief's brings shame and robs him of eternal life; both make others' possessions their own, but the poet gives them new life and enhances their value for others.

Dante's concern with acquisition, deception, and change is reflected in his vocabulary throughout the canto and in his poetic devices. Words of possession and acquiring, of quantity and consumption abound, in literal and figurative uses: *roba*, 7, *ringavagna*, 12, *piglio*, 24, *aggrappa*, 29, *chiappa*, 33, *munta*, 43, *consuma*, 49, *rendo*, 76, *aggiunge*, 80, *stipa*, 82, *produce*, 87, *copia*, 91, *ficcavan*, 95, *raccolse*, 104, *pasce*, 109, *gola*, 123, *colto*, 133, *tolto*, 135, *ladro*, 138, *apposto*, 139, and their opposites, *manca*, 7, *spoltre*, 46, *scipa*, 84, *dimagra*, 143, *spezzerà*, 149. But since possessions can be constricting, there are also many words of oppression: *grave, accascia*, 54, *legate*, 94, *aggroppate*, 96, *annoda*, 99, *oppilazione, lega*, 114, *involuto*, 146. Words that suggest the theme of deception, confusion, disguise, are also frequent: *assempra*, 4, *imagine*, 5, *cangiata faccia*, 13, *sbigottir*, 16, *par*, 26, *tenta . . . s'è*, 30, *mostrandomi . . . meglio . . . che . . . non*, 58–59, *per non parer*, 64, *parea*, 69, *neente affiguro*, 75, *non si vanti*, 85, *pertugio, elitropia*, 93, *smarrito*, 116, *mucci*, 127, *infinse*, 130, *dipinse*, 132, *negar*, 136, *ladro*, 138, *falsamente*, 139. The same themes of acquisition and deception are echoed in the preferred rhymes, core and equivocal. Core rhymes are based on a word that appears itself as one of the rhymes, and as part of the other two; that is, the rhymes are made by acquisition, piling letters or syllables on the core word, or by stripping them away again: *-anno*, 1–3, *-anca*, 5–9, *-oltre*, 44–48, *-èe*, 86–90, *-omo*, 110–114, *-era*, 119–123, *-odi*, 140–144, *-agra*, 143–147. Equivocal rhymes are in appearance the same word but with a very different meaning, a deceptive identity: *tempra*, 2, 6, *faccia*, 11, 13, *piglio*, 20, 24, *porta*, 37, 39, *dimagra*, 143, 145. The canto begins with a heavy concentration of the two kinds of rhyme and returns to them at the end with a flourish, a rhyme that is both at once: *dimagra, di Magra, agra*. Enjambment, which also contributes to an unsettled feeling of confusion in the reader, is similarly concentrated more at the beginning and at the end of the canto, in connection with the change in nature and in Virgil's mood and then with Vanni Fucci's surprising revelations about himself. Dante seems to tease the reader in every way with the problem of deception and reality in this section; the climax of the *bolgia* in Canto xxv—the fusion of serpent and man and the exchange of shapes between the two, man literally becoming the beast—is a translation of Vanni Fucci's metaphorical *son Vanni Fucci / bestia* (xxiv, 125–126) into physical reality, an intentional confusion of literary figure and visible truth.

Yet another level of deception and theft through words is hinted at in this section: The three metamorphoses Dante describes (two of them in Canto xxv) may also suggest fraudulent contracts, fashioned to disguise the practice of usury. Usury was defined as a form of theft, a fraudulent appropriation of others' goods. Pistoia and Florence, the two cities attacked in this section, were both commercial centers, heavily dependent on usury for their success, and of the five Florentine thieves named by Dante, four of them came from major merchant-banking families, whose theft was probably perceived by Dante's audience as commercial. Commercial transactions were *commutationes,* money-changing; one of the three major guilds in Florence was *cambium,* in Italian *cambio,* a word that recurs throughout the episode along with *mutare, trasmutare, cambiare, converte.* Since Dante treats property as a part of the self, something he emphasizes in his definitions and division of the sins of the seventh circle, an exchange of property is a kind of metamorphosis, and the illicit exchange of property is presented in this section as actual metamorphosis.

Within all the intentional confusion, perhaps to counterbalance it, Dante imposes a rigid structure on Canto XXIV:

> nature simile, sun, frost (1–6)
>> peasant-shepherd (7–15)
>>> Dante, Virgil, the climb (16–64)
>>>> sound of serpents, decision to descend (65–81)
>>> serpents, souls (82–120)
>> Vanni Fucci (121–142)
> nature simile, storm, political prophecy (143–151).

Dante begins and ends with nature similes involving the cosmos (planets) and its effects on mankind, the first apparently threatening but ultimately benevolent (to a peasant and his flocks), the other destructive (to political parties and their cities). In between he sets off the peasant, the honest laborer with almost no possessions and no control over his own fate, against the thief, Vanni Fucci, who steals out of malice, not need, and has the power to harm the innocent. The poets, Dante and Virgil, the good thieves, who make their way painstakingly and laboriously up the moat, along the ledge, and down again, in pursuit of fame and a divine mission, contrast with the bad thieves, the souls bound and bitten by serpents, impeded in their every movement by the symbols of their own actions, whose efforts have brought shame and damnation.

The canto begins with the description of a frost covering the earth, briefly giving the impression of snow, until it melts. The aspects of nature are personified: the year is young, the sun warms (or cools) his hair, the frost copies the image of her sister, snow, with her pen, and the earth changes its face. Frost's images disappear very quickly; other images of nature last longer but are destined to disappear; art's image may last longer still. Normally, we think of art imitating nature (cf. *Inf.* XI, 97–105), but here nature seems to imitate art, using its tools just long enough to deceive its audience. The deception is emphasized by the equivocal rhymes in the description of nature (*tempra* [2, 6]) and in the peasant's reaction (*faccia* [11, 13]). The peasant, who has very little to sustain himself or his flock, assumes the worst and can do no more than lament his fate, until the frost disappears and he is able to pasture his sheep; when the world changes its face, the grieving peasant also changes, takes up his crook, and becomes a shepherd. He is the simplest form of human life, responding immediately to the natural world, working with what it gives him, unable to change or control it in any way. Like nature, he seems to exist outside the moral order, perhaps representing the human race within the cosmos, subject to its will, caught up in its flow. He thus seems to be the lowest form of human life, only a step above the animals he tends, and he will continue to seem so until we see Vanni Fucci—the man with all the resources of civilization, who defies the natural order and declares himself, by his actions and his words, a beast.

Dante, like the peasant, is temporarily distressed by the look he sees on Virgil's face, the force he relies on in the universe of his journey. It was Virgil who had got them into the predicament. By thrusting Dante into the sixth *bolgia* to escape the devils (XXIII, 37 ff.), whose directions he had foolishly believed (XXIII, 139 ff.), reason has stranded him among the hypocrites; that is, to escape the charge of barratry, Dante assumed a righteous posture that later embarrassed him. But no one wearing those cloaks, no one carrying the weight of hypocrisy, of a false appearance of righteousness, can make his way out of the moat. Dante has gone out of his way to dissociate himself from certain aspects of fraud: In the fourth section he makes it clear that he is not a false prophet, in the fifth that he is not a barrator as charged. But he does admit to some hypocrisy by allowing himself to be trapped in the sixth *bolgia*. To extricate himself, he must practice another kind of deception, the theft of the seventh *bolgia*, which in Dante's case is the appropriation of words and images. Now Dante's mind must work very carefully (*adopera, estima* [25], *innanzi si proveggia* [26], *avvisava* [28]) to find the way. Virgil has returned to the comforting appearance of their first encounter, recalled by reference to the mountain Dante saw in Canto I to remind us that Purgatory is the ultimate goal of Dante's climb. Virgil, Dante's reason and a major source of his poetry, is now able to cure Dante's ill (18), to find an alternative to the broken bridge (19). This time Virgil does not carry Dante but pushes and guides him, telling him to test each rock to be sure it will support his weight before he relies on it; given the intensity of poetic relations in this and the succeeding canto, and the presence of Dante's major classical sources, it may well be that the rocks represent classical poets, those strong enough and firm enough to take the weight of Dante's poetry without giving way. It is a new direction in poetry that offers Dante the way out of hypocrisy; the works of Virgil, Ovid, and Lucan provide him with the structure and much of the material he needs to fashion his own statement of the reality he sees and embodies. Not the least of their contributions to Dante is the sense of Rome as the center of civilization, and of Roman principles, like self-sacrifice for the common good, as the essential political virtues.

Once Dante has made this move, he will be able to withstand the temptation of fraudulent counsel in the next *bolgia*. He will keep himself from falling into the moat and the sin by holding onto a large rock (*ronchione* [XXVI, 44]), perhaps a reference to the poetry of Virgil, who mediates there between him and Ulysses and who provided Dante with an alternate model to Ulysses. Instead of imitating the man who led his followers to destruction in the pursuit of unreachable goals, Dante aspires to be Aeneas, the exile who journeyed and guided others to a renewed homeland. Even with the support of the classical tradition, however, the climb is possible only because the whole of hell leads downward (34–40); that is, it is easier to climb because in fact Dante is descending toward even greater evil. But that descent to the core, the full knowledge of evil, is necessary for the ascent of Purgatory, the climb of purgation. In hell, one strives in order to fall, whereas in the larger moral universe, one descends in order to rise. Nonetheless, Dante is quickly exhausted by his efforts (*munta* [43], literally "milked," as if all his productive sources had been depleted) and stops to rest. The only weapon Virgil has against Dante's weariness is the thought of fame. Life without fame, which cannot be won either in ease (resting "on down" [47]), or from a protected position ("under covers" [48]), is consumed, wasted, rather than used. To make his point, Virgil uses a subtle reference to his own poetry, a kind of code between himself and Dante, and perhaps the literarily alert reader; such a life, he tells Dante, is like "smoke in air" (50), "foam in water" (51). *Fummo in aere* is a literal translation of Virgil's *fumus in auras* (*Aeneid* V, 740), which describes Anchises' disappearance after he has told Aeneas in a vision to take only the young and brave to Italy because of the struggle ahead. The scene follows the episode in which the Trojan women, weary of the journey and hard labor, allow themselves to be deceived by the disguised goddess Iris, burn the ships, and then furtively hide from the results of their deed. This act separates those unworthy of the great enterprise of founding Rome from those who will carry it out. The reference is not just a call to glory, but specifically to participation in the Roman destiny, which is Dante's divinely ordained mission as it was Aeneas's. Even the devoted Palinurus, who is not deceived by Sleep's disguise, finally succumbs to weariness at the end of Book 5, and is removed from the group that will reach its goal. Virgil's words keep that from happening to Dante.

In order to carry out his mission, Dante must conquer the weariness of his heavy body (54) with his spirit—not allow himself to be beaten down like the women, not relax because he has made some progress. It is not enough to give up the wrong position (56), he must make an active effort to assume the right. Dante responds immediately by pretending to greater breath and strength than he feels, a positive pretense because it supplies what is lacking and enables him to proceed, as if, by speaking what one should feel, one begins to feel it (64); the poet's words are his action. But they also give rise to words from the next moat, which Dante cannot make out. Dante and Virgil have understood each other perfectly; Virgil's "if you have understood, now profit from it" (57), was answered immediately by Dante's suitable action and words—the soul responding to reason, the Christian poet responding to his classical source. But such communication is not possible with the souls of this region who trade in deception, at least not until Dante has seen them in action, for what they are. "I know not what he said" (67), "I hear and cannot understand" (74), Dante complains, asking that they descend (dismount, treating hell as a reverse of the mountain of Purgatory). Virgil's response is immediate action, although he does not miss the opportunity to explain in words that there is no more appropriate response to an honorable request than silent action. The emphasis is on words because poetry is the subtext of the canto, but vision, the other sense on which reason primarily depends, also has difficulty functioning here. "I see down but can distinguish nothing" (75), Dante says, using the word affiguro, which suggests "make a figure for myself," "imagine," as though Dante were calling attention to the creative difficulty of describing this section.

Once he gets down into it, Dante sees the terrifying mass of serpents, the memory of which drains him of blood (84), as the climb had "milked" him of breath. Once again, he is revived by classical sources, although he clothes the reference in a subtle claim of superiority: "Let Libya boast no more about her sands" (85). The Libyan sands and their monstrous serpents recall Dante's two avowed rivals in this section, Ovid and Lucan. Although Ovid is the less obvious source in this case, there are some significant connections between the passage in Metamorphoses IV and Canto XXIV. Ovid describes how, when Perseus flies over the sands of Libya, carrying the head of Medusa, the blood from the head drips on the sand and gives rise to various serpents (IV, 617 ff.). The passage occurs shortly after Cadmus, who had founded a city by sowing the teeth of a sacred serpent, flees his city overwhelmed by its troubles, and is himself turned into a serpent by the avenging gods (IV, 563 ff.), an episode Dante cites in XXV, 97; the contrast between the hero's attempt to create a civilization and the inevitable political corruption and violence and divine vengeance are relevant not only to the entire Comedy but particularly to the end of Canto XXIV. Perseus, like Dante, had been exiled and condemned to death because of his potential threat to his ruler and, like Dante, is aided by a figure of reason (Minerva); Perseus is able to destroy the monster Medusa by looking at her reflection in the shield Minerva gave him (Virgil covers Dante's eyes when Medusa appears), as the poets' audiences can see danger through their poems. Perseus also, albeit accidentally, kills the ruler who exiled him, something Dante might well want to do, at least in the sense of destroying the power of the Black faction in Florence.

The references to Libyan sands in Lucan also suggest political corruption: the first occurs in I, 368, during the debate among Caesar's people over the imminent civil war, when Laelius urges Caesar to lead them even over the hot sands of Libya; but it is of course Cato, the great leader who sacrifices himself to the needs of Rome like Aeneas, the model for Dante's pilgrim-persona, who actually leads his men through those sands in Book IX. Refusing to deceive them about the danger (388), he asks only those Romans who are attracted by the risks and the glory to accompany him. Lucan describes Libya as the realm of Medusa, IX, 626, rugged with stones (like the moat Dante has just climbed); he gives surprising attention to Medusa, as if she symbolized the whole march through the desert, perhaps even the civil war that led to it. He describes the snakes around her neck and brow, and over her back, and notes that men can look at only this part of her and live. That is, the human part of Medusa is the most harmful, because it is the most deceptive, just as the thieves of the seventh *bolgia* were most dangerous as deceptively honorable human beings, when the serpent part of their nature was concealed. With her human face and serpent hair, Medusa may have been one of the sources of Dante's Geryon, the monster of fraud, who is recalled particularly in this *bolgia*. Lucan also lists the various monsters that grew from Medusa's blood, some fourteen, from which Dante selects five for their particular characteristics as Lucan describes them: *chelidri*, whose track smokes as it moves (IX, 711), presumably hiding their bodies; *iaculi*, which fly (720) like Geryon and hurl themselves from trees, through the heads of their victims (822 ff.); *faree*, Lucan's *parias*, which plow tracks with the tail (721), the tail's effect again suggesting Geryon; as does the *cencri*, whose body is more spotted and patterned than marble (713–714); and finally the *anfisibena*, which moves toward each of its two heads (719), suggesting its duplicity. Dante focuses our attention and horror on these monsters not only by their strange names but also by the unusual rhyme-words (*stipa* and *scipa* [82, 84], *Etïopia* and *elitropia* [89, 93]) and the core rhymes (*faree* [86], *ree* [88], *èe* [90], a progressive stripping down to the core word). Dante like Cato passes among the monsters untouched, having no connection with their kind of deception.

In the midst of this throng of monsters, the souls run naked and terrified, totally unprotected, as if they were innocent victims, whereas, we eventually learn, they are simply poisonous serpents, the perpetrators, so to speak, in their disguise. They have no place to hide, no way to make themselves invisible to their pursuers (no heliotrope), no means of deception such as they practiced on their victims. Now their hands are bound behind them by the serpents, who also knot their own heads and tails, the dangerous parts, through the souls' loins. The image of a man covered by hostile serpents recalls Laocoön as Virgil describes him in *Aeneid* II, 199 ff. He has warned the Trojans against the wooden horse (the originator of which will appear in the next *bolgia* as a counselor of fraud) and the deceptions of the Greeks, even bearing gifts, but is interrupted by the appearance of a particularly deceptive Greek, Sinon, who comes on the scene with his hands bound behind him like the thieves in Canto XXIV. Sinon tells his tale of Greek treachery (the entire episode in the *Aeneid* is filled with words for deception, as Canto XXIV is), presenting himself as the innocent victim, swearing falsely by the divine powers who know truth, but the Trojans finally believe him because Laocoön and his sons are attacked and killed by a pair of serpents, which is taken as a corroborating omen. Troy, the future Rome, is destroyed by the stratagem of the arch-counselor of fraud, Ulysses, with the help of the innocent-appearing liar, Sinon, and the evil agency of the serpents, the same combination of human and serpent features that operates to deceive in the symbolic monster of fraud, Geryon, and in the thieves of this section.

Suddenly, at line 97, Dante focuses on one of the thieves, who is bitten by a serpent where "the neck and shoulders form a knot" (*s'annoda*). (*Nodo* in the *Comedy* usually means an impediment, a problem, rather than a binding [cf. *Purg.* IX, 126, and XXIV, 55–56], as if the evil represented by the serpent were the impediment to the proper functioning of mind and body; it is also used for the decorations on Geryon's body in *Inferno* XVII, 15.) The result of the bite is an immediate and total reduction of the body to ashes, a burning that is swifter than *o* or *i* can be written; *o* and *i* are both the basic forms of circle and line on which all construction and writing rely, and also the letters that, in reverse, *io,* express the most personal form of individual existence, "I." The individual seems to have disappeared altogether, but the dust collects itself and returns to its former shape. The return to itself recalls the passage in the *Georgics* IV, 444, in which Virgil describes Proteus, who attempts to escape capture by turning himself into every kind of shape but finally gives up and returns to his own; like Proteus, Vanni Fucci attempted to elude capture by stealth and deception, an effort that apparently succeeded in life, but here, he is finally captured in his true shape by Dante. Once again, Dante's reference to Virgil is so subtle as to be easily missed, while his analogy of the soul's resurrection to the phoenix begs comparison with the description in the last book of the *Metamorphoses,* XV, 392 ff.

Ovid's description is put in the mouth of the Samian philosopher (another voluntary exile from tyranny), rather than directly narrated by the poet, as if Ovid had taken it from him, so Dante's version, which is very close to Ovid's, is like the theft of a theft. (Like Ovid, Dante attributes his information to "great sages" [106].) It is intriguing that the philosopher asks his audience why they are afraid of death and the Styx, the shades and empty names, the material of poets and dangers of a false world: *quid tene-*

bras et nomina vana timetis, / materiem vatum falsique pericula mundi? (154–155). If Dante expects his audience to recognize the reference to Ovid, does he not run the risk of their connecting him with the poets who make up stories about the world of the dead? Is this perhaps another way of raising the issue of deception for good? In fact, the philosopher speaks at length about human corruption and abuse, as well as about change and flux in all life, animals, men, nations, and eras of history. Just before the phoenix passage, he says that some think the marrow in a man's spine, when the spine decomposes after death, changes into a snake, which suggests, in Dantean terms, that the capacity to be a snake, a deceiver, a thief, exists in all of us. But Ovid treats the periodic rebirth of the phoenix as a natural, if unique process, which takes time to complete. Dante, because of the analogy with the soul's resurrection, suggests a highly unnatural, indeed monstrous event, which occurs almost instantaneously. The one set of rhyme-words that is complete within the phoenix passage in Canto xxiv—*rinasce, pasce, fasce* (107–111), that is, birth, life (feeding), and death (winding sheets)— reminds us of the primary symbolism of the phoenix in Christian tradition, the resurrection of Christ and of the human soul after death. The thought of that event, which can come only once to each individual, makes the perverse version that comes to this soul again and again particularly horrifying. When he comes to himself, he is confused, like one who has been possessed by a demon, or by epilepsy (popularly associated with demonic possession), but the demon who possessed him is really himself, that is, another soul of a similar nature. The whole act is God's revenge, but unlike the revenge visited on the victims described by Ovid and Lucan and even Virgil, these souls have brought it on themselves and have made themselves both its victims and its tools: as God's vengeance "showers down" (*croscia* [120]), so the soul fell like rain into this part of Hell (*piovvi* [122]); and the serpents, which are souls, are also the instruments of their fellows' punishment.

The resurrected soul, the only one of the featured souls who does not actually become a serpent, describes himself as a beast: *son Vanni Fucci / bestia* (125–126), the enjambment laying particular stress on "beast," which comes as a shock even though he has already said he preferred bestial to human life (124), like the "mule" he was. This slang word for bastard may be a way of blaming others for his state, something characteristic of the souls in hell from their very arrival, when they curse God, their parents, the human race, and the place and time of their birth (iii, 103 ff.); the same may be true of his reference to his city, Pistoia, as a worthy "den," 126, as if one could be nothing but a beast in such a city, a point that will reecho in the political prophecy at the end of the canto. Dante, who seems to avoid speaking directly to him, tells Virgil to ask why he is in this section, since he knew him as a "man," a loaded word in this context, "of blood and anger" (129). The "sinner . . . turned his mind and face " (130–131) toward

Dante, words that recall *Aeneid* XI, 800–801, when the Volscians turn their eyes and minds to their queen as she is ambushed; Vanni will in fact ambush Dante himself, but nine lines later. For the moment, he answers Dante's question directly, although "painted" with shame; his *vergogna* is *trista* (like the *tristissima copia* of the serpents [91]), which along with *dipinse* casts some doubts on the truth of the feeling. He admits to pain because Dante has found him here, and that seems to be real, since he takes the first opportunity to avenge himself on Dante. But first he explains that he is here because he was a thief (and again Dante uses enjambment to get the full effect of that announcement: in *giù son messo tanto perch'io fui / ladro* [137–138]); he stole from the sacristy articles he describes not as holy but as beautiful, the aspect that presumably attracted him, a crime "falsely" laid to another (139). Since this fact is the last thing he says about his crime, it seems to be a boast of his ability to deceive, to accomplish what he wanted and have another pay for it.

Vanni's final words, and they are the final words in the canto, are a political prophecy, spoken to wound Dante, who has seen him where he got himself and destroyed his cover, so to speak. After what is either a threat or an insult, "if you can ever leave" (141), he tells Dante that Pistoia will first lose her Blacks, using the verb *dimagra*, "strip herself of," that is, harm herself by giving up a part of herself; then Florence will renew her people and customs, making a fairly obvious analogy with the thieves in this section who are constantly renewed (cf. *Purg.* VI, 145–147: How often . . . have you [my Florence] changed . . . and revised [*rinovate*] your citizens!). The sense of upheaval and loss is echoed in the rhyme that is both equivocal and core in lines 143–147: *dimagra, di Magra, agra*. The political struggle is explained in terms of divine and cosmological forces, as if it were a part of the constant flux of human existence, and not a result of individual and collective corruption. Vanni says that Mars, the god of war and rejected patron of Florence, draws a vapor from the Val di Magra, a reference to Moroello Malaspina, marquis of Lunigiana, military leader of the Tuscan Guelphs from 1301–1312, who helped Florence and Lucca to defeat Pistoia, the last White stronghold in Tuscany. That vapor, and the clouds around it, brings a storm to Campo Piceno, where Catiline was defeated and killed with all his soldiers, according to Villani (*Chronicle* I, 32), and which was identified by Dante's contemporaries with Pistoia. This ancient site of defeat and death will also be the source of hurt to every White, everyone of Dante's party, and of course to Dante himself. Thus the canto closes with a natural image of great violence, in contrast to the gentle one with which it began, and even in contrast to the storm in *Aeneid* V, from which Dante drew the inspiration to his climb in this canto. That storm was sent by a helpful god to put out the fire in the ships and enable Aeneas to continue his destined mission to found Rome; this storm is sent by an angry God, who helps to foment civil war and impedes Dante and the Whites and the empire from restoring Rome to its proper position as the seat of world government in Europe and the capital of Italy.

Dante's own political fate, as the victim of factional struggles and the maneuvers of corrupt rulers, ties him to many of the classical figures who appear in his sources, Perseus, Cadmus, Cato, the Samian philosopher, Aeneas. Like them, he tries to oppose the corrupt forces, to further the cause of good, using poetry as his weapon. Unlike the thieves, individuals, and cities, who appropriate others' possessions, money, or territory to satisfy their own greed for wealth or power, Dante only appropriates the treasures of his fellow poets, which exist for the good of all, which he can build on and enhance for the greater good of all. The literary thefts he practices so frequently in this and the following canto, some blatantly, others stealthily, far from impoverishing or threatening the foundation of his society, increase its cultural wealth and contribute to its greater stability.

BIBLIOGRAPHY

Baker, David J. "The Winter Simile in *Inferno* XXIV." *Dante Studies* 92 (1974): 77–91.

Baldassaro, Lawrence. "Metamorphosis as Punishment and Redemption in *Inferno* XXIV." *Dante Studies* 99 (1981): 89–112.

Chapin, D. L. Derby. "Io and the Negative Apotheosis of Vanni Fucci." *Dante Studies* 89 (1971): 19–31.

Chiampi, James T. "The Fate of Writing: The Punishment of Thieves in the Inferno." *Dante Studies* 102 (1984): 51–60.

Economou, George D. "The Pastoral Simile of *Inferno* XXIV and the Unquiet Heart of the Christian Pilgrim." *Speculum* 51 (1976): 637–646.

Ellrich, Robert J. "Envy, Identity, and Creativity: *Inferno* XXIV–XXV." *Dante Studies* 102 (1984): 61–80.

Ferrante, Joan M. "Good Thieves and Bad Thieves: A Reading of *Inferno* XXIV." *Dante Studies* 104 (1985): 83–98 (a longer version of this piece).

Hawkins, Peter S. "Virtuosity and Virtue: Poetic Self-Reflection in the *Commedia*." *Dante Studies* 98 (1980): 1–18.

Hollander, Robert. "Ad ira parea mosso: God's Voice in the Garden (*Inferno* XXIV, 69)." *Dante Studies* 101 (1983): 27–50.

Maier, Bruno. "Canto XXIV." In *Lectura Dantis Scaligera: Inferno,* ed. Mario Marcazzan, 831–838. Florence, 1967.

Rosadi, Giovanni. "Il canto XXIV dell'*Inferno*." In *Lectura Dantis,* ed. G. C. Sansoni. Florence, 1917.

Terdiman, Richard. "Problematical Virtuosity: Dante's Depiction of the Thieves." *Dante Studies* 91 (1973): 27–45.

Vallone, Aldo. "Il Canto XXIV dell'*Inferno*." In *Lectura Dantis Romana,* 1–35. Turin, 1959.

Since this essay was written, the following articles have appeared on *Inferno* XXIV: Rebecca Beal, "Dante among Thieves: Allegorical Soteriology in the Seventh Bolgia (*Inferno* XXIV and XXV)," *Mediaevalia* 9 (1986 for 1983): 101–123; Caron Ann Cioffi, "The Anxieties of Ovidian Influence: Theft in *Inferno* XXIV and XXV," *Dante Studies* 112 (1994): 77–100.

CANTO XXV

The Perverse Image

ANTHONY OLDCORN

> do you not know that we are worms and born
> to form the angelic butterfly that soars,
> without defenses, to confront His judgment?
>
> (*Purg.* X, 124–126)

> I wished to see
> the way in which our human effigy
> suited the circle and found place in it—
> and my own wings were far too weak for that.
> But then my mind was struck by light that flashed
> and, with this light, received what it had asked.
>
> (*Par.* XXXIII, 136–141)

The most dramatically memorable (and controversial) individuals in the *Inferno*—Francesca da Rimini, Farinata degli Uberti, Pier delle Vigne, Brunetto Latini, among those we have already encountered, and Ulysses, Guido da Montefeltro, and Ugolino, to cite a few we will encounter soon— are memorable (and controversial) because of their eloquence, their skillful and intriguing (in every sense) use of speech. Oblivious, if not of where they are or how they came to be there, of the fundamental *why,* they persist in their former earthly assumptions, plead their special causes, syllogize from apparently impeccable premises, not infrequently enlisting the reader's unsuspecting sympathies. The best modern exegesis has consisted in unraveling the watertight self-justificatory rhetoric that blinds each several moral conscience. The prevailing mode of self-presentation is the persuasive, but always suspect, dramatic monologue. Yet Vanni Fucci, by no means the least articulate and eloquent of Dante's interlocutors, is remembered not for a speech but for a gesture. Long before I began to read the *Comedy,* news of Vanni Fucci's scandalous put-down reached me through the "good parts" grapevine. That this should be so is a tribute to the resourcefulness of the narrator, who contrives to divide Vanni's appearance tendentiously into two parts, the first of which the reader tends in retrospect to forget.

Vanni first comes onstage at XXIV, 97, where he is presented as merely one otherwise unidentified casual victim ("one / who stood upon our shore") among the many naked targets of the malice of the innumerable repulsive worms with which the dark and silent *bolgia* teems. Dante calls them "serpents," modern taxonomies would call them "reptiles." Their very memory, let alone their sight, is enough to curdle the author's blood (xxiv, 84), as the very thought of the dark wood in Canto i renews his fear. It is worth stressing that the shades are "naked," with the accent on their defenselessness, and not "nude." There is no suggestion in Dante of aestheticizing these "bodies," as the figures of the damned would later be aestheticized by the poet's illustrators, leading even an attentive critic like Momigliano to project a "Michelangelesque vehemence" (though he was probably thinking not so much of Michelangelo as his nineteenth-century epigone Gustave Doré) onto the impotently defiant figure of the "second" Vanni Fucci in the opening lines of Canto xxv.

Bitten by a snake at the nape of the neck, the Vanni Fucci of Canto xxiv is immediately consumed and falls to dust and ashes, only to rise up again just as suddenly in his former human form. The vision is frightful, but, like the coming metamorphoses in Canto xxv, it is described with "clinical" detachment. Not a word of sympathy for the victim of divine justice, who initially, before Dante learns his name and crime, is identified simply as "the sinner" (xxiv, 118 and 130). Virgil now begins the interrogation, asking the sinner who he is. Vanni Fucci, another of Dante's fellow Tuscans, spits out his name and seems determined, in his swaggering aggressive answer, to pass himself off as one of the violent. The vehemence of his self-assertion could also be read psychologically, we will come to realize, as a form of overcompensation for the extreme precariousness of his sense of self-identity. He refers to himself as a "beast" and a "mule" (a reference not to his stubbornness but to his status as the illegitimate son of a Pistoian patrician: "mule," which designates the mongrel offspring of a jackass and a mare, is a cant word meaning "bastard"—and a particularly appropriate metaphor, we might add, for one who would consort with Centaurs, as well as a hint at the perverse confusion of natures to come in Canto xxv). According to Vanni, his native town, Pistoia, Florence's traditional rival about twenty miles to her northwest, is a worthy "den" for such as him. Unlike the sinners, however, who "rain" into the *bolgia* (the metaphor used by Vanni here will be repeated by Master Adam at xxx, 94; Pier delle Vigne had said that the souls of the suicides fall like seeds into his unnatural forest [xiii, 96]), who, in plain words, are transported directly from the world above to the one place of punishment where they belong, Dante has visited all of the previous circles and he knows that the violent, less guilty than the fraudulent, are punished in the seventh circle; and we happen to be in the eighth. Though he has recognized his contemporary Vanni by now, and though he knows only too well the violent side of this "man of blood and anger," Dante is having none of it. He wants to know (and to let the world know) what offense brought Vanni to this lower than anticipated position on the inverted ladder. Turning to Virgil, in a typical good cop–bad cop routine

(Ask him where he was on the night of March 13, 1295), Dante implacably forces Vanni to confess, "coloring with miserable shame" (xxiv, 132), to his status not as a holdup man but as a sneak thief, which is why he is here and not plunged to some precisely calculated depth in the bloody river of Phlegethon along with the rest of the violent against their neighbors, under the watchful eye of their equally violent Centaur warders. The damning word *ladro* (thief) is deliberately underscored by the poet, who, so to speak, forces Vanni to highlight it by placing it in enjambment at the very beginning of the line (xxiv, 138). In the first line of Canto xxv, it will be made still more prominent and accusatory by placing it in the still more conspicuous rhyming position. *Ladro* in Italian is a difficult word to rhyme. When finally wrung from Vanni, incidentally, it provides the answer to another question that has been bothering the reader since the description of the plight of the sinners in the seventh *bolgia* began: what are these shades here for, what is their offense?

Benvenuto da Imola, Dante's garrulous fourteenth-century interpreter, makes the most of the obvious affinities between covert thief and covert serpent. The attentive reader of the text thus far has already been given more than an inkling of the importance for medieval ethicists of property and its correct use. Property was in a sense an extension of the person (or the community), the natural world having been created to permit the survival of humankind, according to the Aristotelian principle that the less perfect exists to serve the more perfect. The avaricious and prodigal of Canto vii among the incontinent, and, among the violent, the violent against their neighbors of Canto xii ("Violent death and painful wounds may be / inflicted on one's neighbor; his possessions / may suffer ruin, fire, and extortion" [xi, 34–36]), as well as the self-lacerating squanderers, found alongside the suicides in Canto xiii ("A man can set violent hands against / himself or his belongings" [xi, 40–41]), were all examples of the willful abuse of property. Several modern commentators have hypothesized (on purely speculative grounds, mind you, given the paucity of information present in the text) that all the thieves punished in the seventh *bolgia* are guilty, like Vanni, of the theft of public or communal property. However that may be, it is clear that, here in the anti-City of Dis, it is the public face (or facelessness) of theft that Dante condemns, its fraudulent disruption of the political and religious bonds of community.

The last dozen lines of Canto xxiv are occupied, the reader will recall, by a rhetorically complex and mysterious oracle, pronounced by Vanni and cast in the symbolic meteorological mode, whose main point is to prophesy the imminent failure of Dante's political cause and the overcoming (if you will, the *Ueberbietung*), the rout and expulsion of the White Guelphs from Florence, which was to be the occasion of Dante's permanent exile. The acrimony of Vanni's response was in a sense the answer to Dante's deliberate provocation of this former political antagonist, the prophecy's

vengeful motivation being made quite explicit in the snarled last line and reinforced by the virulent and venomous alliteration of its stabbing initial *d*'s:
E detto l'ho perché doler ti debbia! ("And I have told you this to make you
grieve"), while the repetition of the verb *dolere* (to cause pain) with which
Vanni had begun his discourse (*Più mi duol che tu m'hai colto* ["I suffer more
because you've caught me" (XXIV, 133; my italics)]) completed the rhetorical circle and gave his speech and his onstage appearance ringing closure.

The transition from Canto XXIV to Canto XXV is one of the most surprising and cleverly handled in the entire *Comedy*. The encounter with
Vanni Fucci turns out, when we turn the page, not to be over. This narrative carryover will occur once again, between Cantos XXXII and XXXIII,
though its movement will be inverted: from gesture to speech, not as here
from speech to gesture. Here, for the first time in the divisions of the cantos, there is no marked ellipsis between the two units, no slackening of the
tension, no zoom out. The new canto does not begin with a fresh close-up
on the pilgrim and a new narrative departure, or with a rhetorical reflection
upon what has just occurred (as will be the case, for example, with the apostrophe to Florence that balances the apostrophe to Pistoia soon to come
and prolongs the echoes of the present Canto XXV into Canto XXVI). All that
lies between Cantos XXIV and XXV is a (spurious as it transpires) blank space
and the new canto heading—elements of the paratext. Vanni Fucci remains stage front under the spotlight, and the narrative of his oral and ges-
ticulatory discourse continues as if nothing had intervened. We may be reminded, among other things by the expression of exacerbated pain ("*I
suffer more*"), of the earlier dialogue between Dante and Farinata, interrupted at X, 52, and its reprise 24 lines later in words that show that for the
Florentine Ghibelline, as for the Black Guelph from Pistoia, Dante's coming has not been innocuous ("and taking up his words where he'd left off, /
'If they were slow,' he said, 'to learn that art, / *that is more torment to me than
this bed*'" [*Inf.* X, 76; my italics]); but in Canto X the interruption fell within
the canto and was occasioned by the sudden apparition of Cavalcante dei
Cavalcanti, and the hand of the maker was not so arbitrarily, or rather skillfully, evident. Here, Dante the demiurge manipulates not simply his narrative material but also his character, permitting him to speak or silencing
him at will.

In fact it is this interruption that makes the figure of Vanni Fucci so scandalously memorable, dividing his appearance in the poem and especially
the nature of his discourse into two parts, politically vindictive but rhetorically eloquent on the one hand, and blasphemously mutinous but also
crudely inarticulate on the other. So that the "new" defiant Vanni *outdoes*
the "old" in senseless evil, *outdoes* indeed in malicious and ultimately futile
prideful violence not only the overweening titanism of the pagan Capaneus
of Canto XIV but the presumption of the sum total of hell's denizens
("Throughout the shadowed circles of deep hell, / I saw no soul against

God so rebel, / not even he who fell from Theban walls" [13–15]), giving Vanni Fucci a narratively split personality, and Dante the last word.

Pier Paolo Pasolini's belittling characterization of Vanni as "a small-town Capaneus" and, with an appropriative anachronism, "an aging ted-dyboy" (younger generations, read "hooligan" or "skinhead") is a by-prod-uct of Dante's manipulation. And Pasolini was surely wrong to imply that the encounter with Vanni was for Dante in some sense an encounter with an alter ego, similar, we may add, to the encounter between "skald" and "skin" in Tony Harrison's powerful poem "V": "He aerosolled his name, and it was mine." His not unprovoked diatribe and prophecy over, Vanni Fucci remains briefly onstage (and forever in the reader's memory), reduced to gross inarticulateness, to perform his scabrous gesture and be summar-ily silenced.

Seen in this light, the entire canto may be read as a procession of silenc-ings: Vanni's would-be silencing of God, the serpents' silencing of Vanni ("He fled and could not say another word" [16]), Hercules' silencing of the truculent Cacus ("his crooked deeds / ended beneath the club of Hercules" [30–31]), the interruption of Dante and Virgil's exchange by the three Florentine souls' abrupt inquiry as to who they are ("At this the words we shared were interrupted" [38]), Dante the pilgrim's silencing of his guide Virgil ("I raised my finger up from chin to nose" [45]), Dante the rhetori-cian's silencing first of Lucan ("Let Lucan now be silent" [94]), then of Ovid ("Let Ovid now be silent" [97]), all culminating in the silencing of the voice of humanity in the transformed sinners. Silencings and silence. The si-lence that was characterized by Attilio Momigliano as one of religious awe; though he also pointed out elements of sorcery or witchcraft, and some later readers have demurred. A silence, in any case, broken—and per-haps this is true of no other canto—by no dialogue but only, apart from Vir-gil's nine-line excursus on the history of Cacus, by unarticulated words and shrill and anxious shouts and questions. The unarticulated (but nonetheless transcribed) words of the throttling serpent ("I'll have you speak no more" [6]), the unanswered shouts of Vanni himself ("Take that, o God; I square them off for you!" [3]), of Cacus ("Where is he, where's that bitter one?" [18]), of the three new-coming souls ("And who are you?" [37], and "Where was Cianfa left behind?" [43]), of two of the same souls held transfixed as Dante is by the first metamorphosis ("Ah me, Agnello, how you change! Just see, / you are already neither two nor one!" [68–69]), of the vindictive former serpent become a man in the final transformation ("I'd have Buoso run / on all fours down this road, as I have done" [140–141]). This final dis-course, like Vanni Fucci's resentful brag in the previous canto, verbalizes the malicious aggressiveness that possesses the anti-citizens of this *bolgia*, when they are not its hapless and helpless victims.

Vanni's gesture of "giving the fig"—Mandelbaum's judicious solution, "both figs cocked" (2), hints nicely at the ribald connotations—is an archaic, politically incorrect gesture (apparently still in use, since its European isoglosses were mapped as recently as the 1970s and reported in Desmond Morris's *Gestures*). It consists of thrusting a fist in the direction of the recipient with the thumb protruding between the index and second fingers. The resulting signifier may be seen as a evoking either a bawdy or a scatological likeness. In the first place, to what Eric Partridge used to refer to archly as the "female pudend" (whose vulgar designation—the equivalent of the English "cunt"—*fica* or *figa*, has upset the symmetries of Italian grammatical gender by virtue of which the masculine word normally means the tree and the feminine the fruit of the tree [*melo* = apple tree, *mela* = apple, *pero* = pear tree, *pera* = pear, etc.]), to the point that to translate *fiche* as "figs" may actually be a mistranslation, the masculine noun having been compelled throughout the history of the language into double service (*fico* = fig tree *and* fig), and there being no historical instance of *fica* meaning "fig" recorded in Battaglia's authoritative *Grande Dizionario*. In the second place, to a pair of straining buttocks (the Latin *ficus* = fig tree or fig, whose gender was a matter of dispute among the ancients, could also mean hemorrhoids, a person suffering from hemorrhoids, or simply anus. See below the gesture's misdemeanorial association with mooning, as well as Spitzer's speculative linking of the Latin phrase *facere fileccham,* glossed by Lombardi-Lotti as synonymous with *facere ficas,* with the German invitation *Schleck mir den Arsch*). The gesture is ambiguous, allowing the figger to eat his fig and have it, so to speak, since, though the disposition of the fingers may allude to a virtual cavity, the accompanying forearm is clearly phallic and aggressive.

The churlish Vanni makes the gesture not just with one hand but with two (as extratextual examples indeed suggest was customary), accompanying the two "figs" with a formulaic utterance specifying their addressee, in the present instance God himself. The horror of Vanni's double fig may be somewhat attenuated, when we recall that the gesture was apparently common enough to be forbidden explicitly by more than one local Tuscan city statute. In 1297, for example, Florence's closest urban neighbor, Prato, imposed a fine of ten liras or a public flogging upon whoever "should make the figs or expose the buttocks toward heaven, or toward the sacred image of God" (Tommaseo, cited in Lombardi-Lotti). The two gestures may be read as synonymous or complementary: mooning either proffering the signified without recourse to the symbolic signifier, or inviting and daring the reciprocal phallic fig. Since Vanni presents himself as a typical representative of his worthy den, Pistoia, Dante's attribution to him of this sacrilegious gesture may have been suggested by the two marble arms that the chronicler Giovanni Villani tells us were erected atop the tower of Pistoia's defensive fortress at Carmignano, whence they brandished the double fig in the direction of rival Florence.

The gesture, incidentally, survived into Elizabethan and Jacobean times and is frequently mentioned by Shakespeare and his contemporaries, where it is perceived as exotic, Mediterranean, and in particular Spanish and—perhaps for that same reason—associated with braggadocio. It is, for instance, a favorite expression of the scurrilous and irascible Pistol ("When Pistol lies, do this; and fig me like the bragging Spaniard" [2 *Henry IV* v, iii, 118]; "Die and be damned! and *fico* for thy friendship. . . . The fig of Spain . . . I say the fig / within thy bowels and thy dirty maw" [*Henry V* III, vi, 56–61; see Gary Taylor's note in the Oxford Shakespeare *Henry V*]). In addition to its value as an insult, the fig may also have had a protective apotropaic value, like the Neapolitan horns gesture, and other gestures of a sexual nature. If we disregard for a moment this superstitious use, giving the fig to God was presumably part of one's image, intended as much to impress one's cronies and other bystanders as anything else.

As Pistol's words make clear (the Quarto reads "within thy jaw"), the fist was understood to be symbolically thrust into either one of the two principal male orifices. Vanni's scatological eschatology, then, is painting God with our effigy (*Par.* XXXIII, 131), making the Word flesh, with a vengeance. (Though I would hesitate to make too much of contiguousness of the normally theological Latinism *verbo*—otherwise found only in *Paradiso*—here at XXV, 16.) Vanni is, then, going far beyond the Scripture's usual condescension to our human powers, which stops short at "assigning feet and hands / to God but meaning something else" (*Par.* IV, 44–45). In a canto that, as we will see, contains more than twice as many lexical terms referring to parts of the human body than any other single canto of the *Inferno* (De Robertis counts a total of fifty-nine but doesn't say whether he includes *fiche* among them), Vanni's gesture implies a God with private parts. His figs cut God down to size. Father Luigi Pietrobono has further pointed out (and he is frequently cited) that there may even be, in the Italian verb *squadro* (I square off) a suggestion that the proffered figs, made with an all too human hand, are made to measure, fit like a glove! It is as if Edmund were to conclude his soliloquy, "Now, gods, *bend down* for bastards!"

If I may be permitted an aside, however, I would like to point out that Pietrobono's is *not* the sense of the word *squadro* in the sonnet, apparently written in response to an accusation of literary *theft*, which Cino, a prominent jurist and a poet from Vanni Fucci's hometown of Pistoia, addressed to Guido Cavalcanti, "Qua' son le cose vostre ch'io vi tolgo" (What are these things of yours I steal from you), and to which Dante may be alluding knowingly and polemically, when he repeats, in a prominent position in the opening lines of this canto, one of its difficult pairs of rimes, *ladro / squadro* (Gorni). For our purposes here, we may recall the use of similar nonverbal statements—the British V-sign; the ancient, now typically American, *digitus infamis* (or "finger" *tout court*); the Italian "forearm jerk" (as Morris dubs it)—as the final unanswerable retort, cutting short an otherwise heated exchange, or even—from behind the wheel of a pickup truck, say—replacing articulate verbality with a kind of short-hand short-hand. Read thus, the gesture becomes the first in that procession of would-be and actual silencings that characterizes the canto. (And, if we go along with Gorni, its very phrasing implies Dante's own silencing of Cino's disapproval of the *Comedy*.)

Gianmario Anselmi has recently suggested a hitherto unsuspected connection between the thief Vanni Fucci's "figs" and the lewdly comic Latin poems to the god Priapus, the *Carmina priapea*, in which a similar ritual gesture is attributed to thieves confronted with the roughhewn wooden statuette of the ithyphallic garden and orchard god Priapus, used in a gentler age before razor wire and guard dogs to mark off the boundaries of one's property and discourage intruders. One of the principal themes of this profane mock-serious genre is the shameful chastisements that await would-be thieves, not precisely at Priapus's "hands." Modern scholarship gives the *Priapea* for anonymous, but medieval and early renaissance manuscripts had no qualms about ascribing the entire collection—on the basis of allusions in the younger Pliny, Suetonius, Aelius Donatus, and Servius—to none other than Dante's Virgil himself. Virgil does in fact mention Priapus's custodial role against thieves in his canonical *Georgics* (IV, 110–111), as well as in his *Eclogues* (VII, 33–36), while, among the other authors canonized by Dante in Canto IV, Ovid twice tells the same anecdote of how the inflamed desire of ruddy Priapus was thwarted on the brink by the untimely braying of Silenus's ass in *Fasti* I, 391–440 and VI, 319–346, and Horace's *Satires* I, 8 is a monologue spoken in his person. One of the last priapic poems written in Latin is by the fourth-century Christian writer Prudentius.

The short fifty-sixth poem of the eighty *Carmina priapea*, to cite one of a number of possible examples, is a kind of inscription, meant to be pinned to his crudely carved and painted image, putting words into the mute idol's mouth. Before going on to threaten the thief with *irrumatio*, a punishment considered even more humiliating than *paedicatio*, the speaker begins: *Derides quoque, fur, et impudicum / ostendis digitum mihi minanti?* (So, thief, you make fun of me and thrust your shameless finger at me when I threaten you?). A recent Spanish editor, unlikely to have been thinking of Dante as he translated—though possibly influenced by the genre's frequent punning references to such metamophorical fruits—actually renders the proverbial *impudicum digitum* as the fig gesture: *Tú también, ladrón, te burlas y me haces la higa al amenazarte?* (Enrique Montero Cartelle, ed. *Priapeos, Grafitos amatorios pompeyanos, etc.* [Madrid, 1981]). The 1988 English version of poem LVI by W. H. Parker, despite its usefulness, elides in the present instance the notion of exorcistic reciprocality, reducing the thief to a rude schoolboy, by domesticating the sign, with doggerel inversion to boot, to "a snook you cock" (*Priapea: Poems for a Phallic God* [London], 154). If this interesting—possibly subliminal, though hardly sublime—source is added to those already hyperdetermining Vanni's unfriendly gesture, then this first silencing is also interpretable as the first reprise in Canto xxv of the *Über-bietung,* or outdoing topos (in the present case the gestural equivalent of the schoolyard taunt, "my priapus is bigger than your priapus"), a rhetorical motif encountered in the previous canto, in the poet's more purely literary dismissal of the bookish deserts of North Africa. It would certainly not be inappropriate, as the reader will soon see, for the god who was a symbol of nature's generative power, notorious chiefly for his disproportionate display of "the member that man hides" (116), of "what is best not named" (*Purg.* xxv, 44), to be evoked on the threshold of this particular canto.

Be that as it may, the vengeance of the Lord is swift, and Vanni's "glori-ous '*Up yours!*'" (as the incorrigible Almansi somewhat irreverently puts it) does not go unpunished for long. His blasphemous throat is garroted by one serpent, while another tightly rebinds his sacrilegious hands behind his back, as they were bound before his instant pulverization in Canto xxiv, which, distressing though it may have been, had at least served to free them temporarily for the insult or for the outrageous (and futile) gesture of affront and self-defense.

The apostrophe to Pistoia, "the den that suited" Vanni Fucci, has been held back until line 12, unlike the parallel address to Florence, which will open Canto xxvi, where, with five thieves to Pistoia's one, Florence will be complimented for a little outdoing of her own. Dante, who could not have foretold the self-destructive proclivities of the California voter, is of course being sardonic when he invites the Pistoian descendants of Catiline to de-cree their own incineration. That their world should end in ashes would, however, be appropriate *sub specie aeternitatis,* given the split-second disin-tegration of their favorite son we witnessed in Canto xxiv.

The composite monster Cacus has appropriately been called "the heraldic compendium of the canto" (Sanguineti). But it must also be ad-mitted that there is something armorially wooden about his lumbering late entrance, after the bird has flown; and Virgil's digressive thumbnail sketch, coming on the heels of the sarcastic aside to Pistoia, further interrupts the urgency of the narrative flow: an extended marginal gloss, as it were, that has slipped into the text. Cacus's voice may be the voice "not suited to form words" that we heard indistinctly in xxiv, 66 (Hollander). His appearance raises a number of questions. Is the fraudulent Centaur who dragged his stolen cattle by the tail to put his pursuer off his track a warder or an in-mate and, if a warder, are we to take it that he is the only one? It is not clear either whether the serpents on his haunch are passengers, assailants, or a permanent part of his anatomy, like the Gorgons' hair. (Cacus's mother was the Gorgon Medusa, drops of blood and venom from whose severed head, according to an etiologic legend dismissed as apocryphal by the skeptical Lucan, though this does not stop him recounting it in an extremely detailed digression [*Pharsalia* ix, 619–701], seeded the vast uncultivated wilderness of Libya, thereby engendering such a multifarious and ghastly crop of serpents.) In number Cacus's serpents outdo the vernacular *bisce* of Dante's own Tuscan Maremma, familiar local snakes that stand in the same relationship to the catalogue of exotically named fauna of XXIV, 86–87, as Flaubert's *sublime d'en bas* to his *sublime d'en haut.* Unlike them, the flame-throwing dragon appears to be a permanent fixture, a special-order option that the violent Centaurs of Canto XII had to do without. In his presentation of Cacus, Virgil is quoting himself. In the *Aeneid,* he had Evander recount the ruse and punishment of Vulcan's son, "of the half-human Cacus" (*semi-hominis Caci* [*Aeneid* VIII, 193]). It is Dante's interpretation of this last phrase that makes Virgil's ogre into a Centaur, and in the Latin poet the fiery breath came not from a dragon but from the giant's own mouth. Commentators are also quick to point out that, in contrast to the version given in Book I of Ovid's anecdotal *Fasti,* strictly speaking in Virgil's text the scourge of the Aventine receives his final comeuppance not by concussion but by strangulation. Hercules, however, is described by Virgil as setting out armed with his club and as showering a multitude of blows upon the thieving predator with a variety of weapons, so that the summary account given here is not all that unfaithful to Dante's chief *auctor.* Chief author, because of Dante's "figural" reading of the stoically pious pre-Christian Aeneas, and that hero's creator's consequent textualization as Dante's guide. Not surprisingly, however, the poet's envisioning memories, so to speak, of the more graphic Ovid are actually statistically superior, an intertextual presence of which the present canto is about to provide a striking example.

The fifth *bolgia* is the most memorable locus in the *Inferno* of Dante's grotesque expressionistic sublime. It is also the place where Dante (who might have answered Eliot's question "What is a Classic?" much as Eliot himself might, with a curt but courteous "I am"), having been welcomed already in Canto IV into the company (canon) of his five major classical *auctores*—Homer, Virgil, Horace, Ovid, and Lucan—finally puts himself through his paces, overtly challenging, indeed "outdoing," at least two of them.

Vanni Fucci's incineration in Canto XXIV is on a par with, say, the liquefaction of Lucan's Sabellus. In order to set the stage for the final showpiece (the surreal telemorphic exchange of shapes between Buoso and the serpent), the first of the two metamorphoses depicted in hallucinatory detail in this canto (the perverse fusion of man and serpent into a single monstrous hybrid) appears to have been deliberately modeled on an episode from Ovid, a classic in the annals of sexual harassment, implicitly presented as one of the Latin poet's crowning achievements, the outer limits of his art. Dante, having imitated the theme with gruesome (we might call them "Lucanian") variations, will then proceed, with his next descriptive exploit, to go beyond it. Alcithoe, the teller of Ovid's tale, proclaims its novelty ("it is a newer tale that I'll recite" [120]), a challenge our poet will pick

up on later with the leave-taking *novità* (novelty, newness; "strangeness")
of Italian line 144, which echoes the *novitas* of *Metamorphoses* IV, 284, applied this time by Dante to his own creation.

Ovid's story tells how Hermaphroditus, the son of Hermes and
Aphrodite, attacked as he bathed by the amorous naiad Salmacis, coalesced
with her to become the bizarre hermaphrodite, how he went, that is, from
a perfectly normal doubleness, the spitting image of both Mom and Dad
("in his face / one saw his father and his mother traced" [121]), to an unnatural freakish compound ("so were those bodies that had joined / no
longer two but one—although biform: / one could have called that shape
a woman or / a boy: for it seemed neither and seemed both" [124]). As this
sample quotation shows, Dante's description follows Ovid quite closely,
privileging, however, horror and strangeness over beauty, and substituting
for Ovid's mannered eroticism the concretely realistic, oppressively *material*
mode that characterizes Dante's style in lower Hell. The ivy simile, for example, is from Ovid (who also significantly likens the clinging Salmacis to
an entwining *serpent,* as well as to an octopus); the hot wax and the splendidly observed burning paper, whose everyday familiarity serve to render
the grotesque interpenetration even more uncanny, are Dante's own,
though we may recall the melting away of the limbs of Lucan's Sabellus,
compared by the Latin author to that of snow before the warm south wind
or wax beneath the sun. (Outside Hell, incidentally, Dante's use of the
term *cera* [wax] is exclusively metaphorical and designates the earthly subjects disposed to receive the seal of divinely imposed *form.*) The major innovation in Dante's rewriting of this total androgynous *union with the other*
(see Barthes's *Fragments*) to which all lovers claim to aspire (there is already
a suggestion of *contrapasso* in Ovid's cautionary tale) is to have the two
halves of the resultant amphimixis come from two reproductively incompatible species, two species indeed whose very association is the object of
a biblical taboo. One extratextual quotation should suffice: "And the Lord
God said unto the serpent: Because thou hast done this, thou art cursed
among all cattle, and beasts of the earth: upon thy breast shalt thou go, and
earth shalt thou eat all the days of thy life. I will put enmities between thee
and the woman, and thy seed and her seed: she shall crush thy head, and
thou lie in wait for her heel" (Genesis 3:14–15).

Birth, procreation, and death. These are the central mysteries of our being in the world. If, in reverse order, Vanni Fucci's instantaneous falling to
dust can be read as a fast forward parody of death and decay ("dust thou art.
and into dust thou shalt return" [Genesis 3:19]), the coupling of Cianfa and
Agnello (not surprisingly, given the erotic Ovidian subtext) is a monstrous
parody of fecundation, or rather of a failure to fecundate, while the final
parodic transubstantiation, which begins at the umbilicus ("the part where
we first take our nourishment" [86]), simulates a monstrous de-gestation,
a de-*formation* or unbirthing. The word "transubstantiation" has of course

a precise theological meaning and, however apposite to the present circumstance, given the considerable philosophical overlap between the terms "substance" and "nature," is used here ironically. In the eucharistic transubstantiation the inferior species is transformed to the higher, whereas here the opposite is the case. Dante will encounter transformations of a purely theological nature at key points in his upward journey: in the Earthly Paradise, the adamitic Dante will perceive the symbolically alternating hypostatic natures of the griffin mirrored in the eyes of the allegorical Beatrice (*Purg.* xxxi, 121–126), while at the height of Paradise, knowing even as he is known, the metamorphosis will finally become subjective (*mutandom' io* ["even as *I* altered" (*Par.* xxxiii, 114; my italics)]), and the sainted Dante will be vouchsafed the visionary mutability to see the three-personed Godhead for the *Imago hominis* he really is. (See my second epigraph).

Though I stand with those who believe that reptile and human forms alike represent damned shades, that, in the economy of the canto, as Skulsky, puts it, there is simply not enough humanity to go around, and that the panic-striking horror of the thieves' eternal fate lies precisely in the knowledge that they are eternally vulnerable, forever poised on the brink of their own bestiality, their identities precarious, "with no hope of a hole or heliotrope" (xxiv, 93), subject at any time to "change / and rechange" (142–143), back and forth among *any* of the three terrifying mutations (and possibly more), yet, in the order in which the author Dante—merciless here, and as mathematically detached in the construction of his wonderland as any Lewis Carroll—presents them, there is a ruthless escalation, a climax of symbolic unbecoming, which says to the sinners: you died and did not die, you were conceived and misconceived, begotten and misbegotten, better for you had you never been born. Identity is snatched and stolen, but ahead lies an eternity of *survival,* intermittent but inescapable; and the liberation of annihilation, the "second death," will only be proffered—Tantalus-like—and then denied. The immortal soul, with its three faculties of memory, understanding, and now unfree will, lives on, in either of the two material forms, as snake or sinner. "Never to be, never to be, no more," the mutant souls might almost sigh, with Pascoli's riddling *fin de siècle* Odysseus, "but without death, than to exist no more" (*Non esser mai, non esser mai, più nulla, / ma meno morte, che non esser più*).

The text enacts verbally the loss of selfhood it describes. After the disappearance of Cacus, for the remainder of the canto (building to a climax in the final reciprocal transmutation), the repetition of the indefinite pronouns—"one of them" (42, 85), "the other" (42, 92, 111, 120, 121, 134), "one of the three" (51), "the other two" (67, 83), "each one" (67), "the one" (88, 121), "one" (92, 119), "each of them" (123), "the other one" (138), combined with various other merely deictic nouns ("the serpent" [*passim*], "the wretch" [117], etc.) and circumlocutions ("he who stood up" [124], "he who was lying down" [130], etc.)—underscores the completely random and anonymous election and mutation of the victims described in the present canto. Even the bodies themselves, the *corps morcelés*, with their mere *disjecta membra*, alienated from the whole being that is more than the sum of its parts, are subject to an impersonal enumerative gaze. Furthermore, except for Vanni Fucci, who identifies *himself*, and cripple or lame Puccio ("Sciancato" is a nickname not a proper name and should probably be translated as such), who escapes the theft of personhood for the moment only to have his presence among the thieves exposed by the poet himself in xxv, 148, their names—Cianfa, Agnello, Buoso—come up quite by chance and only in the exclamatory speech of their fellow sufferers. The shades named in Canto xxv will in fact be referred to by these first names only— and at that when they are not yet or no longer humanly present (if they can ever be said to be really present). Their identifying patronymics are purposely withheld. The confusion this creates in the reader (Who does what with what and to whom?) is deliberately orchestrated. The earliest commentators, writing only a short time after Dante's death, conscientiously attempted to sort out what they saw as the mess, to put a stop to all this anonymity, but they didn't have much to go on. Four first names, one linked to a nickname, an obscure periphrasis ("the other one made you, Gaville [a minor Tuscan placename], grieve" [151]), and the fact, brought out at the beginning of Canto xxvi, that the thieves of Canto xxv were all Florentines. Their identifications are arbitrary and their glosses for the most part mere embroidery, speculative elaborations on Dante's text. (Benvenuto goes so far as to question lame Puccio's career decision to become a thief, since his handicap meant he was constantly getting caught!) Subsequent editors have equally conscientiously—after all, it's their job—repeated their extremely suspect glosses, completely missing Dante's point, which was to illustrate the biblical *lex talionis* by stealing the thieves' textual identities even as his narrative robs them of their forms.

The second of the two hideous metamorphoses is preceded by Dante's famous explicit challenge to two of his authors. This is in fact Dante the rhetorician's second official silencing of his predecessors, his second recourse to the *cedat, sileat, taceat nunc* topos exemplified in Curtius's classic work (162–165). The first, we earlier reminded the reader, occurred implicitly at xxiv, 85–90 ("Let Libya boast no more about her sands . . . "), where the landscape and its denizens were already purely literary, and Libya's boast was actually Lucan's boast, and Lucan was, for the time being metonymically and anonymously, gone one better. But while the previous reference had been oblique, transparent only to the connoisseur, part of the genealogical striptease by which the poet alternately conceals and reveals his intertexts, here Dante names names. The graphic account that follows, like the one just completed, will combine descriptive traces gleaned from both models, Ovid's fabulous resource of fantasy with Lucan's unflinching (some would say "morbid") pathological curiosity. And, if we set aside

Vanni Fucci's miraculous resuscitation, his reduction to dust in Canto xxiv had been an essentially Lucanian transformation—a competitive variation offered by Dante, on the already extensive catalogue of venom-induced medical freaks rehearsed by Lucan in Book ix of the *Pharsalia*.

An interesting insight into the moralistic strain in American Dante criticism is the recent revival, apropos of Dante's use of the Ueberbietung topos, of the controversy mentioned by Curtius as having taken place in the first half of the twelfth century (antedating Dante's text, then, by a good century and a half) as to whether hyperbolic panegyric is ethically permissible. (The one-upmanship issue is further complicated in Dante's case by the fact the panegyric is directed at himself.) Before accusing Dante of "problematic virtuosity," however, or defending him against the accusation, let us examine more closely the nature of his "boast." Apart from being a variant on the traditional rhetorical armamentarium, what precisely does Dante's claim to novelty consist in? It is not that Dante is claiming to be a better poet or a better inventor of metamorphoses than Lucan or Ovid. Certainly, he is underlining a difference in kind. Whereas Ovid had described the transformation of the same quantity of matter, usually beginning as a person, from one form to another, from an initial to a later form, a before to an after—Cadmus to Cadmus as serpent, Arethusa to Arethusa as spring: fantastic transformations indeed, but nonetheless conceivable within the economy of a materially and temporarily finite universe—what Dante witnesses or claims to have witnessed is the mutual transformation of two individuals, occurring simultaneously at a distance, in which what changes is, he asserts, not merely the external form or disposition of their matter (the Scholastic "act"), but the "matter" itself.

Ovid had described various metamorphoses of X into a new form of X and the case, involving the nymph Salmacis and the boy Hermaphroditus, of the fusion of X and Y into a hybrid $X + Y$ that was both and neither. The latter description had in fact formed the subtext, as we have seen, of the fusion of Cianfa (in noncopulable anguineous form) with Agnello in lines 49–78. What he had never described was the separate and simultaneous "telemorphic" transformation of X into Y and Y into X. Dante subtly underscores the originality of what he is about to let fly by citing in his *taceat* a pair of names from Lucan's *Pharsalia* (Sabellus and Nasidius, both of whom died horridly transformed by snakebite) and a pair from Ovid (Cadmus and Arethusa, the latter chosen in part, it has been suggested, because her subsequent form as fountain, or *fonte,* fits the Italian triple rhyme, though Salmacis—as Curtius remarked to Contini, *Dante war ein grosser Mystificator*—gave her name to a fountain too), but the textual pairings here are quite arbitrary and casual, since the characters referred to, unlike Dante's, underwent *separate* not reciprocal transformations.

Moreover, Dante is, as we remarked, at pains to point out that what the astonished pilgrim witnesses, and what he as poet describes, is not merely a trans-*form*-ation but a trans-*material*-ization. Of course Dante was aware that the two terms are philosophical abstractions, that in fact matter does not in practice exist without form: matter, he might have put it, in scholastic philosophical terms, is *for form*. This is exactly what makes the coming exchange "impossible." Two beings, then, belonging to two different "natures," one human and one ophidian or serpentine, will swap their individualized "matter," inseparable from the principle that determines each of their specific forms, that which makes them what they are, the principle known in technical language as the "principle of individuation." In this reverse-projection parody of fetal growth or generation, a fully formed man is unmade and at the same time develops the physical characteristics of a serpent while, separately and at a distance, but with mysterious mutuality, a serpent loses its identity as a serpent and becomes a man. What is exchanged, moreover, are not the specific forms of the two individuals. Buoso does not become the "blazing little serpent" who attacked him, nor does the attacking serpent become Buoso. Instead, the serpent takes on human form with the specific features of another thief, or, to put it another way, another thief, previously transmaterialized, exactly as Buoso is now, into a serpent, is temporarily restored to his *own* human nature. (That the serpent too would be recognizably different is my inference. Dante's gaze being anthropocentric, he is understandably less interested in the before and after snapshots of the reptile, and his text is silent regarding the alien taxonomy.) In all of this, there is, if we look still more closely, a further paradox. In the fiction of the *Comedy*, neither the "serpent" nor the "man" Dante is describing is or has any matter or material existence at all. They are both *shades*.

It will take Dante a long time to face this last problem head-on, but he will eventually get around to it, and it can hardly be coincidental that he will get around to it exactly one canticle, so to speak, later, in Canto xxv of *Purgatorio*, signaling the connection, and the importance of what is described there to the understanding of what is described here, by the repetition, among other textual features, of the same triple rime, *bocca, tocca, scocca*, encountered at *Inf.* xxv, 92–96, in a different order, *scocca, bocca, tocca* (*Purg.* xxv, 17–21). Here, finally, the explanation that subtends the entire *Inferno*, and *Purgatorio* too, is delegated to another poet, Statius, who was, according to Dante at least, both classical and Christian (who indeed owed his Christianity to his pagan precursor and model Virgil). Perhaps coincidentally (since the formula is not infrequent at didactic moments), his speech ("Open your heart to truth we now have reached" [*Purg.* xxv, 67]) will echo the thief Vanni's injunction ("open your ears to my announcement, hear" [*Inf.* xxiv, 142]). What he will describe, in an extraordinarily beautiful and moving first foretaste of the inspired scientific poetry of *Paradiso*, is the natural generation of the human body and its various metamorphoses within the womb, guided by the inherited *virtù formativa* ("the power that gives *form"* [*Purg.* xxv, 89; my italics; and see also *Purg.* xxv, 41])—which is already the inchoate *soul*—followed by the direct supernatural intervention of God to perfect that soul, to endow it with the capacity for memory and intelligence and will (and we might add, casting a cold eye back on Malebolge, for their fraudulent abuse):

> then the First Mover turns toward it with joy
> on seeing so much art in nature and
> breathes into it new spirit—vigorous—
>   which draws all that is active in the fetus
> into its substance and becomes one soul
> that lives and feels and has self-consciousness.
>
> (*Purg.* xxv, 70–75)

God, to put it another way, makes of "the animal . . . a speaking being" (*Purg.* xxv, 61–62). And suddenly the insistence upon silence in *Inf.* xxv also finds an explanation—the reduction of speech to shouted question, shrill cry, and inarticulate animal-like spluttering ("the other one, behind him, speaks and spits" [138]). Articulate speech, the prerogative of reason, is the sign of what makes us human. These souls, who want discourse of reason, are right to brag they are brute beasts. The informing virtue that survives the first death has been too debilitated to continue to imprint their human seal upon the air. The mutable loss and reappearance of their human identities, their exits and their entrances, as it were, into a finite reservoir of humanness, existing alongside the store of reptilian nature in which they also share, may even suggest that Dante, God, or the Counterpassman is engaged in a parody of the Averroistic heresy of a separate "possible intellect" or communal soul—the very heresy exploded in *Purg.* xxv—comparable to his sport in Canto x with the Epicureans, when he entombed the immortal souls they had thought mortal.

To get back to Dante's "boast," brag, or overbidding. What recent critics, who have alternately accused Dante of and defended him against the charge of "problematic virtuosity" (presumption, hubris, or reprehensible pride in his inventive genius), fail to take into account is that the virtuosity of Cantos xxiv and xxv, as elsewhere in the *Comedy*, is not Dante's but God's. This was in a sense clearer in Canto xxiv, where Dante issued his first challenge, his first outdoing, silencing not a poet but a series of exotic (and ultimately literary) places—the anything but deserted deserts of Libya, Arabia, and Ethiopia—whose herpetological fauna were no match for the "dreadful swarm" (xxiv, 82) of serpents with which the architect of Hell has stocked the seventh *bolgia* of the eighth circle. Within the fiction of the *Comedy* (wasn't it Charles Singleton who said somewhere that the fiction of the *Comedy* is that it is not a fiction?), whose author aspires to be no more than the scribe of God, surely the point is that the imminent third metamorphosis of the thieves will be transcendent, not because Ovid, unlike the better poet Dante, could never have imagined or invented it, but because Ovid was never given the opportunity to describe a metamorphosis comparable to the one to which Dante is now called upon to witness. Because what Dante is about to describe goes beyond and against every scientific principle of the natural world, splitting the Aristotelian atom of the *synolos* and separating the metaphysically inseparable *eidos* and *hyle,* form and matter, and because it was revealed to him in the otherworld by an omnipotent Christian God to whom all things are possible: "Oh, how severe it is, the power of God / that, as its vengeance, showers down such blows!" (XXIV, 119–120). So much should in any case have been obvious from the text, since the *nunc sileat* topos (interpretable as authorial presumption) is canceled out by the *serum deficit* topos of authorial modesty in the closing lines of the canto ("may the strangeness plead for me / if there's been some confusion in my pen" [143–144]). The trouble is—and here's the old catch-22—a boast is a boast is a boast, but a topos of modesty will invariably be read as a topos of *false* modesty. So, Dante, let's face it. As a poet you can't win. You joined the Doctors' and Apothecaries' Guild. Did you ever think of becoming a real druggist?

BIBLIOGRAPHY

The English versions of the lines from Ovid are taken from Allen Mandelbaum's translation of *The Metamorphoses of Ovid* (New York, 1993), to which the accompanying page numbers refer. Dante knew the work as *De rerum transmutatione.* The National Gallery in London has a painting by Cornelis van Haarlem representing Cadmus's followers devoured by a dragon, a visualization of Ovid that would not be out of place as an illustration to this canto. My conviction that the three types of metamorphosis described lie randomly in wait for all the shades, besides being more satisfying dramatically, has the added advantage of making speculative subdivisions among the various kinds of theft punished in the *bolgia*—a problem that has preoccupied a number of commentators—unnecessary.

The classic close readings of this and the preceding canto are those of Attilio Momigliano and Edoardo Sanguineti. Italian exegetes in general tend to highlight the philological, stylistic, narrative, and historical quiddity of the text rather than deploy their ad hoc learning in divinity. Even in a less purely narrative canto, I too would tend to avoid as far as possible foregrounding theological and scriptural precedent, preferring to stick to the letter, (a) because I become ever less convinced of the usefulness of the notion that the allegory of the *Comedy* is that it is not an allegory, and (b) despite, or perhaps on account of, being brought up, like James Joyce, by the English Jesuits (the comparison with Joyce stops there), and having an English Jesuit hero—an associate of Guy Fawkes—in the family, I confess to finding the view of Dante as orthodox casuistical theological whiz-kid somewhat fossilizing and restrictive, and (c) because readers so inclined will find plenty to satisfy their craving in previous (and I suspect subsequent) readings.

Since the very earliest commentators, these cantos have attracted—perhaps because of their uncomfortable contents and the apparent doctrinal aporia in the text—considerable ingenious speculation, for which Virgil's simile in Canto XXIV ("as smoke . . . to air or foam to water" [51]) often seems apt. [No, of course I don't mean *your* reading!] Particularly on this side of the Atlantic, the abstract side of Auerbach's "figuralism" tends to be privileged at the expense of the concrete, and Dante made the victim of a rampant (and ultimately trivializing) intentional fallacy—seamless, canonical (in every sense of the word), and dead, another dish on the buffet of cafeteria religion. Homer may nod and the pope may be fallible, but not our Dante—the Anglo-Saxon Protestant Dante, that is, not for heaven's sake that opinionated thirteenth-century Florentine Catholic with a photographic memory who just happened to be one of the world's greatest poets.

Like war to the generals, Dante—maybe even theology—is too important to be left to the Dantists. It took a classicist, Leonard Barkan, to make the most, not only of Dante's connections to his authors, but also, reading Dante with Dante, of the retrospective light the metamorphoses of *Purg.* xxv throw upon the present canto. Despite the references in Hawkins and Kirkpatrick among others, I had felt till I read Barkan that some of what I was saying was relatively new. Vittorio Russo, for example, who has written important *lecturae* on both *Inf.* xxv and *Purg.* xxv, had failed to exploit the connection. Not so Barkan, whose reading of the first in the light of the second is exemplary.

Having failed to say something new, therefore, I must now fall back on the *pis aller* of trying to satisfy at least Robert Ellrich, who once expressed the hope that someday someone would compile a bibliography for Canto xxv as complete as Bruno Maier's for Canto xxiv. The following list contains only twentieth-century sources, with the exceptions of Moore and Dobelli, who appear to have been the first (so late in the day) to point out, independently, the correct Ovidian subtext for the fusing of Cianfa and Agnello, so frequently rediscovered since. The names of Ovid and Lucan, incidentally, are coupled again by Dante in his *Monarchia* (ii, vii, 10). I take for granted all of the standard commentaries—from Jacopo Alighieri down to Anna Maria Chiavacci Leonardi (Milan, 1991)—and the relevant entries in the *Enciclopedia dantesca,* as well as the antiquarian research on Vanni Fucci and Dante's Pistoia listed, for example, in De Robertis (38).

Ahern, John. "Nudi Grammantes: The Grammar and Rhetoric of Deviation in *Inferno* xv." *Romanic Review* 82 (1990): 466–486.
———. "Troping the Fig: *Inferno* xv, 66." *Lectura Dantis* 6 (1990): 80–91.
Almansi, Guido. "I serpenti infernali." In *L'estetica dell'osceno,* 37–88. Turin, 1974.
Anselmi, Gianmario. "L'incipit di *Inferno* xxv e i *Carmina priapea." Studi e problemi di critica testuale* 48 (April 1994): 83–86.
Anzalone, Ernesto. *Il canto xxv dell'"Inferno."* Caltanissetta: Pietrantoni, 1906.
Auerbach, Erich. "Dante's Addresses to the Reader." *Romance Philology* 7 (1954): 268–278.
Barkan, Leonard. "*Taccia Ovidio:* Metamorphosis, Poetics, and Meaning in Dante's *Inferno.*" In *The Gods Made Flesh: Metamorphosis and the Pursuit of Paganism,* 137–170. New Haven, 1986.
Barolini, Teodolinda. "Arachne, Argus, and St. John: Transgressive Art in Dante and Ovid." *Mediaevalia* 13 (1987): 207–226.
———. *Dante's Poets: Textuality and Truth in the Comedy,* esp. 223–226. Princeton, 1984.
———. "Narrative and Style in Lower Hell." *Quaderni d'Italianistica* 8 (1990): 314–344. Reprinted in *The Undivine "Comedy": Detheologizing Dante* (Princeton, 1992), 74–98.
Batard, Yvonne. *Dante, Minerve et Apollon: Les images de la "Divine Comédie,"* 140–144. Paris, 1952.
Boyde, Patrick. *Dante Philomythes and Philosopher: Man in the Cosmos.* Cambridge, 1981 (esp. chs. 10 and 11).
Capetti, Vittorio. *Lectura Dantis: Il canto xxv dell'Inferno.* Florence, 1913.
Capo, Oreste. "Il canto xxv dell'*Inferno.*" In *Lectura Dantis Romana.* Turin, 1959.
Chiampi, James T. "The Fate of Writing: The Punishment of the Thieves in the *Inferno.*" *Dante Studies* 102 (1984): 51–60.
Ciafardini, Emanuele. "Nella bolgia dei ladri." *Rendiconti della R. Acc. Naz. dei Lincei. Classe di Scienze morali, storiche e filologiche,* 5th s., 32 (1923): 217–237.
Cohen, Louise. "Le mythe du serpent." *Revue des études italiennes,* n.s., 11 (1965): 40–84.
Corsi, Florido. "La bolgia dei ladri (canti xxiv e xxv dell'*Inferno).*" *Quaderni di Cultura del Liceo-Ginnasio Galvani* 3 (1965): 225–246.
Curtius, Ernst Robert. *European Literature and the Latin Middle Ages* (1948). Trans. Willard R. Trask. New York, 1953 (for the "overbidding" [*Überbietung*] topos, see 162–165).

De Amicis, Edmondo. "Il canto xxv dell'Inferno e Ernesto Rossi." In *Capo d'anno: pagine parlate*, 191–208. Milan, 1902.

De Robertis, Domenico. "Lo scempio delle umane proprietadi (*Inferno*, canti xxiv e xxv, con una postilla sul xxvi)." *Bullettino storico pistoiese* 81 (1979): 37–60.

Dobelli, Ausonio. "Intorno ad una fonte dantesca." *Bollettino della Società dantesca*, n.s., 4 (1896–1897): 16–17.

Ellrich, Robert J. "Envy, Identity, and Creativity: *Inferno* xxiv–xxv." *Dante Studies* 102 (1984): 61–80.

Ferrero, Giuseppe Guido, and Siro A. Chimenz. "Il canto xxv dell'*Inferno*." In *Nuova Lectura Dantis*, ed. S. A. Chimenz. Rome, 1954.

Filomusi-Guelfi, Lorenzo. "La pena dei ladri." In *Nuovi studi su Dante*, 197–206. Città di Castello, 1911.

Floriani, Piero. "Mutare e trasmutare: Alcune osservazioni sul canto xxv dell'Inferno." *Giornale storico della letteratura italiana* 149 (1972): 324–332.

Fornaro, Pierpaolo. *Metamorfosi con Ovidio: Il classico da riscrivere sempre*. Florence, 1994.

Forti, Umberto. "L'embriologia fino all'età di Dante (aborto no, aborto sì)." *Cultura e scuola* 15, no. 57 (1976): 209–221 (the author appears to be unfamiliar with Russo 1971).

Gorni, Guglielmo. "Cino 'vil ladro': parola data e parola rubata." In *Il nodo della lingua e il verbo d'amore: Studi su Dante e altri duecentisti*, 125–139. Florence, 1981.

Grana, Gianni. "I ladri fraudolenti (*Inf.* xxiv e xxv)." *Lectura Dantis Romana*. Turin, 1959.

Gross, Kenneth. "Infernal Metamorphoses: An Interpretation of Dante's 'Counterpass.'" *MLN* 100 (1985): 42–69.

Guardini, Romano. "Les métamorphoses dans l'Enfer des voleurs." In *Dante visionnaire de l'éternité*, 229–251. Paris, 1966 (German original, 1958).

Hawkins, Peter S. "Virtuosity and Virtue: Poetic Self-Reflection in the *Commedia*." *Dante Studies* 98 (1980): 1–18.

Hollander, Robert. "Ad ira parea mosso: God's Voice in the Garden (*Inferno* xxiv, 69)." *Dante Studies* 101 (1983): 27–49.

Iannucci, Amilcare A., ed. *Dante e la "bella scola" della poesia: Autorità e sfida poetica*. Ravenna, 1993 (contains, among other important contributions, impeccably documented essays by Violetta de Angelis and Michelangelo Picone on Dante's Lucan and Dante's Ovid).

Jacoff, Rachel, and Jeffrey T. Schnapp, eds. *The Poetry of Allusion: Virgil and Ovid in Dante's "Commedia."* Stanford, 1991.

Kirkpatrick, Robin. "*Inferno* xxv." In *Cambridge Readings in Dante's Comedy*, ed. Kenelm Foster and Peter Boyde, 23–48. Cambridge, 1981.

Kleinhenz, Christopher. "Notes on Dante's Use of Classical Myths and the Mythographic Tradition." *Romance Quarterly* 33 (1986): 477–484.

Lombardi-Lotti, Mansueto. "Facere fileccham." *Lingua Nostra* 14 (1953): 63–64 (and see Leo Spitzer's reply, *Lingua Nostra* 15 [1954]: 13).

Mattalia, Daniele. "Canto xxv." *Lectura Dantis Scaligera*, 1:889–929. Florence, 1967.

Momigliano, Attilio. "Il significato e le fonti del canto xxv dell'*Inferno*." *Giornale storico della letteratura italiana* 68 (1916): 43–81. Partially reprinted in *Letture dantesche: Inferno*, ed. Giovanni Getto (Florence, 1955), 469–488.

Moore, Edward. *Studies in Dante, First Series: Scripture and Classical Authors in Dante*, 213. 1896. Reprint, New York, 1968.

Muresu, Gabriele. "I ladri di Malebolge (*Inferno* xxiv–xxv)." In *I ladri di Malebolge: Saggi di semantica dantesca*, 9–50. Rome, 1990.

Norton, Glyn P. "'Contrapasso' and Archetypal Metamorphoses in the Seventh Bolgia of Dante's *Inferno*." *Symposium* 25 (1971): 162–170.

Pagliaro, Antonino. "La settima zavorra." *L'Alighieri* 6 (1965): 2, 3–26. Reprinted in *Ulisse* (Messina-Florence, 1967), 1:325–370.

Palmieri, Pantaleo, and Carlo Paolazzi, eds. *Benvenuto da Imola lettore degli antichi e dei moderni*. Ravenna, 1991.

Paratore, Ettore. "Il canto xxv dell'*Inferno*." In *Nuove letture dantesche*, 2:281–315. Florence, 1968. Reprinted in *Tradizione e struttura in Dante* (Florence, 1968), 281–315.

Pasolini, Pier Paolo. "Vanni Fucci." *Paragone* 194 (April 1966): 156–164 (including a two-page reply from Cesare Segre).

———. "La volontà di Dante a essere poeta." *Paragone* 190 (December 1965): 57–71 (see Segre 1965; together these two articles, along with Pasolini 1966, constitute a polemical exchange across the chasm that separates a militant from an academic critic. Pasolini, whose view of Vanni Fucci is tributary to the interpretive tradition of Pound and his early model Robert Browning, reprinted his side of the argument with minor modifications in his *Empirismo eretico* [Milan, 1972; now available in English as *Heretical Empiricism*, ed. Louise K. Barnett, trans. Louise K. Barnett and Ben Lawton (Bloomington, Ind., 1988)]).

Pietrobono, Luigi. *Il canto xxv dell'"Inferno."* Florence, 1918.

Porena, Manfredi. "Parole di Dante: il verbo *abborrare.*" *Lingua Nostra* 14 (1953): 36–39.

Robson, C. A. "Dante's Use in the *Divina Commedia* of the Medieval Allegories on Ovid." In *Centenary Essays on Dante by Members of the Oxford Dante Society*, 1–38. Oxford, 1965.

Ronconi, Alessandro. "Per Dante interprete dei poeti latini." *Studi danteschi* 41 (1964): 5–44.

Russo, Vittorio. "A proposito del canto xxv del *Purgatorio.*" In *Studi di filologia romanza offerti a Silvio Pellegrini*, 507–543. Padua, 1971. Reprinted in *Esperienze e/di letture dantesche* (Naples, 1971),103–160 (I drew heavily on this article for my notes to *Purg.* xxv in the 1983 Bantam Classics Dante).

———. "La pena dei ladri." In *Sussidi di esegesi dantesca*, 129–146. Naples, 1966.

Sacchetto, Aleardo. "Il canto delle allucinanti trasmutazioni." In *Due letture dantesche*, 41–72. Rome, 1953. Reprinted in *Dieci letture dantesche* (Florence, 1960), 59–89.

Sanguineti, Edoardo. *Interpretazione di Malebolge*, 199–223. Florence, 1961.

Sansone, Mario. "Il canto xxv dell'*Inferno.* In *"Inferno": Letture degli anni 1973–1976*, ed. Silvio Zennaro, 615–641. Rome, 1977.

Scarano, Nicola. "Le trasformazioni dei ladri." In *Saggi danteschi*, 201–225. Livorno, 1905.

Segre, Cesare. "La volontà di Pasolini 'a' essere dantista." *Paragone* 190 (December 1965): 80–84 (see Pasolini 1965).

Shapiro, Marianne. "*Inferno* xxv." In *Dante's "Divine Comedy," Introductory Readings: Inferno*, ed. Tibor Wlassics, 319–331. Charlottesville, Va., 1990.

Skulsky, Harold. "Thieves and Suicides in the *Inferno*: Metamorphosis as the State of Sin." In *Metamorphosis: The Mind in Exile*, 114–128. Cambridge, Mass., 1981.

Sowell, Madison U. "Dante's Nose and Publius Ovidius Naso: A Gloss on *Inferno* 25.45." In *Dante and Ovid: Essays in Intertextuality*, ed. Madison U. Sowell, 35–49. Medieval and Renaissance Texts and Studies. Binghamton, N.Y., 1991.

Terdiman, Richard. "Problematic Virtuosity: Dante's Depiction of the Thieves (*Inf.* xxiv–xxv)." *Dante Studies* 91 (1973): 27–45.

Tomaselli, Angelo. "Il canto xxv dell'*Inferno.*" In *Miscellanea di studi critici in onore di Vincenzo Crescini*, 399–428. Cividale, 1927.

Vallone, Aldo. *Il canto xxv dell'Inferno.* Naples, 1983. Reprinted in *Lectura Dantis Neapolitana: Inferno*, ed. Pompeo Giannantonio (Naples, 1986), 487–503.

CANTO XXVI

Ulysses: Persuasion versus Prophecy

GIUSEPPE MAZZOTTA

Translated by Allen Mandelbaum and
Anthony Oldcorn

Canto XXVI tells mainly the story of Ulysses' tragic shipwreck as the hero ventures beyond the pillars of Hercules into uncharted seas. It is also true, however, that, perhaps more than any other canto in the *Comedy,* Canto XXVI cannot really be read separately from the others. In fact, so fascinated are the pilgrim and the poet by their encounter with the Greek hero that it will play a pivotal role in the dramatic economy of the entire poem: at key points of the narrative—from Dante's initial hesitation and fear lest his own journey prove *folle* ("wild and empty" [II, 35]) to his final survey, from the heaven of the fixed stars, of "Ulysses' mad course" (*Il varco / folle d'Ulisse* [*Paradiso* XXVII, 82–83; my emphasis])—Dante anticipates or recalls Ulysses' epic journey as the steady point of reference enabling the pilgrim to define the inner sense of his own quest.

Taken by itself, the story of Ulysses as told in *Inferno* XXVI is the focus of a number of Dante's intellectual and moral concerns, and it affords the poet a pretext to reflect on his own poetic strategies and poetic language. That Dante's imaginative stakes are high in this canto is exemplified by his own bold, radical revision of the essential structure of the classical version of the myth. He leaves no doubt that the mythic discourse of antiquity is to be read from a perspective that is alien to it.

According to the ancient tradition, which finds its crystallization in Homer's two epics, Ulysses is the supremely crafty hero who leaves his native Ithaca to fight for ten years in the Trojan war and, after the destruction of Troy, returns to Ithaca. Neoplatonic commentators interpreted Ulysses' journey away from Ithaca and back to Ithaca as a philosophical allegory of the *nostos,* the return of the soul to its place of origin after its descent into the dross of materiality and its subsequent laborious purification from it.[1]

In *Inferno* XXVI Dante breaks with this neoplatonic tradition. In Dante's representation Ulysses is no longer a paradigm of the successful philosophical flight of the soul to its divine homeland. Quite to the contrary: although Dante shows Ulysses as he frees himself from the magic lures of Circe and is about to return to Ithaca, Ithaca will no longer be Ulysses' final destination. Neither love for his wife and his family nor duty to his country can conquer in him the desire to know in their full range the splendors and miseries of the human experience. By this insistence on the necessity of moving into an unfamiliar, unexplored world, Dante breaks open the closed circle of Greek philosophical thought, replacing it with the conviction that harmonious, rational closures are fictions. Accordingly, Dante shows Ulysses as a visionary who arrives home only to set out again on a mad quest (the operative word is *folle,* 125) into the unknown world, in the tracks of the sun and with a few loyal companions.

Dante's Ulysses moves within this large conceptual framework, but Dante's narrative reinterprets the central assumptions of the myth. There is no return home for Ulysses from his new quest, and his journey into the unknown is a heroic, but ultimately tragic, violation of all boundaries and limits. For all his admiration of Ulysses, Dante exposes the limits of Ulysses' heroic vision. Along with Diomedes, Ulysses is the only epic hero among the fraudulent sinners (on either side of Ulysses are the five contemporary Florentine thieves of Canto XXV and the mercenary *condottiere* Guido da Montefeltro of Canto XXVII). Thus Dante establishes a dramatic contrast between the grandeur and singularity of the epic hero of antiquity and the petty, provincial, unheroic world of his own time. And yet, beyond the apparent differences of degree and achievement between them, all the sinners, Ulysses included, belong to the same moral area of fraud: Ulysses is really no better and no worse than a common Florentine thief.

Dante's ambivalent sense of the greatness and the limits of Ulysses (and of Greek philosophical discourse in general) is conveyed by a prodigious deployment of rhetorical machinery, at once complex and detailed. He unveils the covert strategies and subtle techniques of rhetorical persuasion, thereby uncovering also the hidden, murky basis of the seemingly luminous Greek *logos.* Rhetoric, in effect, affords the context within which Dante represents Ulysses' great claims for himself. It also allows Dante to reflect on the pretensions and possibilities of language to produce or adequately represent reality. From this standpoint, Canto XXVI shows Dante interrogating stylistic levels of representation, and the relation between political rhetoric and prophecy, and the links between rhetoric and ethics. More important, it shows Dante as he comes to terms with his own poetic claims and poetic authority.

The rhetorical substance of the canto comes immediately to the fore. The story it tells is that of a mind-bewitching orator who moves men by the power of his speech to the pursuit of the good and the true. Human beings, Ulysses claims, are not made to live like brutes but to follow virtue and knowledge (118–120). In making this statement, Ulysses casts himself as the rhetorician who fashions moral life: an Orpheus or a civilizing agent who assuages the beast within and sees life as an educational process. Ulysses, in short, embodies the values of Ciceronian rhetoric that reached Dante primarily through a text of political rhetoric composed by one of his ideal teachers: Brunetto Latini's *Retorica*.[2]

For Brunetto, as for Cicero in his *De inventione,* rhetoric is the foundation of history, in the sense that the political order of the city is rooted in the gift of language. Within their humanistic visions, the orator's language is a cohesive force that persuades men to move away from their original bestiality. Both Cicero and Brunetto are aware, to be sure, of the damage eloquent men can cause the state unless they possess wisdom and are moved by ethical ends. There is no doubt that one thematic strain of Canto xxvi focuses precisely on the concerns both Cicero and Brunetto articulate regarding politics and rhetoric.

The canto enacts an extended reflection on the fates of secular cities: Florence, Prato, Thebes, Troy, Rome and the quest for a "new land" (137) constitute the historical points of reference within which rhetoric emerges as a discipline capable of fashioning history. More specifically, the canto's opening lines (1–12) feature Dante's prophecy that the city of Florence will soon reach its apocalyptic end; while in its closing lines (136–142) Ulysses' vision of a new land climaxes in a catastrophe. Dante's understanding of rhetoric shuttles between the promise of a new city and the prophetic announcement of the destruction of the old one.

Furthermore, Dante casts Ulysses—for all his craftiness—as the rhetorician who lacks the attributes of wisdom called for by Cicero and Brunetto. Ulysses is shown at Troy as he steals the Palladium (63), the icon of Minerva or the simulacrum of wisdom and, grasping at its *appearance,* undermines his extended claim (98–99) of experience with the world as well as the vices and worth of men. Dante even seems to place Ulysses' experience within an ethical context:

> "When
> I sailed away from Circe, who'd beguiled me
> to stay more than a year there, near Gaeta—
> before Aeneas gave that place a name—
> neither my fondness for my son nor pity
> for my old father nor the love I owed
> Penelope, which would have gladdened her,

was able to defeat in me the longing
I had to gain experience of the world
and of the vices and the worth of men."
(90–99)

It has long been acknowledged that Ulysses dramatizes himself in this speech as another Aeneas. As he recounts his departure from Circe at Gaeta he explicitly mentions Aeneas: "before Aeneas gave that place a name" (93). The interpretive twist given by Ulysses to Aeneas's journey is remarkable. The hero's mission to be the carrier of tradition from Troy to Italy emerges as an activity of naming, his history-making a "poetic" mission as he names the island in memory of his dead nurse. Apparently, naming is the process by which man memorializes his world, marks his losses, as the world comes to be history, the place of man's nostalgic recollections. For Ulysses, however, to mention Aeneas's naming of places discloses a further irony: he disguises himself as Aeneas and identifies himself with the latter's *pietas*. Yet the priority he claims over the Trojan hero (*before* Aeneas, he says) reveals the illusoriness of the identification and underscores Ulysses' own failure to name. The canto, in general, exemplifies Ulysses' excessive rehearsal of geographic toponyms (103, 104, 110, 111), but as he comes closer to the unknown world, that world remains unknown to him, and his language collapses into merely temporal specifications.

But Ulysses' speech goes on to evoke the line of domestic affections that should have kept him at home but in which he cannot acquiesce. The lexicon is charged with ethical resonances—"fondness for my son" (94), "pity / for my old father" (94–95), "the love I owed / Penelope" (95–96)—that invoke public duty and private responsibilities in order to justify the supposedly higher moral imperatives of the journey. Yet Ulysses' journey is not an ethical quest nor is it a case of rhetoric joined to ethics. A sharper intimation of the divorce between rhetoric and ethics in the canto occurs when Ulysses defines the object of his quest as worth and knowledge (*virtute e canoscenza* [120]).

In effect, by having Ulysses equate virtue and knowledge as if they were the same thing, Dante retrieves the fundamental error of Socratic thought: the illusory belief that to know a virtue is tantamount to having that virtue. More than that, by making virtue the object of rhetoric Dante lays open the intrinsic error of rhetorical language: virtue is contained within the statement but its fulfillment lies outside that statement. In Canto XXVI Ulysses attempts to travel the distance that separates words from facts and to fill those words with reality.

The speech in which Ulysses narrates his experience forces on us Dante's sense of language. Ulysses evokes his journey between the shores of Spain and Africa, his trespassing beyond the pillars of Hercules, and then he recalls the "brief address" (*orazion picciola* [122]) he made to his companions:

> "'Brothers,' I said, 'o you, who having crossed
> a hundred thousand dangers, reach the west,
> to this brief waking-time that still is left
>   unto your senses, you must not deny
> experience of that which lies beyond
> the sun, and of the world that is unpeopled.
>   Consider well the seed that gave you birth:
> you were not made to live your lives as brutes,
> but to be followers of worth and knowledge.'
>   I spurred my comrades with this brief address
> to meet the journey with such eagerness
> that I could hardly, then, have held them back;
>   and having turned our stern toward morning, we
> made wings out of our oars in a wild flight
> and always gained upon our left-hand side.
>   At night I now could see the other pole
> and all its stars; the star of ours had fallen
> and never rose above the plain of the ocean.
>   Five times the light beneath the moon had been
> rekindled, and, as many times, was spent,
> since that hard passage faced our first attempt,
>   when there before us rose a mountain, dark
> because of distance, and it seemed to me
> the highest mountain I had ever seen.
>   And we were glad, but this soon turned to sorrow,
> for out of that new land a whirlwind rose
> and hammered at our ship, against her bow."
>   (112–138)

Ulysses' brief address is set within the imagined area beyond the known world, an open and unbounded region. The strategy of isolating language in a spatial vacuum discloses its peculiar feature. There is no necessary correspondence between *res* and *signa,* between things and their signs, nor is a sign the receptacle of a reality. Tragedy creeps into Ulysses' epic quest as he ventures from the known world to the forbidden land he approaches but never reaches. The vision of the mountain dark because of distance heralds a tragic denouement, couched in a stylized rhetorical definition of tragedy: "And we were glad, but this soon turned to sorrow." The line translates *verbatim* the formula "tragic song begins in joy and ends in grief."

The tragic reversal that shatters any illusion of a possible *return* of the hero is the truth underlying Ulysses' rhetorical seduction of his companions. The phrase "brief address" (*orazion picciola*) affects modesty; the apostrophe "Brothers" (*O frati*) draws Ulysses' companions into a state of complicity and flatters their worth by making them akin to the hero. The speech, moreover, is marked by hyperbole that throws into relief the grandeur of the quest and by a *captatio benevolentiae* that celebrates their common past achievements. The frequent and conspicuous enjambment (112–113; 114–115, etc.) and the cosmic dimensions of the directions (*giunti a l'occidente* ["reach the west"]; *di retro al sol, del mondo sanza gente* ["beyond the sun, and of the world that is unpeopled"]) stress the epic expansiveness of the experience. The recurrent sounds and alliterative modulations of the Italian text (*cento* [hundred, 112], *giunti* [reach, 113], *occidente* [west, 113], *sensi* [senses, 115], *rimanente* [lies beyond, 115], *esperïenza* [experience, 116], *mondo sanza gente* [world unpeopled, 117]—as well as *cento . . . occidente, sensi . . . sanza, rimanente . . . mondo*) create the persuasive harmonies of Ulysses' speech: the repetition of the same sound compels the rhythm to return on itself and creates an incantatory, suspended effect.

It is within this general belief of Ulysses that his language can bend the wills of his listeners and move them to action (as in fact it does) that we appreciate Dante's ironic stance regarding his hero's claims. One such irony is clearly visible in the choice of Virgil as the privileged interlocutor of Ulysses. Virgil provides the clue to the irony that will invest both himself and Ulysses when he insists that he—the author of "noble lines" (82), that is, Virgil's epic—should be speaking to Ulysses, the epic hero. The implication of the detail is clear: formal propriety ought to be observed, the epic poet is the proper interlocutor of the epic hero. Yet, in the canto that follows, Guido da Montefeltro's apostrophe, "O you to whom I turn my voice, / who only now were talking Lombard" (XXVII, 19–20), retrospectively undercuts the possibility of rigidly formalized levels of representation. In point of fact, Dante exemplifies and simultaneously abrogates the juxtaposition of the lofty language of the epic with the realities of the vernacular dialect. Separations of style, which classical rhetoric upholds in the conviction that to every subject matter corresponds a fixed level of style, is an empty fiction in Dante's Christian world.

The irony does not invest Ulysses alone: it also invests Virgil and his claim, made earlier in the poem, that he has written an *alta . . . tragedìa* (XX, 113). That claim, it may be remembered, was advanced in the context of the canto of the soothsayers, the sinners who perverted prophecy. The more immediate context was a debate on the origin of the name of Mantua, a city founded, as Virgil now affirms, by Manto, daughter of the Theban Tiresias. This statement contradicts the one Virgil himself made in the *Aeneid*. The privileged epic of Rome in other words contains errors that need correction, and by this token Virgil places in question his own authority.

For Dante, Ulysses' error far exceeds Virgil's. Whereas Virgil corrects himself, Ulysses is blind to the fact that he does not control language but is, to all intents and purposes, controlled by it. The detail of the tongues of fire that envelop and conceal the sinners and by means of which Ulysses tells his story (42, 48, 87 ff.) draws attention to Dante's ironic representation of the Greek hero. The tongue of fire in which Ulysses is enveloped is to be primarily construed as an instance of Dante's *contrapasso*. Ulysses had a fiery inward longing (*ardore* [97]), from which his desire to know originates. Now, ironically, he is *inside* the flame, trapped by it. There can be no doubt, however, that this tongue of fire has a number of other crucial resonances.

Commentators have traditionally stressed that the flames Dante sees in Canto xxvi are a pointed parody of the descent of the pentecostal tongues of fire upon Christ's disciples, and that Ulysses' sin of evil counseling is primarily a sin against the good counsel of the Holy Spirit. It might be added in this context that the production of sound through the metaphor of the wind (88) ironically recalls Acts 2:2 in which the descent of the Spirit is described as occurring in tongues of flames and to the sound of a mighty wind. The allusion to the inspirational *afflatus* prepares a sustained reflection on Ulysses' language and its relation to the prophetic word. It prepares, more important, a reflection on Dante's own poetic language, wavering as it does between prophecy and rhetoric.

The opposition between prophecy and rhetoric is underscored by the implied antithesis between Elijah and Ulysses obliquely announced at lines 34–39. As the pilgrim approaches the flame-wrapped sinners he recalls Elisha watching Elijah, the prophet who was borne up by a whirlwind in a chariot of fire. The terms of the comparison are such that Elijah is presented as the antitype of Ulysses, while Dante is like Elisha. These thematic contrasts are concerned with the contrast between spurious and genuine prophecy. This contrast is made more cogent by the fact that the tongue of fire is an image that describes both the gift of prophecy and the rhetorical craft. In Acts (2:30), for instance, the cloven tongues of fire designate the apostles' prophetic language. At the same time fire is the adornment of rhetoric in Alan of Lille's *Anticlaudianus*. In Canto xxvi the tongue of fire holds the rhetorician Ulysses as it did the prophet Elijah.

The double exegesis of the flame in terms of rhetorical and prophetic allusions dramatizes Dante's sense of the proximity of prophecy and rhetoric. It would seem that Ulysses' rhetoric, then, is the degradation of prophecy, or that prophecy is the norm from which Dante denounces the lies of rhetoric. Nonetheless, it is clear that Dante is also interested in showing the kinship between them, their dangerous sameness. Why would this be the case?

The opening lines of Canto xxvi feature Dante's own prophetic wrath against the city of Florence:

> Be joyous, Florence, you are great indeed,
> for over sea and land you beat your wings;
> through every part of Hell your name extends!

Among the thieves I found five citizens
of yours—and such, that shame has taken me;
with them, you can ascend to no high honor.
But if the dreams dreamt close to dawn are true,
then little time will pass before you feel
what Prato and the others crave for you.

(1–9)

Dante's poetic outburst is followed (23 ff.) by a moment of self-reflex-iveness on the part of the poet: threatened by the danger of his own poetic imagination, Dante is intent on bridling his creative powers: he will curb his talent (*'ngegno* in line 21 translates the Latin *ingenium,* the word for the po-etic faculty) lest it run unguided by virtue. The willed curbing of his talent or *ingegno* betrays Dante's suspicion that his own poetic undertaking may bear a likeness to Ulysses' rhetorical venture. Once again, as in Canto II, Dante fears that he may be reenacting Ulysses' mad quest.

But Dante's self-reflexiveness and self-government also reflect the prophetic outburst he voices against the city of Florence. At stake in the act of curbing his *ingegno,* then, there is Dante's consciousness that his voice constantly balances the claim of speaking with fiery prophetic self-assur-ance and the awareness that his prophecy is a contrived rhetorical act. Doubt accompanies the poet throughout his journey and it is the sign of the authenticity of his claims.

We can understand, finally, why the figure of Ulysses exerts such a sin-gular fascination on Dante and why the memory of Ulysses haunts the pil-grim long after he has moved beyond Canto XXVI. In spite of his fascination, however, Dante draws a sharp distinction between himself and Ulysses. Ulysses' journey ends in tragedy, and his deception ends up being a self-de-ception, a way of succumbing to the literalness of his language, of being trapped by his own tongue, of himself believing in promises on which he cannot deliver. Ironically, this craftsman of persuasion is spellbound by his own song, the way he is caught within the tongue of fire, the way he was spellbound by the song of the sirens (cf. *Purg.* XIX, 22).

Dante's posture in Canto XXVI is neither that of Ulysses nor that of Eli-jah. He forces on us another term of comparison for himself when he evokes the story of Elisha watching Elijah's ascent (34 ff.). Like Elisha, the witness to the ascent of Elijah, Dante now comes through as the fascinated spectator of mighty events and horrors. But, as every reader of the *Divine Comedy* knows, this self-contained spectatorial posture is not real. Unlike Ulysses and like Elijah, Dante will ascend beyond the sun and will see God face to face. And he will be gifted with the virtue the Greek hero lacked: the hard virtue that will allow him to make his way back from the loftiest jour-ney ever taken.

NOTES

1. The neoplatonic interpretation of Ulysses is advanced by John Freccero, *Dante: The Poetics of Conversion* (Cambridge, Mass, 1986), 136–151. Another important perspective on Canto XXVI is that of Bruno Nardi, *Dante e la cultura medievale* (Bari, 1949), 153–164.

2. A more detailed account of the rhetorical substance of the canto is available in Giuseppe Mazzotta, *Dante, Poet of the Desert* (Princeton, 1979), 66–106. Cf. also Giorgio Padoan, "Ulisse *fandi fictor* e le vie della sapienza," *Studi danteschi* 37 (1960): 21–61, reprinted in *Il pio Enea, l'empio Ulisse* (Ravenna, 1977), 170–204.

CANTO XXVII

False Counselors: Guido da Montefeltro

JENNIFER PETRIE

In Canto XXVII of *Inferno,* Dante and Virgil are in the same *bolgia* as in Canto XXVI, usually called the *bolgia* of the fraudulent counselors, although the sin punished in this section is never explicitly stated: We hear rather of the specific sins of individuals. Fraudulent counsel is, however, the sin of the main character here, Count Guido da Montefeltro, hidden like his fellow sinners in a tongue of "thieving" flame (127). Guido, count of Montefeltro and lord of Urbino, was a Ghibelline military leader, active mainly, but not exclusively, in Romagna, where he was a constant opponent of papal interests, and famous for his cunning and astuteness. He conducted a number of successful campaigns in the teeth of papal opposition, excommunication, and even a crusade mounted against him by Pope Martin IV. In his old age he made his peace with the Church and became a Franciscan friar. He died at Assisi in 1298.

In *Convivio* IV, xxviii, 8 Dante extols Guido as an example of the virtues of old age. In discussing the way in which innate nobility (*gentilezza*) develops over a lifetime, Dante describes the noble soul in old age as turning to God, like a ship coming into port. His most noble fellow Italian, Guido da Montefeltro (*lo nobilissimo nostro latino Guido montefeltrano*), lowered the sails of his wordly activities (*le vele de le mondane operazioni*) and entered religious life, putting aside all wordly delight and activity (*ogni mondano diletto e opera disponendo*). Here in *Inferno,* however, the *Convivio* judgment is reversed, probably on the basis of the early fourteenth-century chronicler Riccobaldo da Ferrara's account, which Dante may have known at first or second hand. Boniface VIII, warring against the Colonna cardinals, who had contested the validity of his election to the papacy, is said to have sought Guido's advice over finding a way of destroying the seemingly impregnable fortress of Palestrina. Guido allegedly advised generous promises that could subsequently be broken, a recommendation the pope adopted with success. In *Inferno* xxvii we learn that with this piece of fraudulent counsel, Guido returned to his "former sins" (71). He tells his story to Dante the pilgrim, never imagining that the latter is alive and can report it back on earth. Guido's long revealing monologue contains two grimly humorous pieces of dialogue with something of the tone of a morality play: the scene between himself and Pope Boniface and then the grotesque conclusion in which Saint Francis is deprived of Guido's soul by a devil-"logician" who leads the sinner before a raging Minos.

The pairing of Guido da Montefeltro with Ulysses in this episode, with its parallels and contrasts, has often been remarked upon. Ulysses, according to the fourteenth-century commentator Benvenuto da Imola, is guilty of dishonest astuteness in his own dealings. To it Guido adds fraudulent counsel in his dealings with others. Each tells his story, which is primarily a story of his last years and death. Ulysses is the proud Greek who must be invoked by Virgil; Guido is *latino* and may converse with Dante. In each case there is a misuse of old age, the time, as Dante says in the passage of the *Convivio* already mentioned, of lowering the sails and returning to port. The *Convivio* offers Guido as an example of one who did just that. Therefore, it is appropriate that Guido himself recalls it here:

> "But when I saw myself come to that part
> of life when it is fitting for all men
> to lower sails and gather in their ropes,
>   what once had been my joy was now dejection."
>   (79–82)

Ulysses, far from sailing quietly into port, wanders out beyond the known, populated world, while Guido's adoption of the virtues of a noble old age turns out to be a delusion.

The sins of this bolgia—*astutia,* misuse of intelligence, fraudulent counsel—however they are interpreted, seem to have a particularly strong effect on Dante. We see it particularly clearly in a passage in Canto xxvi, in which author and pilgrim seem unanimous:

> "It grieved me then and now grieves me again
> when I direct my mind to what I saw;
> and more than usual, I curb my talent,
>   that it not run where virtue does not guide;

so that, if my kind star or something better
has given me that gift, I not abuse it."
(XXVI, 19–24)

While this sentiment may apply especially to the case of Ulysses, it would
hardly be too far-fetched to relate the moral reflection to Canto XXVII as
well, in which the lesson to be learned involves the revision of a previously
held opinion.

As with Ulysses, though not to the same degree, the figure of Guido has
given rise to conflicting interpretations. Guido is one of the impressive ambivalent figures of the *Inferno*—either a tragic figure or a grimly comic one.
The former view sees him as the hapless victim of the scheming pope Boniface VIII, the true protagonist of the canto and Dante's main target. The
latter stresses the black humor of his situation—the deceiver deceived—and
the repeated irony of Guido's unavailing calculations.

A conspicuous feature of Canto XXVII is its use of direct speech, indeed
of dialogue. In the previous canto, Ulysses tells his story in a classical
"tragic" Virgilian manner. He speaks following a markedly formal invocation by Virgil. But there is no real exchange between Ulysses and the
poets. In Guido's case, the situation is different. He initiates the dialogue,
provokes a reply from Dante, answers a question. A relationship of sorts is
established. Meanwhile, Guido's story contains two lively examples of dialogue: the exchange with Boniface, and the taunting words of the devil.
Perhaps it is possible to see here an instance of a contrast between the high
"tragic" style, associated with Virgil, and the lower, stylistically mixed
"comic" manner of Dante.

Guido is presented as a figure of note and as a soul in pain. His *dolore* is
stressed as that of Ulysses is not, perhaps because Ulysses belongs to the
number of the *magnanimi* like Farinata or Jason who seem to despise the
pains of hell. Guido does not achieve this stature; an emphasis on pain
marks his appearance in the canto. He is first described by means of the
horrible simile of the Sicilian bull in which victims were burned, their cries
transformed into the bull's bellowing. The simile has a complex function,
as was noted very early (by Benvenuto for example). The use of a classical
analogy perhaps bestows a certain distinction on the as yet unnamed figure,
but this is offset by the emphasis on pain and its expression, and by the brutal, animalesque image. At the same time, the story alluded to, of the de-
signer becoming the bull's first victim, anticipates the case of Guido himself, a victim of his own deviousness. The authorial comment, "and this was
just" (8), implies already a certain distancing on Dante's part, a moral condemnation and a lack of sympathy. As the canto continues, it bears out the
impression.

Guido's first words (19–21) raise a problem of interpretation for modern
commentators. They express, like other such passages in the *Inferno,* the

recognition of the speaker as a fellow Italian. In Canto x, it is Dante who is recognized as Tuscan, but in this case Guido recognizes Virgil as speaking Lombardo and, rather oddly, quotes his dismissal of Ulysses as a piece of near dialect, uncharacteristic of the normally elevated style assigned to Virgil in the *Inferno*. While the early commentators did not apparently register any sense of incongruity, modern commentators have expressed surprise: Does it say something about Guido that he quotes—or perhaps paraphrases—Virgil's words in such a way? Or is Dante merely giving us a rather clumsy signal that this canto will involve a shift in style from the tragic mode of the previous one? Terraccini relates Guido's words to his own condition in hell, as they onomatopoeically suggest the hissing of flames, with the word *adizzo* perhaps creating associations with the similar *atizzo* (kindle a flame; poke a fire).

What is clear from the rest of Guido's opening speech is his passionate involvement in the Italy he has left behind, and perhaps his use of dialect indicates it. For him, as for many of the damned, it is the *dolce terra*. The memory seems not merely a nostalgic and beautiful contrast with hell but in some way part of the torment, because bound up with the sin ("from which I carry all my guilt" [27]). His eager question about the inhabitants of Romagna—are they at war or at peace?—expresses both this entanglement with his own world and also his state of ignorance of the present that is the lot of the souls in hell (x, 100–105). At the time of Guido's death, there had been the possibility of a peace settlement in Romagna through the mediation of Pope Boniface VIII. Guido wants to know what has come of it.

In its density of information, especially information about the speaker, Guido's opening speech is characteristic of Dante's skill in the use of direct speech and dialogue. Guido is, after all, a tongue of flame, and his tongue, literally, is everything. But a similar skill is evident in Dante's reply (36–54), which provides a shift in perspective. Guido's words are eager, passionate, and can invite sympathy: Dante's reply creates a distance and a certain coolness. Romagna becomes *Romagna tua* (37), a place with which the sinner is involved but, the pilgrim's words seem to imply, one alien to Dante. Its rulers are unsympathetically depicted as *tiranni*, always at war in their hearts, at present only deceptively making a show of peace. The account of the ruling families that follows uses their coats of arms to suggest both the imposing heraldic formality of *signoria* and a sinister, dehumanized, or bestial power: Images appear of hovering or brooding, of claws or talons. The impression of hostility and detachment on Dante's part is reinforced when the tone changes to one of formal courtesy as the pilgrim asks the sinner's identity, invoking, as often in the *Inferno*, his probable wish for fame on earth (55–57).

Guido's reply takes up the idea of fame but turns it into a possible fear of infamy (65–66). The introduction to his longest speech, in which he tells his story, is immediately revealing, all the more conspicuously because of the dramatic irony:

> "If I thought my reply were meant for one
> who ever could return into the world,
> this flame would stir no more; and yet, since none—
>   if what I hear is true—ever returned
> alive from the abyss, then without fear
> of facing infamy, I answer you."
>
> (61–66)

Dante is silent and remains so for the rest of the canto. He does not undeceive Guido. This silence seems a continuation of the distant hostility expressed towards Romagna and its lords. The ironic situation of the calculating man falling into the trap he thinks he has avoided is coldly surveyed, both at this point, and later as Guido's account unfolds.

Against the silence of Dante the character, Guido's words are extremely animated. He constantly interrupts himself or comments on what he has said. There is a certain angry bewilderment at all his plans being thwarted:

> "I was a man of arms, then wore the cord,
> believing that, so girt, I made amends;
> and surely what I thought would have been true
>   had not the Highest Priest—may he be damned!—
> made me fall back into my former sins;
> and how and why, I'd have you hear from me."
>
> (67–72)

What might seem a bitter assertion of his own credulity (68) is followed by the confidence that his plans would have succeeded if it had not been for Boniface. Similarly, in line 84, he claims that his repentance would have "helped." Guido gives the impression of constantly turning over the question of why his tactics failed. Calculation appears to be a substitute for morality.

Guido speaks for himself, and so for different readers or commentators he can appear as more or less persuasive. By his own account, he has been thwarted by the immoral and hypocritical cynicism (perhaps even moral and spiritual blackmail) of the pope. Yet equally apparent in his words are both his calculating deviousness and his awareness of what he is doing. There is a curious ambiguity in the style and tone of Guido's language, which gives rise to divergent descriptions of it. Bosco and Reggio draw attention to the Latinisms, to a tragic dignity of style. Kirkpatrick, on the other hand, sees linguistic convolutions or lapses of taste or tact as reflecting the speaker's wrong moral orientation; he quotes the ugly line 73, with its debasement of human bodily dignity: "While I still had the form of bones and flesh" (according to Bonora, who quotes another instance in Dante's poem "Tre donne 'ntorno al cor," line 84, this periphrasis belongs to ordinary colloquial speech).

Ambiguity, in fact, runs through Guido's speech. His words draw attention to his skill and fame as a tactician but tend to undermine any heroic image. His works, he tells the poets, "were not / those of the lion but those of the fox" (75). The lion and the fox, with their flavor of an Aesop fable, join the other animals of the canto. The foxy Guido's skills are, however, dignified by the biblical lines 77–78: "my renown / had reached the very boundaries of the earth" (ch'al fine de la terra il suono uscie), which recalls verse 4 of Psalm 18, as well as the words of Guido's opponent Pope Martin IV, in his proclamation of a crusade against the Ghibelline general. In the lines quoted above, the colloquial and abusive a cui mal prenda! coexists with the intellectual precision and the almost pedantic sounding choice of the Latin word in the phrase e come e quare.

In lines 79–84, Guido sums up his "conversion" in words that both recall Convivio IV, xxviii and hark back to the previous canto.

> "But when I saw myself come to that part
> of life when it is fitting for all men
> to lower sails and gather in their ropes,
>   what once had been my joy was now dejection;
> repenting and confessing, I became
> a friar; and—poor me—it would have helped."
>
> (79–84)

Guido avoided the error of Ulysses, of sailing into the open sea in his old age instead of returning peacefully to port. Nevertheless, performing the activities appropriate to old age has turned out to be no guarantee of a Christian death.

Guido lays the responsibility for the frustration of his plans at the door of Pope Boniface VIII, "the prince of the new Pharisees" (85), and for many commentators, the pope at this point comes to the center of the stage. Nevertheless, he is always seen through Guido's eyes—even though it may well be assumed that this perspective coincides largely with that of the author. Guido's words about the pope recall Inferno XIX and indeed anticipate the denunciations found in the Paradiso. Boniface scandalously "wages war" against fellow Christians (86); he forgets his own sacred office and orders as well as Guido's religious profession (91–93); he is in a fever of pride (97). There is no need to question the moral reliability of Guido's judgments in these lines, as they are so much in keeping with the rest of the Comedy. (The damned in hell rarely falter, when condemning the evils of

others.) However, Guido's account of his own part in the episode is more
ambiguous, precisely because he tells his story from what appears to be a
moral standpoint, of one severely critical of the pope.

By his telling, Guido was wisely silent when the pope first asked his advice, as the pope's words seemed mad (98–99). Boniface has been ironically
compared to Constantine (94–97), a comparison that perhaps highlights
that pontiff's imperial claims to universal temporal sovereignty. Guido, like
Pope Sylvester, had to "cure" him. The verb *guerir* (95, 97) carries considerable moral ambiguity, as the analogy hardly holds: Constantine was gen-
uinely cured of his leprosy, but Boniface's "cure" will in fact feed his pride.
This remark may be pure sarcasm or may reveal a flaw in Guido's moral
outlook: while the analogy holds in the case of the sickness, the opposite
is true in the case of the cure. At the same time, the simile offers a significant reversal of roles whereby the pope becomes emperor and the ex-war-
rior becomes pope.

In the dialogue that follows, Guido presents himself as persuaded to
commit his sin by the pope's "grave arguments" (106), that is the promise
of absolution and possibly the veiled threat of excommunication. His
words to Boniface indicate that he knows that what he is doing is a sin
(108–109). The pope, as he appears in his part of the dialogue, seems coolly
in command of the situation. Moreover, he evidently sees through Guido.
His preposterous proposal of absolution in advance will, he knows, be sufficient to overcome the latter's hesitations. He insists upon his powers with
an air of easy, even offhand arbitrariness:

> "You surely know that I possess the power
> to lock and unlock Heaven; for the keys
> my predecessor did not prize are two."
>
> (103–105)

While there is no explicit threat of excommunication, there is a somewhat
sinister, allusive tone in Boniface's words that might allow a listener to infer it. And yet we may ask whether Guido is an almost helpless victim of
spiritual blackmail or rather, as he himself implies, one who simply assumes
that to follow Boniface's *argomenti gravi* is in his best immediate interest.

The two keys represent the power of absolution and that of discern-
ment: Boniface is misusing both. The early commentators insist on this
point: as Benvenuto says, the pope can bind and loose, but not "with an
erring key." Dante himself in the *Monarchia* insists that the power of the
keys cannot be understood in an absolute sense: otherwise the pope "could
absolve me without my being penitent, which even God Himself could not
do" (*Monarchia* III, viii, 7). Perhaps if Guido misses the point it is because
God does not enter into his calculations.

While a hint of a threat may be present in the pope's words, what is more apparent is his cavalier tone: the almost casual reference to the power of the keys, and the sardonic allusion to Pope Celestine V, who failed to value them. This last slighting remark is relevant to the political background of Boniface's crusade. The election of Boniface following the abdication of Celestine had been contested by two Colonna cardinals, and it was against these that Boniface was fighting. The question of the validity of his election is raised by implication in a context in which Boniface is proposing an undoubtedly invalid use of his spiritual power.

Dante's own position on the question seems hard to determine. In the *Purgatorio*, the indulgences granted by Boniface in the jubilee year of 1300 have effect in the other world. Hugh Capet presents the arrest of Boniface by Philippe le Bel as the arrest of Christ in the person of his vicar. Yet in the *Paradiso* Saint Peter speaks of Boniface as a usurper: His throne is vacant in the sight of Christ. This may imply merely a moral judgment on Boniface's abuse of papal power rather than an invalid election, but the language is strong. The present context of *Inferno* XXVII seems to raise at least a doubt and to reinforce it with the spurious promise to "absolve" Guido.

Guido now realizes that his policy was the wrong one: Silence would have been more advisable. Instead he adopts the proffered escape clause:

> "*Padre, da che tu mi lavi*
> *di quel peccato ov' io mo cader deggio.*"

> "Since you cleanse me of the sin
> that I must now fall into, Father . . . "
> (108–109)

His escape clause is carefully spelled out. Bosco and Reggio note the irony of the word *Padre* (thus placing the focus back on Boniface). But we may note also the slow, cautious rhythm of his speech, somehow heightened by the repeated assonance of *Padre . . . lavi . . . peccato,* which highlights the key words. Guido's explicitness is a mark of his caution and a testimony against himself: he knows that he is about to commit a sin.

These words conclude Guido's life story. The scene shifts to introduce a new drama, after his death. Saint Francis comes to take him to heaven: appearances have been kept up so well, evidently, that even the saint is deceived! But one of the *neri cherubini* (i.e., an intellectual devil, as the cherubim represent wisdom) forestalls him: Guido is condemned for giving a fraudulent counsel (116). The devil then sets out the moral with sardonic logic:

> "one can't absolve a man who's not repented,
> and no one can repent and will at once;
> the law of contradiction won't allow it."
> (118–120)

Guido, we are to assume, with his intelligence, should have been equal to such basic rules of logic as the principle of non-contradiction. But perhaps he thought the devil could be fooled. "How I started / when he took hold of me and said: 'Perhaps / you did not think that I was a logician!'" (121–123).

The final character to appear and speak is Minos, consumed by a "great anger" (126), who consigns Guido to his place. The *gran rabbia* (126), has been variously interpreted. Commentators who see this canto as directed mainly against Boniface, see that pope as its object. Minos, then, is frustrated in that he cannot condemn the real villain. Yet Guido is condemned to a lower place in hell than Boniface, and a more obvious reading would see the anger as directed against Guido himself.

When Minos is introduced in Canto v, he utters a warning: take care whom you trust (19). The inhabitants of hell are not always to be relied on: appearances may be impressive but the reality otherwise. Appearances are deceptive in the case of Guido, a man who apparently died a holy death, and who finally tried to deceive the devils themselves. Minos's rage may well be at the man who dared try to outwit him.

The canto ends with Guido's pain and regret. Neither Virgil nor Dante (as poet or as pilgrim) makes any comment. Almost as if to underline this attitude of coolness the final lines introduce the next *bolgia*.

Guido then is left to the reader's judgment, or to that of the black cherub and Minos. They have no doubt about Guido's guilt. Guido himself blames Boniface, eloquently, and for some, persuasively. But a great deal can be brought against him.

For the early commentators, too, there is no doubt about Guido's guilt. Nevertheless, they anticipate the objection that Guido is merely obeying the pope, who has the power to bind and loose. Pietro Alighieri sees fit to summon a number of authorities to support his argument that just as God cannot sin, so the pope cannot legitimize sin. The devil's principle of non-contradiction is appealed to. In Benvenuto's allegorizing commentary, the devil represents Guido's bad conscience: Guido himself knows that his position is illogical. In fact, Benvenuto adds grimly, commenting on the words *come mi riscossi* ("how I started" [121]), Guido has sinned against the Holy Spirit in presuming on the hope of salvation.

The pope seems to receive Dante's censure, in this canto as elsewhere, for abuse of his office: crusading against Christians and pronouncing absolution when he cannot do so. He puts temptation in Guido's way, lending it weight with his "grave arguments." At least as far as appearances go, Guido's predicament is a difficult one: to remain silent would require moral courage—even though in the past, as a Ghibelline leader who twice incurred excommunication, Guido had shown that he was not a man to be afraid of going against the pope. Perhaps Guido views his "conversion" mainly in political terms, from being the pope's enemy to being his ally, from Ghibelline to Guelph as it were.

Dante's own political attitudes may provide a further comment on this canto. Dante opposed Boniface's ambitions in Tuscany, and in Florence in particular, and spoke against giving armed assistance to the pope. He refused to do what Guido did, that is, support the pope's political and military ambitions. Later, in the *Monarchia,* he was to take issue with Boniface's claims to universal temporal supremacy. This stand meant tackling the question of submission to the pope and the limits of the latter's powers, and it is interesting that in the context of this canto he illustrates the impossibility of absolving an impenitent sinner.

Dante's stand in the *Monarchia* is close to the Ghibelline position, of strict separation of temporal and spiritual power. Yet he remained critical of the Ghibelline party, as is clear from Justinian's words in *Paradiso* VI. The Ghibellines appropriated the Roman eagle, the "universal emblem" (100), for partisan ends; they should adopt another sign:

> "Let Ghibellines pursue their undertakings
> beneath another sign, for those who sever
> this sign and justice are bad followers."
>> *(Par.* VI, 103–105)

Justice is all-important for Dante: It is central to the *Monarchia* as it is to the *Comedy.* Guido's fraud serves to bring about "injustice" (*Inf.* XI, 22–24). Had he held fast to justice, he would not have been in hell. And just as the word *arte* applies to the Ghibellines' undertakings—*faccian lor arte (Par.* VI, 103)—it serves aptly here too, as Guido speaks of his own ingenious strategic exploits:

> "The wiles and secret ways—I knew them all
> and so employed their arts that my renown
> had reached the very boundaries of earth."
>> *(Inf.* XXVII, 76–78)

These observations may help to account for the element of coolness in Dante's characterization of Guido. Guido belonged to the warlike tyrants of Romagna. He was a Ghibelline noted for his *arte,* lacking the justice essential for the imperial cause. If his conversion was as far divorced from true repentance as his Ghibellinism from justice, perhaps it is not after all so surprising that he returned to his "former sins" (*Inf.* XXVII,71).

In this canto as elsewhere in Malebolge, Dante offers an indictment of the corrupt politics of his time, whether Ghibelline or Guelph. Boniface and Guido both lose sight of the meaning of justice and the true functions of temporal and spiritual power; they are both symptomatic of "that world which / lives badly" (*Purg.* XXXII, 103–104), with its false values. For this, satire is the appropriate treatment, and it accounts for the vein of black humor in the canto, from the dramatic irony of Guido's first cautious words to the grotesque morality play at the end. It is not the only note: Guido is a strong figure, angry, in pain, occasionally passionate, with a certain courtesy and at times with greatness. To many commentators he is tragic, even if most admit that he falls short of the stature of Ulysses. This combination of pathos and possible tragedy with grim comedy gives moral weight to Dante's satire against a world gone wrong, in which defying the pope may be necessary to save a believer's soul, where popes engage in crusades against Christians and abuse the sacraments, where an apparently holy penitent becomes damned in hell, and devils have to remind humans of elementary logic. It is a world in which appearances cannot be trusted.

Dante achieves his effects of pathos, irony, black comedy, and moral satire almost entirely through the skillful use of direct speech (and his own silence): the opening words of Guido, the brief exchange between Dante and Virgil, Dante's account of the "tyrants" of Romagna and his question to Guido, the latter's cautious reply followed by his story, in a long, uninterrupted monologue containing two rapid pieces of internal dialogue. Comments are reduced to a minimum: the implicit judgment in Dante's use of the word *tiranni*, Guido's indignant diatribe against Boniface VIII, and the sharp comments of the devil. Anything further—the search for the truth, for the reality in the maze of words—is left to the reflections of the silent poets, and to the reader.

BIBLIOGRAPHICAL NOTE

For this canto, I have drawn especially on the commentaries of Bosco and Reggio (Florence, 1979) and Sapegno (Florence, 1955). Of the early commentators, I refer to Pietro Alighieri, *Il "Commentarium" di Pietro Alighieri nelle redazioni ashburniana e ottoboniana*, ed. R. della Vedova and M. T. Silvotti (Florence, 1978), 373–377; and Benvenuto da Imola, *Comentum super Dantis Comoediam*, ed. J. P. Lacaita (Florence, 1887), 2:295–331. On the historical circumstances, there is a useful discussion (with bibliography) by Aldo Rossi, in *Enciclopedia dantesca* (Rome, 1971), 3:1020–1021. Readings of the canto offer a spectrum of positions from those largely sympathetic to Guido, which see Boniface VIII as Dante's main target, to those that emphasize Guido's own responsibility. Of recent instances, Bosco and Reggio's commentary (see above) provides a clear instance of the first position. A more qualified example of a similar viewpoint is the sensitive and balanced reading of Benvenuto Terracini in *Letture dantesche: Inferno*, ed. Giovanni Getto (Florence, 1955, rev. 1964), 539–567, with its careful analysis of the language of the canto. Another balanced account of the canto and its language is that of Ettore Bonora, in *Lectura Dantis Scaligera: Inferno*, ed. Mario Marcazzan (Florence, 1967), 967–96, which considers the problem of Dante's revision of his view in the *Convivio*. Judith Davies, "*Inferno* xxvii," in *Cambridge Readings in Dante's Comedy*, ed. K. Foster and P. Boyde (Cambridge, 1981), 49–69, places the stress on the ambiguity of Guido's character. Ambiguity, with a relatively negative reading of Guido, is again emphasised in the interesting discussion of the canto by Robin Kirkpatrick in *Dante's "Inferno": Difficulty and Dead Poetry* (Cambridge, 1987), 348–362: reassessment (on Dante's part) is seen as a characteristic note, while difficulty lies in the fact that "clarity and control are themselves rendered problematical" (351).

CANTO XXVIII

Scandal and Schism

THOMAS PETERSON

After the exordium of *Inferno* I–III, the first five circles of Hell are presented in as many cantos (IV–VIII). The subsequent sins of heresy and violence require progressively longer treatments. Once Dante and Virgil reach lower Hell and Malebolge (Cantos XVII–XXIX), the relation between text and terrain has become roughly that of one canto for each of the ten forms of fraud. Though the reasons for this dilation are formal and expressive, they are also ethical and reflect Dante's conviction that the sins of malice require particularly scrupulous attention, also because those who commit them are the most potentially noble among us. In particular, fraud, malice aided by reason, is dangerous to the intellectual and the artist, as it involves deception by distortion of the word or image.

In cataloging the fraudulent, Dante reveals the centrality of ethics to his worldview. Ethics has a pivotal role in a correct understanding of justice, a status formalized in the *Paradiso,* where ethics is placed over metaphysics in the celestial hierarchy. Here in the eighth circle Dante's ethical view, which presupposes the complementarity of aesthetics and history, finds its paradigmatic poetic treatment. This deceptively simple canto retains an exceptional symbolic importance—forward and backward—to the rest of the *Comedy.*

The main theme of Canto XXVIII is that of secular and spiritual schism. Those who foment discord within justly unified religious, political, or family groupings, "the sowers of dissension and scandal" (35–36), are punished by the splitting of their bodies. The canto is widely known as that of

Bertran de Born, the twelfth-century Provençal troubadour praised in *De vulgari eloquentia* as the exemplary poet of arms and in the *Convivio* for his liberality. The most degraded example of a hideous form of fraud, Bertran, who glorified war as the justly heroic means by which man guarantees his survival and health (*salus*), has been decapitated and carries his head like a lantern, the eyes now sources rather than receivers of light. The canto closes with Bertran's pronouncement of the principle of retribution commonly accepted as the central juridical principle of the *Inferno*:

> "And thus, in me
> one sees the law of counter-penalty."
> (141–142)

The structure of the canto is fairly straightforward: a lengthy prologue, including a periphrastic list of wars fought on Italian soil, and then encounters with five "sowers of dissension and scandal." Each of them is mutilated in a different manner, though each is forced to walk a circular path and be riven anew by the sword of a devil upon completion of the circuit. The characters relish the act of speaking. What was in life their stock in trade, the power of words to alter reality, is countered here by the brutal fragmentation of their bodies and the frustration of their desire to communicate with the living, in history. As if to complement this, the rhetoric of the canto is artificial and segmented; the phonic register is that of "crude and scrannel rhymes" (xxxii, 1) rather than the melic; the lexicon is arduous and military in nature; and the numerous historical references encompass a metatemporal domain.

The named schismatics and sowers of discord are Mohammed, according to legend an apostate from the Christian faith (accompanied by Alì, his son-in-law); Pier da Medicina, "a sower of scandal among Bolognese citizens and among the tyrants of Romagna" (Buti); Curio, a Roman tribune (as told in Lucan's *Pharsalia*) who prodded Caesar to cross the Rubicon and thus enter into civil war; Mosca de' Lamberti, the Florentine who, by advocating the execution of Buondelmonte, started the factional strife between Guelphs and Ghibellines; and Bertran de Born, who advocated the rebellion of the "fledgling king," Henry III of England, against his father, Henry II. In naming the *contrapasso* Bertran provides a gloss on the entire exercise of commutative (or retributive) justice in the *Inferno*: one "suffers back," quantitatively and qualitatively, as one has sinned. The enigma that gives density to this concept, and bestows a paradigmatic quality on the canto as a whole, is that a sinner names it. Like those before him who enunciate their respective truisms, Bertran is a shade and thus lacks all moral knowledge of his sin.

The deeper moral structure of the canto belongs to Virgil and Dante, whose succinct comments and thoughts give structure to the expressive mimetic fragments of the above figures. The architectural importance of their laconic interventions produces the following outline:

1.   Prologue and figure of Mohammed, 1–45
2.   *Virgil's* speech and reaction of the throng, 46–54
3.   Prophecies of Mohammed and Pier; Curio, 55–102
4.   *Dante's* retort to Mosca and reflection, 103–117
5.   Bertran de Born, 118–142

The "pillars" of rectitude, Virgil and Dante, stand in symmetrical contraposition to the perverse monumentality of the canto's two major figures, Mohammed and Bertran.

The idea of the *contrapasso* is biblical but derives, along with the entire moral architecture of the *Inferno,* from Aristotle's *Nichomachean Ethics* and Aquinas's commentary on it. And yet we recognize the freedom Dante exercises in numbering and presenting the forms of fraud. In this canto he tends to conflate the clerical and lay forms of schism, and the sowing of discord. As Reade states, "Dante does not preserve the most accurate sense of *schisma:* for the word should refer only to divisions within an ecclesiastical communion . . . The examples of *schisma* show, in fact, that *seditio* or *contentio* or *discordia* would have been almost more suitable terms" (344).

Confined to the darkness of the ninth pouch are more bodies than Dante can realistically recount or count. As a lengthy opening to an important canto (1–21), his pretermission has a particular weight. It is unlike most other such disclaimers in the *Comedy,* in that the poet is not affectively overwhelmed; instead he is limited by the mode of extension itself, that is, by the finitude of "our speech" (5), where *nostro* has the same sense of collective identity as proposed in the first line of the *Comedy.* Greater by far than all the battles Dante can name is the scene before him, which defies his or anyone's "tongue" (4) to tell. After diminishing his own abilities, Dante names Livy, the chronicler of some of the wars cited, as an authority whose word never deviates from the truth. More than a *topos* of modesty, this mention introduces the theme of an objective reportage, in contrast to Bertran de Born's *planh* glorifying war, "Si tuit li dol," which these lines openly imitate. It also suggests the unerring authority of God, and the increased severity of this canto. The lengthy pretermission sets the stage without giving any literal information about the scene. It would seem that Dante realizes that, in order to "gain full experience" (48)—the reason Virgil will give for his mission—he need not "recount in full" (2–3) what he sees, but simply grasp its essence. Thus the canto is organized in a series of truncated descriptions of sinners' bodies riven by the sword of a devil. The wounds are to be seen literally, and in terms of their particular scandal ("stumbling block" is the usual English translation of the biblical *skándalon*).

When the ninth pouch was announced at the end of the previous canto, it was in the low mimetic, or comical, register. The monetary metaphor of "the ditch where payment is imposed on those / who, since they brought such discord, bear such loads" (XXVII, 135–136) exploited the double sense of *scommettere* (to disjoin; to bet) and *acquistare* (to acquire; to buy). That tone is now absent, as if to emphasize the gravity of parlaying strife, a sin that dooms one to be riven like Prometheus on the rock: immediately, repeatedly, and without pity. This scenario necessitates a more detached or sublime tone on the part of the poet. Only at the opening of Canto XXIX will Dante express empathy, and this upon seeing his father's cousin, Geri del Bello. Here, rather, he observes Virgil's paradoxical monition of *Inferno* XX, 28: "Here pity only lives when it is dead."

As a veteran of the battle of Campaldino (1189)—the last of three major battles that left the Guelphs victorious over the Ghibellines (Benevento, Montaperti, Campaldino)—Dante was not naive about war. Nor, in the celebrated scenes of torture that precede this canto, does he ever display a lust for dismemberment or gore. Yet, in order to understand the ethical importance of the sowing of discord, he must take his poetry where a fluid and "untrammeled prose" (the *parole sciolte* of the first line) cannot go: into a pitiless presentation of anatomical disfigurement.

Even such a complex ideological figure as the founder of Islam is reduced to a graphic, frontal description of his mutilation. Mohammed is riven from chin to crotch; his viscera hang below him and are described in a periphrasis that does not diminish but emphasizes the fetid atmosphere (and, M. Picone argues, continues the scatological opening of Canto XXII, also a calque of Bertran):

> one whom I
> saw ripped right from the chin to where we fart:
>   his bowels hung between his legs, one saw
>   his vitals and the miserable sack
>   that makes of what we swallow excrement.
>
>   (23–27)

Mohammed is considered a religious schismatic, though as suggested, Dante's use of *scisma* is general and polyvalent. Having divided a sacred institution, in his own words, Mohammed now splits himself: ("See how I split myself!" [30]). The reflexivity of the punishment reveals the nature of the *contrapasso*, understood as opposite suffering, that is, suffering back for what one has done. Dante translates this law of retribution onto a dramatic level, that of the *figura*. Thus Mohammed is left to explain the common punishment endured in this pouch: the "road of pain" where one's healing wounds are perpetually reopened by a sword-wielding devil. As Fubini notes in his *lectura,* this devil is purely expeditious and allows the focus to remain on the figures.

Like all the rest of the damned, Mohammed ignores the basic fact of sin, seeing it as a breach of a moral code. By reenacting his sin (sins of *malitia* are always portrayed through a specific act by Dante, unlike sins of incontinence) he becomes an emblem of it. His entrails are pushed outwards, meaning that his inner disposition to divide, which wrought havoc in the world, is all that remains of his soul. Knowledge of sin would imply repentance and this is absent. He suspects Dante himself is a tarrying shade, to which presumption of doom Virgil responds.

> "But who are you who dawdle on this ridge,
> perhaps to slow your going to the verdict
> that was pronounced on your self-accusations?"
>   "Death has not reached him yet," my master answered,
> "nor is it guilt that summons him to torment."
>
> (43–47)

Virgil's response informs all those within earshot that Dante is neither "dead" nor "guilty"; upon hearing this, "more than a hundred" (52) souls react in wonder (this number lies midway, in the vague demographics of the canto, between the countless masses of the opening and the complete solitude of Bertran de Born at the end). Virgil's speech opens up the narrative to the theme of the world above. Told that Dante is among the living, Mohammed dispatches a message to the world, in the form of a warning to the heretic Fra Dolcino (a religious schismatic still alive in 1300). Regardless of its tone, which commentators have debated, the essential fact of any such warning in Dante's cosmology is its impotence (save of course in its didactic value to the reader); the use of *forse* (perhaps) further underscores the lack of any truly prophetic vision.

The next figure Dante sees, Pier da Medicina, is mutilated in the face and neck; he is missing his nose and one ear and must speak through a hole in his throat that he opens with his hands, exposing the inside, bloodred. His speech is the longest of the canto (70–90); like Mohammed's (30–45), it is followed by a rejoinder. The symmetry of the two episodes reflects a point-counterpoint structure, also evident in the two prophecies of demise. Yet Mohammed's message to Fra Dolcino (in his rejoinder to Virgil) and Pier's to Guido and Angiolello (in his main speech) are only superficially similar. First of all Pier's prophecy lacks a warning; second, his addressees are not sowers of discord but its victims; third, Pier brackets his message with a hypothesis, "if the foresight we have here's not vain" (78). Certainly the foreknowledge of matters on earth *is* vain and is a constitutive part of the punishment: the "foresight" (*antiveder*) of the damned is also, adversatively, their "anti-sight."

Pier's elaborate speech concerns a conspiracy by the (unnamed) tyrant Malatestino (called the "new mastiff" by Guido da Montefeltro in Canto XXVII), whose sowing of discord he calls "betrayal." This use of *tradimento* and *traditor* reflects Pier's desire to be superior to someone who has committed the same sin as he (betrayal is the only sin *below* fraud). Both Mohammed and Pier seek to displace their torment by prophesying a catastrophe on earth; Pier is particularly elevated in his oratorical evasion. In contrast, Curio has his tongue cut out and Mosca de' Lamberti and Bertran are blatantly laconic. The former woefully repeats his fatal accusation of Buondelmonte; the latter's words emerge like objects from his detached head and identify him as one who divided father and son.

Dante's two remarks (91–93; 109) accomplish in the latter half of the canto what Virgil's speech does in the former. In the first he promises to deliver Pier's message to the men of Fano, Guido and Angiolello, if Pier will identify the "bitter" figure he has alluded to (Curio) who wished he had never seen Rimini; in the second he reminds Mosca that he brought not only strife to Florence but death to his own family. The episodes of Curio and Mosca together comprise a condemnation of factionalism. The Roman told Caesar that if he was ready to attack it was self-defeating to wait (an action Dante cites favorably elsewhere in support of his desire that Henry VII invade Italy). The Tuscan claims that by denouncing the Guelph Buondelmonte to the powerful Amidei family he himself had sown "the seed of evil for the Tuscans" (108).

It is important to Dante's political vision that the two figures are contiguous and that the paradigmatic lemma, "evil seed," is one of three in the comedy and that it lies midpoint on the universal-personal axis delimited by the other two. The phrase is found in *Inferno* III ("the evil seed of Adam" [115]), in Virgil's description of how the shades, descendants of Adam, descend into Charon's boat; and in *Purgatorio* XXX, 119, immediately after Virgil's departure and the *Comedy*'s only mention of Dante's name. There, in Beatrice's first speech, the "evil seed" is a metaphor for Dante's *own* sin, the weed most apt to prosper in the greatest soil or souls (a principle paraphrased in the opening of this *lectura*).

Elucidating the intermediate "Tuscan" context of this evil seed is the obvious reminiscence of *Inferno* VI, where Dante asks the glutton Ciacco what has become of Mosca, Farinata degli Uberti, and others. The respect Dante accords Mosca is negated in Canto XXVIII, where he pays the price for his betrayal of Florentine unity. The use of *tosca* (Tuscan) cited above also recalls Farinata's opening address to Dante ("O Tuscan" [*Inf.* X, 22]); that factionalist is punished for his heresy, a sin related to schism (as Reade advises, all schism is heresy though all heresy is not schism). Another unavoidable reminiscence is that occasioned by the common etymons of trunk and truncate; four occurrences of the noun *tronco* and one of the verb *troncare* in *Inferno* XIII regard the bleeding trunk of the suicide Pier delle Vigne whose self-destruction is a thematic trait shared by the sowers of discord, from Pier da Medicina, "his nose hacked off (*tronco*) up to his eyebrows" (65), to Bertran de Born. Noting the common thematics shared among cantos, we must stress the brutality of lower hell, where the fragmentation of bodies is presented with greater dispatch and psychic violence.

After his retort to Mosca, qua Tuscan, Dante pauses to reflect on his incipient fear at telling what he saw. He then gains strength from the purity of his conscience:

> But I stayed there to watch that company
> and saw a thing that I should be afraid
> to tell with no more proof than my own self—
> except that I am reassured by conscience,
> that good companion, heartening a man
> beneath the breastplate of its purity.
>
> (112–117)

The simile of armor is appropriate, since it is conscience that "arms" the pilgrim against the hideous figure of Bertran. The complementarity of this speech with the canto's opening pretermission, based on humanity's inability accurately to recount certain horrors, is reflected by humanity's reluctance to believe such horrors exist. Dante's fear is that his readers will be incredulous. He is not wonderstruck, but implacable, before the monstrous shade he now encounters, seemingly without Virgil; the wonder (*maraviglia*) in this canto belongs to the sinners only. Dante's reflection and the subsequent rendering of Bertran and his speech is peremptory and matter-of-fact and fits within the rhetorical and procedural flatness of this canto. Confronted with the terse documentary style, the reader is apt to wonder about Dante's apparent change of position on the virtues of Bertran.

Dante engages a raw, even vulgar, language in order to literalize the defective characters of those condemned to the ninth pouch. The concrete and repelling imagery is essential to the canto's ethical and polemical message, yet so is the poet's disinterestedness, as reflected in the arduous and highly technical versification. An example of this technique is the presence in filigree of several lexical correspondences: pairs of the same word disposed symmetrically with respect to other such pairs. It is first apparent in the chiasmus formed by the terms "guilt" and "wonder."

There are, as is known, a variety of literary typologies present in the *Comedy*. Dante owes his detachment from the events he reports to the full absorption of his vision, whose raw materiality confers irony on the sinners who presume to have vision and strenuously desire to communicate with the world above. Dante is not impervious to what he sees, but he is not scandalized. His affective suspension relaxes only at the beginning of Canto XXIX, where he sees his father's cousin, Geri del Bello. Once again it is the play of point-counterpoint that makes the transition effective, reinforcing the paradigmatic nature of the canto just completed.

It is obvious that this penultimate grouping in the penultimate sin has a particular intellectual and polemical weight in the *Comedy* as a whole. The circular route of the schismatics, who heal only to be split again, is a wheel of fortune from which all fortune has been removed. Their juridical fate is limited to the perversity of the carnal evidence, the frontality of the perception. In addition to factionalism, the canto intimates the dilemma faced by Dante in *Paradiso* XIX regarding the destiny of virtuous non-Christians, and the inscrutability of divine justice. It also addresses the dialectic of aesthetic craft versus morals, which regards every poet named in the *Comedy* (we think in particular of the episodes of the classic poets, of the minstrel Casella, and of Sordello), and in the immediate context concerns Dante's earlier pronouncements on Bertran de Born. The canto addresses the theme of the desire of the dead to communicate with the living and connects by way of negation to the figure of Guido da Montefeltro. Whereas Guido, a former "man of arms" who became a fraudulent counselor, dreaded that others might know of his fate (*Inferno* XXVII, 61–66), two of this canto's denizens, Mohammed and Pier da Medicina, wish to communicate on matters of arms to those in the world above. There is obvious irony in these vain *communiqués,* as there was in Guido's speech. The presence in Purgatory of Guido's son, Bonconte, himself a genuine man of arms, is generally recognized as an indication of the indifference of divine justice to questions of family relations. That dialectic, while absent in this impersonal and polemical canto, emerges at the opening of Canto XXIX where Dante sees his father's cousin.

Giuseppe Mazzotta has called Canto XXVIII Dante's "farewell to arms," arguing—in a fashion consonant with Picone—that the poet's view of war had changed, and that a poetry glorifying war could no longer be condoned. The power of poetry itself mandates a higher ethical end. If in the Aristotelian order ethics was a practical (lower) science, and if for Brunetto Latini it is simply the "mechanical" branch of philosophy, in Dante ethics was intimately involved, though not synonymous, with justice. "Ethics, which is grounded in justice, designates the sphere of the duties and obligations attendant upon man's concrete actuality; but justice is not simply equated with the sphere of human actions. There is a Platonic theory of the Good and of Justice operative in Dante's imagination, as there is in Aquinas's" (79).

Dante's access to the imagination is by means of poetry. The force of metaphor to teach ethics is at the center of this canto's message about commutative justice, which concerns a penalty equally weighted to the crime (as in the biblical injunction, "an eye for an eye, a tooth for a tooth"), and not distributive justice, which also involves "reparation" and the extra weighting of the judgment in consideration of an individual's greater or lesser importance in the society.

The sins of lower hell are committed by illustrious persons; yet they are banal to the point of being disgusting. Lest the living be deceived by the eloquence of the fraudulent (Pier da Medicina, for example), Dante reduces their words to crude material, and their material remains to an anatomy lesson. Their consciousness is revealed in their language, which ranges from the executive (Mohammed) to the oratorical (Pier) to the almost remorseful (Bertran). The sinners persist in their delusion of nobility. They are at once self-naming exemplars and self-damning judges.

The fraudulent complicate in order to deceive. Thus Dante represents them in a series of pouches divided from one another by walls of moral darkness. The civic nature of the inadequacy is particularly apparent in sins resulting in factionalism. The sowers of discord were neither irreligious nor outwardly rebellious of political authority but caused schism and discord from within the Church or court. These in turn subverted the legitimate "corporeal" unity of the body politic and the body of Christ, which is consubstantial with the true Church.

The canto is also paradigmatic in its linguistic violence and expressionism (a Dantean style first explored by Gianfranco Contini). Most obviously it places an extraordinary emphasis on the organ of sight. Dante's frequent use of "I saw" has Apocalyptic overtones, while the use of the same verb by the shades attests to their utter lack of vision. The verb *vedere* (to see) has a very broad usage in the *Comedy;* Canto xxviii contains more uses than any other (20). The act of seeing presents a kind of filter that unifies various oppositions: unity and fragmentation, truth and words, simplicity and complication, conscience and self, prophecy and blindness. The infernal perversion of sight is sealed in the eyes of Bertran, flames that light a lantern but presumably cannot see. Bertran's poetry is also parodied extensively— as it is in the opening of Canto xxii.

Every *contrapasso* has its irony and each represents a further development of that before it. This dialectic presupposes the interaction of diverse (historical, aesthetic, moral) systems. In Canto xxviii the irony is that those who divided sacred unions are joined with one another. Dante is not concerned with casuistries but wishes to literalize the split as something disgusting toward which the appropriate attitude of pilgrim and guide is that of a detached elevation. As Francesco De Sanctis states in a summary of the canto, "it is not disgust purified in the sublime but the sublime that is fouled in disgust" (267). The text of the schismatics, like the figures, lies disposed around us in a series of finite segments, truncated and dovetailed. Our involvement, through Dante and Virgil, is to "observe." And in the final line Bertran, passive and unknowing, observes the truth: *Così s'osserva in me lo contrapasso* (142).

BIBLIOGRAPHY

Abrams, Richard. "Against the *Contrapasso:* Dante's Heretics, Schismatics, and Others." *Italian Quarterly* 27 (1986): 5–19 (equates the *contrapasso* with the vengeful wrath of an anthropomorphic God, that is, an illusion of the damned).

Della Vedova, Roberto. "Dinamica lacaniana del *corps morcelé:* ipotesi per una lettura d'*Inferno* XXVIII." In *Psicoanalisi e strutturalismo di fronte a Dante,* 2:119–133. Florence, 1972 (locates in the "morbid psychology" of the Bosch-type mutilations a "neurotic" Dante whose mystic *visio* involved projecting his pilgrim's progress along a pathway from the "mirror stage" to the present "dynamics of the 'fragmented body'" [as occurs in dreams] to the eventual paradisial union of mother and child).

De Sanctis, Francesco. *Lezioni e saggi su Dante,* ed. Sergio Romagnoli. Turin, 1955.

Fubini, Mario. "Il canto XXVIII dell'*Inferno.*" In *Lectura Dantis Scaligera: Inferno,* ed. Mario Marcazzan, 999–1021. Florence, 1967 (an authoritative reading that examines the canto's mixture of crude frontality and high rhetoric. Dismissing readings that stress psychological nuances or tone, Fubini concentrates on the novelty and appropriateness of Dante's arduous metric and lexical choices).

Mazzotta, Giuseppe. "Metaphor and Justice (*Inferno* XXVIII)." In *Dante's Vision and the Circle of Knowledge,* 75–95. Princeton, N.J., 1993 (focuses on the encyclopedic nature of Dante's use of poetry, and on the power of metaphor to configure a theory of justice, in this case commutative justice).

Picone, Michelangelo. "I trovatori di Dante: Bertran de Born." *Studi e problemi di critica testuale* 19 (1979): 71–94 (ties Dante's changed evaluation of Bertran [from his exalted position in the prose to his condemnation] to an evolved moral stance, and to the loss of the belief in man's ability to gain happiness "within the limits of the historic here and now" [80]).

Reade, W. H. V. *The Moral System of Dante's "Inferno."* Port Washington, N.Y., 1969 (this canonical work details Dante's moral and theological system as it derives from Aristotle, Aquinas, and other sources).

Sanguineti, Edoardo. *Interpretazione di Malebolge,* 287–310. Florence, 1961 (conducts a detailed reading of the entire Malebolge, connecting local aspects of syntax, lexicon, and versification to the macroscopic structure of the work, and specifically to the "most profound law of Dante's poetry, its narrative articulation" [358]).

CANTO XXIX

Such Outlandish Wounds

LINO PERTILE

Strictly speaking, Canto XXIX of *Inferno* has no narrative unity of its own. It consists of two segments: the first (1–39) is a continuation of the matter of Canto XXVIII, while the second (40–139) is a preamble to the matter of Canto XXX.

As the canto begins, Dante and Virgil are on the point of leaving the ninth ditch of Malebolge where the sowers of discord, who spread division within the Church, the state, and the family, are punished by being literally cut, cloven, divided in their own bodies. The last voice to be heard was that of the Provençal poet Bertran de Born, and it issued from his severed head, which he held high by the hair: "thus, in me / one sees the law of counter-penalty." In the opening lines of the new canto Dante stares with unusual intensity at the gruesome landscape of the *bolgia*. The sight of so many bloody mutilations has so filled his eyes that he just wants to stop and weep. But Virgil rebukes him. Why does he keep looking down there—he asks impatiently—amongst the maimed shades? He has not done so in the other pouches, and if he intends to count all the dead one by one, he should know that this *bolgia* measures two and twenty miles, and the time left to inspect the rest of Hell is getting short.

Something similar happened in the fourth *bolgia* when, at the sight of the diviners' twisted bodies, Dante starts to weep and Virgil reproaches him with the memorable line, "Here pity only lives when it is dead" (XX, 28). This tension between pilgrim and guide is not uncommon in the *Inferno*, but in our canto it emerges, unexpectedly, in a particularly problematic way. What is more, it remains unresolved.

To begin with, Virgil's enjoinder does not lead to Dante's compliance. On the contrary, Dante replies that, if Virgil had paid more attention to the reason for his interest, perhaps he would have allowed him to linger a little longer; then, moving away from the bloody scene, he adds that in the ninth *bolgia* he believes that a shade of his own blood is weeping for his sins. This remarkable revelation does not seem to concern Virgil in the least, nor to affect his determination to press on. He brushes aside Dante's visible anguish, urging him not to let his thoughts be diverted by the plight of his relative; he should attend to other things and let the sinner get his just deserts. He then explains that, while Dante was still all absorbed by the sight of Bertran, he had seen the shade of the poet's relative at the foot of the bridge, pointing his finger at him menacingly, and he had heard the others call him Geri del Bello—a first cousin of Dante's father who had been murdered in 1280, or soon afterwards, by one of the Sacchetti, a Florentine family.

The issue that compels Dante's interest is complex. For Dante reveals that what makes Geri so disdainful is the failure of the Alighieri to take revenge for his *violenta morte* ("it was his death by violence / for which he still is not avenged" [31–32]). And so Geri went off without talking to Dante, making the latter only "pity him the more" (36).

This line has caused much debate in the exegetical tradition (see Salsano, 53–78). Dante's quiet but firm declaration of increased pity for his kinsman stands in sharp contrast to Virgil's hasty dismissal of Geri; moreover, this time, contrary to what happened in Canto xx, it is the pilgrim who has the last word. But does Dante's sympathy imply that he chooses the law of private revenge against the Christian imperative of forgiveness? Or is it just Dante the character who does so, while the vigilant judgment of Virgil disapproves and spurs him on?

The right to, and duty of, private revenge among the nobility was stipulated in the statutes and customs of Dante's times, as can be seen, for instance, in Brunetto Latini's *Tesoretto* and *Trésor* (see Mariani, 1034–1036; Mazzotta, 84–86). In addition, it was enshrined in Cicero's notion of *jus naturae* where *vindicatio* is placed on a par with *religio, pietas, gratia, observantia,* and *veritas.* Through *vindicatio,* Cicero argues, "by defending or avenging we repel violence (*vim*) and insult from ourselves and from our relatives (*a nostris*) who ought to be dear to us" (*De inventione* II, xxii, 65–66). In the same passage, Cicero defines *pietas* as a natural law that compels us to do our duty toward our country, our parents, and our blood relations (*patriam, aut parentes, aut sanguine conjunctos*). These are the principles Geri implicitly appeals to when he points his accusing finger at the son of his father's cousin. Justice, pity, and custom demand that he be avenged. And yet

Christian ethics totally prohibit the exercise of private revenge; the new law is a law of love, not of fear, and revenge belongs only to God (see Thomas Aquinas, *Summa theologica* II-II, 108, 1). As for the *pietas* toward parents and blood relations, this is secondary to the devotion we owe to God (*religio*); in case of conflict between *religio* and *pietas,* our duties toward God take precedence over duties toward our family (ibid., 1 and 4).

So much was clearly implied in what Virgil had said, as we have noted, in *Inferno* XX, 28, and in what the poet himself will repeat, with different words, in *Inferno* XXXIII, 150 ("and it was courtesy to show him rudeness"), and in *Paradiso* IV, 105 ("not to fail in filial / piety, he acted ruthlessly"). Furthermore, it must be remembered that in Dante's times private revenge was a determining factor in the continuation and aggravation of fierce feuds within families and communities. Indeed, Benvenuto da Imola writes that, among Italians, the Florentines were known as extremely vindictive people. Therefore, it was right for Dante to evoke the custom of revenge within the *bolgia* of the sowers of discord, provided it was done unambiguously to condemn it, with all the rigor of which we know him to be capable. And yet here, on the contrary, the poet constructs a profoundly ambivalent episode that culminates in one of the most perplexing and disturbing sentences of the entire *Comedy:* "and this has made me pity him the more" (36).

Contrary to what is usually said, what makes the pilgrim pity him *the more* cannot be the fact that Geri is still unavenged, for Dante was aware of this before coming to Hell, and therefore it could not now heighten his feeling of pity. What increases his pity must be something new: it is the fact that Geri chooses not to speak to him. The withdrawal of speech between members of the same family, or former friends, was a clear signal of the existence of some serious grievance between them. Dante knows this very well: he is able to decipher immediately and unambiguously Geri's gesture. Indeed, after Dante's explanation, Geri's lonesome stance acquires a dignity that Virgil had failed to perceive. With his silence and his threatening finger, Geri peremptorily demands revenge from his living kinsmen. This and this alone is the passion that sustains him in Hell, as though he could not even begin to pay for his crimes so long as his death remains unavenged. In his craving for revenge the essence of his sin is caught and perpetuated as a form of suffering almost independent of his punishment. It is an affliction he shares with his living relatives, thus showing to what extent, although dead and in Hell, Geri's ghost is still alive as a projection of his family's sense of guilt.

Dante's understanding of his kinsman's passion does not mean, of course, that he either sympathizes with, or condemns, Geri's dreadful demand. But herein lies the problem. Dante's apparently neutral reaction, besides contradicting Virgil's rational voice, leaves entirely open the kind of moral question that the *Comedy* is by definition expected to resolve. The closer we look at this episode, the more disturbing it becomes. To list the most pressing questions:

1.   Why does Dante choose to isolate Geri's case by placing the episode in a separate canto?

2.   Why does he fail to mention either Geri's crimes or the mutilations that, we must presume, afflict him?

3.   Why does he choose Geri, such a distant relative who had been dead for about thirty years when the poet came to write the last sections of *Inferno*? Could this choice be linked with the fact that, according to Benvenuto, an Alighieri did indeed avenge Geri around that time (in 1310)?

4.   Why involve Virgil in the episode, if it is Dante who this time knows and understands more than his guide? How do we explain this reversal of their normal roles?

5.   How do we explain Virgil's sudden loss of telepathic powers whereby, again exceptionally, he fails, or does not bother, to read Dante's mind? Why portray an inadequate Virgil in the context of the Alighieri's private squabbles, when, as we will see, Virgil was very familiar with the notion of revenge?

6.   What is the reader to make of such contrasting reactions as displayed by Virgil and Dante?

7.   What is the nature of Dante's *pietà*? In any case, now that he has found Geri deep in Hell and obsessed by thoughts of revenge, is it not paradoxical that Dante's pity for him should grow instead of turning into its very opposite? And finally an extraliterary, though legitimate, question: what were the Sacchetti family to make of such pity? For we know that they and the Alighieri kept feuding until 1342, when the duke of Athens persuaded them to make peace.

In answer to the first three questions, I suggest that Dante's strategy is to focus not on the eternal punishment, but on the still pending revenge of his dead relative: hence the deliberate isolation of Geri in the new canto and the silence on his crimes and mutilations; hence also the choice of Geri as the only dead member of the Alighieri clan still caught in his vendetta at the time of the fictional journey. Why raise the question of private revenge? In all likelihood because, in a society in which the right to private justice was an unmistakable sign of nobility, Dante's allusion to it was an indirect but sure way to let the Florentines, and particularly the Sacchetti, know that the Alighieri were a noble family (Carpi, 240–242) and that they did not forget an injury.

As for the role of Virgil, it is his link to the episode's literary associations that remains surprisingly unknown or unexplored. A dead shade who in the underworld, against the custom of his kind, refuses to speak to a living visitor can also be found in the *Odyssey* and in the *Aeneid*. As we surmise from Servius's commentary on the *Aeneid* (VI, 468), it is a topos of epic poetry, and Dante adapts it to suit his own poetic ends. His dependence on the classical model appears even more clearly if we recall that, in all three narratives, while the thematic focus is on the silence of the shade, the psychological focus falls on the visitor's sense of guilt. We need not pause on the *Odyssey*—Dante almost certainly did not know the poem, though he had probably read Servius—where it is Ajax who stubbornly refuses to forget his anger toward Odysseus (XI, 541–567). Nevertheless, Virgil's use of the topos in the *Aeneid* is highly pertinent and illuminating.

Emerging from the wood of the suicides in Virgil's underworld, the soul of Dido refuses to answer Aeneas's plea for reconciliation and forgiveness, and as a consequence Aeneas is obliged to go on weeping and pitying her but with his guilt undiminished (VI, 450–476). Aeneas's tragic plight is clear: he can no more undo Dido's death than he could resist the power that, when she was alive, drove him away from her and caused her violent end. He had to sacrifice his private passion to his public duty, the divinely willed foundation of the Roman empire. Similarly, because of the moral imperative that drives him forward, Dante cannot undo Geri's death through an act of revenge; he, too, must sacrifice his private blood feud to his prophetic mission. Dido's silence, as much as Geri's, is an appeal, more eloquent than words, to a primitive notion of natural justice that Aeneas and Dante understand but left behind when they undertook their journeys. In both cases, the laws of the natural, human world stand in conflict with the divine will, and in both cases the two heroes choose to abide by the latter, even if that means taking upon their shoulders the burden of guilt that a moral choice inevitably entails.

The analogies between the Virgilian and Dantean episodes are not only structural and psychological; many textual elements prove the deep connections between the two narratives. For example, Virgil calls his spirits *maesti* (435) just as Dante calls his *l'ombre triste* (6), and he insists on their and Aeneas's weeping (*flentes* [427]; *lugentes campi* [441]; *lacrimas* [468]; *lacrimans* [476]) just as Dante stresses his own desire to weep, and believes Geri to be weeping for his sin. More to the point, the rare, Latinate verb *dimettere,* which Dante uses here in the sense of "to let, to allow" (*forse m'avresti ancor lo star dimesso* [15]), appears also in Book VI of the *Aeneid* where it describes how Aeneas, on recognizing the dead Dido, lets tears fall from his eyes (*demisit lacrimas* [455]), a detail that in its turn reminds us of the pilgrim's initial desire "to stay and weep" (3).

Moreover, there is Dante's use, hardly fortuitous in the context, of that most Virgilian of epithets, *pio.* Its meaning here is said to be "compassionate, pitiful" (see Lanci); however, the presence of the Virgilian intertext suggests that the adjective's semantic connotations may be more complex and disturbing (see Ball), alluding perhaps to the care that the living must take of their dead, and consequently to the persistence of a poignant conflict in the pilgrim's heart between duties to family and duties to God.

Dante's intertextual discourse is indeed likely to be even more complex than I have so far suggested. There is one occasion in Virgil's poem when Aeneas has to face the alternative between revenge and compassion. It is another locus classicus of epic poetry, based on the final stages of Achilles' duel with Hector in the *Iliad*. At the end of his duel with Aeneas, the wounded Turnus sinks to the ground pleading for mercy, if not for himself, at least for his father, the aged Daunus (*Dauni miserere senectae* [XII, 934]); with outstretched hands he implores his victor not to press hatred further (*ulterius ne tende odiis* [XII, 938]). At first Aeneas holds his hand, but when he sees Pallas's baldric on Turnus's shoulder, the fire of passion overwhelms him, and he plunges his sword into Turnus's breast (XII, 948–950). Thus, finally, Aeneas chooses revenge instead of compassion, his *pietas* for Pallas prevailing over his pity for Turnus.

It is interesting to note that, on referring elsewhere to this episode, Dante states that Aeneas's clemency was such that, had he not noticed Pallas's baldric, he would have spared Turnus's life (*Monarchia* II, ix, 13–14). Thus Dante in the *Monarchia* seems almost to justify Aeneas's vengeful deed. But what does the pilgrim do in *Inferno* XXIX? Between an Aeneas who, in Dido's case, sacrifices his private passion, and one who, in the case of Turnus, in keeping with pagan standards, yields to it, Dante seems to opt for the only model that is consistent with Christian doctrine: that of an Aeneas who pities Dido but in the name of a higher authority refuses to be diverted from his fateful journey. However, the manner of this choice is essentially evasive in that it does not result in the denunciation of the other option. In other words, Dante's treatment of Geri is profoundly equivocal. On the one hand, by leaving Geri behind and unspoken to, the poet portrays himself as Christian hero, a new *pius Aeneas;* on the other, by so pointedly failing to reprove his relative's craving for revenge, indeed by so emphatically pitying him, he shows himself to be still clinging to the aristocratic model of the avenger. What is astonishing is that, of all conflicts, this should be the one that shows Virgil incapable of understanding!

The presence of so many Virgilian echoes, clustering in and around such a powerful thematic focus, confirms beyond any doubt the "tragic" significance of the episode of Geri del Bello. And it explains the episode's formal and structural isolation from the rest of the ninth *bolgia*. For, if the dreaded memory of his unavenged relative is to bear "tragic" connotations, Dante cannot place Geri in the space assigned to family schisms, next to a Mosca de' Lamberti (XXVIII, 103–111) where, in terms of narrative logic, he belongs. The poet must construct an artistic space in which both the personal and ethical aspects of the conflict find proper expression and resonance. And so he does, albeit at a high price for both the moral significance of the episode and the coherence of Virgil's character. Indeed, Virgil's character seems to be the principal casualty of a strategy that allows the poet to safeguard the right of his family to seek revenge without openly taking a stand on the moral merit of exercising such a right. And how could he? To approve the ancient custom of vendetta on the basis of Virgilian *pietas* meant to contradict the sacred principle of Christian *pietà* and endorse, however indirectly, the bloody Florentine feuds the poet bitterly condemned elsewhere; but to disapprove of that custom was tantamount to suggesting that the nobility of the Alighieri family, as much as that of old Florence, was polluted in its very foundations. Both options were internally self-contradictory and in the last analysis incompatible with a worldview founded upon Christian fundamentalism and the traditions of a mythical Florence.

The transition from the first to the second section of the canto is effected by means of a brief reference to the two pilgrims' continuing their conversation until they reach the tenth and last *bolgia* of Hell.

> *Così parlammo infino al loco primo*
> *che de lo scoglio l'altra valle mostra,*
> *se più lume vi fosse, tutto ad imo.*
>
> And so we talked until we found the first
> point of the ridge that, if there were more light,
> would show the other valley to the bottom.
> (37–39)

It is almost a new narrative opening. We recall the beginning of Canto v:

> *Così discesi del cerchio primaio*
> *giù nel secondo, che men loco cinghia*
> *e tanto più dolor, che punge a guaio.*
>
> So I descended from the first enclosure
> down to the second circle, that which girdles
> less space but grief more great, that goads to weeping.

Or the first tercet of Canto xxi, the only other canto that begins with *Così*:

> *Così di ponte in ponte, altro parlando*
> *che la mia comedìa cantar non cura,*
> *venimmo . . .*
>
> We came along from one bridge to another,
> talking of things my Comedy is not
> concerned to sing.

This new opening insulates Geri del Bello from the ninth and tenth *bolgia* alike, creating a peculiar textual space reserved exclusively for him. But, of course, the function of the transitional tercet is also to project our attention forward to the new landscape that, though still engulfed in ominous darkness, is now looming before the pilgrims' eyes.

This is the *bolgia* of the falsifiers, who are divided into four categories: falsifiers of metals, or alchemists (the subject of the rest of Canto XXIX), and falsifiers of persons, of coins, and of words, who occupy the next canto. The remainder of the canto can be subdivided into three narrative segments. In the first we are given a general overview of the tenth *bolgia* and of the punishment meted out there (40–69). Then, two souls are singled out and addressed first by Virgil and then, on Virgil's prompting, by Dante (70–108). Finally, these two souls identify themselves as Griffolino d'Arezzo and the Florentine Capocchio and, together with Dante, they make fun of the vanity of the Sienese (109–139).

As he comes close enough to the ditch to begin to make out its inhabitants, what first strikes Dante is not what he sees but what he hears:

> When we had climbed above the final cloister
> of Malebolge, so that its lay brothers
> were able to appear before our eyes,
>   I felt the force of strange laments, like arrows
> whose shafts are barbed with pity; and at this,
> I had to place my hands across my ears.
>
> (40–45)

The new narrative opening concentrates on the sense of hearing, just as the opening tercet of the canto had highlighted the sense of sight; and just as then the pilgrim's eyes were brimming with the sight of "so many souls and such outlandish wounds," so now his ears are so full of the piercing, pitiful lamentations of the damned, that he has to cover them with his hands. There is no further mention of this fact in the canto, but we should take notice that, by the time he comes to the end of this *bolgia*, the pilgrim is to be found listening to Master Adam squabble with Sinon (XXX, 130); he will be so engrossed, in fact, that Virgil will have to reprimand him for his base eavesdropping (XXX, 147). At first, then, the pity that earlier affected the pilgrim seems to spill over into the next episode; he cannot bear to hear the heartrending lamentations of the falsifiers. However, as he moves on, pity seems to give way to a kind of participation, a morbid interest that Virgil will later show to be as dangerous as pity.

The introduction to the new *bolgia* is somewhat slow. It begins with a simile that, extending over two tercets (46–51), evokes in one hypothetical sweep all the sufferings contained in the hospitals of Valdichiana,

Maremma, and Sardinia in the hottest time of the year—all their sick gathered together in a black ditch stinking with the foul smell of festering flesh; however, nothing as yet that we can precisely visualize.

The next two tercets (52–57) still keep us waiting; the narrative focus shifts to the two pilgrims as they move down the last bank of Malebolge to gain a clearer view of the falsifiers—and we will return to this point presently. Meanwhile, what follows is not a direct description but a new simile, extending over three tercets (58–66), in which through a fabulous, literary reference we are led to imagine heaps of bodies languishing one on top of the other.

The first direct, visual picture of the *bolgia* only now emerges in the tercet that follows. Yet we come to it imagining what to expect. The two previous similes, one hyperbolic and the other fictional, have strong narrative contents that point in one direction: while the former evokes a dark ditch crammed with crawling diseased bodies, the latter, nearer the bottom of the ditch, presents bodies languishing in heaps as lifeless sheaves of wheat. Only now are we ready to take in the sight of individual shades, lying one upon the other, or dragging themselves on all fours along the dismal way:

> Some lay upon their bellies, some upon
> the shoulders of another spirit, some
> crawled on all fours along that squalid road.
>
> (67–69)

The rhythm of Dante's verse effectively depicts the painful heaviness and slowness of the damned souls. The *bolgia* is a huge, dark, nightmarish hospital ward, full of diseased bodies (*li ammalati* [71]) that have been drained of all energy. Dante and Virgil, too, move along it slowly, without uttering a word, much as healthy people do among the sick.

Before looking at the next section of the canto, we must pause to consider an apparently marginal remark inserted between the two similes. As he moves down the last bank of the long ridge, Dante recalls:

> *fu la mia vista più viva*
> *giù ver' lo fondo, là* [there] *'ve la ministra*
> *de l'alto Sire infallibil giustizia*
> *punisce i falsador che qui* [here] *registra.*

> my sight could see more vividly
> into the bottom, where unerring Justice,
> the minister of the High Lord, punishes
> the falsifiers she had registered.
>
> (54–57)

The question raised by these lines is: where is it that God's infallible justice registers the names of the falsifiers who are punished *là* (there), in the depth of the tenth *bolgia*? In other words, where is *qui* (here)? The exegetical tradition has given two answers: "here" means "in the tenth *bolgia*" (but then here and there would, confusingly, indicate the same place), or it means "in this world," thus implying that God's justice punishes *there,* in the tenth *bolgia,* the falsifiers whose names it registers in its book when they sin *here,* in this world. The latter explanation, which through Daniello's commentary goes back to Trifon Gabriele's exposition of *Inferno* in 1525 (see *Annotationi*), has prevailed in the last thirty years or so, having been adopted by all the most recent commentators (Bosco and Reggio [1979], Pasquini and Quaglio [1982], Vallone and Scorrano [1987], Chiavacci Leonardi [1991]; but contrast Hollander [1982]).

There is a downward gradation as we move further into the *bolgia* of the alchemists:

> We journeyed step by step without a word,
> watching and listening to those sick souls,
> who had not strength enough to lift themselves.
> (70–72)

First they are lay brothers in a cloister (41), then rotting lepers in a huge hospital ward (46–51), finally quasi-inanimate objects, like sheaves of wheat piled together in scattered heaps (66). Dante insists on their lethargic state: they cannot raise themselves, they can only crawl, dragging themselves slowly around—like grotesquely huge slugs, we may be tempted to add. Thus, perhaps, those who pretended to transform lead into gold now find themselves transformed into heavy and worthless things, their skin hardened to an unbearably itchy crust they are forever and in vain trying to scratch off with their nails. The degradation of the human form here reaches new depths—we are indeed very close to ultimate materiality, the frozen bottom of Hell—and Dante has no qualms about descending into the kitchen and the stable to evoke in minute detail suitable images for the scene he has in mind: two bodies are propped against each other as pan on pan to warm; they are plying upon themselves the "bite" of their nails as furiously as a stableboy, hurried by his master, plies his currycomb to a horse; their nails are scraping off their scabs, as a knife the scales of a bream (73–84). And, continuing with Virgil's shocking *captatio benevolentiae:* sometimes they use their fingers to rip open their crust of scabs as though it were a suit of mail; at other times they pull each scab away from their skin by using two fingers as pincers (85–87). The sound of Dante's rhymes is as hard and harsh as the images he evokes are vulgar and low; his enjambments are shocking (*il morso / de l'unghie; la gran rabbia / del pizzicor*); his alliterations biting and cutting (*e sì traevan giù l'unghie la scabbia /*

come coltel di scardova le scaglie): it is a supreme example of technical mastery in the low style.

Two hundred years later Pietro Bembo was to ban this kind of imagery and language from Italian literature. If Dante, he argued, felt unable to express his images with less vile, harsh, and offensive words, he should have omitted them, as we must omit from our writing all the things that cannot be said in a seemly manner (*Prose della volgar lingua* II, v). Fortunately, Dante thought otherwise. Whenever the low life is the only one capable of providing a body of metaphors suitable for his expressive needs, he resorts to it without the slightest hesitation. What is even more shocking is the fact that he makes Virgil himself use this low language and insist on using it, as when he addresses one of the two falsifiers thus:

> "O you who use your nails to strip yourself,"
> my guide began to say to one of them,
> "and sometimes have to turn them into pincers,
>   tell us if there are some Italians
> among the sinners in this moat—so may
> your nails hold out, eternal, at their work."
>
> (85–90)

All the rules of *convenientia* are here broken. The *sommo poeta* is made to speak the language of the gutter, thereby lending authority to the style Dante has just employed, deliberately, to describe the condition of the falsifiers.

This, however, is not all; we are about to witness another sharp shift in the style of this canto. One of the two souls, addressed by Virgil, says, weeping, that they are both Italians; then, as they hear that Virgil is guiding a living man through Hell, they break their position of mutual support and with others, who had overheard the conversation, turn trembling toward the pilgrim. In his turn, the pilgrim asks them to reveal their identities: their unseemly and loathsome penalty—he adds—should not deter them from declaring their names to him (107–108).

What follows is somewhat surprising, for it is in a tone consistent neither with the gravity of the alchemists' sin nor with their lethargic state. One of the two lepers, Griffolino, says that, though Minos has rightly sentenced him here as an alchemist, he died for another reason, as the result of a *beffa*, a joke that ended badly. Hearing Griffolino's claim that he could raise himself up in the air and fly, the vain and stupid Albero da Siena took him at his word and demanded to be shown the art of flying, and, since Griffolino could not turn him into a Daedalus, Albero had him burned by the bishop of Siena. The substance of the story is tragic, of course, but witty Griffolino turns it into a comic, albeit learned, little sketch, that shifts the attention to the capricious vanity of the Sienese Albero. Surprisingly, Dante is ready to play the stooge to Griffolino by turning to Virgil with a playful question: "Was there ever / so vain a people as the Sienese? / Even the French can't match such vanity!" (121–123). Virgil does not answer, but his silence is enough to involve him too, willy-nilly, in the proceedings. In fact it is "the other leper" who, quicker than Virgil, answers in his place, and lists, in the same lighthearted and frivolous tone as Griffolino's, four more examples of Sienese citizens well known for their "fatuous megalomania" (Bosco and Reggio, 435). Having done that, he invites Dante to look hard, if he wants to know who backs him here against the Sienese: the face he sees will tell him it's Capocchio, the alchemist counterfeiter of metals. And Capocchio adds, "if I correctly take your measure / recall how apt I was at aping nature" (138–139). Thus, in medias res, our canto ends.

This narrative is perplexing. When they are first introduced, the two falsifiers can hardly shift their own bodies about, and one of them is weeping over their disfigured state (91–92). But, as soon as they realize that one of their visitors is still alive, they too seem to come alive again and find unsuspected new energies; they become sparkling and quick-witted, incapable of taking anything seriously. Griffolino's six-line account of how he died under the wrong imputation is full of roguish winkings, its tone hardly different from that of the *beffa* for which he was burned at the stake:

> "It's true that I had told him—jestingly—
> 'I'd know enough to fly through air'; and he,
> with curiosity, but little sense,
>   wished me to show that art to him and, just
> because I had not made him Daedalus,
> had one who held him as a son burn me.
>
> (112–117)

This is in the style and form of a regular little *novella,* with some lively direct speech and various quick, masterful strokes of character: altogether, a story more apt to be told in the sunny squares of this world than in the dark and sorrowful ditches of Malebolge. Moreover, Griffolino seems to accept Minos's judgment with equanimity, and even of Albero, who was responsible for his death, he speaks without any special animosity: briefly, Hell does not seem to have changed much this soul's cheerful disposition. Similar observations could be made with regard to Capocchio's ironies at the expense of the Sienese. The two seem to be well suited to each other, making up together a good double act; and all the signs are that they enjoy performing at least as much as we, and Dante, enjoy watching them. In fact, far from eliciting any further sympathy for their pain, their behavior reminds us of that other spirited troop, the Malebranche of the fifth *bolgia.* Until, of course, we cross over to the next canto to find, beyond an extensive mythological interlude, Capocchio bitten in the nape of his neck by

Gianni Schicchi's piercing fangs, and then made to scrape the hard bottom of the ditch with his belly (xxx, 28–30)—while Griffolino is spared only to chronicle the event. There is no escaping Dante's penal colony. And just as the poem's unifying moral force arrives, eventually and inevitably, to punish Capocchio, so it does not fail to strike a blow against the temporary lapse in the pilgrim's moral vigilance. When the measure is full, Virgil bursts (xxx, 131–132). But by then, of course, the pilgrim's *voglia* is quite satisfied.

Canto xxix of *Inferno* cannot be said to be a major canto. The tension between formal structure and thematic organization of content, which we mentioned at the beginning of our reading, remains unresolved until and beyond the canto's last line. Indeed, this tension is further complicated, as we have seen, by the remarkable shifts in Dante's stylistic register. The canto is an excellent example of the poet's unique ability to synthesize in one structural unit figurative elements and levels of language and style that the literary tradition, before and after him, treated as utterly incompatible: the tragic silence of Geri del Bello, the comic storytelling of Griffolino, and the ironic gossiping of Capocchio; the *popol tutto infermo* of mythical Aegina and the repugnant lepers of contemporary Valdichiana, Maremma, and Sardinia; the pitiful tears and lamentations of the damned and their grotesque and loathsome punishment; the high-sounding, civilized conversation of the two pilgrims and the harsh, detailed realism of the alchemists' degraded condition. It is precisely to the vast range of this scandalous *contaminatio* (Contini, 447) that Pietro Bembo so bitterly objected, when he wrote:

> It would have been far more praiseworthy if he [Dante] had set out to write about a less lofty and wide-ranging subject matter, and kept it to its appropriate middle ground; having chosen, however, to range wide and high, he could not help demeaning himself by writing very often about the most base and vulgar things.
>
> (*Prose della volgar lingua* ii, xx, 178)

Thus Bembo was to regret that Dante had not been another Petrarch. What he failed to foresee is that, following his advice, the search for a dignified middle ground was bound to produce, as with few exceptions it did, a mediocre literature.

BIBLIOGRAPHY

Ball, Robert. "Theological Semantics: Virgil's *Pietas* and Dante's *Pietà*." *Stanford Italian Review* 2 (1981): 59–79.
Bembo, Pietro. *Opere*. Ed. Carlo Dionisotti. 2d ed. Turin, 1966.
Bosco, Umberto. "I due stili della decima bolgia dantesca." *Romanic Review* 62 (1971): 167–182.

Carpi, Umberto. "La nobiltà di Dante (A proposito di *Par.* xvi)." *Rivista di letteratura italiana* 8 (1990): 229–260.

Chiari, Alberto. *Letture dantesche,* 83–120. 2d ed. Florence, 1946.

Contini, Gianfranco. "Sul xxx dell' *Inferno.*" In *Varianti e altra linguistica,* 447–457. Turin, 1979.

Gabrieli, Francesco. "Il canto xxix dell'*Inferno.*" In *"Inferno": Letture degli anni 1973–1976,* ed. Silvio Zennaro, 705–719. Rome, 1977.

Hollander, Robert. "Dante's 'Book of the Dead': A Note on *Inferno* xxix, 57." *Studi danteschi* 54 (1982): 31–51.

Lanci, Antonio. "Pio." *Enciclopedia dantesca,* 4:525. Rome, 1973.

Mariani, Gaetano. "Canto xxix." In *Lectura Dantis Scaligera,* ed. Mario Marcazzan, 1027–1060. Florence, 1967.

Mayer, Sharon E. "Dante's Alchemists." *Italian Quarterly* 12 (1969): 185–200.

Mazzotta, Giuseppe. *Dante's Vision and the Circle of Knowledge.* Princeton, 1993.

Pertile, Lino, ed. *Annotationi nel Dante fatte con messer Trifon Gabriele in Bassano.* Bologna, 1993.

Salsano, Fernando. "Il canto xxix dell'*Inferno.*" In *Nuove letture dantesche,* 3:52–82. Florence, 1969.

Sanguineti, Edoardo. *Interpretazione di Malebolge,* 311–336. Florence, 1961.

Sapegno, Natalino. "Canto xxix, *Inferno.*" In *Letture dantesche,* ed. Giovanni Getto, 589–603. 1939. Florence, 1965.

Tench, Darby. "Canto xxix." In *Dante's "Divine Comedy," Introductory Readings: Inferno,* ed. Tibor Wlassics, 373–387. Charlottesville, Va., 1990.

Virgil. *The Eclogues, Georgics and Aeneid of Virgil.* Transl. C. Day Lewis. London, 1966.

CANTO XXX

Dante among the Falsifiers

ROBERT M. DURLING

The second of the cantos devoted to the falsifiers occupies a special place because it is the last of the thirteen cantos of the Malebolge. As we shall see, it ties together and develops with particular intensity themes and motifs that have been important throughout this longest section of the *Inferno*. If Canto XXIX was oppressively static, Canto XXX gives a certain interlude of action—utterly purposeless action that gradually turns into a mere exchange of taunts between two of the damned—against the *bolgia*'s background of general hebetude and paralysis. A first phase is introduced by an extended epic simile (parallel to those opening Cantos XXII and XXIV, the former of which has a close structural parallel with this one). In addition to intensifying the hypnotic atmosphere of madness and perverse violence, this simile also connects the events of the *bolgia* with two of Dante's types of condemned polities, Troy and Thebes, the latter of which, with its modern counterpart Florence, has replaced Rome in Dante's adaptation of Augustine's concept of the Earthly City, founded in fratricide and governed by pride, violence, and imperialistic ambition.

Of the two sinners exemplifying impersonation, Gianni Schicchi is an almost contemporary Florentine, while Myrrha is a figure from ancient myth. They are compared to pigs let loose from the sty (lines 25–27), and their manner of seizing on their victims attributes to them something like boars' tusks (*sanni*)

> The one came at Capocchio and sank
> his tusks into his neck so that, by dragging,
> he made the hard ground scrape against his belly.
>
> (28–30)

Heilbronn has pointed out that pigs, madness, and demonic possession are connected in Matthew 8:28–33, where the possessed swine "ran violently down a steep place into the sea: and they perished in the waters." Jacoff has explored the complex association of themes of patrilinear inheritance and legitimacy, incest, and female desire in Dante's female transgressors from Semíramis (Canto v) to Myrrha (an association equally applicable to Potiphar's wife). There are vague sexual connotations, too, in Gianni Schicchi's violation of patrilinear succession for "the lady of the herd," the horse or mule he bequeathed himself when he falsified Buoso Donati's will. It is not really clear why this fury is assigned to impersonators as opposed to other falsifiers in the *bolgia*, except insofar as the impersonator's sin subverts his very identity (cf. the thieves of Cantos xxiv and xxv), or why they are worse than anything in the Theban or Trojan cycles; but the interruption, similar to that of the prodigals in Canto xiii, sets off the main part of the canto very effectively.

The grouping together of alchemy, impersonation, and counterfeiting has a traditional basis. Alchemy, repeatedly condemned as fraudulent by the popes, often involved passing off base metals as gold, as Contini points out; the connection with counterfeiting is obvious. The traditional association of counterfeiting and impersonation goes back at least as far as Gottfried von Strassburg's *Tristan*, to Brangäne's impersonation of Isolt on her wedding night (ed. Ranke, 12601–12670); it is possible that Gottfried's passage derives from one in the lost portions of the Old French *Tristan* by Thomas, which Dante probably knew.

Master Adam, the chief focus of this canto, is introduced in a manner parallel to the two alchemists of Canto xxix: "I saw two" (xxix, 73), versus "I saw one" (xxx, 49; and cf. xxii, 31–32, a parallel noted by Contini), in one of the most vivid passages of the poem:

> I saw one who'd be fashioned like a lute
> if he had only had his groin cut off
> from that part of his body where it forks.
>   The heavy dropsy, which so disproportions
> the limbs with unassimilated humors
> that there's no match between the face and belly,
>   had made him part his lips like a consumptive,
> who will, because of thirst, let one lip drop
> down to his chin and lift the other up.
>
> (49–57)

Obviously based on direct observation (especially the graphic details of the disproportion between head and body—though this description is thematically motivated—and of the fevered person's extension of the lips), the passage is also, in medieval terms, a technically exact account of the physiology of dropsy, and, as we shall see, is laden with figural significance, even beyond the fact that by Dante's time dropsy was a traditional figure for avarice (Contini). Dante coyly notes that Master Adam would look like a lute if he were cut off "from that part of his body where it forks": since he is utterly immobilized by his disease—spiritually immobilized by his sins—Master Adam essentially has no legs.

Following without transition on this introduction comes Master Adam's first speech, a brilliantly compressed portrait that deploys the facets of this forceful personality, from his eloquent self-pity and the imaginings that deepen his suffering, to the nature of his sin and the fierceness of his desire for vengeance.

> "O you exempt from every punishment
> in this grim world, and I do not know why,"
> he said to us, "look now and pay attention
> to this, the misery of Master Adam:
> alive, I had enough of all I wanted;
> alas, I now long for one drop (*gocciol*) of water."
>   (58–63)

The antithesis between the luxury Master Adam knew in life, suggested by his association with gold, and his present yearning for a single little drop of water governs the whole passage. The abundance alludes, as the commentators have observed, to the parable of the rich man and the beggar (Dives and Lazarus) in Luke 16: the rich man, now burning in hell, begs the beggar he disdained at his doorstep, now in heaven, to dip his fingertip in water and bring it to him.

Master Adam's opening words echo Lamentations 1:12, a passage also echoed by Dante in *Vita nuova* VII, 3 and *Inferno* XXVIII, 132:

O all ye that pass by the way, attend, and see if there be any sorrow like to my sorrow: for he hath made a vintage of me, as the Lord spoke in the day of his fierce anger.

Dante almost certainly means that Master Adam intends the allusion (Contini showed that Master Adam's academic title, like his elaborate and learned rhetoric, identifies him as a clerk, probably a nobleman or high bourgeois; the idea that he is of low social origin is a misconception), and the lines matchlessly convey his self-pity. In the biblical passage, the personified city of Jerusalem is speaking after the sack of the city and the enslavement of the population by the Babylonians; the biblical allusion thus refers to a major instance of God's wrath (the Day of Judgment reminds us that Gianni Schicchi and Myrrha are God's instruments as well as his victims); finally, just as Jerusalem personifies the body politic, Master Adam represents a whole condition of society.

The echo of the personified Jerusalem calls attention to the exemplary nature of Master Adam's punishment (this motif figures also in the parable of Lazarus and Dives: the rich man begs that Lazarus visit his five brothers and warn them of his own fate [Luke 16:27–28]), but in his desire for revenge Master Adam apparently forgets God's anger and the warning that "Revenge is mine, and I will repay, saith the Lord" (Romans 12:19, recalling Deuteronomy 32:35), just as he disregards the reminders of God's mercy. A salient quality of his opening speech is the transition from the lamenting, self-pitying first half (six tercets) to the second (five tercets, beginning at line 76), which is dominated by his desire for vengeance against his employers, who led him to sin, a desire so great that he would not give it up in exchange for the water he so desperately craved a moment before ("Fonte Branda" is of disputed identity). What he would do if he found either of the counts of Romena is unstated but clear enough from what follows between him and Sinon: he would gloat over them and claim to be better than they. And in fact his desire to intensify the suffering of another of the damned is gratified in the case of Sinon, but at the price of undergoing the same process himself. In this respect Master Adam foreshadows the inhabitants of Cocytus, like Count Ugolino, whose rejection of salvation is associated with the desire for vengeance that has him gnawing the skull of his enemy.

As Sally Musseter and others have shown, the figural associations around Master Adam are particularly rich. Adam seems to be the name of an actual person burned at the stake in Florence in 1281. This name, and Master Adam's memory of the streams of the Casentino, establish a connection with the first Adam and the Garden of Eden, but Master Adam's fate is the reverse of that of the first Adam, who, expelled from Eden because of his sin, believed God's promise, repented, and was saved (we meet him in *Par.* xxvi, 82–142). Master Adam, then, is a type of Adam unsaved, the "old man" of Pauline tradition (see Romans 5:12, 17, and 6:6)—as are all the damned, but his case brings the idea into sharp focus.

> "alas, I now long for one drop (*gocciol*) of water.
>   The rivulets that fall into the Arno
> down from the green hills of the Casentino
> with channels cool and moist, are constantly
>   before me; I am racked by memory—
> the image of their flow parches me more
> than the disease that robs my face of flesh.

> The rigid Justice that would torment me
> uses, as most appropriate, the place
> where I had sinned, to draw swift sighs from me.
>   There is Romena, there I counterfeited
> the currency that bears the Baptist's seal;
> for this I left my body, burned, above."
>
> (64–75)

Part of the richness of the passage lies in the suggestion, conveyed by the plurals, that the Casentino has a multitude of "little streams" and fresh, moist streambeds; the diminutives (*gocciol* [little drop], *ruscelletti* [rivulets]) intensify the emphasis on the familiarity and simplicity of the element water, as well as contrasting with Master Adam's swollen bulk. The antithesis between health and disease is particularly strong in the implicit parallel between the earth, conceived as a healthy organism essentially immune to the corruptions brought by man, and Master Adam's diseased body, particularly in the greenness of the hills and the use of the term for softness of the cool, moist streambeds, in contrast with the rigid distension of Master Adam's belly and with the "rigid Justice" that probes him. That the little streams descend into the Arno reminds us that they are part of a system of rivers, an important aspect of the parallel between the earth and the human body.

That Master Adam sinned by falsifying "the currency that bears the Baptist's seal" (74)—the florin of twenty-four-karat gold whose genuineness was guaranteed by the image of John the Baptist stamped on one side, a lily on the other—makes unmistakable the allusion to baptism implicit in the description of the streams. The diminutives mentioned above have a further function in this connection, for baptism restores the soul to health and a childlike "newness of life" (Romans 6:4). The image of childhood, and the innocence and everyday simplicity of water, as well as its connection with natural fertility, are emphasized in the traditional blessing of the baptismal water in the midnight Easter service (*Inferno* xxx takes place during the evening before Easter; Dunstan Tucker has demonstrated the frequency of references to the Easter liturgy in all parts of the *Comedy*):

> Let the Holy Spirit, with the secret admixture of its divinity, make fertile this water prepared for the regeneration of men; so that, sanctification conceived, a heavenly offspring may come forth from the immaculate womb of the divine fountain: and so that grace may give birth to all, though they may be separated by sex or age, into the same infancy . . . [Touching the water with the hand:] May this creature be holy and innocent, free from all incursions of the adversary. . . . All-powerful God, be present in your mercy; breathe upon us kindly. Bless this simple water

with your mouth; so that, beyond the natural cleansing which it offers
bodies that are to be washed, it may be effective also in cleansing minds.

(Liber usualis, 776y)

The baptismal aspect of the water imagery does not touch Master Adam,
who is engrossed by his suffering and the rigidity of God's justice, but its
function is far from external or generic. The poignancy of the lines derives
also from the fact that at the moment of Master Adam's sin both his natural surroundings and the very coin he was counterfeiting were offering
him salvation, calling him to repentance (the Baptist, saying "Do penance:
for the kingdom of heaven is at hand" [Matthew 3:2]), had he only been
able to understand them correctly and to respond.

Even Master Adam's grotesque shape has a figural meaning. As Denise
Heilbronn has shown, behind the comparison of Master Adam's shape to
a lute there lies a long tradition comparing Christ on the Cross with a
stringed instrument. In other words, Master Adams's punishment is a distorted, parodic parallel to the Crucifixion, one that has no redemptive
power, though it may serve as a warning (the echo of Lamentations in Master Adam's first speech also recalls the traditional exegesis of the fall of
Jerusalem as a type of the Crucifixion).

The intensity of Dante's portrait of Master Adam, and the importance
of its figural dimension, should not distract attention from Dante's careful
analysis of fraud. The last two *bolge,* those of the sowers of discord and the
falsifiers, include climactic effects Dante has reserved for their final position,
effects that derive from his view of the social effects of fraud. In Canto
XXVIII, 7–21, he imagines the agglomeration of the wounded from the
bloodiest battlefields of Italy; in Canto XXIX, 46–66, the massing together
of all sufferers from malaria—it is compared to the plague in Aegina. The
grandiose horror of these scenes has only been approached so far, in the *Inferno,* by the mass effects of the cantos of the thieves. In these sweeping
spectacles of war and disease we have something like direct representation
of the body politic; perhaps nowhere else is it made clearer that fraud is a
disease of society as a whole.

The individual souls in these *bolge* suffer punishments that correspond to
the effects their sins have had on the body politic; thus they are figures of the
body politic individually as well as en masse. This idea is made explicit by
Bertran de Born when he says that his decapitation is the specific *contrapasso*
for having sown discord between father and son; interestingly, he speaks of
his trunk as the origin of his head, thus indicating a double valency in the
punishment: Henry II was both the origin of the young king, whom Bertran
incited to rebellion, and the head of state and family. That the sinner suffers
in his own body the effect he has produced in society is appropriate for reasons beyond the symmetry and the traditional view that the deceiver is
caught in his own devices (conspicuously the basis of many punishments in

the Malebolge). It is a representation of the essential inseparability, even, at a certain level, the identity, of individuals and their society.

For Dante hell is a giant projection of the human body. The myriad parallels are based on the traditional idea of the body of Satan, the infernal correlative—and parody—of the body of Christ, the community of those who are saved. Dante and Virgil begin their descent at what corresponds to the head (Limbo, which represents humanity's memory of the ancient world); we pass the devouring gullet among the gluttons, the spleen with the sullen. Within the City of Dis we reach a river of blood, the forest of the heart, and what should be a fountain or reservoir of life but is instead an arid, burning plain: the circles of violence correspond to the breast, where the intellectual and bestial natures are joined. Hell is divided, and Dante requires transportation, at points roughly corresponding to the major divisions of the human body: neck (Phlegyas; the walls of the City of Dis correspond to the ribcage), diaphragm (Geryon). Antaeus and the other giants are in a location that corresponds to the genitals, and they are like grotesque, rebellious penises. Cocytus, finally corresponds to the large intestine.

Throughout the *Inferno,* and with particular clarity in the Malebolge, Dante associates sin and its punishment with bodily malfunction and disease, for hell is Babylon, or confusion (hence Satan, the head, is at the bottom). The Malebolge, where fraud is punished, correspond to the belly and are based on an elaborate parallel between the digestion of foods and the work of the mind, for truth is the food of the soul, fraud its poison; their concentric circles have an obvious relation to the labyrinth of the intestines. References to food, to cooking, to the various parts of the digestive tract, to excretion and excrement, are legion, along with allusions to some dozen diseases that in Dante's time were considered results of malfunction of the digestive system. Punishments like those of the barrators, who are boiled in pitch (Cantos XXI–XXII); the thieves, who undergo changes and exchanges of form, incineration, and agglutination (Cantos XXIV–XXV); the simoniacs, who are burned by oily flames (Canto XIX); and the flatterers, who are immersed in excrement (Canto XVIII) involve sharply focused parodies of cooking and digestion (on this whole question, see Durling 1981).

Counterfeiting is a branch of fraud with particularly important social repercussions due to the peculiar character of money. As Shoaf has shown, Dante, like other fourteenth-century writers, is intensely concerned with the ambiguous nature of money, both a good (gold) and a universal signifier. Money is involved in a general crisis of signification felt in the fourteenth century, the more so that deliberate debasement of the currency, such as Master Adam's addition of three carats of dross, creating twenty-one-carat rather than twenty-four-carat gold, was not uncommon.

Dante's treatment of Master Adam rests on a technically precise parallel between the minting of coins and the digesting of food. In both cases, the cooking of raw material must break down its form, allowing the separation of impurities and at last the shaping of the purified material. After the so-called first digestion in the stomach, according to the received theory, the second digestion, in the liver, converts the usable food, now liquid, into blood that it then shares out to the members, each of which assimilates what it needs (there was no conception of the circulation of blood at this period). The moment at which Master Adam adds three carats of base metal to the purified gold corresponds closely to the second digestion, and, in fact, the dropsy of which Master Adam complains results from the liver's not properly converting liquid food into blood: "unassimilated humors" (53).

In terms of the body analogy governing the Malebolge and hell as a whole, the *contrapasso* is particularly interesting. Master Adam's metallurgy has caused a disproportion between the face of the coin (proclaiming its genuineness) and its contents, just as in dropsy "there's no match between the face and belly" (54). Furthermore, in debasing the florin Master Adam has introduced impurities into one of the vital fluids of the body politic: He has inflated the currency, and his distended belly is itself the figure of a distempered economy. Behind Dante's conception lies a particular variant of the Roman historian Livy's fable of Menenius Agrippa, which relates the rebellion of the members against the greedy belly (*Ab urbe condita* II, 32–33). Dante uses John of Salisbury's twelfth-century version (*Policraticus* 5 and 6), which introduces the notion of the malfunction of the organs, including the stomach. In John's influential discussion of the Platonic idea that the health of society depends on harmony and balance among the classes, the head of the body is the king, the heart is the senate (the repository of wisdom), and the stomach and intestines are the tax-gatherers and treasurers (these would include the minters of coin), not, as in Livy, the ruling class. John implies the parallel between money, portable wealth, and bodily humors, especially blood—digested (thus portable) food—though, to the best of my knowledge Nicole d'Oresme, later in the fourteenth century, is the first to make this connection fully explicit. Dante almost certainly got the idea from John; he, too, leaves implicit the parallel between money and blood. Master Adam is thus in many respects the climax and summation of a basic theme of the Malebolge; we might call him the very belly of the belly of hell.

The possibility of hostile interaction between Master Adam and his companions in misery is already implied in his scornful references to them, *questa gente sconcia* (85), the adjective translating variously as "shameful, obscene, indecent, or mutilated," and "Because of them [Guido and his brothers] I'm in this family" (88). Both of these lines imply that Master Adam would have considered himself superior to his companions during his life. The term *famiglia* referred to the household servants of a lord: he would have scorned to serve a lord who had such servants, but now he and they alike are household servants of the devil.

Presumably Sinon—Potiphar's wife, too, though she will remain silent, perhaps in allusion to the volubility of her accusation of Joseph—has been listening to Master Adam's entire speech. Dante's question about them follows naturally on Master Adam's reference:

> And I to him: "Who are those two poor sinners
> who give off smoke like wet hands in the winter
> and lie so close to you upon the right [*a' tuoi destri confini*]?"
>
> (91–93)

The reference to Master Adam's "frontiers" (*confini*) is a sardonic allusion to his deformed bulk, but it derives an added force from its relation to the counterfeiter's symbolic status. The vivid image of the vapor rising from the "two poor sinners," in addition to the tension introduced by the reference to winter where everyone is so feverish, contributes to the impression of hebetude and helplessness and makes Sinon's sudden blow the more surprising and effective. The immobility of his neighbors, Master Adam says, is equal to his own:

> "I found them there," he answered, "when I rained
> down to this rocky slope; they've not stirred since
> and will not move, I think, eternally.
>   One is the lying woman who blamed Joseph;
> the other, lying Sinon, Greek from Troy;
> because of raging fever they reek so [*per febbre aguta gittan tanto leppo*]."
>
> (94–99)

Master Adam's last remark is the first reference to stench in this canto, but XXIX, 50–51 introduced it as basic to the *bolgia*; etymologically related to words for fat, *leppo* seems properly to refer to the smell of burning fat, and we are meant to connect it with the visual image of rising smoke or steam, with vivid, disturbing effect.

The stench of dead bodies is frequently mentioned in the prophets' description of the Day of Judgment (e.g., Isaias 3:24, Joel 2:20, Amos 4:10), and the stink of the damned is the antithesis of the biblical notion that an acceptable sacrifice smells sweet to the Lord (e.g., Genesis 8:21). Odor is also a common figure for reputation (e.g., Ecclesiastes 10:1), and as such is particularly relevant to Sinon's reaction to Master Adam's words:

> E l'un di lor, che si recò a noia
> forse d'esser nomato sì oscuro,
> col pugno li percosse l'epa croia.
>   Quella sonò come fosse un tamburo;

e maestro Adamo li percosse il volto
col braccio suo, che non parve men duro.

> And one of them, who seemed to take offense,
> perhaps at being named so squalidly,
> struck with his fist at Adam's rigid belly.
>   It sounded as if it had been a drum;
> and Master Adam struck him in the face,
> using his arm, which did not seem less hard.
>
> (100–105)

And so the flyting (exchange of taunts) begins, the two physical blows immediately replaced by verbal ones. Master Adam quickly forgets Dante in his quarrel with Sinon. This is an unusual event in the *Inferno:* almost all Dante's and Virgil's interlocutors are so intent on the conversation that even if briefly distracted their attention soon returns. This will not be the case with Master Adam; his only interest in Dante and Virgil is to have them witness his woe. Sinon's blow to Master Adam's most conspicuous feature is described with technical precision: whether *li percosse l'epa* means that the blow fell on the location of the liver or is a metonymy, which seems more likely, we are reminded again of his particular digestive disorder, the focus of his status as a figure for the body politic. The learned term *epa*, along with the unusual word *croia*, maintains the scornful tone of the first description. The mention of a drum brings in the nomenclature of dropsy, one type of which is called *tympanitis,* and perhaps shows that Dante was drawing on a particular passage in Bartholomaeus Anglicus, as Contini argued, in the term *tamburo:* "the belly swells and resounds like a drum . . . the neck and the extremities become thin." Sinon's blow is also particularly appropriate to Sinon; it echoes, even verbally (*sonò, insonuere*), the famous passage in the *Aeneid* where Laocoön warns the Trojans against the Trojan horse:

> *"Equo ne credite, Teucri!*
> *quidquid id est, timeo Danaos et dona ferentis."*
> *sic fatus validis ingentem viribus hastam*
> *in latus inque feri curvam compagibus alvum*
> *contorsit, stetit illa tremens, uteroque recusso*
> *insonuere cavae gemitumque dedere cavernae.*

> "Trojans, do not
> trust in the horse. Whatever it may be,
> I fear the Greeks, even when they bring gifts."
> And as he spoke he hurled his massive shaft
> with heavy force against the side, against
> the rounded, jointed belly of the beast.

> It quivered when it struck the hollow cavern,
> which groaned and echoed.
>
> (II, 68–75)

The Malebolge began with Geryon, a spatial representation of the diachronic structure of fraud; Trojan horse and counterfeit coin, paired in this last Malebolge canto, are two of Dante's most fundamental, recurrent figures for the synchronic structure of fraud. They exemplify the disparity between the surface (or face) of a container/vehicle—the horse as offering to Minerva, the imprinted faces and the color of the coin—and its contents (or belly)—the armed men, the debased gold: "There's no match between the face and belly" (54). Both bellies are wombs pregnant with social disaster. Master Adam's and Sinon's blows strike belly and face and themselves refer to the dual structure (fundamental to language, in Dante's view) that makes fraud possible.

The emphasis on hand and arm both in the blows and in Sinon's taunts is part of the system of allusions to coining in the canto: to mint a coin, one placed a sphere of gold of the appropriate size within an engraved die, to which one then gave a sharp blow with a heavy hammer. The traditional range of metaphors involving coining is very large, as Marc Shell has shown; coining is an important instance of the imposition of form on material; as such it was used metaphorically of the influence of the heavens on the sublunar, the imposition of resemblance to the father on the fetus (the Aristotelian theory of human reproduction assigned only a passive role to the mother, based as it was on analogy with agriculture), the assimilation of food to the various organs, and the achievement by a writer of individual style.

A striking aspect of the quarrel in Canto xxx is that these two arch-deceivers say nothing to each other that is not strictly true, but of course these are truths that do not nourish but rather poison them: *lo 'nferno li attosca* (VI, 84), as Dante says to the glutton Ciacco, in one of the first instances in the poem of the food/poison antithesis. It has often been pointed out that the lower we descend in hell the more reluctant the souls are to be remembered among the living, the more desirous of concealing their identities—this is true especially in the Malebolge and in Cocytus. The cause of this concealment is partly shame that the blackness of their sins should be known, but it should be remembered that in the two lowest circles of hell we are witnessing the punishment of fraud, and Dante shows that this punishment requires those who forfeited salvation by suppressing the truth to make it known and hear it made known by others. That the truth-telling is malicious and futile is also part of its sting.

Much has been made of the vivid vulgarity of the exchanges, whose point lies in the degradation of intellect in persons of a certain social standing (Sinon, like Master Adam, is no plebeian, nor is Potiphar's wife).

That the last taunt in the flyting is Master Adam's reference to Narcissus is significant:

> "*tu hai l'arsura e 'l capo che ti duole,*
> *e per leccar lo specchio di Narcisso,*
> *non vorresti a 'nvitar molte parole."*

> "you have both dryness and a head that aches;
> few words would be sufficient invitation
> to have you lick the mirror of Narcissus."
> (127–129)

There is an implicit dog image in *leccar;* it connects these lines with the bestial images applied to Gianni Schicchi and Myrrha, as well as to Hecuba (20), whose barking looks forward to the "faces / made doglike" (XXXII, 71) of Cocytus and the doglike barkings and gnawings of Bocca (XXXII, 105) and of Ugolino (XXXIII, 78). The reference to Narcissus functions on several levels. The beauty of Narcissus sharpens our sense of the deformity of these sinners. The reference brings the episode to a conclusion with an echo of the references to the streams of the Casentino, which are, as we saw, a negative reflection of Master Adam, increasing his torment by reminding him how different he is from them. The knowledge of their own deformity is a chief suffering of the damned. Augustine of Hippo's classic account of his conversion shows the impact of the moment in which the sinner for the first time gazes steadfastly at his true state and recognizes that in it God's image has been defaced.

> But you, Lord, as he [Ponticianus] spoke, were forcing me to turn back to myself, taking me from behind my back, where I had placed myself while I did not wish to attend to myself, and you were placing me before my face, so that I might see how ugly I was, how distorted and filthy, stained, and ulcered: and I saw and was horrified, and there was no place where I could flee from myself.
> (*Confessions* VIII, 7, 16)

In Augustine's view this moment is actively produced by God in his effort to bring the sinner to repentance. Its negative narcissism is critical because if the soul refuses grace it becomes petrified in horror and despair. Here almost certainly is the ultimate significance of the Medusa for Dante, as we see in cases like Master Adam and like Ugolino (see especially XXXIII, 46–49), and it governs the entire presentation of Cocytus.

Dante's treatment of the counterfeiters thus focuses sharply on the problem of imagery and its debasement. Dragonetti and Shoaf have explored a complex set of parallels, centering on references to Narcissus, that relate *Inferno* xxx to the thirtieth cantos of the other canticles: Dante must transcend his sinful fixation on "counterfeiters of goodness" (*Purg.* xxx, 131) and on his own image, eventually to reach the ultimate—the redeemed—narcissism of seeing *nostra effige* (our image, Christ's human nature) in the sealike depths of light in God (*Par.* xxxiii, 127–133).

At the beginning of Canto xxix, after two cantos of watching the mutilation of the sowers of discord, Dante is drunk with the spectacle of blood and wishes to go on watching and weeping. Virgil rebukes him with the need for haste, and the pilgrim defends himself, not altogether ingenuously, according to the first three lines (xxix, 1–15). At the end of Canto xxx a similar fixation on the damned is interrupted by an even more severe rebuke from Virgil, one that seems more disproportionate than the last: "To want to hear such bickering is base" (148).

That Virgil reproaches Dante for a base desire ought to puzzle readers. The poet has obviously taken much pleasure in his sardonic representations. The Italian critics traditionally regard the passage, and Virgil's rebuke, as the poet's exorcising farewell to the mode that had fascinated him in his *tenzone* with Forese Donati. Shoaf urges that the sequence of rebuke, prayer for forgiveness, and forgiveness acts out the redemptive pattern that Master Adam and his associates rejected; this is the case, but it overlooks a difficulty. No doubt we are meant to dissociate a correct way of reading the passage from the hypnotized fixation attributed to the pilgrim. But if the rebuke seems both excessive and, on the poet's part, disingenuous, just as the pilgrim's excuses seem fulsome, it is because in such moments the paradox of the poem comes very close to the surface: the disparity between the *Comedy's* theological fiction—that after his journey to the beyond the poet expresses moral attitudes that are entirely "correct," worthy of heaven—and the human delight he and we take in the vivid spectacles of evil anatomized that he provides.

BIBLIOGRAPHY

Augustine. *Confessionum libri viii.* Ed. I. Capello. Turin, 1948.
Avicenna. *Liber Canonis,* ff. 300r–305v. 1507. Reprint, Hildesheim, 1964 (on dropsy).
Barkan, Leonard. *Nature's Work of Art: The Human Body as Image of the Cosmos.* New Haven, 1975.
Bigi, Emilio. *Il Canto xxx dell'"Inferno."* Florence, 1963.
———. "Adamo, Maestro." *Enciclopedia dantesca,* 1:49–50. Rome, 1970.
Brownlee, Kevin. "Dante and Narcissus (*Purg.* xxx, 76–99)." *Dante Studies* 96 (1978): 201–206.
Contini, Gianfranco. "Sul xxx dell'*Inferno*" (1953). In *Varianti e altra linguistica: Una raccolta di saggi,* 447–457. Turin, 1970.
Dragonetti, Roger. "Dante et Narcisse, ou les faux-monnayeurs de l'image." In *Dante et les mythes: Tradition et rénovation,* ed. Etienne Gilson, 85–146. Paris, 1965.
———. *Dante, pèlerin de la sainte Face.* Ghent, 1968.
Durling, Robert M. 1981. "Deceit and Digestion in the Belly of Hell." In *Allegory and Representation: Papers from the English Institute,* ed. Stephen Greenblatt, 61–93. Baltimore, 1981.

Fumagalli, Carlo. "Poesia addominale di Malebolge." *Annali dell'Istituto di studi danteschi* 1 (1967): 359–372.

Heilbronn, Denise. "Master Adam and the Fat-Bellied Lute (*Inf.* xxx)." *Dante Studies* 101 (1983): 51–65.

Jacoff, Rachel. "Transgression and Transcendence: Figures of Female Desire in Dante's *Commedia*." *Romanic Review* 79 (1988): 129–142.

John of Salisbury. *Policraticus*. Ed. C. Webb. 2 vols. Oxford, 1909.

Martinez, Ronald L. "Dante, Statius, and the Earthly City." *Dissertation Abstracts* 38 (1979): 6707a–6708a.

McMahon, Robert. "Autobiography as Text-Work: Augustine's Refiguring of Genesis 3 and Ovid's 'Narcissus' in his Conversion Account." *Exemplaria* 1 (1989): 337–366.

Musseter, Sally. "Inferno xxx: Dante's Counterfeit Adam." *Traditio* 34 (1978): 427–435.

Ogilvie, R. M. *A Commentary on Livy*. Books 1–5, 312–359. Oxford, 1965 (on the fable of Menenius Agrippa).

Rahner, Hugo. "Flumina de ventre eius: Die patristische Auslegung von Joh. 7,37–38." *Biblica* 22 (1941): 269–302, 367–403.

Shell, Marc. *The Economy of Literature*. Baltimore, 1978.

Shoaf, Richard A. *Dante, Chaucer, and the Currency of the Word*. Norman, Okla., 1983.

Singer, Charles, and E. Underwood. *A Short History of Medicine*. 2d ed. New York, 1962.

Tucker, Dunstan J. "In exitu Israel de Aegypto: The *Divine Comedy* in the Light of the Easter Liturgy." *American Benedictine Review* 11 (1960): 43–61.

CANTO XXXI

The Giants: Majesty and Terror

MASSIMO MANDOLINI PESARESI

In his *prologo* to Valéry's *Le cimetière marin,* Borges comments on the fact that Christian poetry feeds on our amazed incredulity. He observes that Dante, ignoring our ignorance, had to stick to the *novelesco* and the extraordinary varieties of destiny.[1] The defiant certainty required by the author of otherworldly fiction is thematized in Canto XXXI and developed in a varied and complex way.

After an initial reference to the crucial ambivalence (or ambiguity) of life and death ("The very tongue that first had wounded me . . . was then to cure me with its medicine" [1–3]), the canto unfolds a series of reversals of sensations, feelings, and modes.[2] The reversals create a comedy of errors that underscores the transitional character of this canto, placed on the threshold of the anticlimactic epiphany of evil within the frozen marsh of Cocytus in Canto XXXIII. Devoid of damned souls and inhabited by the solitary figures of the towerlike giants, Canto XXXI is a canto of dim twilight and silence, rent by the horn and the cry of Nimrod and by the shaking of Ephialtes: a sinister interlude in the tragic despair of the final circles of Hell.

Dante already confessed the extreme difficulty of describing visions of ever increasing horrors and atrocities in Hell. In the opening of Canto XXVIII, the rhetorical question "Who, even with untrammeled words and many / attempts at telling, ever could recount / in full the blood and wounds that I now saw?" is followed by a hypothetical simile "Were you to reassemble all the men," which probably derives from the powerful incipit of the *planh* for the death of the young king, "If all grief and sorrow and

406

dismay," where words similarly fail.[3] A comparable rhetorical gesture comes when Dante deems the horrors of Greek mythology an inadequate term of comparison for his own ghastlier phantasmagoria (xxx, 22–27). Later, Dante drastically negates his hypothesis that he can master a suitable means for expressing Hell's *tristo buco* ("melancholy hole" [xxxii, 2]). Apophasis, or expression by silence, leaves no space for figurative imagination. The pilgrim has known all sorts of torments and evil and is now approaching "the emperor of the despondent kingdom" (xxxiv, 28). It would seem that the tragic has exhausted all its resources, from the doom of Paolo and Francesca to the false repentance of the courtier Guido de Montefeltro. The only locus left for true pathos is Ugolino's episode, and it strikes us because of its forbidding tone. The narrative of the atrocious event has the dismal dryness we expect from one who has poured all his tears, has fathomed the horror of the human condition, and cannot find appeasement even in revenge. Dante's soul too is parched by pain and grief, and the pilgrim is ready to distance himself from those ghastly visions and to ascend.

Essential to this transition at the end of the canticle are the giants of Canto xxxi. Frightening and comic, huge and stupid, deafening and speechless, they seal the intrinsic ambiguity of the episode.[4] Although deprived of majesty, the giants still preserve an undiminished aesthetic grandeur. They are impotent and brutish creatures; their arcane, towering shadows in the misty plain will haunt our memory. Their ambivalence mirrors the ambivalence of evil as depicted in the last cantos.

Evil, if we are to overcome it, must be deprived of its allure and appear devoid of any seductive or majestic power: Lucifer must therefore become a ludicrous monster, which seems to come out of a child's nightmare of hairy and horned beasts. And yet such evil can damn our souls for ever. Seemingly harmless as a caricature, it still has the power to shatter our lives. Dante's insight into the nature of sin (which we may call weakness, or error, or confusion) bears on this fundamental duplicity. "Virtue itself turns vice being misapplied, / And vice sometimes's by action dignified," says Friar Laurence (*Romeo and Juliet* ii, iii, 17–18). A comparable proximity, difficult to disentangle at times, characterizes damnation and salvation.

In this canto the quest for truth takes the form of an endeavor for the right vision. Dante devotes a long and detailed description to the gradual vanishing of his optical illusion. He gains a true view, but the ancient error lingers in it. The moral tension of the episode hinges on the unremitting effort required to grasp the truth: It is terribly easy to go astray, and only grace can save us from the grim mechanism of evil. Salvation may appear as a warm and friendly guidance ("Then lovingly he took me by the hand" [xxxi, 28]) that leads us across the bridge, as narrow as a sword's blade, overarching the deadly dangers of our life. (Of the few studies on this canto, Peter Dronke's "The Giants in Hell" stands out for its vast erudition and sensitive reading.)[5]

The visual delusions of Dante the pilgrim, who, at the embankment past the tenth *bolgia,* mistakes the giants for towers add a sinister but not fearsome ambivalence to the whole episode.[6] The delusory image of the towers lingers as an obsessive leitmotiv throughout the canto.[7] Besides being an allusion to "the scientists' modes of explanation," Dante's insistence on such "illusions"[8]—as actual sensory misjudgments or as simile or comparison—appears to me deeply functional to the comedy of errors that he is creating. The pilgrim's grasp of reality is shaken, and the poet's mastery over his own expressive means is blurred as well. Misconception and misrepresentation seem to be the fate of one who is about to confront the utmost horror just before he escapes from it. Dante's journey is unequivocally oneiric in its beginning ("I was so full of sleep just at / the point" [I, 11–12]). His prolonged nightmare makes the dreamer suspect that the giants are also a dream. The monsters he encounters *are,* in a certain sense, towers. They are as lifeless and harmless as immobile shadows. The allusion to scientific theories perhaps shows the elemental rationalization that Dante brings to the texture of his own vision, in order to exorcise its horror. Dante demythologizes the giants to tame them. Huge, humanlike beings, they are devoid of all the fabulous attributes of mythical tradition. Dante goes as far as having Virgil contradict his own statement, in the *Aeneid* (VI, 287 and X, 565–568) concerning the fifty bodies of Briareus. This giant is not unlike Ephialtes (in other words, he has human features) but is more ferocious in his countenance: "The one you wish to see lies far beyond / and is bound up and just as huge as this one, / and even more ferocious in his gaze" (XXXI, 103–105).

In the Middle Ages, such explanation was a form of rationalistic criticism of pagan mythology. Guido da Pisa, in his commentary on the canto, juxtaposes the classical giants not only with Nimrod and Goliath, but even with Saint Christopher.[9] Dante, however, emphasizes his demythologization with some humorous remarks: "Surely when she gave up the art of making / such creatures, Nature acted well indeed, / depriving Mars of instruments like these" (49–51). Unlike the original euhemerism, which used a rationalistic interpretation of the gods as outstanding humans to explain the godlike cults attributed to the Hellenistic monarchs, Dante's aims at dispelling the fearsome shadows of the fiction he has created. The monsters who challenged the gods and could have defeated them (119–121) are simply colossal creatures that can be measured in palms or contrasted with the stature of tall men. Dante is thus preparing a background for Lucifer, the rebel par excellence, who defied not the false pagan deities but the true God and nevertheless appears more grotesque and undignified than the giants themselves, outstripped as he is even of the grim majesty of a tower seen in murky air ("The emperor of the despondent kingdom / so towered from the ice, up from midchest, / that I match better with a giant's breadth / than giants match the measures of his arms" [XXXIV, 28–31]). The reassuring effect of misperception and misrepresentation is paradoxically achieved with the ambiguity usually found in the quiet, domestic horror referred to as the "uncanny." The uncanny is characterized by the perception of a frightening aura in a familiar object or situation—if what looks like a tower turns out to be a fearful giant. But no accompanying sense of mystery inhabits the infernal scene. The horror immediately sinks to a grotesque level, emphasized by means of such images as the pine cone, which adorns St. Peter's (58–59), and the three Frieslanders (61–64).

The sense of a progressive liberation from the ominous suspension at the beginning of the canto to the subdued fear in Antaeus's episode is mirrored in the shift from "the dense and darkened fog" (37) to the picture of a bright sky run through by clouds ("Just as the Garisenda seems when seen / beneath the leaning side, when clouds run past" [136–137]). Nevertheless, there are some moments of sheer terror in the canto, as when Ephialtes suddenly shakes or Nimrod blows his horn. Their hubris against heaven (Jove or the Lord) still appears in motiveless and frustrated gestures, which can scare but not harm the pilgrim. Among the giants, Nimrod stands out as a powerful and original artistic invention. In fact, while Ephialtes is a rather plain citation from Virgil (*Aeneid* VI, 577–584) and Ovid (*Metamorphoses* VI, 151–155), Dante's Nimrod is different from the strong hunter of the Vulgate. Augustine had shown Nimrod as the giant who instigated the building of the tower of Babel (*De civitate Dei* XVI, 4) and Dante accepts this tradition both in the *Comedy* (cf. also *Purg.* XI, 34–36) and in *De vulgari eloquentia* (I, vii, 4–8).[10]

In the Latin work, Dante retells and reinterprets the *Genesis* story, drawing in part on Augustine's reading (*De Genesi ad litteram* and *De civitate Dei*). At the very beginning of the treatise (chs. iii and iv), the author argues that language was given to man alone, because only to him—not to angels or animals—it was necessary (*De vulgari eloquentia* I, ii, 2). This pragmatic interpretation of the origin of language, conceived as a means to convey a rational content in a sensory medium[11]—is confirmed in the story of Babel: "Later, from this tripartite language (which had been received in that vengeful confusion), different vernaculars developed, as I shall show below" (*De vulgari eloquentia* I, viii, 3 [*Ab uno postea eodemque ydiomate in vindice confusione recepto diversa vulgaria traxerunt originem, sicut inferius ostendemus*]). The different idioms emerging from the confusion did not stem from Hebrew (the descendants of Shem, in fact, did not partake in the sinful enterprise). They were new languages given according to the different tasks performed in the construction:

> Only among those who were engaged in a particular activity did their language remain unchanged; so, for instance, there was one for all the architects, one for all the carriers of stones, one for all the stone-breakers, and so on for all the different operations. As many as were the types of work

involved in the enterprise, so many were the languages by which the human race was fragmented.

(*De vulgari eloquentia* I, vii, 7)

Here Dante goes beyond Augustine's statement on language as the instrument, par excellence, of social and political power (*De civitate Dei* XVI, 4). He defines power through the organization and division of labor. This kind of "corporative" origin of languages (in which there is a memory of the medieval *arti*) is tinged, however, with the *contrapasso*'s grim theodicy: "and the more skill required for the type of work, the more rudimentary and barbaric the language they now spoke" (*et quanto excellentius exercebant, tanto rudius nunc barbariusque locuntur*).

In order to interpret the enigmatic cry of Nimrod, we must place it within this system of counterbalances. If the giant had the greatest responsibility in the blasphemous challenge—a crime ranked by Dante on a par with original sin and with the moral depravation punished with the Flood (*De vulgari eloquentia* I, vii, 1)—his speech must show the utmost barbarity. Since language is originally and intrinsically the primal communicative instrument, Nimrod's words should be synonymous with unintelligibility. On this ground, we might easily concur with Dronke (and with Virgil) that *Raphèl maì amècche zabì almi* has no meaning and thus rule out all attempts at ascribing these words to a particular language.[12] The interpretation of the giant's cry as a *gramelot*—a glossolalic invention—of "dazed proto-Semitic" with inevitable comic effects, leaves unexplained the Arabic resonance of Nimrod's words. In fact, if he assumed that the post-Babelic languages did not originate from Hebrew, Dante could have set apart Nimrod's language of sin from the language of salvation of the "elect people," contriving a barbarous-sounding idiom without such evident Semitic features to convey Nimrod's language of separation and dispersion. Its Arabic cast recalls the fearfully graphic depiction of Mohammed and Alì in the bolgia of the sowers of discord three cantos earlier. It seems that, for reasons still to be investigated, Dante, who was such a sympathetic admirer of Averroës (Ibn Rushd) and Saladin (Salāḥ al-Dīn), believed that the Muslim religion should be presented with a character of emblematic laceration: the schism par excellence.[13]

Going back to the giants, the real protagonists of Canto XXXI, we may conclude our reading with a seemingly playful question. In which forge of the imagination were these monsters created? With all their improbable and arrogant reality, they are alone and unjustified in their world as we are in ours. Perhaps Dante is playing with the mirages of his own fiction or contemplating in a cracked mirror the distorted reflections of his meditations. The discourse that he is weaving on the very meaning and legitimacy of his creation may refer to a deeper ontological perplexity. At the end of the *Comedy*, Dante's brooding on the elusive nature of the poet's vision acquires a dramatic ring: "So is the snow, beneath the sun, unsealed; / and so, on the light leaves, beneath the wind, / the oracles the Sibyl wrote were lost" (*Par.* XXXIII, 64–66). Here the fading of memory is perhaps a trope for the more radical vanishing of existential certainty. In *Inferno* XXXI the poet, approaching the end of his infernal journey, rehearses in an almost comic vein the enigma that will have later its final, sublime orchestration.

NOTES

1. "Christian poetry feeds on our amazed incredulity, on our desire to believe that nobody disbelieves it. . . . Dante, who ignored our ignorance, had to abide by the fictional, by the extraordinary varieties of destiny. He possessed only a straightforward certainty; he always lacked hope and negation. He was not cognizant of propitious insecurity: the insecurity of Saint Paul, of Sir Thomas Browne, of Whitman, of Baudelaire, of Unamuno, of Paul Valéry" (Juan Luis Borges, *Prólogos, con un prólogo de prólogos* [Buenos Aires, 1975], 166; my translation).

2. See André Pézard, "*Manche* et *mancia,*" in *Dans le sillage de Dante* (Paris, 1975), 263–283.

3. Rather than Bertran de Born, the author of the *planh* "Si tuit li dol e.l plor e.l marrimen" is probably Rigaut de Berbezill: see *The Poems of the Troubadour Bertran de Born,* ed. William D. Paden Jr., Tilde Sankovitch, and Patricia H. Stablein (Berkeley, 1986), 93–94.

4. For the medieval belief in the historical character of the Genesis narration, see Arturo Graf, *Miti, legende e superstizioni del Medio Evo,* ed. Giosuè Bonfanti (Milan, 1984), 56–77.

5. Dronke, "The Giants in Hell," in *Dante and Medieval Latin Traditions* (Cambridge: 1986), 32–54. Alberto Chiari's "Nuova lettura del Canto dantesco dei Giganti (*Inferno* XXI)," *Critica letteraria* 11, no. 1 (1983): 3–25, is a new version of his 1930 reading published in *Letture dantesche* (Bergamo, 1973). See also André Pézard, "Le chant des géants," *Bulletin de la Société d'études dantesques—Annales du Centre universitaire méditerranéen* 12 (1963): 53–72; E. F. Jakob, "The Giants (*Inferno* XXXI), in *Medieval Miscellany Presented to Eugene Vinaver,* ed. F. Whitehead, A. H. Dinerres, F. E. Sutcliffe (Manchester, 1965), 167–185; Christopher Kleinhenz, "Dante's Towering Giants: *Inferno* XXXI," *Romance Philology* 27 (1974): 269–285; and Giovanni Cecchetti, "*Inferno* XXXI," in *Dante's "Divine Comedy," Introductory Readings: Inferno,* ed. Tibor Wlassics (Charlottesville, Va., 1990), 400–411.

6. In *Medieval Latin,* 34–35 Dronke shrewdly contrasts this episode with similar events in comparable moments of the dramatic structure of the *Comedy:* the heavenly host, first perceived as a flash of light, then as seven trees of gold, and eventually as walking candelabras, in *Purgatorio* XXIX; and the sight of the celestial rose, in *Paradiso* XXX, similarly attained with a gradual overcoming of delusion.

7. Cf. *torregiavan di mezza la persona / li orribili giganti, cui minaccia / Giove del cielo ancora quando tuona* (*Inf.* XXXI, 43–45); *Non fu tremoto già tanto rubesto, / che scotesse una torre così forte, / come Fïalte a scuotersi fu presto* (106–108); *Qual pare a riguardar la Carisenda / sotto'l chinato, quando un nuvol vada / sov'r essa sì, ched ella incontro penda* (136–138).

8. Dronke (*Medieval Latin,* 36) quotes Alhazen's *Optica* and Witelo's *Perspectiva.*

9. *Expositiones et Glose super Comediam Dantis* (ca. 1328), as mentioned in ibid., 136.

10. Further evidence of medieval execration of the Vulgate's *robustus venator* Nimrod can be found in Boccaccio's *Genealogia deorum gentilium:* "belua illa Nembroth" (XIV, viii) (*Opere in versi, Corbaccio, Trattatello in laude di Dante, Prose latine, Epistole,* ed. Pier Giorgio Ricci [Milan, 1965], 954). It should be noted, however, that in *De vulgari eloquentia* I, vii, 4 (*Presumpsit ergo in corde suo incurabilis homo sub persuasione gigantis Nembroth, arte sua non solum superare naturam, sed etiam ipsum naturantem, qui Deus est* ["Incorrigible humanity, therefore, led astray by the giant Nimrod, presumed in its heart to outdo in skill not only nature but the source of its own nature, who is God"]), "Nembroth" appears in the Berlin codex and was rejected by Pio Rajna ("Approcci per una nuova edizione del *De vulgari eloquentia,*" *Studi danteschi* 14 [1930]: 5–78). (All translations from *De vulgari eloquentia* are from Steven Botterill's edition [Cambridge, 1996].)

11. "It was necessary that the human race, in order for its members to communicate their

conceptions among themselves, should have some signal based on reason and perception. Since this signal needed to receive its content from reason and convey it back there, it had to be rational; but, since nothing can be conveyed from one reasoning mind to another except by means perceptible to the senses, it had also to be based on perception. For, if it were purely rational, it could not make its journey; if purely perceptible, it could neither derive anything from reason nor deliver anything to it" (*De vulgari eloquentia* I, iii, 2).

12. The interpretation of line 67 has been the object of several investigations. See, for instance, Richard Lemay, "Le Nemrod de l'*Enfer* de Dante et le *Liber Nemroth*," *Studi danteschi* 40 (1963): 57–128 (the second part of a study titled "Dante connaissait-il l'arabe?"); and Bruno Nardi's response, "Intorno al Nemrod dantesco e ad alcune opinioni di Richard Lemay," in *Saggi e note di critica dantesca* (Milan, 1966), 367–376.

13. For further Arabic echoes in this canto, note the similarity between the description of Ephialtes (86–88) and the portrayal of Satan in the *Liber Scale Machometi: Die lateinische Fassung des Kitāb al mi'radj,* ed. Edeltraub Werner (Düsseldorf, 1986), 192: "et cathenis ferreis ligaverunt, unam manum ante et alteram retro et similiter in eandem manerium pedes ejus" (and fastened him with iron chains, one hand to the front and the other behind his back, and likewise his feet).

CANTO XXXII

Amphion and the Poetics of Retaliation

JOHN AHERN

> The principle of poetry is a very anti-levelling principle. It aims
> at effect. . . . It has its altars and its victims, sacrifices, human
> sacrifices. . . . Carnage is its daughter.
>
> <div align="right">(William Hazlitt, on <i>Coriolanus</i>)</div>

> Whatever Book is for Vengeance and whatever Book is Against the
> Forgiveness of Sins is not of the Father, but of Satan the Accuser
> and Father of Hell.
>
> (William Blake, speaking of Dante)

> A speech produced without the least violence would determine
> nothing, would say nothing, would offer nothing to the other; it
> would not be <i>history,</i> and it would <i>show</i> nothing.
>
> <div align="right">(Jacques Derrida, <i>Writing and Difference</i>)</div>

1–15.   Following many classical writers on rhetoric, Dante believed that speech generates society. Brunetto Latini, whose works he admired in his youth (*Inferno* xv, 79–87), states the position succinctly: "Tully [i.e., Cicero] says that the greatest science of governing cities is rhetoric, which is the science concerned with speaking; without speech there would be neither cities, nor stabilized justice, nor an established human society" (*Li livres dou trésor,* iii, 1). In this canto Dante's subject is the "foundation of the entire universe" (xxxii, 8), an expression to take in its fullest possible sense, not merely as the center of the Ptolemaic universe. Cocytus, Hell's ninth and final circle, contains the constitutive principle of unredeemed human society: violent, self-destructive betrayal of family, community, guests, and benefactors. Here a special problem faces the poet: if speech creates human society, what kind of speech can represent its disintegration?

Dante the narrator takes as his model Amphion, the ancient Greek poet who founded Thebes, and whom he knew from Statius's *Thebaid* and Horace's *Art of Poetry.*

> Orpheus, who was a holy man and interpreter of the gods, deterred men
> of the forest from slaughter and eating polluted food, and for this was said
> to tame tigers and maddened lions, and Amphion, the founder of Thebes,
> was likewise said to move rocks where he wished by the sound of his

413

voice and gentle prayers. In days of old, wisdom consisted in separating public property from private, the sacred from the profane, in checking promiscuity, in laying down rules for the married, in building cities, in inscribing laws on wood.

(Art of Poetry, 391–400)

"By the sound of his voice and gentle prayers" Amphion made huge rocks form the walls around Thebes and also instituted a complete cultural order based on codes of legal, economic, religious, dietary, and sexual differentiation. Some take the phrase I render as "slaughter and eating polluted food" (*caedibus et victu foedo*) as a reference to cannibalism (Brink, 387). Brunetto Latini developed at greater length Amphion's role as a civilizer:

> Tully says that in the beginning men lived like beasts, without proper homes and without the knowledge of God, among woods and rural glades, and no one observed matrimony nor distinguished between father and son. Then there was one wise, well-spoken man who advised the others, and little by little showed them the importance of the soul, and dignity of reason, and discretion, so that he drew them from their wild surroundings and encouraged them to inhabit one spot and to maintain reason and justice. And thus through eloquence, which was in him with sense, this man was like a second god who brought the rules of human society to the world. And so history tells us that Amphion, who founded the city of Athens, charmed the stones and timber through the sweetness of his song, that is, through good words. He drew the men from the savage rocks where they lived, and made them common inhabitants of that city.
>
> <div align="right">(<i>Li livres dou trésor</i> III, 5–8)</div>

Brunetto mistakes Athens for Thebes—a significant error. Athens, of course, was the traditional model of the great city, whereas Thebes was the quintessential city of suicidal civil war. Brunetto, reluctant to see the nonviolent Amphion as founder of so violent a city, changed its name, probably unconsciously, to a more noble one. The lower part of the Inferno is a kind of Thebes (xx, 1–3; xxv, 15; xxvi, 52–54; xxx, 2–22). Briareus, one of the towerlike giants at the edge of the ninth circle (xxxi, 98), is from the *Thebaid*. The history of Thebes will be invoked three more times in this and the next canto (xxxii, 130–131; xxxiii, 76, 89). Amphion, *conditor Thebae*, would seem to be a natural model for the narrator of the Inferno. But if "sweetness of song" can found social order, it hardly seems suited to describing its collapse into cannibalism and violent reciprocity.

The narrator comports himself in a manner most unlike Amphion. His tone is sarcastic and bitter. Imitating the violence of the traitors, he makes language the object of violence. He wishes he could squeeze the juice out of his thought more completely (4–5). He needs violent language to represent violence. It is not, he says, a task "to take in jest" (*pigliare a gabbo* [7]). *Gabbo* refers to mimetic verbal aggression, often apparently humorous, between opponents who try to defeat one another by imitating and surpassing each other's offenses. The pilgrim engaged in one such exchange with Farinata (x, 40–51, 73–84) and was rebuked by Virgil for becoming too entranced by another between Master Adam and Sinon (xxx, 100–129). In this canto he will participate in a most violent *gabbo* with Bocca degli Abati (85–105).

His scornful reference to babytalk (9) anticipates the world soon to be encountered where parents and children murder one another and draws attention to the early stages of human development, when children acquire language and are integrated into society. These stages correspond to the primitive stages of history when cities are founded. But Dante here is concerned with the disintegration of language and society, not their institution. Not by accident, Nimrod, another of the towering giants who guard Cocytus, speaks an incomprehensible fallen Hebrew (xxxi, 67). We have reached the bottommost limit of language where verbal signs (*il dir*) and reality (*il far*) do not correspond. There exist no words to imitate acoustically the violence that must be narrated. *Convenientia,* or fittingness, a fundamental principle of classical rhetoric, posited on the assumption that reality is imitable in language, no longer applies (Varanini, 6).

The narrator wants but knows he will not find words harsh enough (*rime aspre* [1]) to imitate the violence of betrayal. Classical rhetoric divided words into the "harsh" and the "sweet." Dante himself advised against "harshness" (*asperitas*) except when mixed with "smoothness" (*De vulgari eloquentia* II, xiii, 12–13) but admitted it when the subject matter was not "smooth" (*Convivio* IV, ii, 13). After his early "sweet" love poems, he composed (ca. 1294–1296) the *rime petrose,* or "rocky rhymes," in a harsh, violent language for a cold, indifferent woman, Lady Rock, who refused his love. He chooses to repeat here the winter landscape, the ice, cold, and stone, the savage lexicon and behavior (Blasucci). In this all-male world, erotic desire exists solely as a parody of itself. In the *rime petrose* the poet-lover's desire degenerates into violence against its object as he imitates that object's brutal "hardness." Here in Cocytus the traitors are each other's objects as they give way to mimetic violence.

At the beginning of his journey Francesca, the sinner of erotic desire par excellence, said that Caïna (the first division of Cocytus) was awaiting her husband for murdering his brother, her lover (v, 107). In the second circle our attention focused on the rapport between Francesca and Paolo, but the relation was in fact a classic triangle: two brothers are rivals for the same woman. This triangle extends from one end of Hell to the other, two points in the second circle, the third in the ninth circle. Although Francesca tastefully understated the violence of Paolo's death and hers (v, 90, 102,

106–107), her desire cannot be understood apart from the violence it engendered. Dante again underlines the link between Francesca and the ninth circle when he has Ugolino's speech begin in a manner strongly reminiscent of Francesca's (XXXIII, 4–6; V, 121–123). Dante connects the ninth circle with Francesca and the *rime petrose* to make the same point: the mimetic violence of the traitors is the most advanced, or degenerate, phase of mimetic desire.

The narrator wants rhymes that are also "crude" or, more literally, hoarse (*chiocce*), an epithet more properly applied to the voice or throat. Such rhymes make the voice that utters them sound hoarse. The narrator's disclaimers are anaphrastic. Hoarse and harsh rhymes fill this canto— *chiocce, rocce; suco, buco, conduco; abbo, babbo, gabbo; Osterlicchi, Tambernicchi, cricchi; ghiaccia, faccia, procaccia; becchi, orecchi, specchi; Pazzi, cagnazzi, guazzi; riprezzo, mezzo, rezzo; teste, peste, moleste; lagna, cuticagna, rimagna; ciocca, Bocca, tocca; buca, manduca, nuca; pecca, secca*—constantly reminding the reader that the poem is, among other things, sound uttered by his mouth. (In the Middle Ages reading includes saying and hearing the words.) The human mouth, whether Amphion's, the narrator's, the sinners' or the reader's, is the true locus of this canto. Hell itself is a mouth, "a bottom that devours" (XXXI, 142; my trans.), and "this savage maw" (XXIV, 123), a place where "it's hard to speak" (XXXII, 14). The mouth reverts to cannibalism, the condition from which Amphion's potent, civilizing song saved society. Shortly we will meet a traitor named "Mouth" (Bocca degli Abati) and another traitor who is a cannibal.

Amphion, then, is the narrator's antimodel. His "closing," or walling, of Thebes (11; my trans.) marked a splendid, absolute beginning of cultural order. The narrator's closing of his Thebes, the Inferno, marks a terrifying absolute end, the reversion of cultural order into primeval anarchy. There is no question of the narrator imitating the "sweetness" of Amphion's song, just as there is no question of his successfully applying the canons of mimetic classical rhetoric. A more violent language, a harsher and hoarser language than any now in his power, is what he needs. In his frustration at falling short of his goal he takes on some of the resentment of the traitors.

16–39.   The narration resumes as the pilgrim looks up at the soaring walls of Cocytus. An anonymous voice admonishes him not to kick any of the thousands of heads protruding from the ice (19–21), a warning he will soon violate. He responds with violence to the violence of the damned. His own behavior, both as pilgrim and as narrator, imitates the violent behavior he condemns. It is almost impossible for him to divorce himself from the values and codes of the family-based, vendetta-torn world of fourteenth-century urban Italy (Herlihy; Martines; Brucker, 62–74, 97–130). The long-standing feud of his own clan, the Alighieri, with the Sacchetti was not settled until two decades after his death. A few cantos earlier he interpreted his kinsman Geri del Bello's silent gesture as a call to avenge a murdered relative (XXIX, 13–36). He implicitly accepts the logic of the *lex talionis*. In the precise, two-edged language of the anonymous warning, the protruding heads belong to "brothers." Some of the traitors we are about to meet are in fact brothers or close relatives, and the pilgrim will reveal himself as their "brother" in violence.

Cocytus, the frozen river of human tears and compassion, is a mirror of contemporary Italy, an extraordinary number of whose cities figure in these cantos: Montereggioni, Faenza, Bologna, Rome, Siena, Genoa, Pisa, and Florence. Betrayers of kinsmen are in the first section, Caïna, named after Abel's murdered brother. When the narrator imagines a rock falling with enormous impact at the edge of the circle of ice and describes the sound it does *not* make (*cricchi* [a faint thud—another harsh and hoarse rhyme]), he is anti-Amphion moving rocks with his voice at the edge of a city (25–30). Most commentators identify Tambernic as Mount Tambura in the Apuan Alps north of Lucca not far from Pietrapana. The girl gleaner in the frog simile (31–36), together with the muses and the *mamma* of babytalk constitute the minimal female presence in Cocytus. Her gender and the harvest she dreams of define by contrast the sterile violence of this all-male world. Some of the souls imprisoned in ice make a storklike sound. Brunetto Latini says that storks, having no tongues, make odd clacking sounds (*Trésor* I, 160, 1). Some traitors do lose the power of speech. They have fallen beneath the subhuman edge of language and behavior. In the canto's final line, the pilgrim takes an oath that alludes to the possibility of his losing *his* tongue. The imitation of the violence of the traitors first roughened his speech, it will soon threaten it altogether.

40–72.   On earth Alessandro and Napoleone degli Alberti murdered each other in a dispute over their patrimony. Here, paralyzed from the neck down in ice, their entwined hair indistinguishable, they struggle in a travesty of a lovers' embrace. Freezing tears shut their lips together in eternal silence—a gruesome kiss. The most common form of conflict in mythology is struggle between brothers usually ending in fratricide. Their near identity jeopardizes family-based social order by obliterating the distinctions that generate it (Girard 1977, 61). In the struggle over their inheritance, the moral distinctions between brothers vanish. Each is aggressor and victim as they merge into a monstrous, bipartite unity. The simile of wood on wood (*con legno legno* [49]) underscores this lack of difference.

The insolent Camiscion de' Pazzi murdered his cousin to acquire his castles (52–69). His asymmetrical frostbitten face matches his abrupt truncated speech. A born informer, he reveals the names of the Alberti brothers and many others. His head is frozen in a permanent downward angle. Unable to look each other in the eye, he and the pilgrim gaze down, their glances meeting at the same point on the ice. Like all the sinners, he assumes that everybody else is guilty of his sin. He asks the pilgrim accusingly, "Why do you mirror yourself in us so long?" (*Perché cotanto in noi ti specchi?* [54; my trans.]). He speaks of his fellow traitors as "stuck in gelatin" (*fitta in gelatina* [60; my trans.]), almost like morsels in jellied broth, sarcastically suggesting that they are potential victims, not aggressors, something to be eaten instead of ferocious eaters. He names Mordred, slain by his uncle (or incestuous father, according to some), King Arthur. The spear and sunlight penetrate Mordred's body at the same time. As with the sowers of discord in the ninth *bolgia*, the human body is an emblem of the body politic. Mordred rent the unity of Arthur's kingdom and family by attempting to wrest power from him. Focaccia, or "flat, sweet bread," is the edible nickname of Vanni dei Cancellieri, who in 1293 murdered one family member to avenge another, initiating a blood feud that polarized his clan, then Pistoia, Florence, and Tuscany into the White and Black Guelphs. (Feuding between the recently formed Blacks and Whites was a factor in Dante's exile.) Little is known of Sassol Mascheroni, a Florentine of the Toschi clan, who murdered his brother's only son to seize the inheritance. Carlino de Pazzi, a kinsman of Camiscion, will betray a castle to its enemies in 1302, two years after this encounter. In the eyes of the status-conscious Camiscion, this betrayal makes his betrayal look less serious. The traitors are rivals in everything, even betrayal. This speech is part of the radical reevaluation of contemporary politics that began when the pilgrim learned from Ciacco that the leaders he most admired were among the blackest souls in Hell (vi, 77–87).

73–123.   At the battle of Montaperti (1260) exiled Florentine Ghibellines, led by Farinata degli Uberti (*Inferno* x), massacred thousands of Florentine Guelphs and their allies when Bocca degli Abati changed to the Ghibelline side, creating panic among his former comrades. The effects of the battle haunted Tuscan civic life for the next half century. The division of political life into Guelphs and Ghibellines began with the killing of Buondelmonte dei Buondelmonti in 1213 in Florence. Although in theory, supporters of the pope and emperor, the two factions pursued their own interests. There was as little difference between them as between the Blacks and Whites at the end of the century. Earlier, among the sowers of discord, Mosca de' Lamberti (xxviii, 103–111; vi, 79–85) held up the stumps of his lopped-off arms, reminding the pilgrim of the now proverbial phrase with which he had instigated the murder of Buondelmonte: "What's done is at an end" (*Capo ha cosa fatta*), meaning that the murder would *end* a family feud once and for all. The opposite occurred: a series of reprisals perpetuated the violence down to the horrors of Montaperti and the vendettas of Dante's day. What was done was a *beginning*, not an end. *Capo* has both meanings. Mosca's proverb unwittingly enunciated the dynamic principle of sinful human politics: violence to end violence engenders more violence.

The various parts of the head (skull, brain, eyes, eyelids, ears, cheeks, scruff and nape of the neck, mouth, lips, tongue, throat, and hair) appear obsessively in this and the next canto. The head (*capo*) is the principle of unity in the body, where the brain reasons and remembers and the mouth utters those acoustic signs that create society. Since the body is subject to the head, leaders of political "bodies" are commonly called *capi* or "heads." For Christianity the head of redeemed human society is Christ. The reduction of the traitors to heads sticking out of the ice mocks their mockery of the unity of the body politic under a single head.

Political violence has been on the pilgrim's mind since he and Farinata traded insults in a discussion of Montaperti (X, 40–51; 73–93). The pilgrim, we have seen, does not repudiate the logic of vendetta. It hardly seems by chance, then, that after a pointed warning he kicks in the face, among the thousands there, the man who betrayed his side (the Guelphs) and his city to forces led by Farinata. This apparently inadvertent act of violence avenges the betrayal of Montaperti. At first, victim and avenger do not recognize each other. The guilt-ridden Bocca assumes that a stranger's kick was intended to punish him for his treason. Still living by earthly codes of honor and shame (the very unwritten codes that produce violence), Bocca (mouth) refuses to give his name. Once again betrayal ends in silence. After a violent verbal agon, recalling in form the stichomythia of Greek tragedy, the pilgrim, determined to learn finally the traitor's name, in an act of frightening sadism rips out handfuls of Bocca's hair—a clear but significantly nonerotic parody of the erotic violence of a passage in the *rime petrose*:

> When I had taken the beautiful tresses,
> which have become my whip and lash,
> grabbing them before Tierce,
> I would continue with them until Vespers and the bells
> and would be neither compassionate nor courteous,
> but would act like a bear at play,
> and even though Love whips me with them now,
> I would avenge myself more than a thousand times.
> In fact, those eyes which sparks come out of
> and which set my heart on fire, so that I carry it around dead,
> I would look at them from close up, and fixedly,
> to take vengeance on her for running away from me,
> and then I would give her, together with love, peace.
> ("Così nel mio parlar voglio esser aspro," 66–75)

Kicking Bocca in the face may have been accidental, but ripping out his hair on the unconfirmed suspicion that he betrayed Florence and the Guelphs thirty-five years earlier cannot be justified even as vengeance. We feel now the full force of Camiscion's question to the pilgrim: *"Perché cotanto in noi ti specchi?"* (literally, "Why do you mirror yourself so much in us?" [54]). There is little difference between his violence and that of the traitors. They reflect each other.

When Buoso da Duera divulges Bocca's name, Bocca vengefully betrays his betrayer's name as well as others. We have by now entered Antenora the second subdivision of Cocytus. The circle of traitors to *patria* or community takes its name from Antenor, who betrayed Troy to the Greeks. Most of the men whom Bocca names were active in the years around Montaperti. Buoso betrayed the Ghibellines by allowing the French army to pass through his territory in 1265. Tesauro di Beccheria, a churchman and Florentine by adoption, was beheaded for plotting with the Ghibellines in 1258. In that same year Gianni de' Soldanieri, a member of an expelled Ghibelline clan, betrayed it by rebelling against one of its leaders (as Ganelon betrayed Charlemagne's nephew in the *Song of Roland,* an incident recently alluded to [XXXI, 16–18]). In 1280 Tebaldello, a latter-day Antenor, opened the gates of his city, Faenza, to the Guelph opponents of some personal enemies who happened to be Ghibellines.

124–139.   The rival Alberti brothers "came out of one body" (58) and, after killing each other, became a single body once more, locked in a fratricidal embrace. They anticipate a second pair "frozen in one hole" (125) at the end of the canto—a count and an archbishop, heads *(capi)* of political and ecclesiastical communities, a final instance of violent reciprocity, indistinguishable not in their hair but in their heads. One head *(capo)* wears the other like a hat *(capello).* The matter-of-factness of the simile underscores the horror of one man eating another's brain. The single hole *(buca)* in which they are trapped parallels the pit *(buco)* of Hell itself, which is a kind of mouth *(bocca),* an all-devouring foundation (XXXI, 142). Speech, the activity of the mouth that creates community, yields to cannibalism, the activity of the mouth that destroys community. Because they are almost indistinguishable, the count's cannibalizing of Ruggieri has the appearance of autophagy. At the end of Hell Satan uses his three mouths not for speech but to devour three traitors. In the next canto one head will hint that it cannibalized its children.

Count Ugolino eats Archbishop Ruggieri's brain as a hungry man eats bread. The unusual word for eating, *manducare,* is the same word that the Latin Bible employs when Christ tells his disciples to eat his body in order to be saved (John 6:52). In Christianity eating Christ's body under the form of bread creates and maintains the collective body of the redeemed that is the Church. Here, by contrast, a secular head quite literally consumes a spiritual head in vengeful ingestion, not loving communion. Ugolino repeats in eternity the law "eat or be eaten." He the victim is now *sovran,* "on top," "sovereign." Dante compares these two Pisans to two Thebans, citizens of the city Amphion built. In the *Thebaid* Tydeus, mortally wounded by Menalippus, killed him and then bit into his skull (VIII, 732–736).

From Bocca the pilgrim learns that the traitors want no publicity for their sins. Now, in a cunning piece of rhetoric, as antiphrastic as the narrator's opening words (1–15), without allusion to any guilt of Ugolino's, the pilgrim invites him to explain the hatred that leads him to eat Ruggieri, to narrate *Ruggieri*'s sin (as if their two sins were any more separable than their two bodies) and to identify himself. He wins Ugolino's trust by encouraging him in his role of victim. In this world of broken agreements the pilgrim makes a pact (*convegno*) to publicize the sinner's self-justifying portrait.

Contrary to his intentions, Ugolino betrays his character if not his specific sin. Ignoring the multiple betrayals for which he is here, and concentrating on Ruggieri's inhuman cruelty, he inadvertently reveals himself as a child-devouring father, another Saturn. In keeping the pact with Ugolino, Dante betrays him. His betrayal of Fra Alberigo will be far less subtle, when he refuses to honor the equivocal promise to remove the ice from his eyes (XXXIII, 115–117, 149–150; Bárberi Squarotti).

The pilgrim concludes his *captatio* with a traditional oath or curse (may my tongue dry up if this is not true) turned into a periphrastic proviso: "if that with which I speak does not dry up" (139). The canto ends where it began, in Dante's mouth as it utters violent rhymes (*pecca, secca*). In the descent to the place where language dies, the pilgrim risks losing the powers of speech. Soon the narrator will not write down what the "faint and frozen" pilgrim experienced—a Satan *in piccolo* as mimesis comes to a dead end (XXXIV, 22–24).

The ninth circle brings Dante's essentially mimetic poetics into unavoidable danger. The imitation of violence obliterates distinctions between the imitator and the violent men he condemns. Both pilgrim and narrator catch the contagion. Ripping out Bocca's hair cannot be justified as the high-minded execution of divine justice, as many commentators would have it, unless we posit a vengeful God siding with the Florentine Guelphs. Likewise, when the furious narrator, after Ugolino's speech, calls on the islands near the mouth of the Arno to dam up the river and drown *everyone* in Pisa, the "Thebes renewed," for the suffering of Ugolino's innocent children (XXXIII, 79–90), he becomes an anti-Amphion of apocalyptic vengeance, moving enormous masses with his voice, a destroyer rather than a builder of cities. Both incidents are reprisals. The poetics of mimesis has inevitably degenerated into the poetics of retaliation.

Dante the maker of the poem (in contradistinction to the pilgrim and narrator who are both, after all, fictions he created) does not abandon mimesis as an informing principle of his poetic practice but does, in the figure of Amphion, introduce into the narrative values it comes near to repudiating. Yet by and large Dante criticism has neglected the role played by Amphion in the economy of the *Inferno*. From Statius and Ovid Dante knew that mythology gives Thebes another more famous founder, Cadmus, who slew the dragon and sowed his teeth, which grew into armed men (letters of the alphabet in some versions). These men engaged in murderous conflict with one another, their survivors becoming the chiefs of the first Theban clans (Vian). The myth of Amphion in comparison with those of Cadmus and Orpheus (his companion in Horace) attracted few writers in the Middle Ages. Unlike most foundation myths, it locates the origins of society in "sweetness of song" rather than murderous violence (Girard 1978). Cadmus, the founder in violence of Thebes and inventor of the alphabet, would seem to offer a more fitting model for a narrative obsessed with mimetic violence and the relation of language and violence. But here, precisely, is the disadvantage of the Cadmus myth: it is too easily imitable. Had Dante decided to invoke Cadmus rather than Amphion, he would have so completely identified the narrator with violence as to make the poem an apology for Hell. By contrast, the atypical myth of Amphion, being inimitable in this context, breaks the spell of mimetic violence by implying a judgment on the vengeful narrator and pilgrim. In this way the maker of the *Comedy* keeps the margin of safety or difference that is at once the poem's esthetic and theological salvation and its goal.

BIBLIOGRAPHY

Ahern, John. "Apocalyptic Onomastics: Focaccia (*Inferno* xxxii, 63)." *Romance Notes* 23 (1982): 181–184.
Bárberi Squarotti, Giorgio. "L'orazione del conte Ugolino." In *L'artificio dell'eternità*, 283–332. Verona, 1972.
Blasucci, Luigi. "L'esperienza delle *petrose* e il linguaggio della *Divina Commedia*." In *Studi su Dante e Ariosto*, 1–35. Milan, 1969.
Brink, C. O. *Horace on Poetry: The "Ars Poetica."* Vol. 2. Cambridge, 1971.
Brucker, Gene, ed. *The Society of Renaissance Florence: A Documentary Study.* New York, 1971.
Davis, Charles T. "Brunetto Latini and Dante." *Studi medievali* 8 (1967): 421–450.
Derrida, Jacques. "Violence and Metaphysics." In *Writing and Difference*, trans. Alan Bass, 79–153. Chicago, 1978. Originally published as *L'écriture et la différence* (Paris, 1967).
East, James R. "Book Three of Brunetto Latini's *Trésor*: An English Translation and Assessment of Its Contribution to Rhetorical Theory." Ph.D. diss., Stanford University, 1960.
Ferrante, Joan. "The Relation of Speech to Sin." *Dante Studies* 87 (1969): 33–46.
Freccero, John. "Bestial Sign and Bread of Angels (*Inferno* xxxii–xxxiii)." *Yale Italian Studies* 1 (1977): 53–66. Reprinted in *Dante: The Poetics of Conversion*, ed. Rachel Jacoff (Cambridge, Mass., 1986), 152–166.
Girard, René. *Des choses cachées depuis la fondation du monde.* Paris, 1978.
———. *Violence and the Sacred.* Trans. Patrick Gregory. Baltimore, 1977. Originally published as *La violence et le sacré* (Paris, 1972).
Hazlitt, William. *The Complete Works of William Hazlitt: Characters in Shakespeare's Plays*, ed. P. P. Howe, 4:214. London, 1930.
Herlihy, David. "Family Solidarity in Medieval Italian History." In *Economy, Society, and Government in Medieval Italy: Essays in Memory of Robert L. Reynolds*, ed. D. Herlihy, R. S. Lopez, V. Slessarev, 173–194. Kent, Ohio, 1969.
———. "Some Psychological and Social Roots of Violence in the Tuscan Cities." In *Violence and Civil Disorder in Italian Cities 1200–1500*, ed. Lauro Martines, 129–154. Berkeley, 1972.

Hollander, Robert. "Babytalk in Dante's *Comedy*." In *Studies in Dante,* 115–129. Ravenna, 1980.

Martines, Lauro. "Political Violence in the Thirteenth Century." In *Violence and Civil Disorder in Italian Cities 1200–1500,* ed. Lauro Martines, 331–353. Berkeley, 1972.

Pézard, André. "Le chant des traîtres." In *Lectura Dantis internazionale,* ed. Vittorio Vettori, 308–342. Milan, 1963.

Romilly, Jacqueline de. *Magic and Rhetoric in Ancient Greece.* Cambridge, Mass., 1975.

Varanini, Giorgio. *Il canto XXXII dell'"Inferno."* Florence, 1962.

Vian, Francis. *Les origines de Thèbes: Cadmos et les spartes.* Paris, 1963.

CANTO XXXIII

Count Ugolini and Others

EDOARDO SANGUINETI

Translated by Charles Ross,
Richard Collins, and Tom Harrison

Bridging the space between Antenora and Ptolomea, Canto XXXIII contains the poet's final conversations with the souls of the damned (Virgil will merely point to the three sinners in the jaws of Lucifer in the *Inferno*'s ultimate canto). The canto features the bare tale of Count Ugolino, whose earlier introduction allows him to be isolated here along with Fra Alberigo, who points out the silent presence of a third soul, that of Branca Doria. Each of the two sections of the canto (the technical term "canto" is included in the text at line 90) is followed by an invective against a municipality. These invectives replicate earlier attacks on Pistoia and Florence in the Malebolge and prefigure an extended attack on Italy in the next canticle, an attack that will return again to Florence. The tone here differs from the satire and sarcasm found elsewhere. Therefore it is useful to notice that Ugolino recognizes the poet by his voice as a Florentine, although he ignores his personal identity and the reason for his unusual presence:

> I don't know who you are or in what way
> you've come down here; and yet you surely seem—
> from what I hear—to be a Florentine.
>
> (10–12)

Ugolino's recognition of the pilgrim's origin seems to justify the poet's moral curses by collapsing the separation of narrative and frame, pilgrim and poet. Ugolino tells his story in a similar way, leaving out information that

424

"there is no need to tell" (16) to one who is among the living. The revelation of his name and that of Archbishop Ruggieri, his "neighbor" (15), suffices to clue Dante to what he already knows. Yet something is added, in these compact tercets, by the shift in verbal tense between the past of Ugolino's "I was" (13) and the present "this [is]" that he employs for the archbishop (14). Dante's style allows this rhetorical shift, which the paradoxical insistence on good manners exaggerates, creating an eternal present of the two souls, one of whom chews the other's skull. The effect is to orient the "now I will tell you why" of Ugolino into the mode of a narrative recounting of a death that was hidden to the world but that will now be posthumously revealed. This is the fundamental ideological mode of the *Comedy,* according to Dante's letter to Cangrande Della Scala: the entire subject (*subiectum totius operis*) is the state of souls after death (*status animarum post mortem*) insofar as justice rewards and punishes them (*iustitie premiandi et puniendi obnoxius est*).

The structure of the canto alternates between narration and imprecation. At the center, in the transition from one zone of Cocytus to another, Dante will investigate the wind that afflicts and congeals the deep well of the traitors in order to prepare for the terminal portion of the canticle, which features the appearance of the servants of Lucifer. At this point Virgil only tells him that soon his "eye will answer" (107) his question of the source of the wind.

I want to insist on a rigorous division of the canto and on the presence of damned souls in couples in the predominantly narrative portions, even if the couples are diversely motivated. With Fra Alberigo it is possible to find a conceptual supplement to will: an indictment from traitor to traitor, an indictment that touches a presumably living person and yet fits onto the mechanism, normal to the poem, of a deceased person who spontaneously undertakes the role of guide and illustrator for companions of punishment and of reward. The reader is aware of the rule, in the present abysmal "valley," that the desire for fame is not permissible and what dominates is instead a radical desire for "the contrary" (XXXII, 91–96). Ugolino clearly exhibits a desire to disseminate "seed from which the fruit / is infamy" for his neighbor (XXXIII, 7–8). But we also know that the appearance in the story of the "two shades frozen in one hole" (XXXII, 125) belongs to that pattern of duplicitous pairing that has marked, earlier in the crowd of the damned, "those two who go together" (Paolo and Francesca [V, 74]) and those two who shared one "flame / with horns" (Diomedes and Ulysses [XXVI, 68]). The pattern assigns Ugolino at once to the great gallery of infernal couples who speak with a single voice.

Even within Cocytus this typology is represented by the Alberti brothers, "locked so close" in Caïna (XXXII, 41), who "came out of one body" (58). In the fashion of Cocytus, they are singled out and discovered by Camiscion de' Pazzi, a dispenser of infamy and slander. The presence of this couple is enough to establish the pattern of the following canto, which ends with a couple held fast by frost, in the compulsory hug that links them, and begins with the couple who are bestially marked as eater and eaten in such a way "that one's head served as the other's cap" (XXXII, 126).

In fact, the allusion to the myth of Tydeus and Menalippus would not have such force if it were not linked, at the conclusion of Canto XXXII, to the periphrasis of the opening, where the Muses are invoked as "those ladies . . . who helped Amphion when he walled up Thebes." In a poem where the allusions to Thebes are as many and varied as the echoes of Statius—even before he assumes, in the *Purgatorio,* the privileged role by which we know him—the memory of the walls of Amphion (see *Thebaid* x, 873) would not have the impact it does, if it did not contribute to such a marked constructive function, ripe with consequences.

The same invocation to the muses is linked, then, at the very source, with the episode of Capaneus that gave Dante one of his major heroes of evil. Statius's text (*Thebaid* x, 829) transcends the typical and traditional poetic sermon ("No more may I sing after the wonted way of bards" [*non mihi iam solito vatum de more canendum*]). The text also makes a request "from the Aonian groves" for "a mightier frenzy" (*maior ab Aoniis poscenda amentia lucis*); that is, the text asserts an astonishing boldness in writing: "Dare with me, goddesses all" (*mecum omnes audete deae!*). Dante has already widely demonstrated the "inexpressibility" topos with his "Let Lucan now be silent" and "Let Ovid now be silent" (XXV, 97). Here his reference to the "tongue that cries out, 'mama,' 'papa'" (XXXII, 9) suggests the difficult assimilation of language to event. Those "ladies" who helped Statius conclude his *Thebaid* are necessary to assist Dante, if we may put it that way. Since he is unaware of the *Silvae,* Dante cannot know that "after Statius the panegyrical formula of outdoing, together with the *cedat*-formula, becomes a permanent stylistic element." (For the formula and history of "overbidding," see Ernst Robert Curtius, *European Literature and the Latin Middle Ages,* trans. Willard R. Trask [1948; Princeton, 1973], 160.) Even less can he focus directly on the formula of Claudian, although he applies it derivatively, *taceat superata vetustas* ("let antiquity be silent" [*In Rufinum* 1, 280 ff.]).

From Statius Dante has learned not only the negative imperative not to compete with the divine *Aeneid,* but to follow in its footprints, as he does when he addresses Virgil as "master" and "author" and proclaims him the source of his "noble style" and model for his calling as a poet (*Inf.* 1, 85–87). In the process he has also learned that the epic style, whether of Ovid or Lucan, is better emulated than imitated, whether in elevating or lowering the diction. Cyrrha (one of the peaks of Parnassus, standing for Apollo, god of poetry) "may answer" (*Par.* 1, 37), just as "crude and scrannel rhymes" suit the "melancholy hole" at the bottom of the world (XXXII, 1–2).

Thus in the canonical form of the "no differently" (in whose Dantean version the epic *non* and *haud aliter* and the *non secus* and *non alias* converge into one), what surfaces is an evocation of Statius at whose overcoming this entire place of narration is aimed. The line "no differently had Tydeus gnawed" (XXXII, 130) is not merely an illustrative term but a term of imitative confrontation, of canonical *aemulatio*—which should be the true descriptive epigraph of the Ugolino episode. In short, we would like to suggest here that the definition of Pisa as "Thebes renewed" (XXXIII, 88) is more than a moral characterization in the mode of *imprecatio* (or curse, further refined by the sophisticated *anadiplosis* of *novella/novella*); it follows models of *prominatio*, which would reward in-depth study. We might recall, in the *Comedy,* the prophetic devolution of the figure, from the "second Jason" (*Inf.* XIX, 85) to the "new Pilate" of *Purg.* XX, 91, or, in the *Epistles,* the *proles altera Isai* (VII, 8) on the positive side and, on the negative side, the *alteri Babilonii* (VI, 8), twins to the "new Pharisees" of *Inf.* XXVII, 85. Most relevant of all, precisely on account of its own documentary and probative origin, is the *Totila secundus* of the *Vulgari eloquentia* II, vi, 6, constructed as a model of the most distinguished *gradus constructionis,* which is that defined as *sapidus et venustus etiam et excelsus.* All this, we would like to stress, is relevant and still in need of exploration in the light of a well-established tradition of eloquence. Here, however, the matter of greatest interest is different. The figure of a second Thebes is above all a stylistic hint, as a *novella Thebais,* the sign of a hidden "Let Statius now be silent."

As in a kind of miniature *Thebaid,* the gestures of Ugolino frame his tale. He interrupts his "fierce meal" (XXXIII, 1) to wipe his mouth over the hair of the destroyed head of a damned soul—atrocious but irreproachable table manners (in the *Noie* Pucci affirms his disgust for dolts who do not keep their mouths clean at table). He vigorously lowers his caninelike mouth again over the skull (the gesture recalls the line "insatiable, he ate the head of his hapless foe" [*miseri insatiabilis edit . . . caput* (*Thebaid* XI, 87)]), as if he were starving, the situation suggested by the last term of the narration, the crucial "fasting" (*digiuno*).

Ugolino's own first words, which justify his oration, suggest a suspicion. The phrase "You want me to renew / despairing pain" (XXXIII, 4–5) is certainly indebted to the opening of Book II of the *Aeneid;* it echoes the memorable *Infandum . . . iubes renovare dolorem* ("too terrible for tongues the pain / you ask me to renew"). From Aeneas's exordium also proceeds the oppression of thought before every word ("my mind, remembering, recoils in grief") as well as that necessary union of words and tears that renews the embrace of pain and thought ("pain . . . even as I think" [XXXIII, 5–6]). These emotions will be projected from the narrator to the listener in the center of the tale in such a way as to lead us to the apex of Ugolino's questioning:

> "You would be cruel indeed if, thinking what
> my heart foresaw, you don't already grieve;
> and if you don't weep now, when would you weep?"
>
> (41–42)

It is reasonable to think that an abundance of both precise and loose Virgilian references does not indicate either an unawareness or a forgetfulness of Statian echoes. Dante's imitation of the *Thebaid* relies upon Virgil, as it must. Dante overgoes Statius by tracing backwards to the *Aeneid*.

Let us leave aside for a moment the question of the second Thebes. We have touched upon the connection of speaking and weeping (a theme anticipated by Francesca [*Inf.* v, 126] and reflected, as if in a zero degree, in the line "he said / in tears," referring to Cavalcante [*Inf.* x, 58]). This theme is also directed at the reader, who is urged to weep too. Weeping and speaking contrast to the petrified silences and barren faces of Ugolino and his sons during their long agony. When the poet calls for tears, he reechoes the weeping of the innocent children between their waking and their calls for bread ("They wept" [XXXIII, 50]), which contrasts with the behavior of the father, who says he "did not weep" (49) as he watched his sons "without a word" (48).

And yet there is more, beginning with the moment that Ugolino's silence is confirmed by a total absence of locutory self-citations within his narrative, where, in second-degree direct discourse, all that is registered, along with the two interruptions of Anselm and Gaddo, is the central Senecan moment, as Contini puts it, of the apostrophe to the father. We can see, without being accused of being overly scrupulous, the pathetic possessive of the dying Gaddo's *padre mio* ("Father, why do you not help me?" [69]) as balancing Ugolino's "my poor little Anselm" (50). Yet it may be more appropriate to focus on the metaphorical opposition between dressing and undressing, insofar as the flesh is metaphorically understood as clothing (as in the wood of the suicides [XIII, 104], or "the weight of Adam's flesh as dress" [*Purg.* XI, 43], in which the poet dresses himself, or the "flesh" that—"glorified and sanctified"—will be "once again our flesh" [*Par.* XIV, 44], completing the desire by which all the blessed will arise, chanting with "new-clothed voices" [*Purg.* XXX, 15] and enjoying the advantage of a "double garment" [*Par.* XXV, 92 and 127]).

Now, it is precisely Seneca, the moral Seneca before the tragic Seneca, with the famous passage from *Epistulae* XIV, 92, 13, who provides us with a type of automatic gloss, which he provided to all of Latinity, when he says that when he speaks of clothing, he intends the body. The image was readily adapted by Christianity thanks to several scriptural authorities, such as the "coats of skins" that God makes for Adam and Eve as he expels them from Paradise (Gen. 3). By relying on Matthew 6:25 for a link between the body and clothing, Augustine is able to confirm that clothing is an image of the body (*vestem audis, coopertorium audis, et aliud quam corpus intelligis?* [*Enarr. in Ps.* CI, 11, 14]). And Gregory guarantees the same thing, again interrogatively (*quid enim vestimenti nomine nisi hoc terrenum corpus exprimitur, quo induta anima tegitur?* [*Moralia* IX, 36, 58]). At this point it may be more maniacal than scrupulous to recall that for the dying Capaneus, in *Thebaid* x, 937, it is written that "his earthly frame deserts the hero" (*membra terrena relinquunt, / exuiturque animus*).

Let us return now to the pathos of Ugolino to see how strictly tied it is to horror, where the gnawing of someone's head is, for Dante, the "bestial sign" of "hatred" (xxxii, 133–134). It is easy to regard these verses as a supreme exercise in synonyms, where the word-choice and circumlocutions include chewing, gnawing, feeding, and digging one's teeth into another's brain. The episode also has a vaguely determined framework of time. Through a "narrow hole" Ugolino saw "several moons" (xxxiii, 22, 26) before he had a prophetic dream, whose oneiric uncertainty accounts for verbs like "appeared to me" (28) and "it seemed to me" (34). Pietro Alighieri derived the time a man could live by starving from David's experience, fasting for his son in 2 Kings 12. The hypnotic bestiary of the hounds and the wolf and its whelps (29, 32) is important insofar as it leads to the "flanks torn by sharp fangs" (36). To evoke a nightmare from Statius (*Thebaid* ix, 574) and to suppose that Dante fully transposed this dream is to validate the idea that the archetype to be emulated is insinuated even in the less important turns of the discourse. If Ugolino perceives his own appearance "reflected in four faces" (57), it is difficult to imagine that the poet is not recalling Tydeus as he contemplates the severed head of Menalippus and, in this way, receives a pungent premonition (*Thebaid* viii, 753).

As for Dante's imitation of the cannibalism in Statius, it is sufficient to notice the internal references, which lead, for instance, from the innocent prisoners "asking for bread" (39) back to the first description of Ugolino gnawing "just as he who's hungry chews his bread" (xxxii, 127). The echo reveals the essential feature of Dante's thematic and stylistic attitude in this place, namely, the homogeneous remixing and leveling of the manner of the "cruel" death and "fierce" penal meal, beginning, once again, with the oneiric inscription of the central image of phagic violence.

The key interpretive crux of the canto is the last line of Ugolino's speech, when he says that "fasting had more force than grief" (75). Does he cannibalize his children or mourn their deaths? We ought not to sacrifice in any way the indications, certainly more topical than referential, suggested by Contini with the *Thyestes* in hand. We must, however, note that the formulation of Ugolino's cry ("O hard earth, why did you not open up?" [66]) presupposes, in the memory of Dante and of his reader, the fall of Amphiaraus in the *Thebaid,* for whom the earth opened. This Theban echo supports the larger one, the anthropophagic resolution of Ugolino's destiny. Therefore, what is more powerful than the oneiric prefiguration is the anticipation gathered in the equivocal gesture around which the entire operation of the damned soul revolves. For when he bites his own hands out of grief (57), his children believe he is trying to eat himself. The final victory of fasting over grief is indeed already marked and decided precisely by the distorted but horribly anticipatory interpretation that the innocent children give to the bizarre behavior of this mad soul of Cocytus. The children seem to opt, atrociously and deliberately, for a reading of the final line as a reference to cannibalism.

Therefore it does not seem doubtful that under the veil of harsh and scrannel rhymes, sane intellects might perceive what is restated figuratively in the ferocious and ferociously allusive canine behavior—the *metacontrapasso*—of Ugolino returning to his meal. Nor will we forget his "eyes awry" (76), which, if they can be internally explained as a horrifying variant of the gluttonous Ciacco's gaze ("twisted and awry" [*Inf.* VI, 91]), do not necessarily need to be referred to the "wrathful eyes still flickering" of *Thebaid* VIII, 756. They can be correctly referred back to the *trahi oculos* of Menalippus, if we are not content with the formulaic Statian models, *obliqua tueri* and *obliquo lumine* (I, 447; III, 377; IV, 606).

One final annotation is indispensable, even within the necessary sobriety of this reading, and it involves the revelation of those Luciferine foretastings that Ugolino's episode provides. Recall the sufferers chewed in "each mouth" (XXXIV, 55) of Dis, almost "like a grinder," in that gnawing and gnashing with the teeth, even as such chewing was nothing when compared to the "clawing" (59). The penal scheme of the two shades frozen in one ditch is but the preparation, in a minor key (fittingly in the profane terms of a second Thebes), of what is expanded in the following canto into a major, theologically triplicated, and enlarged Lucifer.

In fact, the demonic quality of the episode of Ugolino, in the spectacular representation of cannibalism as well as in the veil through which Ugolino's story is perceived, is the very demonicity of Cocytus at large. That demonic quality appears in the legal and ethical surface of Dante the pilgrim, the betrayer of traitors. He operates with sacred cruelty and just fraud before the "exhausted, wretched brothers" (XXXII, 21), protected by an ambiguously calculated mixture of desire, destiny, and fortune but ultimately guaranteed by the implacability of divine vengeance in that "eternally cold shadow" (XXXII, 75). The contrast of the "long promises and very brief fulfillments" (XXVII, 110) in the episode of Fra Alberigo, and the resolution of "rudeness" into religious "courtesy" (XXXIII, 150), thus seal the infinite variety of emotive attitudes displayed as Dante explores the reign of evil. The narrative denies the merciful gesture. Its most perverse formulation is the sibylline *jeu de mots*, the deprecatory "may I go to the bottom of the ice" (117).

It is unnecessary to inquire into the "weeping [that] won't let them weep" (94), where the "grief" (95) turns within to "increase their agony" (96) once the canto has insisted so much on the theme of "tears" (97). Figuratively, it is an open invitation to readers to situate themselves in a moral region that, in some way, is beyond crying and beyond the expression of grief. It is sufficient to remember that—because of the "privilege" (124) of

Ptolomea, whereby the bodies of the damned survive in the world above thanks to demonic possession, as a devil takes over and dresses himself in human flesh—there arises an ingenious variant of the chronological antic- ipation of a sentence that the determined temporality of Dante's voyage would otherwise suspend. The first commentators already noticed the scriptural authorization of the descent of one living to Hell. The demonic variation is mentioned in Luke 22:3 ("And Satan entered into Judas") and in John 13:27 ("Satan entered into him"). It is yet another trick that leads di- rectly, by figurative means, to the soul "who has to suffer most" (xxxiv, 61). And here, even if we are right to illustrate Dante's solution by adducing the self-commentary of *Convivio* IV, vii, 10 ("one who is dead yet goes on earth" illustrates a man who remains a beast), still the shift here—specifically de- termined by the demon who erupts and "keeps that body in his power" (xxxiii, 131)—should not be lost. In fact, if the page in the treatise thor- oughly illustrates the sequence of one who "eats and drinks and sleeps and puts on clothes" (141), it obviously does not explain the words of Fra Al- berigo, who refers us back to the ditch of the Malebranche for the similar fate of Michele Zanche, the last victim of betrayal.

Obviously the real point is not the mere sensible survival in itself but the way Dante orders the demons in hell. With a small amount of highlighting, we might affirm that, if the first part of the canto is a barely dissimulated exercise in outdoing Statius, the final part is a different but no less impres- sive example of overbidding previous medieval narrations of demonic pos- session. But here an adequate inquiry has yet to be conducted, and Dante's "privilege" can only be postulated. At least we can quietly affirm that, only from this similar position, with Dante finished cursing someone, the tale can now confidently address itself to the supreme figure of evil.

CANTO XXXIV

Lucifer

REMO CESERANI

Translated by Charles Ross, Rala Potter,
and Martha Craig

Most of the last canto of the *Inferno* is devoted to the grandiose depiction of Lucifer—the enormous antihero, emperor of the world of Hell, and genuine incarnation of evil—immobilized in the midst of a dark and frozen landscape in the deepest recesses of the abyss. The canto also contains a narration of the difficult and painful progress of Dante and Virgil, as they make their way out of the infernal world and ascend toward the more serene regions of Purgatory.

Here we encounter the most original and inventive part of Dante's cosmography. Although the Ptolemaic system is his representation of the heavens, he locates his Hell and Purgatory in the universe and in time according to a forceful combination of physical science and religious history. In this construction, God and history determine the extreme moment of sin and redemption. He conceived the idea that Hell formed following the fall of Lucifer, when the infernal chasm opened right below the point where Christ was crucified on Golgotha. On the same axis, at the opposite pole, the Mount of Purgatory arose, organized from the gigantic mass of earth displaced by Lucifer's body, with the Earthly Paradise of Adam and Eve at its summit.

The solution provided by Dante in the *Inferno* to the cosmological problems of the origin of the world, the separation of land and sea, and the location of Hell and Purgatory is different than that put forward in one of his shorter Latin works, the *Questio de aqua et terra*, dedicated precisely to these problems. The contrast between the two positions has prompted some scholars (such as Bruno Nardi, who specializes in the philosophy of Dante) to doubt that Dante wrote the work; its incoherence clashes with the orderliness of Dante's thought. Others (such as Giorgio Padoan, John Freccero, and Giovanni Mazzoni) maintain that it is perfectly legitimate that one author set forth different opinions and claims in two different works. Dante, in the *Questio,* gives a "natural" cause for the emergence of land in the southern hemisphere, while in the *Inferno* he gives a theological one: the world assumed a new shape when Lucifer's fall upset the original order of nature.

The themes treated and the tone and progression of the discourse allow the canto to be divided into two equal parts of sixty-nine lines each. The first section, where Dante and Virgil encounter Lucifer, is descriptive and dramatic. The second half is narrative and informative and may be subdivided into two parts at line 127 on the basis of a slight narrative shift and change in tone. In the first part, the perspective of Dante and Virgil reverses unexpectedly, and they now see Lucifer upside down. Virgil unfolds a syncretistic, typically Dantean lesson of Lucifer's role in the biblical and cosmological history of the world. In the second part, we hear of the movement of Virgil and Dante through the long narrow passageway that brings them to the other hemisphere and back to the light, a culmination prefigured by an accumulation of signs—the "sounding stream" (130), the "things of beauty" (137–138), and the "stars" (139)—that herald the emergence of the travelers into the "bright world" (134).

Critics of widely differing perspectives have questioned the artistic effectiveness of the canto, confessing disappointment in the way the account of the infernal voyage is brought to its final crescendo. Regarding the scene in which Dante stands before Lucifer, a perceptive commentator of the *Divine Comedy,* Attilio Momigliano, has spoken of "sporadic weaknesses":

> Dante, in the face of the most gigantic character in hell, finds himself ill at ease. His artistry abandons him: hyperbole and exclamation replace the ill-defined vision of the monster enveloped in the infernal night.

Another commentator, Natalino Sapegno, has stated,

> Only in part does the artistic force of the writer respond to the grand scale of the conception; it spends itself in details excogitated more by the intellect than by imagination, accumulating elements of the scene without blending them together, and retreats into arid digressions.

And an interpreter like T. S. Eliot, while his outlook is that of another culture and sensibility, has spoken of "failure," advising his English readers "on our first reading of the *Inferno,* to omit the last canto," because it is

probably the most difficult on first reading. The vision of Satan may seem
grotesque, especially if we have fixed in our minds the curly-haired
Byronic hero of Milton; it is too like a Satan in a fresco in Siena. . . . I feel
that the *kind* of suffering experienced by the Spirit of Evil should be represented as utterly different. I can say only that Dante made the best of a
bad job. In putting Brutus, the noble Brutus, and Cassius with Judas Iscar-
iot he will also disturb at first the English reader, for whom Brutus and
Cassius must always be the Brutus and Cassius of Shakespeare.

What these critics condemn as artistic lapses, however, are intrinsic elements of Dante's art. More recent criticism praises the figure of Lucifer as
a composite of many disconnected parts, including his immobility, and his
grotesque aspect. They also defend the way Dante constructed the canto
from intellectually opposed elements.

No doubt Dante intended to surprise even readers familiar with Christian liturgy when in the first verse of the canto Lucifer appears as a giant
with six great wings. Virgil intones in Latin a processional hymn, one normally sung for the office of Vespers during Easter week, when Dante's journey was imagined to have taken place (between Good Friday and Easter
Sunday). The hymn was composed by Venantius Fortunatus, bishop of
Poitiers (ca. 530–600). In it the Church celebrates the relic of the cross do-
nated by the Byzantine emperor Justinian II to the saintly Queen Radigund.
The hymn compares the arms of the cross to banners: "Abroad the regal
banners fly, / Now shines the Cross's mystery; / If upon life did death endure, / And yet by death did life procure."

Dante's rhetorical intent is evidently to make the king of Hell an infernal parody of the king of Heaven. He does this by putting the first line of
the ecclesiastical hymn into the mouth of Virgil and adding the word *in-
ferni*. Next he changes the metaphor of Fortunatus, who refers to the arms
of the cross as banners. Dante compares the wings of Lucifer to windmill
vanes. The triumph of the king of Heaven becomes the false triumph of
the king of Hell.

If the rhetorical procedure seems clear, its interpretation has proven
rather controversial for the commentators and readers of this canto. (We
will leave aside the irresistible comparison to Don Quixote.) That Dante introduced his encounter with Lucifer by putting a line from a solemn hymn
into the mouth of Virgil has given rise to radically opposing interpretations.
Francesco d'Ovidio has called this procedure of applying a hymn of the
Passion to the suffering of Lucifer a dark parody. Scartazzini, another nineteenth-century commentator, was of the opposite opinion. In his view
Dante, without ironic intent, applies the words of the hymn to Lucifer to
signify the contrast between the prince of darkness and the prince of light.
Brugnoli, a scholar very sensitive to rhetorical issues, warns against hasty

conclusions. It is not clear whether the tone assumed by Dante as he parodies the liturgical text is ironic. Even admitting irony, we may still wonder
how to understand the passage ethically and aesthetically.

The problem of interpretation extends beyond the first line to the whole
encounter with Lucifer. Of those critics who find a coherent parody, Gorni
has concentrated on rhetorical and intertextual aspects, while Freccero has
accented the ideological and allegorical elements of the scene. Together
they furnish the ethical and aesthetic coordinates demanded by Brugnoli.

Freccero finds in the conflation of Lucifer with an image of the Cross a
reminder of the Christian doctrine of the "necessary" crucifixion. He also
registers the Platonic-Christian doctrine of the "imitation of Christ," a
program of education and salvation that aims to restore the image of God
in man. The great narrative, structural, and allegorical theme of the canto,
for Freccero, is the image of Satan crucified. (We must not forget that Satan occupies, in the center of the earth, the midpoint of the line that connects the two poles of the fall and the redemption—the Earthly Paradise,
at the summit of the Mountain of Purgatory, and Golgotha, on whose summit Christ was crucified.)

The climax of the episode is the moment when Dante and Virgil confront the crucifixion of Satan and manage to transform it into an instrument of salvation. The parodic reversal evident here in terms of the imagery and allegory is paralleled by a similar reversal on the linguistic plane.
To clarify this point, Freccero calls our attention to line 82 of the canto. To
Freccero, the "stairs" to which Dante and Virgil cling represent the Cross,
rendering the cross of the devil a cross of salvation:

> By turning upside down at the center of the universe, the pilgrim and his
> guide right the topsy-turvy world of negative transcendence from which
> they began. Satan, the prince of this world, seems right side up from the
> perspective of hell; after crossing the cosmic starting-point, however,
> Dante sees him from God's perspective, planted head downward with re-
> spect to the celestial abode from which the angel fell.
>
> (Freccero 1965a, 37)

Lucifer is undeniably the focus of the canto. Dante's vision of Lucifer's slow
appearance is effectively rendered by the rhythm of the lines. The vision
seems to have a deformed or unreal quality, almost as if it results from the
observer's estrangement or "perspective of incongruity," to use a rhetorical term dear to Kenneth Burke. The effect recalls in some ways Dante's
perception of the approaching giants in Canto XXXI. There, an optical effect
causes Dante from far off to mistake the distant figures for tall towers. The
giants are fixed in our imaginations before Lucifer appears, giving them a
narrative connection to the final canto. At the end of their respective
episodes, both the giant Antaeus and Lucifer serve as mechanical means for

Dante and Virgil to overcome the obstacles in their path. Antaeus transforms himself into a kind of forklift, and Lucifer resembles a flight of stairs. There is also a typological connection between the giants and Lucifer. Lucifer has the same physical and moral characteristics as the giants— arrogance, violence, deformity—qualities that make him seem inhuman. Peter Dronke has pointed out that Lucifer is immersed more deeply in ice than the giants are in their pit, that he is larger than they are, and that his supreme rebellion against God overgoes the rebellion of the pagan giants against the divine kingdom of Jupiter. His end is the same as theirs, however. All receive the punishment of perpetual immobility.

Immense silence surrounds Lucifer, fixed in ice. The absence of sound seems to extend to everything, even to the wind, to the dripping tears of Lucifer, to his jaws forever grinding the three traitors, and to the reactions of Dante, so that we find all the more striking, almost as if accompanied by high-pitched trumpets, the opening verses sung by Virgil. And thus it should be. If God is the Word, Lucifer is nonspeech, the non-Word. The descriptive strategy that Hegel attributed to Dante's poem (in a well-known passage that forms the basis of Erich Auerbach's essay on Dante) reaches its culmination here. According to Hegel, the poem plunges the living world of action and suffering, or more precisely, the deeds and destinies of the individual, into an eternally fixed existence. In our episode, the immutability of Lucifer, that is, his obstinacy in evil and error, finds its poetic expression in ice and infinite silence.

Ten lengthy tercets are devoted, piece by piece, to a description of Lucifer, whose massiveness corresponds to the number of lines he occupies. (The description draws on a well-established cultural and figurative tradition and also forms the point of departure for a new and influential one, as seen, for example, in the frescoes of the Campo Santo of Pisa, a mid-fourteenth-century painting cycle directly inspired by Dante's poem and its commentaries.) Scholars have applied themselves diligently to reconstructing the cultural and figurative traditions that inspired Dante's depiction of Lucifer, arriving at sometimes conflicting results. The diverse sources that he draws upon begin with the Bible, where Lucifer or Satan is called the "adversary" in Hebrew and the "slanderer" in Greek (Isaias 14; Matthew 25:41; Luke 10:18; Apocalypse 12:9–12). Lucifer is a being who intervenes in the lives of men, setting temptations before them, either directly or indirectly by means of demons. He uses his power and intelligence to thwart God's plan. He was identified with the serpent of Genesis.

Portrayals of the devil are absent from the classical tradition; Hades and Pluto, kings of the dead, are represented without a monstrous aspect. There are, however, descriptions of giants and monstrous creatures such as Homer's Polyphemus and bifrontal beings such as Janus. The medieval theological tradition that continually stressed the allegorical meanings of the biblical account developed an interpretation of Lucifer that attributed to him the overwhelming sin of pride (Saints Bernard, Bonaventure, and Thomas; Peter Lombard). The folklore tradition was figurative and narrative. Depictions of Satan as a mixture of animal forms were well diffused in the Middle Ages in bas reliefs, frescoes, portals, manuscript miniatures, stories, histories, and chronicles from the Romanesque and Gothic periods. A good example of this influence is the *Visio Tnugdali* (Visions of Tondal), a text written in Bavaria around 1150–1160, reproduced in numerous manuscripts, which presents a gigantic Lucifer and another diabolical and beastly figure by the name of Acherons. From the East, lands populated by dragons according to Baltrusaitis, came the devil's sneering animal mask, withered trunk, hairy feet with talons, and bird wings or bat wings appropriate for a fallen angel.

Christian iconography, moreover, has combined classic and folklore elements to create a correspondence between the triumphant Trinity of heaven and an infernal trinity. If we accept the reconstruction of Baltrusaitis, it follows that Satan himself (as here in Dante's canto) should take on a tripartite form, adopting a triple nature and triple face and, as in Dante, a triple meaning. The folklore of pagan and oriental sources contributes the figures of many-headed genies. Bifrontal Janus was made popular in calendars. He is sometimes pictured before a laden table as he presides over an infernal banquet. When he appears in the form of Kronos, the bifrontal version (meant to indicate his link to past and present) is joined by another with three faces (linked to past, present, and future). From there the figure leaves the calendars and becomes part of more complex and metaphorical symbols. Satan reflects the three faces or natures of the Trinity when set before them as a deforming mirror.

Dante gives each of the three faces a mouth devouring a famous traitor. In this way the Church and the empire, the two great pillars of the world, get equal shares of revenge in the deepest, darkest point of the universe. The presence of Brutus and Cassius should not surprise us. As regicides, they opposed the providential establishment of the empire, the unification of the world in that period that prepared for the coming of Christ. They are placed at the same level as Judas, the supreme betrayer. Throughout Dante's entire description, Lucifer is presented as a mechanical and grotesque creature, more of an imposing presence than an animated one. Each iconic element of the description has a symbolic value, and the resulting web of correspondences has unleashed the interpretive fury of the commentators, even from the time the poem first circulated. That Lucifer is half within the ice and half without suggests a symbolic personification of passion that dulls the intellect; his bat wings represent brute force devoid of intelligence while his tears mixed with slaver express the impotent anger of the defeated prince. The three faces of three different colors are thought to have meanings as well. The ruddy face embodies hatred or anger, the pallid one impotence, and the black one ignorance. It is not the most abstruse of interpretations that contrasts these colors to the three virtues of prudence, love, and constancy. More interesting are the possible links between the three-way figure of Lucifer and the numerological symbolism that governs Dante's poem. A structure based on threes dominates the division of the poem, the narrative technique, and many thematic elements. Some commentators have suggested possible links between the triple aspect of Lucifer and the three savage beasts of Canto 1. Others have remarked on the division of the sins, again based on threes, which determines the zones of the Inferno. Many have called attention to the three circles of *Paradiso* XXXIII, 117–120, establishing yet another structural correspondence between the last cantos of the first and third canticles.

As we have seen, we can also divide this canto into three parts. If the first part is dominated by the monstrous figure of Lucifer, in the second part that figure is transformed as Dante recalls his great fall from the heavens and depicts him as the gravitational center of the world. Lucifer becomes a great universal power, the incarnation of ineradicable evil. And his frozen shadow lingers menacingly in the minds of the two poets as they struggle upward toward the stars.

BIBLIOGRAPHY

Baltrusaitis, Jurgis. *Le Moyen Age fantastique: Antiquités et exotismes dans l'art gothique.* 1955. Reprint, Paris, 1972.
Brugnoli, Giorgio. "Venanzio Fortunato." *Enciclopedia dantesca,* 5:913. Rome, 1976.
Cervigni, Dino S. "*Inferno* XXXIV." In *Dante's "Divine Comedy," Introductory Readings: Inferno,* ed. Tibor Wlassics, 428–438. Charlottesville, Va., 1990.
Ciotti, Andrea. "Lucifero." *Enciclopedia dantesca,* 3:718–22. Rome, 1971.
Dronke, Peter. *Dante and Medieval Latin Traditions.* Cambridge, 1986.
D'Ovidio, Francesco. *Studi sulla "Divina Commedia,"* 2:562–563. Milan, 1901.
Eliot, T. S. "Dante" (1929). *Selected Essays,* 237–277. 3d ed. London, 1951.
Freccero, John. "Infernal Inversion and Christian Conversion (*Inferno* XXXIV)." *Italica* 42 (1965a): 35–41. Reprinted in *Dante: The Poetics of Conversion,* ed. Rachel Jacoff, 180–194 (Cambridge, Mass., 1986).
———. "Satan's Fall and the *Questio de aqua et terra*." *Italica* 38 (1961): 99–115.
———. "The Sign of Satan." *MLN* 80 (1965b): 11–26. Reprinted in *Dante: The Poetics of Conversion,* ed. Rachel Jacoff, 167–179 (Cambridge, Mass., 1986).
Gorni, Guglielmo. "Parodia e scrittura in Dante." In *Dante e la Biblia,* ed. G. Barblan, 323–340. Atti del convegno internazionale promosso da "Biblia." Florence, 1988.
Gorni, Guglielmo, and Silvia Longhi. "Canto XXXIV: La parodia." In *Letteratura italiana: Le questioni,* ed. Alberto Asor Rosa, 5:459–487. Turin, 1986.
Grabher, Carlo. "Mostri e simboli dell'*Inferno* dantesco." *Annali della Facoltà di lettere e filosofia e di magistero dell'Università di Cagliari* 21 (1953): 20–22.
Leo, Ulrich. "Lucifer and Christus." In *Benedetto Croce,* ed. Francesco Flora. Milan, 1953. Reprinted as "Sehen und Wircklichkeit bei Dante," *Analecta Romanica* 4 (1957): 121–131.
Momigliano, Attilio. Commentary to canto XXXIV. In *La Divina Commedia: Inferno,* ed. Francesco Mazzoni, 705–726. Florence, 1972–1979.
Musa, Mark. "There is a place down there (*Inferno* XXXIV)." In *A Dante Symposium,* ed. W. De Sua and G. Rizzo, 151–158. Chapel Hill, N.C., 1965.
Nardi, Bruno. "L'ultimo canto dell'*Inferno*." *Convivium* 25 (1957): 141–148. Reprinted as "La caduta di Lucifero e l'autenticità della *Questio de aqua et terra*," in *Lectura Dantis Romana* (Florence, 1959), 3–14.

Padoan, Giorgio. Introduction to *De situ et forma aque et terre,* by Dante Alighieri. Florence, 1968.

Palgen, Rudolf. "La 'Visione di Tundalo' nella *Commedia* di Dante." *Convivium* 37 (1969): 129–147.

Pasquazi, Silvio. "Canto XXXIV." In *Lectura Dantis Neapolitana: Inferno,* ed. Pompeo Giannantonio, 623–641. Naples, 1986.

———. "Sulla cosmologia di Dante (*Inferno* XXXIV e *Questio de aqua et terra*)." In *D'Egitto in Gerusalemme: Studi danteschi.* Rome, 1985.

Petrocchi, Giorgio. "Il canto XXXIV dell'*Inferno.*" In *Lectura Dantis Scaligera.* Florence, 1963. Reprinted in *Letture dantesche,* ed. Giovanni Getto (Florence, 1965), 653–665, and in *Itinerari danteschi* (Bari, 1969), 295–310.

Pézard, André. "Le dernier chant de l'*Enfer.*" *Bulletin de la Société d'études dantesques—Annales du Centre universitaire méditerranéen* 15 (1962): 245–264. Reprinted in *Letture dell'"Inferno,"* ed. Vittorio Vettori (Milan, 1963), 397–427.

Rossi, Vittorio. "Il canto XXXIV dell'*Inferno.*" In *Saggi e discorsi su Dante,* 177–204. Florence, 1930. Reprinted in *Letture dantesche,* ed. Giovanni Getto (Florence, 1965), 635–665.

Sapegno, Natalino. Commentary to canto XXXIV. In *La Divina Commedia: Inferno,* ed. Natalino Sapegno, 377–387. 1955. Florence, 1985.

Scartazzini, Giovanni Andrea. Commentary to canto XXXIV. *La Divina Commedia: Inferno,* 429–444. Leipzig, 1874.

Stabile, Giorgio. "Cosmologia e teologia nella *Commedia.* La caduta di Lucifero e il rovesciamento del mondo." *Letture classensi* 12 (1983): 139–173.

Vallone, Aldo, "Il canto XXXIV dell' *Inferno* e l'estremo intelletualismo di Dante." In *Nuove letture dantesche,* 3:189–208. Florence, 1969.

Venturi, Vittorio. "Il canto XXIV dell' *Inferno.*" *Lectura Dantis florentina.* Florence, 1928.

Bibliographical Note
and Suggestions
for Further Reading

We possess no single authentic manuscript of Dante's poem. The accepted critical edition, which supersedes all previous attempts to reconstruct the text as Dante wrote it, including that published by the Società Dantesca Italiana in 1921, is contained in the four volumes of *La Commedia secondo l'antica vulgata*, edited by the late Giorgio Petrocchi (Milan, 1966–67): it constitutes the letter of the *Comedy* expounded by the most recent Italian and American commentators. The English quotations in the preceding essays are taken from *The Divine Comedy of Dante Alighieri*, translated by Allen Mandelbaum, originally published by the University of California Press— *Inferno* (1980), *Purgatorio* (1981), *Paradiso* (1982)—and now available in the Bantam Classics series. (The Italian text translated by Mandelbaum and appearing on facing pages is of course Petrocchi's.)

Since the Latin Vulgate was Dante's Bible, the Old and New Testaments are cited in the Douai-Rheims version of Jerome's text. For Virgil's major work, line references are to the University of California Press's 1981 *The Aeneid of Virgil*, a verse translation by Allen Mandelbaum, subsequently issued by Bantam, which also carries the Latin line numbers at the top of the page. Other works by Virgil are cited from the Loeb Classical Library editions, as are Ovid's *Metamorphoses* (*Met.*), Lucan's *Pharsalia* (*Phar.*), and the *Thebaid* (*Theb.*) of Statius.

English citations from the *Convivio* refer to *Dante's Il Convivio (The Banquet)*, trans. Richard H. Lansing. New York, 1990.

REFERENCE WORKS

Brieger, Peter, Millard Meiss, and Charles S. Singleton. *Illuminated Manuscripts of the Divine Comedy*. Princeton, 1969.

Lansing, Richard, ed. *The Dante Encyclopedia*. Associate editors Teodolinda Barolini, Joan Ferrante, Amilcare Iannucci, and Christopher Kleinhenz (in preparation).

Lovera, Luciano, ed. *Concordanza della Commedia di Dante Alighieri*. Con la collaborazione di Rosanna Bettarini e Anna Mazzarello. Premessa di Gianfranco Contini. 3 vols. Turin, 1975.

Petrocchi, Giorgio, and Ignazio Baldelli, eds. *Enciclopedia dantesca*. 6 vols. Rome, 1970–1978 (directed by Umberto Bosco, with Petrocchi as chief editor, joined, from vol. 4 on, by Baldelli. The first five volumes are ordered alphabetically. The sixth volume includes Petrocchi's biography of Dante; a unique collective series of essays on Dante's language and style; an extensive bibliography; and the texts of all of Dante's works—as well as works that may be Dante's. The *E.D.* is one of the finest examples of a collective scholarly critical enterprise that our times have produced, but the individual bibliographical notes to the alphabetically ordered entries contain many references not found in the general bibliography in vol. 6).

Toynbee, Paget. *A Dictionary of Proper Names and Other Notable Matters in the Works of Dante*. Revised by Charles S. Singleton. Oxford, 1968.

Wilkins, E. H., and T. G. Bergin, eds. *A Concordance to the "Divine Comedy" of Dante Alighieri*. Cambridge, Massachusetts, 1965 (less detailed than the Lovera edition and not based on Petrocchi's critical text, but in a single convenient volume).

THE TRECENTO COMMENTARIES

The task of the interpreter of the *Comedy* is a venerable and cumulative one, and, while the dates and order of composition of the earliest manuscript commentaries are uniformly controversial, the first glosses on the *Inferno* by Dante's son Jacopo Alighieri have been dated as early as 1321, the year of his father's death. A date of 1324 has been proposed for Graziolo de' Bambaglioli's Latin commentary on the *Inferno*. The first commentary to cover all three *cantiche*, by the Bolognese Jacopo della Lana, may have been written between 1323 and 1328. The Ottimo (or best) Commento, the second to elucidate the entire *Comedy*, probably composed by the notary Andrea Lancia, is usually assigned to 1333. The date and influence of Guido da Pisa's Latin exposition of the *Inferno* are particularly moot, though at least one recent scholar (Luis Jenaro-MacLennan) would place it as early as 1327–28. Dante's other son Pietro Alighieri's Latin commentary exists in more than one redaction and belongs to the last decade of the first half of the century, 1340–50. The author Giovanni Boccaccio's unfinished *Esposizioni*, which explicate the text as far as the opening lines of *Inf.* XVII, are the product of his public lectures on the *Comedy* (the first Lectura Dantis) delivered in his native Florence in 1373. Similarly, Benvenuto Rambaldi of Imola's lively Latin commentary began life as a course of lectures given in Bologna in 1375, while Francesco da Buti's Pisan lessons were also transcribed in the last quarter of the fourteenth century. Buti's is one of the few important keys to Dante's text not so far included among the forty-seven ancient and modern commentaries available online via the Internet at the important Dartmouth Dante Project conceived and directed by Robert Hollander:

<http://milton.mse.jhu.edu:8001/research/italian/dante.html>

The early commentaries may also be consulted in the following, for the most part rare, nineteenth- and twentieth-century printed editions.

Latin Commentaries

Alighieri, Pietro (Pietro di Dante). *Petri Alleghieri super Dantis ipsius genitoris Comoediam Commentarium.* Ed. Vincenzo Nannucci. 3 vols. Florence, 1845.
Benvenuto da Imola. *Benevenuti de Rambaldis de Imola Comentum super Dantis Aldigherij Comoediam.* Ed. Giacomo Filippo Lacaita. 5 vols. Florence, 1887.
Guido da Pisa. *Expositiones et glose super Comediam Dantis facte per Fratrem Guidonem Pisanum.* Ed. Vincenzo Cioffari. Albany, New York, 1974.
Serravalle, Giovanni di. *Translatio et comentum cum texto italico totius libri Dantis Aldigherii Fratris Iohannis de Serravalle.* Ed. Marcellino da Civezza and Teofilo Domenichelli. Prato, 1891.

Italian Commentaries

Alighieri, Jacopo (Jacopo di Dante). *Chiose alla cantica dell'Inferno di Dante Alighieri scritte da Jacopo Alighieri.* Ed. Jarro (G. Piccini). Florence, 1915.
Anonimo Fiorentino. *Commento alla Divina Commedia d'Anonimo del secolo XIV.* Ed. Pietro Fanfani. 3 vols. Bologna, 1866–74.
Bambaglioli, Graziolo de'. *Il commento dantesco di Graziolo de' Bambaglioli dal Colombina di Siviglia con altri codici confrontato.* Ed. Antonio Fiammazzo. Savona, 1915.
Boccaccio, Giovanni. *Esposizioni sopra la Comedia di Dante.* Ed. Giorgio Padoan. Milan, 1965 [vol. 6 of *Tutte le opere di Giovanni Boccaccio*, ed. Vittore Branca].
Buti, Francesco da. *Commento di Francesco da Buti sopra la Divina Commedia di Dante Allighieri.* Ed. Crescentino Giannini. 3 vols. Pisa, 1858–62.
Chiose anonime alla prima cantica della Divina Commedia di un contemporaneo del poeta. Ed. Francesco Selmi. Turin, 1865.
Lana, Jacopo della. *La Comedia di Dante degli Allagherii col commento di Jacopo Della Lana bolognese.* Ed. Luciano Scarabelli. 3 vols. Bologna, 1866.
[Lancia, Andrea?]. *L'Ottimo commento della Divina Commedia: Testo inedito*

d'un contemporaneo del poeta. Ed. Alessandro Torri. 3 vols. Pisa, 1827–1829.

RENAISSANCE COMMENTARIES

Of the four major Renaissance commentaries—by Cristoforo Landino (Florence, 1481), Alessandro Vellutello (Venice, 1544), Bernardino Daniello (1568), and Lodovico Castelvetro (1570)—only the last two have been reprinted since their first editions:

Castelvetro, Lodovico. *Sposizione di Lodovico Castelvetro a XXIX canti dell'Inferno dantesco.* Ed. G. Franciosi. Modena, 1886.

Daniello, Bernardino. *L'espositione di Bernardino Daniello da Lucca sopra la Comedia di Dante.* Ed. Robert Hollander and Geoffrey Schnapp with Kevin Brownlee and Nancy Vickers. Hanover, New Hampshire, and London, 1989.

See also the previously unpublished commentary of Daniello's mentor Trifone (or Trifon) Gabriele, recently made available by the Commissione per i testi di lingua:

Gabriele, Trifone. *Annotationi nel Dante fatte con M. Trifon Gabriele in Bassano.* Ed. Lino Pertile. Bologna, 1993.

SELECTED MODERN COMMENTARIES

The following works are listed alphabetically for ease of reference. It should be noted, however, that the exegetical tradition is cumulative and that the most recent commentaries are, theoretically at least, the most complete and accurate.

Biagi, G., G. L. Passerini, E. Rostagno, and U. Cosmo, eds. *La Divina Commedia nella figurazione artistica e nel secolare commento.* 3 vols. Turin, 1924–39.

Bosco, Umberto, and Giovanni Reggio, eds. *La Divina Commedia.* 3 vols. Florence, 1979.

Chiavacci Leonardi, Anna Maria, ed. *Commedia.* Milan, 1991–97.

Chimenz, Siro A. *La Divina Commedia.* Turin, 1962 (vol. 1 of *Opere*).

Del Lungo, Isidoro, ed. *La Divina Commedia.* 3 vols. Florence, 1924–26.

Durling, Robert M., ed. and trans. *The Divine Comedy of Dante Alighieri.* Introduction and notes by Ronald L. Martinez and Robert M. Durling. Vol. 1: *Inferno.* New York and Oxford, 1996.

Fallani, Giovanni. *La Divina Commedia.* 3 vols. Messina-Florence, 1964–65.

Garavelli, Bianca, ed. *Commedia.* Con la supervisione di Maria Corti. Milan, 1993.

Giacalone, Giuseppe, ed. *La Divina Commedia.* Rome, 1988.

Gmelin, Hermann, ed. *Die göttliche Komödie übersetzt von Hermann Gmelin: Kommentar.* 3 vols. Stuttgart, 1954.

Grabher, Carlo, ed. *La Divina Commedia.* 3 vols. Florence, 1934–36.

Grandgent, Charles Hall, ed. *La Divina Commedia di Dante Alighieri.* 3 vols. Boston, 1909–13.

Mattalia, Daniele, ed. *La Divina Commedia.* 3 vols. Milan, 1960.

Mazzoni, Francesco. *Saggio di un nuovo commento alla Divina Commedia, Inferno, canti I–III.* Florence, 1967.

———, ed. *La Divina Commedia. Inferno.* Con i commenti di Tommaso Casini-Silvio Adrasti Barbi, e di Attilio Momigliano. Introduzione e aggiornamento bibliografico-critico di Francesco Mazzoni. Florence, 1972.

Momigliano, Attilio, ed. *La Divina Commedia.* 3 vols. Florence, 1945–47.

Montanari, Fausto, ed. *La Divina Commedia.* 3 vols. Brescia, 1949–51.

Padoan, Giorgio. *Commento all'Inferno (canti I–VIII).* Florence, 1967.

Pasquini, Emilio, and A. E. Quaglio, eds. *Commedia.* 3 vols. Milan, 1982–86.

Pézard, André, ed. *Oeuvres complètes.* Paris, 1965.

Pietrobono, Luigi, ed. *La Divina Commedia.* 3 vols. Turin, 1924–30.

Porena, Manfredi, ed. *La Divina Commedia.* 3 vols. Bologna, 1946–48.

Sapegno, Natalino, ed. *La Divina Commedia.* 3 vols. Florence, 1955–57; 2d ed. 1968, 3d ed. 1985.

Scartazzini, Giovanni Andrea, ed. *La Divina Commedia.* 3 vols. Leipzig, 1874–82. Rev. ed. 1900.

Scartazzini, Giovanni Andrea, and Giuseppe Vandelli, eds. *La Divina Commedia.* Milan, 1903 (and subsequent editions).

Singleton, Charles S., ed. *The Divine Comedy.* 6 vols. Princeton, New Jersey, 1970–75.

Steiner, Carlo. *La Divina Commedia.* Turin, 1926.

Tommaseo, Niccolò, ed. *La Commedia di Dante Allighieri.* Venice, 1837.

Torraca, Francesco, ed. *La Divina Commedia.* 3 vols. Milan-Rome, 1905–6.

Vallone, Aldo, and L. Scorrano, eds. *La Divina Commedia.* 3 vols. Naples, 1985–87.

Vandelli, Giuseppe. *See* Scartazzini and Vandelli

LECTURAE DANTIS

The format followed in the present volume, as in the forthcoming companion volumes on the *Purgatorio* and the *Paradiso*, conforms to a well-established exegetical tradition that goes back to Boccaccio and is still the most common hermeneutical approach to Dante's masterwork. For the one hundred cantos of the *Comedy* an equal number of international experts were identified and invited by the editors to contribute a reading of a single canto. Modern collections of comparable canto readings include (in chronological order):

Nuova Lectura Dantis. Ed. Siro A. Chimenz. Rome, 1950–59 (sponsored by the Casa di Dante, Rome).

Letture dantesche: Inferno. Ed. Giovanni Getto. Florence, 1955.

Lectura Dantis Romana, nuova serie. Ed. Giovanni Fallani. Turin, 1959–65 (sponsored by the Casa di Dante, Rome).

Lectura Dantis Internazionale. Ed. Vittorio Vettori. Milan, 1963–70.

Letture classensi. Ravenna, 1966–.

Nuove letture dantesche. Florence, 1966–76 (sponsored by the Casa di Dante, Rome).

Lectura Dantis Scaligera: Inferno. Ed. Mario Marcazzan. Florence, 1967.

Inferno: Letture della Casa di Dante in Roma. Ed. Silvio Zennaro. Rome, 1977.

Lectura Dantis Neapolitana: Inferno. Ed. Pompeo Giannantonio. Naples, 1980.

Lectura Dantis Modenese: Inferno. Modena, 1984.

Lectura Dantis Newberryana. Ed. Paolo Cherchi and Antonio Mastrobuono. Chicago, 1988–.

Lectura Dantis Virginiana: Dante's "Divine Comedy," Introductory Readings. Vol. 1, *Inferno.* Ed. Tibor Wlassics. Special issue of *Lectura Dantis* 6 (1990 suppl.).

Three volumes have so far been published in the monographic *Lectura Dantis Americana* series:

Cassell, Anthony K. *Inferno I.* Philadelphia, 1989.

Jacoff, Rachel, and Stephany, William. *Inferno II.* Philadelphia, 1989.

Simonelli, Maria Picchio. *Inferno III.* Philadelphia, 1993.

MORE ON DANTE IN ENGLISH

Consultation of much of the foregoing material presupposes a knowledge of Italian. For the reader who lacks fluent reading skills in that language, there follows a far from complete list of useful titles in English.

Asin Palacios, Miguel. *Islam and the "Divine Comedy."* Trans. and abridged Harold Sunderland. London, 1926.

Auerbach, Erich. *Dante, Poet of the Secular World.* Trans. Ralph Manheim. Chicago, 1961.

———. *Mimesis: The Representation of Reality in Western Literature.* Trans. Willard Trask. Princeton, 1953.

Barbi, Michele. *Life of Dante.* Ed. and trans. Paul G. Ruggiers. Berkeley, 1954.

Barkan, Leonard. *The Gods Made Flesh: Metamorphosis and the Pursuit of Paganism.* New Haven, 1986.

Barolini, Teodolinda. *Dante's Poets: Textuality and Truth in the "Comedy."* Princeton, 1982.

———. *The Undivine Comedy: Detheologizing Dante.* Princeton, 1992.

Boyde, Patrick. *Dante, Philomythes and Philosopher: Man in the Cosmos.* Cambridge, 1981.

Cachey, Theodore J., ed. *Dante Now: Current Trends in Dante Studies.* Notre Dame, 1995.

Cambon, Glauco. *Dante's Craft: Studies in Style and Language.* Minneapolis, 1969.

Carroll, John Smyth. *Exiles of Eternity: An Exposition of Dante's "Inferno."* London, 1903.

Cassell, Anthony K. *Dante's Fearful Art of Justice.* Toronto, 1984.

Curtius, Ernst Robert. *European Literature and the Latin Middle Ages.* Trans. Willard Trask. New York, 1953.

Davis, Charles T. *Dante's Italy and Other Essays.* Philadelphia, 1984.

Dronke, Peter. *Dante and Medieval Latin Traditions.* Cambridge, 1986.

Ferrante, Joan M. *The Political Vision of the "Divine Comedy."* Princeton, 1984.

Foster, Kenelm. *The Two Dantes and Other Studies.* London, 1977.

Freccero, John. [Various *lecturae.*] In *Dante: The Poetics of Conversion,* ed. Rachel Jacoff. Cambridge, Massachusetts, 1986.

Giamatti, A. Bartlett, ed. *Dante in America: The First Two Centuries.* Binghamton, New York, 1983.

Gilson, Etienne. *Dante the Philosopher.* Trans. David Moore. New York, 1949.

Hollander, Robert. *Allegory in Dante's "Commedia."* Princeton, 1969.

———. *Studies in Dante.* Ravenna, 1980.

Iannucci, Amilcare, ed. *Dante: Contemporary Perspectives.* Toronto, 1997.

Jacoff, Rachel, ed. *The Cambridge Companion to Dante.* Cambridge, 1993.

Jacoff, Rachel, and Jeffrey Schnapp, eds. *The Poetry of Allusion: Virgil and Ovid in Dante's "Comedy."* Stanford, 1991.

Kay, Richard. *Dante's Swift and Strong: Essays in "Inferno" xv.* Lawrence, Kansas, 1978.

Kirkpatrick, Robin. *Dante's "Inferno": Difficulty and Dead Poetry.* Cambridge, 1987.

Mazzotta, Giuseppe. *Dante, Poet of the Desert: History and Allegory in the "Divine Comedy."* Princeton, 1979.

———. *Dante's Vision and the Circle of Knowledge.* Princeton, 1993.

Moore, Edward. *Studies in Dante.* 4 vols. Oxford, 1896–1917.

Morgan, Alison. *Dante and the Medieval Other World.* Cambridge, 1990.

Musa, Mark. *Advent at the Gates: Dante's "Comedy."* Bloomington, Indiana, 1974.

Shapiro, Marianne. *Women Earthly and Divine in the "Comedy" of Dante.* Lexington, Kentucky, 1975.

Shoaf, Richard A. *Dante, Chaucer, and the Currency of the Word.* Norman, Oklahoma, 1983.

Singleton, Charles S. *Dante's "Commedia": Elements of Structure.* Cambridge, Massachusetts, 1954.

Thompson, David. *Dante's Epic Journeys.* Baltimore, 1974.

Vossler, Karl. *Mediaeval Culture: An Introduction to Dante and His Times.* Trans. William Cranston Lawton. 2 vols. New York, 1929.

PERIODICAL AND ELECTRONIC RESOURCES

Two current American periodicals—the annual *Dante Studies* (published by the Dante Society of America, founded in 1881) and *Lectura Dantis* (published at the University of Virginia since 1987)—are entirely devoted to Dante. A number of other periodicals in the field of modern languages regularly publish articles on Dante. Since 1953 *Dante Studies* has published an annual annotated bibliography, first (1953–84) under the editorship of Anthony L. Pellegrini, then (1984–90) under that of Christopher Kleinhenz. An Italian Dante bibliography for 1988–90, prepared by Federico Sanguineti, was originally published in *Dante Studies* 112 (1994).

All these bibliographies are now accessible in a searchable electronic format developed by Richard Lansing—The American Dante Bibliography—either through the Dante Society of America's homepage:

<http://www.princeton.edu/~dante/>

or at Brandeis University:

<http://www.brandeis.edu/library/dante/index.html>

More online Dante bibliographies are displayed at the ORB (Online Reference Book for Medieval Studies) website:

<http://www.ilt.columbia.edu/projects/dante/index.html>

Links to these and other websites, as well as additional Dante materials, are conveniently located on Otfried Lieberknecht's extremely useful homepage for Dante studies:

<http://members.aol.com/lieberk/welcome.html>

Contributors

John Ahern, Dante Antolini Professor of Italian at Vassar College, has written widely on Dante and other Italian authors, mostly of the twentieth century.

Teodolinda Barolini, Professor of Italian at Columbia University, is the author of *Dante's Poets: Textuality and Truth in the "Comedy"* (Princeton, 1984) and *The Undivine "Comedy": Detheologizing Dante* (Princeton, 1992).

Philip R. Berk, Professor Emeritus of French Literature at the University of Rochester, has written on Dante and the authors of the French seventeenth century.

Giuliana Carugati teaches at Emory University. She is the author of a study of the mystical aspects of Dante's work, *Dalla menzogna al silenzio* (Bologna, 1991).

Letterio Cassata, Professor of Italian Philology at the University of Rome II, recently published a critical edition of the poetry of Dante's "first friend," Guido Cavalcanti (Anzio, 1993).

Remo Ceserani, Professor of Comparative Literature at the University of Bologna, has taught at Brown, Harvard, and Berkeley. Among his recent books are *Il fantastico* (1996), *Raccontare il postmoderno* (1997), and *Lo straniero* (1998).

Paolo Cherchi has been Professor of Romance Languages at the University of Chicago since 1965. His critical works include *Andreas and the Ambiguity of Courtly Love* (Toronto, 1994). He is coeditor of the *Lectura Dantis Newberryana*.

Caron Ann Cioffi, Assistant Professor of English at the University of California, Davis, is currently finishing a book on the influence of Ovidian mythology on Dante's *Commedia* and Chaucer's *Troilus and Criseyde.*

Charles T. Davis was Professor of Medieval History at Tulane University until his death in 1998. His *Dante and the Idea of Rome* (Oxford, 1957) and *Dante's Italy* (Philadelphia, 1984) brought a historian's perspective to Dante studies.

Dante Della Terza, formerly Irving Babbitt Professor of Comparative Literature at Harvard University, has been, since 1992, Professor of Italian Literature at the Università Federico II in Naples. He recently published *Strutture poetiche, esperienze letterarie: percorsi culturali da Dante ai contemporanei* (Naples, 1995).

Robert M. Durling, Professor Emeritus at the University of California, Santa Cruz, is the author of *The Figure of the Poet in Renaissance Epic* (1965) and, with Ronald L. Martinez, *Time and the Crystal: Studies in Dante's "Rime petrose"* (Berkeley, 1990).

Steve Ellis is Professor of English at the University of Birmingham, England. Among his books are *Dante and English Poetry: Shelley to T. S. Eliot* (Cambridge, 1983) and Dante's *Hell* (London, 1994), a verse translation.

Joan M. Ferrante is Professor of English and Comparative Literature at Columbia University and a former President of the Dante Society of America. Her latest publication is *To the Glory of Her Sex: Women's Roles in the Composition of Medieval Texts* (Bloomington, 1997).

Eugenio N. Frongia is Professor of Italian and Humanities and Chair of Foreign Languages and Literatures at California State University, Chico. He specializes in Renaissance humanism, regional Italian literature, and cinema studies.

Robert Hollander, Professor of Comparative Literature at Princeton University, is the author of *Boccaccio's Dante and the Shaping Force of Satire* (Michigan, 1997). He won the Gold Medal of the City of Florence in recognition of his work on behalf of Dante.

Amilcare A. Iannucci is Professor of Italian Studies at the University of Toronto and a former Vice President of the Dante Society of America. He developed *Dante's "Divine Comedy": A Televisual Commentary* (University of Toronto Media Centre).

Scholar-poet **Allen Mandelbaum** is the William R. Kenan, Jr., Professor of Humanities at Wake Forest University and the translator of *The Divine Comedy* (Berkeley, 1980–84).

Giuseppe Mazzotta is the Charles C. and Dorathea S. Dilley Professor of Italian Literature at Yale University. He is the author of *Dante, Poet of the Desert* (Princeton, 1979) and *Dante's Vision and the Circle of Knowledge* (Princeton, 1993).

Susan Noakes, Professor of French and Italian at the University of Minnesota, Twin Cities, is the author of *Timely Reading: Between Exegesis and Interpretation* (Cornell, 1988).

James Nohrnberg, Professor of English at the University of Virginia, has also taught at Toronto, Harvard, and Yale and given the Gauss Seminars at Princeton. He is the author of *The Analogy of "The Faerie Queene"* (Princeton, 1976) and essays on Homer, allegory, the Bible, Dante, Boiardo, Spenser, and Milton.

Anthony Oldcorn, Chair of Italian Studies at Brown University and a contributor to the 1996 *Cambridge History of Italian Literature,* is currently editing the *New Penguin Book of Italian Verse.*

Lino Pertile, Professor of Romance Languages and Literatures at Harvard, is the coeditor, with C. P. Brand, of the *Cambridge History of Italian Literature* (Cambridge, 1996). He recently published *La puttane e il gigante: Dal Cantico dei cantici al Paradiso Terrestre di Dante* (Ravenna, 1998).

Massimo Mandolini Pesaresi is Assistant Professor at Columbia University and the author of *Grecian Vistas: Giacomo Leopardi and Romantic Hellas* (forthcoming).

Thomas Peterson is Associate Professor of Italian at the University of Georgia. His monographs on Pasolini (*The Paraphrase of an Imaginary Dialogue*) and Fortini (*The Ethical Muse of Franco Fortini*) won the annual book awards from the Northeast Modern Language Association (1990) and the South Atlantic Modern Language Association (1996) respectively.

Jennifer Petrie is College Lecturer in Italian at the National University of Ireland, University College, Dublin. She has published on Petrarch and Dante, her most recent work being an edition, in collaboration with June Salmons, of Dante's *Vita Nuova.*

The late **Giorgio Petrocchi** was one of Italy's most prominent authorities on Dante. Chief editor of the *Enciclopedia dantesca,* he also edited the standard critical text of the *Commedia* (Milan, 1966–67). A literary polymath, Petrocchi was a prolific critic and theorist who made significant contributions in all areas of Italian literary studies.

Charles Ross, Professor of English and Comparative Literature at Purdue University, is the translator of Boiardo's *Orlando Innamorato.* His latest publication is *The Custom of the Castle: From Malory to Macbeth* (Berkeley, 1997).

The late **Vittorio Russo** studied and taught medieval romance philology at the University of Naples. A contributor to the *Enciclopedia dantesca,* he was the author of important volumes of essays on various aspects of Dante's thought and culture.

Edoardo Sanguineti, a leading Italian poet, is Professor of Italian Literature at the University of Genoa and the author of *Interpretazione di Male-*

bolge (1961), *Tre studi danteschi* (1961), *Il realismo di Dante* (1965), and *Dante reazionario* (1992).

John A. Scott is Professor Emeritus of Italian and Honorary Senior Research Fellow at the University of Western Australia. The author of books and numerous articles on Dante, Petrarch, the Italian Renaissance, Leopardi, and Baudelaire, he is a Fellow of the Australian Academy of the Humanities and has taught at leading universities in the United States, Britain, Canada, and Australia.

Maria Picchio Simonelli, Professor at Boston College (1967–84) and the Istituto Orientale in Naples (1984–96), has published a critical edition of Dante's *Convivio.* Her many publications include a volume of essays on the figure of Beatrice, *Beatrice nell'opera di Dante e nella memoria europea* (1994).

Manlio Pastore Stocchi is Professor of Italian Literature at the University of Padua, a member of the Venetian Academy of Arts and Sciences, and a contributor to the *Enciclopedia dantesca.* In addition to his Dante scholarship, he has edited texts by Boccaccio, Poliziano, Goldoni, and other medieval, Renaissance, and modern Italian authors.

Alfred A. Triolo is Professor Emeritus at Pennsylvania State University, where he continues to be an active scholar-teacher in late medieval and Renaissance Spanish and Italian literature.

Paolo Valesio, Chair of the Italian Department at Yale, has been a Guggenheim Fellow and a Fellow of the Whitney Humanities Center at Yale University. He is a poet, narrator, and literary critic, the founder of *YIP: Yale Italian Poetry,* and Associate Director of the Italian Poetry Society of America.

Tibor Wlassics, William R. Kenan, Jr., Professor of Italian at the University of Virginia, is the author of *Interpretazioni di prosodia dantesca* (Rome, 1972) and *Dante narratore* (Florence, 1975), as well as founding editor of *Lectura Dantis: A Forum for Dante Research and Interpretation.*

Index

The index contains the names of all persons (including fictional characters) and premodern works mentioned in the text. Works are listed under the author's name or, if anonymous, under the title.

Designer:	Steve Renick
Compositor:	Integrated Composition Systems
Text:	10.9/12 Dante
Display:	Castellar MT
Printer:	Edwards Brothers, Inc.
Binder:	Edwards Brothers, Inc.